Axel-Ivar Berglund

Zulu Thought-Patterns
and Symbolism

Axel-Ivar Berglund

Zulu Thought-Patterns and Symbolism

Indiana University Press
Bloomington and Indianapolis

Text and photographs © Axel-Ivar Berglund, 1976
This volume is No. XXII in
"Studia Missionalia Upsaliensia"
Indiana University Press edition, 1989

Library of Congress Cataloging-in-Publication Data

Berglund, Axel-Ivar.
  Zulu thought-patterns and symbolism.

  Reprint. Originally published: Uppsala : Swedish
Institute of Missionary Research, 1976. Originally published
in series: Studia missionalia Upsaliensia; 22.
  Bibliography: p.
  Includes index.
  1. Zulu (African people)—Social life and customs.
2. Zulu (African people)—Religion.   I. Title.
DT878.Z9B45   1989   306'.0899639860684   89-11039
ISBN 0-253-31175-6
ISBN 0-253-21205-7 (pbk.)

1 2 3 4 5 93 92 91 90 89

Printed in Hong Kong

To three Women

My Mother,
who first taught me to trust God and respect human beings

Kerstin,
mother of our four children

Monica Wilson,
who taught me to listen to peoples' self-interpretation

Contents

Acknowledgements

Zululand friends behind this book are so many that it is quite impossible to mention them all by name. But I nevertheless wish to express my heartfelt thanks to them for much kindness, gracious hospitality, patience and willingness to assist me. I am particularly grateful to the many who went out of their way to be helpful in giving representative material towards this study.

I have had the exceptional privilege of being led and guided in African studies by renowned scholars. Professor Carl-Martin Edsman, Uppsala, introduced me into the exciting world of comparative religious studies. His learned insights and personal attention given so freely to his students kindled the desire to know more about people and their thought-patterns. Professor Sture Lagercrantz, Uppsala, taught me the ethnographic fascinations of the African continent. With his keen awareness in regard to the importance of detail and his profound knowledge of the literature on Africa, he made the African continent both alive and truly engaging. Professor Bengt Sundkler, also of Uppsala, filled the continent with living and attractive people. With him, African men and women, the history of which they are an integral part, the Church and its programme of crossing frontiers were essentials which captured and involved his students. Lectures given and seminars led by these three scholars coupled with warm personal friendship, have been of great importance in my studies. I thank them most warmly for what they have meant to me.

In South Africa it is to Professor Monica Wilson of Cape Town, that I owe more than I can account for. Her untiring constructive criticism and her constant encouraging pressure on me to see the study to an end have been a source of great inspiration. Her standards of research, reflected in her publications and in her supervision of studies, have set goals in anthropological achievement which, for most of us, are inaccessible. But her kindly guidance constantly drove one to further detailed research and to attempt to penetrate deeper than merely the descriptive and general. It is Professor Monica Wilson who taught me to regard the thought-patterns of men from their own points of departure, trying to understand people as they see themselves. The lessons have been many and have proved greatly rewarding. I thank Monica Wilson for more than I can express.

I have received financial and other aid from Statens Humanistiska Forskningsråd (Stockholm), Lutheran World Federation (Geneva), Svenska Institutet för Missionsforskning (Uppsala), the Church of Sweden Mission (Uppsala), the Ernest Oppenheimer Memorial Trust (Johannesburg) and the Theological Education Fund (London). I acknowledge these gifts with much gratitude, for without them the study would not have been possible.

I should like to thank those who have read the manuscript and given me so much useful constructive criticisms. I am also grateful for their help in

11

making necessary grammatical and language corrections in the writing up of the thesis.

I wish to express my appreciation to the Board and staff of the Church of Sweden Mission, Uppsala, fellow missionaries, relatives and a great many friends who have followed the growth of the study with interest and encouragement. Their moral support has meant more to me than they might have realised.

The contents of this book was presented to the University of Cape Town as a thesis for a Ph.D. under the title "Zulu Ideas and Symbolism". I gratefully acknowledge the university's kind permission to publish the study. It is with a deep sense of gratitude that I acknowledge the honour of having the material published in the Studia Missionalia Upsaliensia series.

Preface

The Zulu, numbering about 4 030 000 persons, are a Nguni people who live mainly in the province of Natal in the Republic of South Africa. It is this people that is described in the present study.

The anthropological ethnographic literature on the Zulu people is extensive. So is the linguistic and historical material. Written evidence has been made use of, particularly in instances where differences in rites, rituals, customs, ceremonies, symbols, etc. have been recorded. But because the study is focused on an understanding of patterns of behaviour, thought, and expression rather than a description of them, the material on which the study is based is to a large extent my own fieldwork. The data presented is, from this angle of approach, original.

Comparative evidence published on neighbouring Nguni peoples and other African peoples has been used as a guide in my own investigations and analysis of material collected in the field.

There are different ways of understanding a people's thought-patterns, behaviour, and means of expression. In this study historical approaches and interpretations which may have arisen in the minds of anthropologists (including myself) have been ignored, and every effort has been made to obtain Zulu interpretations of their own words and actions.

As other students who have undertaken the same sort of project elsewhere in Africa have found, such a study has proven to be a time-consuming undertaking, a test of patience, and an exercise in evaluating material and information gathered. No matter how wholeheartedly one tried to identify oneself with the people one was studying, there was always the gap between the student and the object of study caused by a great number of social, economic, religious, etc., differences. In the South African setting the cultural and ethnic difference between people is strongly underlined, and was experienced very keenly on several occasions.

To attend e.g. ritual celebrations, or to be allowed to associate with people freely and naturally, in order to see what was being done and hear what was being said, proved to be only one step towards reaching the goal of the investigation. The second, that of acquiring the actors' and the speakers' understanding and interpretations of their underlying ideas, was a far more difficult undertaking. Not only did people view the student and his keen questioning with suspicion, at least to begin with. But sometimes I had the definite feeling that people, when asked about a particular issue, posed the unspoken question: "What does he want me to answer?" or, "What would he himself have replied to such a question?" To the interviewed it was a matter of giving an answer which the interviewer would find meaningful and logical from his (the interviewer's) cultural point of view, rather than accuracy in terms of the setting in which the interviewed lived. Hence the ne-

13

cessity of careful evaluation of information and data collected, so that material presented would be as exact and as representative as possible.

The time-consuming interviews and the many efforts made to reach the goal of the investigation have proven rewarding. The reward lies in the overall picture of a people who have a system of thought that is not only intelligible, but also logical. It is these intelligible and logical ideas, expressed chiefly in rites, rituals and symbols, which the study presents. It thereby depicts the wealth of systematized thinking in a people that once, unfortunately, was regarded as "primitive" in an evaluative sense of the word. It is shown that intelligible and logical methods of reasoning are not limited to scientific ideas.

Umpumulo, Mapumulo, in August 1972

Axel-Ivar Berglund

List of Illustrations

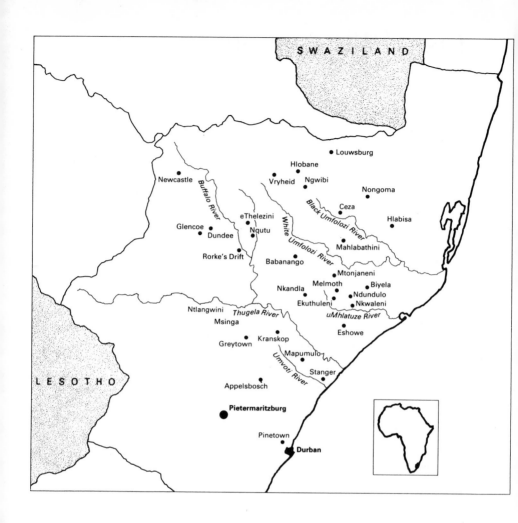

SWAZILAND

LESOTHO

Louwsburg

Hlobane
Newcastle   Vryheid   Ngwibi
                              Nongoma

Ceza
                    Hlabisa

eThelezini
Glencoe   Nqutu
        Dundee   Mahlabathini

Rorke's Drift   Babanango

                    Mtonjaneni
              Melmoth   Biyela
Nkandla   Ndundulo
        Ekuthuleni   Nkwaleni

Ntlangwini   Thugela River   uMhlatuze River
Msinga   Eshowe

Greytown   Kranskop
                  Mapumulo

                  Stanger
Appelsbosch

Pietermaritzburg

Pinetown
        Durban

Buffalo River
White Umfolozi River
Black Umfolozi River
Umvoti River

16

Chapter I

Introduction

Scope of the Study

Since Professor Evans-Pritchard published *Witchcraft, Oracles and Magic a-mong the Azande* in 1937, followed by *Nuer Religion* in 1956, there has been a growing interest in examinations of thought-patterns and symbols in a specific society. These studies, which analyse rituals and symbols as important parts in the working machinery of the society in which they appear, have, to some extent, replaced general descriptions of societies with interpretations of rituals and symbols suggested by scholars themselves. The examination of ideas and methods of expressing them (through rituals and symbols) have proved useful. For the studies have shown how moral values and qualities express realities, and that symbols and rituals are meaningful to members of the society in which they are found.

Anthropologists of the structural-functional school have convincingly shown that there is a clear relationship between rituals and social realities expressed in the political and economic activities of a society. Within the smaller societies the integrations between the political, economic and ritual aspects of life has been shown to be closer than in larger societies. In the latter, a certain autonomy between the different aspects exists, isolating the one from the other more than in the smaller societies.

Recently, attention has also been drawn to the relationship between symbols and ritual. Symbols and a translation of them from the point of view of the people who use them, prove to be keys to a fuller understanding of the rituals in which they occur: they make a ritual intelligible to the men who are involved in it. This aspect has received attention in this study.

Contributions towards Ndembu symbolic ritual understanding have been made by Professor V. Turner who has produced major studies on the subject.[1] Professor Monica Wilson[2] and Dr T. O. Beidelman[3] have analysed field material in the Tanzanian context, Professor Wilson dealing with Nyakyusa in a series of important books and Beidelman in a number of articles. Professor Mary Douglas has carried out research work among Lele (Congo).[4] Dr G. Leinhardt has written on Dinka concepts[5] and M. Griaule on Dogon.[6] Other contributions are those by Drs Audrey Richards.[7] P. Rigby[8] and C. M. H. White.[9] Professor Marja-Liisa Swantz has discussed changing symbolic ritual expressions and their reflections on developments in a society, particularly among women. Her field of examination has been Zaramo of Tanzania.[10]

Among the Zulu people, as in much of Africa, there are forces which very obviously act and react on men and the society which they constitute. Industrialization and subsequent urbanization, Western cultural influence, Christian missions, new economic values, the presence of whites and Asians (the latter particularly south of the Thugela river) and many other pressures all contribute to the changes of life approach which, of necessity, must take place in a society such as that of Zulu men and women.

The various pressures which put their weight on Zulu give rise to situations of conflict. On the one hand there is, in Zulu society, a national pride which is felt everywhere among people. Based partly on a short but dramatic and impressive historic period of greatness, the national pride is encouraged also by nation-building elsewhere in Africa and, in the South African setting, by local political views. Proud of being just Zulu, people have a strong desire to build on their own traditional culture. There is, partly, a deep sense of love and admiration of the past, partly, a growing appreciation of traditional thought-patterns expressed in rituals and symbols.

On the other hand, pressures of our day force men to face new conditions of living and new approaches to life which sometimes differ considerably from traditional ones. In the situations of conflict which arise, there takes place an adjustment of the old, acceptance of new ideas and even a repudiation of traditional thought-patterns to allow for Christian, medical, agricultural, mechanical and other rational empirical scientific approaches. For these have come also to Zulu society to stay. Some of these new thought-patterns and symbols which arise from cultural cross-influences are described in the study.

The study also shows that much of traditional thinking is not only still found in Zulu society, but, in fact, is receiving increasing attention, especially among people who live in rural areas. This is particularly true in times of crisis in the lives of men and women.

However, the study, in describing and analysing thought-patterns and symbols found in Zulu society, is designed to show how these concepts, in their specific settings, are logical and intelligent. The relationships between men expressed in the rituals and symbols of their society, make living in that society a meaningful experience. In other words, a main concern of the thesis is to show how thought-patterns and symbols are not only a means of communication, but that the rituals and symbols are logical and intelligible to the members of that society.

It may be true to state that symbols to a greater extent express thinking in societies where rational and scientific values have not yet gained a strong foothold. This is a quantitative distinction between symbolic expressions and scientific ones, not a qualitative comparison. It does not follow that a rich symbolic thinking is necessarily pre-scientific or a forerunner to rational expressions. The need to express values in symbolically meaningful formulas is not of necessity a stepping-stone towards a rational science. Nor does this need indicate an inability to reason rationally and/or scientifically. To express concepts by way of symbols is simply another way of expression. The symbols are vehicles whereby it is possible to voice thoughts, experiences and concepts, and to do so intelligibly. When, therefore, the study describes and analyses Zulu thought-patterns and symbols, it does not presuppose that these are inferior to rational and scientific approaches to life. The point of departure is that there is more than one way of expressing life and its circumstances of living.

There are numerous limitations to the study. First, in writing, I have constantly asked myself: "How do Zulu themselves understand this their particular expression? How do *they themselves* explain it?" The emphasis has continually been on the Zulu interpretation of expressions found in their society. This accounts for the sometimes lengthy quotations of discussions with informants and the comparatively small attention paid to interpretations given in ethnographic records. However, ethnographic records have been referred to from time to time, and where similar thought-patterns and symbols have been noted among other Bantu people, particularly Nguni, these have been indicated.

The study addresses itself to a description of thought-patterns and symbols relevant mainly to commoners. Should material descriptive of chiefs, kings and authority have been included, the study would have become unduly large and the handling of the material difficult. There are other limitations also. For only those thought-patterns and symbols which are in the minds of people daily and those which play a significant role in a man's thinking at a crisis in life have been elaborated on. Much could have been added about concepts of the moon, rites of passage, agriculture, fertility and husbandry, but these ideas will have to be dealt with at a later stage.

A third limitation is the temporal aspect. Appreciating the fact that no society is static in the sense that it remains what it has been previously, I have attempted to describe Zulu as they are today. I do not try to account for concepts and thought-patterns which were found previously. But ideas which are relevant today and which were found in Zulu society earlier are taken up, and the historic ethnographic sources noted. It follows that I have not gone out of my way to trace Zulu who still cling keenly to traditional patterns of thought for the purpose of tracing them. Rather, the experts who know and have an overall view of Zulu thinking have been approached to gain information. These informants have included conservative thinkers, e.g. two diviners who had a systematized thinking, and others who had not consciously adopted either Christian modes of life or otherwise become westernized.

Because the study is one which describes Zulu and because emphasis lies on Zulu understanding of their own thought-patterns and symbols, no attempt has been made to relate findings to the wider African context. Judging from earlier records on Zulu it appears that the Lord-of-the-Sky did not play that significant role in Zulu thinking previously that it does today. Similar developments have been noted from elsewhere in Africa and have been elaborated on in various studies. These latter studies have not been taken into account in the present thesis.

Field Work

I was born at Ceza and grew up at Ekuthuleni, at which places my parents were missionaries. So I spoke Zulu from early childhood. Language, when communicating with Zulu-speaking people, has, therefore, not been a problem.

Before attending school my play-mates were Zulu children. With them I was introduced into Zulu society in a very real and natural way. I recollect a great many occasions and incidents which not only fascinated me and remained in my memory, but also have proven to be useful points of departure when, at a later stage in life, I collected material towards a study on Zulu thinking. Ekuthuleni, where my parents were stationed from 1931 to 1947, is situated in the very close vicinity of the royal homesteads of eNthembeni and kwaMabovula, and living there gave me access to knowledge of behaviour towards Zulu royalty and communication with royals. Partly because of close ties with many friends and partly because I am a missionary, a great number of contacts have been made without great effort.

Fieldwork for a thesis was commenced in the Vryheid–Louwsburg–Mahlabathini (including Ceza) area early in 1959 and was concluded in the Mapumulo district in late 1970. While stationed at Rorkes Drift (January 1960–October 1962) many contacts were made with the local population. The presence of Sotho-speaking people in the Nqutu district proved a useful field of observation where Zulu concepts could be studied in contrast with Sotho influence. Frequent visits were made to the eMthonjaneni district, particularly Ekuthuleni and Biyela parishes and their outstations. Working here was like being at home. Much valuable information submitted in the thesis has been collected in the Mapumulo district (October 1962–November 1970, except for ten months absence 1963/1964). The complete Mapumulo district is inhabited by Zulu with the exception of some whites in the Mapumulo village, the Umpumulo parish and hospital, and occasional shopkeepers who are either whites or of Asian background.[11] The present tense used in the study refers to the time when fieldwork was carried out, i.e. January 1959–November 1970.

Recording conversations with people, once trustworthy and cordial relations had been built up, proved to be the best method of obtaining accurate information. In the beginning of collecting material notes were made mainly in notebooks, while, towards the end of the time, when I had acquired a tape-recorder, this was used extensively. Often discussions arose from incidents that I had witnessed. It goes without saying that gaining access to many of these occasions was a time-consuming encounter. Also getting informants to speak freely was not always an easily reached goal, particularly if informants did not feel free to talk because of accompanying friends, or visiting neighbours, or when sentimentally bound information was sought. But personal field-work proved most fruitful, although sometimes tiring and slow in producing results. Recordings were made in Zulu and only very seldom in a European language.

As far as possible, any information concerning rituals gained through accounts given by informants was checked by attending such rituals. It was not that informants were doubted, but their accounts were sometimes idealized. Often they gave very useful points of departure which, when followed up by personal observation, opened wide avenues to underlying thought-patterns.

The use of questionnaires was discarded at an early stage, partly because people were suspicious of them, partly because many who had valuable information found giving a full answer too laborious a task, partly because many questions which arose while conversing with informants never would have appeared on the questionnaire.

Experience soon underlined the need to check and recheck information again and again, thereby testing both accuracy and representativeness of material collected. Information referred to in the study has been sifted in this way. When material has been obtained but not verified, or doubtfully verified, this has been stated. Any material which may be the product of a lively imagination rather than accurate knowledge has not been used, unless it has cast light on other information.

It would be unrealistic to assume that any single person is versed in all knowledge pertaining to rituals, concepts and symbols. Zulu themselves admit this from time to time, saying that they do not know. Diviners sometimes refused to express themselves about medicines and the attached symbols, claiming that herbalists were the ones who knew, and very few people knew much of the doings of the heaven-herds beyond what they saw these men doing when they practiced in the various homesteads or treated people with medicines. But few diviners would confess lack of knowledge about the shades. Again and again I found myself discussing with the specialists in various fields in order to gather as much information from them as possible. Verification of material thus collected would, of necessity, be limited to other specialists within the similar field.

Sometimes informants themselves became assistants in finding the reasons *why* things were done in a particular manner, *why* certain words were used, etc. For evidence soon revealed that although a man was acquainted with procedure in the rituals, i.e. the *hows* were known, and often conservatively adhered to, the underlying dogmas and interpretations of happenings, words and things involved in the happenings, i.e. the *whys*, were not equally well known. I owe much gratitude to many such friends who went out of their way to find out the underlying meanings.

For obvious reasons informants are anonymous, only three allowing me to quote their names. Laduma Madela in fact insisted that he be quoted! Qedizwe Ngema, a traditionalist in the best sense of the word and a very knowledgable informant, most unfortunately is no longer alive.

Some Informants

To give an exhaustive account of informants and people who have been of assistance when collecting material, would become a thesis on people. During the course of the years a great many people have been helpful in many ways, some in connection with some incident which I followed up, their contributions being limited to that particular happening only. Others have proven valuable sources of information during a definite period of time while another group who have had knowledge of a particular area, have been of assistance while working in that area. Others, again, have been excellent informants because of their positions in society, while some, the experts in specific fields, have been people to whom I have returned again and again. It is particularly from among the latter that I would like to introduce a limited number of informants.

a. Laduma Madela has attracted the attention of several scholars, some of whom have given us their findings in writing.[12] It is possible that more will be forthcoming.

Madela is, no doubt, a philosopher who, when one meets him, immediately brings to one's mind the writings of Paul Radin. Madela lives in his own individual and creative world of thoughts, fascinating because they bear witness to vision, imagination and a systemizing of thinking in a remarkable way. Very self-conscious, alert to things happening in his surroundings and equipped with a remarkable memory, Laduma Madela is in one way a traditionalist in a conservative manner, in another a progressive in the sense that nothing new is by-passed as if it were insignificant. He has the ability to ab-

21

sorb various impressions and happenings and relate them to his own particular setting.

It would not be correct to say that Madela's views always are representative of Zulu society. But his thinking and statements are fascinating because they come from a man who is well versed in Zulu history, customs and rituals: a man who at the same time is not only a smith in the traditional sense, but also a heaven-herd and herbalist. He also divines. Madela's views are often coloured by his own creative and imaginative contributions.

In one sense Madela is very eager to share his thinking and views with serious scholars. Sometimes he forces material on one without hesitation. I recall an incident when several people had gathered outside his homestead to seek his assistance. They were allowed to sit and wait for him for several hours while he was engaged with me. After speaking to me, he sent word to the people gathered under some trees that they could return the following day, retired to another hut in the homestead where he drank fermented porridge (*amahewu*), and returned to me to discuss his ideas for another two hours. In another sense he is very secretive. It has, for example, been quite impossible to obtain a full and clear picture of Madela's associations with the local Ceza church and school other than through church and school records. Sometimes he says that he has been taught a little writing at school, on another occasion he claimed that his teacher was *uMvelingqangi's* angel!

b. Qedizwe Ngema lived in the Mapumulo district. Equipped with a lively intellect, Ngema himself desired to know as much as possible. He belonged to the category of people who, had they been given the opportunity of schooling, would have become scholars. With him one could discuss seriously. Learning from Ngema was not, in the first instance, a tapping of a useful source. This would have been against Ngema's personality. To him it was rather a giving and receiving of information. Often our discussions ended with my relating and trying to explain the life-approach of whites and Christians in return for Zulu information Ngema had given me.

Travelling in the car with Ngema was a memorable experience. A perfect gentleman, he would arrive at our meeting-place well ahead of time, and, on each occasion, take his place in the back seat, occupying the front seat only on being asked to do so! He would eagerly follow every movement of the driver, watching what was done to control the vehicle's movement. At the same time he would be describing the country through which we were travelling, pointing out places of historic interest and adding a host of interesting details. Once we stopped at the top of a high hill overlooking the Thugela valley and Zululand on the other side of the river. Ngema pointed out various places in Zululand with great accuracy, described roads to follow to reach these places and adding information about what to expect on arrival there, who to approach, and what to say so as to obtain as much information as possible. I was utterly amazed to learn that in spite of the fact that Ngema had never been north of the Thugela river, he possessed such accurate information not only of places, but also of people living there, their professions and personal inclinations.

c. X lives in his homestead overlooking the uMhlatuze river. Approaching his home and entering it one does not realize that one is in the home of a renowned and honoured ventriloquist diviner, a man of considerable standing. His wives go about their daily duties in much the same way as any Zulu wives would do. There are not many huts in the homestead which would give one the impression of a large family or many kinsmen living together. Neither does the cattle-enclosure indicate any great wealth in cattle. On the other hand, the homestead is always neat and clean, its inhabitants well fed and hence healthier than many neighbours who often suffer because of insufficient food.

X's wealth lies in his knowledge. But gaining access to this wealth proved a tiring and, in the beginning, a hopeless undertaking. Although I had known of him when I was a boy and he accepted me as an old acquaintance, he at first refused any further associations. But with time mutual respect and trust grew, and on my seeking his advice on a number of issues because friends indicated him as an expert, X gradually allowed me into his particular world of thinking. The strenuous test on patience experienced in the beginning of serious studies of Zulu thought-patterns and symbols, turned into a most rewarding contact with a man who not only held a great wealth of information as far as details and their interpretation is concerned, but who also had an overall systematized view. Unselfish with his information, I owe X much gratitude for his patience with me, gracious charm and true Zulu hospitality.

d. Z at eThelezini was another source of much information. His home is surrounded by an atmosphere of awe-inspiring quiet, characteristic of renowned diviners. Contrary to many popular colleagues, Z does not handle medicines other than such as are related to divination. Further, he is one of the few male diviners of standing operating in Zulu society.

Unlike X who is very stable and steady, Z is irritable at times, impulsive and excitable. As with X, building up ties of friendship and mutual trust proved to be a time-consuming effort, although the approach was somewhat different, due mainly to the very different character of Z. X is nearly always down to earth, with a matter-of-fact approach to our deliberations, calm and realistic. Z is emotionally highly strung and, once he could react freely without fear of being embarrassed by my presence, would even cry bitterly. He gave free play to his feelings, sometimes reacting violently, sometimes with great tenderness and personal involvement. With him there is no apathy, callousness, or want of feeling.

With X one gained mainly in discussions. Whether these were related to some witnessed ritual celebration or incident was not important. But with Z the best results were obtained when one could refer to happenings and rituals which, preferably, we both had attended, or matters with which Z was intimately connected. Z often introduced matters himself, indicating their specific values and significant roles. It was he that without much ado, introduced me into the realm of the shades, drawing my attention to a number of details which might otherwise have been missed.

Having made acquaintance with Z is having associated with an intelligent and excited Zulu who, in his divination, made frequent and in my presence amazingly open use of his knowledge. Z was a master at *ukuhlonipha*, particularly when speaking of the shades, and it was a constant source of joy to find that one had understood him correctly! His ability to express himself in figurative language was also a constant source of inspiration and a never-failing reminder that there is always room for increasing one's knowledge in expression, even in the restricted area of a single language. Z also has a thorough command of proverbs—also a cause of anxiety lest one miss the point in discussions, and a cause of further admiration.

e. M at Ekuthuleni represents the progressives of Zulu society. His homestead consists of three square houses roofed with iron and, in the sitting room, there is a ceiling. The home is surrounded by very well worked fields. M sells considerable quantities of maize and other produce from his gardens. His cattle-enclosure is one of the larger in the area and the animals are carefully looked after and much admired. Despite unsuitable climatic conditions M keeps a few sheep for slaughter purposes, looking after these also with great care.

M is a distinguished member of the local community and although his schooling is limited, he is a member of many committees, frequently being chosen chairman, treasurer, or secretary. His ability and his natural air of dignity and authority has focused attention to him.

Although a progressive and a staunch Christian, M is very Zulu, clinging proudly and with great zeal to that which is particularly Zulu. He is ashamed of nothing traditional, without hesitation rejecting that which he thinks bad and pursuing with great diligence that which he regards as useful and good. Being the authority and leader of the community which surrounds him, he has a valuable knowledge of local history, people, and their circumstances of living. His knowledge becomes apparent when one listens to him arguing with people who come to seek his advice. He knows the ins-and-outs of court procedure and is a councillor in the local chief's council with good reason. People desired to have him as the local dip-officer because of his intimate knowledge in matters pertaining to cattle. But M declined, offering his assistance outside the dip and its associations—for M has never been able to convince himself of the usefulness of plunging cattle into a dipping-tank when the ticks could be removed by hand!

f. Three single women, all at Ekuthuleni, deserve an introduction. Two, with limited schooling, nevertheless became teachers and did outstandingly well in their work, gaining not only the confidence of school-inspectors, parents and children, but of the whole community. Of these two ladies another informant said: "It is fortunate that they never married, for their husbands would have had difficult times!" He was referring to their authority and wide experience. The third served in homes for many years and eventually became matron of a boarding institution. From her mother, a dignified lady of a distinguished clan, she inherited the vast amount of knowledge of Zulu etiquette and life approach, as far as possible abiding by it herself and teaching girls at the boarding institution to do so also, applying much to Christian conditions of life. What she could not absorb, she bore within her as information of the pagans. All three women had their own homes, the two teachers living together for considerable lengths of time, especially during holidays. It is from them that I have learnt much, particularly in matters pertaining to women, fertility, and the heavenly princess.

Literature on Zulu

A number of factors drew attention to the Zulu-speaking people at an early stage. A glance at the bibliography of any representative book on Zulu reflects the amount of ethnographic, linguistic, historic and missiological material that is available. I do not propose to give a full evaluation of literature available. The aim of this section is merely to draw attention to some of the significant ethnographic studies.

 a. The earliest accounts on Zulu were those of N. Isaacs, *Travels and Adventures in Eastern Africa*, Vol. I & II (1836) and H. F. Fynn's Diary, edited by J. Stuart and D. McK. Malcolm. A. Gardiner's book, *Narrative of a Journey to the Zoolu Country*, appeared in 1836. Although not directed towards descriptions of the Zulu the publications contain valuable information on Zulu life at the time of writing. Fynn was a pioneer settler, arriving in present-day Durban in 1824. Gardiner's main concern was that of a missionary although he held a civil appointment, and Isaacs traded in Zulu country. The Rev. J. Shooter published *The Kafirs of Natal and the Zulu Country* in 1857, having in mind a book describing Zulu life. The publication contains much valuable information collected both through reading descriptions given by other authors and personal observations.

 b. In 1868 Canon H. Callaway published his first major collection of Zulu material, *Nursery Tales, Traditions and Histories of the Zulus*. Urged by a desire to speak Zulu beyond "a miserable gibberish, composed of anglicised Kafir, and kafirised English and Dutch words, thrown together without rule but the caprice and ignorance of the speaker" (p. i) in order to achieve "communication of mind with mind", he set about to write at the dictation of Zulus. Twelve years sedulous, critical, and inspired writing accumulated into a mass of material, "full of interest to the missionary, the philologist, the ethnologist, and antiquarian, as well as to a large portion of the general public". From it emerged his first collection of Zulu narratives. Callaway was unselfish, and, characteristically, what had started as a study to penetrate the barriers of linguistic communication on a personal level, became a class-book "to teach the English Zulu, or the Zulu English". Hence both the original Zulu texts and an English translation.

 Realizing the wealth of information and significant value in Callaway's writings, the Folk-Lore Society (London) published, in 1870, three previously completed and issued studies from Callaway's pen, *The Religious System of the Amazulu*. Prior to publication the fourth section dealing with "Abatakati; or Medical Magic, and Witchcraft", had been added, both Zulu and an English translation appearing side-by-side as in the first volume.

 c. The name of A. T. Bryant, missionary, linguist, historian, and anthropologist, cannot be bypassed. Born in England, he came to Natal in 1883 at the age of eighteen years. He associated himself with the CMM (Congregation Missionariorum de Mariannhill) brothers at Mariannhill, Pinetown, where he opened the first boarding school for boys in Natal. In 1887 he was ordained priest in Rome and at the age of twenty-two read his first Mass at no less distinguished a place than the high altar of St. Peter's of that city. After spending some years in the Transkei, Bryant returned to the Zulu people, building a mission station on the Ngoye range, near the Indian ocean, between the uMhlatuze and uMlalazi rivers. Here he worked for many years, collecting the vast amount of material which later was to result in important books on Zulu, and eventually lead him to a post as lecturer in Bantu Studies, University of Witwatersrand, in 1920.

 Already in 1903 Bryant established himself as a Zulu linguist when he published his Zulu-English Dictionary. Noting that at the time of publication he had run the boys' hostel at Mariannhill, spent time in Europe and at least three years in the Transkei, and mindful of the wealth of information in the dictionary, one begins to appreciate Bryant's working ability and genius. Beside more than 20 000 entries in the dictionary, there is an introduction which contains a thought-provoking historical description of clans that make up the Zulu nation; here are botanic references and ethnographic details, linguistic and dialectic notes on differences in speech between Zulu of Zululand proper and people living south of the Thugela.

Bryant remained a lecturer in Johannesburg for three years and worked thereafter on an historical study on the Zulu. In 1929 *Olden Times in Zululand and Natal* appeared. Bryant describes the history of clans which constitute the present Zulu nation rather than the history of a nation. This, I suggest, is an important contribution made by Bryant, for although the Zulu speaking peoples were, in theory, a nation already at the time of Shaka, the national sense of togetherness appears to be of later date.

Bryant's major contribution to ethnographic knowledge of the Zulu people is collected in his exhaustive study *The Zulu People,* completed about 1935, but not published until 1949. In this study Bryant reveals his extensive knowledge of Zulu, and, through many comparisons, draws attention to similar findings elsewhere in Africa.

Beside the three studies referred to by Bryant, there are a large number of articles, essays and lectures, both in Zulu and in English. His unpublished writings are to be found in the Killie Campbell Africana Library, Marriott Road, Durban.

d. It was not until 1936 that an overall study on the Zulu people was made available. Before embarking on the ambitious task of describing, with her husband, the Lovedu people of Transvaal *(The Realm of a Rain-Queen)*, Professor Eileen Jensen Krige furnished anthropologists with *The Social System of the Zulus.* No study of the Zulu, particularly anthropological research, can bypass this important contribution. Although the study is a compilation of information found in various books and periodicals and also unpublished material, there is also material which results from Professor Krige's own research. An important section of the book is an extensive description of kinship thought-patterns of the Zulu, which is the particular and exact contribution of Professor Krige herself. Evidence shows the importance of a clear understanding of kinship relationships in society, not only for an evaluation of social relations, but also towards an appreciation of thought-patterns and symbols, which often are closely linked to kinship relationships.

e. Of necessity a lesser known study on Zulu is that of G. Asmus, *Die Zulu.* Asmus arrived in Natal as a missionary from Germany in 1903, serving mainly at two stations, Muden and Georgenau. He retired shortly before the Second World War. Due to the destruction of the book early in the war, before many copies had left the publishers in Essen, Germany, and due, partly, also to linguistic factors, this contribution on Zulu has not received the attention it deserves. Living in isolation on a mission station and with very little comparative material on which to base his studies, Asmus nevertheless succeeded in producing a study which reflects enviable linguistic and anthropological knowledge. Asmus was well grounded in the local tradition and had obtained a total conception of Zulu thought-patterns which indicates an intimate knowledge of the people whom he describes. *Die Zulu* is filled with detail, placed in a setting which makes reading this study fascinating and thought-provoking.

f. A great wealth of detail is to be obtained in *The Collector,* collected and edited by Fr. W. Wanger of the CMM community, Mariannhill, between 1911 and 1913. It is unfortunate that this material is so difficult to obtain due to there being very few copies of *The Collector* available.

g. The Rev. J. E. Norenius, a Swedish missionary who worked among Zulus from 1897 to 1934, wrote several short but important studies, describing Zulu religious ideas, ritual celebrations and concepts. It is unfortunate that Norenius did not write more, and that the little that there is, appeared in a language not known to very many, for no doubt he also had attained considerable insight into Zulu thinking and had gained an overall picture of life-approach at the time he worked among the people.

Definitions

Magic

In anthropological literature the word magic has been used extensively—and unfortunately also misused. If by magic we define, with Ch. Winick, "the techniques of coercion, based on what we would consider false premises, by which persons, usually non-literates, try to obtain practical ends",[13] then we are saying exactly what this study tries not to do. If we associate magic with certain substances, rites and rituals, symbols of people, there may be room for magic in the sense that a certain substance (i.e. magical materia) or an act in ritual (magical act) may become isolated from an intelligent appreciation of symbols, due to changing situations brought about by various pressures on society. Professor Mary Douglas, underlining the communicative aspect of symbols in rites and rituals, appears to differentiate between ritual acts which contain a meaningful and appreciable symbolic interpretation and acts which are magic because they lack interpretation.[14] Adopting this view and relating it to the aim of this study, i.e. to describe intelligibly Zulu thought-patterns and symbolism, the use of the word magic automatically falls away.

Ceremony, Ceremonial and Ritual, Rite

While in Western cultures and among westernized people there may arise doubt between what is a ceremony or a ceremonial act on the one hand, and a specific rite or ritual on the other, because of the role played by faith, the difference in Zulu society is quite clear.

The English words ceremony and ceremonial are used to translate the Zulu term *isiko.* An *isiko* is a conventional and traditional action which does not of necessity involve religious engagement. Behind *amasiko* (plural form) stand conventional forms of behaviour, not necessarily sanctioned by the shades. Ceremony expresses sentimental and emotional feelings, and is frequently found together with rites and various ritual celebrations. At e.g. marriages, puberty rites, birth, burials, and other occasions of celebration, some acts are ceremonial, others are ritual.

Ritual refers to celebrations which aim at a communion with the shades. The various rites of the complete ritual are religious in content and conservatively sanctioned by both age and the shades with whom communion is sought: while ceremony is a conventional and sometimes an elaborate form of voicing one's feelings, ritual aims at a communion with the shades which is efficacious.[15]

Although, in theory, the distinction between that which is ceremonial and that which is ritual is clear, in practice a great amount of overlapping must be allowed for. Zulu do not emphasize a distinction in practice between that which is religious and that which may be described as secular. To quote an informant: "What is there that is not religious? Has not God made everything?"

Sacrifice, Offering and Communion

Zulu are explicit that there is no *worship* of the shades in the sense that there is a veneration of them. If there is a worship, then it is the veneration of the Lord-of-the-Sky. But with the shades there is an association, a togetherness, which takes the honour and respect of seniors for granted but allows for intimacy and an atmosphere of mutual trust as expressed and experienced in the sharing of food. This togetherness of the lineage, those beyond the rite of passage of departure from the living with their survivors, is, to quote J. Kenyatta: "communion with ancestors".[16]

I maintain that there is no worship of the shades, neither is prayer addressed to them. On the other hand there is a speaking (*ukuthetha*) to them, a "telling them everything". Likewise, if sacrifice and offering assume a transcendental dimension, neither are terms applicable to Zulu thought-patterns relating to the shades. If, however, sacrifice and offering describe gifts of food (beer and meat in particular) that are given to the shades, gifts such as are given by juniors to seniors in the lineage, and the food shared by seniors and juniors, then sacrifice and offering are acceptable. This meaning is expressed here by the word *communion*.

Symbol

A symbol is that which represents and/or typifies another thing, action or sound. A symbol is more than a sign, for it involves associations. When men use symbols, they operate with articles, acts, colours and sounds in a given setting/context which are meant to be associated with that which they represent and/or typify, thereby becoming meaningful to those who feel, see, hear and/or act in the ritual containing the symbol.

There is an intentional generosity attached to the use of symbols which excites the imagination of the onlooker (or feeler, hearer, participant), giving room for wider experiences and sensations than those expressed in words. The experiences and sensations which arise in the minds of men will, of necessity, be related to the systematic thought-pattern and the particular context in which the symbol is used, if these symbols are to be meaningful. Allowing for flexibility, variations in emphasis and even differences of opinion in reactions towards symbols—for humans are not automatons—thought-patterns governing a particular context are systematized sufficiently to make symbols intelligible and pregnant.

Elaborating on relationships between a symbol and its interpretation, two points require to be underlined. Firstly, the role of the individual. It is beyond doubt that symbols are the collective representational characteristics of a given society. But it is equally true that it is the persons of that society who express themselves, either as individuals or members of groups, through symbols. It is natural that the knowledge which the persons have pertaining to the symbols and their interpretation varies. This allows for the experts in any given context who have a fuller knowledge of the symbols of that context and their use, as well as the experiences and sensations they are expected to arouse. It also allows for such as are not at all exact in knowledge, and, avoiding the embarrassment of not knowing, explain symbols by way of tradition: "It has always been done like this."

Secondly, the role of the symbol in relation to the particular context requires attention. Sometimes similar things are symbols with different meanings in different settings. Heaven-herds sometimes use stones when preparing medicines to protect homesteads against violent storms. The blackness of the stones is associated with the dark of storm-clouds, and the spark brought by throwing one dark stone against another is a symbol of lightning. But at burials stones are placed in, and sometimes on, the grave because "dead people are like stones". In both cases stones are used, and I have witnessed burials when the same type of stone was used in the funeral as those which a local heaven-herd claimed he used when preparing medicines. But in the two contexts the symbolism of the stone was different.[17]

On the other hand, symbols remain relatively similar within a given setting. If at funerals stones are not available, sods of earth are used to replace the stones. In the Mapumulo area I saw chips from clay vessels used to replace the stones and informants made it clear that the corpse was like the hard clay of the vessel; this in turn was associated with stones.

Shades, Elders, Seniors and Survivors

The term ancestor is avoided in the study and the word shade used instead. One reason for not using the word ancestor is that the English idiom suggests ascendants who are dead (according to Western concepts) and, as a result, there is a distance between them and the living. There is, in other words, a separateness between the living and the dead. This is not descriptive of Zulu concepts which, as the study will be showing, assume a very close and intimate relationship and association within the lineage between the departed and their survivors. To quote an informant: "My father is departed, but he is," the idea being that the father is present and active although he is no longer living as the speaker was.

Professor Mbiti speaks of "the living dead".[18] The terminology is challenging insofar that the departed are expressed as living realities, albeit they no longer associate with those still living on the earth's surface. But the combination of the extremes, living and dead, seems exaggerated, and hence the avoidance of this idiom also.

Describing Nyakyusa, Professor Monica Wilson speaks of "senior relatives, living and dead", "senior kinsmen, living and dead", and "the cult of senior relatives".[19] By so doing, she bridges the gap between the departed and the living seniors. This approach to Nyakyusa thought-patterns is valid also among Zulu, for also among the latter the distance between the departed and the living is not great at all, and, sometimes, non-existent. Further, the departed are felt to be as real as the living senior relatives. No Zulu doubts that the shades exist—in dreams, various manifestations, omens, they are both seen and experienced.

But as there nevertheless is a difference between the foetus and the born child, between the bride and the married woman, between the mother and the childless, the married and the widow/er, so there is a difference between the living (*abaphilayo*) and the departed. To mark this difference the term shade is used to describe those who no longer in humanly visible forms are seniors in their lineage.

The term senior refers to elder kinsmen still living in the lineage who, because of their status and age, are the ones that are the officiants at ritual celebrations. Because Zulu are patrilineal, seniors of a homestead will of necessity be male kinsmen.

The word elder refers to those who act as advisors to seniors and/or chiefs, and merit this particular position either because of age, ability or, sometimes, profession.

Survivors, in contrast to the shades, are those who have not yet departed life on earth, i.e. the humanly living members of a particular lineage.

Traditional, Traditionalist and Pagan

The terms are used to describe people who to a greater extent than others live in forms of life which have evolved in a Zulu setting. The idioms do not exclude Western (and sometimes Asian) influence. But they do assume that the people concerned are neither schooled or members of Christian congregations. The emphasis lies in their differing from Zulu who have attended school, or who consciously have adopted Westernized patterns of living, or who are Christians. There is emphatically no classification of traditionalists and pagans as inferior to or less advanced than any other member of society. The words merely describe those who rigidly and conservatively have tried to adhere to that which traditionally has been Zulu.

Notes

[1] Turner, V. W., *The Drums of Affliction; The Forest of Symbols;* 'Ritual Symbolism among the Ndembu'.
[2] See bibliography for Monica Wilson's contributions.
[3] Beidelman, T. O., 'Pig (Guluwe): an essay on Ngulu sexual symbolism and ceremony'; 'Right and Left among the Kaguru: a note on symbolic classification'; 'Three Tales of the Living and the Dead'.
[4] Douglas, Mary, 'Social and Religious Symbolism of the Lele of the Kasai'; 'Animals in Lele Religious Symbolism'; 'The Lele of Kasai'.
[5] Leinhardt, G., *Divinity and Experience.*
[6] Griaule, M., *Conversations with Ogotemmeli.*
[7] Richards, Audrey, *Chisungu* (London 1956).
[8] Rigby, P., 'Dual Symbolic Classification among the Gogo of Central Tanzania'; 'Some Gogo Rituals of Purification'.
[9] White, C. M. N., *Elements in Luvale Beliefs and Rituals.* See further studies in bibliography.
[10] Swantz, Marja-Liisa, *Ritual and Symbol in Transitional Zaramo Society.*
[11] For a sociological survey of the Mapumulo district see Berglund, A.-I., *Church and Cultural Change in a Zulu Tribal Community* (Lux Mundi No. 3, Pretoria).

[12] Bodenstein, W. & Raum, O. F., 'A Present Day Zulu Philosopher'; Schlosser, Katesa, 'Die Ahnen des Blitz-zauberers Laduma Madela'; 'Zulu Mythology as Told and Illustrated by the Zulu Lightning Doctor Laduma Madela'; *Wandgemälde des Blitz-Zauberers Laduma Madela.*

[13] Winick, Ch., *Dictionary of Anthropology,* p. 334. See, however, a different approach in G. & Monica Wilson, *The Analysis of Social Change,* pp. 72–72 and 88–95.

[14] Douglas, Mary, *Purity and Danger,* pp. 22 f. and 58–72.

[15] Wilson, G., 'Nyakyusa Conventions of Burial'. See also Evans-Pritchard, E. E., *Witchcraft, Oracles and Magic among the Azande,* p. 12.

[16] Kenyatta, J., *Facing Mount Kenya: The Tribal Life of the Gikuyu,* pp. 265–268.

[17] Turner, V., *The Drums of Affliction,* p. 2, thought-provokingly argues in terms of symbols as "storage units" in which are stored a maximum capacity of information. Hence, he continues, the total significance of a symbol is only gained once it has been viewed from each ritual context in which it is found. Turner sees three levels of interpretation: i) an exegetical, given by the participants themselves, ii) an operational which is drawn from the context in which the symbol is found, and iii) the positional meaning, which is obtained by way of comparisons (Turner, *Ritual Symbolism among the Ndembu,* pp. 82 f.). The three levels of interpretation suggested by Turner have not been distinguished from each other in this study, although his approach to the questions raised in understanding symbols has been borne in mind in the latter part of the field study, in order to obtain that maximum capacity of information that symbols no doubt often represent.

[18] Mbiti, J., *African Religion and Philosophy.*

[19] Wilson, Monica, *Rituals of Kinship among the Nyakyusa,* p. 3 and p. 226.

Chapter II

Divinities

The aim of this chapter is to describe Zulu concepts of sky deities. It will also discuss rituals associated with the deities.

The Lord-of-the-Sky

In the following the idiom Lord-of-the-Sky will be used as a translation of the Zulu term *iNkosi yaphezulu* or *iNkosi yezulu.*

Reading studies by Callaway[1] one is given the impression that Zulu of his time made no clear distinction between a sky divinity and the shades. However, modern Zulu are emphatic in expressing a very clear distinction between the Lord-of-the-Sky and the shades.

INkosi yaphezulu is said to live in the sky which, in the minds of many Zulu is not very much further above the clouds. "When the clouds come low, then the sky is coming down over us. Sometimes it is fearful. Sometimes it is good. It (the sky) moves up and down as he wishes it to move." Another said: "When the clouds are high up, then the sky is far away. When the clouds come low, then the sky is low. This time is awesome because he (the Lord-of-the-Sky) is close. Then people should be indoors and keep quiet. The great one is near."

The sky is believed to be a rock, blue in colour, which stretches from the one end of the flat surface of the earth to the other. The great vault of rock rests on the edges of the earth, while the earth itself, being a flat surface, is held up by four bulls, "carrying the earth on their horns. When one of them shakes its head, then the earth also shakes." This is how earthquakes are accounted for.[2]

The sky is above the sun and the moon. Both the sun and the moon move "along their paths underneath the floor of the sky. They do not reach up to the sky because they must shine on the earth only."

Zulu thought-patterns describe the sky as having perpetual light and that the stars are small holes in the floor of the sky through which the light filters through at night. An old Zulu woman described the stars thus: "When it has rained and the cattle are driven to the grazing grounds, they sometimes tramp through the mud and their feet go through the floor of the sky. Then the light comes through." Asked to comment on falling stars, she said that these were caused by the cattle being in a hurry when running to the grazing and thereby dragging the foot which had trodden through the mud. "That is the time when this thing is seen. The light is seen before the mud fills in again. So it is clear that *iNkosi* there has cattle." The statement about the cattle was added as evidence to her belief that there indeed is life in the sky. "How else could there be movements there if there be no life in the sky?" She described the Milky Way as being the main entrance to the cattle-enclosure.

Because the heaven is the dwelling place of the Lord-of-the-Sky one must not point at the sky. "Not even my child points at me. How can we point at the greatest one?" If reference is made to the sky, one can indicate it by lifting one's eyes or by speaking indirectly of it. If circumstances force one to do so, one points at the sky with the right hand fist, the tumb enclosed in the fingers.

The Lord-of-the-Sky and Creation

In Zulu society there are various creation narratives. The following was recorded when a member of the royal clan related the clan- and national name Zulu to the sky, *izulu*. The issue being discussed at the time was the question of the origin of the clan-name Zulu and the praise-name *abaNtwana* (lit. children) of this particular clan.

"It so happened that when *uMvelingqangi* was sitting outside his hut, it was reported to him that a certain young man been mischievous in that he had been riding the favourite white ox of *iNkosi*. Being tired of complaints about this man, *iNkosi* decided to send him down to earth so that he would not cause trouble in the sky any more. The young man was brought before *iNkosi*. He (*iNkosi*) ordered that a hole be opened in the floor (of the sky). Then *iNkosi* himself tied *ithumbu* (lit. intestine) around the waist of the man. He was lowered to the earth through the opening. When he came onto the earth he looked around. He saw all the things that were there. But he was still tied to the cord (lit. navel cord, *inkhaba*). He took a reed nearby and cut off the cord. He found himself being free, the cord merely hanging down from his waist. After one month (lit. one moon) *iNkosi* said: 'How is that young man living there on the earth?' So the hole was opened again. He (*iNkosi*) looked to see where the man was. He saw him lying under *ukhova* (banana plant), being very thin and weak. He was troubled, seeing his child thus. He said: 'What is it with my son? Was there no food and no water (for him on earth)? Why does my son appear in this state, as if he is suffering?' Then *iNkosi* remembered that the man was still young and alone, and he said: 'Now I understand the ailment of the child. He is lonely, having nobody. I shall give him somebody, so that all may see that I, being the father, is the one that gave my son a wife that she may live with him.' So he called upon the most beautiful girl in the sky, saying: 'Today you must leave this place and go to another place and live with your man, so that he may have somebody (with him) who will make him happy.' So he took the cord again, tied it around the waist of the maiden and lowered her down to the earth through the hole in the sky. She came down on the earth. She stood up on her feet and walked close to the banana-plant. The young man woke up and was very much amazed to see such a beautiful maiden. He said: 'Surely, I have never seen anybody so fair since I came to this place. It must be my father that gave me this maiden because who else can give such beautiful gifts?' Then he took a reed again and cut off the cord from the stomach of the maiden, freeing her from the cord. *INkosi* returned the cord into heaven and closed the hole in the sky so that they (the people on earth) could not look up into heaven, nor the people there look down on them, seeing the thing that they did in that they multiplied. That is how people came from the sky to the earth. Furthermore, that is why there are known as *amaZulu*. It is because they came from that place (i.e. the sky)."

Besides forming a logical setting to the praise-name *abaNtwana*, the narrative contains several elements of interest. Firstly, it offers a divine origin of the Zulu clan which, as history shows, became the royal clan of the Zulu nation. Secondly, the cord, associated with the intestine and hence also with the navel, is cut with a reed in both instances. The reed as an instrument for separating mother and child occurs again and again in Zulu thought-patterns. Again, there is the more generally known creation narrative which describes men as coming out of reeds. It may be worthy of note in this connection that the heaven-herds have a whistle made of reed which they use when driving off lightning and hail. The fact that the young man was sleeping underneath a banana-plant is also noteworthy. For it is evident that the banana fruit and the plant itself is playing increasingly important roles in fertility rites and healing in terms of treating the childless.

Bryant,[3] Callaway,[4] J. W. Colenso,[5] C. M. Doke and B. W. Vilakazi,[6] Gardiner,[7] and D. Leslie[8] all agree that the name of the Lord-of-the-Sky, *uMvelingqangi*, is a word with roots in *vela* (come forth, appear, come into view), and *nqangi* (the first, the origin). Yet, I suggest, that their interpretations of the latter word falls short of an essential understanding of the term. *Nqangi*, as is correctly pointed out by Bryant[9] and Doke–Vilakazi,[10] refers to the first-born of twins. "It is not simply the first one. It is always the first one of two which are twins," said one informant. Continuing on this issue he said: "The sky and the earth always go together. They are one, but the one is above the other. The sky is the first-born (of the two), but they are the same kind. That is why the one that lives in the sky is called the first-born of twins. He is the first to come forth. Then came the earth. They belong together. They have their children. They are men (*abaNtu*)." Another informant said: "You cannot speak of the sky without thinking of the earth. The sky stands on the earth at the uttermost ends. If there is no earth, then there would not be a sky. There would be simply a great falling, because there is nothing underneath. So that is the reason why they belong together. They are the same age, but the sky came first and the earth second. That is why he is above and the earth below. They belong together like twins belong together, coming from one mother."

UMvelingqangi is without exception referred to as masculine. Suggesting that the Lord-of-the-Sky is a woman caused amazement among informants. But suggesting that the earth is feminine brought about positive reactions, the diviner at eThelezini saying that "the earth is a mother". Laduma Madela called the sky and the earth "husband and wife. Is it not from the sky that men came in that *iNkosi* there is the one who is the father, producing people? Where do men get their food? Is it not from the earth? So it is clear that one is the husband and the other the wife". A little later in our conversation he argued thus: "The sky is like a husband because the sky is above the earth. They are not only twins. Yes, they are twins, but they are also husband and wife. We call them twins because we do not know which one is the more important. If we say twins, then we do not say that one is greater than the other. But they are different. It is like humans. The one is this way. The other is another way. But they have their similarities."

The Lord-of-the-Sky and the Shades

Zulu are emphatic that the Lord-of-the-Sky is not a shade.[11] A man in the Mapumulo district said: "The shades are underneath (the earth). But *uMvelingqangi* is in the sky. They know each other, the shades bowing and praying on behalf of their children before the face of *iNkosi yezulu*. But they are not one and the same. They have each their place. It is like you and I. You live at Umpumulo and I live at N. We know each other, but we look different and we live in different places." Another informant said: "The shades are people. They are of us. One day we will be shades, living that life of the shades. The shades have their work to do, like all other people have their work to do. But *uMvelingqangi* is not a man. He is the heaven. Have you ever seen the heaven in a dream? If you have, then tell me what you saw, so that I also may know what the sky looks like inside. I have never heard a man who has seen *iNkosi* as we see the shades."[12] A third informant, with whom I replaced the name *uMvelingqangi* with *idlozi* (shade), said: "Why do you continually confuse things? They are two different ones, as I have been saying. The one is in heaven. The others are just here with us. You must not confuse things and bring about misunderstandings. That just brings about trouble."

It is true that also the shades are addressed with the title *iNkosi*. If used in the singular it is applied either to some person known by those to whom one is speaking or otherwise clearly defined. "Otherwise we think of the sky." But used in the plural without specification, the term is applicable to the shades.[13] "We always speak of them as *amaKhosi* (pl.) because a shade is not alone. When we speak to them, we always speak to them together, knowing that they are together as we always are together. There is not one shade and then another and another, in ones. They are together. That is why we say *amaKhosi*, not *iNkosi*."

Modern Zulu make their thinking clear when they refer to the Lord-of-the-Sky as *iNkosi yamaKhosi* (Lord of Lords). An informant said: "A shade cannot be *iNkosi yamaKhosi*. This is only one—he that is above. But of course today things have changed. Now the great people from Pretoria and Pietermaritzburg (national and provincial capitals of South Africa resp. Natal) are called *Nkosi yamaKhosi*. But this is not Zulu. It is to please them and make them feel happy. That is why they are called this name."[14]

The Praise-Names of the Lord-of-the-Sky

To *iNkosi yezulu* are attached a number of praise-names, each descriptive of some particular characteristic which one wishes to emphasize when using the praise-name.

Very common are the praise-names *uMdali* and *uMenzi*, both referring to origin and creation. "When we say that he is *uMdali* and *uMenzi*, we say that he is the source of everything. From him came everything, even the animals." Closely associated with these is the name *uHlanga*, meaning reed. No traditionalist Zulu doubts that the Lord-of-the-Sky caused a reed to bring forth man and beast as is recorded in popular Zulu creation narratives.[15] An old woman said: "He (the Lord-of-the-Sky) is the father of all things because it is he who brought them forth from the reed. The earth is the mother on which the reeds were found, but he is the one that is the father, putting them there. That is why he is *uHlanga,* being *uhlanga* (origin) of every-thing." Neither Bryant nor Doke–Vilakazi mention these praise-names in their dictionaries.

Alice Werner mentions the praise-names *Qamata* and *Luqwitela.*[16] Neither of the words appear to be known today, many informants claiming that the terms are not Zulu. Neither Bryant nor Doke–Vilakazi mention either of them.

As the praise-name *iNkosi* in its plural form is applicable to the shades, so is also the term *Nkulunkulu* applicable to both the Lord-of-the-Sky and to the shades. It can refer to both the Lord-of-the-Sky, a particular shade, or even an old person. "When we say *Nkulunkulu* we do not only think of the shades. Today when people use this word, then we think of the one who is above. He is *uNkulunkulu.* But if a man is speaking of his fathers, then he says *oNkulunkulu.* Then it is known that he is speaking of his fathers. But *uNkulunkulu* is the one above. He is the same one as is worshipped in the church."[17]

While the term *Nkulunkulu* encompasses an atmosphere of antiquity and age, the priority sense of the Lord-of-the-Sky is emphasized by his praise-names *uMpande* and *uNsondo.* Both refer to the origin, but in different as-pects. While *uMpande,* which is formed from the stem of the word meaning root, underlines the aspect of originality in that "no tree can live without roots", so *uNsondo* gives the notion of everlastingness. "The name *uMpande* causes us to think of seeds and of growth. If you observe all things, you will see that it is always the root that comes first from the seed, then the stem and the branches. But first it is the root. This is true of all seeds. So that is why we speak of him in the sky as the one that is like the root that comes first."

uNsondo implies one whose actions are repeated again and again, the ac-tions always being of positive and good attributes. "*uNsondo* is like a wheel which is returning to its starting place and then repeats again. This is what we speak of when we call him *uNsondo.* We say that he repeats good things again and again." A particularly well built man or a beautiful woman are spoken of as "a person of *uNsondo,* because the creator has repeated a beautiful thing again". Another informant suggested that if a hunter returns with meat, then the fortune in hunting is attributed to *uNsondo.*[18]

The most common praise-names of the Lord-of-the-Sky are *uSomandla* and *uMninimandla,* both implying almightiness, having all power. "He has all power. He can do what he wishes. Nobody can do what he does. That is why we call him *uSomandla.*" Another informant said: "We call him *uSomandla* because he has all the power. If a man wants power and cannot get it from the shades or from medicines, then he can obtain it from the one above only, if he is willing (to give it to him). He is very powerful, far more powerful than even the shades or medicines. Indeed, we say that the shades have pow-er. But there is a place where they also are defeated and cannot do what they may like to do. Then he is the only one that has greater power than they." Of some forty instances when the Lord-of-the-Sky was the topic of discussion, no less than twenty-eight informants referred to him as either *uSomandla* or *uMninimandla.* The figures give some indication of Zulu thought-patterns re-lated to the Lord-of-the-Sky.

In Zulu thinking power, *amandla,* is related to wisdom and knowledge. To these there are two approaches. Firstly, they are related to a particular ability given to a specific clan, i.e. those who are the iron-workers as are *ama-Shezi*, the *Nzuza* clan having the particular ability of preparing men for warfare, while rain-makers were of the *Ntlangwini* clan. Secondly, there is the concept of *ukuhlakanipha*, cleverness or profound wisdom, which is regarded as a special gift to a particular person of any clan and not necessarily limited to specific tasks. Informants agree that both kinds of knowledge and wisdom "come from above". They are referred to as *ukuphiwa* (to be given), while being abnormally foolish is spoken of as *ukuncitshwa*, to be denied. "It is *uSomandla* who sees what he wants to do with people. Some are given, others are denied. We do not know why he does this, but it is clear that it is he that works with men in this way. Some are given ability (*mandla*) to do certain things, others are given nothing."

Sometimes the shades are looked upon as intermediaries between the Lord-of-the-Sky and men, passing on knowledge from *uSomandla* to humans. A wife of a particularly knowledgeable informant said of her husband's knowledge: "He gets it (the knowledge) from them (the shades). They see things that we do not see. When a person (*umuntu*) is a shade, then he has left *isidumbu* (physical body) behind. Shades go everywhere, even to that place. (She lifted her eyes respectfully towards the sky.) They come before him. They kneel before his countenance, asking him the things they have in mind in a respectful voice. When they have heard (his reply) they depart from his presence and return to their place. They give the knowledge to their children in a dream or a vision. That is how clever people get their knowledge. It is given to them by the shades. But they fetch it from him who is in the sky."

Bryant,[19] Doke–Vilakazi[20] and Norenius[21] mention the praise-name *uGuqabadele*, meaning he who stoops and they are satisfied. Informants claim that this name has become popular since the arrival of missionaries, old people saying that in their childhood it was not known. Although not commonly used today, it is certainly known among Zulu, particularly among Christians. On the other hand, the praise-name *iSando sezwe* (the earth's pillar) recorded by Norenius,[22] is known among old people. A very old informant at Louwsburg (estimated age about ninety-five years) said that this name was commonly used in his childhood, when reference was made to the Lord-of-the-Sky. It is seldom heard today.

The Lord-of-the-Sky, Thunder and Lightning

Without exception Zulu attribute thunder to the Lord-of-the-Sky. Distinction is made between two types of thunder, one said to be male, *elenduna,* and the other female, *elesifazane.*[23]

Male thunder is characterised by long, drawn-out and deep thunder without lightning and hail. It is generally heard at some distance as a murmuring sound, becoming increasingly loud as it approaches. This kind of thunder is not feared, although looked upon with awe and respect. "We do not fear it with trembling knees because we know it. It brings only rain and will not bring something bad."

Elenduna is spoken of as "the playing of the sky". "When we say that *iNkosi* is playing, we wish to say that he is in a jocular mood. It is the same as with a man when he has decided to slaughter or do something good in his homestead. That is why it is called playing . . . It is like a man who has decided to do something good because he becomes very boastful, walking about everywhere in the home and speaking loudly all the time because he has made up his mind and knows that the people are happy. There is going to be meat. *iNkosi* and the man are the same in that they have made good decisions. The Lord-of-the-Sky had decided to give us rain. That is the cause of his playing."

An informant at Ekuthuleni gave the following description of this kind of thunder: "When we hear this thunder we say in our hearts: 'Today we hear the sky of *Phunga* and *Mageba,* the sky of *Shaka* and *Sitheku* and *Nkanthini.*' It is clear that they (the shades of the royal people enumerated) have spoken for us in that they have seen the drought in the land of their children. So now the sky will open its containers and let its daughters descend on us in that rain falls. 'The sky is good this year because he (the Lord-of-the-Sky) is just making noise and not destroying.' That is what is said that year. They say it because there is just noise and no lightning and hail."

The second category of thunder is referred to as *elesifazane* and described as being sudden and cracking thunder, accompanied by forked lightning and very heavy rainfall, often with hail. Informants say that forked lightning and subsequent sudden cracks of thunder is like "the tongue of an angry woman who speaks frightful things, saying unexpectedly things you did not think would be said by her. But the woman speaks in this manner because she is angry. Anger causes people to speak evil, smiting here and there with their tongues."

Sudden and violent storms are attributed to the Lord-of-the-Sky's bad temper or his anger. "When he appears in this way, then it is fearful because he is angry. He desires to destroy somewhere. Sometimes he comes to that one whom he wants, sometimes he is like an angry man who simply destroys everywhere. So where there has been this violent thunder, somewhere you will hear of some evil. Sometimes among people, sometimes among the fields, sometimes among the animals. Somewhere lightning will have caused damage."

Other informants say that after violent storms there will follow a time of intense heat and drought. They say that this is what can be expected of women who are in the stage of life when they cannot bear any more children. "They look back at what was, seeing their sons and their daughters growing up. Then they remember the pains when giving birth and also the sweetness of the children. They remember this and desire very much to give birth again. The heat in them becomes fearful. But their striving for children does not help. The time (of child-bearing) is past. So it is with this thunder which we say is like women. We say that it is like a woman because it makes much noise and shows great heat, but it brings no rain. That is the saying of people pertaining to this heat and drought."

Lightning is claimed to be a bird, *inyoni yezulu,* sent to the earth by the Lord-of-the-Sky. Others say that lightning is fire, but that the fire is brought to the earth by the bird. A third view is that the bird is fire, but as flames of fire have different shapes, so "the fire that comes from above is in the shape of a bird". Some people, especially south of the Thugela, claim that the name of the bird is *iMpundulu.* Doke–Vilakazi say that it is a "bird supposed to be used by women in witchcraft".[24] Bryant does not appear to mention it.

A man at Rorkes Drift whose home had been struck by lightning claimed that he had seen lightning come into the hut where he and the family were gathered. He described it thus: "We were all in the house when suddenly the door was flung open and lightning came in, taking this one and that one. All fell to the ground, but I stood up because of the medicines I had taken and desiring to defend the home with the medicines. I was holding them in my hand. So I stood up. Looking, I saw the thing. It was fearful to see and moved very quickly. But I saw it clearly. It was a bird. The feathers were white, burning. The beak and the legs were red with fire, and the tail was something else, like burning green or like the colour of the sky. It ran quickly, saying nothing, simply snatching those whom it took. Then it touched the grass with its fire. It vanished through the door again. When it had left, there was one who shouted, so we all ran out of the hut except those whom it had taken." (An old woman and two children were killed by lightning on this particular occasion. They were referred to as having been taken by the lightning.)[25] Informants agree that the description given me by the man at Rorkes Drift is a true description of "this fearful thing". Other friends have said that the bird is known to be very fat "because there is much food in that place from where it comes". Others say that the bird is not small, "like a hen, but tall like a stork", others again adding that it is always sent when it comes.

Inyoni yezulu is referred to as a hen. Sometimes it comes down to earth to lay its eggs. "It is not always looking for somebody. But we do not know its reason for coming, so we are always afraid when we see it." When coming to lay its eggs, it sweeps down over the earth, and in order to stop its speed it digs up a furrow in the earth. "Where the furrow ends, there its eggs will be found." Forked lightning is said to be occasions when the bird intends laying eggs and in order to confuse the heaven-herds who seek the eggs, the bird "dives down this way and that, so that they do not find the eggs, not knowing where it (the bird) came down".

Laduma Madela of Ceza claims that he once not only got hold of the eggs, but actually killed the bird itself and used its fat in his work as a heaven-herd. He described it thus: "When I saw the clouds of the bird coming, I climbed up Ceza mountain and waited there. The bird knew that I was there. I had told *uMvelingqangi* that I was to meet it there. So it flew this way and that, going up and down, and looking for a way to deceive me. But the egg was pressing, so at last it came down. When it stopped at the end of the furrow, then it just sat down for a short while. It laid three eggs. When it laid the third egg, I was on it with this stick (he held up a short stick, white in colour with a small knob (of brass) at one end and used when warding off lightning and storms. It is possible that the stick was a branch of *umVithi*, Maerua angolensis, and referred to by Doke–Vilakazi as *umuNka*[26]) and beating it on the head and everywhere until it fell down. Then I cut its throat so that the blood might come out on top of the hill, knowing that other birds would come to look for their friend who did not return. Then it (the bird) became cool. When it was cold I went home with it. I carried it in this bag." He produced a plastic bag which appeared to have contained chemical fertilizer previously. Madela claimed that he kept the bag for similar purposes in the future and two reasons were given for his choice of bag. Firstly, the bag did not leak. This was important, for nothing of the bird should be lost on the way and no blood should fall elsewhere other than on the mountain or in his hut. Secondly, the bag was white—a detail of importance in this particular case. Madela was emphatic that no other bag than a white one could be used. "How can you carry the thing from the sky in another bag than a white one? Or do you wish to draw evil upon yourself?"

Two traditions account for the fear of lightning. "It happened that when *uSomandla* was angry with the children of men and wished to punish them, he said: 'I shall send fire on them.' So he sent the bird of fire from the sky onto the children of men and whomever the bird touched was taken. Sending the bird, he said to it: 'Go to the earth and burn the homestead of so-and-so. They have vexed me with a certain thing. Strike down on the houses and burn them! Carry away those that are inside so that they do not continue living!' The bird departed. It did the thing, burning and taking away the people. So even today, when this thing happens we fear very much saying: 'What have we done that has caused anger? Who is the person who brings calamity over us? Would it be that the bird takes only those that do wickedness, leaving the others to live.' That is what people say about this thing."

The second narrative is thus: "When *izulu* wishes to have a human, then he (the Lord-of-the-Sky) calls his servant. It is the bird. He says to it: 'Today you are to go to such-and-such a place and fetch so-and-so for me, taking that person from that place and bringing him here.' So the bird prepares to go from the sky to that place and fetch whomever the *iNkosi* wants to come there. The bird itself is fearful to see. It cannot be seen lest the one who sees it dies, or has medicines so that he is strong. So the bird hides in the great clouds that are known as the clouds of thunder. When we see these clouds, the ones that are filled with power and come as if they were aiming at a certain place, then we say in our hearts: 'Who can it be this time? O, that it not be somebody just here nearby!' We prepare very thoroughly, doing everything so that the bird does not see the place or feel attracted to us. We say in our hearts: '*Nkulunkulu,* let it be somebody other than us whom the sky wants!' We say this to the shades. We trust them that they will help us in this danger. We say it not knowing what will happen. To be fetched is a fearful thing. We try to prevent this thing happening by doing all those things that we are told must be done. It is a fearful encounter to come before the Lord there in the sky. The one that goes there does not return. This is the reason of fear, because we have never seen anybody returning from there."

As soldiers who were killed in battle were not brought home to be buried, so a man struck by lightning must not be buried in the vicinity of the homestead. "He will never become a shade, so he has no room with us any more. He is somewhere else." He should be buried in damp earth "so that the fire in him may cool and the body become cold seeing that the breath has left him". If at all possible, a heaven-herd should bury the corpse, thus enabling the relatives of the dead to avoid touching the body. This is regarded as dangerous and heaven-herds claim that it can bring about insanity.

The body is not doubled up in the embryo position, but stretched out. Explaining this, an informant said: "In the past when a king was approached, he was approached by people crawling on their stomach. When people spoke to him, or he spoke, they would lie on the stomach and not look at him. But if it was dark in the house they would role over and lie on the back, if the king spoke for a long time. The person would merely lie there, saying nothing but agreeing to everything that was said by the king. So also a person that is taken by *iNkosi* in the sky. He must be stretched out as a sign of respect to the king who has called him." Suggesting that the corpse then ought to be buried up-side-down, the face turned toward the bottom of the grave, my informant reacted: "No, a grave is a dark house. So he can lie on his back, lying as whites do when they are buried."

The corpse is buried in the dress worn by the deceased when he was struck by lightning, without coffin or other wrapping. Burial in red soil must be avoided at all costs. "Red earth is hot. It makes the man even hotter. Then he will simply burn and there will be no rainfall." In one instance recorded (Dundee and Nqutu area), three attempts to find a suitable graveplace in the vicinity of a small stream were made. On two occasions red earth was reached before the grave was deep enough for interment. The body is not buried deeper than that the right arm of the corpse can be raised and kept in position with earth, the forefinger allowed to stick out of the earth "so that people may see where he has gone". Expressing amazement over the fact that the corpse actually pointed with the finger in the direction that the deceased is believed to have gone, I was told that "his finger is merely like a road sign. He is just pointing out a direction. He is not pointing at the king. He is merely showing where he has gone. That is all. So this thing causes no trouble. It is just a custom showing where he has gone." There is no mound, or, if there is one, a small and insignificant one over the grave of a person struck by lightning. "We do not wish to remember the place of his burial. He is not there. He was taken. So we do not wish to remember him."[27]

There is no mourning for one struck and killed by lightning. Mourning would be regarded as an arrogant act of rebellion against the Lord-of-the-Sky. "Who can do anything against his wish? If he takes a man, then there must be something that he wants with this man. So how can there be mourning?" Neither does one speak of the deceased. Should somebody inquire about him, the reply would inevitably be: "He has been taken."[28]

Neither is there an *ukubuyisa* ritual for one struck by lightning. "If he has taken somebody we cannot ask to have him back again."[28] Widows of a man killed by lightning are not automatically taken over by the deceased's brothers in order to raise children for their dead brother. The shades are consulted first, some informants claiming that a heaven-herd ought to be approached also to obtain his views. Laduma Madela stated quite categorically that in his capacity of a heaven-herd, he always told the people that widows should marry elsewhere and children not be raised. "*UMvelingqangi* has shown that he does not wish this man to live any more." Madela's assistant commented: "It is clear that if the sky has taken a man, that is the end of him. Even if there remains nobody to carry on his life, it does not matter. It is the decision of the sky, so what can we do?"

One struck by lightning is not thought of in terms of being or becoming a shade. He is not spoken of as one who has gone down, *oshonileyo. Ukukhothama* and *ukuthatwa* describe death through lightning. The former term refers to kneeling, and immediately brings to mind one who behaves "in an orderly fashion in the presence of the *iNkosi*".[30] *Ukuthathwa*, as has already been indicated, refers to being taken away from the earth.

The Worship of the Lord-of-the-Sky

It has been stated that the Zulu do not have a worship of the Lord-of-the-Sky and that little attention, if any, is paid to him.[31] It is true that prayer seldom is directed to him, other than the occasions described below. It is equally true that no immediate attention is paid to him. But it would not be true to claim that he therefore is not in the minds of people and that no respect is attributed to him. One informant said: "We do not speak much about him. That is true. It would be bad manners to speak of him as were he our acquaintance. So we simply keep quiet and say nothing." Zulu again and again stress that their not speaking out in clear terms on matters pertaining to the Lord-of-the-Sky is not of necessity an indication that they do not have a notion of him. Other informants add that one may deny knowledge because one desires to safeguard the integrity and honour of the Lord-of-the-Sky.

Zulu state quite categorically that the Lord-of-the-Sky is in their minds from time to time. "We wonder what he is like and what he is going to do." "I think of him as I would think of Dr Verwoerd in Pretoria. I have no direct interest, but I think of him because I live under his rulership." "I know that he is there (in the sky), but I know nothing more about him. So how can I think of him, when I know nothing about him. He does not appear to us at night (i.e. in dreams). We simply hear people talking softly sometimes, whispering that he has shown himself in that somebody has been taken (i.e. struck by lightning). That is all we know of him." Another informant said: "We do not love him as we love the shades. He is too far away to love. One can only love the one that is near. But we fear him. That is what we do. We fear him. He has *amawala* (a haphazard way of acting). We do not know what next he will do to us. So I speak correctly when I say that one cannot love one who is not trustworthy. He is not trustworthy in that we do not know what to expect of him."

Many informants, although not all, are convinced that the Lord-of-the-Sky was the centre of attention in the now obsolete annual festival of the first fruits. The fact that the king played an important and integral part in the worship of the Lord-of-the-Sky at this occasion was explained thus at Ceza: "The king is the child of the sky. That is what I have said previously. Even you agreed saying that the children of the king are *abantwana* (children of the sky). Who then speaks better to a father than his own children? So when our king speaks, he speaks to the father in the sky for his children on the earth. That is what was done at *umkhosi*."

Professor Krige has described the festival of the first fruit, *umkhosi*.[32] Zulu agree that the description is correct. But many argue that the king in this particular function "is not simply the one who is the greatest among the Zulu. He is also the child of the sky. That is the reason why he does all these things." No informant suggests that the role of the shades at the occasion was unimportant. They most certainly formed essential participants in the festival. But they wish to underline that the Lord-of-the-Sky was also brought into the picture, possibly indirectly, but certainly in a conscious way. Said a

42

man at Ekuthuleni: "Who is it that makes the seasons if not he? I agree that the shades do much, but they do not make the seasons. What would men be if there were not the seasons? There would be no reaping in the autumn and no planting in the spring." Another man, listening to the observation, added: "We call this festival umkhosi because it is the festival of iNkosi in the sky. Even by way of the name you can see that it is his festival."[33]

Many Zulu say that the Lord-of-the-Sky is approached through the shades. "If there is something we wish to be brought before him we say to those who look after us, 'We salute you, you of our people, you who see the kings we do not see! We say to you, go and kneel on our behalf! We need not mention the thing because you have seen it. So why should we mention it to you. We are just requesting you, our fathers, we say to you who know the manner of approaching him (the Lord-of-the-Sky), bring this thing before him so that we do not die of hunger.' Then they (the shades) get together and say among themselves, 'How shall we do this thing for our children? They discuss and discuss, at last finding the way of approach. Then they follow that way. When they return they let us know the reply. That is the way we reach him when there is something that troubles us."

Mrs Esther Roberts has made similar observations and says that "informants from the Nongoma district say that, having approached Nkulunkulu through the amaThongo, they pray to the God himself at the Umkhosi festival, and have done so for years."[34] Certainly general opinion among Zulu is that the shades do approach the Lord-of-the-Sky on behalf of their survivors.

A great number of Zulu have underlined that there is an important difference between ukukhonza and ukuthetha. The former, claimed to be misused in ritual terminology of today, is not descriptive of the cult of the shades. The word, in its strict sense, refers to what one in English would term a veneration in a vertical and transcendental dimension. Ukukhonza, according to Bryant and Doke–Vilakazi,[35] means to be subject to or dependent on. Information suggests that the term, when applied to ritual matters, is associated primarily with the Lord-of-the-Sky. Christian Zulus have emphasized that this is the correct word chosen to express the cult of the Christian God and His worship.

Ukuthetha is related to the cult of the shades, the terminus technicus ukuthetha idlozi referring to a ritual celebration involving the shades. Informants state quite categorically that it is impossible to khonza a shade. "That is not the word to use. There is no inkhonzo of the shades. There is only ukuthetha idlozi. This is correct Zulu."[36]

On the occasion of the funeral of a man's only son at Ekuthuleni, the father left the grave during the filling in of it and fled to his hut, overcome by grief and sorrow. No longer able to control himself, he threw himself down on the floor of the hut after entering it, buried his face in his hands and shouted out, hysterically: "My Lord, why did you do this thing?" The people who had assembled for the funeral and were still at the graveside became very silent when they heard the man call out thus. One of the bereaved's brothers was instructed to go and quieten his brother in the hut. Discussing the incident with some neighbours after the funeral two details emerged. First, everybody was convinced that the man had addressed the Lord-of-the-Sky, not the shades. Secondly, he did it in a manner that brought about concern among

Fig. 1. One of the mountains which *uMvelingqangi* is worshipp[ed] when the need arises.

those who heard him. They were alarmed by what they called his *isibindi*, courage. "His courage was dangerous. He could have brought further misfortune over himself by addressing him (the Lord-of-the-Sky) in this manner." The understanding and sympathetic added a word of explanation though, saying: "Well, when a man loses his only son it is clear that he sees no future. So what does it matter if he calls on the sky, asking what this thing is."

Evidence shows that one can call on the Lord-of-the-Sky in times of dire need, but then in an orderly fashion and with appropriate preparations prior to approaching him. There are, scattered around in Natal and Zululand, certain characteristic hills and mountains on which nobody builds and where cattle are preferably not grazed. These have, on the summit, an *isiguqo*, a kneeling place. Frequently *isiguqo* is not marked, but the particular area is known to the local people. On two mountains visited the kneeling-place is marked with a ring of stones, informants claiming that similar rings are found on other hills too. Although a limited number of people claim that the stones have been placed around *isiguqo* by Independent church groups, others say that the same kneeling-place is used by pagans as well as members of the Independent groups. Hills with *isiguqo* are never pointed at with the finger. The clenched fist is used instead.[37]

On occasions of severe drought, when communion with the shades has not led to rain, the local chief or another person of authority (including Zionist group leaders, rain-makers) may appoint a day when people are to mount the hill and pray for rain. For at least a day prior to ascending the hill one abstains from food. "How otherwise will he (the Lord-of-the-Sky) see that we are hungry?" One also abstains from sexual relations "so that he can see how weak we are". There is a marked preference for white clothing on this day—in the case of prayer on N hill at E a large number of the men who attended the ritual wore white or predominantly white loin-skins. When the people have assembled and the leader thinks the time ripe, the people gather in the close vicinity of the *isiguqo*, those wearing shoes having removed them. Kneeling at a distance from the circle of stones, the congregation creeps to the place of worship for some five meters and then stoops down on hands and knees very reverently, men coming closest to the circle of stones, while women kneel behind the men.[38] When everybody has settled down and there is perfect silence, the leader prays with a loud and clear voice. Eloquence of language and a dignified behaviour by the man that prays is looked upon as important. One prayer was thus: *"Nkosi, siphambi kwobuso bakho! Nkosi, silethwe isikhalo sethu esikhulu! Wena wezulu, wena okona njalo-njalo, sibuke usilekelele! Wasibulala, wena wezulu, singazi ukuthi senzeni! Sizilahla phansi kwobuso bakho, wena Nkosi! Sithi, mawusihawukele usilethele amantombazana akho! Sithi, Nkosi yamazulu, ungasibulali!"* (Lord, we are in your presence! Lord, we have been been brought here by our great cry (i.e. our great need)! You of the heaven, you who are everlasting, look upon us and assist us! Why do you destroy us, you of the sky, we being unconscious of what wrong we have done. We cast ourselves down before your countenance, you Lord! We say, have mercy on us and give us your daughters (i.e. drops of rain)! We say, Lord of the heavens, do not destroy us!)

I once accompanied a childless woman to the top of a hill in order to pray there. She had approached me, assuming that because we had spoken of *isiguqo* in her particular area and because we had discussed her personal problem of not having children, I would understand her need and would be willing to assist her in prayer. We were to ascend the hill on a Thursday, at noon. Meeting her at the appointed place, I found her dressed in white. Her hymnbook which has a black outer covering, had been covered with newspaper "so that it might look nice". She wore a white towel around her head and had bought a pair of cheap tennis-shoes for the occasion. We ascended the mountain, I leading. On arrival at the *isiguqo* she knelt very humbly. Creeping up towards a stone that appeared to mark the central part of the kneeling place, she stopped short of it and fell prostrate in front of the stone. She remained in this position for about ten minutes in perfect silence. Then, quietly yet under control she started weeping bitterly. I was amazed by her weeping, for she had hitherto not given any indication of being moved to tears. She soon stopped crying and turned to a long and intense prayer in which she poured out her life of profound unhappiness and utter meaninglessness in that she had no children. She mentioned the scorn she had experienced when arguing with another woman and the ridicule that the other woman had made of her because she had no child. Then, after closing her prayer and calling upon me in a whisper hardly audible, to pray for her, she sang two verses of a very well-known Zulu hymn. We said the Lord's

Prayer together and I closed with the benediction whereupon she rose up and left the *isiguqo* without further ceremony.

She did indeed have a child, and when it was to be christened we spoke of the occasion on the hill. She remarked: "I could not slaughter for the shades. I know that this is not allowed in the Church. But I know that God in heaven hears prayer, especially if it comes to him from that hill. I know of others that have been cured by prayer from that very hill. Even the Zionists pray from that hill and people are healed."

It is on occasions of great need such as severe drought, childlessness, possible famine or epidemics, after in vain having consulted the shades, that one ventures to approach the Lord-of-the-Sky personally. Places of worship are appointed and easily recognizable hills and mountains to which one goes either individually or in community, depending on the cause occasioning the prayer. Informants claim that the Lord-of-the-Sky can also be approached in other places, some mentioning the main hut in a homestead because "God is everywhere". But suggesting that prayers to the Lord-of-the-Sky be conducted in the cattle-byre caused amusement and was sometimes openly resented. A heaven-herd once said: "The shades are called upon in the cattle enclosure, not *iNkosi yezulu*. If you wish to pray to him, then you can go to the main hut (*indlunkulu*) or to the Church. But not in the byre. That is the place of the shades."

The Lord-of-the-Sky and the Heaven-Herds

The term heaven-herd is adopted in this study as a useful translation of the Zulu *abelusi bezulu*. They are also known as *izinyanga zezulu* (lit. the experts on the sky), the word *inyanga* referring to a skilled professional.

Unlike diviners who receive their calling and subsequent instruction in very close relation to the shades, the heaven-herd have no relations to the shades as far as their office of herding the heaven is concerned. In theory anybody can become an heaven-herd, but in practice it is required that a possible candidate be able to refer to some incident whereby he can prove that the sky has called him for service. A man who has seen lightning both enter and leave his hut without being killed is received for preparation to become a heaven-herd. Poeple who have had narrow escapes from lightning or whose relatives have been involved in electric storms are regarded as suitable candidates for the duties allotted to heaven-herds. Correctly Violet Sibeko writes that sons of heaven-herds often follow in their father's footsteps although this is not a prerequisite for becoming one.[39]

A novice initiation is known as *ukusoga* or *ukugoma*. The former term refers to the many cuts and scarifications that the candidate receives while being prepared for his coming duties (cf. *ukusoga,* to circumcise), while *ukugoma* addresses itself to the medicines he is to take.

Having been accepted by an experienced heaven-herd for treatment, the novice leaves his home and stays with the heaven-herd for some time while the latter both treats his apprentice and teaches him what to do when he is to drive off lightning, hail and violent storms. It is imperative that the apprentice arrives at the home of the heaven-herd at the first signs of new moon. When the moon is full, "his wisdom and knowledge is full also. It grows with the moon. When the moon is full, then he should be fully prepared to carry out his duties. That is how we know that he is ready, by looking at the moon."

Laduma Madela related the details of preparing a novice, his apprentice being L who had narrowly escaped being struck be lightning. After extensive preparations of the required medicine, Madela took his apprentice to the top of Ceza mountain so that "we could work in the presence of the great one (i.e. the Lord-of-the-Sky)". The medicines were carried by the heaven-herd himself in a clay vessel. They were white in colour. Madela claims that they are carried in the right hand, the left carrying a very blunt spear, the stick referred to earlier and a small broom prepared of white cattle-tails attached to a short handle, *umshanelo wezulu* (lit. the broom of the sky). There are ten white beads in the hairs of the broom. On arrival at the top of the mountain, the novice was made to kneel and Madela offered a prayer, saying (Madela dictated the prayer in his hut): "Lord, look after this boy (L must have been over fifty years old) and help him in his work of looking after people." Then, L still kneeling, Madela placed the pot containing medicines in front of him and, putting a piece of newspaper in front of L "to collect the medicines that may be dropped on the ground", L was instructed to remove all his clothing and finery. Madela stirred the medicines in the pot with the spear and then began applying them onto L with the spear. He began with the forehead, between the eyes and above these, immediately under the hair. He smeared a coat of medicine down the forehead and onto the nose, then from the chin to the throat and down over the chest, between the ribs, as far as the navel. The medicine was smeared about an inch in width. From the right ear Madela smeared medicine over the neck and onto the shoulder, using the blade of the spear. L was told to lift his right hand and arm, and the medicine was smeared down the upper right arm as far as the tip of the long finger. Starting again under the armpit, Madela smeared medicine down the right side of L as far as the hip-bone. He proceeded down the right side of the novice, over the loins and down the right leg, past the knee, over the calf of the leg and over the ankle-bone along the right side of the foot and stopping with the right foot little toe-tip. The same procedure was repeated with the left side. Then the back was treated. From the neck, just below the hair, Madela smeared a line of medicine towards the last vertebrae of the neck, the candidate kneeling and bending forward. Then two strokes were made above L's eyes, about 40 mm. in length, covering both eyes and stopping just below the eye-lids.

Madela proceeded with making incisions on L's body. To such an extent are these regarded as essential that they in fact name the whole treatment, *ukusoka*. Two parallel incisions were made at the following parts of the body, the incisions being cut diagonally with the line of medicine: on the temple, on the cheek-bone, on the shoulder, next to the elbow, on the wrist and on the tip of the little finger. On the chest incisions were made on the upper end of the breast-bone and just above the navel while on the back they were made just above the last vertebrae and between the shoulders. Some of the incisions bled somewhat. Madela claims he was careful to collect the blood on a small white stick that he had kept in his pocket. The incisions were thereafter extensively smeared with medicine from the pot, the blunt spear being used to rub the medicine onto the wounds. Neither Madela or L spoke during the process. When the bleeding had ceased, Madela went some distance away and planted the stick with blood in the earth saying: "Here is the blood of the boy (umfana). If you want something, come here and fetch it. Do not touch the boy himself but take this blood where I am placing it now." Madela then pushed the stick into the ground, with the end covered with blood facing upwards. Thereafter he returned to the novice who was still kneeling, naked.

In a whispering voice L was instructed to stand up and take a mouthful of the medicine. He did so, holding the medicine in his mouth. Madela told him to spit out the medicine in a westward direction and say: "Go there to the desert, you fire, and cool yourself in the sand. Do not come near me or my place of work. You will merely work where there is not work." L spat out the medicine and repeated what Madela had told him to say. L was instructed to turn eastward and proceed to a small brook running down Ceza mountain, not looking back. He was to wash in a named pool, known to Madela and him, and dress with the clothing that he would find on a log overhanging the pool. Madela returned home to await his novice' return.

The fortnight following the initiatory rituals, the novice is given instruction as to methods of driving away violent storms, knowledge pertaining to medicines and repeatedly treated with medicine as was done on the mountain. Medicine is smeared into the wounds and some is taken orally. He is also furnished with horns containing medicine and tools for driving away storms and lightning.

The horns that the heaven-herd novice receives must of necessity be black and the colour of the medicines must be black. Because the choice is not great, these horns more often than not are either of dark-coloured goats or black sheep. Madela claims that the horns should not be straight ones. These look as if they are inviting the lightning to come. They should, if at all possible, be curved, "showing the lightning that it must turn away". The medicine, also of necessity black and coloured thus through the addition of soot and through a process of charring, are named insizi because of the charring of them.[40] This process of charring and addition of soot to blacken the medicine is important.[41]

The candidate is given a broom of black cattle-tail ends attached to a handle about forty centimeters in length, ten black beads attached to some of the hairs. Madela explained the black colour. "The sky of thunder is black. But when it sees black on earth in the hand of its herdsman (umalusi), it withdraws and goes to another place where it does not see this colour." Two other heaven-herds interviewed had the same opinion as Madela on the interpretation of the black symbolism. But a heaven-herd in the Louwsburg–Vryheid area said that the tail ends should be white "because lightning is white. So this white chases away another white thing." Whatever the colour of the broom, the future heaven-herd is to sweep the sky with it, "sweeping away the clouds in which the lightning bird hides".

He receives, further, a very blunt spear and a stick of the branch of the umuNka, Maerua angolensis, which is white. When it is used to ward off storms it is blackened with the medicines contained in the horns by heaven-herds who have black brooms. The spear must be blunt "so that the sky can see that we do not wish to stab it. We merely carry the spear as does any man. But being blunt the sky sees that we do not wish to harm it." The stick is looked upon as a herdsman's stick and is named accordingly, eyokwelusa. "With it the heaven-herd drives away the anger of the sky." He is also given a flute of reed on which to blow when driving away storms. Although Madela himself blows an old bugle, probably one formerly used in a cadet band, he insisted that "it is the same as *umtshingo* (flute) taken from the reeds." The reed is explained thus: "The sky knows this thing. It was the thing used in the creation of the first humans. So he (the Lord-of-the-Sky) knows it well. It is the thing of *uMvelingqangi* here on earth. That is why we use it in the work of *uMvelingqangi*." (Madela quoted, verified by other heaven-herds.) Professor Krige says that the whistle can also be made of "the tendon of a vulture",[42] but heaven-herds claim they have no knowledge of this today. On the other hand, feathers, bones and flesh from a vulture can very well be used in the preparation of medicine.

Two details concerning heaven-herds require underlining. Firstly, no woman can become a heaven-herd for "where have you seen women tending cattle? Now is not the heaven-herd *umalusi* (herdsman) tending the sky as a herdsman looks after the cattle? So how could a heaven-herd be a woman?" Secondly, whatever the age of the heaven-herd, he is always referred to as a boy, *umfana*. Informants say that this is done because it is boys who look after cattle. Hence this "herdsman is also just a boy". Madela, on the other hand, said that he himself, being a heaven-herd, was known as *umfana* as a token of respect toward the sky. "The sky is very old. It is a sign of respect if someone is old to be attended to by a boy. So the people are honouring the sky when they call me *umfana*. It is also an honour to me. For being a servant (*inceku*) of the aged is a sign of trustworthiness."

During the fortnight of training, the novice is introduced into the art of making medicine for driving off storms and the methods of using them. These are described by Professor Krige.[43]

An important ingredient in the medicine is the fat of *inyoni yezulu*, also known as *impundulu*, and regarded as coming from the sky. Of animals on the earth which also form ingredients, is the fat of *umonya*, Python sebae (Natal rock snake); *imbulu*, Varanus albigolaris (large land iguana), and that of a black sheep. It is imperative the sheep is black. If its horns are fully black and curved, they will be used as medicine containers. Fifthly, is used the fat and skin of *imbila*, Hyrax capensis, the common rock-rabbit and, also, the skin of an otter, *umanzini*, Lutra capensis. Lastly, of living animals, there should be some feathers of a peacock and the flesh of a tortoise, *ufudu*. Should the fat of *inyoni yezulu* not be obtainable due to there not having been thunder for some period of time, or that one cannot obtain the fat from another heaven-herd, then it can be substituted with the fat of *ingqungqulu*, Terathopius ecaudatus. This bird makes a sound which much resembles thunder when it flies. There are two vegetary ingredients, partly the crushed stem of *umunka*, partly the crushed bulb of the red Ifafa lily, Cyrtanthus stenenthus Liliaceae, in Zulu called *impingizana encane ebomvu*, which gives the medicine a greasy consistence. The total number of ingredients are ten, a matter that at least Laduma Madela made clear is an important factor. Other heaven-herds agreed that the ingredients ought to be ten, but did not put great emphasis on this aspect. Said Madela: "As there are ten fingers which makes a complete handful and which makes a man able to work well (i.e. completely, fully), so there must be ten fingers in the medicines. Then they can work together to a full protection against the sky."

Medicines to be used in driving off thunder and violent storms are prepared at a place outside the heaven-herd's homestead. The place is generally a secluded spot, known as *isolo* or *iziko lezulu* (lit. the hearth of the sky).[44] All heaven-herds are emphatic that medicine must of necessity be prepared outside the homestead, preferably on an overcast day "so that the sky does not see the thing we are doing". Another informant said: "A home is a hot place. There are hot people in a home. But these medicines must be cool. They cannot be prepared in a hot place. Then their power is lamed. That is why they must be prepared in a cool place where there are no hot people."

Animals to be used in the preparation of medicine must not be stabbed to death. "The sky will be troubled by seeing its blood come out. It (the animal) must be spoken to in a nice manner, *inyanga* saying, 'Friend of the sky, now you are going to do your work. So do not trouble me. Just remain quiet, helping in every way.' Then the animal is touched with the stick and held down, not breathing until it is dead. All the time *inyanga* is apologizing. When it is dead it is taken to the shadow of *iziko lezulu* and prepared there." Likewise one apologizes when a branch of *umunka* is to be cut off from a tree. The complete tree is not cut down. Heaven-herds claim that one also apologizes when digging up the lily, saying: "I am sorry, think of *iNkosi!* But is this not your work? So I am not troubling you. I am just working with you, doing that work with you which is yours."

Fat from *inyoni yezulu* is regarded as essential because the bird is looked upon as coming from the sky. "If it is killed and made into medicine, it shows the sky how painful it is to die suddenly and unexpectanly as one does when being struck by lightning. The death of the bird by way of the white stick which hits it and the death of men through lightning are the same thing." Others underline the importance of the bird's fat. "The fat says, speaking through the medicines, 'Look, you of the sky! If you destroy through lightning, what fat will there be for you here on earth?' It just brings about trouble. That is all. There is no fat in trouble." *Umonya* is regarded as "the animal of the sky. If it is used in medicines, the sky will recognize its animal, saying, 'No, but this is painful. I cannot hurt people as they have hurt this my animal.' Again, this animal is slow to anger. So if the fat of this animal is used, the heaven-herd is saying, 'Excuse me, Lord! Just look at this thing of yours that is slow to anger. Why is it that you do not resemble it and take away your anger? Instead, be like it and let your great heat just cool off.' That is what is said of this animal." *Imbulu* is looked upon as the most unafraid animal that exists, fleeing from nothing, "not even thunder does this animal fear". Heaven-herds claim that it is in connection with thunder that *imbulu* cries, and it cries "in disgust over what the sky is doing". Smearing oneself with fat of *imbulu* is said to make one unafraid. The black sheep is like the dark clouds of thunder and opposite to the colour of lightning. Further, sheep are silent which again is antagonistic to the crack of thunder when lightning strikes in the vicinity. The skin of the rock-rabbit is said to drive off the violent rains that accompany thunder because "this animal always hides when it rains. So the sky does not agree with it. If it is in the medicines, the sky will not send rain because there is the animal that does not agree with rain." The tortoise is claimed to spout out water upwards when it is to thunder, the spouting occasioned by anger in the tortoise. "So the medicine with this animal in it says to the storm, 'Go the other way! Let your anger go the same way as the anger of the tortoise!' The lightning goes upwards and does not come downwards." Peacocks are said to be the birds of kings, eaten by them only. "So therefore *iNkosi* in the sky is given this bird in the medicines to make him happy, removing the anger." Others claim that the peacock ruffles its feathers when it feels a storm approaching and hence its association with the medicines. (Madela claimed that he did not use otter skin in his medicines, "because the animal smells very bad. It makes the medicine desagreeable for *uMvelingqangi.*" He used the skin of a black cat instead, claiming that "cats fear rain".)

The Thunder tree, *umunka,* "is white inside the bark, just like the heaven is white (lit. light) inside with no darkness". When its thorns are broken off, a red sap comes out said to resemble blood. Hence the tree is spoken of as being human-like and planted by the creator himself. Madela claims that this particular tree is the one referred to as the "tree of life" in Genesis. Also known as *esasezulwini* (that of the sky), it is not cut down even if it grows in fields. The red Ifafa lily comes into flower after the grass in which it grows has been burnt. Hence it is closely associated with fire. "It can even be seen in its flowers. They are red like fire. They are long, like flames." A heaven-herd in the Kranskop area said: "If it is used in medicines the heavens see that this place has already been burnt. So there is nothing more to burn. Then it (the sky) goes elsewhere with its fire (i.e. lightning). It does not strike where this medicine of this plant has been used."

In popular Zulu folk-lore *imbulu* is the fabulous animal that deceives others to do stupid things and thereby gain good results itself. Suggesting to heaven-herds that the use of the animal in the preparation of medicine may possibly have something to do with the element of deceiving the heaven in not bringing a storm, they have all denied this possibility, making it clear that the heaven is not deceived. "It is not possible to deceive the heaven. We discuss with the sky with the medicines. But no one can deceive the sky. The Lord-of-the-Sky is too clever for that."

At full-moon the novice is expected to have learnt everything that pertains to his forthcoming duties as a heaven-herd. But he does not qualify before showing what he is worth. When, therefore, thunder-clouds arise and one is sure that a violent storm is at hand, the heaven-herd who has given the novice instruction calls his student and they each climb a mountain. At Rorkes Drift there are two such hills which offer suitable sites for the test. One hill is the Rorkes Drift mountain itself, the second is the hill at the foot of which is situated the Lutheran Old Age home. The novice contests with his teacher and if he is able to divert the thunder and subsequent storm away from both his particular hill and the area as a whole, he will be accepted into the guild of heaven-herds. But before the test he is not a heaven-herd. If he is unable to divert the storm away from the hill and the surrounding area, he can either undergo renewed treatment and schooling, or, as often happens, abandon further hopes of becoming an efficient heaven-herd.

The Lord-of-the-Sky, Black and White

Zulu informants are emphatic that everything in the sky is white. The Lord-of-the-Sky himself is regarded as being white, some informants saying that "perhaps he is white like water (i.e. transparent). But we do not know because he has not been seen by anybody." When thunderstorms are gathering, everything white must be either covered up or removed. Water, looked upon as white, is thrown out at some distance from the homestead. All shiny metal tools and containers are brought indoors, "so that they do not attract the fire from the sky". Cattle which are white or have much white skin are removed from the cattle-enclosure and driven away and a dark-coloured blanket placed as a covering over the box containing any white cloth. Mirrors, also regarded as white, are stored away. White fowls are either chased away or driven into a hut where they can be kept. Enamel dishes which are white are taken into an uninhabited hut and stored away, preferably under an inverted black cooking pot. Great care is taken to remove everything white or of a light colour. Every form of fire is extinguished. There arose a heated argument once, when a man had lit an electric torch during a thunderstorm and been very strongly reprimanded for this action. He claimed: "A torch has no fire, simply light." His senior argued: "Everything that gives light is fire. Even the globes in the houses of whites are hot when they shine. It is quite clear that a torch has fire!" All the people listening to the senior judged him right.[45]

Light is claimed to be the colour of the sky and thus attracts lightning. Identified with the sky, white is the colour of the heaven-herd when there is no storm. Madela at Ceza regularly wore a white handkerchief tied with four knots over his head. Often the interior of heaven-herd homes are white-washed "because this is our colour". The brooms made of cattle-tails are white when there is no storm and the medicine used in preparing a novice for office is white in colour, although fetched from animals which definitely are not always white. "But their fat is always white. That is why we insist on the fat. It is white." The timber of *umunka* is whiter than other timbers and hence identified with the sky.

When a storm is at hand, the reverse colour is assumed. A man wearing a white shirt will put on a dark one and people gather in the dark sections of the hut, away from the door. The door is closed carefully to let in as little light as possible. When about to drive off storms, the heaven-herd removes everything of a light colour from himself and rubs his herding stick with black medicines. He frowns at the sky when he sees "what it is doing, saying, 'No, but what are you doing now? Are you bringing calamity over us?' He becomes horrified in the face, showing the sky that he is disagreeing to this thing that it is planning to do." Black, being associated with the dark thunder-clouds, is adopted to drive off the "darkness of the thing that the sky is planning to do". With the black one hopes to drive the lightning either to the East, "where there is much water. Is not water white (ref. to Indian Ocean)?" or towards the West, where the "great desert is found. That is the place of sand. Sand is white." Madela said: "I say to it, 'Go in that direction!' pointing towards the West because in that direction is Johannesburg. That is the place of gold. Gold is white." Whether the thunder goes East or West, it is associated with white, the colour of lightning. In the case of the black medicines driving off the dark clouds and the light colour of water and of gold attracting lightning, the associations are sympathetic.

The Lord-of-the-Sky, Rain and the Rain-maker

No Zulu doubts the close relationships between clouds and rain. "If there are no clouds, we know quite well that there will be no rain. So it is clear that it is the clouds that bring rain to us."

Zulu are equally emphatic that rain is sent to the earth by *iNkosi yezulu*, although a large number agree that the shades are closely related to both the quantity and the time of rainfall. "The shades can withhold rain and they can also send it at the wrong time. But we say (i.e. claim) that they do not make the rain. Rain was there like all other things were there. But they use the rain, taking it away or sending it at a wrong time. That is why we speak to them first when we do not get rain. A drought can be caused by their anger. When their anger cools, then the rain is restored by them. That is what we say is the use of rain. But the creator of rain is the Lord-of-the-Sky."

The fact that the king was looked upon as playing an important role in the timely and good fall of rain is documented in the ethnographic literature on Zulu.[46] Present day Zulu are so emphatic on this issue that some attribute what they regard as an increase in drought to the fact that the king no longer functions ritually as was the case previously. One informant said: "The trouble is that our kings do nothing today. They simply sit in an office, dressed nicely and writing letters."

Many are convinced, as one was previously, that it is the king of the royal clan that has the control of rain, for "he is the child of the sky and knows it (the sky) well. So he knows what to do to get rain for his people." Consequently, rain-makers were not many in former Zulu society, as is indicated in the literature on the Zulu from the time. Nevertheless, King Mpande called rain-makers when he was unsuccessful in procuring rain.[47] Rain-makers from among Swazi and Pedi[48] were looked upon as particularly successful, although local Zulu rain-makers were not unknown. This is still the conviction of many Zulu also today.

According to Shooter the rain-maker's profession was hereditary.[49] It has not been possible to verify this statement, because practising rain-makers are few among Zulu. Historic evidence shows, however, that a now unknown rain-maker who originally came from Transvaal found a ready area of activity at Ntlangwini where had settled an offshoot of the Dlamini clan who called themselves amaNtlangwini. Partly due to drought at the time, and partly due to the fact that the amaNtlangwini were originally of the Dlamini clan which has its roots among Swazi, the rain-maker encouraged rain-making in this area and among its inhabitants. Hence the amaNtlangwini became the rain-makers of the Zulu people.[50] But besides rain-makers from this particular clan it is evident that there are rain-makers also from other Zulu clans.[51]

The following material is based on findings among three rain-makers who have been available for information. Two of the informants were women, both married and of the Dlamini clan. The third is a male who calls himself Nkosi, the praise-name of Dlamini. Two claimed that they had learnt their profession from their mother (the male and one female), while the third had taken it from her father. The latter claimed: "My father told me this thing and that, but it was the sky that taught me everything. To hear is one thing, but to learn is another. I learnt from the sky." She claimed she had hitherto never been unsuccessful in bringing rain.

Although my informants admitted that they were related to the shades "like all other people", they were explicit in stating that their special duties of bringing rain was a duty given them by the Lord-of-the-Sky. "When we are sick we call the diviner who speaks to the shades. Then we take the medicines of the herbalist. These two know their work. I for one know nothing of it. But I have my work. They know nothing of it. So we leave each other's work to the one who knows it. We live peacefully. I speak to *uMvelingqangi* about my work. They speak to the shades about their work. That is the difference between them and me."

The three rain-makers each had four horns containing medicine. The horns all appeared to be of goats, although the male informant claimed that two of his horns were of sheep "because they (sheep) are like women". He actually called these two horns *abazifazane* (females), the other two being males. On mentioning this to the other two rain-makers, they claimed that this approach is correct. "But it is a thing that must not be spoken of. It is not for everybody." When not in use the horns are kept in the rain-maker's hut, tucked away in the far back of the hut, preferably behind beer-containers or other equipment stored away there. They are to be kept in the semi-dark, "so that they remain cool and do not become hot".

uMonya (Natal rock snake) is claimed to call from time-to-time to the homestead and lie on the horns "so that they remain cool. It is the Lord-of-the-Sky that sends the snake. It comes from him to this place in order to do its work." Another rain-maker said: "We do not know when it comes, but suddenly we simply see it lying there in that place of the medicines. Then we become very silent, because there is a great messenger in the house. We tell nobody. We simply remain silent, saying nothing. Then, at another time we see it is no longer there. Then we say, 'It has done its work of cooling and strengthening. It has left us. We thank you, *iNkosi* of the sky, that you have not forgotten us and this work that you have given us.' We say all this in the heart, letting nobody hear the words of the heart."[52]

The two male horns contain male medicine, while the two female horns contain female medicine. "To make female medicine, there must be the fat of a female sheep. Sheep are like men. Their fat is like the fat of men. So the fat of female sheep is like the fat of women. That is why a female sheep which has given birth is slaughtered to obtain its fat. Its fat is like that of a woman. So when there is no woman's fat, then it must be that of this sheep." The two horns containing male medicine are treated with fat from a ram.

When making rain, the rain-maker chooses a secluded place either in the homestead or, more frequently, away from home. Two details are emphasized when choosing the place. Firstly, it must be a cool place. Secondly, it must be a quiet one. The second aspect was emphasized strongly by all three rainmakers and differed from heaven-herds in this detail.

Having prepared the place and brought with him things that he requires, the rain-maker pours a little medicine from a male horn into one of the holes of the horizontal stick used in fire-making. This stick is said to be feminine. The stick held between the hands in a vertical position and rotated in the female hollowed stick, said to be masculine, is dipped into the medicine contained in the female horns. "The stick must be dipped into the medicine. The medicine must not be put into the hole of the (female) stick. The male stick must be pushed into the horn of the female medicine. Then he takes it out." While the rain-maker revolves the male stick in the female one he says: "*Nsondo,* here is your thing. It is your medicine that I am making use of. Look upon it. Here there is to be warmth so that your people may warm themselves when you give them the thing that you are withholding from them. Give it to them now, so that they may live and not die." My male informant said that the first ones he called upon were the shades of the royal lineage, Mageba, Shaka and Mpande. But when he had mentioned the names of all the Zulu kings he knew then "it is time to speak to *iNkosi,* saying, 'Give us rain so that we may till the earth and not die. Why do you withhold this thing? Who has made you angry? No, do not be angry. Just let this food that I am preparing for you make you cool so that you give them (the people) rain.' "

As soon as there is a fire, green branches are added to the fire so that the smoke becomes black. Informants claim that the branches and leaves of *umQanda-Nyoka* (lit. egg of a snake), also known as *isiNyembane,* Cassia occidentalis, produces the best smoke "that is liked by the sky".[53] "When the sky is covered with smoke, then *iNkosi* says, 'Who is suffering? Is it my children?' Then he lets the rain come. It comes in these very clouds that come from this fire. So the people become very happy when they see this smoke rising, because they know that this is the smoke of rain."

The male rain-maker, by far the easiest of the three to get along with, gave me the following description of his method of making rain. When the men of a drought-stricken area had decided to approach him, they would do so through their chief or headman, *induna.* The latter would appoint two or three men to go to the rain-maker and ask him "to plead with the sky (*ukuncenga izulu*), giving them either a black sheep or a goat to take with them to the rain-maker (*inyanga yezulu*)". On arrival the men will state their cause and the rain-maker will look very carefully at the animal they have brought along with them. If it has any white or brown, it will not bring rain. Further, it must be fat, "for only fatness will bring rain". In the afternoon the animal is slaughtered by the men who brought it. If they brought a goat, its mouth has to be held tightly while being killed, so that it does not bleat. The men themselves work quickly and quietly. If they have to communicate with each other, they will do so whispering. Immediately the animal has been skinned the rain-maker is sent for. He emerges from his hut where he has been sitting, "praying to *uMvelingqangi* in the darkness, speaking in the heart". He takes the skin and, with his medicine-horns rolled into the skin, goes to a particular black rock in a local stream. The rock is surrounded by water. Having passed through the water to the rock, he lies down on the rock, places the medicine-horns next to himself, and then draws the wet skin over himself. He lies in this position the complete night "without moving once". At dead of night when everything is still and quiet, *inhlwathi* (another name for *umonya*) emerges from a very deep pool in the river, approaches the rain-maker and licks the fat off the skin which covers the rain-maker. It then lies down on the medicines "for a long time until the horns are as cool as it is cool. Then it returns into the water from where it came, without making any sound. I just suddenly find that the snake is no longer there on the medicines." At crack of dawn the rain-makers gets up, takes the medicine-horns and "makes rain just there next to the river". My informant was reluctant to let me know what he actually did at the river, "for these things are fearful things and not spoken of". But he claimed that he caused a mist to rise out of the water, "then the mist made the clouds and the rain came down very heavily". He claimed that on each occasion he had done this he had returned home in pouring rain. For his services he would receive a number of animals and/ or money, depending on how serious the drought had been and the quantity of rain that fell.

The male rain-maker always kept the grass around his home burnt. Commenting on this he said: "When *uMvelingqangi* sees the black around the home, then he knows that I am there, looking for rain. He sees the black and then he knows that I am weeping because he is withholding the thing that everybody is looking for." He would burn the grass regularly when rain was expected and during the months when the services of a rain-maker would be required. (No rain-maker is approached during the autumn and winter when no rains are expected.) When burning the grass, the rain-maker would take great care not to burn the grass immediately east of his homestead, "because that is the road for the great snake when it comes to my home to do its work". He claimed that the snake always approached his home from the east but could not give an explanation for this other than draw attention to "*inthaba encwele yeNkosi yamazulu* (the holy hill of the Lord-of-the-Sky)" and the river from which the snake was claimed to emerge, both being east of the homestead. But one of the female rain-makers also had the grass east of her homestead growing, although the river to which she ascribed the presence of the snake was west of the home. It is possible that east coincides with the direction from which the rainbearing winds come. At least the ventriloquist diviner found this a possible explanation.

Ingredients in the rain-making medicine are to a large extent material from the Indian ocean. *Ukhuningomile*, sea-weed, fetched from the rocks in the ocean form an essential part of the medicine and without it the medicine is of no avail. Equally important is *ikwindi*, mussel shell-fish,[54] and *isikhu-khukhu* sea-urchin,[55] without which the medicine is not efficient. Other useful ingredients are pieces of vegetation cast up by the waves on the shore which have been picked up before they have dried. Two informants said that bone or fat from a whale, *umkhomo*, is an essential, making it as important an ingredient as sea-weed or any other produce of the sea. "This animal is very big. When the sky sees the fat of this animal it will say, 'Surely the drought must be very great when even this animal is dead.' For if a whale dies and its body is found on the shore, then it is known that there will be a very great drought." The male medicines also contain very well ground black pebbles picked up along the sea-shore, while the female medicine contains the fine produce of white stones found on the shore.

The medicines are prepared either in the rain-maker's private hut or in a secluded spot outside the homestead where privacy is found. "Everything must be silent. There must be no talking. Just silence. Also, the place must be cool. That means that there must always be much (i.e. deep) shadow." The medicines are ground together and burnt on a piece of chipped clay-pot. When they blacken, they are made completely black with soot. Ocean-water is added "to make the medicine cool". The medicine is then deposited in the horns where they are kept for use in the future. Rain-makers claim that they collect medicine-ingredients continually and that when the need arises, they will prepare new medicine and add this to their supplies.

Informants were emphatic that from time to time they must go to the ocean to see "the great waters". They said that if they did not see the great masses of water, their spirits would run low and they would not be able to produce much rain. "I forget what much water looks like. In the drought I think that an *ukhamba* (earthern-ware water container) is a lot of water, whereas it is nothing. So I must imprint this image in my mind, remembering what to ask for when I am asking *uMvelingqangi* for rain. When we ask him to send rain, we think of how much rain he should send, adding words about the manner in which he should send it, saying, 'Just let it fall nicely, not damaging anywhere.' So it is this image that we have of great quantities of water which we bring with us, when we return from the ocean." My informants claimed that they would have a special place where they would sit, staring out over the sea for considerable lengths of time. One claimed that he sat there a whole afternoon, the following night (which was full moon) and part of the next morning.

Two birds are closely related to both the sky and rain, *insingizi* (Buceros Caffer, common ground-hornbill) and *ingqungqulu* (Terathopius ecaudatus, an eagle). The former is looked upon as a messenger of the sky, sent to earth to bring a favourable report. "It (ground-hornbill) brings good news. The news is that it will rain. So people rejoice when they see this bird in the spring when they expect the rains." General ideas are that it is able to fly very high and appears on earth prior to rains only. It does not foretell drought, as does *ingqungqulu,* and when it flies about, wailing, people say: "Is this not *insingizi,* the bird of the sky, that is crying today? So the rains are just close by." Its walking about particularly in reaped fields is also a sign of forthcoming rain.

Informants claim that when neither the king nor they could produce rain, they would go "to another land where there is rain" in order to catch a ground-hornbill. Care must be taken to catch a multicoloured bird, so that the sky sees "that we are taking away the friend of the rainbow".[56] The bird is carried alive to the rain-maker's home. Very early in the morning it is taken to a river, preferably one which still has flowing water. There it is destroyed without spilling any of its blood. One informant said that the neck of the bird was broken, another indicated that it was suffocated. When the body has cooled a large stone is tied to its legs and feet and it is lowered into a deep pool in the river. "The sky will weep because of its animal with the beautiful colours. It (the sky) says, 'Are there no colours (i.e. is there no rainbow) in that land?' Then it remembers that there are no colours in that land, there being a great drought in it. So it sends rain to the land which has lacked colours, so that the killing of its animal be not repeated. To the sky the death of this bird is painful."

Insingizi is said to be a female bird and a favourite animal of the Lord-of-the-Sky. He likes it "because of its beautiful colours. It reminds him of the rainbow. The bird and the rainbow are beautiful ladies, his children, whom he loves." *Ingqungqulu* is also regarded as a messenger from the sky. "But

57

we do not know what kind of message it brings. It can be a good message and it can be a bad one." While droppings from *insingizi* falling either on a homestead or even on a person are regarded as special signs of forthcoming blessings, droppings of *ingqungqulu* are regarded as evil omens. The sound produced by its wings when flying are said to remind people of thunder. "This bird is a male, so it may be foretelling male thunder." (i.e. thunder without lightning but with good, yet heavy downfalls of rain.) Another informant added: "This kind of rain is better than drought. So if we get no other rain, we choose this kind."

If it proves difficult to find *insingizi* which can be killed at a river, *ingqungqulu* can be made use of. But it is known, however, that the subsequent rains need not of necessity be soft, soaking rains. One expects heavy downfalls. The procedure with *ingqungqulu* is the same as that with *insingizi*, with the exception that the bird sometimes is allowed to drown instead of being killed first and that a shallow pool is chosen instead of a deep one. The shallow pool is associated with the amount of water expected in the downpour. "If the pool is shallow, then the rain will not be so violent." Drowning is chosen because "the breath (*umoya*) goes upwards, bubbling through the water, and reaches the sky. There it reports that it has suffered at a certain place. Then the sky weeps, mourning this strong bird known for fearlessness."[57]

Popular thought regarding rain relates also to sharp sticks, protruding stones and boulders lying on hills. When there is a drought, people are sent out to remove all upright and protruding sticks and stones, especially on elevated hills and mountains. Explaining this, a man said: "It (the sky) sees these sharp things resembling spears. It becomes afraid to come down over us to give us rain. So to avoid causing fear, these things are removed. They are not a sign of respect towards the sky, resembling pointers just being pointed at it (the sky)."

Big boulders are rolled down hills in times of drought. A rain-maker explained it thus: "These stones become very hot. Even putting the hand on them is like putting it on a stove. They are very hot. When they are hot, the sky withdraws, saying, 'Why is there heat on the earth?' But if these stones causing heat are removed, then the sky will soon come, bringing rain. The heat of the stones is the anger of the earth. Heat and anger are the same. If there is anger, then nothing good can come. So the stones are rolled into the shade, removing the heat in them. Sometimes they are rolled into water, if it is possible. Or they are just simply covered up with earth. They become cool. Surely it will rain after this great work has been done."

Several reasons are given for the sky withholding rain, besides the fact that irritated or angry shades do so. If it is the Lord-of-the-Sky that is withholding rain, one of the following can be the cause of the drought: a man struck by lightning has not been buried in damp soil and is "burning the earth with drought": one of twins has not been destroyed and "is causing anger in the sky because it is still alive": a woman has undergone violent abortion and not reported the matter as she ought to have done. The premature child has been buried in dry ground: a man struck by lightning has been buried in red earth, a child that has cut one of its upper teeth before the lower has not been destroyed and/or not buried in damp earth near a river or stream: a person has taken an oath by the sky which was not true: a barren wife has gone to some unknown man to have a child with him and then deceived her husband saying that the child is his: a woman in the area continues to suckle her child although she knows that she is pregnant again, hoping to bring about an abortion by prolonged lactation.

Experience shows that in all cases where there are abnormalities in children, thought-patterns are that it is the Lord-of-the-Sky that is offended in the first instance, thereafter the shades. "He is angered because he is the creator of men. It is true that the shades work in procreation, but the life (*i-mphilo*) is already there from the beginning in the man when he does the work of procreation. The life comes from the creator." Unless necessary steps are taken to rectify the wrong, the wrath of the sky will remain and there will be no rain. The only instance of exhumation on record was an occasion of severe drought claimed to have been caused by a mother who had buried an aborted child immediately outside the homestead. Informants say that a diviner eventually traced the reason for the drought to this particular homestead and under pressure of other women, the unfortunate woman confessed. When the remains of the child had been buried in the vicinity of a river some considerable distance from the home and water from the river had been poured over the place where the body of the child had been buried previously, the anger of the sky was stilled. Three days later it rained.

In the case of the man who had taken an oath without support of truth, one said that the sky had been vexed by being offended, the offence expressing itself in a withdrawal of rain. Not until the man had confessed and slaughtered a white goat did rain come.

The role played by sheep-fat has been mentioned in connection with rain-making. One rain-maker associated the quietness of sheep with soft and penetrating rains. "This fat of sheep is used because it brings soft rain which has no noise. Again, a sheep is steady, not being like a goat. So its fat brings about steady rain."

Heat and coolness are thought-patterns applicable to Zulu ideas about rain. Heat is closely associated with anger. "When he (the Lord-of-the-Sky) is angry, he is hot. That is the time when the sun burns over us and there is no rain. But when he is at ease, there being nothing (that irritates him or angers him), there is no bad heat and the rains fall nicely. But the heat of his anger is a bad heat. We feel it in the shining of the sun very much." There is no indication that the Lord-of-the-Sky is identified with the sun or that the heat developed by the sun is identified with his anger. Proposing this to Zulu friends brought about amazement. "No, indeed not. How can the Lord-of-the-Sky be the sun? Who has said such things?" Further, it is never the rains that of themselves refuse to come. It is either the Lord-of-the-Sky or the shades that have interferred, their action caused by anger or irritation. Sometimes rains can also be delayed by witchcraft or sorcery.

In order to bring about "coolness in the sky" which, once achieved, will cause rain to fall, symbols which reflect coolness are made use of. The medicines and the horns which contain them are kept in cool places, one avoids sunshine at all costs when preparing the medicines, and one assumes a quiet attitude towards them. Quietness is regarded as a cool temperament as opposed to the heated debate which takes place when people quarrel and are angry. The Zulu expression *inhliziyo epholileyo* (lit. a cool heart) indicates one who does not speak much and is of a quiet disposition. Coolness, as heat and anger, are understood to be both physically expressed and a definite state of mind. Rain-makers claim that people who quickly become angry and have a very short temper cannot become rain-makers.

Rain-making medicine is stored away in a cool nook of a hut. They are also hidden under overhanging rocks and cliffs,[58] great care being taken that they are so well tucked away that no sunshine or heat will reach them. Rain-makers claim that this is common procedure (although none was willing to disclose such a place or show me the medicines). The male rain-maker explained it thus: "We do it to keep the medicines cool. If the medicines become hot, they do not do their work." One rain-maker operating in the Umvoti valley said that she kept her medicine cool by "burying them in the sand underneath a very big tree with a deep shade. The tree grows next to the water." All rain-makers agree that "the coolest place is underneath a very great rock (i.e. a cave)". Two rain-makers underlined that there must not be the possibility of a great amount of wind at the secluded spot where the medicine is hidden, for the wind would blow away the clouds of rain. But all were of the opinion that a small breeze was a good thing, because it kept the containers of the medicine cool, and "it is this kind of breeze that brings the good rains". One female rain-maker said that she placed her medicine in a cave where she knew that "the snake of the sky" would find it, claiming that it would come and lie on the medicine, keeping it cool. She hid her container in a cave overlooking the Thugela valley where pythons are found.

Closely associated with coolness is *inhlwathi* or *imonya,* the python. The two understandings of coolness referred to above are said to be embodied in this snake. Firstly, it is physically cold. Zulu are convinced that it is "the coolest of all the animals in the whole world". Several informants, including rain-makers and heaven-herds, agree that the coolness of water, especially that of deep pools, is brought about by the coolness of the python which is believed to live in the pools. Secondly, there is the coolness related to calmness and an even temperament. A python is said to have no *amawala* (careless, hasty and haphazard action). "This animal is never seen working hastily or in anger. It is always slow and steady, thinking a long time before it does something. So it is clear that it has no *amawala* at all. That is why we say that it is cool."

The python is also the symbol of great power, expressed in physical strength and ability. A man in the uMhlatuze valley where pythons are found said: "It is the strongest of all, only he (the Lord-of-the-Sky) being stronger. It is stronger than all the animals, being able to kill anything. Even bulls are killed by it." The very fact that a python squeezes its prey to death is a sign of power and ability not given even to men. "Even we, when we slaughter, we spill blood. We kill in this way because we lack *amandla* (ability) to kill in another way. So we do it in the way of spilling blood. But this animal kills in a manner which does not spill blood. That is a very dignified way. It kills nicely. There is no blood spilled. So the death is a dignified death in that there is no blood that is spilled."

The python itself is said to be very difficult to kill "because of its coolness all the time, even when it is facing death". A renowned diviner said; "It remains peaceful, doing nothing. So many times people think that it is dead and commence working (i.e. removing the skin). But when they look inside (the skin) they find that it is living. They fear very much and take it very quickly to the shadow of a tree. There they cut off the head, letting the blood run out on the earth under the tree, the animal all the time just remaining quiet and doing nothing."

Pythons symbolize togetherness, undivided oneness. The diviner at eThelezini used the word *inzongolozelwane* when referring to this characteristic. "We admire a man who can sit down in the evening and when the cocks crow in the morning he has eaten a whole goat. We admire him because he has shown that he is a man, simply sitting down and eating piece after piece until the complete goat is finished. But this thing (a python) is worse. It swallows everything at once, merely opening its mouth steadily and swallowing the complete goat in one mouth-full. That is why it is more fearful than a man, even a man who eats a whole goat without rising from his seat."

The thought-pattern of togetherness is the underlying idea in the use of a python's skin in the *inkhatha yesizwe,* the emblem of national unity and loyalty. It is only when the *inkhatha* has been enveloped with the skin of a python that it is really and truly the national emblem, even though it could lack other ingredients. But under no condition may the skin of the python be omitted. "How else could we say, 'We are the children of Mageba and Zulu' if this thing was not there, binding us together."

If the place where a python is rolled up is known, people avoid the place. It is looked upon as bad-mannered to stop and look at it. "If you meet it, just walk past it. Do not look at it. Just look in another direction as if you did not know that it is there." One informant said that if one looks at a python it will "catch the eye and you will never be able to look away again". Another said that if one stared at the reptile one's eyesight would be damaged and one would be dazzled "as when you look into the sun. You see simply nothing, just sharpness of light and white."

Talking ought to be avoided in the presence of pythons. The quietness is said to be like that which prevails "when there is thunder, because both come from the sky". Another said: "There is no talking because the great one is present." On the verandah of a local shop in the Mfolozi valley there had been placed two boxes, each containing a python which had been captured and were awaiting transport to Durban. While this particular verandah on other occasions was the meeting-place of people from the neighbourhood, all talking and laughing, it was completely void of people on this day, except for some inquisitive children from a nearby school who wished to see the reptiles.

Walking in the Nkwaleni valley with friends and our conversation being lively, their silence became very noticeable when they all at the same time stopped talking and the foremost man quickened the pace considerably for some five hundred meters. Then the pace was slowed down again and the conversation continued as if nothing had happened. My friends explained their behaviour thus: "Did you not smell something?" I admitted that I had smelt nothing. I was told that had I been attentive I would have noticed a smell "like sour milk". Curious to see whether it really was so, I suggested that we return to the place, but under no circumstance would my friends accept this, the smell having been that of a python. They claimed that the snake has a very characteristic smell. All the men, six in number, were fully aware of the fact that they had refrained from talking while passing the place where the snake was, and they were very conscious of the fact that our pace had been increased. They all denied being afraid of it and claimed that they had been silent as a sign of respect, passing by it quickly because they were close "to the animal of *iNkosi*". Other informants have said that pythons smell like lactating women, a limited number saying that the smell is that of women "when they are hot" (reference to sexual relations).

Lastly, no commoner, unless he is a heaven-herd, rain-maker or especially authorised to do so, is allowed to destroy a python. Traditionally, it was only members of the royal clan that had this privilege. When destroying pythons, one must avoid looking into its eyes. No blood ought to be allowed to run onto the ground. Either its neck is broken or else it can be suffocated to death.

All three rain-makers were emphatic that vessels used to prepare and store away medicine for rain-making should be of clay from a place that is always damp, even in times of severe drought. No emphasis was placed on the kind of clay used, although the male rain-maker claimed that dark clay was preferable to light-coloured material. All rain-makers said that after the pots had been burnt, they had to be cooled in a deep pool where they knew that "the snake of the sky" dwelt. "We cool the pots in the pool so that the snake recognizes them the time it comes out and seeks them." The pots are burnt on an overcast day "so that they see what thing is expected of them and the medicine they are to carry within themselves".

Rain-makers say that the horns containing medicine must never be removed from one another.[59] "It is like telling a wife to leave the home. What home is that which has no mother? Or it is like telling a man to leave his home, saying this without reason. If he goes, there is only trouble because he is missing." When the horns are not in use they are generally bundled together and kept in a bag or hidden in a secluded place at the back of the hut. Wherever they are kept, they must not be separated. One female rain-maker said: "If they are separated, then the clouds will never come together and cover the sky, bringing rain. They will just remain separated from each other, travelling over the sky and bringing no rain. That is why they must be together."

Rain is regarded as a fertilization of the earth by the sky. The male rain-maker expanded on this thought-pattern thus: "The sky and the earth are twins like my two fists are twins or my two feet are twins. The right fist and the right foot are stronger than the left. But they came from the womb at the same time, both the right fist and the left one. That is the condition of the sky and the earth. They are twins. They are both from the beginning. One is like the right fist and the right foot. That is the sky. The other is weaker, like the left fist and the left foot. That is the earth. Being twins, they are also husband and wife. The strong one is the husband. The weaker one is the wife. The husband fertilizes the wife. The fertilizer is the water. That is how it is with this thing of rain. It is the water of the sky which causes something to happen on the earth. Like no woman can bear a child without the assistance of a man, so the earth cannot produce food if the sky does not work with water on it (reference to sexual act)." Enlightning further on this issue, my informant said: "When a man does his work with his wife, we say, 'He is working with water.' It is the same with the sky. When it gives rain, it is working with water. If a man is angry with his wife, he does not go to her. She remains dry, producing nothing. It is the same with the sky. When it is angry, it leaves the earth dry. Nothing grows. We say to it, 'What has made you angry, since you have withdrawn your water from us?' Then perhaps the reason for the anger is found. It is cooled. Then the rain comes again." At least with my male rain-maker informant he was very conscious of sexual symbolism in his efforts to produce rain and readily admitted such knowledge. Whether the two female rain-makers were equally conscious was not easy to ascertain. Although their approach to rain-making was much the same as that of the male rain-maker, evidence did suggest that their interpretation was not as advanced as that of their male colleague.

The sexual symbolism may account for the fact that there are no unmarried rain-makers in Zulu society, the three with whom contacts were made all being very emphatic that a rain-maker must be married. The male rain-maker said: "How can an unmarried person know the work of water, not being married? Either the person must know how to work with water (male reference) or she must know how to receive water (female reference)." It may be a matter of co-incidence but certainly interesting, that both female rain-makers were esteemed mid-wives. Both claimed: "This is our work. We know it." Commoners chose not to comment on this observation, the male rain-maker saying: "That (midwifery) is the work of women. But these know it better than others." He would not expand on whom they were better than!

The Heavenly Queen

In the following section the term the Heavenly Queen is used as a translation of the Zulu names *iNkosikazi yeZulu, iNkosikazi yaseZuluwini* or, simply, *iNkosikazi*.

Although literature on the Zulu gives one the impression that in former times there was no clear distinction between the Heavenly Queen and *Nomkhubulwana,* modern Zulu are convinced that there is a very clear distinction between them. An informant at Ekutuleni said: "One is *inkosikazi*. She is the elder of the two, being the mother. The other is *inkosazana* (lit. a maiden). She is the younger."

Although Zulu are emphatic that there is a definite distinction between the two, local, personal and traditional thought-patterns on *inkosazana,* the Heavenly Princess, vary in detail. But they are to be found throughout Zulu society, also in towns and cities. This can, on the other hand, not be said of the Heavenly Queen. The conception of the Heavenly Queen has been lost to that extent that a large percentage of the population of Kwa Mashu township near Durban claimed never to have heard of her. Only a very limited number said that they had heard of her, mainly from old people. But apart from the name, they knew nothing of her.

However, the Heavenly Queen is known in different rural areas, although obtaining any significant details proved more-or-less fruitless. At Ekuthuleni an informant said: "We know that she is there (in the sky). She is the wife (*inkosikazi*) of the Lord-of-the-Sky, cooking his food for him and looking after him. That is all I know." Another informant said: "The old people say that she is the wife of *iNkosi*. He is white (i.e. transparent), so she must surely be like him in that they are not seen with the eye." Madela who claimed to have seen her in a vision, described her thus: "She is very big and has great dignity, being the great wife. She has many servants. She knows the work of women and attends to those who cook. She is fearful to see, being very strict. Everything in her house is beautiful. She is a real *inkosikazi*. The rest of the vision I am not allowed to reveal." A very old lady at Ekuthuleni claimed that in her youth *inkosikazi* was not spoken about, but people had knowledge of her. "People knew who she was, being the mother of the Princess (*inkosazana*). Today nobody knows her. Yes, there is a difference between the knowledge of former times of my childhood and to-day. Today the people know the things taught in the schools. In those times they knew the things taught in the homes. So there is a difference in knowl-edge."

Several old people, particularly women, agreed with the claim of the quoted old lady. It is therefore possible that the present-day concepts are shadows of what previously may have been clearer ideas about the Heavenly Queen.

Norenius states that there is a small plant with white and red flowers associated with the Heavenly Queen.[60] Two, possibly three, reliable inform-ants have said that they know of the plant. But it has been quite impos-sible to obtain any further information about it. Norenius also states that there were special office holders whose duties were to attend to rites in con-nection with the Heavenly Queen. The old Zulu lady quoted above claimed that in her childhood there was a man in the royal homestead of Prince Sitheku near Ekuthuleni called *inceku yeNkosikazi* (servant of the Heavenly Queen) whom she associated with the queen. She could not recollect what his duties were, but remembered him being dressed in a gaily coloured coat on a few occasions and that on these occasions he was very much hon-oured and respected.[61] The multi-coloured coat was mentioned to Madela at Ceza on an occasion when he were talking of the Heavenly Queen. He merely looked up alarmed and asked where I had got the information from. "These things are not spoken of. The person that told you will die of in-sanity. That is all I say."

The Princess and her Cult

Nomkhubulwana, described as *iNkosazana yeZulu* or *iNkosazana yasezulwini*, is the heavenly princess. Although interest and subsequent attention paid to her is by no means comparable to that of the Lord-of-the-Sky, she plays a far more prominent role in thinking, particularly among women, than does the Heavenly Queen. Professor Krige argues that "these rites, long thought to have died out, have not only survived in outlying parts of the country, but have lately been revived in many areas, some quite close to Durban".[62] Ex-perience supports this statement, although the traditions and information are definitely localized. This localized character, I suggest, accounts for the varie-ty in traditions and differences in the cult of *Nomkhubulwana*.[63]

Certain characteristics of *Nomkhubulwana* and her cult described in the ethnographic literature are found in the various local traditions and rites. These indicate the essential attractions to the deity. Firstly, the Princess is looked upon as being a virgin. As such she is closely related to the young marriageable girls as well as to fertility in mankind, animals and groups. Secondly, she is associated with the sky. To a number of Zulu she is the daughter of the Lord-of-the-Sky. It is in this capacity that she is regarded as being everlasting in that she neither becomes older nor changes. For time to time she gives advice and rules which have neither been sanctioned by society nor derived from the shades.

An informant at Mapumulo described her thus: "She is *inthombi* (a virgin) and must be honoured as a maiden. That is why men must not look at her. This would be a bad thing." Another informant at Ekuthuleni said: "She is *inkosazana* who comes down from heaven. She lives there (in the sky) with her father. She comes in the mists and is the one seen by children and maidens. A man must not see her. It would be like looking at the daughter of a king." But girls are friendly with her because she is always their *inthanga* (age-group). "She is *inthanga* of all girls. She does not grow old." In several areas one agrees that *Nomkhubulwana* can appear also to men, "but then they must look away immediately". One underlines that men looking at her will either become blind because they have looked where they ought not to see, or they will become very ill and no herbalist will be able to heal them. "That sickness is too strong for medicines. It comes from the sky. That is why it is stronger than medicines." But as a rule the Princess is said to reveal herself only to maidens and children. They also avoid looking at her as if they were inquisitive, but merely listen to her, noting what she wants them to know.[64]

Zulu women relate that the Princess is dressed in white, although a limited number say that she may also reveal herself in a multicoloured gown. A fair number of Zulu women say that *Nomkhubulwana* is naked except for a small string of white beads around the waist. (The latter informants have all been pagan women.) No informant knew of her appearance as being "of a beautiful landscape with verdant forests on some parts of her body, grass-covered slopes on others and cultivated fields on the rest", as described by S. O. Samuelson in the early 20th century,[65] or as "a very little animal as large as a polecat and marked with little white and black stripes; on one side there grows a bed of reeds, a forest and grass; the other side is that of a man", as described by Callaway in the 1860's.[66] At Ekuthuleni the Princess is described as being "a very beautiful girl of twenty years with shiny skin and white attractive teeth. She is always smiling, except when something bad has happened or she brings news about droughts or famine." She is looked upon as shy and bashful in a becoming manner, neither talkative nor inquisitive, "merely interested wherever people wish her to see things". All informants agree that *Nomkhubulwana* appears in the morning mists and that she is closely associated with the rainbow, a small number saying that she is the rainbow itself. They are equally convinced that the Princess has the ability to bring about steady and frequent rains, these brought by pleading with her father, the Lord-of-the-Sky. An old woman at Ceza claimed that the cause of the frequent droughts recently is the fact that people no longer honour *Nomkhubulwana* as they did in former times. "I say to you, when also those who honour her today no longer do this, then we shall all die because of drought."

A group of girls in the N valley said that they annually celebrated *Nomdede,* a festival described by several authors.[67] Their description of the ceremony differs somewhat from that related by ethnographic accounts, reflecting a difference in local custom. The local procedure described by the girls was verified by people in that area. Information gathered elsewhere had more in common with descriptions of the occasion in literature, and will hence not be accounted for in detail here. Because of the difference between the celebration of *Nomdede* by the girls of N valley, their description of the festival will be related.

Secretly the girls brew beer known as *uNomdede*. It is brewed on the occasion when the first mist in spring is noticed on the local S mountain, indicating that "now our friend, *inkosazana,* has come down from the sky onto the mountain". They claim that in this particular area the heavenly Princess would not descend anywhere else except on the mountain from where she would make occasional strolls to spruits in the close vicinity of the hill, preferably such as had vegetation growing over the water. Because of respect toward the Princess men avoid the mountain, especially in the early spring. "The men do not fear her. They merely respect her by not going to places where she is known to appear. It is not good for men to see her."

The beer is brewed of millet brought from their respective homes, each girl contributing a quantity which is given to the girl appointed for the purpose of brewing the beer. They claimed no longer to practise the old custom of *ukuphukula umlomo,* although they admit having heard of it. Elderly women in the area claim that it is recently that this custom has been discontinued and that only some fifteen years ago it was still practised.[68] While the beer is fermenting the girls borrow their lovers' every-day wear, dancing shields and sticks. The dress is not of necessity the traditional loin-clothing, but often merely a pair of trousers and a shirt. While Bryant says that the *Nomdede* was celebrated in December, my informants maintained that "at Christmas we have long ago completed our work".

On preferably a Thursday, at the crack of dawn,[69] the girls, dressed in their lovers' attire, would enter their fathers' cattle-enclosure and drive out two or three cows to be herded by them on the slopes of the hill. One of the beasts ought to be a heifer while another ought, if possible, to be a milk-producing cow, the calf of which would be left with the other calves. The girls were reluctant to indicate the grazing ground, presumably fearing that they would be spied upon on some later occasion. At the grazing ground they would leave the cattle under the care of two of the girls while the rest would climb a little further up the mountain to a known place, each carrying with them a calabash containing the beer they had brewed, some maize, millet, pumpkin seeds and beans. Some of the calabashes containing beer would be placed on a large overhanging stone "where *inkosazana* can see them clearly". The packets containing the seeds would be placed next to the beer-containers. Then the girls would sing a song, inviting *Nomkhubulwana* to come and partake of her food. "Come, our sister! It is for you that we have prepared! Here is food prepared for you! Come, our sister! We have brought it here for you!"[70]

The rest of the beer would be drunk by the girls during the course of the day. The seeds would be removed in the afternoon when they returned home and used in the field tilled in honour of the Princess elsewhere at a later stage. From time to time two girls would leave the company and release those that were hearding the cattle, thus allowing all girls to participate in the festivities. The girls maintain that it is not essential that all of them herd the cattle. But it is essential that all be given a chance of "being with *Nomkhubulwana* who is our sister so that she may see her friends". The day would be spent in gossip, amusement, beer-drinking and talk about their lovers and hopes of an early marriage. They would relate to each other secrets and intimate news they had of other girls who were being courted. Now-and-again they would sing and dance around a small fire made of sticks found on the mountain, clapping their hands as they performed. They would also compose songs to be sung on the occasion of their marriage. Vile and obscene language would be shouted at anybody who came near the place where they were and was not involved in their festivity. Should the person not leave immediately, the girls would hide among boulders and rocks, throwing stones at the person, urging him to leave unless some serious ill should befall him.[71]

Prior to their departure in the late afternoon, the girls would pour out the beer placed on the overhanging rock onto the stones, saying: "Here, sister, is your food! It is the food eaten by men. Look after us that we may soon feel horns around us! (ref. to male member)." The girls return home unseen by anybody and thus avoid the regular paths. On arrival at the homesteads, they steal into their huts and change their clothing immediately. The cattle are left immediately outside the main gate and turned into the cattle-enclosure by the herd-boys. The cows are milked in the regular way by the boys or menfolk. "Sometimes a boy may say: 'Where has this cow been all this day? Has it been with our sister who also has been away?' Then we simply remain silent. Or we may say, if the boy asks again: 'Oh, we have just been somewhere to see a friend.' Then they think that we have been at a party, knowing nothing."

With the return of the cattle and the change to normal dress, the girls do not participate in further *Nomkhubulwana* celebrations that year. The girls interviewed claimed that the celebration in their particular area never occupied more than a day, nor was there any festivity carried out in their homes.

The girls made it clear that their getting together for the occasion on the local hill was a secret known to them only. They admitted that sometimes women would know that they were preparing for the festivity and that they sometimes were asked when they were planning to ascend the mountain. Sometimes they would reveal the planned date to women newly married and who had recently been participants of the occasion themselves. They would decide among themselves on a suitable day to celebrate, whom they would invite to participate with them, choosing new participants from girls who had lovers and who would possibly marry in the near future. When a girl married or had a child prior to marriage she would automatically be excluded from the celebrations "because our sister is an *inthombi*". The girls laughed heartily when asked whether girls who had not commenced monthly periods would be allowed to participate. "What do they know about these things of our sister, being children?"

The girls were emphatic that they met on the hill to celebrate *inkosazana*, assuring me that she is *Nomkhubulwana*. They celebrated her in order that "things may go well during the coming year. We wish to marry but we do not know whether our lovers will remain faithful. So we do this work of our sister. We take the seeds with us so that she may see that we are planning for her garden. Then she will bless (*ukubusisa*) the fields so that they give a (good) harvest. The money from the towns is becoming less and less."[72]

Explaining their being dressed in their lovers' clothing the girls said: "How can we, being girls, herd cattle? Cattle are the animals of men, herded by men. So how can we herd them dressed in our (own) clothing? It is this that causes us to wear men's clothing. That is all. There is no other reason." Asked why they wore their lovers' clothing and not their brothers' as apparently was done previously, they replied: "It is because they are in the towns. Some are in Durban. Some are in Stanger. Some even in Johannesburg. These are the places where they work. That is the reason. Further, if we wear our brothers' clothing, then we would be remembering them (the brothers), whereas the ones we are thinking of when we do this thing are the men who love us. We wish to think of them." One of the girls added later: "If we wear the dress of our lovers then *Nomkhubulwana* sees that we want her to assist us in marrying them. We wish our sister to agree with us, telling us that the men are good choices. She is our sister. She will tell us whether they will be faithful or whether they will be bringing some fearful sickness from the towns (reference to venereal diseases). That is why we do not wear the clothing of our brothers today."[73]

All the girls emphasised that the millet used in brewing the *Nomdede* beer should not be millet bought in a store but be from the previous year's own supply. "If we use any other millet then *inkosazana* will be disappointed in that we simply have bought something for her, not remembering her when we took the last of the millet (in the stores) but simply eating everything ourselves. So we must show her respect in that we keep some millet for her, preparing the beer from it. It is the way she likes it prepared." Another girl of the group disagreed, however, saying that if the millet was bought in the store "our sister would really see that we honour her. If that is the reason for keeping some millet, why do we buy Christmas presents? We buy these because the store has better things than we have. How then can we say that our millet is better than that in the store?" But having voiced her opinion, she was opposed by the other girls who argued that if that be the case, then why not buy meat at the local butcher for ritual celebrations. "But when have people bought meat at the butcher for such work? So it is clear that when it comes to work, the things must come from the home." Such emphasis is given to the beer taken to the hill that the beer not only has a special name given it, *Nomdede*, but this specific name in fact is the term used to describe the whole celebration.[74]

Nomkhubulwana is closely associated with the mist which, according to Zulu, is a certain sign of the advent of spring. The girls were emphatic that the sole reason for their celebrating *Nomdede* after the arrival of the first mists on the local hill was its close relationship with the princess and her connections with fertility of the coming year. One of the girls said: "When we see the mist for the first time, then we quickly spread the news to those of our age-group who do not see the hill from their homes, saying, 'Now the princess has come. We have seen her on the hill.' Then we know that it is time to prepare (for the festival)." Asked whether she regarded it a misfortune if it rained on the day of celebration, the girl laughed and said: "No! Then we will not be seen." Another added: "On a rainy day we would say, 'Today our sister is meeting us in a nice way.' So we would be happy, laughing much." "Even if we are cold because of the rain on this day, we would not feel it. There is nobody who feels the cold because of happiness." I suggested that being out-doors in rain may bring about colds; one of the group replied: "No, there can be no illness after *Nomdede. Nomkhubulwana* is the one that removes all sicknesses from her friends. So when we have been with her there can not be any sickness."

There is no fixed quantity of seeds that must be taken to the celebration on the mountain. As much millet and maize as can be scooped up in one handful is taken or, as one girl put it, "we take one cob and one ear of millet". About 25–30 beans are taken and about an equal number of pumpkin pips. "We take these seeds so that *inkosazana* can see them and give us good crops. She knows that they are for her garden. Then she drives away *ingcokolo* (common maize grub), so that we may reap good crops." Asked whether they also took along potatoes to the mountain, seeing that this crop is becoming increasingly popular in the area, the girls said that *Nomkhubulwana* did not know potatoes. "This food has been brought by the whites." Nor did they take with them either sweet-potatoes (Ipomoea batatas) or *amadumbe* (Colosia antiquorum), although these have been staple foods in the district for generations. Commenting on this observation one of the girls said: "It may be that our sister does not know them because they grow under the earth. But I do not know."

The presence of cattle in the close vicinity of the girls' celebration of *Nomdede* is, according to the girls, also to be interpreted as a fertility symbol. "If we did not have cattle with us, then *inkosazana* would say, 'Sisters, have you no cattle any more? Is there no bellowing in the byres? How do you eat now, there being no sour milk in the calabashes? Or is *uphuthu* (dry, boiled maize meal) eaten dry these days?' So we must have cattle with us." In connection with the choice of cattle taken to the grazing ground one of the girls said: "We take a heifer so that *Nomkhubulwana* sees that we are looking at this animal to see when it is in calf so that there may be milk in the calabashes. Again, it (the heifer) is like us in that it has not given birth. So we are all hoping. She (*Nomkhubulwana*) can help us." Commenting on the fact that not the complete herd is taken along as was the custom previously, the girls said that it was sufficient to take only two or three animals with them. But bulls and oxen were not considered. "They do not give birth. It is the cows that are made pregnant, not the male animals. When have you heard that men take part in *Nomdede*? Why then should these animals be present?" They did, however, admit that they were aware of the fact that previously the herd in its totality was driven away by *Nomdede* participants.[75]

Some ethnographic records point to a close relationship between the rainbow and the princess, saying that the rainbow is "regarded as an emanation of her glory".[76] Samuelson expressly states that the rainbow is an emanation of the Heavenly Queen and draws at the same time a very clear distinction between the Queen and the Princess. Bearing in mind the localized ideas relating to both the Heavenly Queen and the Princess, it is perhaps not surprising that present-day Zulu do not have consistent ideas about whom the rainbow is attached to. Some of the girls in the N valley were convinced that the rainbow not only was an emanation of the princess but, in fact, was the princess herself, dressed thus for the occasion. On other occasions she was the mist. A of Ceza said that the rainbow, *uthingo lwenkosazana*, is a bundle of supple sticks that formed a part of the Princess' hut in the sky. She continued her description of the Princess' hut thus: "She loves human beings. So she opens the heaven, allowing them to see things in there. That is when the rainbow is seen. It is when she (*Nomkhubulwana*) lets them see it. The arches are the colours. They are beautiful having all the colours. Then people are happy, saying, 'The Princess surely loves us. Now the rain will stop and give us sun-shine. Then after a time she will bring rain again.' That is what people say when they see this beautiful thing of the Princess." On another occasion the same informant said that huts were built as they were with soft wattle sapplings which are bent into arches, "because the Princess has taught us to do it this way in that she opened the sky and showed us the hut of the sky where she lives."

At least one end of the rainbow always stands on the earth, the base buried deep in a pool of water in which lives a snake with as many colours as the rainbow. "That is why snakes and animals with many colours are always very much feared. They come from the rainbow." Diviners and heaven-herds are said to take careful note in which pool in a river the arch of the rainbow ends, so that they know where the snake is to be found.

Should a male find himself immediately underneath the rainbow he is sure to become seriously ill and no herbalist will be able to help him. If the man finds himself near the pool where the rainbow enters the earth, traditions say that the snake will come out of the water and swallow him whole. If a woman, on the other hand, should find herself immediately under the rainbow she can speak "softly to the Princess, asking for the thing she wants. That is why women who have no child always watch carefully for the rainbow. When nobody is looking they will run naked to the place where it enters the pool to ask of the princess for the thing that they desire very much. They become happy, knowing that the husband will sleep with them that night, saying, 'Wife, how is it that you are beautiful like the rainbow today?' He will desire her very much, more than at any other time and go to her even before everybody is asleep. The Princess will give the woman the child that she has been longing for because she made the wife beautiful so that her husband worked very much." Girls who are said to be ugly also seek to come close to the rainbow and thereby become fair to look upon. "They do not become beautiful in that they change their skin or their appearance. It is simply that the men look at them and then see that they are beautiful. Then they have become beautiful. This is the work that she (*Nomkhubulwana*) does for her sisters."

A, quoted above, was emphatic that the Lord-of-the-Sky was *Nomkhubulwana*'s father, adding that 'the father loves his daughter very much because she is beautiful and good and trustworthy". He (the Lord-of-the-Sky) is claimed to tell his daughter everything she wants to know and hence she is able to tell her earthly sisters things they wish to know. My informants said that the Princess loved human beings very much and that this was the reason for her giving them good advice from time-to-time, introducing new customs and teaching people "the new ways of behaving in a proper way". "To those who do not believe (i.e., pagans) she is what the angels are to me. She gives them advice as to their behavior so that they may be looked upon as good and reliable girls. She tells them which young men are good to marry and which the girls must avoid. She tells them many things which we do not know of. It is like this. I am old now but I know no man. I would never been able to live like this had it not been for God's angels who constantly appeared to me, telling me what to do and how to behave. So the angels are my friends who helped me through everything. It is the same relationship between *Nomkhubulwana* and the pagan girls. She tells them everything in order that they do not transgress the rules and cause trouble."[77]

An old woman in the Mapumulo district said of *Nomkhubulwana*: "She is the friend of all the people who behave properly. She comes to them from the sky. She helps them in every way with the children, giving them advice when they should be weaned and what other food they should be given. It is because of her that we today give them *incumbe* (sour fluid porridge) because she has agreed to this food."

My informant from the Mapumulo area continued: "*Inkosazana* is always young because she has no children of her own. She never grows old and becomes like one of us. She is always beautiful, having a handsome body with strong legs. Her breasts are always uncovered (i.e. she is never pregnant), showing us that it is not disgraceful to walk about in this way. It is the white man like yourself that has brought disgrace in saying, 'Cover up yourselves!' Now we cannot see when a girl has been up to mischief or not. But in the days of *Nomkhubulwana*'s teaching it was not like that. What she taught was better than that which was brought by the white people." Another informant said that the Heavenly Princess was like the Lord-of-the-Sky who did not become old or degenerate. "He is always the same. So is *inkosazana* of whom you are asking. She does not change." An informant at Ceza said that she could not visualize *Nomkhubulwana* as becoming either older or unattractive. "She is in the sky. Up there everything is the same year after year. The Princess only knows when the year starts and then she reveals herself. But she does not know any number of years (i.e. she does not count years)."

Nomkhubulwana as advisor and instructor has been hinted at. Several informants underlined that the Heavenly Princess' main duty when coming to earth was to assist womenfolk and especially marriageable girls in matters pertaining to choice of partner, children, cultivation of fields, preparation of foods and general welfare. A, quoted above, felt strongly along these lines and was of the definite impression that the chief reason for a temporary loss in interest in *Nomkhubulwana* was the fact "that today one learns everything in the schools. So *inkosazana* has nothing to teach our people. That is why she does not appear very much these days and people have been forgetting her.[78] If the white people had not brought schools then *Nomkhubulwana* would have remained our teacher." My informant's thoughts were generally those of most people of that area, although she possibly had views stronger than most of her fellow women-folk.

An analysis of the *Nomdede* ceremony as conducted by the group of girls in the N valley does not stress *Nomkhubulwana* as teacher and advisor. To them the Princess was in the first place a fertility deity, strongly anchored in their life of constant fears of living unmarried, the daily struggle for sufficient food and a strong conservative background and setting in which they lived. In the valley there is a majority of women. The men, until recently, nearly all go to towns and cities to seek work and, once a man finds a job, he will stick to it for fear of losing it and being without work and subsequent

income. Being a heavily populated valley, the soil is tilled to maximum capacity. Should rains be delayed or devasting thunderstorms wash away the
crops, or hail damage the gardens, then the prospects for the coming season
are indeed gloomy. To this must be added that *Nomdede* is celebrated at a
time of the year when supplies are running very low and people are expecting the rains with growing excitement. Against this background a fertility
ritual as that of *Nomdede* certainly fills a living function. One appreciates the
setting aside of millet to brew the beer in quite a different way when one
understands what the setting aside of this millet means in terms of a lost
meal or possibly a calabash of beer for a lover when he returns from work in
a neighbouring town or city over a weekend!

Nomkhubulwana's revelation requires two additional notes. Firstly, in areas
where the fertility aspects of the Princess are stressed one finds that the princess reveals herself in the mists, in the soft rains, in the rainbow, at spruits
and rivers with much overhanging vegetation, preference being given to places
where the water flows freely over stones in the bottom of the river causing
the water to murmur and bubble. I was taken to such a place by a woman
from U. It was in a deep valley. The water ran over solid rock and made
its way to a larger river through dense indigenous forest. The air was cool
and moist, although the day itself was hot. There was much moss growing
on the rocks and the under-growth was at places so thick that it was impene-
trable. Several small waterfalls caused the water to murmur continuously.
"This is the place of the daughter of the Lord-of-the-Sky", said my escort
when we came to an open place in the valley. "The girls sit on the rock
and wait for her here." She spoke in a low and very respectful voice,
bending down over her walking-stick continually and only occasionally lifting
her head. Having shown me the place she was keen to leave as soon as possible. "Now you have seen the thing you have been asking for. Let us leave
now. It is getting late." *Nomkhubulwana* is said to appear in fields, especially when these are being tilled by women alone and when the mists are
present.

All informants but one assured me that the Princess appeared to people
in such a way that they could hear her distinctly but not see her. This is
said to be the reason for her choosing millet and maize fields or the dense
vegetations surrounding brooks and spruits, "so that she may hide in the
grass or in the fields. She is naked and must not be seen."[79] Both in areas
where the princess is accepted as advisor as in the Ekuthuleni area, or where
she is regarded as a fertility deity as in the N valley, this holds true. One
single informant said that *Nkomkhubulwana* appeared to people in dreams.
But this was denied vigorously by all other informants. A said: "No, the
Princess does not come in dreams. If people dream about a young maid, then
it is the shades that are speaking to them about that woman whom they see.
Never has it ever been heard that *inkosazana* appeared to anybody in
dreams. It is impossible."

Bryant describes a ceremony performed in the fields when the plants are
some two feet high, this ceremony associated with *Nomkhubulwana* through
the *Nomdede* beer.[80] Each girl, carrying with her some red clay powdered in
order to be readily spread, and a twig of *ulethi* bush, assembles with her
comrades at a point in the fields nearest to their home; they pass through
the fields and sprinkle the plants with the powdered clay, touching the plants

with the twigs and crying: "Grant us corn! What shall we eat? Oh, what?" On a later occasion they will pass through the fields again, uprooting plants which have been attacked by the maize-grub. After passing through all the fields, in the company of elder women on this occasion, they will go to a remote place and bury the ears of millet in the earth while the grub-eaten stalks will be thrown into a river. This ritual has also changed through the course of the years, although it appears to be practised far more widely over the country than is the *Nomdede* festival. Secondly, it seems to have been separated to a large extent from *Nomkhubulwana*, at least in many places, and become a purely medical treatment of the plants in the fields.

Informants agree that red soil, powdered for the purpose, is mixed with ash of the *ulethi* (Myrica conifera) and strewn over the plants as a treatment against the maize-grub. But few informants associated this treatment of the fields with the Princess. Old women, on the other hand, said that formerly *Nomkhubulwana* was called upon by the girls who strewed the mixture on the fields: one of them gave the words of the song composed for this occasion: "Sister, what is happening? What is this thing in the fields? Have you forgotten us, our sister? What shall we eat, our food being eaten by animals? Oh, what shall we eat?"

A stressed the importance of removing all stalks with maize-grub in them from the fields. She was convinced that if they were left in the fields the cattle would get ill from eating the smitten stalks and that the grub would spread to further areas in the coming year. Explaining the burying of the millet ears, she said that food should never be thrown away, "because the shades would think that we have too much food and they will not give us what we ask for". Other informants said that no food should be thrown into the river because "the water carries away everything that is bad. The food in the ears is not bad. It is the grub that is bad. That is why we bury the ears and throw the stalks into the river." According to A's opinion there was no direct connection between the *Nomdede* festival and the attention given to the fields in terms of the maizegrub, unless "it was that *Nomkhubulwana* on some occasion previously has taught our people to treat this disease in this manner. Otherwise there is nothing between *Nomkhubulwana* and this treatment of the fields." Curiously, *ulethi* is also a medicament used against cough. A said that *ulethi* is used for this ailment because "cough is caused by small worms that look like the maize-grub. So one and the same medicine is used." According to Doke–Vilakazi *ulethi* is "burnt among the corn in order to induce a good harvest. . ."[81] A large number of informants agree to this information, saying that the shrub causes a bluish smoke which, if it settles over the fields, is regarded as strengthening the plants. The shrub is hence burnt in the fields in the late afternoon when the smoke tends to spread over the fields rather than rise.

Nomkhubulwana is known in Swazi thinking. According to B. A. Marwick the Swazi equivalent to the Zulu *Nomkhubulwane* is known as *Nomku6ulwane*. Marwick writes that "the deity is a female one, and it appears to have no relation to Mkhulumnqande or Mlentengamunye", the Swazi equivalents to the Zulu Lord-of-the-Sky. According to Marwick *Nomku6ulwane* is "capable of sending sickness to human beings." Both these characteristics of the Swazi deity are different from the Zulu equivalent who is strongly associated with the Lord-of-the-Sky and who, under no circumstances, sends sickness. She is, on the other hand, able to prevent sickness. Being looked upon as thoroughly good, she is not able to cause any evil or damage.[82]

Professor Hilda Kuper writes that *Umkhulumcandi* (of the Swazi) "had a messenger, *Umlenzengamunye* (One Leg) who occasionally descended from the skies in a thick mist and was visible only to women and children. His appearance heralded fever, and it was customary to propitiate him." Mothers would "bury their little ones up to their necks in the river sand for a few minutes, then dug them up again and, without looking back, hurried them home".[83]

Notes

[1] Callaway, *The Religious System of the Amazulu and Izinganekwane*. However, see pp. 50 and 53 f. in the former where the creator is stated to be in the sky.

[2] For further discussion see Krige, *SSZ*, p. 410.

[3] Bryant, *Dict.*, p. 397. Cp. also Döhne, *Zulu–Kafir Dict.*, p. 364.

[4] Callaway, *The Religious System of the Amazulu*, pp. 7–9.

[5] Colenso, *Ten Weeks in Natal*, p. 59.

[6] Doke–Vilakazi, *Dict.*, p. 517.

[7] Gardiner, *Narrative of a Journey to the Zoolu Country*, p. 178.

[8] Leslie, *Among the Zulus and Amatongas*, p. 207.

[9] Bryant, *Dict.*, p. 444.

[10] Doke–Vilakazi, *Dict.*, 764.

[11] Farrer, *Zululand and the Zulus*, p. 130, writing in 1870's, says that "in addition to *Unkulunkulu* and quite distinct from him, the Zulus speak in their traditions of a Lord of heaven, whom they call 'the king which is above'". By 1911 Bryant, Wanger and van Oordt were arguing that *uMvelingqangi* should not be confused with the shades. See *The Collector*, No. 365, pp. 49 ff. Sikakana, 'Review of *Zulu Woman*', p. 97, states that Zulu definitely have had a God in the sky. African authors from both East and West Africa argue along similar lines, e.g. Mbiti, *Concepts of God in Africa* and Sawyerr, *God: Ancestor or Creator?* See also Moore, 'God and Man in Bantu Religions'.
For evolution of changing thought-patterns among Balovale see White, 'The Supreme Being in the Beliefs of the Balovale Tribes'.
See also Dammann, 'A Tentative Philological Typology of some African High Deities'.

[12] Informants claim that the Lord-of-the-Sky has only one name, *uMvelingqangi*, and a number of praise-names. Although Madela used the name frequently, Zulu in common hesitate to use it. Nobody doubts that *iNkosi yezulu, iNkosi yaphezulu* and *uMvelingqangi* are the same.
Very little attention is given by Zulu to a distinction between the sky itself and the Lord-of-the-Sky whom they believe to live in the sky. While scholars of comparative religions debate this issue, the Zulu say that "the one living at that place is that place. So what is the difference?" Compare Schmidt, *Der Ursprung der Gottesidee* and Pettazoni, *Dio*.

[13] See further Doke–Vilakazi, *Dict.*, p. 405.

[14] See discussion on the issue of *uNkulunkulu* as shade, founding shade, creator, etc. in Wanger, 'The Zulu Notion of God', pp. 351–385 and Schebesta, 'uNkulunkulu', pp. 525–526.

[15] For extensive material on creation myths and an analysis of these see Baumann, *Schöpfung und Urzeit des Menschen im Mythus der Afrikanischen Völker*. Baumann argues that myths dealing with creation of the world are not original African myths, the traditional myths presupposing the existence of the world on which takes place the creation of man. Creation in African mythology is, according to Baumann, wholly an anthropo-genesis, man being the measure of everything in creation and existence.
For Zulu creation myths relating to a reed see Callaway, op.cit., pp. 1 ff.: Shaw, *The Story of my Mission in South-Eastern Africa*, pp. 451 f.: Bryant, *Dict.*, p. 758:

Bleek, *Zulu Legends*, pp. 2 f.: Norenius, 'Något om zuluernas religiösa föreställ-ningar', p. 104.
[16] Werner, A., 'Some Notes on Zulu Religious Ideas', pp. 31 & 32. For Xhosa usage see Kropf, *Kafir–English Dictionary*, p. 347.
[17] Wangemann, *Ein Reise-Jahr in Süd-Afrika*, p. 225, writing in 1850, says that he is of the impression that there is not another God among the Zulu other than the shades. Shaw, op.cit., p. 225, states that "the Kaffirs had extremely vague and indistinct notions concerning the existence of God before the missionaries and other Europeans had intercourse with the natives".
See also Campbell, *Travels in South Africa*, p. 513. Krauss, 'The Zulu', writing in 1839/40 says that "in the past their ancestors had believed in the existence of an all-governing spirit which they called 'Villenangi' (literally, the first apparition). He was supposed to have created another being of great power, called "Koolukoolwani". This being was supposed to have come to earth in order to divide the sexes and colours of men."
[18] Cf. Callaway, op.cit., pp. 13–15, who gives the impression that *uNsondo* is applicable to the shades. Modern Zulu deny this emphatically.
[19] Bryant, *Dict.*, p. 209.
[20] Doke–Vilakazi, *Dict.*, p. 278.
[21] Norenius, 'Något om zuluernas religiösa föreställningar', p. 98.
[22] Norenius, 'Något om zuluernas religiösa föreställningar', p. 98.
[23] See also Callaway, op.cit., p. 401 and Farrer, *Zululand and the Zulus*, p. 146.
[24] Doke–Vilakazi, *Dict.*, p. 513.
[25] Zulu are explicit that *ukuthathwa* in this particular setting always refers to being taken by the Lord-of-the-Sky.
[26] Doke–Vilakazi, *Dict.*, p. 574.
[27] *The Collector*, No. 365, p. 55, says ·the finger above the earth indicates the deceased's "saluting, as it were, the Lord in heaven, in his grave for the honour conferred by him".
[28] Brownlee, 'A Fragment on Xhosa Religious Beliefs', p. 38, says that a person struck by lightning is not mourned among Xhosa.
[29] See Stuart, *Kulumetule*, pp. 215–218, for a description of the burial of one struck by lightning.
[30] *Ukukhothama* is not limited only to such that have been struck by lightning. Members of the royal clan, when deceased, are also referred to as *abakhotheme*, those who kneel. People at one of the royal homesteads at Ekuthuleni said that "those who are *abantwana* (royal clan) return to the one who sent them. That is why we say that they are kneeling. They are kneeling in front of him (the Lord-of-the-Sky), pleading for us who are still here (on earth)". An informant said in connection with the burial of the late King Cyprian: "It is only nowadays that it is said even of kings, 'They are dead', This is bad. Formerly it was said, 'They are kneeling'. Then people knew that he was pleading for us who are his children."
[31] Cf. e.g. Fritsch, *Die Eingeborenen Süd-Afrikas*, p. 98: Wangemann, *Ein Reise-Jahr in Süd-Afrika*, p. 225.
[32] Krige, *SSZ*, p. 249 ff.
[33] Cf. Bryant, *Dict.*, p. 319.
[34] Roberts, E., *Shembe, the Man and his Work*, p. 5. Cf. with Sikakana's statement that "Zulus propitiate the spirits (*ukuthetha amadlozi*) which to them, are a celestial liasion between the people and the Supreme Being whom they worship". (Sikakana, Review of Zulu Woman, p. 96.)
[35] Bryant, *Dict.*, p. 317: Doke–Vilakazi, *Dict.*, p. 405.
[36] Bryant, *Dict.*, p. 624: Doke–Vilakazi, *Dict.*, p. 792.
[37] See also Tyler, *Forty Years among the Zulus*, p. 111.
[38] Women participate in large numbers when Christians or members of Independent groups gather on the hills and mountains for prayer.
[39] Sibeko, A. V., 'Imilingi neMithi yokwelapha yaBantu'.
[40] Doke–Vilakazi, *Dict.*, p. 761.
[41] See further Chapter IX, Medical Treatment and Symbolism.
[42] Krige, *SSZ*, p. 313.
[43] Krige, *SSZ*, p. 317. See also Sibeko, 'Imilingo neMithi yokwelapha yaBantu', pp. 200 ff.

[44] *The Collector*, No. 470, p. 79.

[45] *The Collecotor*, No. 136, p. 12, says that everything white is removed during a thunderstorm. See also Sibeko, 'Imilingo neMithi yokwelapha yaBantu', p. 200.

[46] For the role played by the king in rain-making see Callaway, *The Religious System of the Amazulu*, pp. 409, 319, 375: Gibson, *The Story of the Zulus*, p. 91: Kidd, *The Essential Kafir*, p. 114: Holub, *Sieben Jahre in Süd-Afrika*, Vol I, p. 329: Shaw, *The Story of my Mission*, p. 461.

[47] Shooter, *The Kafirs of Natal and the Zulu Country*, pp. 212 f.

[48] See Schoeman, 'The Swazi Rain Ceremony': Beemer, H., 'The Swazi Rain Ceremony': Krige, *The Realm of a Rain-Queen*, pp. 271 ff.

[49] Shooter, *The Kafirs of Natal and the Zulu Country*, p. 212.

[50] For further historic information see Bryant, *Olden Times in Zululand and Natal*, pp. 248, 364 & 366.

[51] A reputed rain-maker in Northern Natal is said to have been a woman called Madungudu, living among the Ndwandwe clan and most probably of this clan herself. Fokoti was a male rain-maker, living in the regions of the Mkuze river, while Maqabisi was a woman operating in the Ngoye area.

In the Izude region of the umZinyathi (Buffalo) river there is a spring from which tradition puts it that rain-making in Zululand originated. Tradition also puts it that Dingane destroyed the rain-maker who lived at this place and that since that time there has been no rain-making there again.

For a description of a rain-maker and his duties, medicines, etc., see Sibeko, 'Imolingo neMithi yokwelapha yaBantu', pp. 202 ff.

[52] See also Shooter, *The Kafirs of Natal and the Zulu Country*, p. 212.

[53] See Watt and Breyer–Brandwijk, *The Medicinal and Poisonous Plants of Southern Africa*, p. 68.

[54] Doke–Vilakazi, *Dict.*, p. 427.

[55] Doke–Vilakazi, *Dict.*, p. 410.

[56] Informants claim that when they speak of the colours of the bird they are referring so the "colours seen in the black feathers. It is true that the feathers are black, but the colours of the sky (i.e. the rainbow) can be seen in the black (ref. to colour refraction)".

[57] See Callaway, *The Religious System of the Amazulu*, pp. 407 f. for further information on *insingisi* and *ingqungqulu*.

[58] Krige, *SSZ*, p. 320.

[59] Krige, *SSZ*, p. 320.

[60] Norenius, 'Något om zuluernas religiösa föreställningar', p. 99.

[61] Norenius, 'Något om zuluernas religiösa föreställningar', p. 100.

[62] Krige, 'Girls' Puberty Songs and their Relation to Fertility', p. 173.

[63] See e.g. Pettersson, *Chiefs and Gods*, p. 184: Gluckman, 'Zulu Women in Hoecultural Ritual', pp. 255 ff.

[64] Cf. Callaway, *The Religious System of the Amazulu*, p. 253. This characteristic has been underlined also by Prof. Krige, 'Girls' Puberty Songs and their Relation to Fertility', p. 179 ff.

[65] Samuelson, *Long, Long, Ago*, pp. 303 f. Cf. Bryant, *The Zulu People*, p. 667. Also Norenius, 'Något om zuluernas religiösa föreställningar', p. 100, who says; "she has many ways of revealing herself, often followed by a number of children".

[66] Callaway, *The Religious System of the Amazulu*, p. 253.

[67] Asmus, *Die Zulu*, pp. 37 ff. who gives a detailed description of the *Nomdede* festival and attached rituals: Bryant, *The Zulu People*, pp. 665: Norenius, 'Något om zuluernas religiösa föreställningar', pp. 100–102: Samuelson, 'Some Zulu Customs', pp. 191–192.

[68] For descriptions of this custom see Bryant, *The Zulu People*, pp. 665 & 668: *The Collector*, Nos. 929 & 288.

[69] Thursday as a second day of worship in the week is becoming increasingly important among Zulu. In Christian as well as other circles Thursdays are looked upon as set aside for worship. A Zulu in Stanger who seriously considered becoming a Moslem decided against it "because I am free on Thursday evenings and can go to the meetings in the church in the township. But I am not free on Fridays. So I cannot go to the Mosque on that day. This is the trouble with these people (Moslems). They should worship on Thursdays. Then many would join them."

[70] The girls pointed out that the most important ingredient of the day was the beer which had to be prepared exceptionally well. On a few occasions they referred to the festival as *isonto lethu,* our Sunday, or, our ritual.

[71] Asmus, *Die Zulu,* pp. 37 ff. quotes some of the obscene songs that are sung by the girls.

[72] A large percentage of the girls' lovers were migrant labourers, most of the men working in Durban while a small number worked in Johannesburg on the gold mines.

[73] Compare with Gluckman's views on the *Nomkhubulwana* ceremonies which, he claims, is an expression of rigid suppression of men. Gluckman, 'Zulu Women in Hoecultural Ritual'.

[74] Previously this has been pointed out by Bryant in *The Zulu People,* p. 665.

[75] Cf. Kidd, *The Essential Kafir,* p. 112, says "they rush into the cattle kraal, seize the oxen, and drive them out to graze, herding them all day and night".

[76] Samuelson, *Long, Long, Ago,* p. 304. See also Samuelson, 'Some Zulu Customs and Folklore', p. 50: Norenius, 'Något om zuluernas religiösa föreställningar', pp. 98–100: Norenius, *Bland Zuluer och Karanger,* Vol. I, p. 48, relates the rainbow to the Heavenly Queen and not to the Princess.

[77] Callaway, *The Religious System of the Amazulu,* p. 255, indicates that *Nomkhubulwana* reveals herself also to men-folk. Modern Zulu stress that as a general rule the Princess is heard by women and children only.

[78] Norenius, 'Något om zuluernas religiösa föreställningar', p. 101, writing 1912/13 says: "The old people saw her often. But to the younger generation she reveals herself more seldom."

[79] Norenius, 'Något om zuluernas religiösa föreställningar', p. 101, says that "she is to be seen in the fields and gardens. When she approaches (people), she conceals herself as much as possible and calls out, 'Do not look at me, I am naked!'"

[80] Bryant, *The Zulu People,* pp. 666-f. See also Gluckman, 'Zulu Women in Hoecultural Ritual', pp. 257–258.

[81] Doke–Vilakazi, *Dict.,* p. 455.

[82] Marwick, *The Swazi,* p. 230.

[83] Kuper, *An African Aristocracy,* p. 191.

Chapter III

The Shades

Introduction

While the previous chapter described Zulu thought-patterns related to the Lord-of-the-Sky and other divinities which, to a large extent, play varying roles of importance depending on local thinking and behaviour, the present section of the study is devoted to an introduction to Zulu thought-patterns pertaining to the shades.

The importance of the shades in Zulu life and thinking cannot be overestimated. Contrary to Professor Gluckman who, in 1942 observed that "in Zululand, on the whole, the ancestral cult has largely died out while beliefs in sorcery and magic have survived" with the addition that "there has been a greater tendency for the ancestral cult of chiefs to survive as it marked Zulu opposition to Whites",[1] evidence today in a very definite manner points in exactly the opposite direction as far as the survival of shade cult is concerned.

Due to the overall importance of the shades, it is not astonishing to find that approaches to them in Zulu society are remarkably uniform. The few variations in thinking that may be traced are related to differences in rural and urban settings and the tendency for urbanised Zulu to be more sophisticated in their thinking. It is true that the symbol through which thinking is expressed at times may change, largely due to local conditions of life. But the interpretation given to the symbol is, again, remarkably uniform. Zulu living in the stone-covered areas of the Msinga district bury their dead with a stone placed at the feet, over the head and under the knees of the corpse, while people in a district where stones are not plentiful will use pieces of broken clay vessels for the same purpose. But both the stones and the pieces of burnt clay are interpreted similarly. "He is like a stone. So we are burying him with stones," was said in the Msinga district, while people living in the stone-lacking area, defining their symbol, said: "The dead man is like the hard clay which is the vessel. It is stone-like (*njengetshe*). That is why we bury him with these things. They are no good to us any more. His body is no good any more. The clay and the corpse are the same." Likewise, there are differences in procedure and the various officiants at different celebrations may vary their practices. But the interpretation given to the procedures and practices offer little material as far as differences in symbol interpretation is concerned.[2]

While a Westerner, schooled in a rational manner of life-approach, can experience tension between knowledge and believing, the gap between these two to the Zulu is either non-existent or very small. The existence and presence of the shades is not doubted. They are a reality which is so strongly interwoven into kinship relations that a world without them is not possible. Faith is not in the first instance approached critically. It is generously inclusive. It is only of recent date that scepticism is finding its way into Zulu thought-patterns and expressed essentially among intellectuals, particularly those in urban settings.

Zulu interpretations of reality are likewise generous. Reality is not only that which is definable in rational terms or acceptable because of proven conclusions. Reality includes experiences which require interpretation and subsequent action. We shall in the course of the following chapters see how dreams are a piece of living reality, how the inborn medicinal powers are realities which act upon men and society, and how evil is accepted as a reality with a personal cause as origin. Explaining dreams an informant said: "To dream is to see the truth at night. If a man says something and you dream about it at night and see it differently at night, then you know that the man is misleading you. It is the dream that shows the truth, because the shades never deceive their children." To him the dream was a reality to that extent that it was preferred to a man's statements because the dream was an experience with a lineage shade.

A study on Zulu concepts of the shades must of necessity be related to thought-patterns on death. Hence a section is devoted to understandings of death. Secondly, the shades must be related to the survivors as well as to man himself. Of crucial importance to Zulu patterns of life is the realm of shade manifestations. These will be discussed prior to a description of shade activities.

Death

There are essentially two concepts of death. Firstly, a timely death which presupposes a number of children and grandchildren who survive the deceased. Secondly, there is death which is untimely and is regarded as a serious interference in a human's life. The quality of such a death is included in the English idioms annihilation or extinction. A timely death is in the Zulu language expressed by terms such as *ukugoduka, ukudlula, ukuhamba* and *ukuqubeka,* which all give notions of a passing on, a continuation. An untimely death is described as *ukufa, ukubhubha,* and *ukugqibuka* which imply a breaking off of life.

Ngema was emphatic that physical death, when it comes at the correct time in life, is in itself not evil.[3] It is to be regarded as a natural continuation of man's existence. "When a man has completed his work in that he is old and of ripe age, then he is happy because things have gone well with him. He sees that there will be those that will do his work for him (ref. to ritual killings) when he has passed on. So he is not fearful because of death. He can even say to his people, 'No, I am now tired of living.' He says this because there is nothing more he can do." Discussions with a great number of Zulu on the issue of death at a mature age indicates that Ngema was not expressing only personal views but ideas representative of the people.

When old people die they are not mourned. "To the old death does not come unexpectedly. We do not mourn them because we knew that it was coming. They were not taken unaware." People expressing sympathy with friends whose aged parents or senior relatives have passed away show no signs of grief and will say: "We do not say anything. He was of ripe age." Or they may say: "Do not complain. It was her turn now. Even the teeth revealed that eating was painful." "You must not weep. Did you not know that he was ready for this thing? So why are you distressed?"[4]

Death of an aged person is not of necessity considered the work of sorcery or witchcraft. It is a natural development and accepted as such.

Literature on the Zulu makes mention of the now obsolete custom of *ukugodusa*, sending the aged further.[5] Informants who have knowledge of this custom agree that it was by no means common although done occasionally. It was certainly not looked upon as cruel. Informants themselves accepted the custom as intelligible, saying that they did not see anything wrong with it other than that "today the magistrate and the police do not allow it." An old man who had been messenger at the battle of Ulundi said that one of his father's brothers had been treated thus. He recollected hearing the man asking his sons to *godusa* him "since he had no teeth and not even the sun could warm him any more". After a few days the old man was no longer seen in the homestead and nobody inquired about him, "everybody knowing what had been done".

It has been difficult to ascertain whether those who in former times were sent further through *ukugodusa* were attended to in forthcoming *ukubuyisa* rituals, but information suggests that this most probably must have been the case. Certainly old people who die of natural causes have *ukubuyisa* rituals.

Death prior to maturity is, on the other hand, taken very seriously and is automatically related to witchcraft and sorcery. "When a man dies before the grey hairs appear, still being full of vigour (*esaqinile*), then the people say, 'What is this thing in our midst? We knew nothing. Suddenly we see *umhlola* (any strange, extraordinary, awe-inspiring thing or occurence causing one to wonder)[6] working among us.' The people become very troubled about the death." A woman whose eldest son had passed away very suddenly during a brief visit at home during Christmas holidays, equally unexpectedly became a widow about a year later. Her reflections were these: "It is clear that somebody is working to kill us. Was it not shortly, only about a year ago, that we were doing this thing of burying? Now it is here again. Who is this person?" A sympathizer, sitting near the widow, added: "This is a fearful thing, in truth. It is destroying them, today even killing the head of the homestead. Yesterday the bull-calf. Today the bull itself. No, this is fearful." Returning from a funeral of a thirty-five year old mother with a sister to the deceased, I tried to express my sympathy by saying something about the unhappy future of the children. Said the woman walking immediately behind me: "The most terrible thing of all is that she could still bear children, there being one already (the deceased was pregnant). But now there will be no more children by her." I said something about the existing four boys and two girls and added that, after all, these were healthy children. "Yes, it was simply because she was strong in giving birth that they directed death to her (*baphonse yena ngokufa*). It would have been better if it had been another who did not give birth easily like her. But good people do not stay long. It is they that die first."

Discussing untimely death with informants, they all most emphatically underline the tragedy involved. Hence the reluctance in speaking about death. "It is an evil. It must not be talked about as if you wish that it came over you." The reluctance, however, must be related to the cause of the death and its subsequent consequences rather than to anything else. The cause is always witchcraft or sorcery and hence viewed with extreme suspicion and anxiety. *Ubuthakathi* and *ukuthakatha*, terms which express witchcraft and sorcery, are associated with *ukubulala nokuqeda umuntu,* to kill and annihilate a person.

"When a man dies young, then there is one who is the cause of the death. The aim of the killer is to kill utterly (*ukubulala nya*). That is why he is working with the man when he is young." Reflecting further over the term *ukubulala nya* with my friend, he defined his expression thus: "I mean this. The man must die. He must die without children. Why? Because they would do his work for him (ritual killings), giving him food when he is hungry. That is what I mean when I say *ukubulala nya.* It is killing him and all the children he carries inside (himself)."

Ethnographic records describing Zulu funeral customs mention the habit of watching the grave for some time after the funeral.[7] Informants are convinced that the watching of the grave is a precaution against any further evil that may befall the deceased beside an untimely death, i.e. an interference with the shade. "The grave is watched because we know the work of *abathakathi.* They come at night and dig up the grave. They take out the man and give him medicines. They drive a stake through his body. He becomes small. They pull out his tongue and slit it so that he speaks like one of them in a tongue understandable only to them. It is the language of the evil snakes, the ones that kill. Then they give him medicines again so that the man becomes their servant. They send him everywhere to do their work."

B: "Can a man who has been dug up become a shade?"

"He was becoming a shade (i.e. under the process of becoming a shade), one that is with us. But they killed him. So he cannot be a shade. That is why the grave is watched at night. It is the fear of *abathakathi* that causes us to watch."

B: "Why do *abathakathi* dig up the man?"

"They dig because they see that the man is dying. So now they want to kill him utterly. If they do this thing with him, then he cannot work with his people. If the shade is dead, then the man is finished (*uma kubhubha idlozi, umuntu usephelile*)."

B: "Can a shade die?"

"It is clear that it can die as I have been saying. It dies if it is taken by *abathakathi.*"

Informants claim that horrifying as untimely death may be, the disturbance of the life of the shade is far more serious and must be avoided at all costs. No evil could surpass that of the destruction of the shade.

The length of time a grave should be watched varies considerably, depending on the social status of the deceased. "If it is a child the grave is not watched. It was but a child. But men with dignity like chiefs and doctors of reputation are watched for a long time. *Abathakathi* work for a long time, trying to kill them. Their shades are strong and killing them is a great thing." One informant said that the grave of a commoner ought to be watched "until the shade appears in a dream or has revealed himself. Then we rejoice, knowing that he is (*ukona*). Then the watching ceases because the shade has revealed itself." Another informant attributed all disasters of recent time (the drought, frequent changes of teachers at the local school, his grand-child's death, the local Lutheran bishop's resignation, the shooting of a local store-keeper, etc.) to the fact that "today there are not many shades but a large majority of *abathakathi*. They are increasing in numbers because there is no watching any more. Not even putting medicine into the grave. Nothing there is done. Nothing. So the shades are dying. They are being taken (lit. eaten up) by *abathakathi*. So what can we expect these days except bad things." I asked my informant for a solution to the difficulties he referred to. He said: "If we watched the graves the shades would be happy. They would feel security. Then things would go well. They would soon appear in dreams, being happy that we were doing their work nicely. But today we are simply forgetting them very soon. Even their food. They appear, saying, 'Children of our fathers, we are hungry.' But there is nothing done. They are dying of hunger."

Man

Zulu are very conscious of the fact that when they speak of *umuntu,* man, they are referring to an entity which is the living human being. A Zulu medical practitioner, operating immediately outside Durban said at a consultation on the Church's responsibility to the sick Zulu: "Whites have failed to see that in Africa a human being in an entity, not in the first instance divided up into various sections such as the physical body, the soul and the spirit. When a Zulu is sick it is the whole man that is sick, his physical as well as his spiritual being that which is affected." Evidence has strongly underlined how correct the consultation participant was.[8]

Reacting to Bryant's statement that "according to Zulu philosophy man is composed of two parts, the body (*umZimba*, pl. *imiZimba*) and the spirit or the soul (*iDlozi*, pl. *amaDlozi*)"[9] informants agree that there is the body and the *idlozi*, but they are hesitant to accept a clear division between the two. "We do not say, 'Here is the body and there is the shade'. They are together." The unity within man is underlined far more emphatically and consciously than is any division of a human into a possible material and visible part and a spiritual and invisible part.

Suggesting that the spiritual components of a human are invisible caused amazement among many informants. Their immediate reaction was a questioning of what that was which was spiritual and invisible. To gain their thinking I suggested *idlozi.* "No, we see it. It is not unseen. It is seen. Sometimes we see it often, sometimes less often. But we see it." Shades appearing to survivors in dreams, visions, omens or through the medium of a diviner are regarded as being seen, experienced, in a very real sense. Their being very much experienced through their means of manifestation is sufficient evidence of their being obvious and real. They are not abstract or very far away. The shade is the man, not a part of him.

Underlining the oneness of the human being, Zulu readily agree that various parts of the body are recognizable as are various characteristics of the person. Thought-patterns in this respect, however, are tangible. While schooled Zulu will far more readily accept e.g. *umoya* as a component of the human and Christians accept it as an essential, conservative traditionalists will go so far as to deny that *umoya* has anything to do with man's composition. Indeed among Christians *umoya* is defined in a wide range of approaches. A Roman Catholic Christian at Mapumulo said that *umoya* "is the thing that goes to God when I die", adding that "*umzimba* is a dirty thing which must just simply be buried in the earth". A Congregationalist was of the impression that "*umoya* is the breath. God gave it to us in the creation. He breathed it into us. We can use it nicely or badly. When I die the breath goes somewhere. God knows where it goes." His reflections on *umzimba* were the following: "The *umzimba* is the body. It goes to heaven. The flesh becomes earth. But the body goes to God."

Umufi, Isidumbu and *Umzimba*

While *isidumbu* refers to a corpse or carcass of either a human being or a slaughtered animal, in the former case suggesting that the body has not yet been buried and in the latter that the meat has not yet been consumed, *umufi* is strictly associated with humans. Unless otherwise defined the word is generally applicable to males.

When a person is dead, he is referred to as *umufi,* the body of the *umufi* termed *isidumbu. Umufi* implies that the *isidumbu* has not yet decomposed and hence lost its identity. While *isidumbu* describes the physical corpse which is being prepared for burial and is placed in the grave, the term *umufi* describes the person who has died. If one says that there is an *umufi* in a homestead, one is saying that there is a dead person in that particular home. Some time after the funeral one ceases to call the deceased *umufi* "because he is somewhere else."

A diviner-informant compared *umufi* with a bride. Asked where the *umufi* was immediately after death, he said: "He is like a bride who has left her father's house and goes to the bridegroom's house. She belongs nowhere. She does not belong to the father. She does not belong to the bridegroom. So where is she? The same with *umufi.* He has left the place where he lived. But he is not in the earth. So where is he?"

B: "He is on the way, going somewhere."

"He is going somewhere. He is going into the earth. But he has not entered yet."

B: "When does he enter?"

"He enters when they put him into it (refers to the burial)."

B: "But is it not *isidumbu* that is put into the earth?"

"It is the thing that they put into the earth. That is true. It is the *isidumbu* of the deceased man (*umuntu ongumufi*) that is put into the earth. The *isidumbu* just simply rots. It is rubbish (*izibi*). But the *umufi* goes somewhere."

B: "Where does *umufi* go?"

"He goes into the earth. That is his new place."

B: "Is *umufi* still *umuntu*?"

Some time for thought. "I could say that he is still *umuntu* because he still is. But he is *umuntu oshonileyo* (a person who has gone down)."

B: "Is it correct to say that *umufi* is *umuntu* without *isidumbu*?"

"Sometimes it can be said. But when *isidumbu* is in the grave, then it rots. *Umufi* cannot rot. He is the one that has gone down."

Umzimba is more than merely the material body of a living human being. It implies the bodily appearance of a person. The physical features of a person are identified as *umzimba,* the phrase *umzimba womuntu othile,* the physical features of a certain person, being used.[10]

The idiom *umzimba uzwiwa umniniwo* covers a human's feelings as well as his health. At a hospital a patient suffering from what he referred to as *isifo sabantu* (an ailment characteristic of Zulu only and believed to be not fully appreciated by white medical practitioners) said, when told that the doctor had found nothing wrong with him: *"ngavela ngasho ukuthi umzimba uzwiwa umniniwo kuphela* (I said already from the beginning that the body is known by its owner only)."[11]

Inzimba describes a person's social status, dignity and prestige. These, in turn, can be related to the physical body, a big person carrying a certain amount of personal prestige and dignity in the size of the body. I have on an occasion seen *inzimba* used in a report, the writer of the report referring to the scholar's ability. A man who had lost a court-case which he was convinced should have had a favourable outcome said: "It is clear that he (his opponent) had more *inzimba* (i.e. ability of arguing the case) than I." Discussing the issue further with some friends, the man referred to his opponent's ability and related it to the man's physical size and strength. "It is certain that he is powerful. Just look. I reach merely to his arm (i.e. he was shorter than the man's armpit). So what was I? Merely nothing."

Umphefumulo

There is a difference in understanding of *umphefumulo* between on the one hand traditionalists and, on the other, schooled people and Christians. While the former emphasize that *umphefumulo* is the breath of humans and animals, the latter will accept this explanation but add that it also is the soul. A teacher said: "It is the breath of a man. That is true. But it is a special breath. We read in the Bible that God breathed into man His breath. It is this breath that is the *umphefumulo.*" Another teacher, listening to our conversation, disagreed and said: *"umoya* is the thing that you are talking about, not *umphefumulo.*" The argument led to no final agreement, the two maintaining their different views. "Well, we shall see in heaven if it is the breath or the spirit which is of God. The other will be left behind."

A traditionalist described *umphefumulo* thus: "It is the breath. We eat it. It is like food. We cannot live without it. A man eats the breath. He takes it in through the nose and then he rejects that which he does not want. It is just like food. We eat it and then we reject some of it. Some stays inside, giving strength. The breath is the same."

B: "Is the air (*umoya*) the same as the breath?"

"They are the same. But when we eat the air it is the breath. It is like water also. A man drinks water. Water is life. He dies if he does not drink. But when he has drunk, he rejects some. Some stays inside. It is his strength." My informant associated food, breath and water to death thus: "When a man dies, he does not eat. He does not drink water. He does not breath air. That is why we say that all these things are the same. So it is quite clear that eating and breathing and drinking are the same thing. When a man lives he consumes all these things. When he dies he does not touch them. He simply leaves them behind."

Another informant associated *umphefumulo* with work, anger and excitement. When a man works or becomes angry, he does it (breathing) quickly. He becomes hot, and his breath comes and goes quickly. It is the same thing with excitement. Then he does it quickly." His choice of words when describing both work and excitement were suggestive, clearly indicating sexual activity. I drew the observation to his attention, and he readily accepted it, saying that this was what he was indicating. "All these things, working and breathing heavily and excitement, they are a man working with the wife. That is the main kind of work for a man." I asked whether there was any relationship between the breathing and the shades who are believed to be active during the sex act. "It is true that it is their (the shades') work the man is doing when he is hot. But the breathing is the breathing of the man. He is just showing much vigour. That is why he is breathing heavily."

B: "Is the breathing a shade?"

"No, the breath is not a shade. But it is a sign, showing that the shades are near."

B: "When a man has worked hard and breathed heavily, he breathes slower after the work. Is this correct?"

"It is correct. That is what happens. The shades have left him. The breathing becomes smooth again. He is not hot any more."

Experience certainly underlines that Bryant was correct when he suggested that *umphefumulo* as a description of Western concepts of the soul is to be traced to missionary influence.[12]

Umoya

Bryant, supported in his views by Wanger,[13] argues that *umoya* has been used by missionaries as a translation for Biblical concepts of soul, spirit and spirituality in man and of the Holy Spirit. Certainly *umoya* is used far more in Christian circles than in pagan and is far more meaningful to them than to the traditionalists. Among Christians *umoya* generally refers to the Holy Spirit and is used to describe spirituality in man only when defined as such.

Traditionally, *umoya* is air and wind. Various kinds of winds, depending on their origin, were given names accordingly and referred to as *umoya*. The ability of speech is associated with *umoya,* it being well known that "without breath there is no speech." One is also well acquainted with the fact that animals make use of air when producing their various sounds.

Isithunzi

Of far greater significance then any of the former is *isithunzi*. Switching over to discussions on *isithunzi* from e.g. *umphefumulo* or *umoya* revealed a marked difference in reactions and interest. One informant said: "Now you are touching at the thing that is hot. The others are simply small. But this one is the important one."

Bryant defines *isithunzi* as the "shadow of man, the living principle in man, spirit (while living), shade (after death=idlozi)",[14] while Shooter, writing in the early 1850's says that "when a person dies his *ihlozse* or *isitute* survives. These words are translated 'spirit' ... the nature of which ... is identical with the shadow".[15] Doke and Vilakazi say that *isithunzi* is, firstly, the shadow; secondly, moral weight, influence and prestige, while, thirdly, it is the soul, personality.[16] Colenso states that *isithunzi* is the shade or *ithongo* of a dead person, influence, weight, prestige.[17]

Informants claim that *isithunzi* is associated with a clan and a definite lineage in the clan. "The *isithunzi* is different from family to family. I am Mbatha. This is our *sthunzi*. People know that we are heavy (i.e. have dignity). This is the *isithunzi* of our clan. If a man is not of our clan, then his *isithunzi* is of another clan." Informants agree that *isithunzi* is related to the clan *isibongo* (clan name).

Isithunzi is present in the procreation act, but informants hesitate to identify *isithunzi* with the shades. The great majority say that the two are very closely associated "because they are the man". But they are not identical. "It is true that *isithunzi* and *idlozi* are present when the father works. That is correct, Both must be there if there is to be a child. If the shade is not there, then the child will be insane or defective. If *isithunzi* is not there the child will not live."

"When the shades mould a child in the womb, they are moulding one of their people. That is the child of their *amathunzi*. They put into the womb their *ithunzi* which will be in the child. When the child is born it comes with its *isithunzi*."

B: "Has a child *isithunzi* at birth?"

"It has *isithunzi* like its fathers have *isithunzi*. It is inside the child."

B: "Does *isithunzi* grow with the child or is it the same throughout life?"

"Sometimes it grows, sometimes it is the same through life. If a man does something that makes him honoured, like bravery, or cleverness in arguing, or gifted at handling medicines, then we say, 'No, the *isithunzi* of this man is strong. We did not see it in the beginning when he was a small child. But now we see it. His shades love him.' This is said when a man's *isithunzi* has grown."

Isithunzi is associated with clan characteristics. A man of the Masondo clan said that their clan identity was small in stature but strong in the hands and he claimed that this was their *isithunzi*. A woman voiced the same opinion when she spoke of the child of her unmarried daughter. The boy responsible had denied relationships with the girl. "Then we said, having questioned the girl once again, 'Just let us sit down (i.e. wait). When the child is born we shall see its *isithunzi*, whom it is like.' When the child was born the older women came and said, 'Let us see the child. We wish to know its father, who he is.' So we took the child and looked (at it) carefully. We looked at it thoroughly and saw its *isithunzi*. We saw that it was the boy whom the mother had indicated. Then he admitted."

Because *isithunzi* is associated with the clan and a specific lineage within the clan, it does not change either with growth or with social changes in life. When a woman marries her *isithunzi* follows her from the paternal home to that of her husband. "With us the women do not change. Even when they marry, they do not change their name. To call her Mrs is a new thing among us. It has been brought by the whites. But in the Zulu fashion the woman retains her *isithunzi* of her fathers. In the home of the children's father she is ma-Ngema. That is her *isibongo* (clan name)." Women return to their paternal homes for the birth of at least the first child because "that is where the shades of her clan are. They are of the same *isithunzi*."

Isithunzi sesimukile (lit. *isithunzi* has departed) indicates physical death. Doke and Vilakazi translate the expression thus: "He has died; lit. his soul has now departed."[18] Informants accept this translation. "When we say that *isithunzi* has departed we mean that *isidumbu* is left behind. The man has gone to his place. The corpse is left. The corpse is put into the earth. That is the burial. But *isithunzi* has gone to its place."

B: "Where is that place?"

"The place of *isithunzi* is the place of the shades. The *isithunzi* is the man. He goes to the place of the shades in the earth. That is their place."

B: "When a man is about to die one says in Zulu: 'The shadow is becoming short.' Why does the shadow become short?"

"It knows its time. The man does not know everything. But *isithunzi* knows it. Sometimes it will reveal certain things to the man in feelings so that he can say, 'How is it that I do not see the day clearly? Perhaps is there something which is to happen today? There is darkness in the future.' He says these words because he feels that there is something that is going to happen. Then surely there happens something during the day. He is perhaps involved in an accident. Or perhaps somebody stabs him with a knife. He dies. That is the shadow that has become short."

Another informant said that *isithunzi* goes to *emathunzini* (lit. the place of the shadows) when a man dies. "When he goes there, then *isithunzi* goes to that place. The man has left the corpse and gone to the shadows in that place of the shadows." A diviner said that a corpse does not cast a shadow because the shade and *isithunzi* had both left the body and were in the place of the shadows. We discussed this particular issue further:

B: "Does *isithunzi* cast a shadow in the place of the shadows?"

"They cast them. (Pause.) But at another time."

B: "When is that time?"

"It is in the night."

B: "You are speaking of the night which is here with us?"

"That is the night that I am speaking of. That is why we say, 'Let a burial be done at night.' That was the work to be done at night, according to the old people. The burial should be at night so that there be no shadow cast by the corpse. A corpse must not have a shadow. It (the shadow) has left. It is now in that place where the shadow goes when a man dies."

Isithunzi is intimately related to the shadow cast by a person, his image in a mirror and the reflection cast in water. All three are referred to as *ithunzi*. Hence the fear among particularly old and/or conservative people towards photography.

No Zulu doubts that the shadow is connected with the light from the sun. But this fact does not interfere with the associations between the shadow and the human. The shadow is still identified with the person. A Christian said: "The shadow is the man, doing everything that the man does. Even if it (the shadow) is small or big, it is still the man. Please tell me, whose shadow is this? (Pointing at my own shadow.) It is yours. You can clearly see that it is yours. You yourself agree to this. I also agree that it is the sun that causes the shadow. Even my forefathers agreed to this. That is not a new thing among us. But the thing is this, that the shadow is yours. When you move, it moves. It cannot be touched by somebody else. Nobody can take it. It is yours."

Callaway speaks of two shadows, a long one and a shorter. He states that the longer shadow shortens when a man approaches death, eventually to vanish completely in death. But the shorter shadow remains "with the corpse and is buried with it".[19] Despite serious attempts to obtain further information of the two shadows, no informant was able to enlarge on the matter, the large majority of people interviewed saying that they had not heard of two shadows. Two diviners claimed to have heard old people talk about the matter, but knew nothing more than that there was some idea of there being two shadows.

Literature refers to Zulu women standing up their husband's sleeping mats when they are away, and, depending on the shadow cast by the mat, the women will know whether their husbands are well or not.[20] Zulu women agree that this was done, especially when wars were common. They are of the impression that it was not done commonly, being withheld to occasions "when perhaps they had dreamt that something had happened to their men. That is when they did it. But not every day." At Ekuthuleni I met two wives whose husband worked in Durban. They spoke of an occasion when they had expected him back "and he did not come. We were filled with fear. We did not know why he did not return. At last we inquired through a diviner. He said, 'Do this thing and look at the shadow!' We did it and looked at the shadow. It was there. The next day he (the husband) came from Durban." An old woman, living in a neighbouring homestead, knew how the mat was to be raised. She had instructed the two wives, telling them either to raise the mat in the doorway or in the far back of the hut generally occupied by their husband when he was at home. If there was a dark shadow cast by the mat, it would be a sign that their husband was alive. The women had been instructed not to raise the mat in the sun. "Then we would see a shadow, perhaps deceiving ourselves. It must be in the hut."

B: "Is the shadow of the mat associated with the shades?"

"It is clear that it is so."

B: "In what way?"

"If he were not (alive) they would withhold his shadow (*Fihla ithunzi lakhe*)."

A woman associated her inability to give birth to her having allowed a friend to take photos of her. The photos were taken at the wedding which had attracted a large number of visitors. "They took *isithunzi* from me in that there were many photos taken. I see clearly that taking photos (*ukushoota*, from English to shoot) is *ukuthwebula*.[21] They said that they were merely taking pictures (*ukuthatha izithombe*) but in reality they were killing me. Indeed, I see clearly that they were killing me. It is now one year ago and there has been nothing (i.e. no child). So I am dead, killed by those who took photos."

Shade Names

Idlozi

Most common of shade-names is *idlozi*. Wanger associates *idlozi* philologically with *umlozi*[22] which, according to Bryant, is "a familiar spirit of a necromancer which makes itself audible by a whistling voice, said to be produced by ventriloquism; such a necromancer supposedly possessed by such a spirit."[23] Zulu informants all agree that an *umlozi* diviner undoubtedly is possessed by an *idlozi* and support Wanger's statement that the two words are related to each other.

Wanger argues that "properly speaking, the departed spirit is not spoken of as an *idlozi* before he is 'brought back' (*ukubuyisa*) by the customary sacrifice".[24] In this respect informants disagree with Wanger's claim. Old people are sometimes referred to as *idlozi* both in an honorary capacity and jocularly when referring to their advanced age. This is done in the presence of the aged themselves who, amused will say: "It is clear that we are old now. The young people are treating us nicely, respecting us." Ngema said that "*amadlozi* are the old people". On being asked whether still living people could be called *idlozi* he agreed emphatically, saying that this not only was possible but in fact done quite frequently. "When we see the grey hairs and see them becoming weak, then we call them *idlozi*. We say this word respectfully, knowing that they like it." Ngema associated *idlozi* very clearly with age and stated that it was possible for an old person to act as an *idlozi* even prior to death. "We even say this word to them to make them happy, avoiding quarrels and anger. It is difficult to have an aged person in the home who is quarrelsome and difficult. He is not easily quietened." A great number of informants from a large variety of places supported Ngema's view that emphasis is not on the ritual of *ukubuyisa* but rather on age.

Ithongo

Some ethnographic records state that *ithongo* is a synonym to *idlozi*.[25] Kidd, on the other hand, gives a list of thirteen reasons supporting his view that *ithongo* is different from *idlozi*.[26] Zulu say that the two words are used differently but "they speak of the same father". The choice of word appears to be dependent on what aspect of the shade one wishes to speak of. A diviner said that he spoke of *ithongo* when he associated the shades with dreams, thereby relating them with *ubuthongo*, sleep. "That is the time of *amathongo*, when we sleep." On other occasions he would speak of them as *amadlozi*. A man at the Stanger hospital was in deep distress because "*amathongo* have caused trouble. I do not know why they cause trouble." A room-mate, without further explanation, immediately drew the conclusion that the troubled man had dreamt unpleasant things. Asked why he drew this conclusion, the room-mate explained: "No, when he said *amathongo,* then I knew that it was dreams."

Kidd says that "the *idlozi* may enter a snake whatever the totem-animal of the clan may be. The *itongo* never enters the totem, nor does it seem to have anything to do with it."[27] Zulu agree that "we do not speak of *ithongo* in connection with snakes. When we speak of snakes and the shades we say, 'This is *idlozi* of so-and-so, mentioning the person.' The man is correct in saying that *ithongo* is not a snake. But *ithongo* is seen in the night."

There is a difference in the usage of the term *ithongo* between northern Zulu-land and southern Natal. While in the south the term is used quite frequent-ly, including a limited number of references also outside the sphere of dreams, *ithongo* is far less frequently known in northern Natal. Laduma Made-la said, when reference was made to *ithongo* in one of our discussions: "You are talking of *idlozi* when you say *ithongo*?" A woman at Hlobane coal-mines claimed never to have heard the word *ithongo*. She had come to the mine from Transvaal, immediately north of the Natal border. It is therefore quite pos-sible that *ithongo* as a shade-name has come to the Zulu from the south where it is the most frequently used name of a shade.[28]

Abaphansi

Not infrequently the shades are referred to as *abaphansi*, those under (the earth). "When a man dies and we bury him, he goes into the earth. The place is under the earth. That is why we speak of them as *abaphansi*. They are underneath (the earth)."

The realm of the deceased is thought to be a shadowy existence underneath the earth. It is referred to as *emathunzini*, the place of shadows. There are Zulu who are dogmatic about the life of the shades in the underworld. Others, on the other hand, are vaguer. "We have only heard people talk a-bout it. We have not been there ourselves, so we do not know the place. But it is the place of *abaphansi*."

While *abaphansi* has the sense of being under the earth, it also implies white-ness. "When we speak of *abaphansi*, we think of the white ones. *Amadlozi* of *emathunzini* are white." My informant went on to describe how everything in *emathunzini* is white, "like shadows".

B: "But shadows are dark?"

"They are dark. But there they are white. That is why the shades are white."

B: "But can shadows be white?"

"In that place they are white. (Long pause.) You are wondering. I under-stand your question. You have seen only the shadows of this place. You have not seen there. But these, yes these very eyes, they have seen that place. (My informant is a diviner, and pointed at his eyes.) These eyes have seen that place. They saw that colour that you are asking about. They saw white."

B: "Does this have to do with the things that are reversed?"

"That is the thing. You have seen the shadows being dark. But *abaphansi* are white, like the shadow they cast. The shadow and the shade are white. It is the opposite."

B: "Are *abaphansi* of whom you are speaking the same as *amadlozi*?"

"They are one and the same. There is no difference."

B: "Is it correct to say that *amadlozi* are white? Or does one say that *ama-thongo* are white?"

"*Amathongo* are white. That is why we can see them in dreams. It is because they are that colour which can be seen. In darkness you can only see that which is white. As for *amadlozi* I have not thought or heard others speak about them as being white. But I would say that they are white. *Amadlozi* ap-pear at any time, sometimes not even being seen."

Another diviner stated very definitely that *amadlozi* are white, adding that because "they are white, they cannot be seen during the daytime".

Umhlabathi

Umhlabathi is defined by Doke and Vilakazi as "hlonipa word for *amadlozi*".[29] This particular shade-name, when used, is related to the pains in the chest and shoulders which are said to be caused by the shades when they require a person to become a diviner. "When they (the shades) are working with a man or a woman, causing pain in the shoulders and the chest, the diviner will say to the sick person, 'It is *umhlabathi* that is causing this *uhlabo.*' Then we know that the shades are working to get the person. They want that person to divine."

Umhlabathi is also associated with the original founding ancestor. When introducing the idiom among informants a number related it to "the people that came from the reeds". Ngema proved well versed in this thought-pattern also.

B: "Why is this *Nkulunkulu* known as *umhlabathi* (earth)?"

"It is because he came from the earth. That is why he is given this name."

B: "Did not the father of all come from the reeds?"

"He came from the reeds. That is true. But he came also from the earth."

B: "How did he come from the earth?"

"He came (from the earth) like a child comes from the mother. That is the way he came from the earth."

B: "Was the earth the mother?"

"The earth (*umhlabathi*) is always the mother. *uNkulunkulu* who is known as *umhlabathi* came from his mother. She was the earth. She gave birth to him."

B: "What about the reed?"

Amusement. "The reed! The reed is the father."

B: "You must explain this thing to me."

"The reed is the father. The reed and the water of the father are one and the same thing. The water came from it. It put water into the earth and *umhlabathi* was born. That is all I can say."

B: "I know that reeds are found where there is water."

"That is the thing. Reeds and water go together. So it is clear that the reed is the father."

B: "Is it not so that a child should not have the name of its parents?"

"That is so. But a child can have the name of its mother. The child is the child of the father. Since when was this *nkulunkulu* called *uhlanga* (reed)? So the name is the name of the mother. He is *umhlabathi* because he came from the earth."

Isithutha

Wanger says that *isithutha* is used to denote the hopelessness of a shade in that it is unable to supply itself with food and has to rely on its survivors "um ihren Hunger zu stillen".[30] Zulu agree to this explanation. A Zulu preacher belonging to a revivalistic-enthusiastic group said in a sermon: "You yourselves tell us how useless the shades are, not even being able to supply themselves with food. is their name not *izithutha*? Why do you call them this name? If you do not know I will tell you—it is because they are foolish. They are like children, unable even to get food for themselves, merely relying on what is given to them. So you see the foolishness of the cult of the shades!"

Other informants have suggested that the shades are called *izithutha* (the foolish ones) because "they are more foolish than the Lord-of-the-Sky. We wish to say that whereas the creator created something with nothing in his hands, creating everything without anything, the shades cannot do anything except work with the things that are there. They simply mould (*bumba*). That is all they can do. So it is clear that they are foolish when they are seen beside *iNkosi.*" Laduma Madela at Ceza said that when he heard the term *isithutha* he immediately associated the shades with the creator, "seeing their weakness".

Umlwane

Colenso states that *umlwane* is the name "for the *amadlozi,* used only in the following expression: *ezemilwane (izinkomo)*, cattle killed in honour of the *amadlozi.*"[31] Doke and Vilakazi say that it is a "departed spirit", associating the word with "sacrifice to the departed spirits".[32] Bryant indicates that the word is not known in Zululand proper but applied to "an *idlozi* generally" by Natal Zulu.[33]

To a large number of Zulu the word appears to be unknown. Those who have knowledge of it say that a negative attitude to the shades is attached to the word. "We do not use this word often. It is not a nice word, for it indicates that they (the shades) are troublesome. It is not a pleasant thing to say to relatives. 'You are worthless, good-for-nothing.' But sometimes it was said when the shades were continually causing sickness. There was first one slaughtering, then the next and even a third. Each time the diviner indicated them, saying, 'No, I see no evildoer. I see only people who are fathers. They are complaining that they are hungry. They are the cause of this sickness.' We continue slaughtering, but there is no improvement in the sickness. Then they lost their patience with them (the shades). That is the time when they were called *abalwane.*"

Umzimu

As was the case with *umlwane,* a number of informants claimed that they did not know this particular word, *umzimu,* used in connection with the shades.[34]

Some informants suggested that *umzimu* was used in a negative sense. "It is used when they (the shades) continually are causing sickness. Perhaps a man is sick and not improving. Or perhaps a man is sick and gets better, then a child gets ill but improves after some time. Then another child or somebody else gets sick. The diviner continually indicates that it is the shades. At last even the last of the cattle is slaughtered. Then it is said, *'Imizimu,* (i.e. cannibals) that is what you are! Look how many cattle you have eaten! Their horns are on the huts! You can count them yourselves! They are too many for me to count! I cannot count them all! Count them, you who are continually complaining that you are hungry! What are you doing? You are eating us up. But the truth is that you are eating yourselves! Soon you have eaten everything: even now there is nothing left! How foolish you are, eating up everything and forgetting that there is a tomorrow! You are simply cannibals!' That is the time when this word was used."

A diviner of significant standing strongly disagreed with this interpretation of the term and said that *umzimu* is not at all associated with the word for cannibal (*izimu*). "It is true that some think so today. They say this because of ignorance. This word (*umzimu*) does not speak about cannibals. It speaks about heaviness (*ubunzima*). When this word is used, the meaning is that the shade is heavy, filled with dignity." He related how he himself always spoke of the shades as being "the heavy ones".

Bryant argues that the idiom *umzimu* (pl. *imzimu*) was confined to "the great tribal spirits, that is to say, to the departed spirits of the clan's kings". He continues to say that "as these ancestral kings were customarily worshipped together en bloc, this last term was almost only used in its plural form, and in the solitary phrase *iziNkomo zemizimu* (the cattle of the great tribal spirits)".[35] Zulu of the royal clan agree with Bryant's information and underline that the term *umzimu* is not associated with cannibals as popular interpretations put it. With the diviner, they associate the word with dignity.[36]

UNkulunkulu, Inkosi, Abakithi

Possibly even more known and used as shade-names are *unkulunkulu* and *inkosi*. The term *abakithi* is used to describe shades within a clan or a lineage by survivors in the clan or lineage.

While *unkulunkulu* and *inkosi* are heard at practically every ritual killing and can include all the shades, *abakithi* (lit. those of us) expresses mutual close relationships and the intimacy which blood relations have towards each other. *Unkulunkulu* gives an atmosphere of age and seniority, *inkosi* indicates superiority with the shade and humility and allegiance with the survivors.

Isithonga and *isithoza, isithinzi*

Isithonga and *isithoza,* mentioned by Colenso as being "spirit" do not appear to be widely known today and are certainly not used in ritual celebrations. Hardly any information could be collected on these two words.[37]

Isithinzi, although by some urbanized Zulu claimed to be a shade-name, is traditionally not a shade but a "mysterious cause of panic or fear".[38] A limited number of old Zulu men said that *isithinzi* is anxiety. "It is the thing that causes the sweat to come out. The thing is not seen but it is felt everywhere in the body, even the feet." Others claim that *isithinzi* is a bad animal in a man. It has not been seen, but rumours put it that "it is a snake, very small and black. It is too small to bite, but causes fear because it is a snake." A third informant said that *isithinzi* is "simply a power. It is a bad power, causing confusion in the body. It is cast on a man by *umthakathi.*"

Unyanya

Callaway indicates that Zulu used the idiom *unyanya* "in the same way as *itongo*. Thus a man who has been fortunate says, '*Ngi bhekwe Unyanya*', I have been regarded by *Unyanya*." Ethnographic records do not appear to refer to this idiom in Zulu context at all. Two aged men claimed that they had heard the word in their childhood, one of them adding that he had heard it used by a diviner who came from "beyond Mpondo", (i.e. south of Mpondo).[39]

Shade Manifestations

Snakes

Bryant has given us an extensive list of various kinds of snakes which are said to be manifestations of the shades.[40] Zulu informants who have either seen Bryant's list or heard it read to them have agreed that he is correct. Many have added, however, that one is not dogmatic about a certain reptile of necessity being the manifestation of one particular shade. "Sometimes a shade will appear in this animal. But the shade of another family, corresponding to the shade in that animal, will appear in another snake."

Snakes which are manifestations of shades are said to differ somewhat from ordinary reptiles. The latter are termed *izinyoka nje,* simply snakes. Shade-snakes do not have a split tongue and as a general rule they do not shoot out their tongues. Indeed, one of the means whereby one can identify a shade-snake is by its tongue.

A snake which is a shade does not die. But it changes its skin. Informants are emphatic that it is this snake alone that changes its skin, and no other. "Ordinary snakes do not change their skin. They die. But a shade-snake (*idlozi*) changes its skin. So the changing of the skin is its death. It dies in this way, but does not die. It lives." The annual change of skin is regarded as an annual death and rebirth, the new skin being identified with a renewal of life. "We say that it dies from the old skin, leaving it behind," said the diviner at eThelezini. "When the people speak of a snake that changes its skin, then you must know that it is a shade. It is the shade of a man, moving about in our vicinity. The snake is like a child when it (the snake) changes its skin. When it (the child) is ready, it leaves the womb. The shades drive it out. It leaves the mother and the womb, gliding out of it. The shade-snake does the same thing. It is like the child that glides out. It glides out of its old skin. The shade and the child are the same in this aspect."

B: "The snake is a shade. You say that the snake and the child are the same. Is the child also a shade?"

"It is like this. The shades of the father mould the child when he is working (i.e. sexual intercourse). When he is very hot, they drive out the water. The water is the shades. They unite with the blood of the mother and the child is moulded. That is how the shades of the father mould (*ukubumba*) the child. They work in the dark inside (the womb). The child grows for nine months (lit. moons). It is born in the tenth. The shades drive it out from the womb. It glides out, leaving behind its skin (placenta). All this is like the snake that leaves its skin. It (the snake) is like the child when it comes out of the womb. The snake discards the skin as the child discards the placenta. That is the first thing. The second is that it does this thing in water, in the time of the dew. When the grass is wet and the water is on it, then the snake does this thing, discarding the skin. The dew is like the water of the womb. That is why some grass has much dew while all the other grass has no dew. The snake discards its skin at a place where there is much dew. The dew and the water of the womb are one and the same thing. The third thing is that the snake discards (its skin) in the night. That is in the darkness. The child is moulded in the darkness. The darkness is the womb. So the snake is born again in the dark like the child is moulded in the darkness. Nobody except some (reference to some diviners) have seen shade-snakes do this thing. It is not seen because it is done in the dark. It is like the moulding and the birth of a child. Just think for yourself—is not the time of birth the night? So it is with the snake. It is born in the night."

In the subsequent discussion the diviner emphasized very strongly that a snake does not change its skin if there is no dew. "There must be water. Otherwise this thing cannot take place. In winter there is no dew. You have never seen the skin of a snake in winter. But you have seen it in spring when there is much dew. That is the time when the snake does this thing of birth."

Discussing the discarded placenta, the diviner revealed that the placenta is "like a corpse. Both are *izibi,* dirt. When they have done their work they are both dug into the earth. The work of the corpse is to be the house (*indlu*) of the shade of a man. When the shade leaves the body, the corpse remains. It is rubbish, feared by everybody. So it is with the placenta. When the child leaves the placenta it has completed its work. It is rubbish. When it comes out it is buried in the earth." We discussed the term *izibi* at length. I wanted to know exactly what my informant understood with *izibi.*

B: "Are all these *izibi* alike?"

"No, they are not all alike. These *izibi* (corpse and placenta) of which we have been talking are not like other *izibi.* They are not treated alike. There are some that are thrown on the rubbish-heap, others are dug into the earth. The *izibi* that are buried are the ones that are like *amanyala.*"

B: "You are indicating faeces?"

"It is that thing. It must be buried immediately. It must be covered up with earth. It is the thing that is known as *amasimba.* These things must be buried in the earth. They cannot be put on the rubbish heap. They are vileness. Again, they come from a man. That is why they should be buried in the earth. Vileness must never be found. Faeces is vileness. But these other things are not *amasimba.* We do not call them *amasimba.* They have been the house of a shade. We just call them *izibi.* But the thing is one and the same. We have different names simply to honour the house of a shade. But the treatment is the same. They are buried in the earth."

B: "Women have told me that children are taught that everything that has to do with faeces has to be done with the left hand because the right hand is used when eating. Are the other things (placenta and corpse) handled with the left hand?"

"No. Faeces is one kind of *izibi.* The other are of another kind. It is the women who bury the placenta. They can use any hand. It is their work to do this thing of burying. They wash afterwards. That is sufficient. It is a work that requires washing in that it is a dirty work. But it is not the dirt of faeces."

B: "Is the skin of the snake the same as the corpse and the placenta?"

"They are the same. But the likeness of the skin is more in line with the placenta than the corpse. I mentioned the corpse by way of comparison. But they are treated alike. They are put into the earth because they are all *izibi.* But the skin of the snake is more like the placenta."

B: "So the skin of the snake should also be buried, like the placenta?"

"No, it is not buried. As I said, the snake does this thing every year in the spring when the dew comes onto the grass. It does this thing regularly, every year. Now it is clear that it knows its time. The skin of the shades knows its time. It is used as a medicine. It is not buried. It is used for those that do not keep to times (ref. to those that give birth outside normal time of pregnancy)."

B: "What thing is it that is outside time?"

"It is the thing of women."

B: "You mean their monthly periods?"

"That is their months. Again, they have other months. It is the months of pregnancy."

B: "Is the skin of the snake used as medicine for menstruation and pregnancy?"

"It is a medicine when the months are not correct. Sometimes women have periods outside the time of menstruation. They are irregular. They require medicine to return to correct times. Then the skin is a medicine."

B: "And pregnancy?"

"The women count the months on the fingers. They expect for nine months, giving birth in the tenth month. They say ten months because they give birth in the tenth month. But sometimes things do not go well. They give birth before the tenth finger. The child is very small. It is not mature (*vuthiwe*) for birth. The woman gives birth too early. Others, again, count past ten, even coming to eleven or twelve. Then they kill the child in giving birth, even killing themselves. Of these things we say, 'They are outside time.' The skin of the snake is their medicine."

B: "But is not a difficult birth perhaps the sign of marital irregularities? This is the thing that is healed with confession."

"If the difficult birth is caused by something that the woman has done without her husband's knowledge, then there must be confession. But the thing that I am speaking of is not that thing. The thing that I am speaking of is the time. The time is another thing. It has other causes perhaps. Sometimes it can be the woman. But the time has other reasons. Then the medicine helps the time to be restored. It is the skin that helps them."

My informant claimed that he had successfully treated a large number of women who had sought his aid. I asked him whether they themselves knew with what they were being treated. He did not know. But he said that he seldom told his patients what he gave them. "The patient does not know. They simply feel the medicine working in them. It is the best way. There are too many who simply want to know and then kill the work of the medicines. If they do not know they cannot kill."

Our discussion returned to the figure ten.

B: "I know of the great snake which has its head on N mountain. I am speaking of the snake with the many colours. It has ten heads, people say. Is this so?"

"It has ten heads. That is so. But it is not a shade snake. It is another one. The snake of *iNkosazana.*"

B: "Why has it ten heads?"

"Because it is the snake of women."

B: "But how is ten the figure of women?"

"We have ten fingers so that we can count to ten. It is in the tenth month that a woman gives birth. She is expecting for nine months, giving birth in the tenth, as I have been saying previously. So the snake of the women and girls which is not seen frequently and which has its head on that mountain has ten heads as you say."

I was keen to know how my informant would interpret the habit of counting the finger from the left hand to the right. He did not hesitate to reply.

"People count this way because ten is the figure of women. So the counting should start with their side."

B: "But if it is a man that is counting?"

"Now you are marvelling me, asking things that you should know! Is not ten always the figure of women, even if it is a man that is counting? Further, is not the child his, he being the father of it?"

Evidence gathered elsewhere regarding this particular detail underlined that my informant was not giving me his personal views only. They were representative.

Evidence shows that the emphasis in thought-patterns to shade-snakes is not, in the first instance, a concern in the species of snake manifesting the shade. Although this aspect must by no means be disregarded, experience suggests that more important than the kind of snake that visits a homestead is the symbolism attached to the snake.

Shade snakes which differ from other reptiles do not die. They undergo a renewal of life in a symbolic rebirth through the annual change of skin. Because of its annual repetition which is thought to be very regular, the skin plays an important part in upholding the regular times which are associated with fertility in women.

Several symbols suggest themselves very clearly along the lines of thinking as illustrated by the discussion with the diviner. Firstly, the close relationships between the shade-snake and the unborn child, its moulding and subsequent birth. Secondly, the role played by water which is identified with the shade, with male fluid, and with dew. Thirdly, procreation and birth are associated with dark, night and the womb, all these being both the time and the specific places of intimate shade activities.

Besides these symbols, there is the association of the placenta and the skin of the snake with *izibi* which also is associated with a corpse.

Dreams

The important role played by dreams in Zulu thought-patterns cannot be overstressed. Without dreams true and uninterrupted living is not possible. There is cause for anxiety when people do not dream. "These are fearful nights. I do not see anything. Perhaps there may be something (bad)," said a troubled man to a diviner whom he had approached. He felt at a loss as to his condition. Another informant said about dreamless nights that follow on each other: "The thing that is bad is that I do not know. I do not see good things. I do not see bad things. It is like sitting in prison, not knowing when the courtcase will be. What is taking place? This is the thing that is most fearful." A great number of informants have said that when they retire in the evening they expect to dream. But it is not essential to dream every night. Some say they dream about two times a week and are quite content with this. Diviners claim that they dream every night. "Sometimes we (the diviners) also see things in the daytime. We cannot work without dreams. The dreams are our eyes in the work."

Beside the shades who reveal themselves in dreams and visions, dreams can be caused by witchcraft and sorcery.

Dreams are a channel of communication between survivors and the shades. In dreams the shades become very real, intimate and concrete. "They come to us at night, very clearly. They reveal themselves. We see them very closely and hear them saying things to us. They are just beside us when they reveal themselves in this way." Their absence in dreams can, as has been stated, cause anxiety. Not only does one experience the lack of dreams as a vacuum in life. The absence of dreams can also indicate a lack of interest on the part of the shades. Said a young man who had planned to seek work in Durban but, because the shades did not give their assent to his going, preferred to be without work than seek it contrary to their approval: "I was much troubled. I did not know whether I was to go out or not. They did not appear to me at all. Even after consultation (through a diviner) they did not indicate what they thought. There were no dreams at all. So there was nothing to do but stay at home. The magistrate's permit is still with me. I did not go."

The reality of dreams in Zulu thinking does not limit itself merely to the seen and the heard. It includes the experienced also.[41] Pain in the shoulders after a night of dreams is most definitely spoken of as the shades' activities. "In the speaking (i.e. in dreams) they sometimes stab a man in the sides and in the shoulder-regions. The man wakes up in the morning, feeling the pain very much. He calls on the people and tells them what he has seen. Then he says, 'Forsooth, I am not deceiving you in telling you the things that I have seen. Indeed, it is so painful, the stabbing, that I cannot even stand up and go outside.' The people merely listen, well knowing what has taken place. They all know that it is the fathers that have been working with the man."

A limited number of informants claim that the shades enter the head "through the mouth of the dreamer. They visit the eyes so that he (the dreamer) sees them. Then they pass on to the ears so that they can be heard. That is why a man who has dreamt much has a taste in the mouth. It is because they have been passing in and out through the mouth. That is the place through which they enter." Others who were questioned about the shades entering a human through the mouth laughed at it and said that this was just what "the primitive people think" (quoted source speaking English). Others said that they had heard people talk about it. Some said that they had never heard of it.

Note has already been made of thought-patterns which associate *ithongo* with dreams. Informants add that "when *ithongo* appears in dreams it always bring good news. If it (the shade) has something bad to say, then it appears in another way, perhaps merely keeping quiet and not appearing in dreams. But if people see *ithongo* then they rejoice because it has something good to say." A friend became quite excited when he spoke of *ithongo* and its revelations in dreams: "When it has appeared to a man in the night and said the good things, the man will rise quickly in the morning. He will start talking to people, even if it is early, speaking in a boastful manner and saying many things. He walks up-and-down everywhere in the homestead, simply joking with everybody and talking much. The people look at him and say to themselves. 'This man has seen something in the night. What has *ithongo* said to him?' They are also happy with him, knowing that it must be something good. When he has boasted sufficiently, telling the people how his fathers are looking after him, he calls the people together and tells them what he saw in the night."

A herbalist related how his *amathongo* appeared to him and gave him good advice regarding his medical practice. Working in the Pietermaritzburg area, he spoke frequently of *itongo* but always did so in relation to good dreams. I asked him whether he consciously associated *amathongo* with good dreams. He replied: "*Ithongo* always brings the things we want. It brings happiness." His wife, a charming Zulu woman with an outstanding knowledge of Zulu thinking, related how her brother had been given information of a suitable horse on which to place his money at the Durban horse races. "It was his father's *ithongo* that appeared. He appeared in a dream. Indeed, he came home with his pocket so filled with money that those who saw him thought he had bought much tobacco." She related another instance of a man who had lost his cattle. In a dream his "*amathongo* appeared and told him where to look for them. He found them, even calling the police to fetch those that had stolen his beasts from him."[42]

Dreams that come through witchcraft or sorcery can be treated with medicines. But no *ithongo* that chooses to reveal itself through a dream can be either misled or layed.[43] An informant explained the difference in dreams thus: "When we see the shades in dreams, we see the shade. It comes to us in dreams and speaks with us, sometimes even touching us (i.e. causing pain in the chest and shoulders). No one can drive away somebody who comes to talk. That is not done, especially if that is a senior (*umnumzane*). That is not done. But dreams which come from sorcery and witchcraft are caused. Medicines have power. They can cause dreams. Again, *abathakathi* come to us through their mediums. That is why these can be deceived and treated with medicines. They can be driven away with powerful medicines."

Women are said to dream extensively during the first months of pregnancy. They carefully note these dreams, for the outcome of the pregnancy as well as the sex of the expected child is announced through the dreams. The diviner at eThelezini proved to be a useful source of information in these matters. He explained the dreams thus:

"When the woman dreams about the child, it is the child's father's shades that are speaking. The child is the child of the father. It is his shade. So the dreams come from them (the father's shades)."

B: "Cannot the woman's shades speak through dreams to her?"

"They can do it. But they speak of other things. The thing in the womb is the father's water."

B: "Are all dreams related to the child messages about it from the shades of the father?"

"Not all. Some are bad dreams. The woman takes medicines. The dreams disappear. But sometimes the bad dreams continue. Then she fears and takes more medicines."

B: "The medicines do not affect the shades' dreams?"

"The medicines do not touch them. It is the shades that tell us what medicines to use. They cannot chase away themselves."

B: "How does the woman know what dreams come from the shades and which ones come from *abathakathi*?"

"When she dreams white dreams she knows that they are from the shades."

B: "What are white dreams?"

"It is the ones that are clear, being white. Again, they are the ones that are the good dreams."

B: "I have read in a book that if the woman dreams of green and black snakes the child will be a boy. What do you say?"[44]

"That is so. But the snakes are not snakes. They are *amadlozi*. The green one and the black one are the fathers of the child. The woman sees the fathers of the child."

B: "But would they not reveal themselves in the same way if the child were a girl?"

"Sometimes, especially if they already know that she will be a diviner. Then they can come in this manner. But as a general rule when they are appearing in this manner, they are saying, 'We have moulded a child. It is a male, one of us. It is our shade (*idlozi lakithi*).' That is what they are saying."

B: "But is the child already a shade before it is born?"

"It is a shade. That is what the fathers are saying when the woman dreams, seeing the fathers of the child. They are saying that their *idlozi* is there, in her womb."

B: "But are not girls also children of their father's shades?"

"They are also of the shades. But this shade that is in the womb is the one that stays (in the clan), giving birth to that *isibongo* (clan). Girls give birth elsewhere."

B: "The book also mentions buffaloes."

"Buffaloes are males. So when the woman sees a buffalo it is a male child."

B: "Why are buffaloes males?"

"They are strong, like men. A strong man is an *inyathi* (buffalo). When young men dance, wearing *ubunyathi* (ornament of plaited buffalo-skin worn by young men around the head and sometimes around the arms at *umjadu* dances) they are saying to the girls, 'Look at our strength.' They lift their legs high, showing off their thighs. They work very hard throughout the dance, showing off their strength. So the animal is a male."[45]

B: "Are there no female buffaloes?"

"There must be females too. But the animal is a male (i.e. a male symbol)."

B: "The same book says that if the woman dreams of puff-adders and crossing rivers she will give birth to girls."

"If she dreams that she is drinking water, then it will be a male child. She is taking in water. The water she is taking in is the water that the father is putting into her to make the child strong. He must do this so that the child eats its shades. So if she dreams of eating water it is a male. If she dreams of leaving water behind, leaving it or crossing it, the shades are saying, 'It is a girl.' They have moulded a girl. Women fetch water elsewhere."

B: "They carry water (male fluid) for other clans?"

"That is the thing. They go elsewhere to get water, leaving behind their own water."

B: "So crossing water means that they will carry another clan's water?"

"That is what the shades are saying when they tell the woman that she is crossing some water in a dream."

B: "The puff-adder?"

"The puff-adder (*ibululu*) has much fat. It is like a woman. On the other hand, it is short and thick. It is like a male member. But it is not the males of our clan that the shades know. So they (the shades) speak a language known to the woman when they show her a puff-adder."

B: "Is the puff-adder like the buffalo in that they are males?"

"They are males. But they are not the same. The buffalo is strength. The puff-adder is male in appearance. The appearance says that it is another than that of our clan because it is not a shade-snake. So when the woman sees it she knows that it is a girl in the womb."

B: "Does a puff-adder always speak of men of another clan?"

"Not always. Sometimes they speak of fatness. Then it is women, especially our own women (i.e. of our own clan)."

B: "But how do you know which sign the puff-adder is representing in the dream?"

"It does not matter. If it is fat, then it is a girl, moulded by our fathers. If it is a male, then it is a male of another clan (than ours). So it is the same."

B: "So the puff-adder says that the woman bears a child that will be the wife of another clan male?"

"No, the puff-adder does not say it. The puff-adder is the symbol (*isibonakaliso*). It is the shades that are speaking all the time. The puff-adder is simply an animal. It does not speak. The shades speak with it. That is the thing."

I asked whether all dreams from the shades were good dreams. My informant's conviction was that "they are good dreams because the shades are our people, wishing no bad thing." But there were occasions when they would trouble people very much. One such occasion was when a woman had been unfaithful to her husband and not confessed. "Then the shades troubled her very much, even causing her to be sick from seeing them too much." He said that in one case of which he had knowledge, the woman had become completely mad and "the white doctors had taken her to Pietermaritzburg (Fort Napier mental hospital), not knowing that she had become mad from seeing the shades too much." They also troubled people "who did not behave nicely, perhaps drinking too much or not sending home money." But such bad dreams were, according to the diviner, not bad dreams. "They are bad in one way because they trouble the one who is bad. But they are good because they will cause that person to return to a better living (*ukuphenduka*)."

Besides dreams caused by the shades and by medicines or witchcraft, there are dreams which are "*maphupho nje*", ordinary and every-day dreams. These are interpreted by their opposite and are believed to be "the language of some friends or even the shades", and do not require either interpretations other than when the dreamer feels that he ought to have them looked into. When a sick man dreams that he is still sick, he will get better. "Then this is a shade that speaks, because they always say the opposite." If a rich man dreams that he suddenly gets robbed, he knows that his riches "will increase because there is something going to happen, perhaps the horses will run well (ref. to horse-racing in Durban) or something else. It happens like that." Dreams seen in the daytime are often simply ignored "because that is not the time for dreaming". But dreams at night are taken more seriously for "this is the time of the shades and of witchcraft".[46]

The Hut

Three different places of the Zulu hut have distinct associations with the shades; the far back of the hut (*umsamo*), the hearth and the doorway. The latter two also have associations with sexual activity.

1. *Umsamo*

Ethnographic records have underlined the importance of *umsamo* of a hut and the special role played by *umsamo* of *indlunkulu,* a homestead's main hut. "The *umsamo* of every hut is sacred, but that of the chief hut of the kraal is especially important, for here all the offerings to the spirits are made, and here the important guardian spirits of the kraal abide."[47]

Umsamo is marked off in the far interior of the hut by *ufindo,*[48] comprising the saplings of the hut framework, and *umbundu,*[49] which is either an elevation of the floor about three to four centimeters in height or, far more common today, a semicircular raised border. *Ufindo* and *umbumdu* form an elongated oval space which is strictly honoured by all family members. Nobody enters this space other than on specific occasions which will be discussed in the course of the study.[50]

Informants are emphatic that nobody, and least of all strangers, is allowed to enter *umsamo*. "This is the place of the shades." However, vessels, clothing, and articles of both sentimental and financial value are stored away in *umsamo*. The ritual spear and *isipuku,*[51] if a homestead has one, are preserved in *umsamo* of *indlunkulu*. Definite reasons are given for using this place for storage purposes. "We put the things in this place of the shades so that they may know that we are looking after them. If the place is empty, then we are saying to them. 'We do not know you. So we are hiding the things from you.' So to put the things there is to tell the shades that this is their home." Another friend said that putting "our things there is the same as asking them to look after our belongings for us. They are watchful. They see better than we."

Umsamo is the place of the shades "because it is cool and dark. That is the place they like. Even their snakes, when they come, go to that place. So we know that this is the place in a house which they like." A man at Ceza said that the main difference between Christian homes which often are rectangular and pagan huts is the fact that "the proper Zulu hut has no window. But school people have windows. They put windows in the walls because they do not know how to honour the shades any more, simply letting the light come in." The man, very critical of westernization and with definite anti-Christian feelings, said: "Christians are always alone. They have no friends (among the shades) because they have chased them out of the houses. So they (the Christians) are always alone. They do not know where to find friends. Nobody likes them because they have no shades."

Flesh, beer and snuff which are to be used in communion rituals with the shades are set aside in *umsamo* overnight. Nobody expects to find any of it either touched or eaten in the morning. But the shades are expected to "lick their food which we have put away for them. They know that it is theirs. They have heard us speaking and seen their food in that place. So they come at night and taste it."

Pieces of savoury meat, good beer and other luxuries are also placed in *umsamo* from time-to-time, although they are not to be used in celebrations in the strict sense of the word. A man, eating *amadumbe* which had been prepared particularly well immediately after being dug up in the garden, related how he had set aside two or three peeled tubers in the cooking-hut *umsamo*. While eating *amadumbe* he recalled how he, as a boy, had heard his grand-father praise these tubers as to his particular liking. While he now was eating the same kind of tubers, he remembered his grandfather and his words. "I said to myself, 'But why do I suddenly remember him now?' Then I peeled two or three and placed them there (in *umsamo*) because I remembered him." Another said: "If we have good beer in the homestead and I have drunk, feeling the goodness of it, I say to my wife, 'Wife, today you have made it better than any other time. Let it not leave this place.' Then she puts one pot of beer in the place of the shades overnight. She puts on the covering just a little, honouring them. Putting on no covering is like feeding the rats. But putting it on just a little is asking them to come and just taste its sweetness. Then they taste it. They become happy, seeing that we have remembered them. The beer increases because they look after us."

The ritual spear and *isiphuku* are stored in *umsamo* of *indunkulu* because "that is the main place where they live. These things are theirs. They do not belong to a man. They belong to *umuzi* (homestead, of which the shades are family members)."

2. The Hearth

Custom demands that a good housewife leaves the cooking vessels unscraped in the close vicinity of the hearth. Most women say that this is merely good custom without actually knowing any definite reason for doing so. Others said that they did not know of it. But a number said that it was done to satisfy the shades. "The shades lick the pots." The diviner at eThelezini expanded on the issue. "The shades warm themselves at the hearth. When they are warm they become hungry and eat that which is left in the vessels. That is the reason for the women leaving the pots with a little food in each." Not only one pot was to be left at the fireplace. If there had been two dishes prepared in the evening, then both pots should be left at the fire-place. The lids should only partly cover the pot openings. "This is the way they like it. If the pots are wide open, then they (the shades) become displeased, thinking that the women indicate that they are greedy."

If the pots are scraped clean prior to the night, the fields will not produce good crops. "The shades say to themselves, 'What does it help to give them much? They simply eat everything themselves.'" A number of women did, however, relate the custom to future good crops by indicating that if the pots were cleaned in the evening the following year's crop would be poor.

One does not step over the hearth itself because "one does not step over a shade". Suggesting that the hearth had sexual associations, the diviner at eThelezini said that this indeed was the case but added that there, in the strict sense of Zulu interpretations, is no wide difference between sexual organs and intercourse on the one hand and the shades on the other. "So if you call it shades or call it sexual intercourse (*ubulili*) it is the same."

Laduma Madela and several other informants claim that the stone placed immediately behind the first supporting pillar of the hut-roof and being the most important of the three hearth stones is intimately tied to the shades. Bryant says of this stone that it is "religiously left in its place, none ever daring to remove it".[52] Experience shows that this custom is rigidly stuck to in pagan homes also today. Laduma Madela claimed that it is called *umlindaziko* (lit. hearth-watcher) because "it is from it that the shades watch the hearth. That is the place they occupy." Other informants support Madela's view, some adding that if one had eaten roasted mealies in the evening, one cob with at least one full row of maize should be left leaning against this stone as "food for the shades". All said that moving this stone would be regarded as disturbing the shades, a thing that cannot be done other than after communicating with them about the matter. Madela claimed that when he had to move from his old homestead higher up Ceza mountain and settle a little lower down towards the local parish centre and hospital, the moving of this particular hearth-stone was his most difficult undertaking. "They refused to move. I explained, saying that it was not my choice that I had to move, but that I had been ordered to do so. They did not understand. They liked that place where we lived. At least, when there was no other way, I simply had to take them. But they troubled me in dreams very much, complaining of cold and hunger. Not until this place had been made red with heat did they stop complaining."

Certainly few people had the extensive knowledge of the hearth-stone and sentiments attached to it that Laduma Madela had. But very few people did not know that the hearth stone was to be honoured and not touched or moved disrespectfully. Mentioning to many that perhaps the honour of the stone was actually honour devoted to the shades caused no alarm or confusion. Some even went so far as to say that it sounded perfectly logical. One woman said that she had asked people who "knew our customs" after I had told her what I knew. On the following day she verified the views I had related to her.[53]

3. The Doorway Arch

The shades are associated with the doorway arch, especially with the crown of the arch, situated between the doorposts and, as a rule, covered with thatching. The crown and the thatching is called *ikhothamo*. Although not many Zulu are able to give specific reasons for doing so, most, if not all, honour the doorway as they do the hearth. "We do not know the reason. But there is something (i.e. a reason). Maybe others have knowledge. As for us, we only know that it must be honoured." Suggesting that *ikhothamo* may have something to do with the shades did not cause amazement.

The diviner in the uMhlatuze valley gave a detailed account of his views on the doorway arch and its relationships to the shades.

"When I divine I sit here. That is where they (the shades) are." (He had been sitting in *umsamo* of his main hut.)

B: "Is a man allowed there? I have learnt that *umsamo* is not entered."

"It is not entered. But I for one enter it. It is their place and my place."

B: "I thought that the whistling came from the door." (I had attended a seance.)

"It came from *ikhothamo*. That is the place from which it came."

B: "I have read in books that the whistling comes from many places in the hut. Is this not true?"[54] (Early in our discussion he had moved from *umsamo* where he had been seated, shuddering frequently.)

"It is true. Even today it came from many places. It came from this place (*umsamo*). It came from *ikhothamo*. It came from the hearth. It came again from this place. But when it came so that I could understand it came from *ikhothamo*."

B: "Is there a difference when the whistling comes from various places?"

"There is a difference. The first is just noise, like children making noise and saying nothing. Then, when they see that the people are not playing but are serious, then they say the thing properly. They say it from that place (*ikhothamo*)."

B: "Are there people who are not serious when they approach a diviner?"

"There are many (such) people. They are not known until they have been seen in the heart. There are *abathakathi* that play, thinking that they will deceive. So they (the shades) test first."

B: "Did they test today?"

"They were troubled today, seeing a white man in their house. That is the reason."

B: "Would they have spoken directly from *ikhothamo* had I not been present?"

"Maybe. Maybe not. Whom am I to tell them what to do?"

B: "Why do the shades whistle when they speak to you? Is there a special reason?"

"That is the language of *amakhosi*. They choose it for themselves. I cannot choose for them. They teach me how to interpret what they say. That is my work. People come to me for this reason, the reason of interpretation."

B: "Other diviners go out to the people often, carrying their equipment with them. But you do not go out to them?"

"They come to me. The reason is *amakhosi*. They do not follow me."

B: "They speak to you from the arch?"

"That is the place they occupy. I cannot hear them if they are outside. They do not whistle if they must speak elsewhere."

B: "Do they speak through *ikhothamo* to you from the outside?"

"They are not outside of *ikhothamo* or this side of it (i.e. inside the hut). They are in *ikhothamo*. That is their place. They abide there. When they speak, they do so from inside *ikhothamo*."

B: "But *umsamo* is also their place?"

"That is true. It is their place. That is why I sit in *umsamo* when I do the work of translation (*ukuhumusha*) for the people who have come (to inquire)." The diviner went on to explain how he had to sit in the place of the shades so that they would "know their man", i.e. himself, before they felt free to whistle. He would sit, as he had done during today's seance, facing the left hand side of the hut, i.e. the women's side, "thinking very hard on them and telling them that everything was ready for them to speak."

105

B: "You do not face the people that speak to you as do the white men, nor do you face in the opposite direction as I have seen the servants of the Chief at enThembeni do?"

"I face in that direction (the left side of the hut, seen from the doorway of it) because it is the shades that are speaking."

B: "But are the shades associated with that part of the hut also? Is that not the place of women?"

"It is the place of women, that is correct. But when the shades speak I face that direction. They do not speak from that place. Then I would face another direction. But the thing is this. *Amakhosi* are our shades, the shades of our clan. Their place, if they were men, would be the right-hand side of the hut. So I face the opposite side."

B: "You are reversing things when it comes to matters of the shades?"

"I reverse them."

B: "Is it the same reason as that of colour (i.e. shades are white and Zulu people are of a dark complexion)?"

"That is the very reason. Now you see it clearly."

We spoke again of the shades being at various places at the same time, mention being made also of the fire-place, seeing that the diviner himself had mentioned the place. He readily agreed that the shades were "in many places at the same time, even outside the hut". There was, in his thinking, no inconsistency in such thinking. He enlarged on this particular point and compared the shades with water. "If there is water in a woman's hut, and water in another woman's hut, does this mean that there is no water in a third or even a fourth woman's hut? Shades are like water. They are everywhere at the same time. Like the woman's vessel is full in her hut, so the shade is full where it is." (The diviner had a day previously attended a service in which the preacher had pointed out that Christ, in His incarnation, was fully man and fully God. It is possible that the diviner had been influenced by the sermon when making the last statement about the fullness of the shades in a particular place.)

Our conversation returned to *ikhothamo*. At a number of funerals I had noticed that thatching was removed from *ikhothamo* when the corpse had been carried out of the hut and buried with the corpse. Was there any relationship between the thatching, the shades and the burial?[55]

"The grass is removed because the man who lived with his fathers in that hut is not in that house any more. He is in another place."

B: "So the removing of the grass is the removal of the shades?"

"That is so. They are taken away."

B: "But is there a special reason for removing the shades from the hut?"

"The reasons are two. First, when the one who looks after those shades is away, then *abathakathi* can do what they like with the shades. They must be looked after so that there happens nothing that will cause difficulties (*ubuthakathaka*). So the grass is removed. Secondly, the shades are simply accompanying their child. They go with him to his new house."

B: "They accompany him into the grave?"

"They accompany him. That is correct."

B: "Yet they are in the homestead with the others?"

"That is where they are. They do not leave. When we take the thatching

Fig. 2. Diviner's medicines stuck into the thatching of the hut roof immediately above the door. The egg shell, attached to a white stick, was said to remind the diviner of the dangers of eating eggs as these would make her think of men and not attend to her calling.

we are merely telling them that they must go with their child, attending to him in that place to which he has gone."

B: "If *abathakathi* obtain the grass, can they kill the shade?"

"Sometimes they can do it if they are strong. I do not know. But I know that there will be disturbance, much disturbance, the shades complaining that they are not looked after nicely by their people, simply left for anybody to do what they like with them. There is no dignity in looking after them if they are treated badly."

Professor Krige describes how medical pegs are placed in the far back, middle and entrance to the hut. One should not stop in the entrance to the hut "on account of the medicines buried there".[56] The diviner at uMhlatuze as well as a large number of Zulu friends have said that is true that under normal circumstances one should not hesitate when passing through a doorway, very much so pregnant women. But the avoidance of stopping in the doorway is not in the first instance due to the medicines.[57] It is rather a respect towards the shades and a partial avoidance of them. "When everything is well, then they are there in their places and we are in our places. We salute them nicely, giving them everything they desire. We honour them as they ought to be honoured. But when difficulties arise, then we want them close to us. They must brood on us (*ukufukamela*).[58] If a man goes slowly through the door, he is asking them to brood. But he should not. So he passes quickly through the door." Sick people who definitely are in need of the shades' nearness will be seen sitting in the doorway or its immediate vicinity. Although not very many sick people interviewed on the matter could give absolute reasons for sitting there, the general answer being that "sick people must sit there. That is their place," three or four men could give reasons for their being there. A T.B. patient at a hospital once said: "I am longing to sit at the doorway of my hut where they can see me and bring health." He was perfectly confident that if he only was allowed to go home and sit in his hut doorway the shades would soon restore his health. He very definitely associated the shades with the doorway and the arch above it.

Women brewing for purposes of communion with the shades will grind the necessary millet in the close vicinity of the doorway "so that they see their food which is being prepared for them". Again, a large number did not know why they used this specific place for grinding this particular millet other than that custom required this procedure. But a number of diviners were emphatic in associating the place with the shades.

Medicine containers of all kinds and sorts, snuff-boxes, tools of various types ranging from small knives to hoe-blades, letters and other articles of sentimental value are pushed into the thatching of the *ikhothamo*. Informed people say that they are put in this place for the same reason that one places other larger articles in *umsamo*, i.e. for protection and as a sign that the shades are family members and share in the common interests of the household.

Maize-cobs, millet heads, eggshells, pumpkin seeds are also placed in *ikhothamo*, the eggshells often strung up on a white cotton thread. "We place them there so that the shades can see them and bless them." Naturally, there are also practical reasons attached which often are stressed, i.e. that mice and fowls do not easily gain access to the seed in this place. But certainly the presence of the shades in this specific place is suggestive.[59]

The shades who occupy the doorway arch are sometimes addressed by commoners. A man who had recovered from a bad wound in his back caused by an ill-tempered ox while ploughing said, while entering the hut on his return from hospitalization: "*Oh, makhosi!* Today I am returning. The wound is well. Indeed, you have looked after me well! I am praising you by word of mouth now. Perhaps there may be something else later when I have seen things here how they are. Indeed, you have treated me well!" Having entered and been in the hut for a minute or two, he came out again, and said while going out of the doorway: "I am here, ye of my fathers! I am thanking you. See, I am even bending the back when passing through this place (the doorway). You see me walking today. But when I left I was not walking. You see for yourselves your work!" Asked whom he was talking to, he looked up, a little embarrassed, chuckled a word or two of amazement that he had been overheard and said: "Today even white men listen to us talking." But he refrained from revealing whom he had addressed until a later occasion when we had got to know one another. He then said that it was "the fathers in *ikhothamo*".

Skulls and horns of animals slaughtered at ritual celebrations are attached to the thatching of a hut immediately above *ikhothamo*. Generally the explanation of their presence in the thatching is that the skulls and horns are *isihlobiso* (a decoration). Some informants have said that they are *isikhumbuzo* (a reminder). "We remember the thing we did with our animal." Sometimes a number of skulls, as many as four, can be seen next to each other, on one and the same hut. When a number are seen the conclusion may be drawn that the inhabitant of that hut has either been ill or involved in some other personal disaster which required ritual slaughter. A limited number interpret the symbol as a reminder "to the shades that there has been work done for

Fig. 3. Horns of a ritually slaughtered goat stuck into the thatching above the doorway of a hut occupied by a sick man for whom a ritual celebration had been conducted. There is also a cob with some roasted miaize on it. "The roasted maize is food for the shades." The maize had been roasted at the hearth of the hut.

Fig. 4. Horns and skulls of animals slaughtered ritually in connection with a diviner's calling, training and coming out. They were attached to the fence of the byre and had been turned upside-down.

109

the household". That the skulls and horns of the animal slaughtered are placed in the close vicinity of *ikhothamo* is again suggestive.[60]

Cattle and the Cattle Enclosure

There is, according to Zulu thought-patterns, a close association between cattle and men. The diviner at eThelezini said on this particular relationship: "The thing is this. A woman conceives and gives birth in the tenth month. So does a cow. It conceives and calves in the tenth month. So a cow is like a human." He described how cattle live "in the same way as humans", drawing to my attention the fact that both cattle and human beings live in "*imizi* (homesteads) which are the places of cattle and humans". He was referring to the fact that both have their night-quarters in the one and same homestead. Ethnographic records state that in former times calves were kept in the homestead huts with humans at night.[61]

The cattle of a homestead are not the property of the father of the homestead only.[62] They are equally the animals of the lineage shades. "When they (the shades) are complaining of hunger, they are calling for food from their own flock." Hence the very strong feelings that regulate behaviour-patterns in regard to cattle and milk, especially those that involve women and homestead animals. Interference with a household's cattle is not merely an interference with the animals or the father of the homestead. It is an interference with the whole male population of the lineage, including the shades.

In the communion experienced with the shades in a ritual celebration, the gall of the slaughtered animal plays a significant role, possibly more outstanding than the eating of the animal's flesh and blood. My informant in the uMhlatuze valley had substantial views on the gall and the gall-bladder. He referred to the outer appearance of the gall-bladder thus:

"This thing has an entrance but no exit. That is the thing that the shades like. It is like a hut to them, having a door but no exit elsewhere."

Seeing that windows and light apparently play a certain role in terms of the shades, this aspect was introduced into the discussion. His reaction was the following: "That is the thing that is important (lit. hot). The gall is dark. It has an entrance but not another way out. They like this place also. They are all alike, the gall-bladder, the womb and the hut."

B: "Why do the shades like darkness?"

"It is because they work in darkness. It is in the darkness that they do their work. That is all I can say. There is no shade that appears working very much in the light."

B: "The shades lick the gall. But it is very bitter. How can they like it?"

"The shades like bitterness. It is their taste. Indeed, the gall is very bitter, if it is eaten by men. But to the shades it is the sweetest thing."

B: "Is this the taste that is opposite to the sweetness of men?"

"That is the thing. Gall is to them what sugar is to you and I."

B: "The shades lick the gall. But are they in the gall of the animal?"

"The gall-bladder is the place of the shade in a cow or an ox and even in the bull. It is the place where the shades live in a beast. If the shade is not in the gall, then the beast becomes sick. Nothing will be able to cure it because the shades have left it."

B: "Do the shades live in the gall of men also?"

"The shades live in the gall of men. But not only in the gall. But in men that is one place that they like."

B: "When a man is sick and he vomits so much that he even vomits gall (*ukukhipa inyongo*) does he not interfere with the shade?"

"No. He is driving out the thing that is disturbing the shades. As with cattle. If the animal is sick and it (the sickness) is in the gall, the shade becomes disturbed."

B: "Do the shades also lick the gall of men?"

"No! (Very strong disapproval.) How can they eat themselves? No, they do not eat themselves. They only lick the gall of an animal."

B: "So the main thing is that they lick the gall of an animal. Not so much that they live there?"

"I do not know how to say it clearly. But it is like this. They are there in the gall. They are not the gall. They are just simply there. They are of our clan. The cow is an animal. So they only live there. That is where they are found. They also like the bitterness (of the gall) as I said. They eat it because it is an animal and not a man. They eat the animal. The gall is the animal."

B: "Is the gall-bladder the same as the womb of the animal?"

"They are the same in that they carry life. The life (*imphilo*) of the beast is in the gall. But the life of the bull is in the womb. The shade is not in the womb of the cow. That is the place of the bull. The shades have their house (ref. to the female organs and womb)."

B: "When a beast has been slaughtered for somebody, a sick man, or a bride before she goes to the bridegroom, or for a diviner, the gall-bladder is fixed to the person's head. Why is this done?"

"It is to say to them (the shades), 'Look what we have done for this person, telling you to look after him. Look at him nicely.' What we are saying is this, 'This is the person whom we are bringing before you so that you can do your work with him. This is the one for whom we have slaughtered, giving you food and making you happy.' The gall-bladder is the sign that the person the shades must attend to is the one who has it (in the hair). It is just a sign. Nothing more is said about it."

B: "The shades do not live in that gall-bladder?"

"No, they are not in that gall-bladder. It has been eaten. But when they (the shades) see the gall-bladder they will remember the sweetness of the gall and attend to that person."

B: "Sometimes goats are substitutes for cattle in ritual killings?"

"They can also be slaughtered. They are animals like the cattle. Goats are good for slaughtering. First, they make much noise, calling the shades nicely. Secondly, the gall is big and very bitter. So it is a good animal for the slaughtering."

From our conversation it became very clear that the emphasis on cattle is not in the indwelling of the shade in the gall or elsewhere in the animal. What was important was, firstly, the fact that cattle give birth as humans do, in the tenth lunar month. Secondly, the form and contents of the gall is such that it very well fell into thought-patterns pertaining to shades, i.e. their liking for darkness and bitterness.[63] The resemblance of the gall with the womb and the hut underline the Zulu sentiments attached to fertility and prosperity which, as we have seen elsewhere, are major thought-patterns in life approach.

As the Zulu hut is the abode of the shades, so is the cattle-enclosure. "The cattle-kraal is the Zulu temple where the spirits of the ancestors are thought to linger."[64] However, the presence of the shades in the byre is not a generalised pattern of thinking. There are, as in the hut, three distinct places in the enclosure to which the shades are very definitely associated: the gateway, the centre where traditionally the grain-pits were dug, and the far interior of the enclosure.

Isibaya (cattle enclosure) "is like the hut. The gateway corresponds to the door of the hut, the centre corresponds to the hearth, and the upper end, opposite the gateway, corresponds to *umsamo*. So they are the same." A limited number of informants drew the lines of comparison rather more to the relation of the traditional grain-pits which were dug in the centre of the byre[65] and the hearth, both places being "places of food", on the one hand, and the interior of the cattle-enclosure with *umsamo,* thus eliminating the doorway and gateway comparisons. Any further information on thought-patterns related to the grain-pits, *imigodi,* was practically impossible to obtain, due mainly to the fact that these have wholly fallen into disuse today.

As the shades are closely associated with *umsamo* of a hut, likewise are they associated with the far upper end of *isibaya,* opposite the gateway. I have been unable to raise a specific name for this portion of the cattle-enclosure and expressed my amazement that such an important place has no name comparable to *umsamo* of the hut. Informants have suggested that "this place needs no name because it is too well known. When we speak of *umsebenzi* (ritual celebrations) we know that it is this place where the animal will be slaughtered. So we need no name for it." One informant said that the place is called *ematholeni* (lit. the place of the calves) because "they are the offspring of the cattle which are kept there, like the things of human beings (i.e. possessions) are kept in *umsamo.*"[66] The latter explanation appears a little strained, however.

Ritual slaughtering is, when done properly, carried out in the upper section of the byre. Under no conditions may any person outside the homestead lineage enter this part of the enclosure, if traditional regulations are followed. "They may not enter because it is the place of the shades." Informants are emphatic that the shades are present in the cattle-enclosure in this particular section, "as they are in *umsamo*. They (the shades) are in both places."

The Earth, *Imphepho* and *Imphephotshani*

Relationships between earth and the shades is not limited to *umhlabathi* (lit. earth) being a name associated with the original founder ancestor. Nor is it only the abode of the shades. Earth itself is identified with the shades. When pregnant women eat white earth, they do so because "the shades are white as this earth is white. They will assist in the delivery. The white earth is the thing that makes the birth easy." A herbalist who introduced this particular aspect of earth and shades to me was explicit in underlining that "earth is the shades. They are one and the same."[67]

Poor crops are sometimes related to the anger of the shades. "If the diviner cannot point at *umthakathi* who has put medicine into the field, then it is the shades." My informant continued: "That is when people say, 'This year the shades are angry.' Or sometimes they say, 'The earth is angry.' The sayings are one and the same." The associations between earth and the shades in the remark are obvious. The diviner of the uMhlatuze valley said that sometimes the words *umhlabathi* and *idlozi* can be freely interchanged and said that he did so sometimes, being perfectly conscious of what he was doing. "If I say *umhlabathi* or if I say *idlozi* there is no difference. They are just the same."

It was at eThelezini that I was given the following details about the use and understanding of *imphepho* (Helichrysum miconiaefolium), a small everlasting plant, mentioned in ethnographic records from time-to-time.[68]

"This plant is like a shade. It does not die as a shade does not die. The flower remains without withering (*ukubuna*. The Zulu word *ukubuna*, however, is more than wither. It includes a fading away gradually, eventually dying away totally, not to recover). The flowers that I picked when I was initiated when I was young are there to this day. They do not change. They are like the shades."

B: "So the shades live for ever?"

"They live for ever like this flower."

B: "But when people think of their forefathers, they generally think of those whom they have known."

"That is so. But they are still. People eat *imphundu* (a medical plant which is said to cause forgetfulness), forgetting them. But they are. That is why *imphepho* and shades are the same."

B: "Is *imphepho* a shade?"

"It is not a shade. But they are alike in that they do not wither. So they are friends (*abazalwane ngokufanana*)."

The diviner related how *imphepho* should be picked. Under no condition should it simply be ripped out of the earth with its roots unless one specifically required the roots for some purpose. When the diviner himself picked the plant he approached the plant so that his shadow fell over it, assuming that he picked it in the daytime. It was better, however, to pick it in the very early morning, before dawn "when there are no shadows", or in the very late evening, after sunset. When he breaks the stem he says: "Excuse me, thing of my people. It is the work of my fathers that I am doing." "Then it breaks off easily, the plant agreeing to doing its work. But if it does not break off easily, the excuse must be repeated. Perhaps the excuse was not heard the first time." Great care must be taken not to look into the earth, when breaking off the plant. "To look there is to look at a shade. This is not done. A man must not look at his fathers." The diviner was convinced that the shades "were just near the plant in the earth". We discussed the issue of being *in* the earth and being the earth again. "Those two things are the same. If I say 'in the earth' I mean the place where they go. The shades are in the earth, near to the plant. But when I say 'they are the earth' then I am speaking of that earth (i.e. the white earth) eaten by women."

Bryant and Doke–Vilakazi mention the fact that *imphepho* is burnt by diviners and the burning is related to the diviners' connection with the shades.[69] All diviners interviewed without exception stress the importance of *imphepho* in divination and nearly all agree to the method of picking *imphepho* described above. A limited number of diviners, however, say that they do in fact pull up the complete plant, with the roots, because the roots produce a stronger perfume and intenser smoke than does the stem and the leaves. When the plant is removed from the earth they hold the fingers of the left hand flat on the ground with the stem of the *imphepho*-plant between the long-and fourth fingers, and thereby avoid lifting any soil when pulling up the roots.

Besides the fact that the flower of *imphepho* does not wither, diviners stress the fact that it has a very clear colour. "Even at a far distance it can easily be seen." This is one of the reasons given for smoking and inhaling the smoke of *imphepho*, "to give clarity". Thirdly, the sweet smell of *imphepho*, once smelt, cannot be forgotten or confused with others odours. This, again, is the reason given for the saying that *imphepho* "gives us a remembering mind. We do not easily forget. It is given to us by the shades so that we may forget nothing."

It appears as if *izinyanga zamathambo*, bone diviners, use *imphepho* rather more frequently than other diviners do. My friend at eThelezini, who looked down on other diviners rather critically, said that "the many things cause confusion. So they need clarity. That is why they must use this thing very much."

Smoking *imphepho* is common among diviners. Others chew the stem and leaves of the plant while the large majority will also place some plants under their pillows "so that the dreams may be clear".[70] A number of diviners said that placing the *imphepho* under the pillow was more important than either smoking or chewing it "because dreams are the most important thing to us".

Bryant and Doke–Vilakazi give the impression that burning *imphepho* was commonly done at ritual celebrations, the smouldering plants placed with the prepared animal in *umsamo* as an incense. But it seems as if this is not done so frequently today as was the case previously. Older informants agree that this observation is true. One young man suggested that "it was a mistake of the old people to burn *imphepho* in the huts. This thing must be handled only by diviners."[71]

Colenso suggests that *imphepho* and *imphephotshani* are one and the same.[72] Diviners who know *imphephotshani* (probably Gazania longifolia),[73] claim that this is not so, although the two plants resemble one another somewhat.

Imphephotshani is rare. Only on two occasions have specimens been shown to me, once at the home of Laduma Madela at Ceza and once in the Melmoth district. Allowing for differences in geographical area, the one plant was clearly larger than the other. But at both places my informants associated the plant with much dew. "It is the plant of the shades. It has much dew. The dew is their water." Not only is it the plant which, according to tradition, shows the first signs of dew in the spring, but it is the first to have dew in the evenings. In spring it gives the first signs of rain in that a drop of dew hangs on the tip of a leaf. "This is their (the shades') sign that the rain is coming."

Friends say that *imphephotshani*, like *imphepho*, is not eaten by cattle. This is taken as a strong indication of the close relationships between the plants on the one hand, and the cattle on the other. It is clear "that the things of the shades do not eat each other".

Imphephotshani is, according to Madela, used for smoking purposes. It is also charred and possibly mixed with other ingredients, rubbed into the back of the animal to be slaughtered in a ritual celebration while the praises of the shades are being shouted out and they are asked "to look at their food". Madela said that if the back of the beast was rubbed with the ash of *imphephot-*

shani "the shades would come immediately and look at their flesh. They would feel the sweet smell of the ash and become happy."

Man

Zulu thought-patterns do not claim only that the shades are continually near to man. They are also in man.

"They are in the head. When I dream they are in the head, causing me to see the dream. I see my eyes being closed. I do not see things outside (me). I see the things that are inside (me or my head). That is where they are when they cause dreams. They are inside." A man, overhearing the above remark, added: "That is true. They are everywhere. They are in the head, in the whole head. When I wake up there is a taste in the mouth. It is clear that they are in the whole head."

Besides the head, the shoulder-blades and the back are closely associated with the shades. Diviners say that one of the sure indications that the shades are calling people to become diviners is "their stabbing in the shoulders and the back. They stab also in the chest. In the morning the man wakes up, having pain everywhere in these places. Nobody asks him for the reason. It is known that it is the shades. They are there."[74] Practically all informants interviewed on the subject agree that pains in the shoulders, chest and back are caused by the shades, these places being "the place they occupy in a man".

The shades are, however, localised very definitely also to the sexual organs of the human body and take a very active role in the sexual act. In fact, some informants say that no sexual act is possible without the excitement which is attributed to the shades. "When a man and a woman get hot, they are hot because the shades are working heat within them."

Bryant and Doke–Vilakazi state that *ufindo* is not only the framework of the hut which is associated with *umsamo*. It is also the "lower projecting part or lumbar vertebrae of the spine, just behind the hips".[75] With reference to *ufindo* of the human body the diviner of uMhlatuze said:

"This is the place they occupy. They are together with the kidneys and the gall there. When a man thinks of a woman it is the shades that cause him to remember the sweetness of the thing. They cause him to wish for the thing and make him strong in the place (i.e. cause erection)."

B: "Is *ufindo* of the male the same as *ufindo* of the hut?"

"They are one and the same."

B: "Tell me what *ufindo* of the male is."

"It commences in the curve of the backbone. It passes through the legs of the man. It comes out in the front. When the man is hot, it can be felt with the hand. That is *ufindo*. It is the bent arch, reaching from the back to the front. It is like the arch of the hut. They are the same."

B: "Is it the similarity of the arches that brings the shades into *ufindo*?"

"The shades are in *ufindo*. That is their place. Where is *ufindo*? It is in the hut. It is in the man. That is all I can say."

B: "Has a woman *ufindo*?"

"She has it. It is the same thing with her. But in the man *ufindo* comes out. With women it stops in the flesh, coming out only very little."

B: "Are the shades in the woman's *ufindo* as they are in the male's?"

Fig. 5. Construction of *ufindo* in *umsamo* of a future hut. Not only is this an important part of the hut, but it is also the starting point when constructing a hut.

"They are there. The woman's mouth (i.e. sexual organ) is the door. They are there indeed, as the male's member is their place."

B: "Do the shades cause desire in women also?"

"That is their work. When the woman is hot, it is the shades that are working in the heat. They are causing it."

B: "Which shades live in the woman?"

"Her father's shades. They are the ones in her. They stir her."

B: "So in sexual union, both the man's shades and the woman's shades work together?"

"They are working together, the shades of his fathers and of her fathers. They bring more and more heat to both. The man works very much until the water comes. Then he falls back, weak. He is weak because the shades are now out of him, in the woman. That is why the woman still sometimes remains hot. The shades are moulding. They are making the child."

B: "Do the two different clan shades work together intimately, seeing each other?"

"The shades of the woman just bring the blood. They put it there. Then the shades of the man come with the water. They take the blood. They mould (*ukubumba*) the child. That is how they work."

B: "So the shades of the woman do not mould?"

"They simply bring the blood. It is the blood of women, the blood of the months. It is their work to bring this. But they do not mould. That is the work of the shades of the male."

B: "Do the woman's shades go with her from her home to the home of the man whom she marries?"

"That is what they do. They go with her. They are in that place (the womb). They cause the blood to come regularly. It is their work. When they have brought the blood, they give it to the child, if it is there. It (the child) eats the blood. The blood makes it strong."

B: "Are they (the shades) in the blood also?"

"No. They simply give the blood. But they are not in the blood. They remain in the womb, giving blood."

B: "Do the male's shades also continue working after the child has been moulded (ref. to continued copulation after conception)?"

"When the man puts water into the womb the shades make the child strong. It eats the water. The shades are in the water. They enter the child and build it strongly. It is strong when the child kicks in the womb."

B: "Are the movements of the child a sign that it is strong?"

"They are a sign that the shades are doing their work. The woman's shades are giving food. The male's shades are building the child strong. That is when the woman says, 'No, but you have strong shades. The child is kicking very much, even causing pain.' But she rejoices, knowing that the child is strong. That is how the shades work in the womb."[76]

Our conversation took up the moving of the woman's shades with her from her home to that of her husband. We discussed the *ukwendisa* animals which of necessity must follow the bride from her home and, if tradition is followed correctly, cannot be substituted either by other animals (e.g. goats) or money.[77] The second of the animals, *isikhumba,* is slaughtered together with *inkomo yokucola,* the latter furnished by the bridegroom's father or senior guardian.

The symbol underlying the simultaneous slaughtering of the animals is the mutual acceptance of bride and bridegroom by the shades of the two parties. "When the cattle are slaughtered it is a sign that the shades of the bridegroom and the bride agree to work together." Two things, the piercing of the *isikhumba* animal's stomach by the bride and the pouring of the gall of both animals on the feet of the bride and the subsequent fastening of the gall-bladders in her hair, are of importance. My informant had the following to say about these matters: "When the animal (*isikhumba*) has been prepared by the bride's party, except the stomach, she enters *isibaya* (byre) through the gate. She enters quietly, saying nothing. She takes the knife and pierces the stomach near the gall, the men pointing at the place but saying nothing. They are very quiet. Then she walks away, the people of the bridegroom shouting very much and showing joy. She returns to her party outside (the byre). The men cut away the gall. Then they say to the bridegroom's party, 'We are here.' When they (the bridegroom's slaughtering party) are ready they say, 'We are also here.' Then the bride comes again to the cattle-enclosure. The men of the parties go to her. They cut open the gall-bladders of both animals over her feet, over the right foot and over the left foot. She stands quietly, saying nothing. They put the bladders in her hair. The people rejoice very much. She returns to her party outside *isibaya*."

Two details are symbolised in the bride's entry into the byre of her future husband and the piercing of *isikhumba* animal's stomach. "She enters because she must be in the presence of the bridegroom's shades. That is why she enters that place. They (the shades) are in that place." We discussed the bride going to *indlunkulu* for the purpose of being in the presence of the groom's shades and my informant said that sometimes the ritual is indeed performed in *indlunkulu* as far as the pouring of the gall on the feet of the bride is concerned. But for practical reasons the piercing of the stomach could not be done elsewhere as the contents of the stomach would have to be emptied into the cattle-enclosure after the piercing of the stomach.

We spoke of an occasion elsewhere where I had been present at the slaughtering of *isikhumba,* and I related the reason given me for the stabbing of the stomach of the animal by the bride, the symbol being one describing her virginity. I gained further knowledge. There ought to be a ring of white beads to place around the wound and the people outside the enclosure shout only when the bride places the ring around the wound. My informant's interpretation was as follows: "The spear is the male because only men carry spears. So it is their thing. When the spear stabs the women it finds the woman closed. That is what the woman says when she does this thing of stabbing. She says, 'I am closed (i.e. I am a virgin).' That is what she says in doing this thing."[78]
He described the white beads as being a symbol of the shades and their agreement to what the bride was symbolising. "They agree with the white beads." The white beads, in themselves, were not a sign of the bride's virginity, but of the shades.[79]

The pouring of the gall of the two animals on the feet of the bride is a symbol that the shades of the two parties concerned agree "to do their work with the woman". The fact that the gall is to be poured out only on the feet of the bride and not the male must be seen in terms of Zulu concepts of fertility. If there is no child in the union, the fault is to be sought with the woman. "So it is in her that they agree to do their work. When we pour the gall on her feet we are asking them to look at her favourably and to do the thing nicely with her. They must work together. That is the reason for pouring the gall of the two beasts together on her feet." It is clear that the mutual undertaking of the shades in the formation and development of the child has its roots already in the marriage ritual, to be followed up by their activities in the procreative act.

Omens

Professor Krige has listed omens associated with the shades, drawing largely from ethnographic records on Zulu.[80] Besides these, there are a great number of omens, various omens being regarded with different emphasis in different places of the country. Omens are often interpreted similarly but with different emphasis. The whirlwind is generally regarded as a shade, this manifestation being particularly common in autumn and winter. "When they appear in this form they are telling us that we ought to reap or we should make fire. They are cold." On the other hand, a dog that suddenly turns in its track "because it saw somebody there" is interpreted as avoiding a shade south of Thugela. But at Ekuthuleni people said it was the "habit of dogs" and were rather amazed to hear that elsewhere the dog avoids a shade. An informant at Ceza said that a shade is speaking when one hears the wind whistling in the thatch of the hut, while at Appelsbosch one said that it was only *umoya* (the air, wind) and were amused to hear it is associated with shades further north.

The Shades and Kinship

C. Faye's and N. J. van Warmelo's studies on Zulu kinship terminology and systems have drawn attention to the strict patrilineal approaches to kinship in Zulu society.[81] Professor Krige has underlined the importance of the lineage within the clan organization as well as giving us an account of behaviour patterns within the lineage and the closer circle of the family hut. The aim of this section is to show the functions and responsibilities of the shades within the lineage of a clan.

To Zulu all human beings are potential shades. But the importance attached to a particular shade varies very much, depending on social status, and the age and number of children a man may have had prior to departure from the physically living.

All are emphatic that children, including infants, are and become shades, disregarding the fact that they may not have been "brought back" to the homestead in the customary *ukubuyisa* rituals. Asked what happens to children when they die, an informant said: "They become *amadlozi*, but they remain children. No child has power in the homestead. So the shade of a child has no power." People are explicit that even children appear in dreams, particularly to their mothers. "Sometimes even to the fathers, especially small boys. When the father is wondering what has happened with the child, then he sees the child in a dream. The father simply sees the boy. Then he (the father) wakes up." All are convinced that no shade of a child can either give advice or exercize influence of any kind. "That is impossible. It is merely a child. What can a child say?" A Christian woman whose child passed away described with enthusiasm one Sunday at the local church how she had dreamt of her child as "an angel, dressed in white and very happy". Other women, listening to her, shared her joy with her. Excited by their comments, the woman gave details of her dream and returned again and again to the meaningful experience that the dream had been. On her departure home, a group of the women who had listened, remained and discussed, among other things, the woman's dream. One of them said: "It may be that she saw the child's shade. I have never heard of children becoming angels." The question of children becoming angels was discussed at length and various suggestions made. But there was a certain amount of uncertainty about the relationships between angels, children and shades. Nobody doubted or questioned the existence of either the angels or the shades—these were taken for granted. After all had agreed that there was nobody in their group who could answer the question satisfactorily, the final decision was postponed to the following Thursday when the women were to meet with their parish minister "who knows what the answer is".[82]

Evidence from Zulu shows that the emphasis is not, in the first place, put on the question whether one becomes a shade or not. The question is rather, 'What influence has a shade?' in a given situation. It is possible that missionary labours have achieved a shift in emphasis as well as a change in approaches in that human dignity is attributed to the human already from conception. Whatever Zulu thought about the unborn child previously, one is convinced today that "the thing in the womb is a human". Zulu reactions towards abortion strongly underline these sentiments. Said a woman at the funeral of a child which was delivered dead and apparently had been dead in the womb for some time: "It is good that you buried the child nicely. Even if it was like this when it was born, it did live (once)." The grand-mother of the still-born child was emphatic that the child, although dead when born, was a shade. "It was a boy. How great the suffering of the father and mother seeing they have only girls. But it is known today that the mother did bear a son although he is a shade now."

The father of a homestead becomes an influential shade only to his own and junior brother's children as well as to his grar.dchildren through his sons. Only in two exceptional instances does a father's shade exercise any influence on his adult daughters. No man becomes a shade to his sister's children as these of necessity will be the children of a lineage different from his own. It is essential to underline that a man can be a shade only to his juniors. No exception to this rule was found anywhere. The realm of a shade's activity is, apparently, narrowed down to his lineage and family survivors only, the sphere of shade activity being defined by strict kinship rules of behavior patterns.

The two occasions when a child-bearing woman appears to be wholly in the hands of her lineage shades are the following. Firstly, when a woman is called to become a diviner. All Zulu informants, without a single exception, are explicit that no diviner can be called by any other shades than those of her/his own lineage. "When a woman is to be a diviner, then it is her own shades that are troubling her. Her husband can do nothing, if it is her shades that are requiring her. Nothing can be done by them (the shades of the husband). They simply remain quiet. They can do nothing. That is if it is her (i.e. her lineage) shades that are troubling her." If the husband insists, he can furnish animals towards the barring of the shade, but this will only be done on condiction that the woman herself agrees and her people are willing to carry out the necessary rituals. Without their positive reactions, nothing can hinder her from being possessed by her shades as a diviner. Other informants say that often the husband is happy when his wife is called to be a diviner "because now there will indeed be prosperity in the home. The sicknesses will depart and the shades become active."

The second occasion when a woman is under the influence of her lineage shades is at the birth of an illegitimate child. If the woman is married and her husband refuses the child (as sometimes happens today when men work in towns and, allowed home only at specific times of the year, are able to tell whether their wives have conceived during their absence or not), the child is said to be of her lineage and sent to her paternal home as soon as possible after birth. If the biological father accepts responsibility for the child, it may be taken by him or his people and the child then automatically accepted into his lineage, including the shades. In cases when the father is unknown the child remains under the influence of the mother's shades, adopting the clan-name of the woman. However, if the father is known and possibly paid a portion of *ilobolo*, the child falls under the influence of the father's shades. A girl at Rorkes Drift for whom some of *ilobolo* costs had been produced by the male's lineage gave birth to a rather sickly baby, a boy. On an occasion when the child was weaker than usual and one feared that it would not survive, the girl's father put his daughter and her child on the bus to Dundee where the child's father had his home with word that "the funeral is the responsibility of the father". On arrival at the child's father's home a ritual celebration was carried out and the child improved. Discussing the matter with the girl's father, he emphasized very strongly that it definitely was the shades of the child's father that had secured health. "With me the child was always sick. But there in Dundee it was healthy. So it is clear that they (the shades of the child's father) were looking after their child's child."

We have seen how the shades of a woman are regarded as participating to a limited degree in conception in "supplying the blood". They are, however, not regarded as responsible for conception. This is the work of the male's shades. The influence of the woman's lineage shades appear to decrease as time goes on, and by the time that she does not bear children any more, her shades no longer have influence over her. "Old women who no longer bear children are left by her shades. They see that she is drying. So they leave her. The blood becomes less, although they are working very hard. But it becomes less and less. Women also notice this thing. They know it. That is when they commence becoming like men." A woman at Ceza put it thus: "When our daughters commence giving suck, then we dry up. That is the way with women." Asked whether women's menstrual flow and its ceasing was due to the shades or whether they left because the blood "becoming less", my informant said that she did not know. "But that does not matter. It is the same with all women. When they (the shades) leave us, then we cease to give blood."

"When women no longer give birth, they are like men. That is why we call them men." The quotation is representative of a great number of informants. Gradually, the women are accepted into the sphere of influence of the husband's lineage, although there is considerable doubt as to the influence of the shades of the husband over the women. Some informants say without hesitation that the women fall under the influence of the husband's shades, others are hesitant: "We do not know." "We have not thought of it." "The old people have not told us." Apparently it is not a matter of great concern. Old women themselves suggest that they are taken care of by their husband's shades. One old woman said: "Perhaps it is like that. We (old women) are under our men. That is sufficient for us." Another old lady said that as long as her husband was alive she felt perfectly happy "because he is my shade. If he dies today it does not matter. He is still my shade."

A woman becomes a shade to her own children, especially if she dies in a ripe age. Her influence as a shade can even include her younger brother's children. A man fell ill and was said to be troubled by a shade. Several diviners were approached, all agreeing that he was sick "because a shade is hungry", but none of them "could see clearly who it was. Each time they mentioned a name, there would be a certain work done (i.e. a ritual celebration). But health was not restored." Eventually a renowned diviner from elsewhere was called. "The price was paid. She divined and saw somebody. Then she said, 'Is there perchance an old woman in the family?' The answer was given, 'There is one. The daughter of my father's father (i.e. paternal aunt).' She said, 'Just tell me, what was she like? Do you recognize her in this-and-that description,' the diviner describing her. The people were very much amazed when the diviner described the woman. The people said, 'Indeed, is it not the old one who was with us at M?' Then they described her to the diviner. She said, 'It is the one that I see.' So there was work done again. The sick man became healthy. It was the old woman."

Also old, but still living people are regarded as shades and can exercise influence on their juniors. The following illustration is certainly suggestive, although not common. Relating it to some informants to see their reactions, they nearly all expressed their approval, some adding that they, in turn, had heard of similar instances. In a few cases, amazement was expressed. A young man was constantly being troubled by a dream in which he claimed to see his paternal grandfather who still was alive, staying with the elder brother of the young man some three miles away. After discussing the dream with relatives and close friends, he decided to visit the brother's home and find out what possibly could be the cause of the dreams. On arrival at the brother's home, the grandmother saw that the young man was troubled and asked him why he was disturbed. He related the dream to his grandmother who approached her husband. The latter is quoted as having said: "Indeed, it is I that he has seen. I am just saying to my child that I am hungry. I have not smelt the flesh of his home for a very long time. I am hungry indeed." On his arrival home, the young man immediately set about preparing a ritual celebration and invited his grandparents to come to his home. For the purpose of transport he hired a local taxi-driver to take the old people from the brother's home to his own. The old people came and were entertained in *indlunkulu* during the festival. After the celebration they returned again to the brother's home. The young man claimed that he was no longer plagued by further dreams.

Zulu are all most emphatic that although shades cause sickness and dreams, "sometimes even causing disturbances in the hearts of men", they do so with good reasons. Never do they cause trouble for the mere sake of bringing about confusion and difficulties. Pressure, exercised by the shades, although it at times in the first instance appears negative, always turns out to have a positive outcome. If they are hungry they cause suffering in the lineage among members who are their juniors and who are expected to conduct ritual slaughterings. The great difference between sickness caused by the shades and that brought about by witchcraft and sorcery is that the latter is intended to kill and annihilate if at all possible, while the former aims at drawing attention, not only of the person assaulted by the dream or sickness, but of the whole family to the needs of the shades. Hence the saying, *idlozi, alibulali, liyathusa nje*, a shade does not kill, it merely frightens.[83]

Notes

[1] Gluckman, 'Some Processes of Social Change Illustrated from Zululand', p. 258 ff.

[2] Cf. Radcliffe–Brown, *Structure and Function in Primitive Society*, pp. 155 ff.

[3] See also Bryant, *The Zulu People*, p. 711, who writes: "The Zulu idea that the extremely aged 'go home' instead of 'dying', and that the event is one of joy rather than for sorrow . . ." Zulu informants react favourably to Bryant's statement. See also Tyler, *Forty Years among the Zulus*, p. 208.
Describing Tsonga, Junod, 'The Theory of Witchcraft Amongst South African Natives', p. 239, says: "death is only natural when caused by old age."

[4] Bryant, *The Zulu People*, p. 699 ff. and Berglund, 'Fasting and Cleansing Rites', p. 106 f.

[5] Samuelson, *Some Zulu Customs and Folklore*, p. 11 ff.: Samuelson, *Long, Long, Ago*, p. 37: Krige, *SSZ*, p. 160: Tyler, *Forty Years among the Zulus*, p. 211: Doke–Vilakazi, *Dict.*, p. 253.

[6] Bryant, *Dict.*, p. 253.

[7] King Dinuzulu's grave was still watched in 1966 by the last of his remaining wives. The King died 1913. See Binns, *Dinuzulu*, p. 255.

[8] Cp. Junod, 'Essai sur les notions fondamentales de la pensée africaine bantoué', who analyses the Bantu concept of *ntu*.

[9] Bryant, 'The Zulu cult of the Dead', p. 140: Krige, *SSZ*, p. 284: Hochegger, 'Die Vorstellungen von Seele und Totengeist bei Afrikanischen völkern', writing on the wider African ethnographic records finds a dualistic concept and argues in terms of "body-soul" and "free soul". The latter implies an ability to leave the body for short periods and is associated with the shade, while the "body-soul", at least in the West African setting, has a pre-natal existence with God or associated with thought-patterns describing a re-incarnation.

[10] Doke–Vilakazi, *Dict.*, p. 893.

[11] Cf. Bryant, *Dict.*, p. 729.

[12] Bryant, *Dict.*, p. 490. Cf. Doke–Vilakazi, *Dict.*, p. 652, who associates *umphefumulo* with not only the breath but also life and soul.

[13] Bryant, *Dict.*, p. 392.

[14] *The Collector*, no. 665, p. 129. See also Callaway, *The Religious System of the Amazulu*, p. 10: Bryant, 'The Religion of the Zulus', p. 45: Bryant, *Dict.*, p. 392: Doke–Vilakazi, *Dict.*, p. 508: Colenso, *Zulu-Engl. Dict.*, p. 351.

[15] Shooter, *The Kaffirs of Natal*, p. 161.

[16] Doke–Vilakazi, *Dict.*, p. 809.

[17] Colenso, *Zulu-Engl. Dict.*, p. 628.

[18] Doke–Vilakazi, *Dict.*, p. 809: Bryant, *Dict.*, p. 665: *The Collector*, p. 129. See also Callaway, *The Religious System of the Amazulu*, p. 91.

[19] Callaway, *The Religious System of the Amazulu*, p. 126.

[20] Krige, *SSZ*, p. 284, and Callaway, *The Rel. System of the Amazulu*, p. 126.

[21] *Ukuthwebula* is to hypnotize or paralyse while *imithwebula* is a medical charm for killing or hypnotizing. See Doke–Vilakazi, *Dict.*, p. 813.

[22] Wanger, 'Totenkult (Ahnenkult) bei den zulusprechenden Vökern', p. 10.

[23] Bryant, *Dict.*, p. 364. Cf. Doke–Vilakazi, *Dict.*, p. 465.

[24] *The Collector*, no. 664, p. 128.

[25] Bryant, 'The Zulu Cult of the Dead', p. 140: Wanger, 'Totenkult (Ahnenkult)', etc. p. 11: Krige, *SSZ*, p. 284.

[26] Kidd, *Savage Childhood*, pp. 281 ff.

[27] Kidd, *Savage Childhood*, p. 283 no. 5. Cf. also p. 284 no. 7. The other arguments raised by Kidd are all, to a greater or lesser degree, refuted by Zulu. Farrer, *Zululand and the Zulus*, p. 127 f., writing 1879, and apparently drawing on material from southern Natal, speaks of *ithongo* and relating the word *idlozi* only to snake manifestations of shades.

[28] Among Nguni-speaking people south of the Zulu the word corresponding to the Zulu word *ithongo* is used, apparently far more extensively than with Zulu. See Hunter. *Reaction to Conquest*, pp. 227 ff.: Hammond–Tooke, *Bhaca Society*, pp. 228 ff.: Soga, *AmaXosa Life and Customs*, pp. 143 ff.

[29] Doke–Vilakazi, *Dict.*, p. 310. Cf. Bryant, *Dict.*, p. 232.

[30] Wanger, 'Totenkult (Ahnenkult)', etc., p. 12: See also Bryant, *Dict.*, p. 666, who says in connection with *isithutha*: "Whereas the fabled *uNkulunkulu* is credited by the Zulus with having created the first human pair, all subsequent reproductions of the species (i.e. in the wombs of the mothers) is regarded rather as the work of the ancestral spirits of whom it is said, *zikwazi ukubumba umuntu zingaboni,* they can make a man (in the dark) without seeing him!"

[31] Colenso, *Zulu-Engl. Dict.*, p. 331.

[32] Doke–Vilakazi, *Dict.*, p. 472.

[33] Bryant, *Dict.*, p. 370.

[34] See Bryant, *Dict.*, p. 729: Colenso, *Zulu-Engl. Dict.*, p. 705: Doke–Vilakazi, *Dict.*, p. 894.

[35] Bryant, *The Zulu People*, p. 523.

[36] Livingstone, *Narrative of an Expedition to the Zambezi and its Tributaries*, p. 520, says, describing people further to the North-West that "the good spirits of the departed, *Azimo* or *Bazimo* may be propitiated by medicines, or honoured by offerings of beer and meat . . .; and the bad spirits, *Mchesi*, of whom we have heard only at Tette . . ."

[37] Colenso, *Zulu-Engl. Dict.*, p. 594 & 598. Cp. Doke–Vilakazi, *Dict.*, p. 803.

[38] See Bryant, *Dict.*, p. 631 and Doke–Vilakazi, *Dict.*, p. 796.

[39] Callaway, *The Religious System of the Amazulus*, p. 148.

However, *umnyanya* is the word ordinarily used for shades in Xhosa. See Kropf, *A Kaffir-Engl. Dict.*, p. 303 and Jordan, *Ingqumbo Yeminyanya*.

Krantz, *Natur- und Kulturleben der Zulus*, p. 104, mentions the term *imishologu* (among others) as a shade name. Zulu do not appear to have knowledge of this term. A woman, married to a Mpondo, said that she knew of it, apparently having knowledge of the word through her marriage. Cp. Hunter, *Reaction to Conquest*, p. 263, where *itshologu* is mentioned as something harmful. P. 257 gives a distinct difference between it and *ithongo* (which is always good). But when it lies on its back it is *itshologu*.

[40] Bryant, 'The Zulu Cult of the Dead', pp. 140 f. See also Krige, *SSZ*, pp. 285 f. who quotes Bryant extensively in this section.

[41] Cf. Laubscher, *Sex, Custom and Psychopathology*, p. 12: "Thus the domain of phantasy and myth invades objective reality and fuses with it." Laubscher is analysing material from Mpondo.

[42] Wanger, 'Totenkult (Ahnenkult)', etc., p. 15. He says: "*ubutongo* der Zustand ist in welchen sich *i-tongo* offenbart, und umgekehrt, dass *i-tongo* dasjenige Wesen ist, das sich im Schlaf, also durch Traume, offenbàrt".

[43] Professor Krige has misquoted Callaway when speaking of the laying of a dream. Callaway is not speaking of the laying of a dream but the laying of a shade. Cf. Krige, *SSZ*, p. 287 and Callaway, *The Religious System of the Amazulus*, pp. 160 f. *Ukukhipa iphupho* discussed in *The Collector*, no 726, p. 147, refers to dreams through which witchcraft and sorcery make themselves felt and not dreams in which shades reveal themselves.

[44] Bryant, *Dict.*, p. 518.

[45] Cf. Bryant, *Dict.*, p. 466 and Doke–Vilakazi, *Dict.*, p. 622.

[46] Cf. Farrer, *Zululand and the Zulus*, pp. 134 f.

[47] Krige, *SSZ*, pp. 46 & 291: Mayr, 'The Zulu Kafirs of Natal', pp. 456 ff.: Lugg, 'The Practice of Lobolo in Natal', p. 24: Becken, *Am Buschbockfluss*, p. 7: In towns

and when people have built square houses with rooms, evidence shows that generally the bedroom of the house functions as *umsamo*. Here meat of ritually slaughtered animals is stored overnight with a pot of beer. See also du Toit, 'The Isangoma', etc., p. 57.

[48] Bryant, *Dict.*, p. 146. Cf. Doke–Vilakazi, *Dict.*, p. 207 and Colenso, *Zulu-Engl. Dict.*, p. 141.

[49] Bryant, *Dict.*, p. 57 and Doke–Vilakazi, *Dict.*, p. 92.

[50] Krige, *SSZ*, p. 91, who says that "no one ever sits at the *umsamo* of anyone's hut because this is the place for the spirits".

[51] *Isiphuku* is a cloak made of skins from animals slaughtered at ritual killings. It is worn, if there is one available in a homestead, on occasions of communion with the shades. See Bryant, 'The Zulu Cult of the Dead', p. 145.

[52] Bryant, *The Zulu People*, p. 195. See also Bryant, *Dict.*, pp. 357 f.: Doke–Vilakazi, *Dict.*, p. 458: Colenso, *Zulu-Engl. Dict.*, p. 319.

[53] Cf. the role played by the hearth and hearth-stones among Sotho-Tswana in Willoughby, *The Soul of the Bantu*, p. 285 f.

[54] Bryant, 'The Zulu Cult of the Dead', p. 141: Norenius, 'Izanusi', pp. 40 f. Norenius definitely states that the voice heard at a seance with *izinyanga zemilozi* comes from the doorway.

[55] Bryant, *The Zulu People*, p. 707.

[56] Krige, *SSZ*, p. 47.

[57] Cf. Berglund, 'African Concepts of Health, Sickness and Healing', p. 39.

[58] Doke–Vilakazi, *Dict.*, p. 215. Note that the word is used in connection with sickness, childbirth and initiation which all are occasions when the presence of the shades is vitally essential.

[59] Braatvedt, *Erindringer fra mitt misjonsliv*, pp. 48 f. He says that egg-shells are strung up on sticks and stuck into the thatching in order to protect the homestead from disease and encourage hens' further laying eggs. See also Grout, *Zululand*, p. 104 and Ludlow, *Zululand and Cetewayo*, p. 52.

[60] Sometimes the skulls and horns are attached to the byre poles. See illustration which depicts horns on the cattle-enclosure fencing in a diviner's home. Note that they have been turned upside-down. The diviner commented: "With diviners this is the way to place the horns. They must be placed upside-down on the byre fencing so that it is known that they have been slaughtered for a diviner."

[61] See e.g. Mayr, The Zulu Kafirs of Natal, p. 456: Jenkinson, *Amazulu*, p. 69: Grout, *Zululand*, p. 97: Tyler, *Forty Years among the Zulus*, p. 45.

[62] Cf. Plant, *The Zulu in Three Tenses*, p. 53. Plant says that the animals are the "property of one man".

[63] Grout, *Zululand*, p. 135, says that should the slaughtered animal "be found to have but little gall, the *amadlozi* are charged with having come and drunk it while the cow or goat was yet alive".

Lugg, 'The Practice of Lobolo in Natal', p. 25, says: "The importance attached to the gall bladder is due to the belief that it contains the very essence of the animal by reason of the fact that its secretions, unlike those of the stomach and urinary passages, have no observable exit, and for this reason regarded as belonging to the body's permanent structure."

[64] Krige, *SSZ*, p. 42, Jenkinson, *Amazulu*, p. 52, speaks of "the most sacred enclosure" when referring to the byre.

[65] See Krige, *SSZ*, pp. 43 f. Although not expressly stated in the text, no. 37 in the sketch (p. 43) is the location of *umgodi* in the cattle-enclosure. See also Plant, *The Zulu in Three Tenses*, p. 46: Jenkinson, *AmaZulu*, p. 52: Duggan–Cronin, *The Bantu Tribes of South Africa*, Vol. III, Section III, plate XCI: Krantz, *Natur- und Kulturleben der Zulus*, p. 63: Grout, *Zululand*, p. 104: Ludlow, *Zululand and Cetewayo*, p. 75.

[66] Krige, *SSZ*, p. 63. No. 25 in sketch marks the calf-enclosure.

[67] See further on earth-eating in Africa in Anell & Lagercrantz, *Geophagical Customs*.

Bryant, *The Zulu People*, p. 623, states that earth-eating does not occur among Zulu. Informants claim, however, that white clay is eaten in small quantities by women during pregnancy "to make the birth easy".

[68] See Bryant, *Dict.*, p. 496 and Doke–Vilakazi, *Dict.*, p. 658: Colenso, *Zulu-Engl. Dict.*, p. 466.

[69] Bryant, *Dict.*, p. 496: Doke–Vilakazi, *Dict.*, p. 658: Plant, *The Zulu in Three Tenses*, p. 44.

[70] Cf. Krige, *SSZ*, p. 309.

[71] Bryant, *Dict.*, p. 496: Doke–Vilakazi, *Dict.*, p. 658.

[72] Colenso, *Zulu-Engl. Dict.*, p. 466.

[73] Doke–Vilakazi, *Dict.*, p. 658.

[74] See also Callaway, *The Religious System of the Amazulu*, p. 159.

[75] Bryant, *Dict.*, p. 146 and Doke–Vilakazi, *Dict.*, p. 207.

[76] Cf. Vilakazi, *Zulu Transformations*, p. 56, on Zulu concepts of conception.

[77] *Ukwendisa* animals ought to be two or three in number and accompany the bride from her home to that of her future husband. If the animals are two, the second is slaughtered with *inkomo yokucola* which of necessity must be supplied by the bridegroom's father or his senior guardian because "it carries the shade of the bridegroom". According to information the two animals should stand close to each other prior to being slaughtered "so that we can see whether the shades of the bride and the bridegroom agree". If one of the beasts should chase the other away this is taken as a serious indication that the shades of the two parties do not agree to the marriage.

Isikhumba beast is slaughtered and prepared by the bride's party in the bridegroom's cattle-enclosure at the same time that the bridegroom's party is preparing *eyokucola* at the upper end of the byre, opposite the main gate to the enclosure. See further Krige, *SSZ*, p. 137: Reader, *Zulu Tribe in Transition*, p. 205: Grout, *Zululand*, p. 172, who relates these animals to the shades: Tyler, *Forty Years among the Zulus*, p. 202, who states that the beast "is ever looked upon as the ox of the *amahlozi* (ancestral spirits), the loss of which by death would be considered a token of desertation".

The first beast of *ukwendisa* animals is called *isigodo* and represents the bride's lineage and shades in the new home. It may not be slaughtered.

[78] Bleek, *Zulu Legends*, p. 14, gives information of associations between the spear and the male partner in the sexual act.

[79] Ludlow, *Zululand and Cetewayo*, p. 177, writes: "the friends of the bride approach and put a string of beads upon it, reaching from the head to the tail. This is said to 'close the wound'."

[80] Krige, *SSZ*, p. 288.

[81] Faye, *Zulu References*, pp. 101 ff. and van Warmelo, *Kinship Terminology of the South African Bantu.*

[82] Cf. Makhathini, 'Ancestors, Umoya and Angels', p. 158.

[83] Tromp, *De Stam der Ama-Zoeloe*, p. 73, writing in 1879, had observed that shades were limited to their lineage. He says that "met de dooden van anderen, heeft hij niets te maken en behoeft hij dus ook niet te vreezen".

Chapter IV

The Shades Brood over Men

All Zulu are well aware of the importance of the direct and immediate intervention of the shades in life's many ins-and-outs. While their nearness in dreams is taken for granted and their specific abode in the various parts of the homestead as well as in the earth and the body are accepted as natural, one maintains a certain distance from them, unless specific circumstances require their very close presence. It is this specific relationship of intimate closeness and nearness that is described by *ukufukamela*, 'brooding', as a hen broods over her chickens.

It is important to note the distinction between *ukuba kona,* to be present, and *ukufukamela,* brooding. While the former, the presence of the shades, is a necessity for a normal and prosperous life, the latter is required only at very special times of crisis when the presence of the shades is changed to brooding. But when the brooding of the shades is no longer required, or when the crisis is over, the shades are shaken off and the appropriate distance between them and the living which is understood in *ukuba kona,* returns.[1]

Bryant says that *ukufukamela* is sitting "indoors (with *ngendhlu*), properly of certain Native customs requiring it".[2] Evidence suggests that the brooding of the shades is very closely associated with a diviner's occupation and ability as well as being related to the times of crisis which demand the shades brooding as indicated by Bryant.[3]

J. L. Döhne draws attention to the fact that the causative form of the verb *ukufukama* involves "to breed out, to hatch out, to generate, to produce the young".[4] Diviners and lay informants say that this is precisely what happens when the shades brood. Discussing this issue with a friend at Ekuthuleni, he said: "When they (the shades) brood, they are doing the same as fowls, bringing something else out of the eggs. The person over whom the shades brood becomes something else. When they complete (brooding) she is not *inkosikazi* (any more). She has become something else. She finds herself being a woman who is a widow." This view was confirmed by a number of other informants. The diviner at eThelezini, however, both corrected a detail and added further information which, subsequently, was endorsed by a number of other diviners. He said that it was not the shades that behaved like fowls, but the fowls that behaved like the shades! Arguing that fowls are a recent introduction into Zulu society, brought by the whites, and only recently become generally recognised as edible also by women, he continued: "When we saw what the fowls did, just sitting there on the eggs (*ukuchamusela*) and producing other things than eggs, the things being chickens, we said, 'Indeed, is this not the very thing done by our fathers when they brood over us?' So the thing done by fowls was given the same name (i.e. word) for the thing done by the shades." Later in our discussion he added an interesting detail: we had been talking on the issue of shaking off the shades and the party who takes the initiative, the shades or the person over whom they brood. The diviner was explicit that the initiative came from the person over whom the shades were brooding and not from the shades themselves. "So here you see who takes the first step. Is it not the hen that just sits and the chicken makes the hole to come out? So it is with the brooding of the shades. They just sit on the person. When that person does something to separate himself from them, they cease the brooding."

Excess brooding of the shades is very much feared. "It brings about *uku-hlanya* (to rave, go mad, be insane; become wild, ungovernable; act in a wild manner)."[5] Besides being a humiliating epithet, the very thought of becoming *uhlanya* is a matter of great concern and avoided at all costs. Informants have said that the only reason for ceasing in attempts to bar the shade when a person is called to become a diviner is the fear of becoming *uhlanya*.[6] "When the shades call a man to become a diviner and he refuses, he becomes sick. He remains sick and there is no improvement. He may be sick all his life. This is bad indeed. But still it is only sickness, the sickness being that of the shades, which does not kill. But if they (the shades) wish to show the man that they require him and he is stubborn, refusing all the time (to become a diviner), they can cause him to become *uhlanya*, just brooding over him. That is the worst thing, even worse than sickness. When the diviner divines, saying all the time, 'The shades are requiring this man,' but he or his people do not agree, he just becomes sicker and sicker. All the time the diviner is divining, the cattle are slaughtered until nearly all are finished. The sick person simply becomes weaker and weaker all the time. Then the diviner says, 'No, people, today I see a new thing. I see that they are determined (i.e. the shades are determined to have their way). The new thing that I see is that there is *uhlanya* in this home. That is what I see today in the divining.' Then the people fear very much, agreeing immediately to the desire of the shades."[7]

Having been called by the shades and accepted the challenge of becoming a diviner, the question of the brooding of the shades becomes a different matter. No doubt the preparation for a diviner's work in being trained by an experienced diviner is a preparation and an initiation into a life characterised by the constant brooding of the shades over one. Without this constant brooding of the shades, the diviner is not able to divine satisfactorily. But necessary as this brooding is, it is dangerous and to be handled with care. Hence training and initiation not only into the required knowledge which a diviner is assumed to have, but also into a life in that closeness and intimacy with the shades characterised by brooding. Experience shows that Zulu are very anxious to have diviners available when they require their assistance. But one is reluctant to have them lodge in the homestead over any period of time. This is particularly true of diviners of standing who are looked upon with awe and fear. "They are fearful, even causing insanity sometimes. We do not know what it is, but surely if a diviner has lived in a home for a long time, then somebody there will become stricken with the sickness of the head, not knowing what they do or say," said an informant who had turned out a diviner from the homestead. The diviner himself, a renowned man who sought accommodation because he had missed the last bus for the day, said: "They fear me. The thing they fear is the brooding. They feel its weight very much. That is the thing they fear very much, not knowing what they fear." Discussing the issue a little further he added: "They fear to become sick because of the brooding. If one does not have medicines which make one strong, then the brooding brings about great sickness."

B: "Where in the body is the sickness?"

"It is everywhere. First it causes many difficult dreams, then visions also in the day. Then the head becomes painful. That is where it stops."

B: "Tell me more about the sickness when it stops in the head. I would like to know this sickness."

"You have seen it. It is the sickness called *ukuhlanya.*"

B: "You mean that the shades bring about so serious a thing as *ukuhlanya*?"

"That is what I am saying. Sometimes if an *umthakathi* really wishes to cause something fearful he throws (i.e. causes) *ukuhlanya* on a man. But sometimes it is because of brooding. Brooding is fearful if you do not have medicines."

B: "You are a married man, having two wives. Do they (the wives) not *hlanya*?"

"It is because of the medicines that they do not become insane. That is the reason. Again, they (the shades) brood over me. But they (the wives) take medicines which I prepare for them."

Four distinct and definable rites are related to the brooding of the shades. All four are to be found in rituals connected with times of crisis in life, i.e. birth, sometimes ear-piercing, puberty, marriage and funerals. They are also found in the life of a diviner as from the day of initiation when he/she comes out and is officially accepted as a diviner by the community.

Firstly, the brooding of the shades is associated with abstention from washing in water. But washing does take place in the chyme of an animal slaughtered for the shades and on behalf of the person over whom the shades may be brooding, e.g. the *nqwambisa* goat slaughtered at the public appearance of a diviner.[8]

Informants are emphatic that ritual slaughtering is not done merely for the sake of eating the flesh of the animal. "It is true that there is meat. It is important. But there is the gall. It is even more important. Sometimes it is the gall only that calls for the slaughtering. Again, there is the chyme. It is for washing. Sometimes it is this thing (the chyme) that is required most of all. As at burials. There must be a washing. So a goat must be killed. They wash. When they have washed they eat (the flesh). But the washing comes first."

Ethnographic records and evidence shows how important it is to wash the hands in the chyme of the slaughtered animal at ritual celebrations. "It must be this thing (the chyme) of the animal because it alone washes so that the hands become like the shades (i.e. the chyme makes the hands white). They appear like shades when they come out of the washing in the chyme. This thing is better than soap because it gives the colour of the shades, the colour inside the hands." People agree that it is the whiteness which results from washing in chyme that is symbolic and hence of the greatest value. The diviner at eThelezini said: "When a man is experiencing brooding, he washes in chyme because it is the colour of the shades that he wants. It gives this colour. Then they (the shades) see that the man agrees to their brooding. So he becomes powerful."

While washing in chyme is regarded as "washing in the animal of the shades", washing in water is looked upon as a washing away of the shades. "To wash in water when they are brooding is fearful. It is washing them away, they and the gall and everything." Informants again and again referred to washing in water to removing the gall of a slaughtered animal from oneself, and it is evident that one avoids removing the gall once it has been poured onto the body. The ventriloquist claimed that once he had not washed for a period of six weeks. "It was the time when I was sick, being eaten up. Then they caused me to dream about this sickness. I saw them brooding over me, not allowing me to wash. So I did not wash. Only after six weeks I became better. Then I dreamt again about this thing. I saw new gall. Then I knew that I must slaughter. So I washed in the morning, washing very quickly and then pouring the gall (over me) so that the brooding should not cease. Then I became better and better, the strength returning." Other diviner-informants stress that they are careful not to wash before they can be sure of anointing themselves with either gall or ash of *imphepho* which, by several, is regarded as equally acceptable to the shades as gall, immediately after washing. Other diviners, on the other hand, maintain that they retain the brooding of the shades by not removing their *iminqwamba* skins when they wash in water. "Sometimes we must wash. But they do not leave off brooding. They see the skins. So they do not depart."[9]

There is no evidence that would point to the chyme of an animal being associated with the shades as is the gall or the vertebrae or shoulders and sides in both animals and humans. Many informants very strongly disassociated themselves from any such thoughts, emphasising that the chyme "is just like soap. But it cleanses in another way. It is the way that they (the shades) like it. That is the reason for the chyme. But they do not eat it or live in it. The chyme and the gall are different."

Secondly, the fixing of the gall-bladder onto the head of a person indicates the brooding of the shades on that person, the animal naturally a ritually slaughtered one. "When a person has a gall-bladder in the hair, then we know that there is something with that person, the shades brooding," said an informant. "It shows that there has been a killing. If there has been a killing, then the shades have been approached."

Diviners attach considerable importance to the gall-bladders they wear, a limited number claiming that the more gall-bladders they have, the greater their ability. The diviner at uMhlatuze, on the other hand, denied this very emphatically and said that it was a matter of having gall-bladders, not the number that one wore. "Even I, having divined many years, since my youth, I have only these two gall-bladders. I have never had more than two, yet the divining has merely increased." It is perfectly true that his reputation was known afar, people seeking his assistance from as far off as Durban and Pinetown. But a bone-diviner in the vicinity of Mapumulo who did not have great success had as many as seven gall-bladders in his hair, an informant claiming that a number of these had been purchased at the local butchery.[10]

It is essential that the gall-bladder be from an animal slaughtered at a ritual celebration and that the animal should have been killed for the particular person wearing it. The gall-bladder is inflated preferably by the wearer, immediately after the gall has been poured over the person concerned or he/she has drunk its contents. "It must be an animal slaughtered for that person so that the shades know who requires the brooding. That is the reason for the killing of the animal for that person, sometimes being sick, sometimes having some other reason for the killing. The shades know the gall in that it to them is sweetness. They lick that person, brooding when the gall is poured on the skin and the gall-bladder fixed in the hair. It is clearly seen that there has been work (ritual slaughtering) for that person in that the gall-bladder is in the hair and the gall on the body, it being unwashed."

As washing is a sign for the shades to cease brooding over a person, so the removal of the gall-bladder from the head is a symbol of the discontinuation of the shades' brooding and a return to normal living, if the person concerned is not a diviner. If a diviner, the bladders will not be removed other than temporarily. The brooding is expected to continue throughout the diviner's life as a servant of the shades. "When the bladders are removed from the head and the person washes, then the brooding stops. That person can work normally again."

Thirdly, associated with the brooding of the shades is abstention from cutting the hair and, sometimes, the paring of at least one nail, sometimes several. This is applicable to diviners who do not cut their hair or, if males, do not shave at all.

As far as ordinary people are concerned the emphasis lies on the shaving after the time of brooding has ceased, the hair being left untouched during the brooding of the shades. This is the reason given for women shaving after childbirth, the shaving of young people undergoing puberty rites, bride and bridegroom at marriage, the corpse prior to a funeral and the bereaved immediately after the funeral. In all these cases the hair is shaved, either wholly or symbolically, however short it has been prior to the occasion.

With diviners the emphasis lies on the growth of the hair and beard, if males. Under no circumstance may their hair be cut or shaved. It (the hair) is allowed to grow and twisted into long strings, hanging over the whole head. The individual strings are known as *uphotho*[1] while the complete arrangement of the head is known as *umyeko*. Today there are diviners who cut their hair but allow a little tuft to grow on the side of the head, mainly to satisfy employers in the cities and towns, who, for the sake of cleanliness, require their employees to cut their hair. But conservative traditionalists strongly resent this procedure, claiming that it is a modern trend that "just brings disrespect on the work of diviners". The diviner at eThelezini said on this issue: "When I see a diviner having only a little hair I say, 'My fathers! Why do you allow such things? This man is playing with you and with us, simply cutting his hair because white men tell him to cut it!' Then I shudder, thinking how this man can work having no ability."[12]

The diviner at eThelezini had a left-hand little-finger nail measuring about three centimeters in length. I suggested that the nail was a sign of his dignity. But he emphatically refuted this statement. "Do not confuse diviners and chiefs. Chiefs have it as a sign of not working.[13] But I for one, I work, doing the work of divination. (We had been talking of symbols of dignity and hence a discussion on long finger-nails.) This thing (he held out his finger nail) is the thing of brooding, like the hair. They are the same, the nail and the hair. If it (the nail) breaks, then surely I must beg pardon of them that own it (the shades). It is their thing of brooding." Although a number of diviners do not have long fingernails, conservative and traditionalist diviners of standing will undoubtedly have at least one long finger nail. Usually it is on the left hand little finger, although other fingers may be chosen also. A diviner in the Msinga valley had three left-hand fingers with exceptionally long nails.

131

Fig. 6. Diviner with uncut hair as a sign of the brooding of the shades She wore three gall bladders from mals slaughtered in connection wit her calling, training and coming o The white tail hairs are of the bea killed on the occasion of her comir out.

She associated them with "their owners", i.e. the shades, with terminology similar to that used by the diviner in the uMhlatuse valley.[14]

Because the hair, and where applicable also the nails, are intimately connected with life and health, *imphilo*, shaving the hair and paring the nails is a symbol of a new start in life, the climax of the former having been sanctioned by the brooding of the shades. When a child is born, it is shaved because it ceases to be a foetus and becomes an infant as a married woman who becomes a widow ceases to be a wife and commences the life of a widow. These associations of crisis are sanctioned by the very close and intimate nearness of the shades characterised by their brooding. When this particular life comes to an end under their brooding, a new life commences in which their presence is not that of brooding but rather of presence at some distance. Hence the shaving. An informant at Ekuthuleni said: "When a widow shaves, it is a sign that she is no longer *inkosikazi*. She now becomes a widow. She is like the bride (we spoke of) who leaves her homestead and goes to the home of her husband. She shaves to show that she is leaving behind her *ubunthombi* (maidenhood). That is why she shaves."

B: "But what about the brooding (of the shades)?"

"The brooding ceases when she shaves the hair. It is the sign that now the time of brooding has come to and end. The shades must now just be there (be present). But they must not brood."

Fig. 7. A diviner over whom the shades are brooding. Her hair was un-cut; the beads attached to it were not looked upon as finery. She had care-fully covered up her shoulders against the rays of the sun with *ingubo yama-dlozi.* The pin hanging around her neck "kept away sharp things".

B: "Is the shaving a sign for the shades to cease brooding or is it a sign that they have ceased brooding?"

"It is like this. When the man dies, they brood over the widow knowing that she is no longer a wife but a widow. That is the time when they brood over her. But when they have completed brooding over her, then they cease brooding and just simply remain near to her. Then she shaves. She shaves when the time of shaving comes. That time is known. The same with the bride. They brood over her, knowing this time to be the time of departing from the home. When she has left the home and arrives at the new place (i.e. her hus-band's home) they cease the brooding. That is the time when she washes at the river and cuts away some of her hair, leaving some. That is the time of shav-ing. It is known to be the time of shaving. Then the shades cease brooding."

The diviner at eThelezini said that "shaving was a sign of starting another mode of life." He took himself as an example. "If I should cease being a diviner, cutting the bonds between myself and them (the shades), then I would separate myself (*ukuzihlukanisa*) from them. In this separation the hair would be cut, leaving nothing on the head. Then they would cease brooding and I would not divine any more."

B: "Would you shave (the beard) also?"

"I would shave it (off)."

B: "Is this shaving like the shaving of those over whom the shades are brooding but cease the brooding?"

"It is the very same brooding and the very same shaving. It is like people at a funeral. Today they are laughing and eating much food, knowing nothing. Tomorrow they see a corpse in the homestead. They are stricken. They do not laugh. They do not eat. They are heavy in their hearts. The shades come and brood over them. Yesterday they knew of no brooding. Today they experience the brooding. Then they do the work of burying. They find themselves fatherless. Yesterday they were children with a father. Tomorrow they are fatherless. So that is the thing of which I speak when I say, 'Shaving is a sign of starting another life.' That is when they shave. It is the same shaving that I would do, separating myself from being a diviner. It is the same thing. Today I am a diviner. But tomorrow I decide I shall not be a diviner. So I separate myself from them (the shades) saying, 'Today I am not your servant any more'. Then I shave the head and the beard and all the hair off."

B: "What happens when the hair grows again?"

"That is the new hair. It is not the hair of the old time. It is the hair of the new life which has begun. If I cease to be a diviner, then the new hair is the hair of the man living a new life which is not the life of a diviner."

Fourthly, people over whom the shades brood put aside all finery and cosmetics until such time that the brooding ceases. "We put them aside because these things are for people to see, looking at us. But this time people must not look too much. There is brooding. That is the important (lit. big) thing then. So there is not time for people when they (the shades) are brooding."[15]

Practically every diviner interviewed agreed to having smeared his/her face with white clay or ash, sometimes with white-wash, both before and after the coming out as a diviner. They also agree to wearing, either on the head or as necklaces and sometimes in both forms, white beads given them during the time of training. Some diviner also wore tufts of white goatskin attached to the hair or hanging around the neck. All diviners were explicit in their views that their wearing beads or skins and their smearing their faces and bodies with white, was not to be regarded as a wearing of finery or smearing with cosmetics. "These things are not *izihlobiso* (finery, cosmetics). They are the things of the work of the shades. That is why they are worn at this time. They are the things of the shades."

There is a definite avoidance of any kind of skin treatment in terms of rubbing it with fats and other ingredients which cause the skin to become shiny and soft. This avoidance is to a large extent comparable with that of avoiding to wash. "If we put on *amakha* (scented ointment) we would be rubbing off (*ukuthintana*) the gall. This is bad. The shades are disturbed. So the body is not rubbed with sweetsmelling things when they brood." Diviners say that if they use *amakha* their ability to divine decreases due to the shades not brooding over them as they ought. "A diviner who uses these things is not a diviner. He is only playing with people."

The use of white clay or ash when the shades brood differs considerably between diviners and commoners. A great number of commoners do not make use of white clay or a substitute at all. Despite special efforts to trace any use of white at funerals or among the bereaved no evidence of its use has been found. But white is used in the puberty rituals, although not extensively. An informant at Ceza associated the white dress worn by Christian brides with the white of shades "when they are brooding. They are the same colours. Whether the bride has white clay or a white dress does not matter. The shades are still brooding."

Diviners, on the other hand, cannot conceive of an initiation without white. "That would not be the birth of a diviner (i.e. initiation) if there was not any white! How could the brooding commence if this colour was not found?" To the diviner at eThelezini white clay or a suitable substitute was an absolute necessity in the initiation rites of a diviner.[16]

Notes

[1] For comparative material on the brooding of the shades see Wilson, *Rituals of Kinship among the Nyakyusa*, pp. 69 ff.

[2] Bryant, *Dict.*, p. 154.

[3] Notice how widows "shaved their heads, anointed their bodies, put on their ornaments and went out of mourning for their husband" when the witch believed to have caused the husband's death was killed. Jackson 'Native Superstition and Crime', p. 256.

[4] Döhne, *A Zulu Kafir Dict.*, p. 84.

[5] Doke–Vilakazi, *Dict.*, p. 321.

[6] Shooter, *The Kafirs of Natal*, p. 193, relates an instance when a man claimed that the excess nearness of the shades caused madness.

[7] Cf. Farrer, *Zululand and the Zulus*, p. 138, who associates ability to divine very closely to insanity.

[8] On *nqwambisa* goat and its slaughtering see Krige, *SSZ*, p. 306: Bryant, *Dict.*, p. 449: *The Collector*, No. 235, p. 30.

[9] Callaway, *The Religious System of the Amazulu*, p. 262, says that a diviner does "not wash or anoint his body". See also Norenius, 'Izanusi', p. 36: Plant, *The Zulu in Three Tenses*, p. 46.

[10] Krige, *SSZ*, p. 307: Grout, *Zululand*, p. 160.

[11] See Bryant, *Dict.*, p. 510, and Doke–Vilakazi, *Dict.*, p. 672. Also Colenso, *Zulu-Engl. Dict.*, p. 683: *The Collector*, No. 234, p. 30.

[12] Cf. *potula*, shave, after restraint imposed by a diviner, Colenso, *Zulu-Engl. Dict.*, p. 477.

[13] Joest, *Reise in Afrika im Jahre 1883*, p. 482, describes Zulu dignitaries with a long finger-nail.

[14] On long finger-nails see Lagercrantz, *Contribution to the Ethnography of Africa*, pp. 138–144.

[14] My informant said that if a diviner did ever shave, the hair ought to be buried "in the earth where it belongs".

[16] Samuelson, *Zululand, its Traditions, Legends, Customs & Folk-Lore*, p. 131 ff. describing funerals refers to abstention from washing (pp. 132, 133, 136 & 137), cutting the hair and abstention from shaving (pp. 133, 136 f.), from finery (p. 133).

Chapter V

Diviners—Servants of the Shades

A Diviner's Call

Nobody can become a diviner of personal choice, at least not in theory. All diviners interviewed are emphatic that they had experienced a very definite call to the office of diviner by the shades. Hence they regarded themselves as the servants of the shades. In theory anybody can become a diviner, but in practice the overwhelming majority are women. Informants could not give any definite reason for this great number of female diviners. "We do not know the way of the shades. They choose the one they want. That is all we know." One informant suggested that women were more numerous because they could be called to divination by both their own lineage shades and those of their husbands' lineage. Another woman denied this possibility very vigorously, saying that it did not matter from whom the call came. "Whether it came from this side or another, that person would still be a diviner. So the source of the call does not matter."[1]

Dreams are a very important instrument through which the shades call their servants. The dreams are often accompanied by visions which, to the dreamer, are both frightening and obscure. "That is why people shout out and scream when they are being called by the shades. They see fearful things. But the people not knowing the reason simply try to quieten them saying, 'No, but why are you shouting? Is there something?' The sick person is all the time filled with fear, but says nothing." People say that the dreams and visions "simply confuse things, so that we do not know what this thing is."

Typical of the dreams and visions is that they, besides being frightening, are unclear and not understandable. "Other dreams we understand. But these are not known to anybody. They are hazy, the dreamer looking very much to see them clearly. But he sees only like shadows, nothing appearing nicely so that he can see well."[2] A diviner related what he had dreamt thus: "What I saw was this. Sometimes I dreamt I was eating pork. That is when I shouted in the night, causing fear among the people. Then the pork made me very sick. It stuck in the throat and caused great pains in the lungs and the stomach. It was fearful. When I completed dreaming of this animal (i.e. a pig), I dreamt of snakes that were very great, eating up all the cattle of my father. The snakes were everywhere, even entering me. I do not know how, but suddenly I found that I was vomiting snakes. I said, 'This thing is fearful! This sickness I have never seen before, people vomiting snakes!' That is what I said. Then the people started asking certain things. Suddenly I dreamt of a certain mountain, but not seeing it clearly. They asked me which one it was, but I could not say it, only seeing dimly. But on the mountain were certain animals. They had eight legs. I said, 'Perhaps it is the cows of white men with great udders.' But then again they were kicking. So it was not udders, but legs. I found myself just confused. That is what fearful dreams I dreamt."

Attempts at finding an acceptable solution to the dreams and visions leads one to calling a diviner who is to diagnose the cause of the dreams. "Then we call a diviner and tell him the things of the night and their fearfulness. He divines and divines, all the time asking questions and coming to the answer. He says it, saying, 'People, just keep quiet. Just let me speak freely once, you not causing trouble with much noise, all the time troubling me with questions. This thing has now become clear. I tell you this one thing as I see it. It is the shades. That is all.' Then he departs, everybody marvelling at his words. They say, 'Forsooth, is there to be a diviner here among us?' The people discuss what to do, looking at the cattle."

Besides dreams, the shades indicate their calling through frequent sneezing,[3] yawning,[4] belching[5] and hiccups.[6] While sneezing and yawning are said to have their seat in the lungs, sides, shoulders and upper parts of the neck, including the backbone and hence related to pain in these regions of the body, belching and hiccups are localised to the lower back and hips.

"Sneezing and yawning come from the place of the shades in a man. They are caused by the shades when there has been sleep and there is no sickness (umkhuhlane, i.e. everyday ailments such as colds)." Well aware of the fact that yawning is caused by a lack of sleep and sneezing by irritation in the nose, Zulu informants claim that when people yawn without reason and sneeze without having a cold, this is a sure sign of the shades' activity. Localizing both sneezing and yawning to the regions of the body believed to be occupied by the shades is looked upon as further proof to the effect that the shades are active. "When a man yawns, having slept nicely, we say, 'There is something.' Again, of a man who sneezes, it is said, 'Thuthuka!' (increase!). These words are said nicely, because people are suspicious of something that is happening with the person. Why does he yawn having slept? Again, why does he sneeze, having no sickness?"

Belching and hiccups are considered a little more advanced signs of the shades' activities in a person, sneezing and yawning being the preliminary signs. "When a man starts belching very much and having frequent hiccups, then they have sunk down deeper into him. So these are the next places to be occupied, the places of the gall and the lower back, the place from where the belching and hiccups come."

Because of the sour wind belched up, diviners are said to suffer considerably from acidity. The acidity is traced to the gall, the place "where the shades are working". Pregnant women are also said to suffer from acidity "because the shades are working in the stomach, causing this sickness". People stress that there is a difference between belching caused by much food and possible overfeeding and that caused by the shades. While the latter always is sour, the former is said merely to be wind and no cause of alarm.

Further signs of the activity of the shades in a person are realized by the pains experienced in the shoulders, sides, upper back and possibly lower neck. These are known as izibhopho. "When a man has pain in these places, then it is a certain sign that the shades are claiming him. There is no sickness that causes pain in these other than they (the shades). That is the place they occupy in a man. When there is pain in these places, the man knows that it is the shades that are working. Such sickness cannot be treated with medicine if the shades do not agree." When pain is experienced in these regions, then there is no doubt that the shades are requiring the services of the inflicted. "Sometimes we do not even go to a diviner saying, 'It is concerning so-and-so. We do not know this ailment.' We simply say among ourselves, 'Yes, today we are clear. Yesterday we were wondering what this thing was, having suspicions nevertheless. But today we know clearly.' So there is preparation for the work of having a diviner in the home. It is known because of the pains in the places of the shades."

A person called by the shades to become a diviner finds himself being increasingly active at night. Such a person claims that there is no sleep "because there is something in the body". Others tend to become restless, others wander about.[7] Diviners themselves give great importance to these nightly activities. Asked whether one could be a diviner without being awake at night, practically all answered that this would not be possible. "The night is the time of the shades. That is the time when they speak clearly, troubling people whom they call. That is why they cause us to be awake at night. If a man says that he has been called by the shades, but sleeps at night, then he is deceiving us. We know that he is deceiving us because of his sleeping throughout the night."

The nightly activities do not cease once the call of the shades has been accepted. They continue throughout the time of training and, according to a number of friends, tend to increase during this time. After the initiation, the diviner spends much time of the night consulting with the shades, nearly all diviners claiming that the best time for such communion with them being either as soon as people have fallen asleep, i.e. the early night, or, preferably, the very early hours of the morning before any of the homestead's other members have woken up. The diviner at eThelezini said: "We are like Christians who pray every day. But we pray in the very early morning when the cocks crow." One diviner said that "the cock crows in order to wake us up for prayer". All agreed that consultation with the shades ought to take place "at night because that is the time when they hear things we say well. That is why we pray at night".[8]

The ventriloquist diviner said that there was a difference between his speaking to the shades at night and praying "to the God of the Christians. The Christians simply tell God the things they want of him, having a great number of things which they require of him. But with us it is not so. We speak to the shades (ukuthetha idlozi), telling them what we see. We also see things. So we speak to them, mentioning this thing and that, and requesting them to express themselves in the matters." He said that Zulu diviners expect an-' swers, "but they may answer when they please, sometimes not even answering at all. Who are we to tell them what we want, merely heaping our wishes on them?" He added that in his personal consultations with them they would sometimes, especially if it is difficult matters that are at stake, let him know their reply later. "They say, 'Tomorrow, my child, there will be news (izindaba).' Then they speak as they said, telling me the news " It was quite evident that the umkhuleko (prayer) was rather a dialogue with the shades than devotions in the traditional understanding of the word.

Once it has become clear that a person has been called to divination, it is important to gain clarity on which shades are responsible for the calling. This is particularly important with women. Because the great majority of diviners are women, in practice there will nearly always be a tracing of the responsible shade. A woman can be called to divination by either her family lineage shades or, if she is married, by her husband's shades. Experience shows that there is no particular tendency towards either lineage, the number of women called by her own lineage shades and those called by her husband's being much the same in numbers. Older informants, however, say that previously it was usually in the woman's own lineage that the responsible shade was to be found. "But today it is also the husband's. It is because the men are away so much. Then the shades of the homestead are troubled, finding only the wife at home. So they trouble her, seeing that the husband is away."

Normally a diviner traces the responsible shade. If, however, he is unable to trace it, as sometimes is the case, a goat taken from the husband's flock is slaughtered by the attending diviner. The gall of the animal is sprinkled over the patient's head, shoulders and back, while a little is drunk by the patient. The bladder is inflated and hung up in *umsamo* of the hut in which the killing took place. The diviner at eThelezini was emphatic that this was one of the few ritual killings when the gall-bladder was not attached to the patient's head, but in the hut. "The shades are not brooding. It is the goat of questioning, not of food. The killing is done to find out who is causing the sickness of the shades. It (the slaughtering) is not for food. So there is no brooding when this goat is killed." The flesh is eaten by the attending diviner and the homestead people, some saying that the patient may eat of it, others denying this. If the patient has "clear dreams in the night following the slaughtering, or if *izibhopho* increase, then it is clear that it is the shades of the husband." If there is no marked change in the condition of the dreams and the pains, a goat from the woman's father's (or senior's) flock will be slaughtered as was the first goat.[9]

Professor Krige states that the tracing of the responsible shade takes place only when it is "decided not to 'bar' the spirit",[10] while many informants say that tracing the responsible shade takes place as soon as it has become clear that the patient's ailments are due to the shades. Diviners of standing claim that a husband would not consider the barring of his own lineage shades because "they are his fathers. A man does not disagree with his fathers." But the latter informants readily agree that a man may consider barring his wife's lineage shades, very much so if she is his only wife and he would have to abstain from married life with her at least during her time of training. In practice many men disapprove of their wives becoming diviners precisely for this reason. "He does not know them (his wife's lineage shades). They, again, do not know him. So they can do him no harm or trouble him, even if he refuses their work in their daughter."

Evidence shows that there are two major reasons for tracing the responsible shades. Firstly, the lineage of the responsible shade will have to supply the necessary animals for ritual slaughtering as well as bear the strain of the financial involvements in connection with the call, training, and subsequent initiation of the called person. Because these often are quite extensive, a family may try to bar the shades responsible.[11] Secondly, tracing the responsible shade also makes it clear whether barring the shades at all is possible. Certainly, if the shades are traced to the male lineage, there is hesitation in view of a possible barring, while, on the other hand, many men will simply forbid their wives to become diviners, especially if they are newly married and/or the woman is the husband's only wife.

Accepting the Call

To Zulu diviners the experience of *ukuvuma idlozi* (lit. accepting the shade, i.e. accepting the call to become a diviner), is an essential step towards further initiation and subsequent knowledge in matters pertaining to divination. To a great many diviners the occasion of *ukuvuma* is as essential a juncture in their lives as diviners as is the subsequent public acceptance as diviners. A large number will return to their *ukuvuma* with possibly even greater enthusiasm than their initiation.

While the barring of the responsible shades (*ukuwethula idlozi* or *ukuvala idlozi*),[12] once the shades have been identified, is a negative reaction to the call of the shades, *ukuvuma idlozi* is a positive response. If the shade is barred, the patient may, or may not, be restored to full health again. Sometimes, if health is restored, the patient becomes ill again and the diviner identifies the renewed ailments as the work of the shades. It is generally accepted that if the shades repeat their challenge several times, further barring attempts will prove fruitless, and the person embarks on the new life of becoming a diviner.

Assuming that an individual accepts the call of the shades, the next step towards becoming a diviner is training under an experienced diviner. The training has a two-fold aim. Firstly, a restoring to the novice health, which, it is assumed, has been disturbed through the process of the calling. The longer the call has remained unanswered, the greater the physical ailments from which the novice must be cured. Secondly, there is the adaptation of the novice into the living conditions of a diviner. Two aspects are essential in this adaptation, partly an introduction into the knowledge of divination and, partly, a gearing of one's life into one which will allow for the constant brooding of the shades without the diviner becoming mentally disordered. The latter two are, according to many diviners and especially conservative ones, the essential part of a novice training. "There are diviners whose health is never restored", said the diviner at eThelezini. "But they divine well. I for one, I am very sickly. This sickness originates from that time (of the calling). I have never been fully restored." Certainly his knowledge and lively intellect indicated that he had been well trained by his tutor. While he claimed that he had been a novice for two years, the diviner in the uMhlatuze valley said that he had been with his tutor for a period of four years before being initiated.

The ventriloquist described his experiences in connection with *ukuvuma* thus: "I was very sick, having dreamt much for many nights. The body was painful everywhere, especially the shoulders and sides. It was *izibhopho*. The whole body was in sickness. On a certain day, in the evening, I was sitting in the doorway. Just sitting there, there came a beetle (*umzifisi*).[13] It came closer. It was white. It came closer and closer until it was next to me. I heard it saying certain words. It said, 'Stand up! Follow me! Stand up! Follow me! (*Sukuma! Ngilandele!*)' It was saying these words very much, flying around about me. It spoke those words until I stood up. It flew in a certain direction, calling me all the time. I followed it. I walked and walked, following the beetle which was calling me all the time, saying the same words. I simply followed, going in the direction of the beetle all the time. It was flying in front. I was walking behind. I felt strong. The energy returned to the bones. I even followed running. I was amazed, finding myself running but being such a sick man. The beetle flew to a certain pool, all the time calling me. I followed it to the pool. It entered the pool, all the time saying to me, 'Ngilandele!' I walked on the stones, entering the pool. I walked on the stones in the pool until I came to the bottom, all the time following the beetle. There I stopped. I looked everywhere, seeing many things. I saw a very great python (inhlwathi) coiled on medicines. It was surrounded by many other snakes, big ones and small ones. They were the snakes of our fathers. They were just there, at the bottom of the pool, lying there and looking at me with open eyes. The python had a lamp (isikethekethe) on its head. It was shining in the pool, throwing light everywhere and revealing the things there in the pool. There was also a lady there with very big breasts, suckling the children of the python. There were many children of the python. It (the python) put spittle (amathe) into the woman. She became pregnant and gave birth, producing the children of the snake. The python said to the shade-snakes, 'Is this the man?' They agreed, saying that I was the man. Then the snake (python) spoke to me, addressing me clearly, 'Did the beetle bring you here?' I agreed. 'What was the colour of the beetle?' I gave the colour of the beetle. It said, 'Did it speak of medicines?' I agreed that it had spoken of medicines, adding that I had also dreamt of medicines. It said, 'The medicines are under my stomach, just underneath me. Just take some medicines.' So I took some medicines, fearing very much. Then it said, 'Smear yourself with the medicines seeing that you have work (to do).' So I smeared myself with the clay, being naked. Then the snake put spittle on me. I feared very much. It put spittle everywhere. Then it returned, lying on the medicines, leaving me there with the medicines and the spittle. It was hot. Then the python said, 'Look at all these. Do you know them?' I said that I recognized them, seeing all the shade-snakes and the woman with the breasts, just suckling all the time. The python said to me, 'Just take som medicines in the hand.' I took medicines in the hand from under the snake. Then the beetle came to me saying the words as before. I followed it, walking on the stones of the pool. I did not look back, having been told not to look backwards. I walked and walked. I came to the top of the pool, following the beetle all the time, just following it. When it came to the bank of the river it stopped, saying, 'From here I leave you.' It returned into the water. There arose a mist. I found myself on the bank of the river, being naked and having the white medicines of the pool. There was whiteness everywhere on the body. Then I looked in the hand and saw the snake that I took in the pool. I hung it around the neck, its head resting on my head, the body around the neck. I walked home. I came home after walking a very long way. There was much noise, people lamenting very much, simply shouting and screaming (isililo) the death lamentation. I said, 'Surely there must be a corpse, somebody having died, seeing that they are lamenting thus.' I came close to the homestead. I called on them saying, 'People of my fathers, what is this noise, my not having heard that there is death in our place?' They said, 'No, there is the corpse of the one that is not. He left here one day in the evening, just walking in the direction of the great river. Since his departure he has not returned. So we are lamenting him, seeing that he did not return.' Then I knew that they were mourning me. I said, 'No, I simply went to the river being called by a beetle, taking medicines at the river. Even just now I have the medicines.' They came out. They saw me. They were very much amazed, seeing me naked and carrying medicines and with a snake. They said, 'But you were dead. We have heard of them that know (diviners) that you were dead. But now we see you living again. We cannot deny the things that were said. But you are living now, having medicines and carrying this thing. But how is it that you left, leaving no word?' Then they were satisfied, seeing me with the medicines and the snake. They took it (the snake). They carried it to its place. There they kept it. Then they were quiet, having stopped lamenting me. The pains in the side were less. But from that day I could not drink beer, or take beans or food made of beans. They just cause sickness and swelling. Even to this day I do not eat beans or a dish of beans. They kill me."

The diviner's account of his experience resembles, as far as contents is concerned, narratives recorded by Kohler.[14] The only major difference in the description recorded above and those related by Kohler is the python. In the narrative related by the diviner of the uMhlatuze valley the role of the python is significant, the python in fact playing a major part in the activities at the bottom of the pool. In Kohler's recordings the snake playing the major role in the pools is called *ixhanthi*. Both the python and *ixhanthi* are suggestive.

The diviner subsequently gave me his ideas on the python in the pool.

B: "Was the python a shade-snake together with the other snakes in the pool?"

"The snakes were all shade-snakes, being our fathers, that is true. But the big one, lying on the medicines of whiteness, it was *inkosi yamadlozi* (lit. the lord of the shades)."

B: "Who is he that is lord of the shades?"

"As I have said, I have not seen him but this once. He is not seen. It brings insanity to the one that is too near to him too much. That is why we do not see him. He brings this thing of fearfulness on men. So he is in the pool because of the cool of the water. It gives coolness to him."

B: "By way of insanity, I know that also the brooding of the shades brings insanity if it is too long. Is this snake then not a shade?"

"You are speaking the truth, saying that the brooding of the shades brings insanity. But that is only an inferior insanity (*ukuhlanya nje*). When the brooding ceases, then the man becomes well again if they (the shades) wish it. Sometimes the man takes medicines and becomes better, not suffering so much of the insanity. But the insanity of this big one is the great insanity, the insanity which finishes a man (*ukuhlanya okumqedayo umuntu*). That is the bad insanity. There is no healing from it, there being no medicines against it. The person just dies. He is eaten up by that insanity, eaten up completely."

B: "So you are indicating that the snake is not a shade?"

"That is what I am saying."

B: "Who is he?"

"Let me tell you nicely. It is *inkosi yamakhosi omkhulu* (the lord of lords, the great one). (The diviner lifted his eyebrows and glanced upwards a moment.) He is the one. I think that you understand me now?"

B: "You are referring to the one above?"

"That is the very one."

B: "Does he come down to earth?"

"He himself does not come. If he came then everybody would be eaten up by fire. He sends his animal. That is the one that is the snake of the pools. That is the one that he sends."

B: "It was the one that put spittle into the woman, making her pregnant?"

"He is the one. It was a sign. The sign says that the life (*imphilo*) comes from the one above. He was giving fertility to the woman. That was the sign of the woman."

B: "But procreation is the work of the shades. They are the water of men, fertilizing the woman?"

"It is so. But the shade-snakes were there, receiving the power from the big one. They receive the power to fertilize from the one above. But they (the shades) are in the water of men, causing conception."

B: "Was the spittle the water, fertilizing the woman?"

"It was the thing that made her fertile. That is how he puts water into a woman. His mouth is the place where it comes out."

B: "Was the spittle the same as male fluid?"

"They are the same. The spittle of the big one fertilizes the woman. The water of men fertilize their wives, causing conception. They are the same."

B: "So there must be a close relationship between shades and the snake?"

"There is a closeness. They work together. The great snake gives the power to the shade-snakes. They come to men with it, giving power to men. That is how it is."

B: "You were called to the pool?"

"I was called by the shades. They are the ones that called me. They answered the great one that I was the one. So it is they who called me."

B: "What about the beetle?"

"It was sent by them (the shades)."

B: "What were the snakes that the woman was feeding?"

"They were signs showing that the children come from the great one. That is what they were saying. They were just pictures, saying that the children of men come from *inkosi,* as I have said."

B: "So they were not shades?"

"No, they were not shades. They had not been men. So they could not be shades."

B: "Must a shade have been a man (*umuntu*) before being a shade?"

"That is so. If the shades are like the ones in the pool, then they must have been men before being like those shades."

B: "Are there shades which have not been men?"

"I have never heard of such shades. But there are other living creatures (*ezinye izinyamazane*) like the snakes that the woman was feeding. Sometimes they are known. Sometimes they are not known."

B: "Are these snakes known?"

"They are not known. As I said, those snakes sucking the woman were just pictures, saying that life comes from the great one."

B: "Was the woman a sign for something?"

"She was the sign of birth, giving birth to the children of the great one. That is her sign."

B: "She was feeding?"

"She was feeding, like all women who have little ones feed. There is nothing in the feeding. That is the work of women. The sign was the birth of the little ones."

B: "You said she was heavy in the breasts."

"That is what I said. She was heavy in that she was giving the breast (to little ones). All women doing this work are heavy in that way. Even here, every woman doing this thing is heavy. There is nothing in this."

B: "Many things are clear now. But it is not clear why the great one was in the pool."

"He was in the pool because the pool is the place of *uhlanga*."

B: "What is *uhlanga*?"

"It is the origin, the place of the coming out of men."

B: "Did men come out of a pool?"

"That is where they came out. The reeds are the carriers of water. They penetrate the earth, causing conception of mankind."

B: "We are talking of conception all the time. You were sick with the sickness of diviners. How are these things related?"

"They are related because there was a birth. There was the birth of a diviner. That is the thing that connects the snake of greatness and the diviner."

B: "Did you know this when the beetle called you?"

"I knew nothing. I was just sick, having great pains. That is all I knew."

B: "Who told you all these things of the snakes and the medicines?"

"They were revealed. (Long silence.) Yes, they were revealed."

B: "How?"

"In the way of the shades."[15]

Although it was the python that lay on the white clay the diviner very clearly and definitely identified the whiteness of the clay with the shades. "That is their colour. They are the white ones. When a man comes out (of a pool) it is known that he comes from the shades in that he comes out white." Not only did he associate the colour white with the shades in this manner. He said that the shades are white. In the dream which to him was an experience of firm and rigid realism, he had seen that they were white. This was an undisputable fact, based neither on rumours nor hearsay, but on personal experience.[16]

The diviner was convinced that the spittle of a python is an effective medicine against infertility and claimed that he knew of a herbalist who used the spittle with great success. Discussing the issue of fertility and the spittle of the snake, the diviner said that "in the same way that the python puts spittle on its prey, swallowing it whole, it brings back whole (i.e. healthy) children by means of spittle". He used the word *phila* to describe both the whole prey and the healthy children, *izingela eliphilayo* and *abantwana abaphilayo*.

My informant claimed that a python fertilizes with spittle. It has no sexual organs as other animals have. On speaking to a number of other diviners on this particular issue, several of them voiced similar opinions. A diviner of reputation in the Louwsburg district said that all snakes which swallowed their prey whole were useful medicines for barren women. He described how these snakes were observed and their spittle collected. "We watch the snake carefully. When it has put its spittle on its food, we rush forward, taking the prey. We remove the spittle. We put it aside, knowing that there will be somebody coming soon for this very medicine." A popular diviner said that the spittle was used for treating women with insufficient milk for their children,

144

but other diviners strongly disagreed with this. Besides underlining their claim that "pythons give birth (*ukuzalisa*) and do not nourish (*ukuncelisa*) (the two words were used as male and female associations), they drew attention to the difficulties encountered in obtaining the required medicine. "Since when does one work day and night, sometimes a whole week, getting only a little, in order to treat breasts! Are there then no more cattle left among the people?"

Although the ventriloquist very clearly associated the python with the Lord-of-the-Sky, the emphasis in his thinking lay not in the first place with the Lord-of-the-Sky himself, but in the fertility brought through the medium of the python. The python was, according to the diviner's mind, a symbol of fertility. Yet the role of the Lord-of-the-Sky was not unimportant, for it was from him that the python had been sent with fertility and it was this ability in procreation that the python gave to the shades. Whether this is a traditional thought-pattern among Zulu is difficult to ascertain, but certainly it is a view held and accepted by many diviners today. To the ventriloquist and to the very large majority of diviners, and very much so the conservative ones, the Lord-of-the-Sky is a reality. But the role of the Lord-of-the-Sky is placed in the background and emphasis on the local level of humans is given to the activity of the shades. It is possible that a certain amount of effort is placed in drawing the Lord-of-the-Sky and his role into the foreground. Hence a consolidation between his role and the participation and activities of the shades.

Ixhanthi, the snake mentioned by Kohler, is well known among Zulu diviners. Evidence shows that this particular snake plays a greater role in thinking than does the python in areas where pythons are not known or have become extinct. On the other hand, where pythons are found, *ixhanthi* is known only by hearsay, the ventriloquist claiming that he knew of "this animal by way of the ears only". We have here, again, an example of how the symbols through which thinking is expressed sometimes changes due to various circumstances, in this particular case a variety of symbols themselves, but the interpretation given the symbol remains unchanged. We shall see how *ixhanthi,* although definitely not a python, serves equally well the function of being a symbol of fertility.

Ixhanthi is a "snake known to diviners only". Some people say that it is "the snake of diviners", seen and known by them only, while commoners know it by hearsay. Nobody that is not a diviner has seen the snake. The same holds true for the python referred to by the diviner in the uMhlatuze valley. He claimed that only diviners could ever see the snake without becoming insane. However, associations with *ixhanthi* do not bring about insanity and suggesting this to informants caused both amusement and doubts that the inquirer really knew *ixhanthi.*

Diviners of standing were emphatic that they not only knew of *ixhanthi* but had personal experience of it. Some gave vivid and dramatic descriptions of their encounters with the reptile. Without exception all diviners claimed that the snake was to be found in the interior of the earth, the great majority of them associating it with the bottom of pools in rivers. Descriptions of the pools indicate that these generally are thought to be very deep, often immediately below a small waterfall and practically always overshadowed by large trees which cast a deep gloom over the pool. All informants vigorously denied the presence of the snake in pools or collections of stagnant water. A few informants living in an area where ant-heaps are plentiful, said that the snake lived in the earth, its entrance being ant-heaps which wither they or ant-bears had dug up. Diviners along the coast were amused by the idea of entering the earth through an ant-heap, but they did not find it impossible.

Ixhanthi is described as being a large snake, and "fearful, causing anxiety in that it looks very much at the diviner. It has protruding eyes which ever stare forward. The eyes are even worse than the eyes of *indlondlo* (an old and over-grown *imamba,* a venomous snake, very quick and easily irritated)." Some diviners describe it as having very protruding vertebrae, especially along the upper back, nearest the head. "The bones nearly stick out of the skin. When it moves, the skin glides up and down on the bones. It is a fearful sight, see-ing these things." The colour of the snake is always black, although some say it has white spots above the eyes and sometimes around the neck.

Ixhanthi is positively not a shade-snake. "The shade-snakes we know. But this one is seen only by diviners. It is not a shade-snake. It is too fearful to be a shade-snake. Shade-snakes do not harm. But this one could harm a man, kill-ing him." Some informants expressed shock at the very thought of it being a shade-snake. But it is intimately associated with fertility in that it constantly produces snakes of its kind which it eats up again. Informants described how the snake all the time "gives birth, just giving birth all the time, there in the pool of waters. When it has given birth it eats them (the children)." Some in-formants said that the snake just gave birth, but did not know what happened to the offspring. Apparently this detail was not of major interest.

Although the snake is not a shade-snake it is associated with white clay which every diviner seeks in the bottom of pools. Practically all informants said that the snake lay on the white clay and that the diviner had to move it in order to obtain the desired clay. "The snake was lying on the clay. The shade-snakes were telling me to take the clay but I feared the snake very much. Then they said clearly, 'No, but we are telling you to take of the clay.' So I took courage, moving the snake aside gently, and took of the earth. I took it from under the fearful one."

Diviners associate the white clay very closely with the shades. "As I said, the white clay that is under the snake is the clay of the shades. They have one and the same colour. So they resemble one another. The clay is the clay of the shades."

B: "But why did *ixhanthi* lie on the clay so that you had to move it to get at the clay?"

"Because it is the snake of the waters."

B: "What does it mean that it is the snake of the waters?"

"It means that it is the snake of the waters which give life. That is why it is called the snake of the waters."

B: "Are the waters special waters?"

"It is as I said water that is living, running in the river. That is the living water. If the water had been in a dam as you asked (a while ago), then there would not be a snake in it. It is the living waters."

B: "I know that the water of men is living because the shades give it life in procreation. Is the water of the pool at all similar to the water of men?"

"The water of men is one thing. The water in women is another thing. This water is the water of the woman when she is pregnant. The snake is the one we say is in the woman. Sometimes it eats the children, not letting her give birth. Sometimes it gives them (the children) prosperity. Then they grow and become healthy. It is this water that I am talking of when I speak of the living waters. There are these two living waters, the one of men and the other of women."

B: "I know of the snake that women have, but generally it is feared."

"Ah, you said it yourself! Is not the snake of the pool fearful as I have been saying all the time, telling you of its fearfulness! So now you see the combination."

Ixhanthi is to commoners the upper row of dorsal vertebrae in either humans or, in animals, in cattle and goats in particular.[17] It is the precise regions where one claims that the shades cause pain when individuals are called by the shades to become diviners or where animals are rubbed with either *imphepho* or fat prior to being slaughtered in ritual celebrations. In humans and in animals these vertebrae are the seat of the shades. It is because of this close relationship with the shades that some diviners of the bone-thrower type, *ezamathambo,* will have bones from the vertebrae in their sets.

Certain details in *ukuvuma* experiences of diviners are a symbolic death and rebirth. These are the diviner's entry into the pool of water and exit from it, the time he spends in the pool and the white clay with which he emerges from the pool. The vision of the suckling woman and her delivery of further children are also connected with death and rebirth symbolism.

One diviner quoted above very clearly associated the water of the pool with the water surrounding a child in the womb. His thought-patterns were verified by a number of other knowledgeable people who claimed to have been in pools. "When a man comes out of the pool, he comes from the water. It is the water of birth."[18] There is no doubt at all that the exit from the pool is accepted as the diviner's birth, although he still has much to learn before he eventually is ready to practice as a diviner. This idea was stressed again in various ways, many diviners quite consciously looking back to their *ukuvuma* as a definite break with their old life and a start in the new.

No informant had as strong views about the entry into the pool as they had about their exit from it. The diviner at uMhlatuze said, after some hesitation and with a certain amount of amusement, when asked whether the entry into the pool was not important: "I have not thought of it. But it must be important. How can a man come out, not having gone in?" Discussing the issue further and asking him whether there was a difference between beeing buried and entry into the pool, our having spoken of the symbol of birth out of the pool, he became far more serious and said: "Today you have caused me to think deeply. I see that you do not take these things lightly. But indeed, both lead into the earth (*ukungenisa emhlabathini*). Both lead to the shades." But he did not wish to comment further. "These things are becoming too deep even for me." A few days later he returned to the subject. "There is a difference between entry and exit from the pool. When entering I was sick, very sick. When I came out I was quite better. So this is the difference I see. The sickness was left behind. The sickness is like the bad things that are buried. So in this way I can agree that there was a burial in that the sickness was left behind."

The diviner at eThelezini had much the same thought-patterns. It is quite clear that Kohler's informants thought likewise, one of them saying: "I heard that once a certain diviner was dead for a long time, about a month, without breathing or eating anything . . . She woke up then and returned to earth as a great *isangoma,* and went to seek white ochre in the pool."[19]

Both ethnographic records and informants speak of a novice being away from home for a period of time, the family members often not knowing where he/she is. Some diviners have underlined the importance of nobody knowing the whereabouts of the novice. Some have claimed that they were away from home about one month, others quoting considerably shorter periods of time. A limited number of popular diviners said that they had been away for a night only, but claimed that this had been sufficient.[20]

The diviner at eThelezini spoke on the matter of being away alone and one's whereabouts not being known. "The person must be alone. If he is with somebody else he is known as a twin. So to avoid the danger of twins the person must be alone wherever he goes." We discussed twins and it became clear that the diviner was associating the lonesomeness of the novice with the lonesomeness of an unborn child. "These two are the same. The foetus is very much alone. So is the one who is away. They are alone, having nobody in their nearness." I suggested that since the shades mould the foetus, the shades were present with the unborn child. He reacted immediately: "You speak nicely! Yes, they are there. They are there also with the man in the fields. He is not alone in that way. They are moulding him also *(bayambumba naye).*" The aspect of being alone with the shades was stressed by a number of diviners, one of these at Rorkes Drift saying: "When I was alone in this way, I felt them very near, preparing me and making me strong. I did not fear them. They were working their work with me." On being introduced to the thought-pattern of the unborn child's lonesomeness and this parallel to his own lonesomeness he said immedeiately: "Who is nearer to the shades than the child in the womb?"

The majority of diviners interviewed on the subject claim that the time of being away coincided with their entry into the pool (or ant-heap). Two diviners operating in the Hlobane area claimed that they entered the earth through caves in the Drakensberg mountains.[21] Practically all related their entry into the earth with their being in the close vicinity of the shades. "When diviners enter the earth, going into it through the pool, they go to the shades. Those are the ones they seek in the earth", said a diviner at Rorkes Drift who claimed that he had entered the earth through a pool in the local Buffalo river. Our discussion ran thus:

B: "When you were at the bottom (of the pool), did you see the snakes?"

"These very eyes saw them." (He pointed at his eyes with both hands.)

B: "What snakes were they?"

"They are the shades. Then there is the big one. The one which is the Lord."

B: "Is that snake the python?"

"Some say it is a python. As for me I have never seen this snake. Some call it *ixhanthi,* having eyes that are red and with great nostrils. But when I came out of the water I was carrying a snake in the hand."

B: "Was it a shade-snake?"

"No. It was an animal."

B: "How long did you stay in the pool with the shades?"

"I stayed until they returned me, saying, 'Return to the earth'. Then I returned."

B: "Do you know how long you were with the shades?"

"If I am to say the time, then I would say a short time. But the people at home said that I was away many days, simply staying away in the fields."

B: "The snake in your hand, did you catch it?"

"They (the shades) said, 'There is an animal. Catch it and carry it.' I did not do it, fearing the snake. After some days they said, 'There is the animal. Catch it and carry it.' Then I took courage, and took it. They said, 'Now you are strong, catching animals. So now you can return to the earth.' Then I returned to the earth with the snake, carrying it in the hand."

B: "So the visit to the interior of the pool was an important thing?"

"Not important. But the most important. How could I divine not having seen them (the shades)? So it was the most important thing, besides the intiation. These two. They are the important things with diviners."

B: "Is there a special reason for the shades calling a man away and taking him to the earth interior through a pool in the river?"

"There is a reason. It is this. The reason is that it is the pool that changes the man (*ukuguqula ubuntu*). They change him from being a man to be a diviner. The thing takes place in the pool. It must be done in their presence, this work of changing a man when he has agreed."

All informants were more or less unanimous that the period away from the home was an essential in the process of becoming a diviner. They also nearly all agreed that during this period of absence the individuality of the called was changed. One experienced diviner of reputation who had a novice under her care said that immediately after the return from the fields, the novice "eats soft food, like the food of babes, *incumbe* and watery porridge, being weak like children".

Appearing from the earth in a naked state was equally commonly accepted by practically all informants. The diviner at eThelezini in fact claimed that if a diviner had not been naked on his return from the presence of the shades, then there was something vital missing in the training. I asked him why it was essential that the novice returns naked. "Just tell me, who do you see naked around about us? Tell me yourself."

B: "Are you referring to children?"

"So you knew all the time. You knew it was children."

B: "But why is the novice compared with a child? The novice is grown up."

"Yes, he is grown up, as you say. But that is not the thing. The thing is that in divination he is not even a child, not having even seen the things (with which he is to divine). So looking at the matter in the eyes of divination, is he not just simply a new-born?"

Our discussion took us to the smearing with white clay and the important role that this plays in the life of a diviner. Besides being a very close association with the shades, my informant suggested that this colour is "the colour of the child at birth, as we have been saying. You know children how they are at birth, very pale." In order to have the diviner's reaction I tried to stress that white was the colour of the shades "as we have seen many times when we have talked". The diviner commented: "If you say a child or if you say shades, what is the difference? Do not the children come from the shades? Why are they white at birth, if not because of the shades? So I can say the white of the shades or the white of babes. They are one and the same thing, these whitnesses."

Accepting the shades' challenge to become a diviner suggests two important issues in *ukuvuma idlozi*. Firstly, there is the positive reaction to the call realised in the person's accepting the fact that he/she is called to divination, the subsequent entry into the earth and experiences with the shades there. Secondly, there is a symbolic death and rebirth, the death associated with the life of a commoner which as from *ukuvuma idlozi* to a large extent has to be given up, and the rebirth associated with the life of a diviner, albeit in the very early stages of infancy.[22]

Training

Having accepted the shades' challenge to become a diviner, the novice is schooled by an experienced diviner. The tutor is either indicated by the shades themselves in dreams, or chosen by the novice depending on personal inclinations.[23] Evidence suggests that if the tutor is a person of the same clan, dreams have most probably indicated the diviner to whom the novice is to go for instruction. If, on the other hand, the tutor is of another clan, more often than not, the novice has chosen the person because of a large variety of reasons. Some say that the tutor was willing to accept them, others say that they were called to become *eyamathambo* and the tutor is of this category, etc. Evidence further suggests that in the former case, the tutor seldom refuses the novice while in the latter the diviner has greater freedom not to accept the novice. The novice will of necessity become the category of diviner that the tutor represents. In practically all cases looked into the novice stays with the tutor during the time of learning, allowing for occasional visits to his/her homestead, especially if the novice is a woman and her husband requires her. In a few cases the tutor allowed the novice to live at home and come to her for instruction. In a few instances the novice paid a regular fee "like all scholars who live in boarding homes, eating the food at the place of learning". Practically always the novice shares the diviner's hut during the period of training, the tutor being regarded as the senior and the novice called "the child". Sometimes the tutor will give the novice a name by which the tutor addresses the novice. It appears that this name follows the novice during the period of training and is also used when the novice practices as a regular diviner. Besides being introduced into the knowledge and work of a diviner the novice also carries out household duties for the tutor. There are informants who have suggested that some diviners accept novices for training simply because they "want somebody to work and then also pay". Diviners, naturally, refute this statement very strongly!

The ventriloquist and the diviner at eThelezini both said that they personally did not have more than one novice at a time. The former had, in fact, had only two novices for training, keeping them for a period of two years each. One eventually practised in the Thugela valley below Kranskop, the other in the Mahlabathini area. The latter of the two I have not been able to trace. The great and overwhelming majority of novices are taught by *izinyanga zamathambo* and hence become diviners who work through bones, shells, claws, etc. One such diviner claimed that she had trained three novices simultaneously but complained bitterly about their poor character and the great difficulty she found in handling them. Many have one or two novices, although they admit that the best training is given if a novice is alone.

Many people who reacted positively to the call of the shades cease their training. Varying reasons are given. Some said that they lacked the necessary animals for ritual slaughtering and fees. Other claimed that they had been told in dreams that they were no longer required. Two informants said that they were "simply tired of the shades and diviners. They just chase us over the whole country, up and down, everywhere, looking for medicines, looking for certain shrubs, and finding nothing." One novice died of natural reasons during the time of schooling.[24]

While nearly all diviners of standing appear to be popular with trainees, there are those who have no novices at all but very much desire to have one or two. Zulu say that a diviner's prestige and reputation grows with the number of novices he/she has. "It is clear that the shades have seen this diviner. She is able. That is why they (the novices) go to her. So if the novices go to the diviner, then the people will also go to her." A diviner at Mapumulo, very seldom called upon to divine, said that she had lost her ability in divination "because she had nobody to teach. So I have forgotten everything." In one case on record a Zionist group leader claimed that he had trained a diviner. Although an occasional case is known, evidence does not show that novices tend to move from one tutor to another, disregarding the fact that there is a marked and very clear spirit of competition among diviners themselves. Some informants said that the people who quarrelled most among themselves were the diviners.[25]

Life with the tutor has two main concerns. Firstly, the health of the novice must be returned to him/her. Secondly, the novice is introduced to the knowledge of a diviner and to the living conditions under which the brooding of the shades is a constant reality.

Although the sickness that the shades bring upon the person they call to divination comes from the shades themselves, i.e. the seniors of the lineage clan, it is not regarded as in itself either good or acceptable. The novice has to be treated against it in order to restore full health again. "No sickness is good. Even if it comes from the shades, it is not good. It is bad." Neither are the many dreams, especially if they continue to be vague and troublesome, looked upon as particularly acceptable. On the other hand, their total absence is also a bad omen. "The dreams are troublesome if they do not become clearer so that the person can see nicely. So sometimes the person is treated against bad dreams also. But if they become clear, then they are just left alone."

Throughout the period of training the novice undergoes healing cures. The aim of the cure is (i) to remove the sickness caused by the shades (*ukuvala ubuthakathaka* or *ukuhlambulula*) through *amabulawo,* and (ii) to strengthen the diviner's physic and a sharpening of his/her alertness. Sickness and weakness is 'removed' through daily emetics and vomiting known as *ukuphalaza,* while strengthening and alertness is gained through smoking and nibbling at medicines hung around the neck. No novice is assumed ready for initiation until health is fully restored.[26]

Besides medical treatment a novice's health is restored through a dance performed from time to time during the training period called *ingoma yoku-*

vumisa (the confessional dance). It is a dance peculiar to diviners only and if danced by anybody else would bring about serious physical and mental ailments.

I attended one such dance. The novice retired to their tutor's hut after washing and shaving the head. In the hut were the tutor, a number of diviners and four other novices. A number of close friends and relatives of the novice also attended. The tutor who acted as host instructed the visitors where they were to sit. Men were seated to the left in the hut as seen from the hut door, the older men seated nearest the door and the younger towards *umsamo*. Women were seated to the right of the door, opposite the men and facing them, the older women nearest the door and the younger towards *umsamo*. Nearest *umsamo* on the women's side sat a girl about ten years old. The order of sitting was, in other words, reversed from the normal where men occupy the right-hand side of the hut and the women the left, the older people sitting in the inner parts of the hut, towards *umsamo*, while the younger visitors would be seated near the door. The tutor herself was seated in *umsamo*. On entering the hut, the novice had with her a knife which she carried in her left hand throughout the dance. She stood up in the hut and began walking around the hearth and called upon the visitors to start clapping. They did so, and the novice started singing her song which she was composing in view of her forthcoming initiation. When she started singing folded skins were brought forward, these having been placed behind the visitors. I was told that the skins, five in number, were of ritually slaughtered animals. Not all, however, had been killed in connection with the novice's training. The visitors started beating time on the skins. This excited the novice in a marked way and she increased the tempo of her dance. She jumped up and down around the hearth, continually increasing the tempo of her dance. The heat became nearly unbearable and the sweat was running down her body. Occasionally she stopped and took ash from the overfilled hearth and smeared herself with this. The onlookers quickened the pace again, shouting and singing the refrain of the novice's song with extraordinary zeal and enthusiasm, working both themselves and the novice into a state of tense excitement. After about ten minutes the noise was terrific in the hut and the heat and smell of sweat intolerable. Suddenly the novice stopped and everybody quietened. In a high-pitched and very tense voice she started confessing dreams, apparently addressing her tutor. She described her experience in the river pool, describing in detail how she was taken to the pool by a white bird, her fears when she entered, etc. The silence while she spoke was very strained, now and again one of the women exposing her feelings in a shrill, high-pitched voice which was silenced dramatically with a slap in the face by the tutor with her switch and a shout of "Voet-sek!". The novice confessed one dream after another, the atmosphere of expectancy and enthusiasm gradually decreasing and eventually dying away completely. The visitors left, one after the other, eventually leaving in the hut only the novice, the tutor and myself. The novice showed signs of marked exhaustion. The tutor remarked: "The relating of dreams brings back health. She must confess all the dreams. That is why we cause her to confess (*ukumvumisa*). It is to bring back health." She added that the *ukuvumisa* dance would be repeated until such time as full health was restored to the novice. If she did not become completely well again, it was a sign that she had withheld some dreams which must be confessed. 'They (the dreams) must all be confessed. Otherwise there cannot be any strength (i.e. health) in her." Evidence shows that in the large majority of cases the confession of dreams plays a significant and important role in a diviner's training. It is evident that the confession of dreams and sometimes of friction between the tutor and novice is related to the restoration of health to the novice.

The form of the dance is uncommon in Zulu society. Firstly, the novice alone danced and, secondly, she did not merely move her feet but leaped up and down. Informants say that this kind of dancing is practised by diviners alone and may be performed by them only. "The novice must be alone. She is the one confessing. There is nobody but her who confesses." I wanted to know why she jumped up and down as she did and I was told that this kind of activity brought to memory all the dreams the novice had forgotten. Also the clapping and beating of the skins by the visitors was said to assist in remembering dreams. It is clear that the aim of the dance is in the first instance geared towards confession of dreams, the confession to include all the dreams seen during the time of calling by the shades.

Several suggestive symbols are associated with the dance. Like the song, the particular dance has to be learnt, and training commences early during the novice's time of seclusion. A diviner said: "That is why the child must live with me. It is for the teaching. I teach her to dance and to do the dancing nicely. When she has seen how it is done, she continues by herself." The tutor gives the first introductory details to the novice who, thereafter, is expected to continue by herself.

Informants say that the tutor watches the novice's ability to *bikizela,*[27] "to shake tremulously or with a quivering motion, – – – , the body with nervous twitchings". Male novices are said to *likizela,* an idiom connected also to the quivering of sheet-lightning which is said to bring about rain but not violent storms and destruction. In the course of time the novice is expected to be able to quiver the body, and she is not ready for the coming out before she has acquired this ability. "First the novice just simply shakes. She shakes sometimes in the leg, sometimes in the body. But the shaking is little. Then we see that it (the quivering) comes from just a small child. It cannot quiver yet. Then it grows. The quivering also grows. Then one day the child has learnt the thing. That is the day the tutor says. 'Today, my child, I have seen the quivering. The quivering of a diviner is there.' Then the child knows that she has grown up and become a diviner." Another informant said that no novice who did not fully control quivering could be accepted as a diviner.

Quivering is associated with the shades. "They (the shades) bring quivering to the child. When they see the child dancing, then they bring the quivering. It is the quivering which shakes the child so that it remembers the dreams. That is how they (the shades) are helping their child to remember them." Increased quivering is a symbol of the increased activity of the shades in the novice and hence growth in divinatory ability and in health.

The amount of quivering in a novice during the dance is associated with the skill acquired not only in the controlling of the twitchings, but also the novice's skill in dancing. The dance is evaluated by the novice's ability in moving all the limbs of the body, of jumping up-and-down and herself regulating the beat of those that assist her with handclapping or beating of the skins. A diviner said of the beat: "If the child does not control it, just letting people lead her anywhere (i.e. if the novice follows the beat), then she will only divine the things they wish to see, not following the shades."

To the diviner at eThelezini the twitching and control of it by the novice was an essential. He underlined the frequent practice of the dance, saying: "This thing (quivering and twitching) must be learnt. Everything must be learnt. Nobody knows the things of the shades through only dreaming or just thinking of it by themselves. They must be learnt. The way of learning is to listen (to those who know how) and then doing it. It must be done (practised) until it is in the blood. That is the time when the child knows the thing of the shades."

Informants again and again underline the importance of jumping up into the air and the novice stamping her feet on the ground, a movement which reminds one of *ukugiya* at ritual slaughterings. "The dancing of the child is the same as *ukugiya*. They both excite the shades. That is why they stamp their feet onto the ground. They excite the shades." Some informants said that stamping is a symbol of security. "If a man is not secure (*qinile*), then he walks lightly. But when he knows that there is security in that he has power, then he does this thing. It is the sign that he knows the thing that he is doing."

B: "From where does the child get the security? Is it the practice of the dance and the quivering?"

"I could agree. But then I could also say it is the shades. They are causing the excitement in the child. Then the child excites them. That is how it works. They give the power. Then the child shows that she has felt (i.e. experienced) the power and knows its use."

B: "How does she know the use of the power?"

"From the one that she (the child) is staying with."

B: "The tutor?"

"That is the one that she is staying with."

B: "What about the training of the dance?"

"How can the child learn by only listening? The tutor says the thing. Then the child does it. So the training of the dance is also a matter (of importance)."

B: "How often does the child practise the dance?"

"It differs. Sometimes according to the diviner. Sometimes according to the clappers. They must always be there to clap for the novice. So it differs."

B: "For how long?"

"Until it is ready. When the child knows it (the dance) well, then the dance is done. nicely and the quivering is over the whole body, the child being in command of it (lit. the child holding it). Then the child is ready. It will be seen in the dancing and the quivering when it is ready."

Training having commenced, a goat, supplied by the lineage of the responsible shade, is slaughtered at the home of the tutor. The skin and the gall of the animal form important ingredients in the future diviner's equipment. The chyme of the goat is used for washing and cleaning purposes. Sometimes the goat is slaughtered in the byre, sometimes it is killed in the diviner's hut so that the skins may be fixed onto the novice without her having to go outside. The gall of the animal is poured over the head, shoulders, back, feet and knees of the novice. The feet and the knees are strenghtened (*ukuqinisa ama-*

154

dolo) for forthcoming long walks. From the back of the animal is cut a long strip of skin which, while still wet, is tied loosely over the novice's left shoulder in a loop under the right arm, the loop reaching to just above the hipbone. Informants are unanimous that this skin, called *inqwamba,* is the foremost outer sign that a novice has commenced her/his training after *ukuvuma* and is an important stage which no novice can bypass.

Some novices have a second loop over the right shoulder and under the left arm, letting the two strings form an X on the back and on the chest. The skins are known as *iminqwamba.* Diviners of standing say that it is wrong to have the second loop attached at this stage of the training. But seeing that some novices break off their tuition or choose the time of the initiation personally, thereby creating conflicts with their tutors, many have the complete set of *iminqwamba* at an early stage of their training. "But the second skin rightly belongs to the initiation and not to the training."[28]

The gall-bladder is inflated and fixed to the hair of the novice. But when he/she is shaved during the period of training by the tutor the gall-bladder is also removed and burnt in the tutor's hut together with the novice's hair. Some diviners said that the bladder was not burnt although it was removed when shaving. It was put away and used later in the training and when he/she practised as a diviner.

Further ritual slaughtering during the course of the training depends on a number of factors. The animals available for slaughter inevitably play an important role. There are cases when white fowls have been used to replace goats and cattle, simply because the latter have not been available. The tutor's views also play a significant role. Conservative diviners demand far more ritual killings than do some of the popular diviners who, sometimes, are satisfied with money. Generally, however, one expects at least two or three slaughterings to take place during the course of the year, the ventriloquist stating that he expected four and the diviner at eThelezini five. Animals to be slaughtered are usually supplied by the lineage from which the responsible shade has been traced.

During the time of training the novice must catch a wild animal. A limited number of insignificant diviners said, that they had caught now extinct wild animals such as lions, leopards and elephants (one case a crocodile), these having been captured "*emoyeni*", i.e. spiritually, or, preferably, in dreams.[29] The great majority said that they had caught snakes. Some said that they had caught porcupines, weasels and in two cases, *umthini,* a fabulous animal closely attached to the rainbow and waterpools where diviners claim to enter the earth.[30] In the latter case, the two diviners were females of standing, living far apart and with apparently no personal contacts or knowledge of each other. Yet their descriptions of both *umthini* and the catching of the animal were much the same. Their descriptions of capturing it were similar to those of diviners who claimed to have caught snakes in the vicinity of *ixhanthi.* The ventriloquist suggested that *umthini* and *ixhanthi* are the same animal "because they both come from the bottom of the pool, having the same work." Certainly, according to him, *umthini* is associated with fertility.

Of thirty-one novices interviewed, twenty-four claimed to have caught snakes. Of the twenty-four, eighteen had returned with the snakes around their necks.[31] These had given considerable importance to their carrying the snake around the neck and it is probable that this importance is associated with the

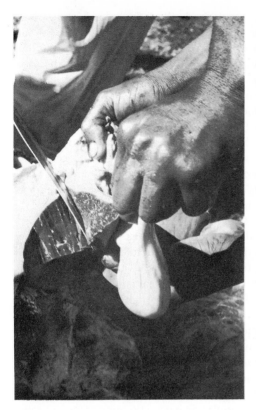

Fig. 8. The gall bladder is removed from the liver of the slaughtered beast.

Fig. 9. The gall bladder is held securely betwe the fore-finger and the long finger of the l hand to avoid spilling its contents. "This (t left hand) is the hand of holding the gall bla der."

fact that the vertebrae of this reptile at a later stage will make the diviner's necklace.[32]

Informants claim that they can hardly visualise a diviner without his/her having caught a wild animal. Besides the necessity of catching it in view of the necklace of snake vertebrae which diviners of standing claim is an important piece in a diviner's equipment, the great majority stressed the importance of courage expressed by the novice's return with the reptile. The diviner at eThelezini gave considerable importance to this aspect. "When we say that the novice must return with a snake, we say it to see what courage she has. If she is a coward, she still have nothing with her. If she is really called by the shades, she will return with the snake around the neck. Then we know that she is not playing but doing her work given her by her fathers."

Although a large number of diviners expressed amazement at the question whether animals other than snakes could be caught, some said that a novice did not know of herself what animal she was expected to catch. "The animal is revealed in dreams. There is nobody that knows that it is to be a snake. Sometimes the shades will tell them to catch other animals." But the diviner at eThelezini and the ventriloquist both said that it was seldom or ever an animal other than a snake. "If there is another animal, then the novice must

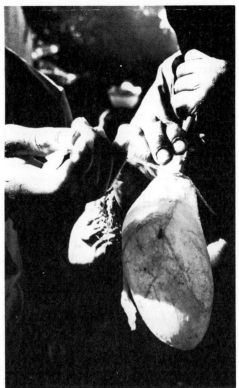

Fig. 10. Inflating the gall bladder by means of a ᵣeed through which the air is blown.

Fig. 11. The opening of the inflated gall bladder is tied securely with a length of string. Sometimes sinew from the slaughtered animal is used.

catch a snake besides catching the other animal. The novice must catch a snake. There must be a snake so that there can be a necklace." All diviners were quite explicit that the snake, once caught, is kept in the tutor's hut until such time as the back-bone is to be made into a neck-lace.[33]

During the time of training the novice must under no condition go outside with the shoulders bare or exposed to the sun. "A novice is like a shade. They have no shadows. They are both like children who must not see the sun. It kills them if the sun shines on them." If, on the other hand, the novice goes outside in the sunshine after some time in training but with the shoulders covered, there would be no harm. Diviners say that the shades work in the shoulders and the back. Hence the novice should avoid the sun shining directly on these parts of the body. "They become sick because the shades are disturbed. Shades do not agree with sunshine. The shades are the people of the night." Also after initiation diviners are careful not to expose themselves to the direct rays of the sun. Either they wear something over their shoulders or do not go out into the sunshine.

When washing, the novice is expected to bathe in cold water. Warm water is said to harm the work of the shades. Further, the water should preferably be fetched from below a waterfall. Waterfalls and murmuring of running water are regarded as signs of *amanzi aphilayo* (living water). Spring water is very acceptable. But water should not be taken from pools or dams. "This water is dead. It does not move." Other informants have said that stagnant water kills the work of the shades. Washing takes place preferably at dawn in a secluded place in the vicinity of a waterfall or the stream from which the water is taken. It is important that the novice fetches the water personally and that it is collected in a special vessel used by the novice alone. This vessel is used for no other purpose than washing. The reason given is that the novice "is weak. She must not touch powerful things." This urge for ritual purity is seen also in the eating habits of the novice.

A novice is particular in the choice of foods that he/she eats. No novice eats eggs, pork or mutton. Bananas are avoided by women particularly, although there are cases of women eating sweet-potatoes but not bananas. "Bananas are like men." Hence they are regarded as being "strong like men". Bananas are also avoided by pregnant women. However, they are readily eaten by women who wish to become pregnant but do not conceive. A diviner once said: "Bananas are like shade-snakes. They enter a person and cause that person to dream very much. Because they (the novices) already dream very much, they do not wish to dream more. So they do not eat bananas."

Food selection varies considerably from novice to novice. Some claim that the shades reveal to them what they should eat and what they should avoid. Others say that the tutor tells them what to eat and what not to eat. Tutors who follow traditional patterns in training the novice maintain that they "should eat food that opens the eyes so that they become alert (kaliphile)". Others claim that a novice should not eat any fat as fat bodies become drowsy and sleepy. "A diviner cannot be a sleepy person, just thinking of sleep all the time and doing nothing."

As bananas, so sweet-potatoes are by some associated with men. "This food reminds me too much of men. That is why I do not eat it. I just become sick as soon as I eat this thing. It is the same sickness as when my husband has desired me. I am sick until the heat (i.e. semen) has left me. In the same way I am sick until I have got rid of this rubbish in my body."

Reasons for not eating pork and mutton were suggestive. A representative diviner said: "Pigs are fat. The fat is not good. It is slippery, causing nothing to remain (in place). The shades do not agree to slipperiness." Others said that pork made one fat and "a diviner cannot be fat".[34] Others said that pork smelt bad and made dreaming impossible, while some claimed that "pigs eat everything, even faeces. So how can this thing be eaten?" Sheep are unavoidably associated with dumbness which, in turn, is related to stupidity and inability. "This thing (a sheep) cannot even object when being killed. It is foolish. It has nothing to say, even when being killed." Another informant said that "eating sheep is bad. It just brings about quiet. Nobody says anything. So there is no clarity in anything, everybody being quiet." One informant said that sheep, unlike cattle and goats, eat emphepho and hence consume "the food of the shades. That is why the shades have forbidden us to eat this animal."[35]

Some diviners and novices say that they abstain for sour milk and a great number claim that they abstain from any food that contains salt.[36] "Salt is bad for the dreams. It makes them hazy. So ithongo has said in dreams, 'Do not eat salt. It is poison, killing people like you.' That is the reason for not eating salt. It tastes bad since that dream."

A novice will make his/her own fire in the hearth, great care being taken to secure a personal match-box from which the fire is made. Only under very special circumstances will a novice borrow matches and this only with the consent of the tutor. Under no condition may a fire be made from live coals in another hut. The novice collects the firewood. "We fear the fire from other huts. This fire has been near people who have been hot. This is bad. The fire is hot, like a man and woman are hot, especially a woman, having the water (i.e. semen) inside." A few have associated coals from a previous fire or from another hut with forgetfulness. "That fire comes from old fire. It is like old people who forget everything. A diviner cannot forget. His mind must always be clear, remembering everything." In this particular case it appears that the thought-pattern which associates the novice with a child maturing is brought to the fore again. The diviner at eThelezini said when asked whether this interpretation was correct: "It is indeed correct. The novice must not forget. She is like a child who must remember all the things that are taught to her by the tutor." Yet, although this view was underlined on this particular occasion it appears fairly certain that in general the avoidance of old fire or coals from another hut is to be regarded as a means of retaining ritual purity.

A novice does not eat food prepared by unknown people or by such as live as husband and wife. "The food is hot, like the people are hot. The food must be cool, giving coolness to the novice. Especially a woman who is pregnant or who carries the thing (semen) inside the stomach is hot. Yet it is she that prepares the food. So the novice cannot eat this food. That is why it must be prepared by a small child or an old woman who has no pleasure in these things any more." Children who have not reached puberty are not regarded as being hot and are therefore allowed to prepare food for a novice. So is an old woman past child-bearing when sexual relations generally cease, on condition that the food is prepared in the diviner's or the novice's personal vessel, on a freshly kindled fire and with water taken from a running stream or a spring.

The fear of contamination stretches to all social encounters. A novice does not shake hands with unknown people, particularly not with married men and women. Some, if at all possible, avoid shaking hands altogether during their time of training and a limited number retain this observance even after their initiation.[37]

In a homestead the tutor and the novice occupy a hut which is entered by nobody besides other diviners and novices, and occasionally guests who have been asked to enter. After the initiation a hut is reserved for the sole purpose of the diviner in the homestead. Not even family members are allowed into the hut without the diviner's consent. "Nobody enters a diviner's hut. It is the place of the shades. They must not be disturbed by people. Only the diviner goes in to them. That is their place of brooding."

A novice attends no social gatherings. The thought-patterns which emerge from this total abstention is that of fear of being ritually soiled. While diviners in general say that *abantu abashisayo* (hot people) must be avoided at all costs (particularly people who have had sexual relations or are menstruating as well as nursing and pregnant women), they are equally explicit that a novice must not allow another person's shadow to fall on them. "This is a very great danger. It kills the work of the shades. The shadow is a very strong thing. It is the person who falls on the novice. It can kill everything that happens in the child. Many diviners have been killed in this way." There is also ritually definable impurity in people who "carry *amakhubalo* (medicines and/or charms) with them. Sometimes they are very strong, having great power. There is something wrong when people carry these things. People are always carrying these things, fearing *abathakathi*. So the novice does not go near them."

Even if married, male and female novices are expected to live a chaste life while undergoing schooling.[38] Some informants have indicated that this requirement has placed such strain on them that it has been sufficient cause to attempt barring the responsible shade. "This is the most difficult thing, especially for women. It is too difficult. That is why we even try to bar the shade, refusing the call. This is the most painful thing, especially for the women because the husband is very demanding."

Difficulties increase when a married female novice is demanded by her husband. If he does not agree to abstain from sexual life with his wife, a goat is supplied by the woman's homestead and lengths of skin cut from the animals back are attached to the woman's legs just below the knee. Sometimes a belt is made which she wears around the waist. These skins, preferably from a white goat, are worn by her throughout her time of training. The flesh is eaten by the tutor and the novice and other inhabitants of the tutor's home. "If she dreams of her husband or feels it nice when he is with her, not being sick when he enters her, then the shades have agreed." Her husband is expected to give his wife some white beads which are added to her collection. These will be made into a necklace or hung in the hair on the occasion of her initiation. Some diviners say that they are not happy with female novices who live with their husbands. "Sometimes they become with child. Then the shades clash, some working the child, others working the divination. This is not good, this mixing up of things." Others maintain that married life prolongs the time of schooling because the novice is away frequently, visiting her husband. Only a very limited number of tutors allowed husbands to visit their wives in the tutor's homestead.

The diviner at eThelezini associated abstention from sexual relations with *ubungane* (childhood) of the novice. "These people are like children, as I have said. They know nothing. They are like small children who know nothing. They are learning. It is the thing of divination that they are learning. That is why they are children. Yet now they want to do the thing of grown ups. That is why the shades have given the rule of abstention. They must not mix childhood with the work of grown-ups. There will only be confusion."

A number of female novices smear themselves with red clay, or, sometimes, red earth over the face, shoulders and back.[39] My friend in the uMhlatuze valley said that this red colour "is the colour of blood. When a woman colours herself with this colour, then we say, 'She is troubled by her fathers,' speaking of the shades of her *isibongo* (clan)."

B: "I have never seen a man with red."

"You will not see one. When a man is troubled by the shades, then they are known. So it is only the women who use it."

B: "Why do you say that the red is the colour of blood?"

"It is because the women carry the blood. The blood is red. So the colour of women is red. It is like *ihlule* (a blood-clot which is believed to develop into the child). I am saying that the novice is like *ihlule*. These two are a-like."[40]

B: "You are associating it with the blood of menstruation and of fertility?"

"You see it clearly. That is the thing. The person with red is like *ihlule*. She (the novice) is still very young, only starting to become something. That is when they put on the red. It is because they are just like children, like *ihlule*."

B: "Would it be incorrect to call the novice *ihlule*?"

"It would not be incorrect if you are the tutor. It is the mother that says to other women, 'I have a suspicion. There is perhaps *ihlule* eating up my blood.' They say this when the months (i.e. monthly periods) have not been, indicating that there may be something in the stomach. So it is the tutor that speaks of the child in his/her care as *ihlule*."

B: "Do the shades recognize the red clay or earth because they themselves are in the earth?"

"They know it. They dwell in the earth. That is their place. So they know the red earth very well."

B: "So there are two things that are important in this matter. It is the colour and it is the earth?"

"That is correct."

B: "So to them (the shades) the red of the woman's blood and the red earth of the novice is just the same thing?"

"Just tell me, please, what is the difference between *ihlule* inside the woman and *ihlule* inside the diviner's hut? Is it not the work of the shades, both of them?"

B: "I see. But is the matter of growth related to the use of red in that the novice does not appear in red on the day of initiation. I have met with no novice who had red on the day of initiation."

"On that day the novice is ready. The novice is like the child that does not eat blood and water any more. It is the time of milk after birth. So the novice and the child are still alike. When they are ready to come out, the child coming from the woman as the novice comes from the tutor, then they cease eating blood and water."

B: "Are you indicating that the white of the novice on the day of coming out is the white of milk?"

"No! (Very audible objection.) No! That is another thing!"[41]

There are essentially two methods whereby the novice concludes the training with the tutor. Either the initiative comes from the tutor or, in less conservative circles, the initiative is taken by the novice.

Informants from circles where divination is conducted along traditional lines underline that the proper procedure is for the tutor to inform the novice of her forthcoming initiation. "Sometimes the novice knows without being told. This is when they have been working together nicely. Then the novice knows without being told." Evidence points to three criteria whereby the tutor concludes that initiation can take place. Firstly, the tutor dreams that the novice has been trained sufficiently to carry on without aid, or that "the novice dreams nicely, being trustworthy". A limited number said that the novice might dream about completing her period of learning soon and tell the tutor of the dream. "Then the tutor may take some steps."

Secondly, if the tutor fears that the novice is attracting away inquirers, training would cease. Diviners of standing claim that this is a very poor way of concluding the training. "It just shows fear. That is all."[42]

Thirdly, when the novice has been restored to health training ceases. Conservative diviners claimed that this is the only acceptable way of judging a novice's maturity. "If the novice becomes healthy it is a sign that all dreams have been confessed. Then she is ripe." Although the confession of dreams is related to health, diviners claim that it is not only a matter of restoring the novice's health. Knowledge is of equally great importance. But no clear lines of distinction are drawn between health and knowledge. "The shades do not give full health before the knowledge is there. It is true that health comes when the dreams have been confessed, but the health will not be complete before the knowledge is there. So these work together."

The ventriloquist said that he watched "the novice's head. When it was soft, then the time is ripe." The softness of the head was not related to any physical change in the constitution of the skull. It was rather the ability to adjust oneself to various conditions and circumstances of work. "A diviner must never think of himself. He must learn to kill his thoughts and desires and just think of the shades. He must do what they tell him. That is to have a soft head."[43]

In a large number of cases the initiative towards terminating instruction is taken by the novice. Evidence suggests two reasons for his step. Either the novice is more active than the tutor and may become bored by the tutor's lack of enthusiasm, or conflict may have developed between them. The latter is not infrequently the case today. An elderly female diviner whose novice had left her after a heated dispute on a matter of expected submissiveness from the novice who refused to run an errand, said: "Today there is no discipline. This is the work of the whites. It was much better before when there was discipline as in the days of Shaka. Those were good days when the youth obeyed. Today there is only trouble with them all. Just look at this thing. She is even refusing to do her work while living with me here in my house. Just think of it how bad it is!"

Coming Out

The idiom *ukuthwasa* describes a coming out afresh after a temporary absence or disappearance. It is generally applicable to the moon and the seasons of the year.[44] *Ukuthwasa* is also applied to a diviner novice who, on having completed the time of instruction with an experienced diviner, appears again on the public scene, reveals divinatory abilities and is officially acknowledged as a diviner. The use of the term *ukuthwasa* reflects something of the importance attached to the occasion. An *ithwasa* is a newly initiated diviner or the person undergoing the final initiation towards becoming a fully accepted diviner while *ukuthwasiswa* refers to the process of being taken through the necessary initiation.[45]

The tutor having decided on a suitable day for the initiation of the novice, word is sent to the novice's home where the initiation takes place.[46] "It is the work of the home to initiate the novice. That is where the shades are. It is the shades that come to the diviner, brooding from that day onwards," said the diviner at eThelezini. At the novice's home beer is brewed and a hut set apart and prepared for the occasion. The beer prepared is set aside in *umsamo* of that hut.

The night prior to initiation the novice is expected to spend *emaphandleni* (in the fields),[47] sleeping on the naked earth. "The novice is coming from the earth. The earth is the mother. The tutor sends her out in the evening from the home (tutor's homestead), saying, *'Buyela kwonyoko!* (Return to your mother!)' That is why she must be away that night, sleeping on the earth. It is because of the earth. The novice goes out, knowing that it is the night of the fields. Then she appears at the house in the home in the early morning." Although, however, most diviners claim that this is the ideal, in practice many a novice spends the night or a larger portion of it in the tutor's home, leaving only very early in the morning.

I attended the initiation of a novice. The novice returned to the homestead at dawn, smeared with white clay[48] and carrying in her right hand an earthernware vessel containing water. In the left hand she carried a knife.[49] The tutor informed me that the water in the vessel had been collected from a waterfall at night and that the water was called *amalotha* (male fluid). On arrival at the homestead, the novice entered a hut, the door of which had a white cross painted on it. I was told that the hut had been pointed out by the senior of the homestead, in this particular case the novice's eldest brother. The hut was said to be furnished with new mats in *umsamo* on which the novice would be seated. Other informants said that sometimes the novice would sit behind a reed-mat which was raised in front of *umsamo*, forming a secluded area between *umsamo* and the rest of the hut. The beer in the hut would not be touched at this stage, the novice only being allowed to drink the water she had brought with her.[50] No food may be taken by the novice and nobody is allowed to enter the hut after her arrival.

Immediately after sunrise the tutor arrived. She entered the hut. A number of local diviners and novices arrived at various times during the course of the morning. They also entered the hut where the novice and the tutor were, the cross on the door apparently being sufficient indication for them to know where to go. Each of these had white beads which, I was told, would be given to the tutor or the novice on arrival.[51] One novice arrived without beads and was being reprimanded by the tutor in no uncertain terms when another novice arrived. The latter shared her beads with her less fortunate companion and the tutor calmed down. Both novices entered the hut. Some twenty people having assembled in the hut, the homestead senior called upon the tutor through the hut thatching that the preparations were completed. Soon afterwards all the visiting diviners and novices evacuated the hut, the diviners clad in their professional dress. They gathered outside the hut door together with a growing crowd of lay visitors.

After a few minutes the tutor appeared and took her place nearest the door. Only a minute or two later the novice appeared, naked but for a minimal loin clothing and resmeared with what looked like white-wash. That the material was white-wash was confirmed later by the tutor. The novice was received by the tutor who shouted out the top of her voice: "*Hrrrr! Shtttt! Hrrrr!* I have given birth! Hear me, I say today I have given birth! This sister is the thing that I have produced! *Hrrrr!* Look! I have given birth!" The surrounding visitors broke out into a jubilant shouting and hand-clapping, a number (probably three, possibly four) of elder female diviners crying out in a shrill, high-pitched voice and running about with short quick steps, waving their knives and divination switches.[52]

The novice walked about the homestead as if lost, inquiring where the entrance to the cattle-enclosure was. On being taken to it, she entered the byre where the cattle had been kept since the evening before, and walked about, looking at the cattle. She stopped at a cow and began rubbing it on the back. Suddenly she started crying very bitterly, the tears streaming down the cheeks. But as suddenly as she had started crying she stopped and shouted out, standing at a little distance from the animal and pointing at it: "*Eyenqwamba!eyenqwamba!*" Withdrawing from the enclosure, she met her tutor at the gate, the tutor taking her to the open space in front of the hut set aside for them. Suddenly, and apparently quite unexpectedly, the novice started running in circles hysterically, jumping up and down occasionally. Very soon a ring of clapping onlookers was formed around her and the tutor, the latter now having joined the novice in jumping and running. The handclapping was definitely adjusted to the jumping of the two, not the other way around. The tutor, being an elderly woman, could by no means compare in enthusiasm and vitality with the considerably younger novice and general interest was with the novice rather than the tutor. The tutor, however, did everything possible to attract attention to herself. Eventually she gave up, shouting quite pathetically: "Today I am being eaten up! *Maye*! What kind of child did I suckle? The breasts being dry have nothing to give, my child is eating me up now! *Maye!*" The tutor retired to a mat rolled out next to the cattle-enclosure some short distance from the exceedingly active dancing and jumping of the novice.[53]

The body dripping with sweat, the novice gradually calmed down the intensity of the dance. The hand-clapping and singing of the onlookers also decreased and the number who formed the circle around the novice gradually became noticeably less. When there were not sufficient onlookers to close the circle the novice left and retired to the hut. After some time the tutor also went to the hut, apparently exhausted and a little irritated.

They remained in the hut about an hour, visitors sitting in little groups in the yard, chatting. Emerging from the hut again, the tutor had not changed her dress. She retired to the mat on which she had been sitting previously. The novice, on the other hand, was noticeably refreshed. She appeared dressed in *inqwamba* skin which hung from the left shoulder and over the right hip. Two gall-bladders were fixed onto the small tuft of her hair remaining above the brow after the recent haircut, and a large number of white beads. There was a necklace of white beads around her neck also and a string of them around her waist. The white-wash on the face and upper trunk had been renewed again. She stopped where she had been dancing previously and no sooner had she arrived at the place than a large number of visitors surrounded her and formed a wide circle. The novice started to sing the song she had composed for the initiation and the visitors joined in with hand-clapping and singing the chorus.[54]

Again the novice commenced a solo dance, consisting of running around and jumping up-and-down. She increased the tempo noticeably and worked herself up into a frenzy, her jumping and running increasing both in height and in speed. The singing and hand-clapping followed suit. Working herself into a pitch that was nearly incredible, the novice suddenly fell down on the

Pl. I. A novice with her face smeared with red day.

Pl. II. A novice dressed in a red garment. Her tutor was a strict and conservative diviner who had extensive knowledge of thought-patterns and symbols. She said: "My children must wear red because they are blood-clots which have not yet been born. They know nothing except the womb."

No other novices dressed in red were traced, although many diviners accepted the explanation of the red dress given by the tutor.

Pl. III. Interior of a diviner's hut, showing beer container's etc. .... The walls of the hut had bee
smeared with red earth which had been obtained at considerable inconvenience. "It (the wall) must b
red so that the diviner may come out nicely."

Fig. 12. A female novice returns home just after dawn on the day of her coming out. She wears *iminqwamba* skins, three gall bladders in the hair and a length of skin around her left wrist. Her face is smeared with red clay.

ground and lay perfectly still for a short while. The sweat was running off her body again. Slowly she started speaking and confessing dreams. Starting with a murmur, she worked up the pitch of the voice so that she was shouting as loudly as she could by the time that she came to the end of the confessions. Visiting diviners listened in tense silence, an occasional visitor breaking the silence with: "*Ngoma! Hrrrr!*" or sometimes: "*Yizwa!*"

While the novice was confessing dreams two men walked up to the tutor who was sitting on the mat in the shade of the cattle-enclosure with a skin, gall, heart, liver and chyme of a goat, the latter enclosed in the skin. On a wooden plate they brought *insonyama*. The chyme was contained in an enamel dish of fair size and placed in the skin. The tutor instructed them to place the skin and contents with the wooden plate at the door of the hut with the cross on the door. They did so. After a while the tutor got up and walked slowly to the novice, still lying on the ground. The novice paid no attention to her, but on the tutor's taking hold of the novice, the latter jumped up and gazed as if amazed into the eyes of the tutor. The tutor said something to the novice which I could not hear, but on hearing the tutor speak, the novice shouted out. The tutor led the nearly uncontrollable novice to the hut and entered, closing the door. She opened the door once to take in the skin and the plate with the goat's meat.

After about an hour the novice emerged again from the hut and was jubilantly received by the visitors. She was now dressed in a second *inqwamba* skin, falling from the right shoulder and onto the left hip. The gall-bladder had been inflated and tied to her hair, thereby making the number of gall-bladders three. The tutor informed me that the gall had been poured over the novice head, shoulders and feet, a little had been drunk and some had been poured onto the hearth in the hut. Both the novice and the tutor had washed their hands in the chyme. Washing completed, the tutor had taken the novice's knife and, after rubbing it in the ash of the hearth, had cut *iminqwamba* from the back of the goat's skin and then tied it in place on the novice. The novice had been crying all the time, sometimes sneezing and belching. At least the belches were clearly audible to visitors standing outside the hut. The tutor claimed that the novice had been seated in *umsamo* of the hut all the time.

Visiting diviners took up the novice's song which they had now learnt. The novice reacted immediately. She jumped high up into the air and fell down on the ground again, quivering and shaking all over. Equally suddenly she rose again and jumped up and down a short while. Then, coming to a sudden standstill, she shouted out: "There is something troubling me! I am like a pierced beast with a pain in the side! There is trouble in this place, things being unclear!" The singing ceased and hand-clapping commenced. The novice stood still and shouted out: "*Bula! Ngizwe!* (Smite! Let me hear!)" She moved in the direction of a grass-heap which was to be used as thatching for a hut under construction. The hand-clapping became nearly deafening and the shouts enormous. Quite close to the grass-heap she threw herself onto it and emerged with a large new billy-can, apparently empty. The enthusiasm of the onlookers was uncontrollable, the novice excited, and the tutor cool and dignified. Encouraged by further hand-clapping the novice subsequently found a hoeblade stuck into the sapplings of the cattle-enclosure, a small metal whistle stuck into the thatch of the hut she occupied (the whistle was immediately hung around her neck by means of a piece of white string attached to the whistle), a vertebrae bone hidden underneath the grind-stone outside a nearby cooking-hut and a bird's claw held in the hand by a visiting diviner. Dripping with sweat and noticeably fatigued, the novice threw herself down on the mat next to the byre where the tutor had been seated previously. Two female children, about nine or ten years old, brought beer and meat to her (I was told that the meat was portions of *insonyama* which had been prepared by the children). She ate meat and drank beer with marked satisfaction. While she was eating the tutor came and sat down on the mat next to her. The tutor also received a plate of meat, but they shared the beer. A large piece of meat, uncooked, the liver, heart and lungs were packed in a plastic bag and these the tutor took with her when she returned home after the meal. Although there was apparently not more meat than that of the slaughtered goat, great quantities of beer were consumed in the afternoon, people gathering in groups all over the homestead. The beer was taken out of the hut by a number of appointed novices who, apparently, were close friends of the newly initiated diviner. Great care was taken throughout the day not to allow anybody into the hut which had been occupied by the novice and the tutor.

Towards evening visitors returned home. There was no more celebration that day, other than beer-drinking and talking. Although the amount of beer prepared for the day appeared to be vast, there were visitors who were not satisfied, stating that if it had been done "nicely, then we should all have had at least our fill of beer, if not of meat". The senior of the homestead ascribed the lack of meat to poverty and claimed that all his acquired animals "had been eaten up by this child of my father. As you have seen, there were two things (i.e. gall-bladders) in the hair. They are my work (i.e. I supplied the animals from which the bladders came)."[55]

Two days after the coming out of the novice I had an opportunity of speaking to her tutor.

B: "Why is it so important that the novice sleep in the fields the night before initiation?"

"It is because she must come from the earth into the home for initiation."

B: "So when you said, 'Go to your mother!' you were not speaking of the girl's mother?"

"I was speaking of the other mother."

B: "Which mother?"

"The earth."

B: "Is the earth the mother of the child?"

"A person has two mothers. The woman and the earth. A diviner cannot be born of a woman. She must come from the earth."

B: "Is it because the shades are in the earth?"

"Sometimes you can say it like that. But sometimes it is because people come from the earth."

B: "So a diviner comes from the earth?"

"That is where they come from. The earth gives birth to them."

B: "Did the novice know this when you told her to go to her mother?"

"What do you think I did all these months teaching?"

B: "I am sure you taught her many things?"

"I taught her many things."

B: "Had you taught her to paint with red and white and carry the vessel with water?"

"I myself painted her with red clay. That was in the beginning when she knew nothing. But I instructed her about the white and the vessel."

B: "I would like to hear more about the white and the vessel with the water of men."

"The white is the colour of the shades. The white says, 'Today she is a servant of the shades.' Everybody who sees that person and knows something says, 'This is ithwasa,' knowing the colour of diviners and shades. That is the colour white and its work. As for the water, it is not just water. It is living water (amanzi aphilayo), meaning that something is happening today. If the water was dead, like water in pools, then they (the shades) would refuse to do their work of making a diviner. That is why the water must be living, so that they can do their work of making a diviner."

B: "Is not the name of the water amalotha?"

"That is true. It is the water of men. But is not the water of men living water?"

B: "Surely it must be living seeing that water of men moulds the child."

"So you are asking me the thing that you know. The water of men carries

167

the shades. That is why it must be water that is living. This water moulds the child which is the diviner. That is why she carries the vessel with water."

B: "But why does she appear naked?"

"It is because she is born a diviner on that day. It is the important day, the day of the birth of a diviner."

B: "If the diviner is born from the earth, ought not the novice return naked from the fields?"

"Sometimes she can come from *emaphandleni* if there is not much time and she is late, the people having arrived. There is nothing wrong in this if she comes from the fields. But now she came from the hut, as you say. This is also correct, to come from the hut. A hut is like a mother in that the child came out naked from it. So if she came from the hut or she came from the fields, it is the same. It does not matter."

B: "Is a hut like a mother in that it gives birth?"

"It is like a woman in that it has the little ones inside it. It is like this. The woman has a stomach (i.e. the womb). A home has a hut. That is how it is. So the diviner (*ithwasa*) comes out of the hut."

B: "Are you indicating that the hut is comparable to the woman's womb?"

"That is the thing that is the truth."

B: "Are the entrances comparable?"

"You mean the entrance to the hut and the entrance to the womb?"

B: "Yes, that is what I mean."

"I do not understand the question."

B: "I know that the shades live in *ikhothamo*. Also you have said this to me. Is also the entrance to the womb a place of the shades?"

"Now I see the question. Yes, they are the same. Did we not once speak of the arch (*ufindo*) in humans? Is this not the place of the shades as is the arch of the doorway? So it is clear that they are both the entrance of the shades."

B: "It is this way that I also have seen it. I merely wished to confirm."

"There is another way, showing the same thing. I will tell you. It is this. A man and a woman must never expose their private parts in the sun. This is not done. Why not? I will tell you. It is because the sun must not shine on these places. They are the places of the shades. That is why the sun must never touch these places. The shades do not agree with sunshine. So a man does his work with the woman in the evening, in the dark."

B: "I did not know this detail."

"So the understanding is clear. There is nothing that speaks against the other. The things are quite clear everywhere, even the hut being a womb (*inimba*)."

B: "So the entrance of the hut, the doorway, and the entrance of the womb are the same in meaning."

"It is as you are saying now. They are the same."

Our discussion took up the brooding of the shades.

B: "The novice had shaved. Is this a sign that the shades were not brooding yet?"

"They were not brooding. But the child will not shave the head again. That was the last time."

B: "Did the shades not brood during the time of learning?"

168

"No, they did not brood. They merely appeared in dreams. Sometimes they appear in other ways also. But mainly in dreams."

B: "Is there a difference between the brooding of the shades and their appearing?"

"There is a difference. The difference is that when they brood they are very near for a long time, sitting there on the person, brooding. That is when they brood. Appearing is when they come and say something and depart. That is appearing. That is the difference between brooding and appearing."

B: "But you have previously told me that the shades brood over a diviner. When do they commence the brooding?"

"They commence on that day. That is when they start brooding, on the day of *ukuthwasiswa*. All the work we do on this day is to call on them to brood over their child."

B: "How are they brought to brood over the child?"

"In the hut that is prepared for the child. This is the hut of brooding. If a person went into that hut without consent, that person would become very ill. Furthermore, they come in the many diviners that assemble on this day. They bring the shades, asking them to brood. Again, there is the gall and the bladder in the hair. It says, 'Come, ye of So-and-so, and brood over this person of yours.' We do not say it in those words. We say it with the thing that is put into the hair. It is their thing. Again, the child sits in *umsamo*. Why? Because she is calling on them to brood. If a man sits in *umsamo* this way, he would die of sickness in the head. But now she sits in *umsamo*, fearing nothing. Nothing happens when the child has been trained nicely for the brooding. But if the tutor has been poor, there may be sickness in the brooding of the shades."

B: "What is the use of the mat in *umsamo*, the one hiding the child?"

"*Umsamo* is for the brooding. The mat is another thing. They are not the same."

B: "What is the purpose of the mat?"

"The mat? It is the thing from the rushes (*emahlangeni*). (Long pause in discussion.) It is the mat of the river."

B: "When you are speaking of the rushes, are you referring to the reed (*uhlanga*) of origin?"

(Marked positive reaction.) "That is the thing. It is the reed of the origin. The mat says that there is a diviner being born today. That is what it says."

B: "Would this message not be said if there was not a mat in front of the child?"

"It would be said. She sits on a mat. It is the mat of the rivers."

B: "You are mentioning rivers. Is there a special river?"

"No, there is no special river. It is that the waters of the river and the reeds of the mat work together in creating (*ukudala*). That is all."

B: "So the mat speaks of the creation of a diviner?"

"You understand it nicely. That is what it says."

B: "You told me once that due to the brooding of the shades you do not wash other than only in the chyme of animals. Will the new diviner do the same?"

"If she does as she has been told. But today one does not know if they obey. This one may obey. Others do not obey. Then they cannot divine nicely, merely deceiving people."

B: "Does a diviner never wash?"

"Only sometimes. Then they smear again. Sometimes they apologize. But they must not wash in warm water. Again, the water of pools kills. They must not even come near it."

B: "Do the shades brood continually over the diviners?"

"They brood all the time."

B: "They do not become *izinhlanya*?"

Amused. "They do not become *izinhlanya*. No. They know the life of brooding and the behaviour when the shades brood. If they were not brooding, there would be no divination. So the power of the shades goes into divination. That is what happens. In other people it goes to the head, making them sick there (i.e. mental disturbances). But a diviner never gets sick in the head."

B: "Are the white beads ornamentation or something else?"

"A diviner cannot have ornamentation. They are the beads of the shades."

B: "What about the whistle that the diviner put on?"

"It is the same thing, having the same colour. It is the thing of the shades."

Our discussion took up *iminqwamba* skins. I drew to the diviner's attention fact that the beast apparently pointed out by the novice had not been slaughtered. In its place a goat had been killed.

"It was a goat that was killed. But it was like the animal pointed out by the novice. It was slaughtered instead of the beast."

B: "Do the shades accept changes like this?"

"If the shades had not agreed the goat would have been dumb. But it made much noise in the slaughtering, everybody hearing it. This is a sign that the shades have agreed to it."

B: "Why was the beast not slaughtered but a goat instead?"

"It was because of poverty. The cattle are finished. They (the homestead people) have nothing. But there are more goats than cattle. Again, the first *inqwamba* strip was the skin of a goat. So this one should also be of a goat to match the first."[56]

B: "Why are *iminqwamba* strips crossed? I have not seen a single diviner without them crossed. It is clear that this is an important thing." (See illustration.)

"When the first skin is put on, we say, 'This person is becoming something.' The people know what is happening. When the second one is put on, we are saying, 'Today the thing has been completed.' When the people see the diviner having both *iminqwamba* (skins) they know that it is a diviner. The second one means that the diviner is ready."[57]

B: "What about the crosses on the door of the hut and the beer-vessels in the hut?" (See illustration of the hut interior, noting the crosses on the beer-pots.)

"They say the same thing. They say that today the diviner is ready. She is coming out, being ripe. There are no crosses when she visits at home only, not being ready. Only when she is ready with the training does she come back with crosses on the door and the beer-pots."

B: "I have been told that at court-cases long ago the accuser would put a

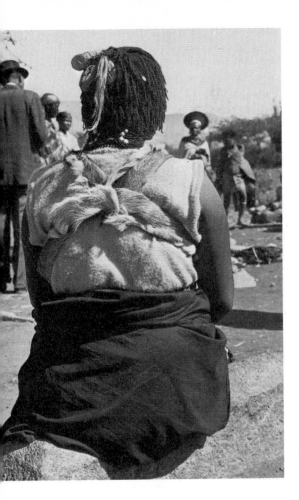

Fig. 13. A female diviner wearing gall bladders, *iminqwamba* skins and *ingubo yamadlozi*. Although the day was very hot she wore a thick pullover to cover her shoulders from the rays of the sun.

stick in front of the judge for each accusation he had. If the accused defended himself satisfactorily, the judge allowed him to place another stick across the one against which he defended himself. The sticks made a cross. What do you say about this cross?"

"It is the same cross. It means that the argument has come to a close. It is complete. There is no more progress in accusing further. The first stick said, 'There is an accusation. We shall see how it goes.' When the people listening at the courtcase saw it, they knew that argument was taking place. Then the defender would argue and argue, calling witnesses, finally showing that there was nothing he had done. Then the judge closed the issue (*ukuvala icala*), saying, 'Cross the stick!' (*Nqamula uthi!*) Then the accused placed a stick across the one of the accuser. The second stick said, 'Now the thing is complete. It is finished, not to be argued any more!' The men went home and there was no more arguing."

Evidence shows that there are not two novices' initiations which are exactly alike. Variations are at times quite noticeable, very much so with popular diviners. Conservative diviners who undergo a lengthy period of tuition tend to adhere to traditional procedure far more rigidly. In a large number of cases the tutor has not been strict in keeping visitors out of the diviner's hut. A large number of diviners said that they did not know about the calabash of water which the novice brings along when arriving at the home for the initiation. But conservative diviners maintain that it is an important item in *uku-thwasiswa*. There are occasions of initiation when there is no animal slaughtered, the novice having been furnished with both *iminqwamba* strips during the period of training. There are initiations which certainly do not take a whole day as did the initiation described above. On the other hand a number of initiations are conducted during the evening, visitors retiring to the homestead huts to sleep until they can go home the following morning.

While a Zulu herbalist achieves a position of social standing through his ability and skill in the use of medicines, a knowledge that he derives from experience, both his own and his tutor's, the diviner looks back on two occasions as the historic moments of his life. Firstly, the occasion of *ukuvuma*, secondly, the occasion of the initiation. Sometimes both occasions play an equally important part in his thinking, in other cases the emphasis is put on one or other of the two, depending on whether importance was given *ukuvuma* or the initiation. In cases where the novice decided on termination of schooling the initiation plays an insignificant role, and one finds that the greater emphasis is given to *ukuvuma*, the diviner claiming that this occasion is the important one and not the initiation.[58]

A friend not very far from the Umpumulo Lutheran Church centre where ordinations take place every now-and-again, had an interesting parallel between Christian ordination and a diviner's initiation. "You have seen the bishop doing the thing with the young men there at the church. That is the very thing that is done at *ukuthwasa*. We ask the shades to brood over the person. That is what we do. As the young men come out, wearing all the things of the ministry, so the diviner comes out, wearing all the things (of divination). Over there (at the church) there is one of them that preaches on that day. So here also with us, the diviner divines. So what is the difference? They are both *ukucoba* (lit. anointing, here ordination)."

Diviners often come back to either both or one of these two occasions in their lives. Talking to them about *ukuvuma* and the initiation, one cannot but note with what zeal and personal engagement they relate details and happenings connected with the occasions. Certainly they return to them with a certain amount of pride and satisfaction as turning-points of no insignificant importance in their lives.

Reading Bryant who speaks of the "*abangoma* fraternity" suggests that diviners form guilds.[59] This is not so. The only occasions when diviners get together are when a novice is to be initiated and at funerals of fellow diviners, the diviners themselves generally standing far away from the grave and under no conditions having anything to do with the corpse.

Certainly not all diviners consciously deceive their patients, although a number undoubtedly do so. Diviners of reputation and standing claim that it is the less able and schooled diviners, i.e. the popular ones, who, when they cannot assist people, rather deceive them than admit that the case is beyond their ability and recommend their inquiring through another diviner. The diviner at eThelezini said that there was a small minority, including himself, who did not corrupt divination. He said that on the few occasions he could not assist folk, he chose to tell them that he did not see his way and advised them to call on another diviner. If they asked him for a recommendation he would give them a name. This had happened three times, he said. The ventriloquist gave me much the same information. He knew of very few diviners who did not occasionally deceive their patients, mentioning some local diviners by name whom he suggested were fully trustworthy. All others were, according to him, to a greater or lesser degree temped to either consciously mislead their clients, or base their findings on previous hints, or, on people's own wishes. The latter he condemned very severely. "What is happening today? People say what they want us to say! Are there then no shades today? I ask again the same thing, are there then no shades today?"

Watching some diviners during their seances it was apparent that the unfolding of a matter at stake left the diviner little room to exercise his/her ability. In some cases it was quite clear that the people who called on the diviner had previously made up their minds and merely required the diviner's approval of their decision. It was looked upon as a 'sanction. On other occasions one was given the impression that the diviner was furnished with alternative solutions to the problem, sometimes only two and seldom more than four, and that, once the problem had been stated, the choice among the solutions offered lay with the diviner. On very few occasions did one feel that the inquirers come wholly void of any suspicions directed to a specific goal, and that the complete matter was left in the hands of the diviner. On equally few occasions one had the impression that the diviner had the ability to stretch beyond the clients' arguments and demands, breaking a new way and approach into the matter. Certainly the diviner at eThelezini and the ventriloquist were of these rare exceptions. There were others, however.[60]

A Diviner's Equipment—Symbolic Associations

Diviners are emphatic that it is not the possession of certain articles in themselves which makes for divination. What weighs far more is the association of the articles with the shades. "When we have these things, then we know that they (the shades) are near us, helping us in the work of divination. But if they are not near the things, then they (the articles) help nothing."

There is no set list of equipment that a diviner is required to have in order to be able to divine. No two diviners will have a similar set-up of equipment. Certainly there do not appear to be two so-called bone diviners who have similar sets of bones, etc., with which they divine. Yet the symbolism attached to a large number of various diviner's equipments is amazingly alike. There is, naturally, a shift in emphasis sometimes, one diviner attaching great importance to his knife, another to the hut in which he/she practises, a third to the use of *imphepho*, etc. But this could be expected. The list below is, therefore, not to be regarded as a compulsary list of equipments. Rather, it is a cross-section of what diviners generally have and the thought-pattern and symbolism attached to the various items. The various items can, on the other hand, be said to be representative of Zulu diviners.

Fig. 14. A diviner sitting in her hut. The mat raised in front of *umsamo* is the one from which she appeared on the occasion of her coming out. Next to the hearth is a pole "to keep the fire-place company. It (the pole) reminds men of warmth and heat. If it is not there, the fire will not burn nicely."

The Hut and its Equipment

Any diviner of standing will have a hut aside in the homestead. This hut is occupied by the diviner alone and such visitors and friends as may be invited to enter it. There are those diviners who are very particular about the people who enter their huts, many others are less particular. Without exception, however, the hut is said to be very closely associated with divination and the brooding of the shades.[61]

More often than not, the hut occupied is situated opposite the place where one would have expected to find it. In the case of male diviners the hut is to be found in the regions of the homestead nearest the main gateway and not in the area of *indlunkulu*. In nine cases of renowned female diviners the hut was situated in the upper parts of the homestead, of these three actually substituting *indlunkulu*. In all cases the hut is known as *eyamadlozi*, i.e. that of the shades.[62]

The diviner's medicines are kept either in *umsamo* or the thatching immediately above the doorway of the hut. (See illustration.) In cold weather a fire is made in the hearth although nobody may intend staying in the hut. Fires are made either by the diviner or, if not available, by children who have not reached the age of puberty, or old women who have passed child-bearing age. "It must be these people so that there is no heat in the hut." The ashes are seldom removed from the fireplace. When excess ash must be removed, only that much which of necessity must be removed is taken away, the greater part being left in the hearth. The excess ash is, according to the diviner at eThelezini, thrown into a river.

As soon as a diviner occupies a hut, a charm (*ikhubalo*), which of necessity

174

Fig. 15. A tuft of grass thatching reversed on the roof of a diviner's hut.

must be white, is hidden in the thatching above the doorway. "It is put there for the shades so that they know their house and their person who works in the hut." The charm may be a single white bead or a cluster of varying size of these beads. Sometimes it is the vertebrae of some animal slaughtered at a ritual celebration. This was the common *ikhubalo* in one area while in another the white beads dominated. In some cases there would be a white pebble hidden in the thatching. In a number of cases a silver coin had been placed in the grass, in one of these instances the diviner referring to the coin as *umnikelo* (offering). In one instance a piece of white china-ware had been inserted into the thatching.

The diviner at eThelezini had a tuft of roof-thatching reversed. The grass was placed immediately above *umsamo*, neatly worked into the rest of the thatching to match with it, yet very clearly noticeable (see illustration). He did not hesitate about its symbolism: "This grass says, 'This is the hut of a diviner who divines by the strength of the shades.' When people see it, they know who works in this hut." He claimed that he had done nothing further with the grass, merely reversing it when he had built that particular hut. He had learnt it of his tutor who, in turn, also had a similar tuft of grass reversed on his hut.

In *umsamo* of a diviner's hut there are often a number of beer vessels. Informants have stressed that these may never ever be completely empty, at least not all of them. At all times there ought to be beer in at least one of them. Thought-patterns all associate the beer with the shades and their demands for beer. "This hut is their house. So they demand something in it. That is why there must be beer in the house of the shades." Several diviners have said that the vessels are owned by the shades and are known, as is the hut itself, as *ezamadlozi*. Sometimes there is a cooking pot near the hearth and on all occasions there has been a little food left in the pot after eating. On a single occasion has the pot been wholly empty.

Sometimes the diviner's sleeping mat may be found in the hut. If the diviner is a male it is frequently found on the left hand side of the hut seen from the entrance of the hut, i.e. the women's side. In a number of instances there has also been a screen of bullrush mats, raised between the floor of the hut and *umsamo*. "The place of the shades should be dark. That is what they like," said the ventriloquist who had such a bullrush screen in his hut.[63] Quite often there will be a small *ilulu* basket in the hut too. The basket, normally used for storing maize and other cereals, is kept either in the cooking hut or store-hut and handled only by women. Diviners, if they have an *ilulu* in their hut, will store it in *umsamo* and claim to use it as a secure place for storing away *imphepho*, divination bones,[6] knife, switch, etc. On two occasions I have been shown snakes that novices have caught being kept in these baskets.

Diviner's Dress

Iminqwamba skins have already been discussed. Undoubtedly they form an essential in a diviner's equipment, there hardly being any diviners who do not have them. But all diviners do not wear them all the time. Most diviners are convinced that divination without them is impossible. A man who claimed to be a diviner, with a small tuft of hair plaited into a tress about five centimeters in length, was the only case I found of a diviner who did not have *iminqwamba* made of skins. His was similar lengths of beans that had been threaded on string. He was, however, the common laughing-stock in his area, people not taking his divinatory abilities seriously. He was neither foolish or otherwise noticeably different from many other diviners although, admittedly, his knowledge of divination and thought-patterns pertaining to divination was based on imagination rather than on knowledge.

A certain amount of importance is given to a square piece of material, black in colour, which a diviner throws over the shoulders when about to divine. Sometimes it is hung over the knees "to cast a shadow", the bones, etc. of a bone-diviner thrown so that they fall in the shadow of the cloth. The cloth is called *ingubo yamadlozi*, the cloth of the shades. When not in use, if owned by a woman, it may be tied around the waist and allowed to hang around the legs.[65] Sometimes it is tied over the shoulders, especially if the diviner has nothing with which to cover the shoulders. Male diviners often include the cloth in their bag which contains their knife, bones, medicines, etc. Diviners say that it may not be tied around the head, many diviners associating their bare heads with the brooding of the shades. Informants are emphatic that the cloth must be either black or of another dark colour. Dark blue or navy are accepted as being black. "We use this cloth so that we can see clearly, in white." The diviner at eThelezini said: "The black is the colour of the night where they (the shades) are." Other diviners confirmed this view, adding that "the black is like the dark of the hut in which we are (we were sitting in a hut with very little light coming through the closed door). No diviner works in the sun. He must have darkness or this black cloth. So they carry the night (i.e. the darkness) with them, where they go." Often there are white beads fixed to the edges of the black cloth, sometimes in considerable numbers. The diviner at eThelezini said: "The beads are their sign if they are white. So when the cloth has the white beads it is clear what cloth it is. It is for divination. Nothing else." Several informants said that the cloth was not to be washed.

Diviners are careful not to expose their shoulders and back to the open sun. If the day is overcast they can appear with the shoulders naked but otherwise avoid going out or, if forced by circumstances, will have something to cover the shoulders and back. Diviners claim that they become sick and cease dreaming if these parts are exposed to the sun. The diviner at eThelezini said that he seldom or ever went out at all during the daytime. If he was forced to do so he would, if at all possible, delay going out until an overcast day or a rainy day. He always wore a heavy army coat, even in very warm weather and said that he was covering his back. The ventriloquist confirmed the diviner's attitude towards going out in sunshine. A diviner who worked as a sugar-cane cutter along the Natal coast was instructed by a foreman to remove the sweater she was wearing on account of the excessive heat on a particular day, but she chose to quit work rather than expose her shoulders to the open sun.

Diviner's Calabash and Carrying-Ring

Besides having separate vessels in which they cook and eat their food, diviners very often have a clay vessel to which they attach considerable importance.

Informants say that the vessel is obtained early during the training of a novice and is kept in the tutor's hut. The diviner is expected to retain the same vessel as long as he/she lives. Destruction of the vessel is looked upon as a calamity. Although some diviners are satisfied with an enamel container today, conservative diviners claim that it should be of clay "because that is the thing the shades know".

Medicines used in the restoration of the novice's health are prepared in the vessel by the tutor. Stored in *umsamo* of her hut, it should, like any of the diviner's equipment, not be exposed to the open sun and hence, if carried about, generally is covered. When the novice is to be initiated, the vessel is moved from the tutor's homestead to that of the novice, the novice carrying the water which he/she brings with him/her at dawn of the day of the initiation in the vessel.

A peculiarity of the vessel is that it can be painted with different colours, conservative diviners using different kinds of clay and earth as colouring material. A few vessels which I have been privileged to see have been of medium size, of the same shape and form as a normal calabash, and coloured with white and red on a black background. The diviner at eThelezini had a vessel with a touching of green, purple and blue, the colours being oil paint. We talked about his vessel.[66] "These are the colours of the rainbow. It (the vessel) is like the rainbow. They bring health."

B: "Is it health generally or is it the health of the diviner?"

"It is the health of the diviner."

B: "How does it bring health to him?"

"It is the water in the vessel. The water comes from the pool in the river where the rainbow enters the earth. The rainbow has many colours. So it is the mother of the colours."

B: "What is the relationship between the rainbow and health?"

"It is the health of women, the health that the women obtain when they stand under the rainbow."

B: "You are speaking of conception?"

"Yes."

B: "How do diviners come into this matter of conception?"

"They (diviners) are people seeking health. If the diviner is sick he cannot see things clearly. So he must always be healthy, having no ailment."

B: "So not being able to divine is the same as being sick?"

"That is so."

B: "Is the barrenness of women and the sickness of diviners the same?"

"They are the same in that they do not see the thing they want. When a woman does not conceive she does not see her chicken (*itswhele*, i.e. child) that she wishes to see. In the same way the diviner who is sick does not see the thing that he wishes to see. He does not see the chickens of the shades properly."

B: "I do not see the relationship between children and the clarity of diviners."

"They are both given (*ukuphiwa*). They come from the outside. Conception comes through water (of men). Clarity comes through water, the diviner having come from water and always drinking the water of the vessel."

B: "I understand the relationship between the water of men and conception in that the shades mould in the womb. This is one thing. I also see that water brings clarity to the diviner, the man of the shades. That is another thing. But what is the connection between them?"

"You have said it yourself. You said that the shades mould the child. That is so. But where does the child come from? (Silence. Then the diviner lifted his eyebrows.) That is where they come from. Where does the water come from? In rain, not so? From above? Is the rainbow not the daughter there, putting the arch (*uthingo*) into the earth at the pool?"

B: "So the connection is the sky?"

No reply. The diviner nods his head. Apparent satisfaction. Quiet for a while.

B: "The medicines of cleansing are also mixed in this vessel, as you said."

"That is so. What is the difference between medicines and water? Do they not work the same thing, giving health?"

B: "When medicines are worked with good thoughts they give health. But is it the same with water, seeing that diviners have this special water?"

(Prolonged yawn and repeated shuddering.) "*Hrrr!* Why are you troubling me today? Reminding me of bad things! You are bringing bad thoughts today! *Aw!* Have you forgotten already the things we spoke concerning the great sea

178

with the monster (*unqanumdolo*)? Are these not evil? Have you today forgotten the greatest snake with the split tongue with no end to the tail? Do you wish me to repeat all these fearful things? Why do you ask whether all water is alike or not. Previously you asked nicely, but today you are asking reminding me of bad things. Why do you confuse the waters? Why do you ask whether all water is alike?"

B: "I am sorry. I was not thinking of the oceans, merely thinking of the waters of the land and the sky, as you were saying."

(Irritation gives way for a smile. Long silence. Deep breath.)

"The waters from above (lift of eye-brow) are like the waters from springs and waterfalls. They are the waters of health. They are powerful, having great energy. They are all the waters from above, as I said."

B: "I see there is a difference between water and water."

"There is a difference, as you say."

It is perfectly clear that the vessel with the colours is associated with health in the diviner's thought-patterns. The interview, verified by a number of other diviners although their thinking was possibly not quite so dogmatic as that of the diviner at eThelezini, emphasized the aspect of water in the vessel. Some diviners said that the vessel must always have water in it. Two claimed that they collected water when it rained for the vessel while one, a truly conservative woman, said that when the rainbow was visible, she would place the vessel outside her hut. No doubt, Western concepts of health (which address themselves to physical ailments rather than those of fertility) would not cover the concept as described by the diviner at eThelezini or his colleagues. To them health is in the first instance related to fertility and productivity. This is the point of departure from which other concepts pertaining to health radiate.[67]

Associated with the vessel is a carrying-ring made of *imphepho,* at least where the latter is obtainable. Informants claim that the vessel should not be placed on the ground without being held in position with the ring, the base of the vessel being fitted into the ring. This is done to avoid spilling the vessel's contents. Some have said that they place the vessel in the ring to avoid its being broken if tipped over. Both reasons seem valid arguments for the presence of the ring. The ring is known as *inkhatha yamadlozi* and is very clearly distinguished from the national *inkhatha.*

The ring is made of *imphepho* wherever available, the circle held in position with the long sinews taken from the back of animals. "It is made of *imphepho* because it is the ring of the shades." It is used solely in connection with the vessel mentioned above and nobody but the diviner, children who have not yet reached puberty and women past child-bearing age are allowed to handle the ring. One diviner said that if commoners handled the ring they would become insane, but this claim could not be verified. The diviner at eThelezini did not approve of the statement and the ventriloquist said that he had not heard of such a case but did not refute the claim. Three diviners said that the ring is coloured with earth "like the vessel so that they agree (in colour)". Asmus also states that the ring is coloured.[68]

179

Knife/Spear

A knife is purchased by members of the responsible lineage and given to the novice during the time of training. Previously, before legislation forbade the use of spears, one of these would be given the novice. Ethnographic records suggest that greater importance was given to the spear in former times than is given the knife today. Old diviners have said that they would have been sick, had they not received a weapon during their time of training, some saying that full health was restored only when they received the spear. Such importance is not given to the knife today. There are several diviners who have been initiated without having either a knife or any other weapon.[69]

There are still diviners who have spears, but these are not used. They are carefully put away in the thatching either above *umsamo* of the hut, or, less often, immediately above the doorway. The ventriloquist had notches cut into his spear shaft, each notch indicating a beast which had been ritually slaughtered on his behalf. On the other side of the handle he had cut X-s into the wood, these indicating the number of patients he had treated successfully.

Diviner's spears were used in ritual killings. They were also used by the diviner for digging up their medicines, peeling bark off branches and in the preparation of medicines. Animals are seldom stabbed in the side today, the general method of slaughtering being stabbing in the neck. For this purpose the diviner's knife is used, if the killing is on the diviner's behalf. In some cases a certain amount of importance is attached to the fact that the diviner's (or novice's) knife is the only instrument used at these killings. On record I have a case where a killing was postponed because the novice, who was being initiated, could not find her knife. Only when it eventually was found, could the slaughtering be carried out.

Evidence suggests that the use of the spear/knife in ritual killings and the preparation of medicines is to be seen in the light of the diviner's fear of ritual impurity. Said the diviner at eThelezini: "Sometimes they fear to have meat from a beast killed with a knife which has cut pork. This is very bad. It would kill the diviner immediately." Another diviner said that on an occasion he had eaten meat cut with an ordinary knife. He had become ill and ceased to dream. He had then investigated the cause of the sickness and found that he had eaten meat which had been cut with a knife "which had cut pumpkin and mixed beans. This is poison to me, making me very sick indeed."

A female diviner at Ekuthuleni who apparently attached a certain amount of importance to her knife related how she had obtained it. "When I was with the diviner at J, I was dreaming of the knife every night. The dreaming troubled me very much, giving me no peace. I told the diviner. She said, 'It is the thing of slaughtering. They are calling for a goat. They want it.' The word was sent to my mother's home (the source of the responsible shade) saying, 'They are calling for something in their work.' A goat was brought by them to the diviner. The diviner sent word to them, 'Since when do they (the shades) eat their meat just like this? Is there then no slaughtering first?' They sent the knife, the very one that I have even today. The diviner instructed the men (about the killing of the goat). They took the knife. They slaughtered (the goat), and brought the skin and the food to the diviner. She cut *iminqwamba* from it with the knife. Then the dreams disappeared, causing no more trouble. That is how I obtained it (the knife)."

Snake-Fat and Snake Vertebrae

Although ethnographic records do not frequently mention a necklace of snake vertebrae, a few diviners of standing attach considerable importance to it.[70]

A diviner of reputation who personally had a necklace of snake vertebrae claimed that the reptile killed for the purpose of obtaining the vertebrae was the snake that he had caught during the time of instruction. His tutor had subsequently prepared the necklace. Asked what diviners who did not catch a snake would wear, my informant said: "There is no diviner who does not catch a snake. If they do not catch snakes, they are not diviners. They must catch a dangerous animal so that it be seen that the shades are preserving him from dangers, giving him courage and strength to handle this thing." He did, however, admit that other animals also were caught and that if the novice caught e.g. a porcupine, the novice would also be required to catch a snake, should he/she wish to have a necklace of snake vertebrae. He also admitted that there were considerable numbers of diviners who did not have these necklaces, but he emphasised that they were not good diviners.

Our discussion commenced with his views on the novice's strength and courage and I suggested that pythons are symbols of strength. But my informant was emphatic that the snake could not be a python. "The snake killed must be just an animal (*inyamazane*). The python is not an animal."

B: "Is the python a shade?"

"Since when are pythons shades? The shade-snakes are known to us. A python is not a shade-snake."

B: "What is the difference between a shade-snake and the snake that is caught and killed by the tutor for the necklace?"

"This snake which is killed is just an animal. It has the tongue which is split. That is how it is known. If it bites a man, then the man becomes sick or even dies. That is the snake that is an animal merely."

B: "Are not pythons animals?"

"Pythons are *amakhosi* (lords)! But the snake that is killed is just an animal."

B: "I have read that among Mpondo an animal is caught. They call it *ityala,* saying that it is a shade that takes the form of the animal which is *ityala.*"[71]

"I know of this animal. A man from Durban spoke of it. But I have not seen it. With us it is only an animal, not a shade. The shades have their animals. We are not the people who are like the Mpondo in having this kind of animal."

B: "So the animal killed has nothing to do with shades?"

"There is nothing that combines them. The shades point out the snake saying: 'That is the animal that you must carry (with you).' But that is all."

B: "Why does the tutor kill the snake?"

"To show courage."

B: "Is it not the novice who is to show courage?"

"That is true. But it is the novice that catches the snake. That is the important thing. To catch it is the thing. To kill is easy. But catching is the thing that is difficult. The novice is a child. A child does not kill. Again, the novice must not see blood. If they see blood their eyes will become red and they will weep much. Children must not weep. So the killing is done by the grown-up (tutor). That is how it is done."

Fig. 16. A diviner holding snake vertebrae strung up on sinew removed from the backbone of a ritually slaughtered beast.

Fig. 17. A popular diviner wearing snake vertebrae to attract attention.

B: "How is the animal prepared?"

"The diviner rises early. He makes fire. He puts the pot on the fire. He goes to *ilulu* and takes the snake. The snake is in it, having been put there by the child. He carries it to the door. He takes the knife and cuts (off) the head. He puts the body into the hot water. The snake wriggles much in the water. He says, 'Just die nicely, animal of the fields! Just die nicely, not spilling the water in the fire!' Then it dies nicely. He puts *imphepho* in the pot. It cooks and cooks and cooks. When it has cooked the meat will float (lit. be on the surface) on the water. He takes the pot off the fire. He digs a hole in the floor. He puts the head (of the snake) in the hole, putting also the flesh of the snake in it. He picks up the bones and puts them inside. He pours the water into the hole. He covers up the hole and puts his foot on it. Then he pours fresh water into the pot and boils the bones again. He takes off the pot and digs another hole in the floor. He puts the meat of the snake into it. Then he pours the water over the flesh and covers up the meat. He takes water again and boils the bones. He does this until they are white, having no flesh at all. When they are ready he puts them aside. When they are dry he wakes up the novice and says, 'Child, look at this thing by the hearth. It came from *ilulu*, from the animal you caught when I sent you out to catch a wild animal.' The child becomes very happy, even smiling, because the animal is in this way. They take sinews and thred the bones onto the sinews. Then they put the necklace into the basket from which it came. When the diviner sends the child home for initiation, he will remind the child, saying, 'Also the thing in the basket.' The child takes the necklace. The people see it and say, '*Maye!* This one has power indeed!' seeing the thing of fearfulness just there around the neck."

While the informant quoted above voiced strong objections in terms of killing a python, Bryant and Asmus both associate pythons with diviners. Asmus has illustrations showing diviners clothed in python skins[72] and Bryant writes: "Soon after initiation the ancestors will appear to her (the novice) in a dream and say, 'Arise, go to a certain pool and you will find a python awaiting you.' She fetches it and carries it to the kraal and places it in the cattle kraal. Next day a goat is slaughtered, eaten in part by the python, in part by the family. After this the python is killed, its spinal vertebrae strung into a chain ornament for encircling the *umGoma*'s body, and the skin, affixed to the back of the head, left to dangle a long stream behind."[73]

The illustration in Asmus' study and the above passage by Bryant were shown and read to the ventriloquist at uMhlatuze. He, like the diviner at eThelezini, was convinced that pythons are not killed. On the other hand they did admit that the snake vertebrae strung into a necklace was sometimes called *inhlwathi* (python). But he claimed that the bones were called this, not because they originated from a python, but rather because they were symbols of courage and strength like that of a python. "When we say *inhlwathi* we do not mean the python itself. We are speaking of the thing that the python resembles. That is courage. So these bones are called *inhlwathi.*"

It is possible that there has taken place a shift in emphasis in terms of thought-patterns concerning pythons from the time when Asmus and Bryant wrote to concepts expressed today. The fact that both Shooter and Bryant who were Zulu linguists refer to female diviners as pythonesses is not acceptable to informants of today.[74] Although diviners reacted against killing pythons they were not indifferent towards associations with pythons as we have seen in their descriptions of entering pools.[75]

Many diviners claim that they smear their bodies with the fat of snakes "in order to make the vision sharp". They say that the fat of practically any snake is useful for this purpose but evidence shows that preference is given to *ibululu* (or *ihobosha*), the common puff adder. Bryant says that the fat of a python is used for this purpose,[76] adding that the diviner anoints his body "in order to secure the favour of the possessing spirit".

Diviners are vague about the use of python fat, a number claiming that they have not heard that this particular fat is used. Two stated that if *inyanga* is a heaven-herd (one of these was Laduma Madela), he has access to python fat and would use it. Madela said that he had given fat to some diviner friends, but he was not willing to expand further on the issue other than say that he did not associate with female diviners. "They cannot take food from heaven (*ukudla okuvela ezulwini*)", seeing that they were women and not men.[77]

Diviners are emphatic that the fat of snakes is a medicine and spoken of as *umuthi*. It is not a cosmetic.

Diviner's Switch

The great majority of diviners carry with them a switch of varying size, known as *ishoba lengoma*.[78] Often it is made of the tuft of hair at the end of cattle tails, preference given to the hair of beasts slaughtered at ritual celebrations. Some diviners said that *ishoba* could also be made of the tail of *inkomo yamadlozi,* the beast of the shades, when it died. Among popular diviners the switch is often carried as a sign of dignity while diviners who also practise in medicines use it to sprinkle medicines.

Ishoba lengoma ought to be either wholly white or wholly black. In the hairs of the switch are attached some of the white beads given the diviner on the occasion of the initiation. The number of beads varies very much, some having only a few, others having considerable numbers. Diviners add beads to their switches in the course of the years as they do with the necklaces and in the hair.

White switches are associated with the colour of the shades. "It is white because it is the colour of the shades." Diviners with black switches maintain that the white beads show up far better against the black background than on the white, emphasising that it is the white beads that attract attention and not the switch itself. The choice of the switch colour is apparently not a very important matter and equal numbers are found amongst conservative as well as popular diviners.

The emphasis is always on the beads, not the *ishoba* itself. As the colour of the switch apparently does not matter much as long as it is uniform, so the kind of hairs is not essential. The diviner at eThelezini had two switches, one of which had been made of horse-tail hairs. But this did not worry him at all. In this particular one he had about thirty beads attached, stating that the hairs with which he had made the *ishoba* were given him by a local Sotho. Ethnographic records account for switches made of cattle tails which appear to be by far the most common,[79] of gnu,[80] wildebeest,[81] and zebra.[82]

Malcolm writes that the "wand which he (a diviner) holds in his hand is used in the many different dances in which with his pupils he engages, and also for smelling out wrongdoers. His initiates, on the occasion of their being accepted into the cult, are patted all over by him with the wand."[83] The ventriloquist maintained that no true *ishoba* could be made other than of the tail of a wildebeest, kudu or possibly a goat. He associated the brush of these animals with their horns and claimed that "even before birth they have them (i.e. the horns)". Their tails, he said, were particularly sensitive to *ububi* (evil) "felt by these animals (reference to flies). These things are the things of evil with these animals. The tails feel the evil (flies) when they settle on the animals. The tail switches them away, exposing them clearly." He described how some insects not only irritate but stick to their prey and suck out the blood. "Is this not the greatest evil experienced by these animals in that their blood is eaten up?" He added that kudu and wildebeest always swing their tails, switching them over the body. Goats do the same when being slaughtered, "feeling the evil of the pain of death with the tail." Hence its use in divination, in efforts to expose evil.

Classification and Numbers of Diviners

The most common word for a diviner is *inyanga*.[84] In the strict sense of the word, it denotes any person skilled in a handicraft or prefession, thus requiring further definition if a specific person or profession is referred to. But in the everyday use *inyanga* is generally accepted as being a diviner/herbalist of some kind. The various types of diviners may be added as a further explanation to what kind of diviner one is referring to, i.e. *inyanga yamathambo* (bone diviner), *inyanga yezinthi* (stick diviner), etc.[85]

Isanusi[86] practically always refers to a male diviner and describes men who have the ability of smelling out evil and *abathakathi*. Bryant and Doke–Vilakazi associate the word with *ukunuka*, to smell.[87] This particular kind of diviner is not common today and some Zulu are of the impression that there are no longer any *isanusi*. A limited number claim that they are still operating, although not in the numbers that apparently existed previously.

One knowledgeable informant said that *isanusi* were related to the kings of old, claiming that *isanusi* were the diviners of the king. They were, therefore to be found in the vicinity of the royal homesteads, in varying numbers. To be accused by *isanusi* of witchcraft or sorcery led to certain death, while an accusation by *isangoma* sometimes left room for further investigations. Influential counsellors also made use of *usanusi* who were regarded as reliable. My informant said that besides merely smelling out the evil and the evildoer, an *isanusi* divined with the aid of ten knucklebones, five of which were from male animals, five from female. He did not know what animals were used to acquire the bones, but suggested apes, baboons, porcupines and antbears. The knucklebones were called *izikhombi*, pointers.

B: "Was there a special reason for having ten knuckle bones?"

"There was a reason. The ten bones are the same as two hands."

B: "You are speaking of the two hands having ten fingers?"

"That is what I am speaking of. Five fingers are male. Five are the female ones. The female ones are the left hand. The male ones are the right hand ones."

B: "Did *isanusi* know the knuckle bones from each other?"

"If he did not know them, then he was not *isanusi*. It is his work to know them. How could he divine otherwise, not knowing his things of divination? No, he knew them."

B: "Were they known as *izikhombi* because they were like fingers which pointed out?"

"They were like fingers, pointing out what they saw."

B: "Who is it that sees?"

"The fathers. They see the thing."

B: "Not the bones of the animals?"

"No! (Very noticeable objection.) When have bones seen? How can they see? They are, as I said, merely *izikhombi* (pointers). They point at the thing that has been seen (by the shades)."

B: "So the shades see the thing and then use the bones to point at it?"

"Now you see it correctly. They are like tongues (*imilimi*) speaking the things of the shades. That is their work. They are just tongues. That is all. Nothing else."

B: "Why are there ten bones?"

"They are ten because ten is the complete life (*imphilo ephelele*). If the bones point in every direction, then it means that there is *imphilo* (health) everywhere. If they point in a certain way in a certain direction, then there is something (evil). The diviner works very hard, speaking nicely to them (the shades) and asking for revelation. Then he throws (*ukuphonsa*) again and they speak the thing that is said to them (the bones). That is how they (the diviners) know the person causing evil."

B: "I have read in a book about death diviners who have these same bones. Are they the same as *isanusi*?" (I read the section in question and described what Samuelson says.)[88]

"It is clear that it must be the same ones. It amazes me that there is a white person who knows this thing. It is true that *isanusi* are *izinyanga zo-kufa* (death specialists) because when they saw a thing, they saw it clearly. So if a man was detected causing trouble with the king, then he died painfully. When they called them *ezokufa* (i.e. these diviners were called 'those of death'), they were speaking of the painful death of *ukujoja* (impalement)."[89]

Ingoma[90] and *isangoma*[91] are terms describing diviners in general. Diviners themselves say that the idiom *ngoma* associates them with the shades from whom they obtain the ability of divining. One diviner claimed that *ingoma* and *isangoma* were, strictly speaking, the same words and denoted diviners who, according to the old Zulu society, divined with sticks known as *izibulo*. These could be of varying length. He claimed that they could be of any shrub or tree but underlined that they should be strong. Often they were prepared by the diviner himself/herself, some having fresh divining-rods for each consultation, some renewing them from time to time. The inquirers would be seated around the diviner in a semi-circle and strike either the ground or a skin which had been folded double, from the tail-end of the animal to the head-end, the striking being vigorous and violent if the diviner was on the correct track and less enthusiastic if he was not correct. The smiting would be accompanied with shouts of *yizwa!* (Hear!), the shouts declining if he was wrong and very loud when he was correct.

B: "Why do they beat a skin?"

"It is because the skin is of the animals of the shades. They know it."

B: "Are they (the shades) in the skin when it is beaten?'

"They are not in the skin. The skins just simply speak for them. That is why it is beaten. But they are not in it."

B: "But the skin must be of their animal?"

"That is correct. It must be their animal. Otherwise they would not speak. They know their animal which was slaughtered for them. So they speak through the skin of their animal."

B: "How do they know this beast from other animals of the cattle-enclosure?"

"It was the one pointed out. They may have pointed it out themselves saying, 'That is the one we require of you today in that it passes water, other beasts not doing it.' Again, they smell it from *imphepho* rubbed on the back before the killing. They ate its gall. They smelt the meat. So they know it well."[92]

B: "Sometimes the people smite hard, sometimes they only tap when the diviner is saying things they do not agree with."

"That is so. But it is not the people who agree or disagree. It is the shades. It is they that are working all the time."

B: "But it is the people that smite the skins."

"They smite them because the shades are exciting them to do it. When the diviner is saying the thing then they excite the people so that they smite, shouting the agreement all the time. Then they become hot and the diviner becomes hot, the shades pointing in the correct direction all the time. But when the diviner does not see nicely, then the shades do not give power (to smite) very much. The arms become weak, they having refused power (*ukuncitsha amandla*). So the smiting is poor. The people do not shout clearly."

B: "But when they smite the earth?"

"It is the same thing as smiting the skins. They (the shades) are in the earth. When the earth is being beaten it is they that are showing the correct way."

B: "Is there any difference in clarity when the smiting is on a skin or on the earth? I know that the one makes much noise and the other causes dust. But is there a difference in the reactions of the shades?"

"No, there is no difference. It depends on what the diviner wants. If he wants dust to help him, then he says, *'Emhlabathini!* (On the earth!)' and the people smite the earth so that the dust is seen clearly coming forth. But if he wants noise, then he says *'Ezikhumbeni!* (On the skins!)' and they beat the skins very vigorously, making much noise. But the divination is the same."

B: "Is the beating of the skin the same in divination and the initiation of a diviner?"

"They are the same. Only in divination the shades point at a certain thing or in a certain direction. But in the initiation it is not the excitement of the shades in their pointing. It is the excitement of the shades so that they can be seen whether the child (the novice) is playing or not. If there is no excitement then the people say, 'This person is playing with us. There is no heat,' speaking of the excitement that they had expected from the shades."[93]

Izinyanga zezinti are also known as *ababhuli*. Today the latter idiom is also used to describe diviners in general, their work of divination being referred to as *ukubhula*.[94]

Callaway quotes *ibuda* as a name of a diviner, adding that it is "an epithet of contempt".[95] Informants stress that *ibuda* is a word that belittles a diviner and used only when he/she is unable to divine or a diviner whose divination has proven to be faulty.

Du Toit, writing in 1960, is of the impression that divination "is in decline",[96] arguing that missionary activity and urbanization have broken confidence in the shades and hence also in the diviner. Van Nieuwenhuijsen, writing at the same time, says that the number of diviners "has strongly increased in the last few years, and in view of the great number of apprentices, it will certainly continue increasing even further".[97] He convincingly states that the increase in diviners has its roots in the breaking up of traditional Zulu life patterns due to urbanization and a subsequent "increase in the number of neurotic personalities among Zulu in general". The overwhelmingly great number of diviners being women he sees as further evidence underlining his assumption, adding that "it confirms the experience also gained elsewhere that emotional disorders are far more frequent among Zulu women than among Zulu men. Expressed in the simplest terms, psychosomatic disorders are manifestations of anxiety-states, and anxiety-states are the result of an incapacity to face certain conflict situations."[98]

Whatever the cause of the growing numbers of diviners may be, evidence certainly shows that there are great numbers of diviners in Zulu society today. Zulu themselves say that there are greater numbers today than there were about twenty years ago. Experience shows that the great majority of diviners are bone-diviners (*ezamathambo*) while there is a smaller number who do not use bones. Only two ventriloquists could be traced and of these two, meaningful contacts could be made with only one after considerable time and patience. Van Niewenhuijsen supports Bryant's observation that the great majority of diviners are women.[99] There is no evidence today to support any opposite tendencies. Of 68 diviners on record, 61 were females.

In Zulu society diviners vary greatly in popularity. Diviners of standing are not very many. Their prices are, contrary to the popular ones, high and they are approached only when the popular diviners have not been successful or when the inquirers have not been satisfied with their views. Popular diviners abound everywhere, their advice being sought frequently but not infrequently disregarded. These sometimes go out of their way to seek inquirers, hoping to make a reasonably successful case for people who accept their services. Quite often popular diviners have either not completed their time of training with an experienced diviner or have been schooled by an incompetent tutor. Conservative diviners resent these trends very strongly.

Few diviners remain only diviners. A great majority also practise medicine, thereby combining divination with medical attention. This is true also of conservative diviners. The ventriloquist diviner at uMhlatuze attended only to his duty as a diviner, recommending his patients to local herbalists. Yet he did have a reasonable knowledge of medicines also and claimed that for personal use he prepared medicines. The diviner at eThelezini, on the other hand, also with considerable knowledge of medicines, said that he never made use of medicines he had prepared himself other than those that were specifically as-

Fig. 18. A male diviner of no reputation. Although he wore no finery he substituted *iminqwamba* skins with strings of beads. His hair was cut except for the plaited tuft at the back of the head.

Fig. 19. A diviner's left wrist.

Many diviners have pins attached to gall bladders and skins from animals slaughtered ritually on their behalf worn around their wrists. Pins are worn so "that no sharp thing may hurt (the diviners)". The illustration shows two gall bladders, a bangle of shells which the diviner associated with fertility in women, and four black rubber bangles which were related to his four years as a diviner.

sociated with divination. When he required medical treatment he consulted a herbalist living some twenty-four kilometers distant. It is quite logical to assume that the common combining of a diviner's services with those of a herbalist has been influenced by legislation which allows traditional herbalists to register for practice, thereby indirectly including also divinatory abilities with medical practice.[100] Many popular diviners emphasize that they are not diviners in the strict sense of the word, underlining that they are herbalists. But popular thinking regards them more as diviners than herbalists.

Notes

[1] Cp. Krige, *SSZ*, pp. 301 ff.

[2] Asmus, *Die Zulu*, p. 79. Asmus mentions the unclear dreams.

[3] Sneezing is *ukuthimula*. Callaway, *The Religious System of the Amazulu*, p. 64: Farrer, *Zululand and the Zulus*, pp. 139 f.

[4] Yawning is *ukuzamula*. Farrer, *Zululand and the Zulus*, p. 138.

[5] *Ukubodla* (belching). Krige, *SSZ*, p. 303.

[6] Hiccups is *i(li)thwabi*. Asmus, *Die Zulu*, p. 80: Norenius, 'Izanusi', p. 36.

[7] Krige, *SSZ*, p. 303: Norenius, 'Izanusi', p. 36.

[8] Bryant, 'The Zulu Cult of the Dead', p. 145. My informants all used the term *umkhuleko* to describe their communion with the shades. But it was perfectly clear that their point of departure was not a transcendental understanding of the word.

[9] Cp. Asmus, *Die Zulu*, p. 83, who says that the gall of the two goats is mixed. Sibeko, 'Imilingo nemithi yokwelapha yaBantu', p. 245, says that the responsible shade announces itself through the ailing person.

[10] Krige, *SSZ*, p. 305.

[11] For costs involved in training and initiation towards becoming a diviner see van Niewenhuijesen, 'The Witchdoctor Institutions in a Zulu Tribe', p. 5.

[12] For a description of barring the responsible shade see Krige, *SSZ*, pp. 306 ff. and Asmus, *Die Zulu*, pp. 81 f.

Norenius gives the following methods of barring a responsible shade, the method verified by a number of informants: First, a diviner applies medicines on the body of the inflicted, particularly where the shades have caused pain. Other medicines are drunk, others nibbled at and chewed when the patient has dreamt of the shade. After nibbling at the medicines, the patient spits on a small stone or stick and throws it away backwards without looking at the stick or the stone.

Failing this, a sheep is slaughtered. Of its stomach and contents a medicine is prepared and the patient drinks of it until he/she vomits. What is brought up is mixed with the remaining parts of the sheep's stomach and contents and taken by a diviner to a cave or a natural shelter where no rain penetrates or moisture otherwise reaches. He buries it in the dry soil, carefully covering it all up with dry soil. Thereafter he turns away and leaves the place running, without looking back. The sheep stands for dumbness, quiet and peace. The dry soil stands for inability of growth, the patient resembling dry earth in which nothing grows.

Failing this second attempt, a third remains. The patient's body is scratched and scarified where pains are felt. Blood from these places is collected and mixed with medicines. The mixture is taken by a diviner to an ant-heap or poured into the mouth of a frog which later is thrown into the pool of a river. The mixture can also be put into tubers in which holes have been made and then buried in some remote spot, preferably a dry one. (Cp. Norenius, 'Något om zuluernas religiösa föreställningar och bruk', pp. 273 ff.)

Ukuhebeza is to scare away, as the troublesome *amadlozi*, Bryant, *Dict.*, p. 227 and *The Collector*, no. 11, p. 2.

[13] *The Collector*, no. 237, p. 30, says that *umzifisi* is "frequently worn by *abangoma* around the neck, also thrown into a river in time of drought in order to cause rain."

[14] Kohler, *The Izangoma Diviners*, pp. 17 ff.

[15] Mofolo, *Chaka, An Historical Romance*, pp. 25–29, describes Chaka's experience

with a snake at a pool. Note, however, that Chaka does not enter the pool but the snake emerges from it and puts spittle on him. A knowledgeable informant said that Chaka's not having entered the pool is the reason for his not having become a great diviner, my having read and translated the passage to him.

On concepts of water and animals believed to live in the water see also Scriba, 'Die Naturerscheinungen im glauben der Zulu', pp. 2–6.

[16] Lee, 'Social Influences in Zulu Dreaming', pp. 271–277, deals with similar dreams in terms of a psychological analysis and refers to the many links between the thought-patterns of water and birth, e.g. p. 272.

[17] Bryant, Dict., p. 770: Colenso, Zulu-English Dictionary, p. 664: Doke–Vilakazi, Dict., p. 862 and Döhne, Zulu-Kafir Dict., p. 374.

[18] See ingcuphe in Bryant, The Zulu People, p. 612, and Doke–Vilakazi, Dict., p. 129.

[19] Kohler, The Izangoma Diviners, no. 102, p. 22. On diviners entering pools Döhne says that "he must often dive deep into the water for the sake of trying whether he can see the bottom, or whether he may there catch sight of amahlozi or obtain some revelation from them". Döhne, A Zulu-Kafir Dict., pp. 83 f.

[20] See Lee, Once Dark Country, p. 60: Kohler, The Izangoma Diviners, pp. 22 ff. Döhne, A Zulu-Kafir Dict., p. 254, says that sometimes the novice falls "into a deep, death-like sleep for several days, from which no one may awaken him, as that state is the very ecstasy he must experience". Informants say that this does happen that the novice does fall into the kind of sleep although they suggest that it was more common previously. The sleep is not regarded as essential today. "It happens when the shades want it to happen."

[21] One diviner said that people can only enter into the earth through caves "if there are shade-snakes and pythons in the cave". He said that he knew of a few such caves but was emphatic that every cave is not one through which one could enter the earth as one could not enter the earth through any pool. "It must be the places of the shades." He argued that ant-heaps were inferior places of entrance although he by no means refuted them. He said that he knew of a great many ant-heaps which "had many and very big snakes. This is a good sign." There appears to be a definite link between the ants and shades.

[22] For a Xhosa parallel to Zulu ukavuma idlozi see de Jager & Gitywa, 'A Xhosa Umhlawayelelo Ceremony in the Ciskei', pp. 109 ff.

[23] See also Callaway, The Religious System of the Amazulu, pp. 265 f.

[24] Evidence shows quite clearly that not all who complete the period of training and undergo initiation practise regularly in divination. Some do it periodically, others cease completely after some time.

[25] Du Toit mentions a 14-year old boy who was sent from the urban setting of Kwa-Mashu, Durban, to a rural diviner for training and refers to at least two diviners in Kwa-Mashu who received initiates. See du Toit, 'The Isangoma', p. 58.

[26] The names of some of the medical treatments that a novice undergoes during the time of training are suggestive:

Izihlazi (Bryant, Dict., p. 245, and Doke–Vilakazi, Dict., p. 324) is a medicine beaten up into froth and then taken as an emetic. It is said to foster the ability of seeing clearly and in great detail as well as giving foresightedness. Cf. ukuhlaziya, meaning to analyse carefully, explain in great detail.

Izimphendulo (Bryant, Dict., p. 494, says that this medicine is used "for changing the sex of children in the womb". See also Doke–Vilakazi, Dict., p. 655) is taken to facilitate the change of character in the novice from the old nature of ubuntu (normal human being) to that of a diviner.

Iziqaluzo (Bryant, Dict., p. 531) is said to break down any resistance in the novice towards wholly committing himself/herself to the services of the shades. Cf. ukuqazula, meaning to crush grain coarsely.

Umvuma is taken in order to remind the novice of all the dreams experienced during the time of calling. Novices who have resisted the call of the shades are said to be particular in taking this medicine, especially if their health is not restored as was expected as any dream not confessed will not allow full and complete health. Forgetfulness is, on the whole, feared by diviners. They regard it as a sign of the shades forsaking them. With diviners ukuvuma amaphupho, confession of dreams, is an important aspect, which goes with restored health.

[27] Bryant, Dict., p. 37.

[28] Krige, *SSZ*, p. 306. *The Collector*, no. 705, p. 141. See also Bryant, A Series of Public Lectures, p. 271, who says that the strips are prepared on the day of initiation.

[29] Shooter, *The Kafirs of Natal,* p. 194, mentions a novice who dreamt of a leopard which was killed and carried home.

[30] Bryant, *Dict.,* p. 629.

[31] Returning with the snake around the neck is suggestive. A diviner at Ceza said: "The snake does not allow throttling." Anger, being an essential in man and which can be used both morally and immorally, is located in the throat and informants agree that the throat must be guarded. Hence it is a great insult and evidence of anger to take hold of people by the throat.

[32] Shooter, *The Kafirs of Natal,* p. 191, says that catching snakes is the normal. See also Norenius, 'Izanusi', p. 36. A diviner-informant of reputation said that even if a novice does catch another animal, as does happen sometimes, it is essential that he/she catches a snake if he/she is to have a necklace of snake vertebrae. Ndebele novices are also expected to catch snakes according to Woods, 'Extracts from Custom and History; Amandebele', p. 19.

[33] On Mpondo novices who catch *ityala* see Hunder, *Reaction to Conquest,* pp. 321 ff.

[34] Certainly a large number of popular diviners today do not justify this statement. The diviner at eThelezini said that far too many diviners drank beer and hence became fat. He tolerated a diviner who drank beer but not those, if they exist, who eat pork. "The shades would just simply kill that diviner, kill him just there where he is eating it. He will die like a dog, not even cared for by anybody."

Cf. Callaway, *The Religious System of the Amazulu,* p. 387, who says that one has no confidence in a fat diviner. Döhne, *Zulu-Kafir Dict.,* p. 253, says that the diviner must "adopt a very spare diet, the more abstentious the better".

[35] Asmus, *Die Zulu,* p. 79, says that diviners associate mutton with ignorance. See also Farrer, *Zululand and the Zulus,* p. 132, "a sheep is foolish and makes no noise".

[36] Cf. Tracey, 'What are Mashawi Spirits?' p. 41, who says that Shona "ancestral spirits show repugnance to salt".

[37] Before I had become sufficiently aware of this detail I once, in eagerness to get to know a novice, more-or-less forced her to shake hands with me. As soon as our hands met the novice screamed at the top of her voice, jumped into the air and fell helplessly to the ground where she remained in what appeared to be a state of unconsciousness. Nobody said or did anything. I was strongly reprimanded when I tried to do something. After a while a grass mat was thrown over her. For some time the novice lay perfectly still without a twitch or single visible movement. Gradually she started quivering when the tense silence which had fallen over the spectators who had surrounded her gave way to comments of hope. "No, she will come back!" The novice started crying bitterly under the mat and suddenly shouted out: "*Maye! Mgathinthwa inkathazo yomlungu!*" (Woe! I have been touched by a white's trouble!) and broke out into quite hysterical crying. Eventually she got up from the ground and, weeping most dramatically, made her way to her hut. The novice remained in the hut for the rest of the day, the event having taken place at about 1.00 p.m. Her tutor said: "Shaking hands kills a diviner. She nearly died. It is clear that she did not agree with this thing."

[38] Cf. Hunter, *Reaction to Conquest,* p. 323, who has made a similar observation among Mpondo.

[39] Should a crab enter a hut, its presence is taken as a serious omen. Crabs are spoken of as "*ababeki bebomvu*" (i.e. those who place in position red earth). The word *ibomvu* is associated with an infant, children smeared with red earth shortly after birth. See Braatvedt, *Roaming Zululand with a Native Commissioner,* p. 180. Informants deny that crabs are looked upon as shade revelations.

[40] Bryant, *Dict.,* p. 259, says that *ihlule* is a blood-clot or an imperfectly formed foetus. However, in Bryant, *The Zulu People,* p. 621, he definitely associates the term with the early stages of conception. See also Döhne, *Zulu-Kafir Dict.,* p. 141.

[41] Cf. Ludlow, *Zululand and Cetewayo,* p. 165, who says that red clay is used in the place of soap. Informants do not deny that clay can be used in this manner but generally associate it with extermination of lice and fleas in the head. They claim that practically any clay can be used for this purpose and not only red.

[42] This second method of judging the novice's ability very clearly reflects the suspicious rivalry which prevails among diviners. "Diviners can never work together nicely. They are always fighting each other."

[43] Cf. Callaway, *The Religious System of the Amazulu*, p. 260. Döhne, *Zulu-Kafir Dict.*, p. 253, says: "In this profession he must be decreased to a low condition in order to become acquainted with the *amahlozi*, i.e. spectres, under whose direction he is expected to act."

[44] Bryant, *Dict.*, p. 669: Colenso, *Zulu-Engl. Dict.*, p. 632 and Doke–Vilakazi, *Dict.*, p. 812.

[45] For a description of *ukuthwasiswa* see Krige, *SSZ*, pp. 307 ff. and Bryant, 'Zulu Cult of the Dead', p. 142. For comparative material from Mpondo see Hunter, *Reaction to Conquest*, pp. 312 ff. and from Swazi see Kuper, *An African Aristocracy*, pp. 164 f.

[46] Asmus, *Die Zulu*, pp. 91 f. Asmus has given a detailed description of a novice's return to his/her homestead and functions attended to at the return.

[47] Asmus, *Die Zulu*, p. 95.

[48] See Bryant, *Dict.*, p. 65 (*ukucaka*) and *The Collector*, No. 709, p. 114. Also novices in urban settings are smeared with white clay in their faces. Cf. du Toit, 'The Isangoma', p. 58 who adds that a novice carries a small drum as a sign of the calling to become a diviner. Drums are playing an increasingly important role among Zulu diviners on the whole.

[49] Ethnographic records and information gathered suggests that formerly the novice carried a spear. However, due largely to legislation, the spear has been substituted with a knife today.

[50] Cf. Asmus, *Die Zulu*, p. 93.

[51] Bryant, *Dict.*, p. 331, says that the giving of these gifts is called *ukukunga*. See also *The Collector*, No. 249, p. 32.

[52] This shrill, pitched cry is called *ukulilizela* or *ukukikizela*. It is particular to births, marriages, funerals and the coming out of diviners. Among Christians it is also heard when parents return from church after baptism and after confirmation services. See Bryant, *Dict.*, p. 305 and 356: Doke–Vilakazi, *Dict.*, p. 457.

[53] Asmus, *Die Zulu*, p. 94, says that although the activities take place at the novice home the host of the activities is, in fact, the tutor diviner, "der Kraalherr ihr gast ist". But it is the senior of the homestead who supplies the beer and meat and who sends out the invitations to diviners and novices.

[54] Norenius, 'Izanusi', p. 39. Norenius has given a penetrating and clear description of the call of a diviner as well as an account of the various kinds of diviners. He says that *igama lokwethwasa* is inspired by the responsible shade. On a Swasi parallel to the song see Kuper, *An African Aristocracy*, p. 164.

[55] Hammond-Tooke, 'The Initiation of a Bhaca Isangoma Diviner', pp. 16 ff., gives interesting parallels to a Zulu diviner's initiation. Note that *ityala* which plays an important role among Mpondo (Hunter, *Reaction to Conquest*, pp. 321 ff.) is apparently not found among Bhaca, while, among Zulu, it is substituted with the catching of snake/s or a wild animal.

Note, further, the role played by dreams, the colour white, white beads and the relationship between these and the shades, the presence of other diviners and novices and their associations with the left side of the hut (p. 19) and the role of the tutor diviner.

[56] According to Asmus, *Die Zulu*, p. 86, the skins to be used as *iminqwamba* ought to be from a white goat and importance is attached to the crossing of the skins on the chest and the back of the diviner. Asmus does, however, not offer any reason for the crossing of the skins. Experience shows that Asmus is correct in stating that the skins ought to be white. But there are many diviners who have skins of other colours because white goats have been unobtainable, or, if obtainable, expensive. See also Schimlek, *Mariannhill*, p. 272, who associates the second *iminqwamba* skin with the initiation and speaks of the slaughtering of fowls.

[57] See Bryant, *The Zulu People*, p. 460, who refers to the fact that also twins wear *iminqwamba* skins.

[58] Discussing the novice entry into a river pool, a python found in the pool, the collection of white earth from under the python, Lee, 'Social Influences in Zulu Dreaming', p. 266, says that the diviner "will then emerge from the water as a new person", the encounter (expressed in Lee's description as a dream) as "obviously one of symbolic re-birth, using symbols found in many parts of the world".

Cf. Berglund, 'African Concepts of Health, Sickness and Healing', pp. 46 f.

[59] Bryant, 'The Zulu Cult of the Dead', p. 145.

[60] Grout, *Zululand,* pp. 138 f says that diviners assist people in making a choice.

[61] Asmus, *Die Zulu,* pp. 93 and 98.

[62] Cf. Laduma Madela's homestead as illustrated in Bodenstein and Raum, 'A Present Day Zulu Philosopher', p. 166.

[63] The ventriloquist said that the screen is called *umgongo* (see also Bryant, *Dict.,* p. 259 and Doke–Vilakazi, *Dict.,* p. 258). He claimed that diviners of standing had similar screens behind which they sat when "they were thinking very deeply" and "when we pray". Retirement to *umsamo* behind the screen he referred to as *ukubuyela ohlangeni* (lit. retirement to the reeds, i.e. to the origin).

[64] Bartels, 'Die Würfelzauber Südafrikanischen Völker', p. 338, has given a description of Zulu divination bones. See also Coertze, *Dolosgooiery in Suid-Afrika,* pp. 15–17. Although Zulu sets contain a large number of other objects which are not bones the term bone is used as a translation of the Zulu *amathambo.* Evidence shows that a large number of popular diviners are *ezamathambo* and that these are increasing in numbers. Cf. Kuper, *The Swazi,* p. 65, who says, describing Swazi diviners: "An increasing number of modern diviners throw bones, a technique associated with Sotho and Tonga influence."

Zulu say that bone divination is an importation from Sotho. Dornan believes that all Bantu originally acquired it from the Bushmen (Dornan, 'Divination and Divining Bones'). It is interesting to note in this context that Ndebele *Izanusi ze 'Nkosi* who were "of Abanguni descent", ... threw no bones. (H.M.G.J., 'Odds and Ends of Matabele Customs and Customary Law', p. 10.)

Zulu also claim that divining sticks, *umabukula,* also known as *izimphengu,* have been introduced recently. (Cf. *The Collector,* No. 242, p. 31.)

It is clear that Zulu diviners, and particularly popular ones, take impressions of other diviners. A woman, returning to her home from Johannesburg brought along four *Hakata* of types used in northern Transvaal and described by Coertze, (*Dolosgooiery in Suid-Afrika*) and extensively by von Sicard, 'The Hakata Names', and used these extensively in her divination. She was, however, not very highly held by the local people.

See also Callaway, *The Religious System of the Amazulu,* pp. 332 ff.

Sotho divination sets which apparently have influenced Zulu thought-patterns are described by Watt and Warmelo, 'The Medicines and Practice of a Sotho Doctor', pp. 48 ff.: Dornan, 'Divination and Divining Bones', pp. 504 ff.: Eiselen, 'The Art of Divination as practiced by the Bamasemola', pp. 1 ff. and 251 ff.: Laydevant, 'The Praises of the Divining Bones among the Basotho', pp. 431 ff.

Pedi sets are described by Watt, 'The Native Medicine Man',: Roberts, 'A Few Notes on To Kolo', p. 367.

Tsonga, who by Zulu are recognised as reliable diviners, are described by Junod, *The Life of a South African Tribe,* Vol. II, pp. 495 ff.: Junod, 'The Magic Conception of Nature amongst Bantu', dealing also with Zulu divination sets, pp. 81 ff.

[65] See illustration in Scriba, 'Hexenwesen bei den Zulu', p. 11. Note that the diviners illustrated carry drums.

[66] Zulu diviners often use a complicated *ukuhlonipha* language which sometimes makes following their arguments a difficult undertaking. This particular interview was exceptionally difficult, due to the diviner being irritated on the day it took place.

[67] Isaacs, *Travels in Eastern Africa,* Vol. II, p. 166, describes a diviner whose one eyelid was coloured red, the other black and the nose black. Informants say that a diviner does not paint his body today. But they do not hold it as unreasonable that it was done formerly.

[68] Asmus, *Die Zulu,* p. 97.

[69] For spears as a part of diviners' equipment see Asmus, *Die Zulu,* p. 98: Norenius, 'Izanusi', pp. 37 f.: Shooter, *The Kafirs of Natal,* p. 179.

Note that Callaway, *The Religious System of the Amazulu,* p. 219, says diviners dig up medicines under prayer. Diviners say that they do this commonly.

[70] Asmus, *Die Zulu,* pp. 90 f. mentions the necklace.

[71] Hunter, *Reaction to Conquest,* pp. 321 ff.

[72] Asmus, *Die Zulu,* illustrations opposite pp. 113 and 240.

[73] Bryant, 'A Series of Public Lectures', p. 272. See also Barter, *A Year's Housekeeping in South Africa,* p. 177, who describes a diviner wearing "a beautifully dried and

flattened skin of an enormous boa-constrictor", the head of which was fastened to the diviner's neck, "its tail some two feet or so on the ground behind her".

[74] Bryant, *The Zulu People,* p. 360: Shooter, *The Kafirs of Natal,* p. 176.

[75] Mohr, *To Victoria Falls of the Zambezi,* p. 36, writing in 1876, and probably speaking of the area around uMhlali river, says that pythons are "quite domesticated and are allowed to lie undisturbed in the hollows of the fields. They serve the same purpose as our household cats."

[76] Bryant, *Dict.,* p. 635 (*intlatu*).

[77] It is quite clear that there was a certain amount of tension between Madela and other diviners in the district. The latter claimed that Madela was a heaven-herd and should attend to his business and not interfere in theirs.

[78] Bryant, *Dict.,* p. 579: Doke–Vilakazi, *Dict.,* p. 743.

[79] Shooter, *The Kafirs of Natal,* p. 177: Stuart and Malcolm, *Diary of H. F. Fynn,* p. 70.

[80] Asmus, *Die Zulu,* p. 97: Krige, SSZ, p. 307: Samuelson, *Zululand, its Trad. etc.,* p. 155.

[81] Birkby, *Native Life in South Africa,* p. 49.

[82] Barker, *A Year's Housekeeping in South Africa,* p. 177.

[83] Duggin–Cronin, *The Bantu Tribes of South Africa,* Vol. III, Section III, plate CIX.

[84] Bryant, *Dict.,* p. 464: Doke–Vilakazi, *Dict.,* p. 620.

[85] Norenius, *Izita Zohlanga,* pp. 10 ff., writing from a very conscious Christian point of view has given a clear picture of the role the diviner plays in Zulu society.

[86] Bryant, *Dict.,* p. 9: Doke–Vilakazi, *Dict.,* p. 12.

[87] Bryant, *Dict.,* p. 456: Doke–Vilakazi, *Dict.,* p. 610. Cp. Colenso, *Zulu-Engl. Dict.,* p. 424.

[88] See also Samuelson, *Zululand, its Traditions,* etc., p. 58, who says: "A death diviner has to take with him ten small knuckle or ankle-bones of various kinds of animals."

[89] For details on *ukujoja* see Bryant, *Dict.,* p. 280: Matthews, *Incwadi Yami,* pp. 49 f. A Zulu medical practitioner who had performed a post-mortem on a person who had been empaled said that there were three distinct ways of doing this: i. Impalement with a stick of considerable length which may reach to the lungs. ii. with several sticks that are driven into the abdomen at various angles and iii. with a branched stick which would split when entering the body.

[90] Bryant, *Dict.,* p. 424: Colenso, *Zulu-Engl. Dict.,* p. 390: Doke–Vilakazi, *Dict.,* p. 556.

[91] Bryant, *Dict.,* p. 8: Doke–Vilakazi, *Dict.,* p. 11.

[92] Burgess, *Unkulunkulu in Zululand,* p. 32, speaks of "rubbing incense over the back of the beast as it stands in the cattle-kraal and at the same time calling upon the spirits of the ancestors to be present".

[93] Cf. Bryant, *Dict.,* p. 8, who mentions the beating of a skin during seance. See also Bryant, *Zulu Medicine and Medicine-men,* pp. 13 f.

[94] Reading Callaway, *The Religious System of the Amazulu,* pp. 259 ff., one is given the impression that these diviners were common in the 19th century.

Mbatha, 'Witchcraft and Ancestor Worship', p. 18, says that this particular kind of diviner had three reeds.

On sticks used in divination see further Bryant, *Dict.,* p. 494 (*impengu*): Doke–Vilakazi, *Dict.,* p. 656 (*phengu*): Bryant, *Dict.,* p. 636 (*inthola*): Doke–Vilakazi, *Dict.,* p. 332 (*hlola*): *The Collector,* No. 242, p. 31.

An informant at Ekuthuleni said that there were eight sticks of about 30 cm in length, one of which, named *inkosi,* was about 5 cm longer than the others and which actually did the pointing, the other seven merely "accompanying their king".

[95] Callaway, *The Religious System of the Amazulu,* p. 280. See also Norenius, 'Izanusi', p. 35, who gives the same associations to the word.

[96] Du Toit, 'Some Aspects of Soul-Concept among the Bantu-Speaking Nguni-Tribes of South Africa', p. 141.

[97] Van Nieuwenhuijsen, 'The Witchdoctor Institution in a Zulu Tribe', p. 4. For further medical studies on Zulu diviners see Lee, 'Spirit Possession Among the Zulu', and his references.

[98] Van Nieuwenhuijsen, 'The Witchdoctor Institution in a Zulu Tribe', p. 5. Barker, *A Year's Housekeeping in South Africa,* pp. 172 f., writing in 1879, made similar obser-

vations. She says that the female diviners raised "their hand as the men do with the low cry of 'Inkosi' in salutation. Their pride is to be looked upon as men when once they take up this dread profession, which is sometimes shared with them by men. They are permitted to bear shield and spear as warriors, and they hunt and kill with their own hands the wild beasts and reptiles whose skins they wear."

[99] Bryant claimed when writing in 1917 that fully 90% of diviners were women. See Bryant, 'The Zulu Cult of the Dead', p. 142. Krauss, 'The Zulu', p. 219, writing in 1839/40 states diviners were "usually women".

[100] Cf. Natal Code of Native Law, Gov. Gazette, 1951.

Chapter VI

Communion with the Shades

Introduction

Zulu society is a community of the survivors and the shades. There is no existence of the survivors separated from that of the shades, nor a realm of the shades separate from the living. The two are closely and very intimately tied together in kinship bonds which make the individuals and shades of a lineage interdependent on each other. A man at Ekuthuleni said: "A man cannot live without shades, wife and children. If one of these is not (i.e. excluded from the community), then the man surely dies."

We have seen how shades are limited in their activities to their lineage in a given clan. It is within this clan lineage that they exercise pressure towards ritual killings when they are hungry, that they actively partake in conception, and from which they call diviners. The shades frequent their own kindred and make known their desires from time to time by various overt signs, the interpretation of which lies with the survivors. The survivors are very conscious of the shades' active participation in the everyday life of the homestead and activities, and, because the shades are seniors, readily conform to their requirements.

In a previous chapter we have seen how the shades manifest themselves to their survivors. It must be underlined, however, that it is well nigh impossible to draw up a dogmatic list of shade manifestations. These vary considerably, geographically, in time, and between clans. Common manifestations are those which express themselves in sickness, a string of physical ailments are mentioned, or delay in conception. The survivor often finds himself in a puzzling situation in which he requires expert assistance—in problems of choice the diviner plays a major role. The shades reveal themselves in a man's ability, or inability, to obtain work, in poor harvests, lost court-cases and also in salvation from many evils; they manifest themselves in the joys of a plenteous harvest, a large family and general prosperity.

Everyday communication with the shades is maintained: they reveal themselves to their survivors in dreams, visions, and a large number of omens which, according to their choice, are symbols of their presence. We have seen how a lack of dreams can cause grave anxiety, this lack being regarded as an absence of communication between the shades and oneself. From the angle of the survivors, communication is upheld by their leaving the unwashed pots in the vicinity of the hearth overnight, placing beer and tit-bits in *umsamo* of the hut for the shades, and by being conscious of their presence and nearness. A woman said: "They are in me. When they are in me, I know that they are there. I feel them. They are happy with me and I am happy with them. I think of them always. They know that I am thinking of them." In winter communication is underlined by there constantly being a fire on the hearth even throughout the night. I recall a visit at a homestead in July 1969. It was raining and the air was cold. Creeping up to the fire in a hut I said something about the comfort which a fire brought. An old lady whom I often had consulted on Zulu thought-patterns immediately remarked: "That is true. Even they (the shades) are warming themselves in this cold." To her the comfort of the shades was as necessary as that of the homestead inhabitants and the visitor.

There is in Zulu society no worship of the shades, if by worship we understand a veneration of them. *Ukukhonza*, popularly translated with the English idiom *worship*, and used in a transcendental sense, is used in relation to the Lord-of-the-Sky. "We do not worship (*khonza*) the shades. We simply speak to them (*ukuthetha*), telling them everything." Another informant said that if the term *ukukhonza* is used in connection with the shades, "then we do not look upwards as one does when one worships the Lord-of-the-Sky". Old people say that the correct term that was used traditionally was not *ukukhonza* but *ukuthetha*. "It is only now that people say *ukukhonza* for everything that is done, even the work of the shades. But we who know this thing of shades, we do not say *ukukhonza*. We say *ukuthetha*."[1]

There is, on the other hand, a fairly complex ritual of communion with them in which the shades and the survivors commune with each other in the widest and most intimate sense of the word. The aim of this chapter is to describe and analyse these rituals of communion, the most far-reaching of them being the ritual slaughter. The communion is a sharing of the slaughtered beast and a renewal of kinship bonds with each other which implies mutual concern for each other. This ritual of communion is at times one of appeasement, at other times one of gratitude, at others, again, of commitment.

The idea of a constant dread inspired by the shades is not true of Zulu thought-patterns today. Perhaps dread was formerly a strong force which acted upon survivors, exerting pressure on them to blind obedience and to kill ritually. But Zulu today accept the shades as their close relatives, the ones with whom one lives intimately together in the sharing of all things, both good and bad. Theirs is the fatherly care of their children, the survivors. There is, in other words, an intimacy and a relationship of mutual understanding and interdependence. Certainly *ukuthetha idlozi* linguistically gives one the impression of an aggressive kind of relationship between survivors and shades. Yet in practice this is not so. Firstly, the idiom *ukuthetha idlozi* is old and hence possibly coloured by former thought-patterns of dread and fear rather than those of intimacy. Secondly, the English translation of *ukuthetha* in the intransitive meaning of the word, i.e. to scold, to find fault with noisily, nag,[2] has, possibly, influenced the transitive which implies giving judgement in favour of, not finding guilty, letting off, offering of praises. Asked whether it is possible to scold a shade, *ukuthethisa idlozi*, Zulu have been most emphatic that this cannot be done. "Who are we to scold our seniors (*abadala bethu*)?" But they readily agree that *ukuthetha idlozi* is a correct expression and implies something quite different from *ukuthethisa idlozi*.

Ihubo, the Clan Song

An outstanding symbol of unity and communion with the shades is the clan song, *ihubo*. While *ingoma*[3] is associated with the national events, particularly with the now obsolete festival of the first fruits,[4] *ihubo* is sung only on occasions related to happenings within a clan or lineage. On discussing the relationship between *ihubo* and the clan with informants and telling them that dictionaries say that *ihubo* is also associated with the various Zulu regiments, a large number agreed that this was done and apparently introduced by Shaka. They are emphatic, however, that *ihubo*, in the strict sense of the word, is the song of the clan only. "It was the king that called the regimental songs *amahubo*. He did it in order to strengthen the regiments. There is nothing like singing. It binds together. So he gave each regiment its song, calling it *ihubo*. But the true *ihubo* is the song of the clan."[5]

Bryant rightly describes *ihubo* as "sacred in character".[6] Zulu are emphatic that when *ihubo* is sung, the shades are in a very real and intimate manner present. "When we sing it (the *ihubo*) we are all present. Even they (the shades) are present, hearing the song." The song also strongly underlines the sense of unity not only with the shades but also among the survivors. "When we sing *ihubo* everybody should be there. If there is somebody absent, not being there, then somebody of the clan should represent him (*ukumela*), singing in his place. But that person must be somebody of the clan. Nobody but people of the clan can sing *ihubo* of that clan."

While the large majority of Zulu songs are accompanied by dancing, *ihubo* is sung standing perfectly still. Shields are raised by men as a symbol of peace. "When we raise the shields we are saying, 'There is nothing between us.' That is why we raise the shields, telling the shades that there is nothing." Everybody is expected to be dressed in festive attire. Informants underline that the correct place for singing *ihubo* is the cattle-enclosure "because in that place the shades are very near. Further, everybody can come into that place, it being large." Evidence shows, however, that *ihubo* can be sung elsewhere as is indeed done when the bridal party arrives at the bridegroom's homestead. But when conditions allow it, preference is given to the homestead byre. Lineage members by birth sing *ihubo* as do also senior wives married into the clan. Junior wives who still give birth generally do not participate in the singing. But they are expected to attend and show due reverence by sitting quietly next to the fencing of the cattle-enclosure.

It is evident that *ihubo* is sung only on very solemn occasions within a clan.[7] At all times it must be held in the greatest respect. Children are not allowed to sing *ihubo* while playing for fear of possible misuse.[8]

Cattle

Communion with the shades is maintained also through the medium of cattle.[9] In some homesteads there is *inkomo yamadlozi* (the beast of the shades) while in traditional marriage in which old customs are upheld and honoured, *ukwendisa* animals play a significant role. In former national rituals *izinkomo zemzimo* were of importance.[10]

Inkomo yamadlozi

Describing Zulu in the mid-nineteenth century, Shooter says that "the largest ox in a herd is especially reserved for sacrifice in case of extreme necessity; it is called the Ox of the Spirits, and is never sold except in case of need".[11] Evidence shows that also modern Zulu who keep cattle may have a beast in the herd set aside as one specifically associated with the shades. It is known as *inkomo yamadlozi* or simply *eyamadlozi*. Not every homestead will, however, of necessity have such a beast.

Although Shooter claims that the beast is an ox, many informants state that the animal should not be a male beast. Asked whether a bull could not be *inkomo yamadlozi,* a limited number of people have been doubtful. But nearly all have reacted against its being an ox. "An ox is for work. This animal *(inkomo yamadlozi)* must not work, being set aside for the shades. That is why it cannot be an ox." Other people have said that they could hardly visualize *inkomo yamadlozi* without its being a cow, preferably one that has calfed at least once and thereby proven its ability of multiplying. Fertility is sometimes significant with *inkomo yamadlozi*. [12]

Informants do not emphasise that the animal should be a large beast. But it ought to be beautiful "so that the shades like it and feel happy". Characteristics of beauty in the animal are fairly long and evenly grown horns, even colouring although not of any specific colour, fatness and docility. No nervous or uncontrollable beast can be considered as *inkomo yamadlozi*. Herdboys are instructed not to beat it, mainly in order to avoid scars and other marks on the skin of the beast. While the brush of some animals may be cut or trimmed, the tail of *inkomo yamadlozi* is not attended to unless one requires hairs from the brush. Milk from *inkomo yamadlozi* is mixed with that of other cows in a homestead but if a calf of *inkomo yamadlozi* becomes one of *ukwendisa* animals and thus accompanies a bride to her bridegroom's homestead, it will be milked in a separate vessel and the milk used by the bride.

When *inkomo yamadlozi* dies, sometimes of old age, often of sickness, it is replaced by one of its calves.[13] The chosen animal merits by its outer appearance and character. I discussed the question of replacement with G of Ceza.

B: "How is the replacing done?"

"When it has done its work (i.e. when it has died), the matter is reported to them (the shades). It is said, 'It is thus, ye of our clan. Your thing is no more. Its dying is known to you. You yourselves saw its sickness and age. So the thing is known to you, what was taking place with this animal of yours. This thing has now happened. It took place in this very cattle-enclosure in which I am reporting.' Then he waits some time, looking (at the calves of the dead cow). Sometimes he dreams. Then it becomes clear which one they want. Sometimes dreaming does not come. So he remains looking at them. Then he sees one. He reports again. He reports in the very same place again, saying, 'Now, ye of our clan! Just look nicely at this young animal *(ithole)*, being the calf of its mother. Just look at its horns and the colouring. To me it seems the best one, even being quiet. Also its udder, it appears to be a plenteous one. So according to my opinion, your beast should be this one, the very one I have been looking at from the time of its mother's illness. That is all I can say. Do not cause trouble now, seeing that I am speaking nicely to you!' If there is a dream, then he knows that they have accepted it. If there is trouble, then they show him which one they require."

B: "Where is the reporting done?"

"Just here in the cattle-enclosure, as I said."

B: "In which place?"

"At this very place we are standing now. (We were standing at the upper end of the byre, opposite the gate.) I stand here, facing that direction (the centre of the enclosure)."

B: "Is there a special time when you report?"

"Sometimes I rise very early with the roosters (i.e. cock-crow) and make the report. Sometimes I can just sit here when the milking is over. Then, when everything is quiet, I can report."

B: "The beast?"

"It stands in its place, the place which it has chosen for itself in the byre."

B: "How do you indicate it?"

"Sometimes I point it out to them (the shades). Sometimes it can be described in the reporting. Sometimes I just rub it nicely, showing its softness (*ukuthamba*)."

B: "Where do you rub it?"

"On the back."

B: "Why do you choose the back?"

"That is the place of rubbing the animal of the shades. It is that place, the back. Just above the shoulders along the spine."

B: "With the hand?"

"With the hand and *imphepho*."

B: "Why do you rub it with *imphepho*? Is not this the medicine of diviners?"

"It is the medicine of diviners, indeed. You know it. But that is the thing for rubbing the animal of the shades."

B: "Do you prepare *imphepho* yourself?"

"It is prepared by the man of *imphepho* (i.e. a diviner). He knows its preparation. I tell him that I have certain work with a certain beast. Then he knows the work that I wish to do with *imphepho*. Then he prepares it in the way of its preparation and gives it to me, telling me its use."

B: "When a diviner gives you *imphepho*, do you use it immediately or do you put some of it away for some time?"

"It is used when the beast has become clear (i.e. when it is clear which beast is to be *inkomo yamadlozi*). Then I take it and use it."

B: "Where do you keep it in the meantime?"

"In the place of the shades."

B: "Where is that place?"

"In *umsamo* of the hut."

B: "Can this beast be slaughtered?"

"No! (Very loud objection.) Who can slaughter this beast? No, they (the shades) being the owners must say if it must be slaughtered. No man can slaughter an animal which is not his."

B: "But do not all the beasts of the herd belong to them (the shades) as well as to the inhabitants of the homestead, the father and the sons?"

"That is so. Nobody can point at the beasts and say, 'These are mine' as if he owned them of himself. They are the possession of *umnumzana* (homestead senior) together with his children and the fathers. But there are those beasts which have a special duty (*umsebenzi othile*) in the herd. Then the animal is set aside for that work. Like this animal. It has its work, being the animal of the shades. Again, there is the beast of the wiping away of the mother's tears when the daughter goes away in marriage. It has its work. These animals cannot be slaughtered without the agreement of the owner. So this *inkomo yamadlozi* cannot be slaughtered."

B: "How do they tell people that they want it?"

"They have their ways. Sometimes by dreaming. Sometimes by sickness. Sometimes by a diviner. Sometimes by another way. They have their ways. They are many."

B: "Have you personally slaughtered such a beast?"

"I for one have not done this thing. No, forsooth, that must be a fearful work, slaughtering for others."

B: "Do you know of others who have done it?"

"Perhaps there are some that have done it. They will know. I have not done it."

In only one single instance did people have knowledge of the slaughtering of *inkomo yamadlozi*. A diviner said she knew of a fellow diviner who had dreamt on several occasions of *inkomo yamadlozi* in her father's herd and that the repetition of the dream was interpreted as an indication from the shades that the beast should be slaughtered. It was subsequently slaughtered on behalf of the diviner who wore the gall-bladder. Two informants who said that they knew of the case claimed that it was wrong to slaughter the beast, even if it was a diviner who had indicated the need for killing it, and that the frequent cases of serious illness in the family after the slaughter were caused by upset shades. "No, the dreaming was nothing. Maybe she (the diviner) did dream of the cow. That may be true. We do not know. But we see her divination. What is she worth? Just playing all the time." The diviner who first related the incident felt that it was correct that the beast had been slaughtered. "When a diviner dreams, the things revealed must be done. Who can speak against the fathers?" She attributed the sickness in the homestead to a wrong distribution of the animal's flesh, maintaining that the flesh of *inkomo yamadlozi* should be eaten by clan members only and not, as happened, also by friends and a large number of visitors. This had offended the shades and hence the sickness.

Similarly, *inkomo yamadlozi* ought not to be sold. "The beast of shades cannot be sold by us. If it should be sold, then they (the shades) must tell us. But we have not heard of their using money." Informants agree that if the beast should be sold, disease would break out in the herd. A convert at Eku-thuleni claimed that on his becoming a Christian and adjusting his ways of life accordingly, he had done away with *inkomo yamadlozi* by giving it to a junior brother in exchange for another beast. The latter did not have *inkomo yamadlozi* in his herd. Christians avoided discussing the issue while pagans accepted the transfer as acceptable.

In selecting a beast as *inkomo yamadlozi*, preference is given animals of old clan stock. There is no hard and fast rule for the choice, differences of opinion on the issue prevailing among different clans. In the royal clan one was quite specific that the animal ought to be of old clan stock. "These are the beasts that they (the shades) know. That is why we choose from them." But an informant of the Nzuza clan, living in the same area as the man quoted above, said that it did not matter from what stock a beast came as long as it was beautiful. He personally had bought an animal from a friend and set it aside as *inkomo yamadlozi* after the purchase, his choice of this particular animal based merely on its outer appearance.[14]

When emphasis is put on old clan stock, a father may give his sons a calf each born by *inkomo yamadlozi* in their homestead of birth. Two occasions on record show that a father gave his sons heifers, indicating that it is not essential that *inkomo yamadlozi* should have calved prior to being set aside.

When emphasis lies with appearance rather than old clan stock and purchasing of suitable animals is practised, preference is still with animals in herds belonging to fellow clansmen. But purchase outside the clan is not unknown.

Popular views are that calves of *inkomo yamadlozi* may be sold or slaughtered. "They are not *inkomo yamadlozi*. Just simply calves of this cow. So they can be sold if a man needs money. They are like his property. When a man has cattle with friends for a long time, the calves of the cows born during the time are the property of the man who looks after them. That is why they can be sold or even slaughtered." But an informant at eNthembeni royal homestead said that the selling of these animals is to be looked upon as unfortunate. "It is true that there are those who sell them. But it should not be done. It is not showing the shades honour when their calves are sold."

No homestead is known to have more than one *inkomo yamadlozi* at the same time, although a number of friends did not rule out the theoretical possibility of there being more than one single beast. By no means all homesteads have this particular animal, but conservative male diviners had one. "They (the shades) have indicated to me that they want one. That is why there is this beast in the byre." All informants objected to the idea of substituting *inkomo yamadlozi* with either another beast or another animal, e.g. a goat. "Such a thing is not possible. There is no such thing. It must be a beast. I have never heard of such things as goats of the shades! That would be an amazing thing! A goat of the shades! No! There is no such thing."[15]

Inkomo yamadlozi mixes freely with other cattle of the homestead herd and is covered by the homestead bull. Should a man decide on hiring out some of his animals in neighbouring homesteads, *inkomo yamadlozi* is under no condition to leave the homestead. "It belongs to that home. It must not go away."[16] It is dipped together with other animals and does not appear to receive any special attention other than not being beaten or having its tailhairs cut or trimmed. The death of a homestead senior or any other family member does not seem to affect *inkomo yamadlozi*.

Inkomo yamadlozi is intimately associated with the shades. It stands for the presence of them in a personified manner in a particular homestead. "It is their (the shades') animal. When he (the senior) reports to them saying that this is their animal, he is giving it to them. So it is their animal." There is no evidence to suggest that the beast is related to the shades other than as possession. Informants object very strongly against any idea of the shades either living in the animal or otherwise being identified with it. "Shades do not live in animals as they live in men. Shades and men go together. But shades do not go together with animals. They simply own the animals as men do."

The beast is looked upon as belonging to all the shades of the lineage, particularly the shades remembered and known by survivors. "We do not say that this animal is the beast of So-and-so, leaving the others with nothing. It is the animal of them all. They all look at it. That is what we say." Some Zulu have suggested that because *inkomo yamadlozi* is common possession of the shades, it cannot be slaughtered as sickness, etc. is traced to a single responsible shade. "So that one shade cannot eat the thing which belongs to all. That is why we kill one beast when a man is sick with the sickness of the shades, leaving this cow alone."

B: "But are not all the shades called upon at the killing of a cow?"

"They are all called upon. That is so. But there is the one shade indicated by the diviner. That is the shade causing the trouble in bringing sickness. So the killing is caused by that shade, the one indicated (by the diviner)."

B: "You mean that one shade is responsible. But they all eat?"

"Yes, it is so. They all eat but there is one only which called for the beast. It is the same with us (the survivors). There is the one that is sick with the sickness (of the shades). But we all eat of the beast. Even the neighbours eat, there being many at the meat."

Evidence shows, however, that certain relationships are upheld with the shades through *inkomo yamadlozi*. "When the cow becomes ill, not being old, it is said, 'What is this thing?' the men giving it medicines and treating it nicely. Sometimes the man (the senior) will see something (in a dream). Then he knows the reason (for its being ill). When it becomes very ill and there may be other things in addition (to the illness of the cow), the diviner may be consulted. Or he may say, after divination, speaking to the people about the sickness of the cow, 'It is anger that is causing the sickness.' Then it is known that there is somebody causing anger among the shades. They are disturbed. That is why the cow is sick, because they are disturbed."

Peculiar and unexpected actions by the beast may be signs from the shades. An elderly woman, her husband's second wife, said: "This cow speaks. It is like this, I can tell you, having watched closely. Once, this very cow that we are talking about, stood near the hut of the eldest daughter. It just stood, refusing to go this way or that way, just merely standing next to the hut. Not even the senior could drive it away when the herdboys failed. We were very much troubled by *inkomo yamadlozi* just standing there and doing nothing. So it was said, 'What is this? The cow is just standing there next to the hut of So-and-so?' Everybody was asking that question. Then, after everybody had asked, it left the hut, walking to the byre. It entered. It stood in its place. Forsooth, the very next morning the daughter of my husband, I am indicating So-and-so, this very daughter became seriously ill. The diviner came. He divined. He saw the sickness. It was the sickness of the shades. That is how she became a diviner. The cow was the first indicator of her call. It said that there was something going to happen. Indeed, the thing took place that very night."

If there is doubt as to which animal is to be slaughtered in a ritual celebration, the animals are all driven into the cattle-enclosure. The beast that passes through the gateway nearest *inkomo yamadlozi* is regarded as the shades' indication of what animal they choose. Some friends have suggested that offspring from *inkomo yamadlozi* are exceptionally suitable animals for ritual killings.

When one wishes to communicate with the shades, one does so in the byre "just near this very cow". N described an occasion of such communion with the shades. "I had been much troubled by dreams. They even led to sickness. But I had nothing, so I could not inquire. If I had had some money, I would have gone to the diviner at X who divines well. But there was nothing (in the purse). Simply poverty. So I remained, doing nothing. Then I went to the cattle-enclosure and sat down. I sat down, just sitting there and waiting.

Then I stood up and went to the cow of the shades. I walked to the place where it was standing. It was standing next to the red cow, there on the left side. I came to it. I rubbed it with ash. I rubbed just nicely with ash.[17] It licked the ash in my hand. I was very happy. When I was rubbing up-and-down I put my hands on the back of it. It stood still, doing nothing. Then I spoke some words. It was the words that I had planned when I was sitting there in the cattle-enclosure before going to the cow. I said, speaking in a pleasant voice, speaking to the shades, I said, 'Oh, ye fathers of my father! What is this thing troubling me? First dreams every night without an interpretation. Then sickness. Yes, even yesterday I was vomiting the whole day without ceasing! Everything came out. Everything, even the gall! That was yesterday. Then today, it is the head. The pains fill the head everywhere. Besides these things there is poverty in this home of yours. I am saying poverty, poverty in this home of Ns. There is not even something for divination that I may know the reason for these things in our midst. That is the reason for my standing at this place, fathers of my father! So I am saying, do not become angry, saying, 'What has the child brought, when approaching us in this manner? We do not see anything (that he has brought).' I have brought nothing but this animal which I have brought before, some time ago, and bringing it, knowing that there would be a gateway to you, Ye of N! That is the reason for my standing here. So do not become angry, asking for something. I am here, speaking nicely, so that I may know (the reason for the illness).' Then I spoke about the poor fields because there had been no tilling due to the sickness (my informant had been ill during the planting season). I begged pardon again for coming empty-handed and bade farewell. All the time I stood there beside the cow, speaking nicely all the time. It also just stood quietly, doing nothing. When I completed the speaking, it still stood in the same place. I knew that they had heard my words in that the cow had stood still all the time, doing nothing, just remaining quiet." N claimed that this ritual of communion had taken place in the late evening when the rest of the homestead people had retired. The following morning he had awoken, considerably better. He attributed his subsequent restful sleep and restored health to the encounter with the shades in the close vicinity of *inkomo yamadlozi*.

Some people say that family events are reported to the beast. A woman related how, when she had received a letter from her husband in Durban with welcome financial assistance for their children's schooling, she had shared her joy and relief with her mother-in-law, a conservative traditionalist, also living in the homestead. The elder woman had, that evening after the cows had been milked, gone into the byre and reported the news to *inkomo yamadlozi*. "We report these things to them so that they may be happy with us. Then they are happy." Evidence indicates that minor matters are announced to the beast as well as major. "When a man has become well again from sickness, it is reported. Health is a great thing. It must be reported so that it (the cow) knows the things of the homestead."[18]

N said that he rubbed the animal's back with ash. Evidence shows that his action was representative. I discussed the issue of ash with him.

"The ash comes from the hearth in my hut. That is where I take it. It must be from that place. From no other place."

B: "Why do you use ash?"

"Because the ash is white. It comes from the hearth, the place of the hearth-stones. It is this ash. It must be this very ash."

B: "So the important thing is the ash. Not the colour of the ash?"

"That is so. It is the ash that is important. It must be the ash from the hearth."

B: "Why must there be ash? Is there some connection between ash and shades?"

"There is a connection. The shades are there, in the place of the ash."

B: "Are the shades in the ash?"

"No. They are not in the ash. But they are near the place of the ash (i.e. the hearth). The ash is the thing of the hearth. It comes from that place. The hearth is the place of the shades. That is the point of connection. The ash comes from the place of the shades in the hut."[19]

The diviner at eThelezini said that diviners have ash in the hearth of their special huts as a symbol of the presence of the shades. "If there is no ash in the fire-place, then the shades are not there. There must always be ash in the hearth."

Of three female diviners who were married, each said that she had *inkomo yamadlozi* which had been brought to her homestead of marriage from her clan home. In each case the responsible shade for the diviner's call was traced to the woman's home of birth. One of the women's husband also had *inkomo yamadlozi* in his cattle-enclosure. This was the only instance when I was able to trace two beasts in one herd that were animals set aside for the shades. Normally, however, lineage members benefit from *inkomo yamadlozi*. They are allowed to take hairs from the beast's tail and make thongs from them. Senior women past child-bearing may also benefit from their husband's animals, but young married women benefit from cows in their own father's herd. Occasionally women return to their homes to obtain hairs from such a beast and make armlets, or, in three cases on record, anklets from the hair.

Ukwendisa or *Imbeka* Cattle

A bride, on leaving her paternal home and settling in the homestead of her husband, maintains communion with the shades of her lineage through *ukwendisa* (or *imbeka*) cattle which of necessity must accompany her from her paternal home if old traditional approaches are upheld.[20]

Professor Krige rightly states that there is confusion about the names of the different beasts of *ukwendisa* animals. Nevertheless, although there is a difference of opinion as far as the naming of the various beasts is concerned, there is no doubt among people as to the function and the understanding associated with the cattle.[21]

The large majority of informants claim that traditionally *ukwendisa* beasts were three in number. But if the bride's father did not have many animals in his herd, two would be sufficient. Animals outside the family stock could hardly be considered. The first of the three could, preferably and if possible, be a calf of the homestead *inkomo yamadlozi*. If this was not possible or the homestead did not have *inkomo yamadlozi*, then the animal should be of old clan stock. The first of the beasts is known as *isigodo* (lit. tree stump), the second as *isikhumba* (lit. skin) and the third *eyokukhulekela ukuzala* (i.e. to request giving birth). While the second animal, *isikhumba*, is slaughtered simultaneously with,*inkomo yokucola* at the wedding and symbolizes the meeting of the shades of the uniting clans,[22] the third beast, *eyokukhulekela ukuzala* is slaughtered ritually by the bride's people, once she has settled down in her new home.[23] The killing is done in the new homestead and the shades requested "to work nicely with her in giving birth so that there be no disturbances." The underlying thought-patterns are that the woman's lineage shades furnish the blood with which the shades of the male, in the male fluid, mould the child in the womb.[24]

It is quite evident that the three beasts are closely associated with the shades. The second name given them, *imbeka,* is suggestive in that the idiom *umbeko,* derived from the same root-word as *imbeka,* refers to beer and meat placed in *umsamo* of a hut for the shades.[25] *Imbeka,* moreover, indicates the meat of an animal slaughtered for a diviner and given him as provision on his return after a successful consultation.[26] Because all three animals are "animals of the shades", each of them can be referred to as *umbeko.* This application of the idiom is wider than that suggested by Professor Krige who applies it to *isikhumba* only.[27]

At this stage our attention will be devoted to the first of the *ukwendisa* beasts, *isigodo.*[28] Different names are given to this particular animal. Generally it is known simply as *isigodo* but may also be referred to as *inkomo neshoba yayo, ishoba,*[29] *inkomo noswazi yayo, ilunga*[30] and *eyobulunga.* All the latter names refer to the animal's tail brush.[31]

Isigodo is not *inkomo yamadlozi,* although its functions are much the same as those of the latter beast. A woman said: "*Inkomo yamadlozi* is for the whole household (*umuzi wonke*). But this cow (*isigodo*) is for one person only. That is why it is not the same (as the former)." As expected, there are a number of details which are applicable to both animals.

Isigodo should be a cow "because of its milk". A generous father will give his daughter a cow that is in milk or very shortly will calve so that the bride can make use of the milk in her new home. Its milk, because it is an animal of her own lineage people, can be used by herself and her children. Milking is done by the homestead herdboys in a separate vessel used by the bride alone. Naturally *isigodo* has value to the bride and her children only.

The animal ought not to be slaughtered. It should die naturally, either of old age or of sickness. Assuming that the cow lives for a number of years after its transfer from a bride's paternal home to that of her groom, the beast is not replaced when it dies. A widow of the late chief Nkanthini of kwaMabovula royal homestead related how an *isigodo* cow which had accompanied a sister to her new home in the Biyela area had been slaughtered after it had fallen down a precipice, breaking its front legs in several places and damaging the flank badly. She described how everything possible had been done to save the animal, the sister's father being called to the scene. He had been delayed in coming and arrived only two days after the accident. Having seen the beast, he gave instructions for its destruction. Although it was perfectly clear to all that it could not live, nobody had dared do anything towards its slaughtering before the bride's father's arrival. The flesh was subsequently eaten by the sister's husband and his clan. But neither the sister nor anybody of her lineage partook in the killing or ate any of the flesh. "They could not eat this beast. It was the beast of the shades. That is why they could not eat it." My informant claimed that seeing the bride's father had given his consent and instructions for the slaughtering of the animal, the killing was possible. It was not wrong either that the husband and his people ate the flesh. "They are Ngcobo. So there was nothing wrong in their eating the flesh of the cow."[32]

Isigodo mixes freely with the cattle of the husband's herd and is attended to by the men of the homestead. It is covered by the homestead bull and its calves are generally regarded as belonging to the homestead "because of the bull". But brides of the royal clan claim that they personally can decide on the future of their calves by their *isigodo* animals. Usually, however, a wife allocates the calves to her husband and her children by him.

Like *inkomo yamadlozi,* the tail brush of *isigodo* is neither trimmed nor cut. But unlike *inkomo yamadlozi* which represents the shades in a herd much attention being given to the hairs of the brush, greater emphasis is put onto the tailhairs of *isigodo.*[33] A bride may pluck hairs from the cow's tail and twist them into thongs which she wears either as a necklace, armlets or anklets. These are known as *izintambo zeshoba.* Hence the various names given the beast which relate to its tail hairs.[34]

A bride described how she had plucked hairs from her *isigodo* while it was grazing outside the homestead. Of the hairs she had made a bracelet to be worn around the arm "to remove homesickness. When I feel it there around the arm, then I do not long home so much." Another newly married woman said that she put hairs from *isigodo* under her pillow so as to have good dreams about her people at home. She feared bad dreams as these inevitably would indicate sickness or "other troubles which I do not know". Other informants say that thongs are made for fortune. "When they (the shades) see these things, they remember us. Then they look after us, giving us nice things."

But thongs play a role in matters far more serious than merely homesickness. A woman who did not become pregnant wore a thong around her ankle. "If I wear it, then surely they will attend to me and give the thing I want. It is the stomach that is not there. That is why I wear it in the evenings when he is coming to me." Another woman at the local hospital at Mapumulo who had had a number of stillbirths wore a thong around the ankle "so that the child may be born living". She claimed that a diviner had given her the advice and her mother-in-law had underlined the effectiveness of wearing a thong. The woman was personally convinced that it would aid her seeing that the cow had "many living calves". A third woman claimed that she had irregular menstrual periods but that since she wore a thong around the waist she had been relieved of much pain and "the blood was flowing nicely (i.e. regularly)". She was assured that her restored health was due, not to any medical powers in the hairs of which the thong had been made, but the shades that "looked at me with other eyes, seeing my suffering".

Experience underlines the positive aspects attached to *isigodo.* This "is a good cow, doing only good things". Besides supplying the bride with milk in her new home the beast stands for moral support and company, retained communication with her paternal shades as well as her paternal home and the shades personal intervention in difficult matters. The animal stands, further, for generosity and thoughtfulness on the part of the bride's father. It is his concern to choose the animal and to introduce his daughter to the purpose of the beast prior to her departure from the home. A woman, reflecting on her *isigodo* and asked to express her ideas about it said: "When I see it, I think of two things. The first is the love of my father. The second is the prosperity (*inhlanhla*). This is what I think of when I see *isigodo*."

Izinkomo zemzimu

Informed Zulu agree with ethnographic records which associate *izinkomo zemzimu* not with cannibals and hence with greed, but with the 'heavy' shades of the Zulu nation, the shades of the royal clan.[35]

Bryants says that the idiom *imzimu* is "confined to the great tribal chiefs, that is to say, to the departed spirits of the clan's kings".[36] He also says that the beasts associated with *imizimu* shades were such that were "drawn from among those belonging solely to the original kraals of the older clan families at Nobamba, esiKlebeni and elsewhere".[37] People from the royal homestead eNthembeni agree with Bryant's statements and add that during the later years of ruling Zulu kings, there were cattle set aside for the sole purpose of being *izinkomo zemzimu*. There was, according to them, no specific choice as far as sex of the animals was concerned. But care was taken to choose good-looking beasts. It was essential that they be of the old royal stock, no beast from other herds being accepted for the purpose. *Izinkomo zemzimu* were ritually slaughtered in honour of the royal shades.

Some old people claim that one of the reasons for the downfall of the Zulu military power was due to the decline and subsequent total ceasing of the slaughtering of *izinkomo zemzimu*. "These cattle from the enclosures of our kings was the greatest sign of communion between them and us. So when we on our side did not give them their food and they did not find their food at their places (the royal burial places), then they forgot us. That is why the whites killed (i.e. conquered) us totally."[38]

Ritual Beer-Drinking

In Zulu society there is a communion with the shades through the medium of beer-drinking. "Beer is the food of men. It is not just food. It is the food of men. It is like meat, eaten by all men." Without any hesitation at all my friend who said that "beer is the food of men" did not think of only living men, i.e. the survivors. To him the idiom men included also the shades.[39]

Evidence indicates that ritual beer-drinking, at least today, is far more commonly practised than would appear to be the case at a first glance. People agree that beer-drinking is not spoken of openly "because Christians and white people do not agree with it, saying that it bewilders (i.e. causes drunkenness)". It is also possible that beer-drinking has increased due to the lack of cattle and goats used in ritual celebrations. At least the frequency of beer-drinking among people who either do not have animals, or only a very few, suggests this assumption.

There appears to be no generally accepted term for ritual beer-drinking. Sometimes it is referred to as *iphathi* (from the English party). Others speak of it simply as *ukudla*, food. Often it is spoken of indirectly. A man at Ekuthuleni spoke of beer-drinking as *ukudla amatshwele*, eating chickens, and was immediately understood by the people surrounding him but not by the white standing nearby. He explained the term thus: "This food is not complete.

The complete food is with meat. Like a full-grown fowl which is slaughtered for food. But nobody eats a chicken. So it is clear that there will be food without meat. That is beer."

Ritual beer-drinking takes place "when somebody has dreamed of it". Besides dreams, diviners may suggest a beer-party or a senior of a lineage indicates it. All minor events within a homestead which are not regarded as sufficiently serious for the slaughter of an animal may be celebrated with beer-drinking. Junior members of a lineage and sometimes women who have married into the clan are attended to with ritual beer. In many instances financial ability does not allow the slaughter of a beast or a goat and beer is brewed instead. Whatever the cause or reason leading to ritual beer-drinking, it is the senior of a homestead or somebody appointed to act in his place who gives the final word for brewing.

There appear to be only very minor differences between the brewing of beer to be used ritually and that which is consumed normally in a homestead. Some informants say that strictly speaking there is no difference and some do not draw clear divisions between ritual drinking of beer and other. "If there is beer that is to be drunk, then there will always be that which is for the shades. Nowhere is beer drunk alone. They are always participating in it."

There are, however, some details which appear to play some role of importance when brewing the beer. Menstruating, pregnant or suckling women should not brew the beer. "They are hot. If they prepare the beer, the shades may take offence. The women who brew should be cool in order that their work may go nicely." A woman who has slept with her husband is also regarded as hot. "When a man decides on brewing, he should leave his wife alone so that she may not be hot. She is preparing the food for the shades." In the royal homestead of eNthembeni it was the duty of the older women past the age of childbearing to brew beer, including that used in normal every-day consumption.[40]

Sometimes the millet used in the brewing is ground either in the close vicinity of a hut doorway "so that they (the shades) see their food which is being prepared for them", or in the close vicinity of umsamo. The shades are closely associated with both places. Further, the water used in the brewing is preferably taken from a running stream. Water from springs or from immediately below waterfalls is looked upon as particularly well suited for brewing. "This is living water (amanzi aphilayo). That is why it is good for brewing."

The amount of beer brewed will depend on the importance of the occasion, the ability of the homestead, the number of people who will partake in the drinking, etc. When ritual beer-drinking substitutes a killing far more beer will be brewed than generally consumed at a party.

A herd-boy at Z, about nine years old, had been badly gored by an ox while yoking the animals for ploughing. (The boy was born two years before his mother's marriage to her present husband. She explained that the boy's father was a former lover who had denied knowledge of her when she had become pregnant. Prior to the boy's birth he had left for Durban and she had not heard of him since his departure.) Immediately after the accident the boy was carried to his mother's hut by his step-father and two other men. On the arrival of the mother in the hut, it was decided that one of the men should go to the local mission hospital and ask for transport to the hospital. While waiting for the ambulance, the mother, step-father and the assistant sat in the hut

with the boy who was groaning in pain. The mother wept bitterly. Her husband comforted her in various ways and said that on the return of the boy
from hospital there would be *iphathi*. The boy was hospitalized for ten days.
He was discharged with plaster-of-paris around the left leg which had been
broken below the knee. After three weeks he was returned to hospital and the
plaster-of-paris was removed. His step-father instructed his mother to prepare beer for a party (although she was suckling a six-month old baby). I
arrived at the homestead at about 9.00 a.m. on the day of the beer-drinking.
Besides the regular homestead inhabitants nobody had arrived yet although we
had been told that the drinking was to take place *ekuseni* (in the morning).
By noon relatives from the boy's mother's homestead and some visitors arrived. The boy sat outside his mother's hut, amusing himself with a younger
brother. There was nothing that suggested his being the key person of the
occasion. About 2.00 p.m. he was instructed by his step-father to come to his
(the father's) hut. He limped into the hut and was called upon to share a
goatskin on which the step-father was sitting. He sat to the left of the step-
father, both facing the hut doorway and seated immediately in front of *umsamo*. Men and women gathered in the hut, men seating themselves to the
right of the door as they entered and the women opposite them. Everybody
faced the hearth, chatting happily.

The boy's step-father greeted the guests as they entered the hut, laughing
and cracking jokes with them. He was very cheerful and invited the guests
"to be happy with him". When the boy's maternal grandparents arrived
they were received with greater hospitality than other guests and seated on
either side of the host and the boy. With them arrived two sisters (married) of
the boy's mother and a brother. In their company were two elderly women
whom I could not place. Little attention was paid to them. They sat with the
other women in the hut, joining in with the talking and the chatting.

At about 2.30 p.m. the step-father rose and, leaning out through the doorway, called to a girl about 12 years old to bring water. She brought it in an
enamel dish, with a towel tied around her waist. She placed the dish with
water in front of her father, gave him the towel and then retired. The
father scooped up water in his right hand and symbolically washed the boy's
head, arms, chest and shoulders. As he washed the chatting in the hut quietened and by the time that he attended to the boy's chest there was perfect
silence in the hut. Some of the people in the hut watched the washing, others
merely looked at the floor. The boy's mother was scratching in a crack in
the floor with a grass straw. After the washing, the step-father dried the boy
with the towel and poured out the water which was left in the dish in *umsamo* where it sank into the earth. Returning to his place beside the boy,
the host asked the boy's mother to fetch a pot of beer. With an atmosphere
of both pride and great reverence she released her baby from her back and
handed it to her mother whom she had not greeted. She fetched a pot containing beer from the hut's *umsamo* and placed it in front of her husband,
creeping reverently on her knees. The silence in the hut was perfect and
everybody followed the various happenings with concentrated attention. The
host removed the lid from the calabash and lifted it to knee-height, his arms
resting on his raised knees. A woman with a child that was waking up and
started crying was asked to quieten the child. She did so immediately but
had difficulty in getting it perfectly quiet. She retired with it and another

woman, sitting close to the door, closed it behind her very dramatically with a bang. Holding the beer-pot in his hands, the boy's step-father described how the boy had been damaged by the ox, paying tribute to the men that had assisted in bringing the boy to his mother's hut and in getting him to the hospital. He then described how it came about that the boy was in his homestead and, although not a lineage child, herded the homestead cattle. He returned to the accident and repeated what had taken place, emphasizing that it was an accident and that nobody could be regarded as responsible, least himself. The men who had been present when the boy was gored all along the address intervened with *kunjalo* (it is thus), *yebo* (yes) and *ushaya kona* (that is the truth). The climax of the speach were details leading up to the beer-drinking. "Today is the day. So now I am doing the work which I promised. It is the food of gratitude in that the boy is not just simply earth today (reference to the boy's possible death) but sitting here with us. So all these people have assembled to this place because of the party." He held the beer-container in front of the boy and instructed him to drink. The boy took a sip. Thereafter the host drank deeply and handed the container to the boy's paternal grandfather, then the boy's paternal grandmother, then his mother and last the men who had witnessed the accident and assisted in the care of the boy. The calabash was returned to a mat placed in front of the host who then said: "So this is the food of the return of the boy which I promised. Today we are eating it." Instructions were given to the boy's mother to hand out the other pots of beer. She placed one in front of the women, another in front of the men and three large calabashes were handed out through the door to visitors who had gathered at the.homestead but not come into the hut. The chatting commenced again and a happy atmosphere prevailed among the people. They remained in the hut, drinking until the beer had been consumed. By 6.00 p.m. they were still there, some of them rather drowsy and sleepy.

Groups gathered in various places both in the huts and the yard and drank beer. The atmosphere was disturbed only by my presence, people asking why I was there and keen to know whether I had been sent to see what was going on. People continued to arrive during the whole afternoon, some of them not obtaining any beer at all and vividly disappointed. Some of the visitors returned before dusk but many remained, although it was commonly known that there was not more beer. Two men who apparently had drunk more than their share argued with the host, telling him that this was a very poor party. "We have walked all this way, thinking of the party. But we find nothing. So we were just wasting our time." While the drinking in the hut appeared to be moderate, this was not the case with those who drank elsewhere in the homestead. None of the latter gave the impression of being at all concerned about the reason for the party. They had been attracted by the beer. The boy drank no more beer than the sip in the hut and after his being let out of the hut, he played with other boys behind the huts.

Although many visitors did not know the exact reason for the party, all were convinced that it was a ritual celebration. People knew that the host had reported the details related to the drinking in the hut and that the boy had been washed ritually. They were equally convinced that the reporting of the accident was necessary so that "everybody may know what happened and that there be no suspicions". Although the speech to an outsider may have appeared to have been addressed to the people sitting in the hut, the host was explicit that he spoke in the hut "so that they (the shades) should hear the words that I was saying". "That is why we were in the hut. So that they may hear well what had happened and that there is no suspicion. They (the shades) cannot stay outside a party. I can say, that in a way it was their party," remarked the host.

Weather permitting, beer may be drunk ritually in the upper area of the cattle enclosure, opposite the main gate. Men will gather here as well as the possible patient, while women will drink in their huts or in the yard of the homestead. Male visitors are allowed into the cattle-enclosure as well as senior women although the latter, more often than not, sit with the other women in the huts.

Addresses are not always given. People say that speeches are made when occasion calls for it. "Sometimes a man may wish to speak, making known certain things. Then he says it. Sometimes he simply remains quiet. Then everybody just respects that he has nothing to say. So if he wants to speak, he will do so. If he chooses to remain silent, he will say nothing, just speaking in his heart."

It is important that the person for whom the brewing has taken place drinks first, even if it is a junior of the home. "That is the person that the shades must attend to. It is a sign to the shades, pointing at the person. Then the senior drinks. They drink first, being the ones closest to the shades."

Many informants, including the diviner at eThelezini and the ventriloquist, claim that there is no clear-cut division between ritual beer-drinking and other drinking. "All beer must be placed in *umsamo* of the hut because it is their (the shades') food. They are always looking for it." The diviner at eThelezini said: "No man drinks by himself. When we eat beer, we eat it with them. That is why a man who goes by himself into a hut, saying nothing, merely to drink because he cannot control his heat (i.e. his desire) for beer, is like a thief. He steals from them (the shades) and he steals from the others (the inhabitants of the homestead). Such a person is a thief. Beer must always be drunk together in that the shades and the people are together. That is *umsebenzi* (ritual celebration). There is no anger when this food is eaten." He claimed that this was the reason for there being no technical term for ritual beer-drinking. "At every brewing, if there is something reported or nothing is reported, there must be *umhlolo* (beer set aside for the shades in *umsamo*)."[41]

It is quite possible that in traditional Zulu society all brewing of beer was solely for the purpose of communion among men and with the shades as suggested by the diviner. But certainly there is a shift of emphasis in thought-patterns in that one does distinguish between a ritual drinking and drinking for other reasons. Some reasons for this shift in emphasis suggest themselves. Firstly, because of the growing lack of animals for ritual killings, another equivalent to the killings is sought. Because of the close associations between on the one hand beer and on the other meat, ritual beer-drinking has come to substitute ritual slaughterings to some extent. Secondly, the intoxicating effects of beer have both changed in the preparation of beer and another evaluation given it. While previously the emphasis lay on beer as being "the food of men" (the expression closely associated with and including the shades), emphasis today is frequently put on the intoxicating effects. A man who readily admitted that he was a slave to drinking said: "To me beer is warmth. I forget everything. That is what I want today. Just simply to forget everything, remembering nothing. That is why I drink so much." Thirdly, there is the pressure of Western thought-patterns which separate secular and religious, allowing for realms within which the religious is not applicable. This thought-pattern is finding its way also to Zulu society and expresses itself, among other ways, in beer-drinking which is not a ritual and drinking which is religious.

Ritual Killing

It is evident that ritual killing does not take place as frequently today as it did previously, mainly due to the lack of suitable cattle. But none-the-less Zulu society regards ritual killings as more important and more effective than any other form of communion with the shades. Certainly the keen interest given ritual slaughter underlines this fact. The lack of animals also gives this communion with the shades a pointed emphasis in the lives of the individuals and society as a whole. Not only are the occasions of ritual killings very much looked forward to. They are also remembered for a long time and treasured as occasions of feasting and, as far as the patient is concerned, of enviable personal attention.[42]

A Ritual Killing

I attended a ritual killing at Y in July. The homestead senior (umnumzana), an elderly man about sixty-five years old, had made a promise of ritual slaughter in December of the previous year. His eldest son, whose wife and children lived in the father's homestead, had returned from work in Durban and become seriously ill. He had been admitted into the local mission hospital. A doctor at the hospital had suggested an operation for gastric ulcers to which the senior had given his consent. On his return to the homestead, after having given consent to the operation, he had made a promise that if the son was to return healthy to the home a ritual killing would be undertaken. The son returned home after six weeks hospitalization and after another month of rest he resumed his work in Durban. In the homestead considerable importance was given to the fact that the patient had been operated on. Visitors who called upon him after his return home all discussed the operation with the patient. A number who knew of the forthcoming ritual killing underlined its importance in view of the operation which was regarded as a matter of great awe and seriousness.

The homestead senior had about thirty head of cattle and said that he could afford a ritual slaughter. He emphasised that he had promised a forthcoming slaughter "because the patient is my inkosana (eldest son). When a man sees this son becoming weak, then surely he does not sit back and do nothing. So that is why I made the promise."

The date of the killing was well known in the surrounding area. The son had returned home for the occasion, arriving two days earlier and planning his return to Durban the following Sunday. Relatives of the patient, including his maternal grandparents, had been informed. His paternal grandparents lived nearby and arrived during the course of the morning, assisted by a junior brother of the host (they appeared to be about eighty-five years old or more, quite grey and not very strong). Other relatives arrived on the day of the killing, one paternal uncle arriving the day after. The latter was a policeman in a neighbouring village and could not obtain leave before the day after the killing.

I arrived at about 9.00 a.m. The homestead was enveloped in an atmosphere of considerable excitement. The cattle had been milked early and driven out of sight of the homestead for grazing. A great amount of beer had been prepared and was stored away in *umsamo* of both *indlunkulu* and other huts. A woman (not identified) was preparing the floor of *indlunkulu*. She later swept the yard around the hut and threw the refuse onto the common heap outside the outer fence of the homestead. Other women and children attended to the tidying of the other huts and the remaining area of the yard. By noon all the huts had been attended to and the complete home cleaned. Heaps of fire-wood had been placed at the entrance to the byre and at the door of each hut, including *indlunkulu*.

At 2.00 p.m. the host instructed two boys to fetch the cattle. They returned after a quarter-of-an-hour with them and drove them into the cattle-enclosure. About thirty minutes earlier the patient had returned from the river where he had washed and dressed in his finery. He took his place in the upper section of the enclosure, opposite the gateway and talked with a number of men who had already assembled there, seated on their loinskins and facing the entrance of the byre. The patient wore, besides his loinskins, a red pullover which was new, feathers and a longsleeved shirt under the pullover. He carried an umbrella in the right hand. When the cattle had settled down, the host entered the byre through a small gate at its upper end (opposite the large gateway), followed by five men. Three of these were close relatives, one a neighbour skilled in butchering cattle and the fifth a messenger from the local chief. The host was also beautifully adorned with feathers and apparently dressed in his best. He carried the homestead ritual spear in his right hand and a thong of hide in the other. People gathered around the fence of the cattle-enclosure, the atmosphere being one of festivity and expectation. They were laughing and very happy.

The host indicated the chosen beast (a large elderly cow) very dramatically. He danced towards it most enthusiastically, describing its size and fatness. Suddenly he came to a standstill and pointed at it with his closed fist. His dancing (*ukugiya*) was supported by the onlookers' handclapping and shouts of admiration. He returned to the other men after a while, and took his place next to his son, quite wet with sweat. The men, seated on the ground, were given the thong and asked to bind the animal. They lassoed it without any difficulty, the beast apparently being quite tame and led it to the upper end of the enclosure, stopping some five metres short of the group of men. The animal was made to face *indlunkulu* and the patient who still was seated on the ground. The host rose and approached the cow with a jam-tin containing beer which had been placed near the fence beforehand. (The ritual spear had been placed against the fence after the host's short dance, the blade facing upwards.) He poured a little beer on the cow's back, calling on the lineage shades with a clear, dignified and very respectful voice. "Ye, of Z clan! Today I am calling on you! I am calling you A (his paternal grandfather), father of B (his father who was seated immediately outside *indlu-*

nkulu)! I am calling you C (paternal great-grandfather) who built across there!" (He pointed out the remains of his great-grandfather's homestead on a hill across a spruit with his closed fist.) He described these three ancestors' deeds, apparently because they were personally known by him. Thereafter he mentioned another two generations whom he knew by hearsay, describing their deeds but with the addition "of whom it is said that you did this-and-that". He then went on to mention paternal uncles and even called on the son's maternal great grand-parents, closing his invocation with a collective invitation to all to attend. "Today I am calling you all, you fathers of your children! Look at this beast! It is here, before you, having been promised! Today I am fulfilling the promise of yesterday! You yourselves have chosen this very beast! So look upon this beast which is your food today, Ye of our clan, ye of Z! To this day there has been no noise (*umsindo*, i.e. quarrelling)! The fire that caused anxiety was extinguished (reference to the patient's sickness). Today there is firewood for another fire! The fire of food and sweet smells! The fire of the stomach and the nostrils! Yea, you extinguished (*ukubula*) one fire indicating another fire through your men, *ababuli* (i.e. diviners. The officiant was playing with words in the address), extinguishing our fears of the fire that could have burnt in our hearts. Here is the fulfilment of the promise." (The officiant pointed at the cow with his closed fist again and then rubbing its back with more beer.)

The cow, all the time facing *indlunkulu*, moved only when the last amount of beer was poured on its back. It was immediately returned to its original position. When the officiant had emptied the jam tin he returned to the ritual spear, walked up to the beast and under the complete silence of the many people who had gathered, continued to call on the shades, saying: "You did well in saving this your child who today is with us!" (The patient rose to his feet and stood perfectly still, holding the umbrella.) "Today he is standing, but then he was lying down!" Patting the beast on the back and following the spine towards its tail, he bent down and carefully, without touching its skin, passed the spear between its hind legs at knee-height. Then he touched its udder with his hand and passed the spear between its forlegs, again careful not to touch it. He patted its dewlap and throat and finished off by again rubbing its wet back and shoulders, all the time calling on the shades. Then, standing erect in front of the cow and facing it, he called for the butcher. The men who had been seated rose while the butcher in a selfconscious and dignified manner approached the beast. The officiant handed him the spear and showed him where he was to stab the beast. An old woman, sister to the officiant, ran into the cattle-enclosure with a small wattle branch in her hand, strutted around the beast and the two men next to it joyfully and crying: "*Ii! Ii! Ii!*"[44] She withdrew when the beast had died. While the officiant showed the butcher the place in the cow's neck, the patient started praising his father and grand-father for their assistance in the restored health. His address was short, less dignified and less fluent than that of his father.

Having handed the butcher the spear and noticing that he was preparing to stab the cow, the officiant commenced calling on the lineage shades with renewed vigour and zeal, but was quiet when the spear sank into the animal's neck. The cow groaned terribly and fell on its front knees. Immediately the host cried out: "*Kala, nkomo yamadlozi!* (Cry, beast of the shades!) *Kala!*" The butcher cut the spear deeper into the neck and the cow fell also on its hind legs. Two men rushed to his assistance and pulled the cow down with its tail, one pushing it so that it fell on its right flank. When it fell, the patient ceased his praises, apparently heard by very few except the men sitting next to him. The onlookers clapped hands enthusiastically, some shouting out and singing joyfully. Immediately the beast had fallen the officiant tied a knot in its tail hairs and took the spear from the butcher. He (the officiant) called on the herd-boys to drive the other cattle out of the cattle-enclosure. Some of them were smelling the slaughtered cow and showing signs of unrest.

After the skinning of the beast by the butcher and the three relatives under the supervision of the officiant and before the carcass was opened, fat from around the navel, pieces of meat from the outside of the right shoulder-blade (*imphukane*), the meat covering the outside of the ribs (*insonyama*) on the right side and blood from the wound in the neck and the spear with which the cow was stabbed, were carried by the officiant to *indlunkulu* on a small wooden plate. The meat and fat were cut from the victim with the ritual spear which, after being cleaned with dung in the byre was restored by the officiant to *indlunkulu* with the meat on the wooden plate. Accompanied by his son, he entered the hut with an atmosphere of awe and great reverence. Again, silence fell over the people who saw them go into the hut, but others did not pay much attention to the quiet and continued talking. A boy was instructed to prepare a fire outside the byre and another boy to make one not very far from the carcass, inside the cattle-enclosure and next to the fence.

In the hut, the host built up a fire from glowing coals in the hearth and firewood heaped up at the doorway. He seated himself to the right of the hearth (men's side) while his son sat down, with crossed legs, between the hearth and *umsamo*, facing the fire-place. The pieces of meat, fat and blood were placed into a chip from a broken clay vessel after the officiant had cut a small piece of *insonyama* from the bigger piece and hung up the meat in *umsamo* of the hut. The chip with the meat was placed over the fire. Nobody said anything. The atmosphere in the hut was one of supreme reverence and a dignified quiet. But outside people were talking and shouting quite audibly. When the smell of burnt meat came from the potsherd, the officiant added a pinch of *imphepho* and said, half aloud: "*Makhosi!*" Rising from his place next to the hearth he took the ritual spear which was leaning next to *umsamo* against the wall and stabbed it through the thatching immediately above *umsamo*, the blade sticking out about ten centimeters through the thatching. He left the spear in this position and sat down again quietly. After sitting perfectly still about five minutes, the officiant said again: "*Makhosi!*" and rose, followed by his son. They left the hut and walked to the carcass where the butcher and the assistants were awaiting their return.

The beast was cut up under the supervision of the host while the son joined a group of men chatting at the cattle-gate. The various sections of the carcass were placed on two large sheets of old roof-iron which had been brought into the byre. The skin of the animal, the right fore-leg (from the shoulder to the knee), the back-bone (but not the tail), the head (not skinned), a large piece of meat from the right side buttock, heart, liver, the fourth stomach and the gall were taken to *indlunkulu* by the officiant and one of the assistants, the meat being carried in the skin. The jam tin which previously had contained the beer which was poured on the animal's back prior to slaughter, was filled with chyme and was carried by a small boy to *indlunkulu*. In the hut, the officiant spread the skin neatly over the floor in *umsamo*, tucking the ends of the skin over so that possible blood from the meat would not run onto the floor. The jam tin with chyme was placed on the skin, next to the meat. Both host and his assistant retired from the hut again, the latter returning to the further cutting up the beast. The officiant fetched his son, still chatting at the gateway of the enclosure and called on the old woman who had appeared around the beast prior to its being killed to bring beer. She met the two men at the entrance of *indlunkulu* and entered with them, placed the calabash containing beer on the skin with meat and retired. She returned with branches of the common tree fuchsia (*indomela*, Halleria lucida) and put them next to the meat. She left the hut, closing the door.

The officiant cut two thin strips of meat, each about fifteen centimeters in length from *insonyama* and placed them on the still glowing coals of the fire. The chip containing the ash of the previous occasion had been set aside, at the upper end of the hearth, reverently lifted from its previous position with both hands. When smoke rose from the strips on the coal, the officiant instructed his son to cross his arms, cut the strips in half, placed a piece of each strip into each hand and told him (the patient) in a whispering voice to eat them. He himself ate the remaining two bits and prior to putting the meat into his mouth said, whispering, yet fully audibly: "*Makhosi!*" Both remained seated until they had completed eating the meat when the host, on his knees, fetched the vessel containing beer which had been placed on the skin by his sister. He handed it to his son who took a mouthful. Thereafter he took a mouthful himself, repeating: "*Makhosi!*" The vessel was returned to its place.

With the knife used in cutting the strips from *insonyama*, the officiant cut a strip of hide from the skin and fastened it to the patient's left arm. Thereafter the gall of the beast was poured into his (the father's) right hand and with it he smeared the patient's head, dipping the fingers of the left hand in the gall, then the shoulders, arms, neck, chest, scar after the operation and the feet. A few drops were dropped into the patient's open mouth. With the rest of the gall the officiant anointed himself, rubbing it onto his shoulders, neck, arms, chest, and legs. The empty gall-bladder was fastened to the patient's arm by means of the piece of the skin attached earlier. The officiant proceeded to cut a strip from the hide and fastened this to himself on the left arm, assisted by his son who tied the knot. The two men rubbed their hands with chyme from the jam tin, the patient doing so first and followed by his father. The chyme was allowed to fall onto the coals in the fire-place. The remaining chyme, about a small cup-full, was splashed by the officiant onto the hut roof, first above *umsamo*, then in the middle of the roof, above the fire-place and lastly above the doorway and to the right of it, i.e. on the men's side, along the door-post to the floor. Last, the meat on the skin was covered with the branches of the tree fuchsia, the officiant again saying: "*Makhosi!*" It was 5.25 p.m. when we left the hut.

The rest of the beast was portioned out to men sitting around two fires, one in the byre and another in the yard, and to women in the various huts. Within a short period of time there was no meat left in the cattle-enclosure. The chyme which had not been taken to *indlunkulu* was spread out in the cattle-enclosure and the spilt blood covered up. The cattle had been returned to the byre, having grazed a little distance from the homestead and the cows milked by the herd-boys.

Some meat was consumed that evening, but the greater part was eaten the following day when a large number of people arrived, far more than on the day the beast was slaughtered. Also most of the beer was consumed the second day, although a fair amount was drunk also on the first day. No doubt some beer had been consumed before the animal was slaughtered as a number of men were noticeably drunk at the time of the killing. They were led away, the man who took care of them saying that their behaviour was disgraceful. "They do not care for anything. All they think of is to get drunk. That is all they think of."

The chief's messenger returned with a piece of meat from the neck, a large piece from a buttock and *insonyama*. Prior to his departure he had eaten of the meat and also drunk a considerable amount of beer. He was one of the last to leave in the evening. On his departure the door of *indlunkulu* was locked with a common padlock, the potsherd with ash having been removed beforehand. The host took the potsherd to the cattle-enclosure after the cows had been milked and scattered the ash and small pieces of burnt meat in the upper section of the byre. He said that sometimes it is spread in *umsamo* of the hut in which the meat is burnt, sometimes scattered at the homestead gateway. "All places are good. There is not one which is better than the other."

Analysis of a Ritual Killing

Discussing this particular occasion and other ritual slaughterings with friends, a number of details were constantly brought to the fore.[45]

1. The Occasion and Participants, the Homestead

All ritual killings are festive occasions in which the main participants are the shades, the patient, officiant and lineage clansmen with the possibility of concerned women's relatives and shades also participating. Although a large number of neighbours and friends also attend and share in the eating, the festival is first and foremost a family concern. "When we are doing this work, then it is the clan members that are the people of the work (*yibona abantu besibongo abanomsebenzi*). Other people come because of the food, being happy with us."

People are explicit that the family concerned includes the shades in a pointed way. "If they are not present, then we are only playing. They must be there. From whom would the blessings come if they are not present?" Another informant said that all the shades "are in the family homestead (*emzini wasekaya*). It is not possible that they are in another place. So if there is food (i.e. a ritual slaughtering) they are certainly there, eating and drinking with us." A third said: "How can it be a festival (*umkosi*) without all the relatives?" His statement no doubt included the shades as well as living relatives.

Hence great importance is given to the presence of relatives at ritual celebrations. At least all homestead family members as well as senior and junior relatives should attend slaughterings. They are generally summoned once the day has been decided upon, a celebration sometimes being delayed in order to make possible the presence of close relatives who work in cities or otherwise are not in a position to come immediately.

Of necessity all ritual killings are done in the homestead "because that is where the shades are". The idea of celebrating a ritual slaughtering elsewhere Zulu find shocking. The only exception to this rule is in the case of a diviner, if the responsible shades are traced to another homestead (in the case of female diviners). But also in their case the killing takes place in the home where the responsible shade is believed to reside.

The many days of preparation, the arrival of relatives who sometimes do not visit at all due to distance, work, or other hindrances, except when there is a ritual killing, and the prospects of a temporary abundance of luxuries such as meat and beer all contribute towards the air of expectation and excitement that is so characteristic of ritual celebrations.

2. Technical Terms and Occasions of a Killing

Ritual slaughtering is referred to as *umsebenzi* (lit. work) or *ukuhlabela amadlozi* (lit. slaughter for the shades).[46] Professor Krige states that Zulu "distinguish two classes of sacrifice. The *ukubonga*, or thanksgiving, takes place when something good has come about, . . . *Ukuthetha,* or scolding, takes place when the people of the kraal die and when things are going wrong, in which case the officiator seriously inquires what they have done to be so persecuted by their ancestors."[47] Informants agree that there are various categories of ritual killing but hesitate to commit themselves to merely two. A variety of reasons lead to killings. Zulu react against the idiom scolding as an equivalent to *ukuthetha*. To them the shades are seniors whose actions are not to be questioned. But they may be requested to consider other points of view which are emphasised by their survivors and possibly change their minds.[48] "Who are we to scold our seniors?"

A great number of occasions give rise to ritual killings. Besides the times of crisis in an individual's life (i.e. birth, puberty rites, marriage, death and *ukubuyisa* rituals which involve the bringing back of a shade to the homestead after burial), sickness, dreams, childlessness, rituals in connection with the call, training and coming out of a diviner, and ill fortune all call for ritual slaughter. "When a person is sick it may be the sickness of the shades. Sometimes they are angry because there is something (i.e. somebody has offended them). Sometimes they are just hungry, wanting food. This is the sickness of the shades."

"The sickness of the shades" which is associated with their hunger is generally diagnosed by a diviner. Sometimes, however, "a man may dream when he is sick, seeing the shades and a certain animal. When he wakes up he knows that the sickness is caused by the shades. They require that very animal that they showed him. So he slaughters it. Then he becomes well again." In other words, pressure is put on the survivors towards ritual slaughtering. The key word, unfolding this pressure, is practically always, *balambile*, they are hungry.

Serious offences, particularly within the clan or against clan members, require ritual slaughter before the guilt is finally removed. Because of the very close and intimate relationships between the shades and their survivors, an offence is always looked upon as a breach of custom also against them. The disgrace lies not only with the offender—it is also borne by the survivors and their lineage shades. Ritual killings which form a part of the restoration of normal relationships within a lineage (in the wide understanding which also includes the shades) is referred to as *ukucacambisa amadlozi* (lit. to put into good condition the shades).[49] The anger of the shades as a result of an offence may reveal itself in sickness, childlessness and general misfortune in a homestead. This pressure put on the survivors towards ritual celebration is different from that which has its roots in hunger.

There are a number of offences which are accepted as more serious than others. Incest and murder are regarded with great indignation. I discussed incest with S with the definite aim of seeing how he would involve the shades in the disgrace. "When a man does a thing with a sister or a daughter[50] he is killing himself by means of the shades (*ukuzibulala ngamadlozi*)."

B: "How does he kill himself?"

"He kills himself by causing strife (*ukuxabanisa*) among the shades."

B: "How?"

"When he does the thing of putting male fluid (lit. ash, *umlotha*) into his own lineage blood (*egazini lakwakubho*)."

B: "The blood is his sister or daughter?"

"That is what I am saying."

B: "What happens then?"

"It is like this. When he puts *umlotha* into the blood, he is planting the shades at home, in their own blood. The shades fight, seeing each other of the same lineage. They fight. They do not mould something. They just fight, finding something different than blood with which they mould. That is what I mean when I say that the man is causing strife."

B: "You are speaking of the shades of the male which mould with the blood of the woman?"

"That is so. So if a man does this thing with a woman of his clan he causes the shades to fight in that they meet each other and are unable to mould. They do not meet their right partners, meeting shades of another clan who simply bring blood. They fight."

B: "What happens when they fight?"

"They become very angry. They say, 'But what is this? Do we meet ourselves in this place of moulding? Did we not expect to meet some other people in this place? What is this thing that we are participating in today?' They complete asking questions. They start looking for a way (to get at the man). They seek and seek and seek. Then they find a way, being very much angry. Then they kill the man. That is how a man kills himself by means of the shades."

B: "How can he save himself?"

"By way of confession (*ukuvuma*). When he suffers under the sickness he pardons himself (*ukuxolisa*). That is all he can do. He pardons himself with slaughter."

B: "Is that the same as *umsebenzi*?"

"It is the same. He pardons himself with confession and *umsebenzi*."

Murder within a clan is looked upon as more serious than murder outside it because "the murder is the spilling of his own blood". Both forms of murder are, however, forgiveable through confession and ritual killing. "The shades see the man that he is weeping. They forgive him, forgetting the evil."

A third category of reasons which lead to ritual celebrations are those of joy or prosperity. When welfare has prevailed in a homestead, the cattle and household animals having increased, the fields having given good crops, absence of sickness and other evils, the safe return of a homestead family member from work in cities, escape from dangers such as road accidents, release from prison, a successfully argued court-case, or in general gratitude directed to the shades, a ritual killing may be arranged. This is termed *enanezela amadlozi* (to applaud the shades).[51] "When a man sees everything going well and has no suspicions (that something evil may befall him), he says, 'No, but the fathers are looking after me well at this time. Truly, I also will do something.' He thinks about a certain work and makes a promise saying, 'Indeed, fathers of my father, I see this thing that you are doing in blessing me. So I say to you in this time of prosperity, I say that you will awaken suddenly one day, being called to a small thing that I have prepared.' Then he sits down and plans the thing he wishes to do."

3. The Promise

Some ritual killings are preceded by a promise (*isithembiso*) of a forthcoming celebration. Every step is taken to fulfil the promise, once it has been given. Sometimes the fulfilment of a promise may be delayed some considerable time, but no person who has given a promise feels free from it before it has been carried out. Much attention is not given to an early fulfilment of the promise—on record I have a case when a killing was carried out two years after the promise had been made.

Slaughter preceded by a promise are generally those with pressure towards the killing attached to them. These are cases of sickness in particular (hunger of the shades), but also when a person is to face a known difficulty (e.g. a court-case) or otherwise be exposed to dangers (travelling to and from work in the cities, imprisonment, etc.). Killings in connection with occasions of crisis in life can, naturally, not be postponed.

A number of reasons are given as cause for a postponement of a ritual killing. There may not be an animal available and one has to be purchased. Sometimes animals are available but the required beast has not been indicated by the shades. On other occasions the reason for postponements lies with the relatives whose presence is essential but who are not in a position to come immediately or who have to travel far. Some informants have suggested that the shades require fat animals and hence killings are conducted in early autumn when there has been much grass and the beasts are in good condition.

Promises are made by the senior male of a homestead "because he owns the animals and knows when he wants to do the work". Having made a promise, he is also responsible for its being carried out. A junior member of a homestead or a wife can, as the following will illustrate, suggest a promise. A woman whose one year old child had accidently rolled into the fire-place of the hut and burnt its legs badly asked her husband to make a promise of a slaughter if the child returned healthy from the hospital. While she was on her way to the hospital with the child, the promise was made and subsequently fulfilled, the victim being a goat.

"If a man joins for Johannesburg (through e.g. NRC) but fears the entry into the earth (i.e. going down into the mine), he can make a promise. He goes to the cattle-enclosure in the evening and sits down. He sits where the men usually sit (at the upper end, opposite the gateway). He remains sitting there for a while, sometimes smoking, sometimes doing nothing. Then he makes the promise. He can say words or he can say it in his heart. He asks them (the shades) for protection, mentioning the fearful thing. He says that if they bring him safely back again and he sees no evil (i.e. encounters no evil), then he will do something for them. He promises the thing they like. When he has made the promise he says, 'Yes, that was all, *Makhosi!*' He rises and returns to the hut. He will sleep without anxiety that night, seeing that he has made a promise."

Evidence shows that promises are also made in *indlunkulu* or, if it concerns a sick person in another hut, in the hut occupied by the patient.[52] Sometimes a short speech or address is made, but generally the senior "just thinks about it". But he will inform the homestead people about the promise at some convenient occasion.

4. Washing

Nearly all promises of a forthcoming ritual killing are followed by a ritual washing, sometimes merely symbolically. This holds true particularly of sick people. Restoration to full health is expected to come soon after the promise has been made. If health does not result from the promise, then the conclusion that the sickness is not of the shades is drawn. "Sometimes it may be that the sickness is too strong for the shades, even for them. That is when the sick person does not get better."

If at all possible, ritual washing is done either in the byre or *indlunkulu* "because this is where the shades work very much". If a patient is too weak to walk to either of these places or cannot be carried to them, then washing may take place in the hut occupied by the patient.[53]

The diviner at eThelezini expanded on the ritual of washing. "When the person is washed it is the work of removing the sickness. That is why there is water and *isichonco* (infusions made by pouring cold or luke-warm water upon medicinal leaves, pounded roots, etc.)."[54]

B: "So the water and the medicines together remove the sickness?"

"They remove it together when there is a promise. The promise must be there. I could say that there are three working together in the removing of the sickness. It is the promise which comes first, then it is the water, then it is *imithi* (medicines). That is how they work."

B: "So without the promise the washing does not work the removing (of the sickness)?"

"That is so. It does not remove it."

B: "But as to the medicines. Do they cure?"

"Not this medicine. It is not eaten (i.e. it is not taken orally). So it does not cure. It is simply the medicine of the shades, removing the sickness of the shades from their children."

B: "What medicine is it?"

"Sometimes it is this. Sometimes it is that. I do not know the medicines of the clans. The herbalist (*inyanga yemithi*) is the one that knows. As for me, I know the medicine of my clan. Each one knows his medicine."

B: "The medicine of your clan?"

"It is known by my clan. (Long silence, indicating unwillingness to commit himself on this particular issue.) Yes, that is so. It is known to those of the clan."

B: "Is there a different medicine for each clan?"

"It may be thus. As for us, we know our medicines. I do not know what others do. They will know their medicines."

B: "Can a washing be done at any place?"

"As I said before, it could be done in the cattle-enclosure or even *indlunkulu*. Those are the places of doing the work of washing."

B: "Could it not be done at a river?"

"I have never seen washing in a river. No, forsooth, I cannot think of such a thing as this work in a river."

B: "But water comes from a river and that is where people wash?"

"That is so. But this is another washing. It is the washing of the shades, removing sickness. So this is another work. As I said, it must be done at those places which I spoke of. There is no other place."

It is perfectly clear that the washing without the preceding promise has no value in itself. Some informants have indicated that washing is associated not only with the promise but also with the forthcoming killing. If "a man makes a promise, and the patient is washed, then the shades are waiting for the thing that was mentioned (in the promise). So there is a debt (*icala*). If the promise is not fulfilled, then the sickness may return with great power, perhaps even killing the man. Also his wife, perhaps, may become sick, also dying." Others have said that the washing is repeated at the killing in order to wash off the debt. "Then there is the second washing at the work with the beast. That is when a man washes off *icala*. There are these two washings. The first one is for the healing of the sick man. The second one is for the removal of the debt."

Medicines vary according to different clans, and presumably, to different geographical areas. Some informants have indicated that no great attention is given to the medicines used, others underline that they are essential. "Sometimes the washing is with water only. There is no medicine. It is the water that removes the sickness." There is, in other words, no dogmatic thought-pattern as regards the medicines.

Evidence does not show that the person who makes the promise must of necessity carry out the washing. If the patient is a male, the homestead senior may do the ritual washing. If, on the other hand, it is a female who is sick, or a child, a senior woman may attend to the patient on instruction of the homestead senior who has made the promise. Emphasis is, on the other hand, put in the person being a senior. "No young person can wash. It must be a ripe person (i.e. an elderly person)." Emphasis is also given to the order of procedure: the washing must always follow on the promise. No washing can precede the promise.

Sometimes the person who attends to the ritual washing says something. A herbalist operating in Stanger said that the following ought to be said at ritual washings: "May they (the shades) cleanse you now. May they restore the health fully now that they shall see something (the future ritual slaughter is referred to)." Other informants indicate that nothing is said. "They know everything. When the promise has been made, they (the shades) know that there will be a washing. So why should there be speaking when they know the thing that is being done."

5. The Officiant and Helpers

The officiant at ritual celebrations is always the homestead senior. But if there is a living lineage senior to him elsewhere, he may act as officiant. When a promise has preceded the ritual killing, the person who gave the promise will be the officiant.

The officiant may approach a skilled butcher who kills the beast. The butcher will also be in charge of the skinning and dividing up of the beast under the supervision of the officiant.[55]

Sometimes an elderly woman past child-bearing age and well versed in the names and praises of the lineage shades, herself of the clan, may be asked to call out the praises of the shades in the presence of the beast prior to being stabbed. Sometimes she will praise the shades with the officiant and at the same time as the latter. This is regarded as a special token of honour bestowed on the old woman.[56]

If a diviner has suggested the ritual slaughter and possibly also indicated the beast required by the shades, the diviner may assist in the slaughtering. But he does not replace the officiant nor the butcher as "a diviner must not spill blood. He does not kill." He will suggest suitable pieces of meat to be set aside for the shades and may be present at the burning of fat and meat in the hut before the beast is cut up and at the ritual communion with the shades when the officiant with the shades and the patient eat in *indlunkulu*.[57]

It is imperative that the officiant and such people who are to assist him in the ritual killing are "cool". "A man that is hot simply destroys everything with his heat. So he must be cool." At least the night prior to the slaughtering the officiant abstains from sexual intercourse, beer, meat, and warming himself at a fire.[58] All these are associated with heat and thus avoided.

The ventriloquist at uMhlatuze expanded on the question of heat. "All these things are the things of the shades. Also dreams. If he dreams something special, then he should inquire. Maybe there is something."

B: "Usually one speaks of abstaining only from sexual intercourse. But now we are speaking of other things also."

"They are all the same. Meat, beer, and the working of men. They are all the same in that they make a man hot."

B: "We have spoken about the heat of men. But how do meat and beer make a man hot?"

"They are the food of men, as we have said previously. When a man eats them, he is eating something special (*okuthile*, i.e. something outside the normal food). These things are eaten also by the shades. Beer and meat are the things they like very much. That is why they make a man hot."

B: "You are speaking of the meat and the beer that are placed in *umsamo* for the shades?"

"These are the ones I am speaking of. But they also eat when people eat. They (beer and meat) are not eaten alone."

B: "Are you saying that when men eat meat and beer they share the food with them?"

"That is what I am saying. A man cannot eat these things alone, by himself. They are there, just very close (*eduze imphela*) when he is eating. When he is eating these things they are working there with him. That is why the thing of men (sexual intercourse) is the same as the eating of beer and meat. They all involve heat."

B: "You said once that fermentation of beer is heat."

"I said so. That is the heat that comes from them. It is a heat. Is not *uku-bila* (lit. to boil, as water: technical term for fermentation of beer) the same as fire? It (the beer) has heat in that it boils. The power to boil comes from them. Again, beer causes desire (*uthando*). When a man has eaten this thing, then he cannot forget it. He desires it all the time until he gets it again. It is these two things. Have you met a man who has tasted beer and does not desire it again?"

B: "No, I have not."

"It is the same with desire for women. That is how they are the same. Both have desire and heat. So you see how you are killing us when you say to us, 'Do not drink beer. Just drink sour-milk and water. This thing is evil, causing the head to turn (reference to drunkenness).' How can you deceive us Zulu, saying this of the food of men?"

B: "Many whites have not yet understood that beer goes with shades."

"Does not *ugologo* (reference to Western intoxicating drink) go with uNkulunkulu? Do you not drink wine there in the church on Sundays?"

B: "To many whites the desire for drink is one thing. But the drinking in the church is another thing. Only very little indeed is taken in church. It stands for presence and remembrance."

"That is the same with beer. It stands for presence. They (the shades) are there. We remember them very much when eating the food they have given us."

B: "So beer always goes with the shades?"

"Yes, that is the truth. It goes with them."

B: "You have said nothing of the fire."

"Did we not once speak of fire and the sticks?"

B: "We spoke of it, saying that it (fire) comes from the two sticks (reference to the traditional Zulu method of making fire with two sticks)."[59]

"It is the two sticks. So you do remember it? Now, is there no heat in the sticks? Just tell me, is there no heat?"

B: "There is heat (i.e. there develops heat) when they are rubbed."

"That is the place (of association). It is the heat. There is heat in the sticks. When they are to make fire, they first develop heat (*ukuveza ukushisa*). When there has been heat, then the fire comes from them."

B: "Is this heat the same as the heat in men?"

"There is no difference. Men are the same. First there is heat in that they show desire. Then they do the thing when the heat is with them. How can a man work with his wife if there is no heat first?"

B: "I see the order. First the heat. Then the fire."

"The heat of the sticks is the same as the heat of men. That is the reason for the sticks being male and female, as I said."

B: "You said so once when we were speaking of these things."

"So the heat in the fire-sticks is just the very same as the heat in the male and female."

B: "I see that they are the same. But as refers to the man who is to slaughter, he just warms himself if he sits next to a fire. Is there not a difference between making a fire and just warming oneself at the fire?"

"No. There is no difference. When a man sits by the fire warming himself he must think of women. He cannot leave women out. He must think of them."

B: "What causes him to think of women when he is just warming himself?"

First response was laughter. "Truly, sometimes you are asking things!" Laughter again. "Are you not a father?"

B: "I am. But I like to listen to the way that Zulu think of these things."

"I will tell you then. When he sits by the fire, he knows from where it (the fire) comes. It comes from the work of the one stick in the other. So when he knows this, how can he escape thinking of himself doing this thing, when he has done it before with his wife? He knows it and the desire is there in him. That is how we Zulu think of these things."

B: "I am grateful. But today, when fires do no longer come from sticks but from matches?"

"He still thinks of women. It is in the blood. Even I, when I sit there by the fire, I think of doing the thing because of the warmth of the fire. It is in the blood. It cannot be removed even by making fire with matches."

B: "So the man that is to work the following day (i.e. be officiant) must not even think of women? Is it not sufficient to abstain from them that night?"

"He must not even think of them. He must just remain quiet, not thinking this way and that way. He must just be straight, thinking of the things of tomorrow. That is to be cool."[60]

Much importance is attached to the officiant's abstention from women and beer prior to the ritual killing, less to his sleeping in a hut without a fire in it and least to his avoiding meat. Some friends said that the matter of meat is never a problem because "if there is going to be meat tomorrow, where does a man find meat to eat today?". There is, in other words, a practical solution to the question of meat.

But if meat is available, traditionalists are emphatic that it should be avoided by the officiant. Meat is very closely associated with the shades, especially if the flesh comes from cattle or goats which normally are the animals slaughtered at ritual celebrations. It is also the food eaten by the shades and shared with them whenever there is a slaughter in the homestead, either ritual or otherwise. Further, people say that meat raises desire for more meat. Once meat has been tasted, men demand it. "That is why children should not eat meat while they are still young. They are too young to appreciate (lit. understand) what meat is. Their desire is kindled for things they do not appreciate." This desire is the same as that for beer and, as the ventriloquist was emphatic to underline, the same desire "which is for women. It must not be awakened too early for they (youngsters) do not appreciate it."

Some people associate the quiet which is expected in a homestead the night after a ritual killing with "coolness". "If there is much talking and laughing, then the people become merry, also drinking beer. The noise leads to heat. That is why there should be quiet when there is flesh of the shades (in a hut)."[61] The diviner at eThelezini said that after a killing and while the flesh of favourite parts of the animal were placed in *indlunkulu*, the shades were eating and should therefore not be disturbed "to attend to other matters". He was undoubtedly thinking of sexual relationships.

Women who brew the beer in preparation for a ritual killing are also expected to be "cool", i.e. they should not be menstruating, nor pregnant, nor suckling. Preferably, only old women past child-bearing age should brew the beer. Certainly women who have been with their husbands should not participate in the preparation of the beer. On one occasion I saw a suckling woman assist in the brewing and wanted to know the reactions to her being there. A woman of her age said: "Suckling is not so bad. It does not give much heat. But the work of the men is the thing that is bad. It gives too much heat. But do not ask me! I am not suckling. Ask her yourself! She will tell you what thing gives most heat, this thing of men or the suckling." An elderly woman said that by right the suckling woman should not participate in the brewing but due to the lack of willing assistants the woman had been accepted. "Today we do not worry much about these things. They just do it, not thinking very much. So I do not know what to say about it. But according to tradition (ngomthetho) she should not be doing it."

6. The Choice of Animal and Slaughter

Either cattle or goats are accepted as suitable slaughter animals. Cattle are regarded as by far the superior animal of the two. But the large majority of ritual killings today involve goats.

Various reasons are given for the increase in the number of goats in ritual celebrations. Often a homestead may not have cattle at all, or only a very limited number of beasts, and goats become substitutes where cattle rightly should have been slaughtered. Sometimes poverty, especially in cases where the animal to be slaughtered has to be purchased, allows only for a goat. If the patient is a junior, a goat may be regarded as sufficiently large an animal for the occasion. Some informants have suggested that since cattle are no longer stabbed in the side as was done previously, "they fall without any sound". Since considerable importance is attached to the "noise of the animal of the shades", goats are preferred by the shades.

If a ritual killing involves a goat, the officiant will generally choose a large and fat animal from his flock. If it has to be bought, the best available will be purchased. No informant indicated that one either dreamt of a particular goat which the shades required or that a diviner suggested one. Callaway, however, states a case in which the shades are claimed to have done so.[62]

Greater attention is attached to the choice of a particular animal when the killing involves cattle. Often the officiant dreams of a beast that the shades require or a diviner indicates it. Sometimes the beast which happens to pass through the gateway to the byre at the same time or nearest a homestead's inkomo yamadlozi when the herd is driven into the enclosure for the killing is chosen.[63] Some Zulu say that if a man has difficulty in choosing a beast, the herd may be driven into the homestead yard in the direction of the hut in which the patient resides and allowed to walk around the hut (or sometimes indlunkulu). The beast that smells at or lifts its head in the direction of the thatching either above the doorway or umsamo is accepted as the animal required by the shades.[64] Another method is to allow the cattle to remain in the enclosure (or the homestead yard) and the beast that passes water or bellows first will be the victim.

Presenting the chosen beast to the shades and invoking them prior to the actual killing, the animal's shoulders and back may be rubbed by the officiant with either charred imphepho or beer prepared for the occasion. It is also possible that both imphepho and beer are used.[65] "The beast is rubbed on this place (i.e. the shoulders) because it is the place of the shades. That is where they like to be." No informants doubted this statement. Nor did people doubt to accept that *imphepho* "is the medicine of the shades. That is why *imphepho* is used in the rubbing."[66]

If the victim is a beast, the killing takes place in the upper section of the byre, opposite the gate, "where the shades are". It is important that the animal, also if it is a goat, faces the correct direction, i.e. *indlunkulu* and the patient, who, if at all possible, will be seated in the extreme upper area of the enclosure if a male, or, if a female, will have been moved to *indlunkulu* for the occasion. It is equally important that the animal falls on the correct side. Should the beast stagger and show signs that it may fall in a manner that indicates misfortune, everything possible is done to throw it on the correct side. A beast falling on its right side and facing *indlunkulu* is regarded as a fortunate omen, while its falling on the left side and facing either the left side or the right side of the byre (seen from the gateway) is looked upon as unfortunate. Falling on the right side but facing the middle of the enclosure is deemed acceptable.

Formerly the beast was stabbed in the side[67] and great emphasis was put on the animal's bellowing.[68] Today animals are generally stabbed in the neck and importance given to any groaning that the beast produces when staggering. Many people, however, indicate that the lack of the beast's bellowing is an offence against the shades. Two butchers claimed that if the officiant asked them to cause the beast to bellow (*ukukalisa inkomo*) the spear (or knife) may not be driven into its correct position between two vertebrae immediately, but be pushed into the animal *eceleni*, at the side (of the correct place). Others, on the other hand, said that they had never heard of this, the aim of having a butcher being the skill he had of slaughtering quickly and causing the beast as little suffering as possible.

Goats may be slaughtered in the cattle-enclosure. But often they are killed in the patient's hut, especially if he/she is too ill to be moved to *indlunkulu* or the byre.[69] Goats have their throats cut with a knife or with a spear. The mouth is not closed and held tight, the animal being allowed to bleat. The victim is sometimes thrown down to lie on its right side and facing either *indlunkulu* or the hut's *umsamo*. Sometimes, if the officiant is alone in killing the goat, it is led into the patient's hut and, facing *umsamo*, the officiant holds the goat standing up between his legs, with pressure on its back from his knees, its head lifted up and then cut. The blood, wherever the killing takes place, is collected in a vessel.

Ritual killings may be performed with a spear reserved for ritual purposes.[70] If one is available, it has been handed down from father to son through the generations, some such spears being of considerable age.[71] Although informants claim that a killing does not suffer if a ritual spear is not used, it will of necessity be used if available in a homestead. "They (the shades) do not first look at the spear. They look first at the beast. Then they look at the thing (the spear), if it is used." When the beast has fallen the officiant may tie a knot in the tailhair of the victim.[72]

The ritual spear is known as *umkhonto wasekhaya* (the homestead spear), *umkhonto yamadlozi* (the spear of the shades) or *ingcula* and is associated with ritual occasions in the lineage, e.g. ritual killings and burials. People are emphatic that the spear would not be used if the slaughtering was not a ritual occasion or the burial one in which the question of succession was not a debatable matter.

The spear is associated very closely with the shades, but it is not identified with them. "We use this spear because it is known by them. So they know that it is their food which is being prepared when we use this spear. Then they are happy, seeing that we are using their things." It does, however, not appear to be essential in ritual killings. "If a man does not have one (a ritual spear), then he uses a knife or another spear. It does not matter. The meat is still the meat of the shades."

On three occasions I have witnessed the officiant passing the spear through the legs of the victim, twice through the hind legs and thereafter the fore, once only through the hind legs. Many people claim that they know of the procedure although they do not practise it themselves. Others said that they did not know of it at all. It appears to be done only when the officiant carries the ritual spear and not when the victim is killed with either a knife or another spear. Further, it does not appear to be done at all with goats.

Evidence suggests a fertility interpretation of the rite. "We do this thing so that the cattle may increase nicely." Another friend said that it is done only when the animal to be slaughtered is a cow and reacted against the idea of it being done with an ox. "No! How can a spear like this one (the ritual spear) look at an ox in this manner! It is not done with oxen." [73]

7. Communion with the Shades

Although the presence of the shades is taken for granted throughout the ritual killing, very close and intimate communion with them is expressed in two, sometimes three, very distinct occasions in the course of the ritual killing. No ritual killing would be valid without the invocation of the shades in the presence of the victim and patient on the one hand, and the burning of *isiko* (choice parts from the slaughtered animal) in *indlunkulu* on the other. Sometimes, when the meat has been eaten and prior to the relatives' and visitors' departure, closing devotions may be conducted by the officiant.

The Invocation

The first and public communion with the shades is the invocation. It takes place in the byre immediately prior to the killing of the animal. If the victim is a goat which is to be slaughtered in the patient's hut, the invocation may be given in the hut.

Technically, the invocation is referred to as *ukubonga*, to give praise.[74] The officiant calls on the shades in the upper end of the cattle-enclosure, in the close vicinity of the victim and the patient.[75] If there is a ritual spear in the homestead he will carry it in his right hand, brandishing it as he calls on the shades and performs the ritual dance, *ukugiya*.

A worthy invocation presupposes dignified language. Friends say that the officiant starts thinking of the words when he has made the promise of a killing. Certainly experience shows that much care is given to choice of words, expressions and gestures to be used in the invocation. Very poetic and extremely beautiful Zulu is often heard at the invocation of the shades. No set pattern is followed in the invocation. Yet there are a number of distinct formulae which are parts of the invocation.[76]

Firstly, the officiant calls on the shades, using their personal names. He commences with the nearest direct ascendant (or, if the killing is in connection with sickness or a diviner's call and coming out, with the responsible shade) and proceeds with the names in the family tree which he recalls, following the order of generations as closely as possible. Special attention is always given to the responsible shade indicated by a diviner or seen in dreams; his (or her) achievements and good deeds are enumerated. The call on the shades may close with a collective address which includes all the shades not personally known to the officiant.[77] Women of standing in the lineage may also be mentioned, particularly if the responsible shade is that of a woman. But children are not mentioned although informants say that in theory they may be addressed. But it is assumed that they are included in the overall invocation.

Secondly, the circumstances and reasons leading to the killing are enumerated in detail. This is known as *ukubika*, to report.[78] Evidence indicates that details and accounts which have given rise to the slaughter are emphasised very much. People say that this is necessary, so that "there is no misunderstanding between them (the shades) and us. So the things must be reported clearly so that everything is known, nothing being hidden."

When a ritual killing aims at restoring normal relations with the shades (*ukucacambisa amadlozi*), the reporting takes the form of a confession. Informants emphasize that the oral confession given by the officiant must include a full account of the matter which is being confessed. Care is taken to obtain all the necessary details which form parts of the confession. A man in the Louwsburg area travelled to Newcastle where a son had information of certain details in a particular case which were necessary as information in a forthcoming ritual killing and attached confession. Although the officiant was certain that his son would be arriving home for the killing, he travelled to Newcastle "because *ukubika* must be planned nicely", undertaking the added expenses to an already strained budget and difficulties in finding the son's whereabout in Newcastle. When the man subsequently addressed the shades at the slaughtering (the victim was a goat), he gave a lengthy and detailed account of what had happened and closed his address thus: "So today we are washing ourselves. There is nothing that is hidden. Everything has been mentioned. Even the hatred (*inzondo*) and the suspicions (*izingabazo*) which were there have been mentioned (lit. placed) here today. So we are washing ourselves." Upon concluding the confession he took a billy-can of water, washed his hands, poured out some water on each foot and took a mouthful which he spat out vigorously over his left shoulder.[79]

Thirdly, the officiant indicates the animal to be slaughtered and may, if it is a beast, expand on its being selected by the shades themselves, its beauty and physical condition, etc.

Lastly, the invocation will contain words about restored health, continued success, or restored good relationships, depending on the nature of the killing. This formula, called *isicelo*, the request, will naturally link up with the reasons enumerated in connection with the slaughtering and its occasion.

Burning of Isiko

The second intimate communion with the shades is the burning of *isiko* in *indlunkulu*, or, sometimes, in the hut occupied by the patient; a ritual in which only the officiant and the patient take part.[80] If there is no patient (as in *enanezela amadlozi*) the officiant will enter *indlunkulu* alone.

The idiom *isiko* refers to the choice pieces of meat and fat as well as symbolically meaningful parts of the victim. Professor Krige rightly states that the "special parts used . . . are not always the same, for not only do different sibs have their own sacred parts, but if a doctor is controlling the ceremony in case of illness, or strengthening a boy who has reached puberty, he may advise the kraal head as to the parts that will be of special advantage for the particular occasion".[81] However, Zulu maintain that *isiko* should always have fat and flesh as well as strips of meat cut from *insonyama*[82] (meat covering the outside of the ribs) of the right side of the victim.[83]

When the officiant, carrying the meat for *isiko*, enters the hut (with the patient), relatives and visitors are expected to observe complete silence. Evidence shows, however, that this is not always the case. A woman at a ritual celebration said on the question of silence: "People today do not know how to behave nicely. They just think about eating (meat) and drinking (beer) and do not respect the work that is being done. They do not know how to honour the work."

I discussed the burning of *isiko* with the diviner at eThelezini. His views proved representative of Zulu thought-patterns.

B: "Why is the fat and the meat burnt? Is not cooking sufficient?"

"It must be burnt. There is the cooking of other meat. But this meat and fat must be burnt. There is no other preparation of this food other than burning."

B: "Why must it be burnt?"

"Because of the fire. It eats the meat and the fat."

B: "What is the reason for the fire?"

"It is their thing. Fire is the gift of the shades to men. So their food must be prepared with their thing."

B: "In what way is it their thing?"

"It is their thing because it is produced (*ukuphemba*) in the way of moulding (*ukubumba*) a child. These two. They are the same, the one producing and the other which moulds (a child)."

B: "You are saying that there is a connection between fire and conception. I have heard this before. But how are they connected?"

"By the heat. Producing (fire) and moulding (men) work through heat. The heat of men in their working you know. Even the matches of white men have heat in making fire. That is the thing that connects them. It is the heat. It comes from them (the shades) if it works for the making of fire or whether it works for the moulding of men."

B: "So the heat of the sticks in making fire and the heat in men when they work with the knife, these two are the same?"

"That is so. Both are the same. They both come from one and the same spring (i.e. source). The spring of this heat is the shades. So when a man is making them happy with flesh, then there should be something on his heat (i.e. fire) which comes from them."

B: "Once you said that the smell is the thing that is important."

"That is what I said. It is the truth. Do you not see the connection between the smell of meat and heat?"

B: "I do not see it quite clearly. But I would like to know it."

"Just remain silent. It is like this. The smell causes the desire (*u-thando*) for meat. It is the same desire that a man feels when he is warming at a fire. The desire is caused by the heat in him. The desire for the meat comes from the fire. That is the connection. The smell and the fire assist one another."

B: "Why is the burning done in a potsherd as I have seen it done?"

"That is of no importance (lit. it says nothing). It (the roasting) could also be on the coals. The potsherd is nothing."

B: "I have also noticed that there is no salt on the food of the shades. People also say that there should be no salt. But I do not know why there is an absence of salt."

"It is because of the shades. They eat without salt."

B: "Why?"

"It is their way. They eat without salt." Long pause. The diviner appeared to be facing an issue which he could not master. Hence he avoided the question.

B: "So the fat, meat and *imphepho* are eaten by the shades?"

"That is so. The burning is for them."

B: "Is it they that are addressed when the officiant says, '*Makhosi!*'?"

"It is they."

B: "Are all the shades there at the food?"

"They are all there. All."

B: "As to the return to *indlunkulu* by the officiant and the patient when the beast has been cut open, why did they not do the burning together with the roasting of *insonyama*?"

"It could be (done) at the same time. The reason for the two entrances (i.e. the two different occasions of entering *indlunkulu*) is that sometimes there is no reverence. People just simply come because of the meat and the beer. That is all (they want). So the burning is done before the cutting up (of the carcass)." [84]

B: "The burning must be done before any meat is eaten?"

"That is so."

B: "Why?"

"Because they (the shades) are *amakhosi*. They eat first. The visitors are only humans (*abantu nje*)."

B: "If all people honoured the customs and had reverence, not eating of the meat before the burning, would then the burning and the roasting of *insonyama* take place at the same time?"

"Yes, if all the people showed reverence. But you do not find people showing reverence today. They just show greed. So there are always two entries."

B: "At the roasting the officiant eats and the patient eats. Do the shades also eat?"

(Very audibly indeed, accompanied with a loud handclap.) "Yes! The beast is theirs! It is their meat! How can they leave their food! Are they not the ones that eat the smell? Why do you amaze me with this question?"

B: "I am sorry. I thought poorly, saying this. But I see that only the officiant and the patient eat in the hut while the people are outside, some eating and others not yet eating but preparing to eat."

"That is correct. That is *isidlo* (communion). They all eat the meat. They are all together, having gathered in that homestead. That is the great party (*idili*) which has been planned for a long time, greater even than Christmas."

B: "When the officiant is in the hut saying, '*Makhosi!*' to them (the shades), does he say this by way of greeting or by way of respect or some other reason?"

"He is not greeting them. He is giving praise, making them happy in that they are honoured and respected. They are the old ones. They must be respected. Here among Zulu it is the younger that honours the older people with words of respect. That is the Zulu way of making a man happy, by way of mentioning him politely. So the officiant says, '*Makhosi!*', making them happy."

B: "I have heard the officiant tell the patient to sit with crossed legs and receive the meat with crossed arms. Is there a meaning to the legs and the arms being crossed?"

"It is because of the health (*imphilo*). If he was ill, still being sick, complaining (*ukukala*) because of certain things in the body, then he would not cross the legs and the arms. But when he crosses them he is saying, 'Today I am not complaining.' So he gives thanks (*ukuphakamisa izwi lokubonga*) in this way."

B: "But I have also seen some patients having become healthy who have not crossed their legs or their arms."

"Women never cross their legs. They cannot be satisfied, not wanting children. But they cross their arms."

B: "Is the crossing not always necessary?"

"Sometimes it is not done. Then the patient does not know the thing of crossing. Sometimes they fear because of the shades and forget to do it. Sometimes there is a reason (for not doing so). I do not always know the reason. Sometimes it is because people do not know how to behave. They receive a gift not even receiving it with both hands and crossing them. That is one reason also. The lack of respect."

B: "I know that the crossed arms are the same as the crossed hands. But on the other hand I have seen sick people receive meat with crossed hands."

"That causes joy to hear that also sick people receive the meat with crossed hands. I am glad to hear it. Then they are receiving the food of the shades reverently. That is the way of saying, 'It is as I already am receiving the health of the work (i.e. the health which will result from the ritual celebration).' So they are not complaining, just remaining quiet and awaiting their health. That is how they are giving thanks in receiving with both hands, crossed."

The ritual spear is put through the hut thatching "to awaken the shades, telling them that their food was being prepared for them". But the spear is not put through the thatching if it is not a ritual one.

The chyme with which the officiant and the patient rub their hands as well as that which is splashed on to the roof of the hut is interpreted in terms of a washing after eating.[85] "When a man has eaten he washes his hands. When he has eaten the meat of the shades he washes in the thing (chyme) of the shades." The chyme flung on to the roof stands for the cleaning "which is with the shades. It means that everything has been completed in a nice way. Everything is clean in that there are no bad thoughts and no ill feelings with anybody. The promise has been fulfilled. So the man who made the promise of slaughtering has completed his work, removing the debt. He is clean. The shades have seen their animal, even feeling the sweetness of the smell and meat. They are happy, in that they still are to eat meat and drink the gall.

So everything is clean. That is what it means when the chyme is flung onto the roof."

Closing Devotion

Norenius says that the officiant may conduct closing devotions when all the meat to be eaten by relatives and visitors has been consumed and when the beer has been drunk, giving an example or a 'prayer'. It contains a short invocation and requests the shades for fertility in animals, fields, and wives in the homestead.[86]

Observation shows that similar devotions sometimes are conducted, but by no means at the close of all ritual killings. They may be conducted either in the byre where men and old women will gather or in *indlunkulu* into which hut will assemble the homestead people, relatives and possibly some of the nearest neighbours. A man in the Mapumulo district referred to this closing devotion as *ukusonga umsebenzi wonke* (a winding up of all the work). Another called it *ukuzicelela izibusiso* (to request blessings for oneself).

At eNthembeni royal homestead two old widows were of the impression that the closing devotions are more common today than was the case in their youth. "Today everybody is praying. Also this prayer is one of all the prayers that people are praying today. Today we hear it. But formerly it was not there in this manner. We do not know it, as to its origin or its purpose, everything having been said." An elderly man, listening to our conversation and possibly afraid that I might feel hurt because of the women's rather harsh attitude to prayer as a whole, said that it was a Christian product, adding: "That is why it is good." He argued: "Christians have taught us to pray often. It is they that brought it to us. The Christians pray when they eat and when they have eaten." He added that formerly missionaries often came and conducted Christian devotions at ritual killings when many people had assembled and that this closing devotion was a copy of what missionaries had done.

8. The Ritual Dance

A great number of Zulu are explicit that a favourable outcome of a ritual killing is by no means to be taken for granted as a mechanical result of a slaughtering. Positive reactions from the shades depend on a number of significant details. For one, the attendance of the lineage relatives is important. Other details which add to chances of a favourable outcome are the preparation of the beer, the choice of the beast, general preparations in the home as well as the attitude of both the officiant and the participants.

Importance is also given to the officiant's ability to address the shades. Hence his careful preparation of the first invocation. The officiant's ability to approach the shades in a convincing manner is also publicly evaluated by relatives and participating visitors. They watch his behaviour in the ritual dance, noting his physical abilities and the manner whereby he relates these to his eloquence in the address to the shades, if the dance accompanies the address.

Technically, the ritual dance is referred to as *ukugiya*. Bryant mentions the officiant wearing a cloak called *isiphuku*, used only on ritual occasions. People agree that formerly *isiphuku* was found in well-regulated homes but that it today has fallen out of use more-or-less totally. No importance is attached to it now.[87] Apparently it was worn during *ukugiya* and removed as soon as the officiant had completed the dance.

Ethnographic records describe *ukugiya* as the officiant's fighting a supposed enemy.[88] Zulu agree that evil (i.e. an enemy) is involved in a ritual dance because "*ukugiya* is to awaken the shades when there is something (taking place)". However, at least today, the emphasis is not so much on a supposed enemy as associations with the shades, the slaughter and the invocation which accompanies the dance. Hence the enthusiasm shown by the onlookers when an officiant excels in dramatic and acrobatic display in the ritual dance. An onlooker said, when an officiant with marked physical strength and great talent had shown his ability in action: "Today they (the shades) have really seen something, awakened like this (*ukuvuswa kanje*)! Since when can a man remain passive (*ukuzihlalela nje*) having seen something like this! Surely something must happen after this dancing (*ukugiya*)!"

Informed Zulu are emphatic that the ritual dance performed by the officiant aims at exciting the shades to action. One informant said that the dance excited the shades, using the term *ukubhibhizela* in his description.[89] "When he does the dancing, then he is exciting (*ukubhibhizela*) the shades. That is why he works very hard." On mentioning the term to other friends, they immediately associated it with *ukugiya*, when we spoke of the ritual dance. Two men used the term *ukuvusa*, to awaken, in their descriptions of the dance.

I discussed *ukugiya* with a friend at Mapumulo.

B: "You are saying that *ukugiya* must take place in the cattle-enclosure. For what reason must it be done there?"

"There is no other place for the proper *ukugiya*. It takes place in the cattle-enclosure. There is no other place."

B: "Why must it be in just that place?"

"As I said, it is the arousing (*ukuhloma*, lit. in the causative to cause somebody to arm oneself) of the shades. That is the work of the man in *ukugiya*."

B: "It is because the shades are in the cattle-enclosure, now that you mention the shades in connection with *ukugiya*?"

"Yes, that is the reason."

B: "Is it not sufficient for the officiant to speak to the shades? Or must there also be *ukugiya*?"

"Sometimes he just says words to them. The people say, having been present, they say, 'There was work at So-and-so. But it was weak work (lit. soft work, *umsebenzi othambileyo*) in that there was no *ukugiya*. So we do not know (the outcome).' That is what people say, having expected to see the officiant doing something but seeing nothing."

B: "When a novice of a diviner dances she says no words."

"Yes, you have spoken correctly. But the responsible shade is known. Again, there is hand-clapping. But this time there is no hand-clapping. So the man must speak and dance himself."

B: "So the man dances before all the shades?"

"Before them all. That is why he dances at the same time that he is mentioning them by name, enumerating their deeds. These two things go together. The speaking to them and then dance."

B: "When a man dances he jumps into the air, brandishes the spear and his weapons, stamps his feet into the ground and many other things. Do these different things have a meaning?"

"They have the same interpretation. They all excite the shades. It is like a soldier who does this in front of other soldiers when they are to fight. He is arousing them to do the thing they must do with vigour (*ngamandla*). That is what the man is doing when he dances. He is arousing the shades to do their work with vigour. He is waking them in that place where they are. That is the reason for the beating of the earth with the feet (i.e. the frequent dramatic stamping of the ground by the dancer)."

B: "Can there be *ukugiya* without arousing the shades?"

"Is there a child that weeps without its mother rushing to it?"

B: "No, the mother comes to it."

"So there is no *ukugiya* without the shades coming to the child that is calling them."

B: "Can there be *ukugiya* without slaughter of some animal?"

"When you call people, saying, 'Come to this place of yours!' do you call them without putting something, even a small morsel, in front of them in order to honour them, even just a small thing that will be like a cheating of the mouth (*ukukhohlisa umlomo*, i.e. just a very small thing)?"

B: "That would be bad manners. When friends and relatives are invited, there should be something (to put in front of them)."

"So you see for yourself that there cannot be *ukugiya* without something, even just a morsel, being a goat."

B: "Is it correct to say that *ukugiya* is a calling of the shades to be present?"

"It is correct. It is a calling of them that they must come and attend to their children (*ukubuka abantwana babho*)."[90]

9. The Carcass—Symbolic Associations

After the slaughtered animal has been cut up, certain portions of it are placed in *umsamo* of *indlunkulu* while the rest is distributed among relatives and friends. The meat placed in *umsamo* is said to be licked by the shades as is also the beer which is placed next to the meat. A limited number of Zulu have said that the meat is placed in *umsamo* "so that the shades may bless it". The meat and the beer which have been in the hut over-night is eaten only by the homestead people and close relatives who, accordingly, "eat the food that has been blessed".

The shades' licking the meat deserves further attention. The technical term for the shades' licking is *ukukhotha*, an idiom that is closely associated with cattle.[91] Bryant defines *ukukhotha* partly as "lick, as one cow licks another", and in examples of expressions in which the word is used refers firstly to *yoz' iyikhothe* (cow licking a strange calf which, after the death of its own, the cow will eventually allow to suck) and, secondly, to *ikhoth' eyikhothayo* (the beast that licks the one that licks it, i.e. reciprocal action of friendly people). Friends agree that "when I hear the word *ukukhotha* I think foremost of cattle. Then I think of licking food from a pot."

Licking is also identified with spittle which, as we have seen, is associated with fertility. Zulu are emphatic that without spittle, licking is quite out of the question. "How is licking possible if there is no spittle (*amathe*) in the mouth?" The spittle of the snake in the bottom of the pool visited by a diviner-novice is "the thing that made her (the woman in the pool) fertile. That is how he (the python) puts water into the woman. His mouth is the place where it comes out."[92]

We have seen the close relationships between cattle and shades. The licking of the flesh placed in *umsamo* of the hut is therefore not merely a question of a physical licking by the shades due to their inability to eat (physically) the meat. Licking is a symbol which stands for the affection of the shades towards lineage members who are to participate with them in the eating of this particular meat (the lineage members are the only people who eat of the flesh), and also it is the sign of fertility and well-being, these, in turn, being symbols of the shades' good will towards their kinsmen.

Sometimes a small boy or an elderly woman may sleep in the hut where the meat has been stored. The person who spends the night in the hut must not be "hot"; the sole reason given for this person being in the hut is to watch the meat lest thieves take it. When the hut is not occupied, the door is securely locked with a padlock.

Meat and beer placed in *umsamo* of *indlunkulu* for the shades are technically known as *umbeko*.[93]

The shoulder of the right fore-leg and *insonyama* of the right flank are automatically set aside for the patient.[94] These are regarded as delicacies, particularly *insonyama*. "When a man eats this meat, then the shades are eating with him. It is the meat which is the tastiest. That is why they are there. It (the meat) is liked most of all the meat on the beast. Then the man gets well again, if he has been sick." *Insonyama* is eaten first, thereafter the shoulder. The latter is hung up in *umsamo* of the hut, attached to either a roof beam or the roof structure, pieces of meat cut from it when it is to be consumed. Sometimes the flesh becomes quite high before being finally eaten by the patient.[95]

Indomela (Halleria lucida tree fuchsia) with which the meat is covered overnight is said to have flowers that "resemble the coming together of people. Some come in groups, others come alone," the quoted informant associating the solitary flowers on some branches with single individuals and the clusters of flowers with the groups of participants who assemble at the homestead where the killing takes place. The morning following the night during which the branches have covered the meat, the branches are removed and deposited in the byre.[96] Should an animal eat of the leaves when the branches are thrown into the enclosure, it is regarded as a favourable omen for the particular animal that eats the leaves. Under no circumstance may the branches be thrown onto the refuse heap. "It is the branches which have covered the food of the shades. They must be put away in a nice place."

The gall of the animal, very closely associated with the shades,[97] is poured over the patient. A few drops are sometimes also drunk by him although people say that this is not absolutely necessary.[98] The bladder is inflated and attached either to the wrist or the ankle of the patient. If the killing was in connection with a diviner's call or coming out, the bladder is attached to the hair, "because the diviner must not cut her hair. So the bladder will not be damaged in this place." If there is no patient at a ritual killing (as in *enanazela amadlozi*), the officiant wears the gall-bladder. Great importance is attached to the gall-bladder and the person wearing it.[99]

Much esteem is also attached to the bracelets prepared from the skin of the victim. These bracelets are worn both by the patient and the officiant as well as relatives, including junior lineage members and old women married into the clan. "When we wear these bracelets we are saying, 'There has been work in which we are involved.' When people see them, they know that we have been doing something." It is with the greatest reluctance that the bracelets are removed by the wearer.

Strips of hide are cut by the officiant from the neck and lower right fore-leg of the victim's skin, "because these are the places of the shades". Some people claim that the strips ought to be attached to the wearers before all the meat of the slaughtered beast has been eaten. Others say that it is sufficient if they are cut and put on before the hide becomes dry and hard, while a limit-ed number indicate that the bracelets should be put on immediately after the killing and before any meat is eaten.[100]

Zulu are explicit that neither the gall, the chyme in which the officiant and the patient ritually wash their hands, nor any flesh of the slaughtered animal are interpreted in terms of having medicinal powers. Some showed marked amazement when I suggested that they might be medicines. Ngema said: "Medicines are one thing. They have their powers. They cure certain sick-nesses. But they do not cure the sickness from the shades when they are hungry. If the sickness is from the shades the patient may eat many kinds of medicines, but they do not help him. There is only this way of slaughtering that cures a man who is sick by the shades. That is another sickness which is cured by the killing. But medicines are another thing. The food of the shades is not a medicine. No, how can food be medicines?"

Ritual slaughter is not associated with the brooding of the shades if it is done to still the hunger of the shades or as a thanksgiving for prosperity. Brood-ing is, on the other hand, related to killings in connection with times of crisis in life (birth, puberty, marriage, death and the subsequent *ukubuyisa* rites). Besides being related to the brooding of the shades, ritual killings at the times of crisis in life are not associated with a promise since, on these occa-sions, the killing cannot be postponed.

Generally, the beast is divided among homestead family members, relatives and visitors according to traditional patterns.[101] If the victim is a beast, meat may often be eaten on the day of the slaughter but the following day is usu-ally associated with the eating of the greater part of the animal. If it is a goat that has been slaughtered it is generally consumed totally on the day of the killing except for the parts placed in *umsamo* over-night.

Rightly, men eat in the byre. They sit in the upper section of it, opposite to the gate.[102] It is important that they are seated while eating. "If they do not sit down, people are amazed and ask, 'What is wrong today, the men not being seated?' If they stand it means that there is trouble somewhere. Per-haps somebody is angry. There should not be anger at a ritual killing (lit. work). Then the blessings do not come." Also women past child-bearing age are allowed to enter the byre to eat there, "because they are no longer hot". Sometimes they eat by themselves, particularly if there are several of them. Women and visitors eat either in the huts or in the yard.

The meat, if boiled, is prepared by the homestead women and such neigh-bours who may have been approached to assist in the work. Roasted meat is attended to by the people who are to eat it. Very little or no salt is used with the roasted meat and sometimes also with the cooked meat. Pregnant women are expected to abstain from preparing any meat as they are said to be quarrelsome besides being "hot". "They are quarrelsome. If they cook the meat, the shades disagree, having heard certain words over their food or seeing certain attitudes. They become offended and do not do their work, having seen somebody with a bad atmosphere (*umuntu onomoya wokuxabanisa abantu*) attending to their food."

The forehead and the horns of the slaughtered animal are stuck onto the thatching of the hut occupied by the patient or, if he/she is attended to in *indlunkulu*, in the thatching of this hut. Occasionally the skulls of animals killed ritually are attached to the cattle-enclosure fencing, as near *indlunkulu* as possible. Skulls from ritual killings in connection with diviners are often reversed, the horns facing downwards (see illustration).[103]

Traditionally, no meat could be removed from the homestead, either by relatives who lived elsewhere or by visitors. This rule is not stuck to rigidly today, particularly if there is a reasonable amount of meat at a killing. But the bones ought to be brought back to the homestead where the killing took place. "The bones come from the food of the shades. So what is not eaten should be returned to their place again. That is why the bones are brought back again. They (the bones) do not belong to the people (who ate the meat). They belong to that homestead (where the killing was done).[104] That is their home." Rightly, the bones should be burnt and the ash spread in the byre.

Ethnographic records underline frequently the quantity of beer consumed in connection with ritual killings. Observation verifies the records.[105] Beer is taken for granted at ritual celebrations. "One cannot eat meat without something with which to swallow it." "These two are like friends, meat and beer. If one appears, then the other must appear. They cannot be separated." "The meat is for the stomach. The beer is for the head. Both the stomach and the head must feel nice. Then a man feels good. So they are both required."

Ngema of Mapumulo stressed the pleasure brought about by beer-drinking and maintained that when the ritual killing was in connection with grave illness or other unhappy events, there should be no beer. "The beer stands for pleasure (*ubumnandi*). So when there is no pleasure in the hearts of men, then there should not be any beer." He readily accepted that, like meat, "it is the food of the shades" and that "when there is joy there must be beer also". But he was most emphatic that when there was sorrow, there should be no beer. "Then the meat is eaten dry. That is the sign of there being drought in the hearts of men." His views were verified by some, others dismissing it and claiming that "Ngema lives too near to the Zionists, listening to them when they say that beer is dangerous for the head".

Notes

[1] Describing parallel thought-patterns among Swazi, Hilda Kuper says that "ancestral spirits are not worshipped. Swazi address them in much the same way as they speak to the living, and the word *tsetisa* (scold) is frequently used to describe the manner of approach." Kuper, *An African Aristocracy*, p. 192.

Fortes, Some Reflections on Ancestor Worship in Africa, pp. 122 ff., elaborating on what he calls a "confusion (which) has long prevailed in the literature through equating ancestor worship with cults of the dead". It is true that Zulu are "vague about the after-life", if we wish them to express thought-patterns in Westernised, rational and critically argued logical definitions which would satisfy a Westerner's questions, but not necessarily be those that occupy the Zulu mind. To the Zulu mind it is relevant to note that the shades, being realities in the richest understanding of the word, are evidence of being beyond physical death.

[2] Bryant, *Dict.*, p. 624: Doke–Vilakazi, *Dict.*, p. 792. Note how Bryant differentiates between *teta* and *tetisa*.

[3] Doke–Vilakazi, *Dict.*, p. 557.

[4] Krige, *SSZ*, pp. 249 ff.

[5] See Bryant, *The Zulu People*, p. 232.

[6] Bryant, *Dict.*, p. 268: Bryant, *The Zulu People*, p. 231.

[7] Bryant, *The Zulu People*, p. 231, says that *ihubo* is sung when a bride leaves her home, on arrival at the bridegroom's home, at funerals and the *ihlambo* (funeral hunt).

[8] Ndamase, *Ama-Pondo Ibali ne-Ntlalo*, p. 58, says that among Mpondo there is a different idiom used for army songs.

[9] Compare relationships between cattle and shades, pp. 110 ff.

[10] Among Zulu there is no parallel to the Mpondo *ukunikela emlanjeni*, described in Hunter, *Reaction to Conquest*, pp. 256 ff. However, Braatvedt, *Roaming Zulu- land with a Native Commissioner*, p. 179, says that "with some sibs it is custom to deposit the umbilical cord of a new-born infant in the nearest stream in homage to the spirits—in this case obviously the crabs". Usually the umbilical cord is buried in a furrow at the back of the hut or put into the wall of *umsamo*, the cord rolled into wet earth or cattle-dung. Members of the Ximba clan bury the navel cord outside the homestead with the placenta, preferably near a river in wet earth, so that "the navel in the mother may not dry up".

[11] Shooter, *The Kafirs of Natal*, p. 165. Jung, 'Im Zululande', p. 114, also men- tions this beast, adding that it is an ox which is not used when ploughing and that it eventually will be slaughtered.

[12] Among Mpondo *inkomo yobuluunga* is comparable to the Zulu *inkomo yamadlozi* (see Hunter, *Reaction to Conquest*, pp. 235 ff.) as is *licabi* among Swazi (see Kuper, *An African Aristocracy*, pp. 187 & 192). Prof. Kuper writes that "every family priest has in his homestead one beast dedicated to the ancestors. It is known as *licabi* (probably from *kucaba*—to offer) and is usually a particularly fine beast. The *licabi* is not killed unless it becomes 'too old', and then it is replaced by a younger beast. When the headman speaks to the dead in his byre, the *licabi* together with the other cattle, is driven in. If a beast is sacrificed, the real victim is shepherded near *licabi* so that by proxy the best goes to the dead." Cf. also Kidd, *The Essential Kafir*, p. 201.

Hughes and van Velsen, 'The Ndebele', p. 102, say that frequently Ndebele have "a beast of the ancestors", and Woods (also on Ndebele) says: "This ox is kept in the kraal and not worked. Natives do not even like dipping it. When it gets too old it is killed and another ox is selected in its place." (Woods, 'Extracts from Customs and History; Amandebele', p. 17.)

For further comparative material see Brown, *Among the Bantu Nomads*, p. 92 (Sotho-Chwana): Stayt, *The Bavenda*, p. 243: Bullock, *The Mashona*, p. 137. On Shona concepts see Chinyandwa, 'Spirit Cattle', p. 92, who says that bulls are most desirable although oxen are acceptable. A particular shade is attached to a cer- tain beast, "a cattle-owner possessing several spirit beasts representing his par- ents", etc.

[13] Tyler, *Forty Years among the Zulus*, p. 202, says the death of the beast "would be considered a token of desertation". This information has not been verified by Zulu today.

[14] Compare a similar procedure recorded by Shooter, *The Kafirs of Natal*, p. 398, note 5.

[15] Hughes and van Velsen, 'The Ndebele', p. 102, claim that among Ndebele a goat might act as a substitute for a beast in the case of a poor man.

[16] *Inkomo yamadlozi* is the special concern of the homestead senior and it would be looked upon as a serious neglect of his duties if the animal left the homestead. Compare the idiom *sisa* in Bryant, *Dict.*, p. 592.

[17] Some informants say that the animal's back can also be sprinkled with beer, very much so if the beer has been brewed in view of ritual communion with the shades.

[18] Compare Hughes and van Velsen, 'The Ndebele', p. 103, who say that "important matters concerning the family should be announced to this animal".

[19] Mindful of the fact that male fluid is very closely associated with the shades, it is suggestive that the Zulu idiom *umlotha* stands for both ash and semen. Cf. pp. 115

[20] Cf. pp. 117 ff. and 126, note 77, where *isikhumba* and *ukwendisa* animals are discussed.

[21] Krige, *SSZ*, p. 391.

[22] See further p. 117 ff. and Reader, *Zulu Tribe in Transition*, p. 205.

[23] This animal is known as *eyokukhulekela inzalo*. The idiom suggests fertility thought-patterns which are associated with the bride.

[24] See pp. 115 f. on the activities of the shades in procreation.

[25] Bryant, *Dict.*, pp. 188 and 129.

[26] Bryant, *Dict.*, p. 28: Doke–Vilakazi, *Dict.*, p. 30.

[27] Krige, *SSZ*, p. 392.

[28] Krige, *SSZ*, p. 392, note 12. Bryant, *Dict.*, p. 188, associates *isigodo* with *eyokukhulekela ukuzala*. He further states that two of the beasts are not supposed to be slaughtered. Practically all informants agree that Bryant is mistaken in this statement, only one of them not to be slaughtered, i.e. *isigodo*.

[29] Cf. Marwick, *The Swazi*, p. 107, who speaks of *ishoba lemngano* among Swazi. Zulu agree that this beast corresponds with the Zulu *ishoba*.

[30] Note that *ubulunga* is defined by Bryant as "a bunch of hair at the end of a bullock's tail". Bryant, *Dict.*, p. 368. Cf. Doke–Vilakazi, *Dict.*, p. 469.

[31] Plant, *The Zulu in Three Tenses*, p. 37, says that *isiboma* is another name for *isigodo*. See also Krige, *SSZ*, p. 392, note 4, for discussion on this issue.

[32] Krige, *SSZ*, p. 392, says that "the bride will never eat its meat, though she would eat that of any other *beka* beast".

[33] Eiselen and Schapera, 'Religious Beliefs and Practices', p. 258, describing Zulu, state that the tail hairs "may be worn round the loins or neck as a powerful protection against evil", but do not give any further details.

[34] Cf. *intambo yobuluunga* among Mpondo in Hunter, *Reaction to Conquest*, p. 237. It is evident that among Mpondo these thongs play a far more significant role than they do among Zulu. Further, while Mpondo appear to emphasize the thongs, Zulu stress the beasts themselves, the thongs made of the hairs from their tails playing a far more insignificant role.

[35] See pp. 92 f. for discussion on *izinkomo zemizimu*. See also Marwick, *The Swazi*, p. 239, who reports on a herd of cattle among Mndzawe called *tinkomo temadloti*.

[36] Bryant, *The Zulu People*, p. 523.

[37] Bryant, *The Zulu People*, pp. 514 ff. Cf. also Shooter, *The Kafirs of Natal*, p. 165.

[38] See Callaway, *The Religious System of the Amazulu*, pp. 92 f. who closely associates *izinkomo zemizimu* with royal ritual killings.

[39] Ritual beer-drinking is also found among Mpondo. See Hunter, *Reaction to Conquest*, pp. 253 ff. for description and analysis.

[40] Women who have been with their husbands/lovers should not brew beer at all. See *The Collector*, p. 86, no. 525.

[41] Bryant, *Dict.*, p. 254: Doke–Vilakazi, *Dict.*, p. 333: *The Collector*, p. 2.

[42] The term patient is used in a wide context to include all the various categories for whom ritual killings are carried out. It also includes the person for whom the ritual slaughter is carried out after the restoration to full and normal health.

[44] See *kikilizela*, Bryant, *Dict.*, p. 305.

[45] Hunter, *Reaction to Conquest*, pp. 240 ff. gives a description and analysis of ritual slaughter among Mpondo which offers interesting parallels and differences to similar Zulu rituals. Note particularly the importance given to a promise, washing and the role of the officiant.

For further comparative material from Nguni see Hammond–Tooke, 'Some Bhaca Religious Categories', pp. 5 ff.: Kuper, *An African Aristocracy*, pp. 186 ff. (Swazi.)

[46] See Wanger, 'Totenkult (Ahnenkult) bei den zulusprechenden Völkern', p. 22.

[47] Krige, *SSZ*, p. 289.

242

[48] See pp. 197 f.

[49] Bryant, *Dict.,* p. 65: *The Collector,* p. 1, no. 9. Note that the Zulu idiom *ukucacamezela* refers to "patch up". See Doke–Vilakazi, *Dict.,* p. 98.

[50] The terms sister and daughter in this context are to be understood in their widest interpretation to include women of the total lineage and clan.

[51] Bryant, *Dict.,* p. 130: *The Collector,* p. 2, no. 10.

[52] Braatvedt, *Roaming Zululand with a Native Commissioner,* p. 180.

[53] Among Mpondo washing appears to take place mainly at the gateway to the byre while Zulu say that the washing seldom takes place at the gateway. See Hunter, *Reaction to Conquest,* pp. 243 ff. On taking the patient to *indlunkulu* see Krige, *SSZ,* p. 292. Professor Krige does not mention the ritual washing.

[54] Bryant, *Dict.,* p. 79.

[55] Callaway, *The Religious System of the Amazulu,* p. 177. See also Norenius, 'Något om zuluernas religiösa föreställningar och bruk', p. 277.

[56] Cf. Krige, *SSZ,* p. 290.

[57] Cf. Krige, *SSZ,* p. 290: Norenius, 'Något om zuluernas religiösa föreställningar och bruk', pp. 279 f.

[58] On men sleeping in hut with no fire in the hearth see Krige, *SSZ,* pp. 290 f. Note that Prof. Krige says that the officiant must "be 'clean'". She does not use the idioms 'hot' or 'cold'.

If an old woman is to invoke the shades she is automatically assumed to be sexually 'cool'. She abstains from beer and warmth of a fire the night prior to the slaughter.

[59] On traditional Zulu methods of fire-making see Callaway, *The Rel. System of the Amazulu,* pp. 26 and 173: Callaway, *Izinganekwane,* etc., p. 173 f.: Bryant, *The Zulu People,* pp. 193 f.: Fristedt, *Tjugofem år i Sydafrika,* p. 181: MacDonald, 'Manners, Customs, Superstitions', etc., p. 137: Stuart & Malcolm, *The Diary of H. F. Fynn,* p. 61: Jenkinson, *Amazulu,* p. 51: Ludlow, *Zululand and Cetewayo,* pp. 165 f.

The wider African context is treated by Lagercrantz, *African Methods of Fire-Making.*

[60] On a previous occasion the ventriloquist had related fire to the hearth in terms of fertility. Fire-sticks and the making of fire he claimed to be associated with men, while the building up of a fire in the hearth and its maintenance was regarded as women's work. "The sticks are like husband and wife. They (the sticks on the one hand and husband/wife on the other) are the same. So the fire is kindled (*ukupemba*) by a man. He kindles it in the female (stick). So this stick in which the fire is kindled is like the wife. The fire burns first in the female (stick). The man puts it into the hearth. Then the woman puts on the small twigs, the bigger sticks and last the big pieces of wood so that it grows. It (the fire) is like the child of the woman. First it (the child) eats the blood (menstrual blood prior to birth), then it suckles, then it eats porridge. Is it not so that the woman feeds the child, giving it what it wants? So she maintains the child. In the same way she maintains the fire. That is why she is the one that gathers the fire-wood. It is the food of the fire, burning there in her hearth."

[61] Braatvedt, *Roaming Zululand with a Native Commissioner,* p. 181.

[62] Callaway, *The Rel. System of the Amazulu,* pp. 368 f.: du Toit, 'The Isangoma', p. 57, refers only to the slaughtering of goats in the urban settings of e.g. Kwa-Mashu, Durban.

[63] Kuper, *An African Aristocracy,* pp. 187 and 192.

[64] Cf. Hammond–Tooke, 'Some Bhaca Religious Categories', p. 5.

[65] Callaway, *The Rel. System of the Amazulu,* p. 174: Norenius, 'Något om zuluernas religiösa föreställningar och bruk', p. 277.

[66] See pp. 112 ff.

[67] Asmus, *Die Zulu,* p. 65: Krige, *SSZ,* p. 293: Shooter, *The Kafirs of Natal,* pp. 165 f.: Bryant, 'The Zulu Cult of the Dead', p. 145: Becken, *Am Buschbockfluss,* p. 7: Norenius, 'Något om zuluernas religiösa föreställningar', p. 277: Liljestrand, 'Något om zulufolkets samfundslif och husliga lif', p. 18.

[68] Braatvedt, *Roaming Zululand with a Native Commissioner,* p. 181: Callaway, *The Religious System of the Amazulu,* p. 177: Krige, *SSZ,* p. 291: Norenius, 'Något om zuluernas religiösa föreställningar och bruk', p. 277.

All ethnographic records quote the officiant as calling out: "*Kala, nkomo yama-*

dlozi!" when the beast bellows. This expression is used widely also today and shouted out when the animal groans.

[69] Asmus, *Die Zulu,* illustration facing p. 177.

[70] For comparative material on ritual spear see Hunter, *Reaction to Conquest,* p. 242 (Mpondo): Hammond–Tooke, 'Some Bhaca Religious Categories', pp. 5 & 8: Junod, 'Some Features of the Religion of the Bavenda', p. 213: Kuper, *An African Aristocracy,* p. 78 (Swazi).

[71] On the ritual spear among Zulu see Krige, *SSZ,* p. 292: Tyler, *Forty Years among the Zulus,* p. 102: Becken, *Am Buschbockfluss,* p. 7.

[72] Although done frequently it has not been possible to obtain a meaningful interpretation of this symbol. But evidence certainly suggests that the knot in the slaughtered beast's tail-brush is different in approach to the tail-hairs of e.g. *isigodo.* See Leslie, *Among the Zulus and Amathongas,* p. 147, who says that a knot is tied in the tail of any animal killed in hunting as this will hinder the meat from giving pain in the stomach. See also Norenius, 'Något om zuluernas religiösa föreställningar och bruk', p. 277: Liljestrand, 'Något om zulufolkets samfundslif och husliga lif', p. 19.

[73] See Hunter, *Reaction to Conquest,* p. 242, where a similar practice among Mpondo is described.

[74] Bryant, *Dict.,* p. 46: Doke–Vilakazi, *Dict.,* p. 84: Krige, *SSZ,* p. 292.

If the officiant calls on a senior (including lineage women) to invoke the shades, he may sit down next to the patient or rub *imphepho* (charred) on the back of the animal. "Women should not touch *imphepho* unless they are diviners. So if he does not invoke, he should be rubbing."

[75] Bryant, 'The Zulu Cult of the Dead', p. 145.

[76] Norenius, 'Något om zuluernas religiösa föreställningar och bruk', p. 275, has underlined this aspect in all Zulu ritual life.

[77] Krige, *SSZ,* p. 293.

[78] Krige, *SSZ,* p. 293.

[79] The billy-can contained about one litre water. I was informed that the water had been fetched from a nearby flowing stream in the early morning by a six-year-old girl. On her arrival at the homestead with it, the officiant had received the can from her, placed it inside the byre himself, care being taken that it would have shade throughout the day. My informant said that sometimes, if the sun is hot, the container with water may be covered up with a branch so as to keep it cool. This aspect of being 'cool' was underlined again and again.

[80] On burning fat and meat see Asmus, *Die Zulu,* pp. 65 f.: Callaway, *The Rel. System of the Amazulu,* pp. 177: Krige, *SSZ,* p. 294: Norenius, 'Något om zuluernas religiösa föreställningar och bruk', p. 277, who says that the smouldering pieces of charred fat and meat are carried from hut to hut in the home. Informants verify this observation but add that it is not commonly practised today.

[81] Krige, *SSZ,* p. 294.

[82] Bryant, *Dict.,* p. 655.

[83] When a beast is not killed ritually, *insonyama* of the right flank is generally sent to the local chief while the left hand side is eaten by the senior of the homestead.

[84] It is quite evident that previously the whole animal was taken into *indlunkulu* after the carcass had been cut up and stored there over-night, the men who assisted in the slaughtering allowed to eat the stomachs of the beast only.

See further Asmus, *Die Zulu,* p. 66: Shooter, *The Kafirs of Natal,* p. 166: Norenius, 'Något om zuluernas religiösa föreställningar och bruk', p. 279.

However, today the practice is to take only the choice pieces such as will be eaten by the patient and the homestead members only to *indlunkulu.*

[85] Shooter, *The Kafirs of Natal,* p. 166.

When slaughtering is for meat only, chyme is not splashed against the hut roof but merely spread out in the byre. Asmus says the chyme is buried in the cattle-enclosure, Asmus, *Die Zulu,* p. 65.

[86] Norenius, 'Något om zuluernas religiösa föreställningar och bruk', p. 279. Norenius says that prayers are said at various intervals during the course of the killing, i.e. when the charred parts of fat and meat are carried from hut to hut (cf. note 80 above), when the gall is poured over the patient. Cf. also Callaway, *The Religious System of the Amazulu,* p. 157: Tyler, *Forty Years Among the Zulus,* p. 103.

[87] Bryant, 'The Zulu Cult of the Dead', p. 144.

[88] Bryant, *Dict.*, p. 185: Bryant, *The Zulu People*, p. 230: Doke–Vilakazi, *Dict.*, p. 250: Colenso, *Zulu-Engl. Dict.*, p. 197 (*gwiya*): Krige, *SSZ*, p. 293.

[89] Bryant, *Dict.*, p. 35: Doke–Vilakazi, *Dict.*, p. 35.

[90] Cf. novice's dance pp. 152 f.

[91] Bryant, *Dict.*, p. 320. Also Doke–Vilakazi, *Dict.*, p. 405: Colenso, *Zulu-Engl. Dict.*, p. 279.

[92] On spittle as symbol of fertility see p. 143.

[93] Bryant, 'The Zulu Cult of the Dead', p. 145.

[94] At times of crisis in life *insonyama* is eaten by the person involved. Eating this particular meat is regarded by many informants as a sign of attention given to that person. At a ritual killing at C I enquired about the person for whom the promise to slaughter had been made. The man who answered me said: "You mean the one who will eat *insonyama* today?"

[95] Callaway, *The Religious System of the Amazulu*, p. 178: Barter, *Alone among the Zulus*, p. 76: Samuelson, *Zululand, Its Traditions, Legends, etc.*, p. 132.

[96] Bryant, 'The Zulu Cult of the Dead', p. 145: Hulme, *Wild Flowers of Natal*, plate 27, no. 2.

[98] Asmus, *Die Zulu*, p. 66: Callaway, *The Religious System of the Amazulu*, p. 178: Krige, *SSZ*, p. 296: Norenius, 'Något om zuluernas religiösa föreställningar och bruk', p. 277. Asmus says that the gall is poured over the meat after it has been placed in the hut. Evidence indicates that this is done, but not of necessity.

Cf. Barter, *Alone among the Zulus*, p. 76, who says that the gall is sprinkled on the hut. This use of the gall has not been verified, although some knowledgeable friends have said that it might be possible.

[99] Liljestrand, 'Något om zulufolkets samfundslif och husliga lif', p. 19, says that if the victim was a beast the gall-bladder is worn around the waist and if a goat in the hair. Hartland, 'Travel Notes in South Africa', p. 483, was given the information that the gall-bladder is worn by an attending "medicine-man" (diviner, or, improbably, a herbalist). But Zulu claim that this is not the procedure today.

[100] Cf. Eiselen & Schapera, 'Religious Beliefs and Practices', p. 258.

[101] Krige, *SSZ*, pp. 294 ff.

The blood of the animal is sometimes cooked on the day of the ritual killing, sometimes left over night next to the meat in *indlunkulu* and prepared the following day. Prepared with small pieces of fat and known as *ububende*, the blood of the victim is eaten as a great delicacy by only close lineage men and, sometimes, by the patient. Very often *ububende* contains also fat from the beast.

[102] Norenius, 'Något om zuluernas religiösa föreställningar och bruk', p. 279.

[103] Cf. pp. 104 ff. The head of the victim is also eaten by the homestead men and/or close lineage male relatives.

[104] Braatvedt, *Roaming Zululand with a Native Commissioner*, p. 181.

[105] Krige, *SSZ*, p. 295: Norenius, 'Något om zuluernas religiösa föreställningar och bruk', p. 276: Shooter, *The Kafirs of Natal*, p. 166.

Chapter VII

Anger and fertility as expressions of power

Introduction

Participation in ritual beer-drinking and in ritual slaughtering is, as the previous chapter has illustrated, an involvement in a communion between the shades and lineage survivors. The communion has been called for: the cause for the celebration being either with the shades or with the survivors. Ritual killing at the times of crisis in life aims partly at reconciling the shades "with a new person who has come. They may become confused finding somebody they do not know among their people." Partly it is requesting them for their future blessings (*izibusiso*). Killings in connection with sickness (or other calamities) aim at satisfaction of the hunger expressed by the shades, or, when the sickness is not "the sickness of the shades" (i.e. caused by the shades), a plea for the restoration of health through the intervention of the shades.

It is important to note that the officiant, at least in the case of ritual slaughter, makes a speech. In it, among other details, he will account for the purpose of the killing and close the address with words of good will and restored harmonious relationships.[1] Although there may not be a speech at all ritual beer-drinking occasions, it is significant that the homestead senior will say something "in his heart". People attach importance to both the speech when it does occur and to the thoughts "in the heart" when there is no speech. "That is the time when he clarifies the aim of the occasion in that he makes friends with everybody." Allowing for also other aspects in connection with the address and the thought "in the heart" at ritual celebrations, I suggest that a main concern attached to these is a reconciliation between the shades and their survivors. This reconciliation is necessary as an introduction to the subsequent communion experienced in the feasting, the feast being a symbol of harmony.

Zulu are emphatic that "there cannot be a participation in food (i.e. meat and beer) if there is something (i.e. a grudge or misgivings among men and shades). That is why the man who takes his beast to slaughter (the officiant) speaks those words. He speaks so that everything is made clear and there be no misunderstandings." Only after this can feasting commence. Hence the importance given to the speech and the officiant's ability in approaching the shades in a fitting manner, the approach including, beside his eloquence, the ritual dance.

In an atmosphere of mutual understanding, everyone being on good terms with one another, the feasting may commence. Through omens such as the beast's groaning, falling on the right side and facing the correct direction—details which are regarded as important—the shades give their approval of the undertaking which culminates in the communion, i.e. the mutual feasting. Their approval is understood as an indication of their also being on good terms with their survivors.

One expects a good outcome of the celebration. The once hungry shade is satisfied and withdraws its anger that caused dreams and/or sickness. If the killing is in connection with witchcraft and sorcery, the intervention of the shades will hopefully lead to both health and the exposure of the source of the evil. When the slaughtering has been occasioned by an event of crisis in life, the lineage member, through the helpful brooding of the shades, will move successfully from the one stage of life to the next. If, on the other hand, the celebration has been caused by the shades' wrath and indignation as a result of an offence, one assumes that normal relations will have been regained in confession and expressions of good-will, the latter realized in one's willingness to confess and slaughter, and, from the point of view of the shades, their being prepared to share food with the offender and his kinsmen.

The sharing of food is an important matter as is the atmosphere in which the sharing takes place. For if there is anger in the minds of any of the participants, including especially the shades, or there is suspicion, "then the spirit of eating is bad. That is not the atmosphere of *umsebenzi* (ritual celebration). Everybody must be cool and pleasant. That is when everybody is happy and can eat nicely without some thoughts." Anger, suspicion and hatred are all geared towards *ubuthakathi* (witchcraft and sorcery), and occasions when many people get together as at ritual celebrations are the occasions par excellence for commiting *ubuthakathi*. "If there is hatred and one man wants to kill another, that is the time when he will put the poison into the beer." "If there is something in the heart of a man (hatred, anger, suspicion), then there cannot be any eating. He must first be seen clearly by everybody so that they may eat in peace. But if he just remains quiet, saying nothing, the bad thing in his heart just being seen in his face and his eyes (unconfessed or suppressed matters of disunity and anger), then the people just look at the food and then walk away. They cannot eat. But when he has spoken and is free, then we are merry. We just eat nicely and do not think of certain bad things. We just sit down, laughing and joking."

Analysis of evidence available does not indicate that Zulu thought-patterns allow for killings in terms of an innocent suffering of the victim. Nor does there appear to be room for a concept of replacement, if by replacement one understands the victims in ritual killings replacing the patient who has occasioned the celebration. Neither is there any indication of the occasion being one of cleansing, if by cleansing we understand a ritual purifying of an unclean patient by virtue of the killing itself. The emphasis is rather on the question of harmonious relationships between men and their shades, expressed in their willingness to share food. Because shades are involved, the choice of food is important, and, therefore, "the food of men", beer and meat. Central to the communion is that host of details which all are meaningful symbols in the drama and the very important preparations which, besides including practical details, assumes the restoration of mutual concern, harmony which allows for no anger, wrath, envy, or suspicion. These must be removed and replaced by 'coolness', that condition which alone allows and gives room for communion in the sharing of food.

This section of the study addresses itself to an analysis of power following a description of it. It is in the manipulation of power (or forcefulness, strength, ability) that Zulu thought-patterns describe the continuation of life and that host of happenings therein. Power, *amandla*,[2] is an important word in Zulu idiom and includes a wide range of various aspects attached to the understanding of force. Two of these aspects will occupy our interest as this stage, that of anger (or wrath, sometimes also hatred) and that of fertility, vitality and the ability of growth. Both are important details in Zulu thought-patterns, affecting a great many aspects of life. They are, in fact, key concepts to an appreciation of Zulu thinking, and as such, linked up with ritual killings also.

The Channels and Character of Power

Zulu thought-patterns distinguish between three channels of power. Firstly, there is the power which is associated with the Lord-of-the-Sky, secondly that which is in the lineage in a clan and, thirdly, that which is found in material substances termed *imithi*, medicines.[3]

The Lord-of-the-Sky

"If a man wants power and cannot get it from the shades or from medicines, then he can try to get it from the one above only, if he is willing (to give it to the man). But if he is not willing, then there is nothing else he can do. The one above is the most powerful one, having more power than shades and medicines." The quotation is representative of Zulu thinking in which the Lord-of-the-Sky plays a significant role, very much so in terms of power. The praise-names, *uSomandla* and *uMninimandla*, reflect this thought-pattern.[4]

Because of the increasingly conscious role that the Lord-of-the-Sky is playing in the minds of people, *uMvelingqangi* is more and more being looked upon as the ultimate source of power "because he has all power. Is he not called since the beginning *uMninimandla* (the all-powerful)?"

Zulu thinking does not allow for a dualism in the source of power, comparable to Biblical teachings which speak of God who, when regarding His creation, "saw that it was good" (Genesis ch. 1), and Satan from whom all evil arises. Zulu informants argue that both good and evil originate in heaven. "That is why we fear him (the Lord-of-the-Sky), just remaining silent so that we do not cause anger." "We do not know his mind. Sometimes he is white (i.e. good). Sometimes he is dark with anger. So from this time to the next we do not know what he is like. Yesterday he was this way. Tomorrow he may show the other way. So that is the reason why we avoid him, in that we do not know what he is like each day." This characteristic of the Lord-of-the-Sky is important to note, for it forms the basis of his being described as partly erratic and unreliable, partly as exercizing both justified and unjustified anger.

Generally, Zulu regard creation as a good act by the Lord-of-the-Sky. "With his power he created everything. That was good. He used his powers nicely in that he created our fathers." Particularly positive is the creation of man, ideas practically always defining man within the own lineage if seen in a narrow sense or, in a wider, the clan and the nation. A particularly well-built man or woman is referred to as "a man of *uNsondo*, because the creator has repeated something beautiful," the idiom *uNsondo* being a positive description of the creator and his creation.[5] While some people associate the creator's good use of his power to timely and sufficient rains, success in work and increase in cattle, others relate it to the fertility of the fields, fortune in hunting or other positive aspects of life.

Although the ventriloquist diviner regarded creation itself as a good thing, he was explicit that the Lord-of-the-Sky had acted unjustly with the young man whom he (the Lord-of-the-Sky) had expelled from heaven. We had been discussing the narrative which relates how the creator caused men to come to earth, expelling a young mischievous man from the sky and later giving him (the expelled) a wife.[6] The ventriloquist was convinced that the motive behind the Lord-of-the-Sky's decision to cast the young man from heaven was bad. "I agree that life is a good thing. Indeed, it is a good thing. But the thing that I am pointing at is the motive. That was the painful thing which he (the Lord-of-the-Sky) did, the spirit (in which he did it). Even today we wonder over this thing."

B: "But was it not a just expulsion from heaven? If I have understood the matter correctly, the young man did the thing that was forbidden in his riding that particular ox?"

"He (the young man) did that very thing that you are mentioning. That is true. Even the riding of the animal was not allowed. That is true. You are speaking well all the time. But what I am saying is that *iNkosi* should have given him a chance (*ithuba*). But he (the Lord-of-the-Sky) did not give him a chance. That is the thing that is painful."

B: "Tell me more about *ithuba*."

"That is the chance of apologizing (*ukuxolisa*). I am saying that he denied him the chance of apologizing. There was no apologizing. He (the Lord-of-the-Sky) just dismissed him. So there was no chance of restoration. It ended badly because of his (the Lord-of-the-Sky) heat."

B: "Why did he (the Lord-of-the-Sky) not give him a chance to apologize?"

"As I said, it was his heat. In another way, it is his anger (*inthukuthelo*) that troubled him." Long pause in discussion. "That is what it was. It was his heat."

B: "Tell me more about this anger that caused the expulsion."

"It is quite clear. There is nothing that is not clear in it. *iNkosi* allowed his heat in anger (*ukushisa kwakhe ngenthukuthelo*) to eat himself up totally. He just gave it freedom (*inkhululeko*) to eat him up totally without stopping it. So when the anger was eating him, he dismissed the man in anger (lit. redness, *ububomvu*). That was when he did the bad thing in giving it (anger) freedom to do the thing that he should not have done. That was the thing that was bad. It is this thing which I said was the painful thing."

B: "Was not the anger of *iNkosi* legitimate (*fanele*)?"

"It was legitimate."

B: "But it was also bad?"

"It was bad in that it was not controlled. The anger should have been controlled (*ukubopha inthukuthelo*). Then perhaps, in controlling it, he would have allowed for apologizing in that the man was given a chance."

B: "So there is anger which is legitimate and anger which is bad and uncontrolled also in the sky with *iNkosi*?" (We had been speaking of moral and immoral anger previously.)

"That is so. There are these two angers also in the sky with *iNkosi*, as you say."

B: "If *iNkosi* had controlled his anger, would the man have apologized?"

"Maybe he would have apologized. Maybe he would not have apologized.

Who am I to know what was in his heart? He alone knew the feelings in his heart."

B: "If he had not apologized he would surely have been dismissed."

"He would have been dismissed. But then he would have been given a chance. If he did not then apologize, having been given the chance, then he would be killing himself and his children. That is another thing. Then he is killing himself. But now it was *iNkosi* that killed him (i.e. punished him with expulsion). If he did not apologize, being given the chance, then he would be condemning himself (*ukuzilahla ngecala lakhe*) in that he could not apologize (*ukuhluleka ukuxolisa*), being guilty of the thing that he did."

B: "If then he did not apologize, having been given the chance, and *iNkosi* dismissed him from heaven, would then the anger of *iNkosi* have been legitimate?"

"That anger is another anger. It is the one that is permissable."

B: "But as things took place, you find the anger of *iNkosi* painful?"

"Truly, my friend of white men, I can say to you this day, speaking of painful things, I say to you that this thing done there (he lifted his eyes), it shows that pain comes from that place. My friend, just think for yourself the tears of that man, being just dismissed. Perhaps there was nothing bad in his heart when he did the thing, just being playful. No, that is what I am saying today, I am saying that the anger of *iNkosi* was fearful on that day of dismissal, just being let loose like an animal destroying everywhere where it saw something. Just think of that beautiful young girl, leaving her people painfully. Surely, even she must have felt the pains. That is the result of anger. It has no end. It just carries on, smiting even those who are not (directly) concerned."

B: "Is it true then to say that the anger which destroys is found also in the sky?"

(Very clearly) "Yes! Yes! It is there in the sky as you see it in that man being destroyed for always, having been thrown out and never to return again."

Besides the above, Zulu visualize the Lord-of-the-Sky's anger in violent thunderstorms. "When he appears in this way it is fearful because he is angry. He desires to destroy somewhere." Differentiating between male and female thunder, it is the female which is regarded as violent and uncontrollable. "That is why he sends them (the female thunderstorms) out of heavens. He becomes very angry at their constant talking and causing irritation. Then they also become annoyed in that they are cast out. So there is hatred on both sides. Then they (the thunderstorms) show us their anger. That is why we fear them. Being the heavens of women, they carry much anger."[7]

The destructive ability of lightning is related to both the power of the Lord-of-the-Sky and his anger emanating from him.[8] "It (lightning) is a great power. It is the greatest power, fearful indeed!" exclaimed a woman, when she was describing the horrors of lightning which strikes down to earth. Informants seem to agree that the power reflected in the destructive ability of lightning emanates from the anger of the Lord-of-the-Sky and that, although sometimes legitimate, "he (the Lord-of-the-Sky) should not act so harshly. It may be that we have sinned. We do not always know. Sometimes we know of it (the sin). Sometimes we do not know of it, not knowing what evil we have done. But he should give us some indications (i.e. warnings) so that people may repent before he strikes us." Another informant, also certain that the powers of lightning were associated with anger, said that the Lord-of-the-Sky had "*amawala* (a rough, thoughtless, careless and hasty way of doing anything),[9] when he wished to destroy. That is the anger we fear because it is bad."

Besides harshness and roughness, the power of the Lord-of-the-Sky in terms of uncontrolled anger expresses itself in an untrustworthiness and an undependability. This particular characteristic thought-pattern becomes very clear in Zulu narratives which describe how death come to exist among men, symbols in the narrative being very representative of ideas one desires to put across. Narratives describe how the creator, after creation, sent a chameleon to inform men that they would live for ever. But on changing his mind, the creator sent a lizard to say that men were to die. Ethnographic records appear to emphasize the role of the two animals concerned and the presence of death attributed to them. "So it came to pass that all men must die, and the Zulus, remembering the wicked trick that was played on mankind by the chameleon, always ill-treat this animal when they come upon it, killing it by filling its mouth with snuff."[10]

Informed Zulu emphasize the role of the Lord-of-the-Sky equally emphatically as that of the animals he chose to send with his messages, underlining his cunning and anger. Some give pointed attention to the creator's choice of reptiles when he decided to send men his message of life and death, claiming that his choosing the chameleon to be one messenger was quite in keeping with his unreliability.

K at Mapumulo became quite excited when a chameleon appeared in the yard in front of a local shop one morning, and gave a lengthy account of the symbolism attached to it. "He (the Lord-of-the-Sky) knew what creature (isilwakazana) he was choosing. I tell you, he is clever! His cleverness is too much for us. We become like rats with which the cat plays when they are half-dead! I repeat, his cleverness! Why did he choose this animal of colours? Because he knew its habits, he himself having created it. He made it with colours (i.e. various colours) so that it could deceive. Just look! Now it is green (the chameleon was resting on a patch of grass on the yard)! But only a short while ago it was mabadubadu (spotted)! Soon it will be uluthuthu (grey) or something else! Have you seen this thing eating? It sits just far from its food (the victim). It (the victim) thinks, 'He (the chameleon) is far away,' not knowing the danger of this thing. It (the victim) deceives itself while it is just sitting still, doing nothing. It is captured by the rope in the mouth (i.e. tongue of the chameleon). So it dies painfully, having been deceived. He! This animal! It is the animal of deceiving! Where did you see an animal with such feet? Since when is there an animal with five feet? Just tell me, since when? (The tail of the chameleon is said to be a leg because it is coiled around a branch and the reptile holds itself with it, like a foot.) Hrrr! Aw! Again, do not go away yet! Just look at these eyes! Where are they looking? You do not know. Up and in front! The side and even backwards! Just look for yourself at this very moment! This one (the right eye) is turning in that direction (in the direction of one of the many people who had come out of the shop to look at the chameleon and was sitting in front of it, the man quoted sitting beside it on the left hand side) and the other eye looking at me. Why is it looking at me? Does it ask for my snuff! Surely it shall get it! (Placing a stick over its neck and pressing down he caused it to open its mouth and poured sand down its throat.) There is the snuff that you are asking for in that you look at me! How can such a thing be created? There could be no sympathy with the one that made such a thing as this."

The group that squatted around the chameleon at Mapumulo is no isolated happening in Zulu society. It is representative and the man quoted is indeed representative of ideas shared by very many people. Chameleons, shunned and despised by everybody, are symbols of unreliability which, ultimately, is traced to its creator "who made it that way, to be unreliable". This unreliability, people say, is a picture of the creator himself, because "if he was fully dependable himself, then he would not have made such a thing."

If pressed to give a reason for the Lord-of-the-Sky's changing his mind after sending the chameleon with the message of eternal life and then instructing the lizard to go with news of death, people are emphatic that the underlying reason is anger, expressed in *amawala*. "He became angry. That is why he sent the lizard, knowing its swiftness (*ijubane*). He knew of the chameleon's lingering. So he chose the lizard so that its (the lizard's) word would arrive first because of the anger." [11]

B: "Why did he (the Lord-of-the-Sky) become angry?" [12]

"I do not know."

B: "If you were to guess, what would you say was the reason for the anger?"

"As I said, I do not know, the old people not having told me. I do not know. But there may have been something. I could say like this, indeed there was something that caused the anger."

B: "You are sure that it was anger?"

"That is what I know."

B: "But you do not know the cause of the anger?"

"It is not easy to say what the cause of the anger was. But everybody has anger. Even he above has this thing of anger. So it is clear that it was anger. What could the reason be other than anger? There is no other reason. But what the reason for the anger was, I do not know. I have not heard anybody talk of it." [13]

A man described the Lord-of-the-Sky's powers of anger in his taking people through the medium of lightning. "In the morning the man rises. He goes to the fields with the oxen and the plough. He inspans the oxen and ploughs. He knows nothing. Then he looks upwards and sees the clouds of anger. He ploughs, not knowing anything. He ploughs and ploughs. Then it (the sky) breaks loose with all its powers and anger. It strikes this way and that. Then it hits him, having just hit around for some time. The man is taken, not knowing anything, just there in the fields while ploughing. So that is how the sky works sometimes, taking men without giving even the smallest indication that there are certain plans of evil in that anger against them has grown into hatred. They are taken because the anger has by now become hatred. That is when the lightning takes a man, simply snatching him where he is."

Evidence puts it beyond doubt that the various acts of hostility as experienced by men and attributed to the Lord-of-the-Sky are outbreaks of his anger. This anger he manifests in exercizing his power which, according to all informants without exception, always is described as both overwhelming and terrifying. When the power exploited in anger reflects itself as outbreaks of uncontrolled anger, despotic cunning or unexpected acts of untrustworthiness, it is always rooted in anger and wrath, this being the centre of the circle which surrounds power. It is quite clear that even if these acts of anger are traced to the Lord-of-the-Sky himself and despite the fact that he is recognised as the all-powerful and fearful, his acts of violence and cunning are regarded as "painful". (People hesitate to use the Zulu equivalent to illegitimate anger or *ubuthakathi*, but very readily accept that the anger is a painful encounter and not good, *ulaka olubhi* or *ongalungile*.) On the other hand Zulu allow for legitimate anger for acts that one today terms *isono*, sins. "Sometimes we sin. Then he (the Lord-of-the-Sky) punishes. This is good anger because when he has punished us, he deletes the sins from his note-book. So that is good anger."

The aspect of the Lord-of-the-Sky's creation as being good must not be forgotten. Evidence indicates that concepts of creation are of an ongoing creation. "We say that he created. That is what people say. But we also agree that it is he who sustains us. When the shades lack power to give people children, then the women go to the mountains and pray. They pray to *iNkosi* in the sky. They tell him that the shades (lit. *amakhosi* below) are not able (*bayahluleka ekubumbeni*). Then, if he wishes, he may do something. They conceive. They become happy, praising him with beautiful words. It is his power that has given them the stomach (i.e. conception). So they remember him for the thing that he did with his power." [14]

The Clan and Lineage

The power of fertility in a clan and lineage is often referred to as heat, *ukushisa*, work, or desire (*ukufisa*). All are enveloped in the general term *amandla*. Anger, on the other hand, is also termed *ukushisa* as in fertility, the subject discussed determining which aspect of the power is being referred to. Other terms for anger are *inthukuthelo*, *ulaka* and *ushaba*, although the latter term is rarely used and is applied to a bad temper rather than wrath.

Previous chapters have revealed how intimately the shades are associated with the concepts of fertility and particularly the sexual act. While the male lineage shades are identified with the male fluid, those of the female are said to be associated with the menstrual blood, both parties playing important roles in procreation. The female's shades continue to feed the foetus with blood while growing in the womb, the continued deposition of male fluid in the woman during pregnancy being accepted as the male shades strengthening of the unborn child. [15]

A mother's ability to breast-feed her baby is a concern of her lineage shades. "When she has given birth, the blood (menstrual) does not come immediately. It is because they (the shades) are working in the breasts. She can even feel them working there. They are forming the food of the child. That is the blood. It is changed (*ukuguqula*) to milk. As they were putting the food of the child into the womb before birth, so now they are putting it into the breasts after the delivery. That is why the bloods of the months (menstrual periods) do not come immediately after birth." The power of growth and development is, in other words, also very closely related to fertility thought-patterns and identified with the shades. [16]

The power of fertility and growth is embodied in each lineage member. Otherwise the individual would not be in the position to participate in the act of procreation. The power is also innate and channelled in and through the lineage. "All men have this power of desire. The menfolk have theirs. The women have theirs." "Each person has desire. It is heat. The desire is the power of heat. It burns in the person. It comes in birth into the person. It grows. It becomes stronger and stronger as the person grows. When the child has grown up it burns strongly in the person. It burns everywhere, but especially in those places of work (sexual organs). That is where they (the shades) put the power. They put it in those places because those are the thing of doing the work of heat."

It is characteristic that the force of fertility, identified with the shades, is their immediate concern with survivors. Men look back three or possibly four generations (in a limited number of cases five generations could be traced) as the chain through which the power of fertility has flowed to them. The generations of shades to which a man refers when speaking of his fertility are the shades known to him or ascendants whom he recollects and memorizes, sometimes through personal recollections, sometimes by hearsay related to childhood memories. Said one man on this subject: "This heat came to me from my father. He received it from grandfather. He got it from my great-grandfather, the very one who died when I was small, living in that place we spoke of."

Pressed to go further than the generations known, informants will either go directly to the founding heroes who, by way of tradition, often are known to their survivors and consciously entertained in the minds of their lineage survivors as *uhlanga lwethu*, our origin. Sometimes people will by-pass the founding hero and claim the coming of men from the bed of reeds as the channel of power.

Challenged to go beyond the founding heroes or the origin of men in the bed of reeds, people unhesitatingly argue that the Lord-of-the-Sky "gave this power to mankind". "He has the power in that he first created men. So it is clear that he gave it to them in order that they may continue living." A man at Ekuthuleni said: "It was he (the Lord-of-the-Sky) that told them (the first man and woman) to multiply. He had the power with him and gave it to them, telling them to multiply. He said to them, 'This is your work, you male, the work of conception (*umsebenzi wokuzalisa*)! This is your work, you woman, the work of giving birth (*umsebenzi wokuzala*)! Just do it nicely and mankind will continue.' That is what he said to them in that he created them, giving them *amandla wokucina umsebenzi wabho* (power to fulfill their work)."

Zulu are unanimous that the power of fertility "is a very great power in man". Because of its potency and exalted position in society it has to be controlled. For otherwise misuse could be detrimental, the power being "greater than man. If it is let loose it can kill a man." It has to be controlled. "This heat in men is a heat hotter even than the fire of a smith. A smith controls his heat, instructing the boy to push the pumps harder or softer, depending on how he wants the heat. He does not let it loose, just letting the boy pump. So how can this heat that is even greater just be let loose? Is it not the whites that have taught us the saying, 'Either the fire is a servant or it is a master.' It is the servant when it cooks the food in the fireplace or it burns the grass in winter. That is the power that is controlled. Or the fire does not prepare the thing that you are to eat, but it eats you yourself. That is when it is eating (i.e. burning) your house and your possessions. It is this that I speak of when I say that this heat must be controlled. If it is not controlled it can cause blackness in a man (i.e. overwhelm a man). Then he does things with this very heat that are not to be mentioned, being fearful."

It is therefore not surprising to find a large number of rules and prescriptions which in great detail regulate the proper use of the power of fertility. Besides convinced views in terms of exogamy, choice of marriage partner strictly outside the lineage and the clan,[17] there are rules that regulate sexual activity and the life of a pregnant woman.[18] It is expected that children be spaced, and their welfare plays an important role in parental care. There are prescriptions which describe the correct manner of their upbringing and introduction to their future life as carriers of the fertility force innate in them.[19]

Another expression of power, different from that which is manifest in fertility and growth, is that which expresses itself in anger. Like fertility, anger is innate in the lineage and clan, and peculiar to each individual member of the lineage. Like fertility, the power which expresses itself in anger is a characteristic of men. "If men did not have anger, they would not be men." "Some people have much anger. Some have little anger. But all people have it, whether it be much or little. It is like the blood. It must be in a man." [20]

Anger as a characteristic of man is traced first through one's nearest senior kinsmen, three of four generations back, thence to the founding heroes or to the origin of men in the bed of reeds. Many people trace anger further to the Lord-of-the-Sky. "They learnt it from the sky. It was God who created them in the beginning. So this thing of anger must have come from him." But although opinions differ on the ultimate source of anger, some claiming that it came from the sky, others saying that it came from "the reeds", all are explicit that anger was given man in creation. "There is nothing in man that was not put into him when he sprang from the reeds in the beginning."

While the power expressed in fertility in men is located in the sexual organs in particular, the power of anger is said to have its seat in the soft palate of the mouth, immediately in front of the uvula and the upper throat. This part of the human body in both males and females is known as *ililaka*. [21] The Zulu idiom is suggestive.

Anger, wrath and passion are all termed *ulaka*, while the plural form of the word, *amalaka*, indicates the inside of the throat or the tonsils which form part, according to Zulu thought-patterns, of *ililaka*. On the other hand, a human's inner feelings and emotions, very closely associated with anger and passion, are also known as *umxwele*, [22] the same term being used to describe the inner parts of the throat. The idiom *ulaka* also expresses man's characteristic of having anger innate in the person, the description *umuntu onolaka* being applied to a person equipped with much anger. Anger is also referred to as *inthuku-thelo, ukuthukuthela* describing the process of becoming angry. It also describes doing something with great zeal and energy, attention being focused on *ukuthukuthela* as an expression of power and ability.[23] A Zulu school-teacher once said that "the opposite to *ukuthukuthela* in the class-room is *ukuvilapha* (to be lazy and good-for-nothing)".

As in the case of anger with the Lord-of-the-Sky, Zulu distinguish between a legitimate anger and an immoral use of it. While the former aims at sustaining order and "a good life", the latter is geared towards destruction and, if possible, annihilation.

Legitimate anger is very intimately related to *unembeza,* by Bryant defined as "the good principle in the heart of man, prompting him to do good and avoid evil, the conscience." [24] Again, *umphimbo* is good will, positive desires and wishes, free will and good memory (i.e. an altogether positive idiom) and *iphimbo* refers to eloquence and fine voice suited for singing or speaking. Song and speech are located in *umphimbo*, the normal internal throat, which, on the other hand, is also the seat of anger and emotions.[25]

Immoral anger is related to *ugovana* which idiom Bryant says is "the bad principle of the heart, spirit of evil prompting within one." [26] He adds that it is "the uvula of the throat. Seat of *ugovana* is pointed out as the same as that of *intliziyo* or moral heart, viz. in the throat." [27] While *umphimbo* stands for eloquence, *unkanka* is obstinate talk and also the nasal passages as well as the upper parts of the throat. [28]

Because anger, being an essential in man and a symbol of life as a human, is seated in the throat, strangling and throttling are regarded as very serious interference in a person's life and dignity. "If a man is touched on the chest or the stomach or the head, then there will be a question, 'What do you want to do, touching me on this part of the body?' But if the touching is on the throat, then the question is not even asked. It is known clearly that the man touching desires to kill. So there is no more speaking. The time of speaking is past. Now the thing has become very serious in that the throat has been touched." Another said: "This thing of strangling (*ukuklinya*) is the most serious thing. That is why it is used in Pretoria with *abathakathi*. When they go to Pretoria they are strangled, being killers (*ababulali*). That is why they are destroyed (*ukunquma*) in this undignified manner by means of the throat." [29]

Material Substances

A great number of material substances ranging from stones, earth and minerals to practically all the various species in vegetation are believed to contain *amandla*, power. Collectively, these are known as *imithi*, generally translated with the English idiom medicines. [30]

Contrary to the power innate in a clan lineage, *amandla* of material substances is neutral. It is sometimes very powerful. "The power is just there in the medicines, doing nothing. It is just there. Then a man comes, seeking this kind of *imithi* which can do the thing that he is planning. He sees it. He keeps quiet, just remembering the place where he saw it. When he is alone he returns, taking with him his hoe and his bag. He digs, removing the medicine. When he has completed digging he puts the medicine in his bag. He returns home. He uses the medicine in the way that he knows (it ought to be used). That is the description of how the power of *imithi* is used by *inyanga yemithi* (lit. specialist in *imithi*, i.e. herbalist)."

Like all power, that of *imithi* can be used illegitimately and legitimately. But contrary to the power innate in man, *amandla* in material substances is manipulated to work good or evil, depending on who the manipulator is and his aims in manipulating the power. "It is like this, if we speak of *imithi* and its powers. The power of a certain thing (i.e. a substance) is known. Now, being known, two men use it. They use it, one being upright (i.e. a just man), the other being an *umthakathi*. The first one takes *imithi*, preparing it very carefully and then giving it to a certain sick person. The power of the medicine combats the sickness, driving it out with much vomiting. The sick person vomits until the sickness is driven out. Then the man ceases giving medicine to the sick man. The sick man becomes well. He rises and gives thanks, being well again. Now *umthakathi* takes the very same medicine of *ukupalaza* (i.e. vomiting) and throws it at a certain person, being sick. The power of *imithi* works with the sickness which was thrown on that sick person by *umthakathi* towards killing that person. There is much vomiting the whole day. Even from the morning through the whole day until dusk. There is only vomiting, until

256

the person vomits the last, even the gall. Then he says, 'No, forsooth, today I am perishing. Yesterday was the day of the sickness in the chest, stomach and knees. But today is the day of death indeed, in that there is only vomiting, even the gall.' When he has spoken, indicating the cause of the death, he dies. That is the power of *imithi* and its use. With one man it gives strength in the knees (i.e. health). With another it gives the bending of the knees (reference to the old custom of doubling up the corpse prior to burial, i.e. it brings death). That is how *imithi* works." [31]

Manipulated correctly and morally, the power embedded in material substances can be used to encourage and support the powers embodied in men. [32] Although fertility and health in a lineage are the concern of the shades, medicines are taken "so that everything may go well". Besides observing traditional rules pertaining to pregnancy, an expectant mother takes certain medicines which are believed to make delivery safer and less painful. A bride takes medicines prior to departure to her new home "in order that she may be received nicely and that she may be fearless and not fear anything". A suckling woman will both take medicines and let her mammary glands be treated so that "the milk may flow plentifully and not be mixed with certain bad things which she may run across". Yet the pregnant mother, the bride and the nursing woman are all conscious of the nearness and positive active support given them by their lineage shades. "When she (the bride) takes the medicines she is not forgetting the shades. It is not so. She is remembering them. They are just there, close (to her). She remembers them in that she is taking the very medicines that they themselves ate when they were in the same situation. Perhaps they even have revealed this very medicine to her or the father or the mother. So she is not challenging them when she takes medicines. The medicines just work nicely together with the shades. They do not disagree." [33]

Again, contrary to the power innate in a lineage and its persons, *amandla* in materials is seldom, if ever, traced to any particular source. It is embedded in the species itself. Many people were amazed at the question when asked from where materials derived their power. "I do not know. I have never thought of it. Is there a source to *amandla* of medicines? I have never heard it being spoken of. There is no source. It is there, in this stone. (My informant picked up a copper-coloured stone from his collection in front of himself.) Do stones have shades? I have never heard this question before." [34] On the other hand, a number of schooled Zulu said that "God had put power into medicines". A school-master differentiated very clearly between what he termed "hospital medicines" and "bad medicines used by my people". "The good medicines used in the hospitals come from God. He gave power to those medicines to heal sick people. The bad medicines used by my people come from Satan. They are just evil, deceiving people that they can heal whereas they are just rubbish. That is all they are, rubbish."

Although herbalists teach their apprentices the manipulation of material powers, each individual herbalist will constantly experiment with new materia and mixtures of these to satisfy an increasingly large demand in varying fields. Herbalists are open to new suggestions and ready to take impressions. Whereas diviners to a large extent are tied to traditional views and approaches to the implementation of their office, herbalists are the progressive who constantly reach for new avenues of manipulating powers entrusted to them.

In part Western medical practice has had great influence on the thinking and work of herbalists, and in part new approaches to life have challenged them to seek and find new medicines that will act and react in response to new cultural and social settings. The powers embedded in *imithi* are today required to act upon an all too successful foot-ball team, and expected to fortify the own team. A gifted lawyer employed by one's opponent in a court-case ought to be stupified and one's own strengthened. Chances of finding a paying job must be supported and the bottle-neck experienced in influx-control must be passed through. Police must be rendered blind to one's lost reference book and the employer charmed by one's ability in work. Examinations must be passed and a better off neighbour must be persuaded to assist in a financial embarrassment. The dangers of modern travel must be guarded against whilst, still, the fears of lightning are very real and have to be remembered. There is in society no limit to both the legitimate and illegitimate usage of the powers of substance, the powers manipulated by those who gave knowledge of doing so towards destruction and strengthening.

Legitimate Use of Power

The legitimate use of power covers a large field. Its use is always, ultimately, a positive act although it may, in itself, include a certain amount of inconvenience, pain, and possibly, even suffering. A diviner's ability is attributed to his close associations with the shades and definitely regarded as a legitimate use of power, although it is well known among Zulu that the life of a diviner by no means always is attractive. "Medicines are always of a bad taste. But it is known that they work good in the body. So they are eaten with ease, remembering their good work." A woman with six hungry children to feed, her husband being in Durban at work and hence the many duties of the homestead resting on her shoulders, said: "Yes, I know of all these troubles. Look, even I have no clothes myself. This torn dress and that for church on Sundays are all I have, because of the hunger and the poverty. But I long for the work he does with me, hoping for another child. I feel the love for it in me, causing me to hope very much each time." Although she could not clearly differentiate between longing for sexual relations with her husband and her craving for further children, she was fully convinced that "that is the good use of power (*umsebenzi omuhle wamandla*)". Consciously or unconsciously she related her own desire to that which she assumed to be in her husband. The combination of her power and that of her husband was moral, legitimate and constructive. But certain as she was of this, equally was she convinced that outside the restricted legitimate boundaries, its use could be "perhaps something that kills everything of this home".

The legitimate use of the powers of procreation are straightforward and need not be discussed extensively. In practice its use is regulated by the many rules and regulations attached to courtship, marriage, birth and upbringing of the subsequent children. Outside these regulations the use of the power of fertility is dangerous. But the legitimate use of anger requires attention. Focus will therefore be placed on this particular issue.

Legitimate anger expresses itself in various ways.[35] Sometimes repeated dreams may be said to originate in a senior's anger, the senior either living or deceased. A young man was troubled by his paternal grandfather who lived with an elder brother of the young man. On the man's preparing a feast for his grandparents, the dreams ceased. I discussed the incident with the parental grandmother on the day of the celebration.[36]

B: "Why did the father trouble his grandson with dreams?"

"He was hungry. That was the reason. Hunger. The hunger caused the father to become angry with the son-of-his-son in that he was not doing something. It was long since he had tasted his child's meat. So he was angry, being hungry. That is what I can say."

B: "Then he caused the son to dream?"

"He caused him to dream. That is so."

B: "Could the old man not have asked verbally for something, I mean something like the meat for which he was craving?"

"He could possibly have done it. But then people would have said, 'Look, he is greedy, asking for meat by way of mouth. Is he not an old man, having dignity?' Some may even have pointed at dreams just mentioning them by name. So he could not do it. Also, he (the son) would have been amazed, having suspicions that the elder brother was not looking after him (the grandfather) nicely. But the son should have known of the hunger of the father."

B: "Are you blaming the son?"

"No, I am not blaming him. But he should have thought just a little. Then he would have remembered his father's father in that he (the grandfather) had not seen a morsel from his homestead. Even since the birth of the first child to this very day."

B: "Was the old man justified in becoming hungry and angry?"

(Aloud with a handclap of amazement) "Yes! Very much so! Do you think that he should have perished in hunger, just keeping quiet? No, he did well in revealing his hunger by troubling him with dreams."

B: "Is hunger and anger the same thing?"

"They are the same thing. But first comes hunger. When the hunger has been felt for some time, the anger comes. But they are one and the same thing. If I say that the son was troubled by the father's hunger or I say that it was the anger of the father, there is no difference. They are the same."

B: "I can see how the hunger was stilled. but how did the anger abate?"

"It started to decline (ukwehla) when the son indicated something (i.e. that he was preparing a feast). Then it went down gradually as the day came nearer. It died totally today when we were sitting at this very table. It died totally just here in this room of the son."

B: "How?"

"When the father heard the words of the son."

B: "You mean the words spoken by the son standing up before he said grace?"

"Those very words."

B: "What did the son say that finally removed the father's anger?"

"It was when he apologized, saying that he had forgotten that we still recognized the smell of meat and referring to the lack of teeth and only eating sweet things." (The young man had occasionally brought sweets and biscuits along with him when he visited his grandparents.)

B: "So the apology was the thing that removed the anger, not the food on the table?"

(Laughter.) "No! It was both. The apology was words. The meat was food. First the son apologizes. When he had spoken those words, explaining clearly, then he put the meat in front of his father. It is the meat that quietens the hunger. That is clear."

Angry shades can cause illness, sometimes prolonged suffering. But they do not aim at killing the smitten person. Sometimes they cause temporary sterility in women, but they are not believed to cause miscarriages and stillbirths. "When a shade is angry, it reveals its anger in sickness. But miscarriages and stillbirths are not sicknesses of the womb that are caused by the shades. The sickness of the shades is painful because all sickness is painful. But they do not kill. That is the difference. If a person is sick with the sickness of the shades, then they are angry because of something. When their anger is cooled, then that person gets well again."

Informants and evidence suggest two main reasons for shades revealing their anger besides that of mutual co-operation and understanding. Firstly, in cases of marital misbehaviour by a wife, the indignation of the shades is revealed in temporary sterility which is lifted only when the matter has been confessed and "washed". Although a wife's secret lover may be unknown to her husband, "the shades know of him because they know the thing that is taking place." The temporary sterility brings about two essentially good things, i.e. it halts the breeding of undesired people and it may force the wife to confession, the confession depending on what the woman may regard to be the cause of her sterility.

Zulu thought-patterns allow for a lively and very real fear of witches and witchcraft and, as we shall see presently, witchcraft is often associated with women.[37] Sterility may be an indication that the woman is a witch and desires *uhlangothi wabathakathi* (the species of witches) to increase by her forthcoming children with her lover. This intention the shades disclose, and, defending the interests of their survivors through the husband, cause sterility. The diviner at eThelezini said on this issue: "They stop the breeding of bad people (*Baval' inzalo yabantu ababi*)."

The sterility may arouse her husband's suspicions of moral misconduct and if he thinks that his wife may be practising witchcraft, he may put pressure on her towards confession. The aspect of pressure towards confession is important because, as one person put it: "Even if she (the wife) is not *umthakathi*, she should not entertain another man. It brings about hatred. Then his hatred becomes the cause of *ubuthakathi*." On my asking him to explain further, he said: "A woman's desire must be like a river, flowing in one direction only. If it divides, then it causes trouble. Her desire cannot go to her husband and the next time to the other one. Why did she accept the other one? Perhaps because he said something nice. So she desires him. Then the desire just grows in her. Eventually she will desire him and not her husband. Then she hates her husband when he comes, wanting her. She hates him with great hatred and decides to kill him. She speaks one night with the lover. They decide to kill the husband. So they do it, becoming *abathakathi*. That is what I mean, when I said that he must beat her until she confesses. She is not dry because of nothing (i.e. sterile without cause). There is a reason that the shades have seen."

Secondly, although all people, including children, are potential shades, Zulu claim that the community of the shades do not accept anybody into their midst if, during some stage of life, serious misconduct has taken place and the matter not confessed and cleared. It has been difficult to trace to what extent that thought-pattern may be influenced by Christian teachings on condemnation after death, but certainly old people claim that this thinking has always been in the minds of Zulu.

An elderly man at H fell very ill (description of his illness suggested pneumonia). A diviner was called to diagnose both the source of the suffering and possible cure. As the underlying cause of the sickness the diviner suggested angry shades. After two days, since the condition of the patient had deteriorated fast, the diviner was called on again and asked to determine the cause of the shades' indignation. The diviner claimed that the trouble lay with the patient's two sons who were in Durban attending to their work. A taxi was hired and the sons called home over the following weekend. On their arrival the diviner left, but the condition of the aged father immediately led to confession and the slaughtering of a goat. The background to the confession was the following. The elder of the two sons was a widower, his wife having passed away two years previously. He lived in a hostel with bachelors. His younger brother was married and was in the fortunate position of having a house, his wife also being employed in the city. The elder brother often visited with his younger brother and on occasions when the younger brother was working on nightshift, the elder slept with his brother's wife. This having gone on for some time and the elder brother seriously reflecting on proposing to the woman to divorce the brother in order to marry him, he claimed in his confession that he had started hating his younger brother. This hatred had caused the indignation of the shades and their subsequent legitimate anger. But the father of the sons, i.e. the patient, also confessed that he should have attended to his elder son's marriage before letting him return to the city after his wife's death; people claimed that he would have acted correctly if he had done so, in that he had foreseen the possible evil that could have arisen between his two sons.

I discussed the case with the diviner who attended to the patient. He claimed that it was correct that both the elder son and the patient had confessed and that both had reason to do so. Had this not taken place, 'the son who did such evil would have become a shade *elizulayo nje* (just roaming about aimlessly)." The diviner claimed that he would not have been accepted in the community of the shades because of the seriousness of the offence. That the elder brother had sought women he did not regard as bad, but that he had 'planted in his brother's garden" was the serious aspect. This, he said, was serious indeed and caused the anger of the shades. That the anger was valid and legitimate was not a matter to be discussed even—so clear did it appear to him, and that it had been reflected in the son's father and not the elder son who, in fact, was the cause of the anger, was a symbol and clear indication of the seriousness of the offence.

Although sickness originating from the shades always is regarded as justified and moral—"who are we to scold our seniors?"—it must be attended to as soon as possible. At least a promise towards ritual celebration must be given if the slaughtering is not possible immediately. Delay may prove fatal, for witches, conscious of the opportunity caused by the "sickness of the shades", may snatch an occasion to further the sickness and turn it to meet their own ends. What, therefore, started off as a seemingly just and moral sickness[38] caused by the anger of the shades, may end in death. A friend said on this issue: "That is the danger with all anger, even the anger of the shades. One does not know whether it will end with the sickness of the shades or whether it will continue."

There is, therefore, always urgency in diagnosing the cause of the sickness.

This is the primary concern of the kinsmen and friends of the patient. "The first thing is to find the cause. We do not know it. That is the work of the diviner. He divines and says it. When he has spoken those words of the source of the sickness, then we know what to do. But first he must point out the direction (i.e. the origin) of the sickness."

An old, spiteful and malicious widow lived with a grandson. She became ill and a diviner attributed the cause of her illness to her husband who had died about seven years previously. His shade was "angry because of the woman's attitude towards her grandson whom she did not respect as she ought". (The old widow was openly spoken of as irritable and very spiteful towards her children and their children. Admiration was expressed for the grandson who, although constantly humiliated, nevertheless had her in his homestead.) The widow dismissed the diviner and his diagnosis as unreliable and called on another to attend to her case. He came to the same conclusion and is claimed to have advised her to *vuma inhliziyo embi* (confess a bad spirit/attitude)." She dismissed him also and his advice and was eventually called upon by a local Zionist-group leader. He is said to have professed having seen her trouble in a dream and that angels had revealed anger in heaven because of her *isono senzondo* (sin of envy). He gave her the advice to confess her sin and be baptised the following Sunday with subsequent prayer for healing. The widow agreed because she regarded the Zionist leader to be *umuntu kaNkulunkulu* (a man of God). She personally claimed to have become better immediately, but on the Saturday before the Sunday when she was to be baptised, the old woman died. Due to tense relations between the woman's grandson and the Zionist leader, the first diviner was called to diagnose the cause of the woman's death, the son suspecting that the Zionist leader had something to do with it. The diviner diagnosed the death as due to "being eaten up by *umthakathi*", but said that he could not see clearly who *umthakathi* was. As far as the grandson was concerned, he felt certain that it was the Zionist leader that had brought death to his home. His mother commented: "It is true that the old woman died painfully. It is clear that the two diviners spoke the truth when they indicated an angry shade. Even we could see that matter quite clearly. But now the death was a different matter. There was *umthakathi* who reached out the hand." The consulting diviner agreed totally, adding: "Yes, *umthakathi* reached out his hand. That is their way. They take the opportunity (*ukubamba ithuba*). She died because of *umthakathi* whereas the sickness started with the wrath of the shades." [39]

Some people say that "this sickness caused by the anger of the shades" can sometimes be recognised without the aid of a diviner. Fainting is one characteristic of their indignation. Also pain that seems to pierce the body from the one side to the other is their pressure on survivors. Patients smitten by the shades do not either cough up or otherwise expel blood, nor do they develop open wounds. "The sickness is just inside. It is not a snake which eats up the man from the inside. Nor is there blood. There is nothing on the body. It is just altogether inside, piercing like a knife, sometimes here and sometimes in another place."

The indignation of the shades is aroused if a lineage member is unduly humiliated as the following case illustrates. A diviner of fair reputation had been consulted by a man. But the diviner had not given him the solution that he had expected and he is said to have risen to his feet and accused the diviner of being an *umthakathi*. (This accusation is serious in the ears of anybody but particularly serious in the case of a diviner who is deemed to be the "great enemy of *abathakathi*".) Friends who heard the man address the diviner thus, reported that they warned him and suggested that he immediately withdraw his statement and confess his anger. But the man did not heed their advice and rode away on his horse. The diviner is claimed to have said that the horse would die as a result of the man's words. The following morning the man found his horse dead for no apparent reason. Inspection of the carcass revealed no wound or other outer cause of the animal's death. Neighbours of the man were excited and shocked, but there was no amazement. One of them said: "They (the diviner's shades) hated him (the owner of the horse) because he had offended their child. That is why they killed his horse." All without exception were convinced that the shades had acted justly, "because the man had offended in a very serious way (*ukuthuka ngendlela emangalisayo*)." "What made it even worse was that he did not listen to the warnings. Truly, in one way he was fortunate in that it was only the horse."

The anger of shades is also manifest in dreams, sickness,[40] and large numbers of ways which diviners reveal. Unsuccessful business matters, death of stock and other domestic animals may be attributed to their anger; misfortune in schools, unexpected unfavourable events, accidents, lost court-cases when everything seemed to speak for a favourable outcome and a great many omens may all be symbols of the anger of the shades.[41]

There is justified and morally defensible anger also among seniors and men of authority over against their juniors.[42] It is used as their tool to enforce correct behaviour and "a good life". Chiefs and magistrates are said to have a large amount of anger and put it into force when they judge cases and punish wrongdoers. But informants are explicit that the anger, although fully legitimate and moral, must, in order to accomplish good intentions with it and hence not cause embarrassment later on, always be under control. "If the anger is not controlled, then the authority is forcing himself on the wrongdoers (*ukuzibuqa*). The wrongdoer may confess. But it does not come from the heart. He is just forcing himself because of his fear of the authority. But as for he himself, he does not wish to confess, not being convinced. It does not come from his inside. It just comes with words because of the fear of the authority."[43]

The anger of a local chief had been kindled against a young man from Durban (born and brought up in the city) who, after seducing a girl living in the chief's area of administration and thus fathering a child, made preparations to marry the girl. He paid the relevant fee of paternity partly to the girl's senior, partly to her mother, but, due to ignorance pertaining to customary procedure, had not forwarded the chief's fee to the chief. In the final stages of the marriage preparations the man found that the local shop-keepers became hesitant in assisting him to obtain the things necessary for the wedding. The area being quite far from other shops, he was dependent on them. He expressed his amazement to the girl's elder brother with whom he was very friendly and the latter explained the cause of the shop-keepers' attitude. He also suggested a suitable procedure in approaching the chief, partly in paying the fee and explaining his ignorance with an additional sum of R5-00. A suitable person was approached who took the apologies of the Durbanite to the chief with R5-00 set aside for the purpose and the fee payable. The chief is said "to have forgotten his anger as soon as he heard the words of the messenger". Shortly afterwards the shop-keepers were willing to assist in the purchase of wedding requirements again!

At least in theory, Zulu society allows for the anger of commoners to be felt over against their seniors if they have been unjustly treated. "A man can feel offended in his heart even against the shades! At even the shades, as I said! So, when he slaughters the animal of the shades, having slaughtered perhaps one or two beasts previously, he speaks to them about this thing. He speaks nicely, asking them why they are eating up all the cattle. But when he is speaking, he is revealing heat in his heart because of the many beasts that he is slaughtering without seeing something (i.e. any results)." In the man's views there was certainly anger and heat in the slaughterer's heart, and that this anger was valid he did not doubt, "because of the many cattle that were no more". The anger was controlled—otherwise he would not have been able to speak "nicely". My friend was certain that the shades would be conscious of his legitimate anger "because they see what is in his heart and can understand the interpretation of the words". The anger being controlled was also reflected in the man's willingness to slaughter a second and third time and, important to note, his willingness to confess his indignation, although covered up in eloquence.

Chiefs who are thought to be unnecessarily strict or harsh in their executing their office, e.g. in judging court-cases, can in theory be subject to their people's anger. Particularly those who exercise authority unfairly and are openly unjust in their handling of matters will experience their subordinates' anger, although it may not break out in open conflict with them. Some informants say that *umzabalazo* (an atmosphere of cool inactivity towards authority) is an expression of anger towards authority. A school-master put it thus in English which he spoke fluently: "This anger is the same as the wall of solid coldness and resistance when people simply do what they must, without speaking or showing any feelings. That is anger." Traditionalists claim that *umzabalazo* is a new way of expressing legitimate anger. Formerly, "if *abakhulu* (authority) became sick, feeling very cold, the feet being cold and the chest being cold, then it was the anger of somebody working this sickness of cold." Others claim that if the authority became weak in the limbs or "felt pain as if there was salt in the joints (rheumatism?)", this was a sign of the anger of subordinates. Others, again, claim that paralysis was caused by the anger of minors but, contrary to pain and cold which could be caused by individuals, was an expression of the indignation of a whole community or group of people who had been mistreated.

Dreams, sickness and misfortunes which befall a person as a result of legitimate anger are always justified in that their cause is moral and their aims are defensible. Besides being a retribution on the wrongdoer, the suffering aims at curing the sidestep from accepted walks of life and is thought to be a warning to the person inflicted against future departures from "the good life".

Equally justified are steps taken by people who suspect immorality by possible intruders. A man fearing adultery by his wife, may, without her knowledge, give her medicine which will bring farreaching and fearful effects on her possible lover. His giving his wife the medicine is a moral act. It is a justified precautionary step taken because he is defending his marital and legal rights. Men who by way of medicine safeguard their homes against malicious people are not responsible for sufferings inflicted on intruders. The following is evidence of this thought-pattern.

A man whose vicious dog one night had torn to bits a passing stranger's clothing was accused of witchcraft by the stranger. The chief who heard the case in which the stranger accused the dog's owner of setting the animal on him, freed the accused "because the stranger had come too near the homestead at a time when normally nobody wanders about (i.e. at night)". The procedure of the case was enlightening on matters pertaining to legitimate and illegitimate anger. The accused, being brought to trial on an accusation of witchcraft (*ubuthakathi*) admitted that he feared the outcome of the case very much indeed, although he claimed that his conscience (*unembeza*) was clear. The accuser, on the other hand, claimed no evil intention at all when passing by the homestead, and it was mere ignorance of its presence in that particular place that had brought him so near to it. His accusation was that the dog's owner "hated strangers, even if they did no harm". The chief had indicated that he did not think the case worthwhile, but on the accuser associating his accusation with hatred he had changed his mind and taken it up. This was also the cause of the accused's anxiety. The latter, however, successfully argued his case, shifting the emphasis from hating strangers to defence against people with hatred (*ukuvimbela abantu abanenzondo*). Having convinced the chief of his good intention in hating strangers, his anger was deemed legal and justified. On no occasion during the hearing did the accused deny his having hatred and anger within himself. This was not the question at stake. What was in question was whether the hatred was directed towards the accuser in which case the court findings certainly would have been different. In a lengthy and exceedingly well prepared speech in which each word had most probably been reflected on, the accused related his anger and hatred, which he readily admitted, to the accuser's declared innocence and lack of evil intention, directing his own hatred to people with hatred. His hatred, addressed towards strangers and realized in the vicious dog had, therefore, been misdirected on this particular occasion towards a stranger who happened to pass the home at a suspicious time. With an amazing ability he led the accuser to admit that he had passed the homestead when anybody would have been suspicious of evil intent and hence the dog's attack on him.

The related court-case and further evidence shows clearly that, firstly, Zulu thought-patterns do not have a fixed code of laws which stipulate boundaries between moral and immoral use of anger. Although, in theory, the divisons are clear, in practice there is room for manipulating the boundaries. Secondly, it is the circumstances related to a particular case of anger that will finally decide whether it was moral or not. A person's depending on *unembeza* is not final, for, as the chief who heard the case related said: "Do these two (*unembeza* and *ugovane*) not occupy the same hut (i.e. the throat)? So which one is speaking when a man talks through the doorway (i.e. the mouth), not revealing who the speaker inside the hut is?"

Thought-patterns allow for a single cure of suffering experienced as a result of justified anger. Confession, which, in practice, involves admission of anger and an expression of a change of spirit is the starting point and may, sometimes, lead to a ritual celebration. But the latter is not always necessary, particularly if the cause of the anger is regarded as a minor one. But whether there is ritual beerdrinking and/or slaughtering or not, confession is essential if the anger is to be stilled and normal relations between people and their kinsmen function again.

Illegitimate Use of Anger

Evidence shows that although legitimate and moral anger is defensible and indeed works towards men living "the good life" on the one hand, and is regarded as an essential in the composition of man on the other, it is feared. The fear is rooted in the devastating consequences of anger. It is caused by the uncertainty, sometimes, of what in a given situation may be judged to be moral anger or may be regarded as illegitimate and, hence, evil anger. The two categories of anger are each other's opposites. Moral anger works for and supports "the good life" in society, while illegitimate anger, realized in *ubuthakathi*, is nothing less than evil incarnate.[44] It is important to note the great range between the two, although in reality the distance between them is very small. In the court-case related above, the accused could, in principle and in practice, have lost the case and, having lost it would not have been a man who in self-defence manipulated legitimate and morally acceptable anger. He would have been condemned as an *umthakathi*.

Hence a great fear is directed towards immoral and illegally applied anger. Not only are the consequences of it far more fearful and devastating than those which result from legitimate anger. As the illegitimate anger is wholly evil and bad, so are its results. Immoral anger and its practical implication in *ubuthakathi* has but one single goal for which it strives, annihilation.

Ubuthakathi and its Reality

The Zulu idiom *ubuthakathi*[45] implies two fields of evil.[46] Firstly, it refers to an incarnate power geared towards harm and destruction which manifests itself through humans and, either directly or indirectly, is addressed to fellow human beings. The manipulators of *ubuthakathi* are termed *abathakathi*. Equipped with power of *ubuthakathi*, they are criminality personified. They and their power are mysterious in the sense that nobody can give an appreciable (from the Zulu point of view) explanation of their frightful abilities (e.g. riding through the air, invisibility) and malicious exercises.[47] While Zulu tales and fables allow for creatures which speak amazing things and beings which have mysterious and fantastic abilities, these are accepted as fictitious and imaginative. But *abathakathi* and their power of *ubuthakathi* are very much a reality and nothing pertaining to them and their evil is doubted or denied. They are real in an undisputable sense.

Secondly, *ubuthakathi* is associated with the embedded neutral powers of materia, *imithi*, the manipulation of which is geared towards evil ends. Assuming that the aims of using medicines are destruction and harm (as opposed to healing and/or self-defence), the manipulator is also termed *umthakathi*. Naturally, this understanding of both *ubuthakathi* and *abathakathi* is believed to be as real and undisputed a manifestation of evil as the former.

It is important to note the difference between *ubuthakathi* and *abathakathi*, for, although the Zulu root in both is the same, the understanding of each is very different. Zulu themselves are very conscious of the differences and in discussing the issue with them, they do not hesitate to distinguish the one from the other. On the other hand the distinctions do not exclude an extensive overlapping.[48]

In keeping with accepted English terminology, *ubuthakathi* in the sense of being an incarnate power in men which may be geared towards harm and destruction is called witchcraft and people who practise this criminal offence are termed witches. The idiom sorcery refers to the use of powers embedded in materia towards evil ends and the manipulator of the powers with evil aims are the sorcerers.[49]

Zulu claim that the idioms *ubuthakathi* and *abathakathi* imply in the first instance evil and the manipulators of evil. In the second place comes the kind of evil and its agent. "When we have seen that there is evil around us and that somebody is killing us, then we say, 'Is there not *ubuthakathi* here in our presence?' That is the thing of importance with us. Only some time later people may ask, saying, 'Forsooth, there is evil. Is there any clarity as to the kind of evil? Was it brought by familiars by chance? Or perhaps it came through medicines?' Whereas we ourselves can see that there is evil surrounding us, it is the diviner who will see what kills us and what person is doing this thing." It is quite clear that Zulu thinking is preoccupied with evil itself in the first instance. Thereafter comes a defining of its course and source.

The uses of power towards evil ends in witchcraft and sorcery are quite distinct. Firstly, witchcraft assumes a supernatural and mystical character of the power and the witch. There is no end to what amazing and incredible things witches can accomplish.[50] In sorcery this characteristic is lacking. In sorcery it is rather a matter-of-fact, based partly on knowledge pertaining to the properties of the great variety of *imithi* and the ingredients of medicines, partly on sometimes very lively symbolic associations.

There is in the witch, as we shall see presently, a physical condition of the body which is characteristic of witches. Although not always recognizable, it is there. People will argue that even if this condition is not evident, it arouses suspicions and is certainly recognised by diviners. But with sorcerers it is different. Medicines can be obtained from a herbalist by practically anybody and the outcome of sorcery depends neither on the sorcerer nor on the herbalist who knows how to manipulate the power of medicines. In sorcery the power is in the medicines. Thirdly, witches are thought to remain witches always, even if they have been identified by diviners or caught in the act of witchcraft. People say that not even confession and expression of a forthcoming "good life" will help. "That is why this kind of *abathakathi* must be killed. They must be removed totally because this thing in them never comes out of them. Sometimes if the witch is a coward it may come out fully in the confession. It comes because of fear. But tomorrow that person if full (of it) again. The witches know their people. They come the following night after the cleansing and return that person to *ubuthakathi*, saying, 'If you do not come with us, we will kill you just in this place you are occupying now.' She becomes afraid and accompanies them, becoming one of them again. It is impossible for a witch to separate from witchcraft."[51]

With the manipulator of medical powers, on the other hand, it is different. A manipulator can one day be the sorcerer who supplies medicines towards harmful ends and assists his client in the manipulation of the powers. But on the following day he is the herbalist who offers *imithi* to cure the harm of yesterday. "This is the way *abathakathi yemithi* (lit. evildoers with medicines, sorcerers) work. That is the fearful thing with them. Today they take money from a man because of the medicines of death. Tomorrow they take money from the sufferer because of the medicines of healing. Today this man is *umbulali* (killer). Tomorrow he is *umsindisi* (saviour) of that very man he was killing.

This is the reason for people of medicines (*abantu yemithi*) being very much feared. It is not known what they are up to. Further, their medicines are frightening."[32]

Various reasons for a herbalist's participation in sorcery are given. But financial interests are brought to the fore again and again. It is possible that this is a major force which puts pressure on both him and society to accept the herbalist who manipulates the powers he masters in this double capacity. Nobody hesitates to attribute to a herbalist, particularly a renowned man of medicines, this capability. Neither does anybody doubt that in a particular situation a herbalist very well can be a sorcerer. The client who approaches him with a view to obtain the required medicines is naturally a sorcerer. But the function of being a sorcerer is dropped with the herbalist as soon as he has completed his part of the work in supplying the medicines, while, with the client, it is dropped when the medicines have accomplished their aim with regard to a particular person. Further, contrary to witches who operate witchcraft "from another place", sorcerers are people with whom one associates daily. They are the men of everyday Zulu society.

Fourthly, witches are very often, though not always, thought to be females. They belong to the community of witches and are strongly inclined towards sexuality. Their breed is the result of offensive and vile sexual relations while their preoccupation is to destroy fertility in men, beasts (particularly cattle) and fields.

This strong emphasis on sexuality is not characteristic of sorcerers and sorcery, if fertility may be distinguished from sexuality. Fertility is, according to Zulu thinking and in accordance with much of Africa, the ultimate good, and accordingly, welfare is geared towards a preservation and sustaining of fertility, if not extension of it. It is therefore quite natural that also sorcery, being evil, aims at the destruction of fertility, either directly or indirectly, as is the case with witches and witchcraft. But sorcery is therefore not preoccupied with sexuality. Sorcerers do not increase through incest and obscenity. Sorcerers do not belong to a community characterised by beastiality and sodomy. Sorcerers arise from a specific situation which requires the ability and possession of medicines which are required to act in a given direction. A friend, defining this distinction between witches and sorcerers, said: "Witches and witchcraft are everywhere, touching on everything, especially the hot places (i.e. the reproductive organs). We do not know from where they do it. We just suddenly feel that there is something in that region, doing something. But medicines *we* can touch. We even know the habits and places of medicines." Sorcery is thought to be the work of men. But witchcraft "is the work of women". Medicines go with men who know the powers of *imithi*. Witchcraft goes with the anger of women (*ubuthakathi buhambisana nolaka lwabasifazane*)."[53]

A fifth and important distinction between witchcraft and sorcery is the fields in which they are said to operate. Witchcraft is seldom thought to operate within a lineage or clan, but generally outside it and preferably, today, outside the nation. Sorcery, on the other hand, knows of no such boundaries and can operate within a lineage as well as outside it. Because of overlapping between sorcery and witchcraft, there are far more cases of sorcery outside a lineage than within it, however.

Lastly, some informants suggest that "witchcraft is worse than sorcery". The quotation suggests a generally accepted evaluation of witchcraft and sorcery.

The far greater fear of witchcraft is due to the wider range over which witch-craft makes itself felt while that of sorcery is limited. Although sometimes one is given the impression that people are evaluating evil itself, claiming that the one evil is greater than the other, this is in reality not the case. Zulu who have systematized their thinking on these matters say that "there is no evil which is worse or less than another. Evil is evil. That is all." The diviner at eThelezini said: "It is because witches are women that they are feared so much. They are cunning and sly in a way which is greater than that of men. Sorcerers are men. Their evils are on this earth. But that of witches comes from Satan. That is why they also are called *amasokoco*.[54] But a man (i.e. a sorcerer) can-not be *isokoco*."

It is also evident that the emotional involvement and the greater fear of witches and their activities rather than of sorcerers and their manipulation of medicines has roots in the community of witches. Being a community "they help each other in doing bad things. But a sorcerer is always working by him-self with medicines."

The presence and gruesome activities of *abathakathi* are not only theoreti-cal for Zulu. It is also reality in its deepest sense. A denial of the presence of sorcery and withcraft is a denial of the existence and activities of evil. A man, on my being introduced to him by a friend as a useful informant on *ubuthakathi* and related matters, said: "You must not start questioning me whether these things are true, as other whites have done. Then we cannot talk. But if you just listen nicely and believe what I tell you, not asking questions of doubt, I will tell you about these things. Just let me ask you, son of a white man, I being a black man, do you believe that *ubuthakathi* exists?" I answered that I believe in *ubusathane*. "That is the same thing as *ubutha-kathi*. *Ubusathane* and *ubuthakathi* are one and the same thing. There is no difference. So I can say that you believe in *ubuthakathi*. I am glad. (He seemed considerably relieved, took snuff and offered me his snuff-container.) Yes, I am glad. So now we can speak about those things you wish to know about pertaining to us Zulu."[55]

Certainly thinking on *ubuthakathi* does not always follow only traditional patterns of expressing itself. Zulu society allows for continual and ongoing ad-ditions to the ideas of the reality of evil. *Ubuthakathi* is inclusive in a remark-able way, no description however fanciful and incredible being too extravagant to be true in the realm of *ubuthakathi*. This belongs to the nature of evil for, "had it been law-abiding (i.e. following set rules and regulations) it could be trapped. But who has caught *ubuthakathi*? Indeed, *abathakathi* are exposed and treated, but *ubuthakathi* is always on new roads."

That *abathakathi* and *ubuthakathi* are altogether evil and corrupt needs to be underlined. While the anger of the shades leads to dreams, sickness and sometimes extended suffering—as does the calling of a diviner for example—the ultimate aim of their inflicting pain on their survivors is never death. It is always the welfare of the individual or the society as such that they have in mind. But with the anger expressed in *ubuthakathi* and realized by *abathakathi* the goal is sickness as an avenue towards death. Death, in turn, manipulated successfully towards evil ends, leads to annihilation which includes interference also with the shades.[56] "There is nothing good in *abathakathi* and their work. They just want to kill. To kill is their joy. That is when they are happy. When a man is sick they are pleased, but when he does not get better they are even more pleased. They are very happy when he dies. That is the great thing for them. So you see that there is no good in them. Nothing! Not even a morsel! We say in Zulu, 'Bamthenele pansi' of abathakathi, meaning that they have killed a man in his youth before even giving birth (lit. they have castrated him in youth). That is when they are most happy, killing a man before he has seen his children." [57]

Zulu find themselves involved in and affected by the realm of the shades on the one hand and that of abathakathi on the other. While, in the lives of men and women, the shades in many respects are the explanation to sickness, dreams, failures, embarrassments, etc., to mention negative aspects only, abathakathi are the answer to all calamities which cannot be traced to the shades. What incidents occur and are not covered by thought-patterns which associate the happening with the shades are, without further questioning, shifted to the activities of abathakathi. Zulu thinking does not recognize a stage in between the two which would be the equivalent to Western concepts of chance, fortune or luck. In Zulu society these do not exist. "There is always somebody (responsible)", as a friend put it.

Mainly old people claim that formerly sorcery was far less common than it is believed to be today. On the other hand there are young people in Zulu society who believe that medicine is a necessity in all ubuthakathi. "How can there be ubuthakathi without medicines?" I was discussing this issue with two young Zulu at eNthembeni royal homestead when a maternal grandmother to them who was listening to us said: "That is ubuthakathi of today. But in the time of the kings (i.e. when the Zulu kings had power) this thing of medicines was only for healing." No doubt the old lady exaggerated somewhat, but her statement nevertheless casts light on thinking pertaining to this issue.

Schooled and sophisticated Zulu often accept sorcery as valid, although they sometimes tend to hesitate to commit themselves to a belief in witchcraft or, as is generally the case, refer to it as "something of the heathens and backward people who believe in such things". A school-teacher said: "Sorcery is the same as poisoning and bad food which is rotten. Of this thing we have plenty, even at this school. Children complain of pains caused by poison. So the matter of medicines is the same as poisoning. But of witches I have only heard. Since I became a man of books and studied very much, I have given up this belief in those things of witchcraft. Today I see that Satan is the cause of all the evil that surrounds us."

Rural settings offer a profound belief in both witchcraft and sorcery, although the cases of either overlapping or only sorcery dominate the minds of people. In the urbanised areas emphasis is put far more on sorcery, only some people being convinced that witches practise in cities. Few denied the existence of witches, but they indicated that witchcraft "is the thing found in the country-side. Here in the cities they do not thrive so well. In this place there are many medicines instead." [59]

Through Anger to Ubuthakathi

Anger is the root of ubuthakathi. Unless the anger is "cooled" it inevitably will express itself in ubuthakathi. The longer anger remains in people and grows in them, the more devastating the forthcoming eruption.

Behind, and as preliminaries towards anger, are a number of emotional feelings which culminate in expressed anger. Professor Evans-Pritchard's description of Azande thought-patterns are applicable also to the Zulu situation: "Azande say that hatred, jelousy, envy, backbiting, slander and so forth go ahead and witchcraft follows after. A man must first hate his enemy and will then bewitch him."[60] One Zulu said that *ubuthakathi* is "like a tree which is bad. When it has grown it starts bearing bad fruit. That is *ubuthakathi* fruit (*izithelo zobuthakathi*). It (the fruit) is poisonous. It kills. The tree is the anger. It is supported (lit. carried) by its roots which are many. These roots are suspicions, envy, misgivings, quarrels, bad talk, jealousy. All these things are roots. There are even other roots also. They hold up the tree."[61]

People who do not show respect to their seniors and superiors are suspects. Disrespect is also realised in a persons not attending social functions such as beerparties, marriages, etc. Today even Christmas celebrations are included in the list of social gatherings. Neglecting to attend funerals is particularly suspect, especially if one lives near to the bereaved. In failing to attend the burial itself, one also fails in expressing sympathy.

Disrespect involves also the shades and a man's neglect in attending to their needs arouses anger. Disrespect towards the shades is reflected particularly in not attending to ritual celebrations. Although people are convinced that death cannot come from the shades unless something exceptionally bad has taken place, one reliable friend said: "Their hunger can cause such anger in them that they just give up hoping. Then they just leave that person, even allowing him to be taken over by *abathakathi* to kill him." Failure in upholding traditional ethical standards and values which have been sanctioned of old by the shades is also a serious reflection of disrespect.

In general, immoral anger also has its roots in selfish greed. Or it may be excited by pride. "It is like this. A man has a favourite wife. The other wife hears the husband praising the favourite one and her food. This causes envy (*umona*) and pride (*ukuziqhenya*). The pride springs from the favourite wife, she boasts about the words of her husband. The other wife hears it. There develops hatred. It comes to the proud wife and it comes to the other one. It fills them both. Sometimes more hatred is found in the second wife who did not hear the words of the husband spoken about herself. Then they just look at each other with hatred in the eyes. They do not speak to each other. One day something happens. That thing that happens is *ubuthakathi*. The bewitching started in the pride of the first one who was praised. It caused jealousy in the other one. It grew in each of them until in the end it became hatred. Then they bewitched each other." Another informant explained it thus: "Two people quarrel. It may be just a small matter of no significance. But they quarrel. The next day they still quarrel, speaking perhaps with even greater heat (*ukushisa*) than yesterday. The third day it is still words which are even hotter. The anger glows in their faces. They carry in themselves nothing but evil thoughts and plans. They just keep quiet and do not speak to each other because of the separation caused by the anger. A man sees the danger that is brooding and he listens to them both when they relate the cause of the silence. He says to each of them, 'Can so small a thing cause such heat? No, my friends, just sit down here beside me and let us cool this matter so that you do not hate each other. There is danger when there is hatred.' But the hatred and the anger has already grown so much that they do not heed the pleasant words of the intervener (*umluleki*). The anger still breeds further in them.

271

When the heart is filled to capacity with anger, then they do the things that should not be done. That thing is *ubuthakathi*. It is the bad thing which should never happen. Perhaps one of them dies. Perhaps both. They bring death on each other because of that thing which grew in their hearts commencing with a quarrel."

Envy and jealousy also cause hatred and attract *ubuthakathi*. An industrious man who has success with cattle is said to awaken envy. In towns or in industry the over-ambitious are warned. Women arouse envy by tilling too large fields or spending more time in cultivating them than others do. Wives who strive for their husband's attention over against co-wives in the polygamous homes that still do exist are said to invite trouble as does over-emphasized conscientiousness in e.g. employees in a hotel or elsewhere where people work together.

A person's behaviour can arouse envy and consequently anger. Greed expressed in not arranging parties, or, if they do take place, in not supplying a sufficient quantity of food (beer and/or meat in particular) is condemned. Pride and boastfulness, a lack of sympathy and hospitality, these and a host of arrogant and humiliating approaches to fellow-men cause people to "look at a man with another eye. Then eventually one bewitches the man who is not good."

We have seen how power is a characteristic of man, a part of his composition, and is found in lesser or greater quantities in all people. Put into negative forms of expression, it breaks out in anger and consequently *ubuthakathi*. Society allows for safety-valves for the outlet of anger. But people also claim that the emotions can be controlled and not allowed to develop into anger. While anger can be sucessfully handled in confessions and not break out in *ubuthakathi*, emotions can be controlled by the individual. But it is important that they are not allowed to develop into anger or hatred. Once having become anger, then the personal attention may not be successful. "Sometimes, if a person feels envy or some other thing in the heart (*inhliziyo*), he controls himself (*ukuzibhopha*, lit. to tie himself up). That is the same as cooling that thing in the heart. He controls himself until he is altogether cooled down (*ukuthamba*, lit. become soft). He does this so that people do not accuse him of anger and hatred. Or he controls himself because he sees that his anger will not lead to any good. Then he cools down."

One informant claimed that children born of witches and which the mother had intended to become a witch but not initiated into the community of witches, were potential witches to a greater degree than commoners. "These people who have not experienced *ukugwemba* must be very careful and control themselves strongly." She claimed that these people, generally women, although not conscious of their mother's former evil intentions with them "felt in the heart of some bad things that they had drunk with the mother's milk", and therefore had to repress any emotions that could lead to anger. "That is why such people often are very cool indeed. They are so cool that it is said, 'What kind of mother did So-and-so have, this person being so soft?' They ask this question, wondering what kind of person the mother was." [62]

There is also a form of *ubuthakathi* which cannot be traced to either witches or sorcerers. It is that which is referred to in the expression *abathakathi bafakhe inhlakanhlaka emzini (abathakathi* have caused general confusion in a homestead),[63] describing general disunity and a tense atmosphere in a family. K commented on the idiom thus: "It is when a diviner divines and sees nothing. He divines again and sees nothing. He divines even a third time and sees only darkness. Then he ceases divining, admitting inability and returns the fee. A second diviner divines. Eventually he also returns the fee, having seen nothing. Both have not seen any cause. They do not see a person (who is the responsible witch or sorcerer). They do not see any animals even (familiars). All they see is that there are bad things. The people themselves who are troubled do not report any suspicions. Then it becomes clear that it is *abathakathi* that are attacking that home. That is the explanation of those words. It means that there is no definite witch or sorcerer. They have just come generally from their place to cause trouble in a home."

Another informant who was very strong on the point that not all evil could be traced to particular witches and sorcerers said: "When they (*abathakathi*) hear of a happy homestead where there is peace, quiet (*ukuthula*) and no noise (*umsindo*), they attack it (*ukusukela*). One goes to *umnumzana* (senior), another goes to his wife, another to somebody else, and so on, each person with his/her *umthakathi*. They trouble them with bad dreams and put bad attitudes (*imimoya emibi*) into them. They wake up in the morning. The husband speaks harshly. The wife does not answer nicely, being disrespectful. The children refuse to obey, being rude and neglectful. They refuse to go to school, saying that they dislike it. That is how it starts. Then the people of that home get hot. There is no more peace. The peace was taken away by *abathakathi* who came to cause trouble that night." [64]

Becoming a Witch

Although witchcraft and sorcery are on the minds of all, and the fear of successfully manipulated powers towards evil and destruction is very real and ever present in people's thinking, there is great reluctance to speak about it. This, from the Zulu point of view, is very understandable. "It must not be spoken of. It is very ill. If a person speaks of it a great deal, it raises suspicions. People say, 'Why does this person speak so much of this thing? Is there perhaps something (that he is doing)?'" Another said: "A man must try to forget his anger and all evil things. Now if he goes about talking of these things all the time, how can he forget them? He just reminds himself constantly and arouses questions with others. He must just keep quiet about such things."

While sorcery is fairly straightforward in that an angered person approaches a herbalist with a view to obtaining the required materia towards sorcery, becoming a witch and hence being in the frightening position of being able to practice witchcraft follows other patterns of development. It is these that will occupy our attention now.

Besides their increase through breeding described below, people can become witches, possibly against their will. Unusual sexual dreams or dreams involving relationships with unknown or suspect people of the opposite sex may be signs of commencing involvement. Dogs barking in the homestead at night in an unusual manner are signs either of somebody practising witchcraft in the home or witches "coming to fetch the person whom they want". Visible evidence to the effect that familiars have visited a home are interpreted likewise, i.e. footprints of cats, baboons and other animals of the night, droppings from them or evidence of their having interfered with the garbage-heaps. "So a man or his wife may be a witch without knowing it. The only sign that they have is that they wake up in the morning complaining of being tired. They themselves do not wish to become witches. Nobody wishes such things. They are simply caught by this power of evil, not being able to do anything (against it)." [65]

M described vividly one method whereby *abathakathi* uphold their kind. "A woman (who is *umthakathi* herself) desires her child to become *umthakathi*. She seduces somebody to have intercourse with her. Sometimes it is her familiar. Sometimes it is *u Tikoloshe*. Sometimes just a stranger who is not known to her. But it is not her husband. It must be another male. When she gives birth to this child of witchcraft (i.e. which is to be *umthakathi*) she breastfeeds it like all other children. The thing she avoids to do is to *gwemba*[66] the child. This habit of *ukugwemba* she avoids at all costs because if she did it the child would refuse of itself to become a witch. So she takes the child one night which is very dark, there being no moon, to a certain place known to her. She takes with her certain medicines pertaining to witchcraft and a knife and goes to that place. On arrival there she commences cutting incisions on the child. She cuts around the anus and rubs in medicines. She avoids *ukugwemba* and does this thing instead. She rubs medicines into the incisions until the bleeding has ceased. There is not as much bleeding as there is in *ukugwemba* for in it (*ukugwemba*) there must be much blood. If the child cries when she is doing the rubbing in of medicines she rejoices because weeping is the thing she likes. Then she wipes the tears of the child with the breast (i.e. she suckles it). Then she returns, having done the work in that place of secrecy. The child grows up. She watches it carefully. If it is weak and soft she refuses it in the society of the witches, saying, 'No. This child is weak. It cannot carry the burdens of *ubuthakathi*.' She does not initiate it into witchcraft. If it grows up being strong and courageous she will commence teaching it the things of witchcraft. She wakes it up at night and takes it with herself to the place of the witches and shows it all the things that pertain to *abathakathi*. Gradually the child gets to know all *abathakathi* of that place whilst they get to know it. One day, when the child is grown, they (the witches) will take it aside and speak, saying certain things. They say to it, 'Forsooth, we see you being grown up now. You have developed nicely. By this time you should know the habits of *abathakathi*. So we wish to remove you from your mother's back where you have been riding to this day. We wish to see you standing by yourself on your feet. Having been on your mother's back to this day you have learnt all things of this work that you have seen her doing all this time. Now, therefore, let us see your ability (*amandla akho*). Tomorrow at this time and at this place we wish to hear what you have done.' The child leaves them. It goes somewhere. Sometimes it is to the brother or to the sister (kinsmen of the lineage). Sometimes it is to one of the fathers (lineage seniors), or even the grandfather himself. If it is a girl, she can go even to her lover. The killing of that person visited is carried out in the way of *abathakathi*. The following night she appears before them (the *abathakathi* who sent the child) again and reports to them saying, 'The thing that I did is this-and-that. The manner of killing was this-and-that,' describing what it (the child) did. Then they say, 'No, we see your work. See, indeed you have today shown what you are able to do being *umthakathi*.' Then they separate the child from the mother, giving it another mate. They do the thing of *abathakathi* just there in the presence of them all. They watch and say, 'Indeed, this child is now grown up, doing this thing in this manner.' Even the mother is watching its child doing it with great zeal (the associations refer to sodomy). From that day they are separated, only meeting each other in the meeting-place of all witches. They work independently from that day. That is how *abathakathi* increase." [67]

Practically all informants agree that *abathakathi* are brought up and reared by women, it being they who decide whether a particular child is to be a witch or not. Whilst the narrator quoted above gave pointed emphasis to the custom of *ukugwemba* others suggest that many mothers indeed carry out the operation with their babies but that not all associate it so strongly with witchcraft and witches. Others, on the other hand, claim that this is the true interpretation of *ukugwema*. "That is taking out the bad blood which sits around the anus. But when women make their children into witches they do not take out the blood of witchcraft but strengthen it with medicines. That is why they make incisions around the anus and rub in medicines." [68]

A witch may introduce close friends into the arts of witchcraft. She does so if she sees a reason for a person becoming a witch, e.g. if she notices hatred and/or anger in a friend and who may wish to become a witch. But the choice is made with care, for, as one person put it, "to be *umthakathi* is a great work. It requires great strength and great courage. No weakling can become one who does frightful things." Informants agree that if people influence each other to become *abathakathi*, the pressure of influence is always put on a person of the opposite sex. With this person there will inevitably be sexual unions outside accepted and recognised standards of marital life.

Witches increase by breeding among themselves. "When they are together in that place of *abathakathi* they are always doing this thing. The females are always either pregnant or suckling. That is their way of increase." [69] Others have underlined the sexual relationships between a witch and her familiar/s and claim that the offspring from such connections are the future *abathakathi*.

Evidence shows that although witchcraft is not necessarily hereditary, witches are often born into the evil society and brought up in it. "That is why sometimes people do not know that they are witches because they have been brought up to be witches. Who knows what it is like to be a thing that you are not brought up into?" People who associate with witches are introduced into *ubuthakathi* "so nicely and cunningly by the witch that they do not know what has happened before they are witches themselves." [70]

The theoretical possibility for practically anybody, including diviners, to become engaged in witchcraft is always pertinent. Diviners themselves claim that it is only jealous and envious people who say that they also can become witches. But the diviner at uMhlatuze said that he knew of one diviner "who was not a diviner because of his deceiving people for whom he divined, whereas he knew nothing," and who actually was a witch "dressed in the clothes of a diviner." Hence everybody can be regarded as a potential witch or sorcerer. Nobody knows who, at a given time, is *umthakathi*. "Nobody knows. If we knew, it would be easy. But we do not know. That is the reason of our great poverty in that our money is eaten up by diviners who expose them. Then we pay for medicines to protect ourselves with. All these things eat up our money."

There is uncertainty as to whether witches are conscious of their doings or not. "Sometimes they know. Sometimes they do not know. But it will be clarified by the diviner or at the court-case (*icala*). People will hear who it is that is causing trouble. Also that person will know for a certainty." Another Zulu, also representative, said: "It is clear that they know what they are doing. There is nobody who does not know what they are doing. All people, including witches, know what they do. But witches hide. They act as if they do not know hoping to deceive people so that they (the witches) are not killed." A second person who listened to the above added: "Even if they do not know it clearly, they know it when they wake up. I would agree that people do not know what they do at night. When I dream, I only become conscious of it after the dream. The same with witches: they become conscious of it later. They wake up in the morning and feel the pains of riding (ref. to riding familiars) and being tired after sleeping. Those are the signs of a person who is a witch without knowing it. When they (the signs) appear, then they may become suspicious of something (i.e. witches). Then they keep quiet, fearing death as my friend here says."

Being a Witch

Whatever the process whereby witches come into being, the ultimate test required by evildoers for fully accepting *abathakathi* novices into the community of witches is the killing of a human being. The human should be a senior, a person in authority, or a strong young man or woman "with much power". Some people claim that the victim ought to be a kinsman, but others resent this very strongly, suggesting that "how can a child kill a father or a mother?" The former reply that they do it "with the fathers simply because that is *ububi*, evil. Are not these people evil? So how could it be that with them they do not kill even their own?" If ideas are divided on this issue, they are not divided on the issue of the victim being a person with vigour. "If they kill an old man or a weak woman, then they are scorned and ignored, themselves being weak."

There appears to be a hierarchy of witches living in a community of their own, the patterns and set-up of this community much resembling Zulu society.[71] This is natural. A woman, describing this community, said: "There is the chairman. That is *umholi* (leader) of their work. Then there are the servants. There are *izinduna* (minor leaders), each having their groups which they lead. That is what it is like." When changes occur in the set-up of the hierarchy, positions of authority and leadership are given those who have committed the most and greatest evils. "Everything is written down in the book (minute-book). When there is a vacancy they look in that book to see who has been the most evil. That one becomes the chosen one." Asked whether positions become vacant due to death, informants became bewildered and some did not know what to answer. The woman quoted above said: "I have not heard of their dying. But maybe they fight. This is the work of *abathakathi*. But in the time of Shaka many witches were killed. The trouble today is that they are not killed. So they become very old and very clever."

Although all witches are believed to have their familiars, senior witches usually travel through the air by virtue of their own ability. The less able ride their familiars, usually facing the tail to which they cling. No uninitiated witch has a familiar and has, therefore, to accompany a skilled witch "riding on the back" and holding onto the male member if the skilled one is a male, or the breasts if it is a woman. Witches are said to be reluctant to lend novices their familiars, but no reason could be obtained for this reluctancy. "It is just like that with them. They do not lend to each other."

Whilst sorcery can be carried out during the day-time, all witchcraft is carried out at night. During the day-time witches sleep or plan forthcoming evil. "Sometimes they just sit and wait for the night to come, being angry that the day is too long for them."

Zulu thought-patterns allow for male witches, and diviners as well as authorities expose men as being witches.[72] But in the minds of people witches are very often described as being females. I discussed this issues with H in the Thugela valley. He said: "It is like this. They (witches) exhume males and make them into familiars.[73] So the familiar is a male. Now this male familiar must have a female. The female is the witch. It cannot live without a male. They are like husband and wife. But whereas I for one, being a man, have two wives, the female witch has two or sometimes three men. They must have men. That is why they exhume men."

B: "I understand. But does not the heat (sexual desire) die also when a man dies?"

"How can it die?" Why does the witch seek this kind of familiar, digging up people from their graves at night? Is it not just because of this very heat?"

B: "I visualized the familiar as a beast of burden (horse was used to describe the beast of burden) to the witch."

"It is the horse of the witch. But it is not like an ox. The ox is castrated to remove this heat so that all its power goes into working and not into cows. Being castrated, it does not remember this heat. The familiar is not like an ox. It is like the bull in the cattle-enclosure. It is kept by the witch for the purpose of this heat."

B: "So the purpose of raising a familiar is to have a partner?"

"That is correct. If it does other work besides this main work, then that is another thing."

B: "If the witch is a male, would he raise a female familiar from a grave?"

(Pause, my informant thinking.) "From what we are saying it could be like that. But I have never heard of a female's grave being disturbed by them (witches)."

B: "A friend in another place told me that witches are the opposite to shades and shades being males, then witches must be females. Is this so?"

"That is very true. That friend of yours knew the thing of witches well. That is so. They (witches) dig up men simply because these men are the shades. So when they make a familiar of a man, they are killing the shade."

B: "Is that what is meant with *ukubulala nya* (kill utterly, annihilate)?"

"You are speaking Zulu now! That is the thing!"

B: "Tell me more about annihilation and shades."

"If a man is killed totally by witches in that he becomes a familiar, then there is not a shade. The shade is no more. It is finished."

"B: "What about its children?"

"It has no children. The children come through the shade. It is the shade that moulds in the woman. If there is no shade, how can there be children?"

B: "So what the witch is after is the moulding?"

"That is what I have been saying all the time speaking about the heat. It kills the moulding of children in the lineage and wakes it to life (*ukuvusa*) in its own lineage of witches. That is the thing that is so bad with witches. They snatch away the power of moulding (*ukuphuca amandla wokuzalisa*) and use it in a very bad way, moulding witches instead of men."

B: "Today you have taught me a great thing, that the heat of moulding remains (in a man) even when he is dead, being a shade."

"I am happy. (Pause.) The heat is in the shade. That is where it is. The man himself is but a stone when he is there in the grave." [74]

The ability of witches includes also the capability of leaving a homestead unseen at night and returning unseen at day-break. A woman described this process thus: "In the evening they wait for everything to be quiet. The husband locks the door. They lie down to sleep. The people fall asleep, one after the other. Then the witch leaves, being naked. It leaves the body in the place of sleeping, deceiving the people of the home. It goes to do its work. At cock-crow it returns again. It slips into the house and returns to its place. There are no windows open and the door is locked. But this does not help. It leaves through the roof or through the walls—I do not know where, not being a witch myself. What I am saying is what I have heard. That is all that I am saying, the things that I have heard." General thought-patterns describe witches as having this supernatural ability of leaving a home. The witches are described as being naked although sometimes some of their familiars are dressed. I once asked a woman whether witches left "in the body (i.e. physically)". She laughed aloud and answered without any hesitation at all: "No! What would the husband do, waking up and not finding the woman there beside him? No, she leaves, the body remaining!"

Familiars

Very closely associated with the belief in witches there is an elaborate faith in familiars who are related to witches.[75] Speaking to people about familiars, one is given the very distinct impression that these are feared as much as witches and sorcerers. Some say that familiars are feared even more than witches because "there are more familiars than witches". Others deny this and say that because familiars are the servant of witches, they are not as bad as their masters.[76]

No witch is thought to operate without the assistance of familiars, although senior witches are said not to use their familiars as much as their juniors. Witches may keep more than one familiar. But if there is more than one familiar attached to a witch, they must be kept apart. The witch ought not, further, to keep more than one species of familiar. The familiars must be given different duties. "If they know of each other they will fight and kill each other." The only reason for witches keeping more than one familiar is said to be a sexual satisfaction of the witch by the familiars.

Zulu idiom offers no technical term corresponding to the English word familiar. Various kinds and species of familiars are referred to by their various names. If familiars are spoken of as a collective they are generally referred to as *imikhovu*, sometimes *izimpaka*. Although not commonly used, there are the idioms *mantindane*,[77] *izikhindimanyana*,[78] and *iziyiyane*.[79] In the singular the terms refer to undefined familiars. Some informants referred to familiars as *iziphokwe* (from the English spooks).

1. *Umkhovu*

Zulu thought-patterns offer three distinct possibilities for witches to procure this familiar.[80]

Firstly, *umkhovu* is produced by the witch who requires a familiar by exhuming a buried corpse and bringing it to life again.[81] Buried men are popular with evildoers in this case, the witch requiring the familiar often being the killer of the man also.[82] Sometimes an ant-bear is used by the witch for the purpose of exhumation. It is claimed that some witches do not even have to dig up the body. They simply strike the grave with a branch of *umdlebe* (Synadenium arborescens),[83] and call the deceased by name. "Then the dead man rises out of the grave, coming out with the feet first." The deceased is crippled by driving a sharpened stick of *umdlebe* through the body, the stick entering the head through the fontanel and coming out of the anus. The tongue is split "to be like that of snakes (*ukunquma ulimi*)," and the eyes made red "so that he can see in the night."[84]

Secondly, *umkhovu* can be exhumed children who are fed on kinsmen's flesh and sexual organs. They are allowed to grow on this diet until they have reached the normal size of familiars which is said to be the height of a man's knee or possibly a little taller. This particular kind of *umkhovu* is believed to be very strong "because they have eaten the correct food of the familiars. That is why they are able to work very much." They are less obstinate and readily handled because they have been brought up by witches from childhood and know the life-patterns of witches.

Thirdly, *umkhovu* is the offspring of a baboon which the witch has caught and tamed. With it the witch has sexual relations and the offspring is *umkhovu*. Further offspring is obtained by the witches' intercourse with the baboon and its breed. Some say, however, that baboons are unreliable familiars and hence, as soon as the witch has become pregnant, she kills the baboon and breeds through its offspring only.[85]

Imikhovu are said to be of small stature and, because they generally are of male sex, are especially fond of women.[86] "*Umkhovu* cannot see a woman without desiring her. The owner (i.e. the witch) gives it medicines to strengthen it so that it can do the thing with women very vigorously."[87] Being shrewd and intelligent, their masters teach them the names of people whom they are to trouble. In a very pleasant and disguised voice they deceive their prey, and once having attracted people to themselves through cunning, they have them in their power.

2. *Impaka*

The Zulu idiom is sometimes translated with wild cat, this familiar resembling wild cats. It is supposed to be the most powerful of the different species of familiars and hence the cause of much fear and anxiety. The fear of *impaka* is very relevant in rural areas.

The familiar is said to be the offspring of the witch and *imbhodla* (sometimes also known as *igola* or *incwabi*),[88] a homeless cat which has become wild and eventually adopted for the purpose of breeding by the witch.[89]

Besides being able to fly through the air with a witch, *impaka* is claimed to be able to go into a house through the thatching and trouble people in the hut. "Especially suckling women are troubled by them. They live on milk, preferring human milk. They suck the women and bite their nipples so that the women refuse to feed their children because of the pain. "Especially woman who have just given birth. They suck them and put poison into them through the nipple until the breasts swell and become very painful. That is the work of *impaka*. Also my wife experienced this thing of swelling and severe pains. (The woman concerned would not speak of it, claiming that it was too terrible to mention.) If the child is sleeping beside its mother they (*impaka*) become very jealous and bite it in the neck, scratch it on the back and on the shoulders. They strangle it by tying the blanket around the throat." Zulu farmers say that *impaka* sucks cows at night too, lacking human milk. If cattle are not available, then the last resort is goats. A peculiarity of *impaka* is that they tend to return to the same homestead, once having become acquainted with it.

The familiar also has the ability of bewitching other domestic animals. Dogs are caused not to bark and oxen bewitched so that they refuse to accept the yoke over the neck when inspanned.[90]

The vintriloquist did not keep cats. His reason for not doing so was that through them he would be inviting *impaka* to his home. "What is the difference between a domestic cat and this thing that you are mentioning? How can you tame it? Dogs I can accept. If called upon, they come. I have never seen anywhere this thing coming when called upon. The only thing that brings it close to a person is meat and milk. What is meat and milk? They are the food of men and children. But this thing eats this very food of men. If that is so, then it is no longer an animal. I tell you, had there not been so many of these animals, there would have been better order in the land. It is this thing that is killing us."[91]

3. Tikoloshe

Tikoloshe is not traditionally a familiar but is increasingly becoming associated with witches. Certainly *Tikoloshe* plays a very important role in the minds of people, more so among townsmen and urbanised people than rural folk.[92]

Traditionally, *Tikoloshe* was a harmless but mischievous character who constantly played tricks on people. Also in this capacity *Tikoloshe* is far more entertained in the minds of people than ethnographic records indicate. *Tikoloshe* becomes harmful when he is caught by a witch. There are those who claim that *Tikoloshe* "is the most sought after of all the familiars because he can really satisfy (sexually) the hunger of the witches".[93]

As a familiar *Tikoloshe* is described as having an exceedingly large male member which, due to its size, has to be carried over the shoulders and around the neck. He is "hairy like a pig", of short stature, and, after treatment by the witch who has caught him, has a split tongue. When not a familiar, he speaks with a slubber, but after the operation by the witch "he speaks that tongue which they understand". Because *Tikoloshe* of necessity is a male, he is the familiar of a female with whom he, like all familiars, has intercourse. He fathers future witches who are brought up by the witch and then becomes the lover of his own children.

Tikoloshe is said never to be ridden by the witch. "He is too mischievous. He may even throw off the rider." Ngema's son, working in Durban, had the most fantastic things to relate of the doings of *Tikoloshe* in the townships surrounding Durban. He explained why *Tikoloshe* is not ridden thus: "*Umtha-kathi* must ride backwards, there being no other way for riding among them.

If *Tikoloshe* is ridden, then the rider must sit on the shoulders. That is, with *Tikoloshe*, the same as having the organ in front of his face. This is bad. He would do no work, only looking at this thing. So *Tikoloshe* is not ridden for this reason."

Because of the very frequent intercourse in which *Tikoloshe* indulges, his right hip and buttock are said to have been worn away. It is commonly believed that he has only one buttock and hip, but when asked whether this is the case, some people were amused and asked: "Where do you get such things from? Perhaps it is like that. We have not seen him."

In many ways *Tikoloshe* resembles humans. He is, hence, said not to favour killing people although he will beat them very thoroughly. Ngema's son described in very lively terms how *Tikoloshe* had beaten one of his friends who had returned to the dormitory late one evening. "He was so badly beaten that he was ill for six days afterwards." He also causes open wounds and sores which fester and become very painful. Contrary to *impaka,* he is said to avoid children altogether and reluctantly attacks women. He is, in particular, the enemy of men and finds considerable joy in harming them. Amazingly enough, he does not do it primarily because of envy. "He does it out of mischief. But now, being in the hands of a witch, his mischief has become worse and very bad."

4. Snakes

There are two kinds of snakes which are looked upon as being familiars of witches, *inyoka yosinga* [95] and *umhlangwe* (Simocephalus capensis).

Although invisible at day-time, *inyoka yosinga* is very real in the minds of people, especially of women who have no children and those who have painful menstruations. If ever seen, the snake appears with a fiery body. Its length varies between twenty and fifty centimeters. Some people say that it is a shade-snake which has been killed by accident,[95] while others maintain that shade-snakes cannot be killed and that *inyoka yosinga* is an ordinary poisonous snake which, having been killed, "is very angry. The witch knows the place where this snake is buried after it has been killed. At night the witch comes and digs up the snake and gives it life again. It (the witch) gives it very strong medicines so that it will not forget its anger. So it remains angry always. Being angry at all times, it is a fearful familiar, very much worse than *Tikoloshe.*" [96]

Ulusinga is believed to be sent by witches to "certain women if there has been some trouble." The snake enters the womb through the sexual organ or through the anus. A limited number claimed that it also could enter through the mouth. "In the stomach the snake rushes around, up and down, everywhere, confusing the days of the month (i.e. the menstrual periods) and making them painful." With married women they consume the male fluid during intercourse, thus making the women barren. The snake also enters pregnant cattle and "causes so much pain in the cows that they abort their calves. Sometimes it causes the cow to run around madly with pain, fighting and jumping so that the owner even has to slaughter the cow. When he opens it, he finds the snake inside." As with women, the snake is said to move about in the womb very viciously and causes the extensive pains through its movements.[97]

Bryant defines *umhlangwe* as being "a large, dust-coloured snake with a prominent spine. It is not poisonous, but regarded as an omen." [98] The reptile is believed to have no intestines, these having been "eaten up by *um-*

thakathi. *Umthakathi* eats them because the snake is known to linger on the way, looking for food. So if it has no intestines, it does not linger any more." Because it is not poisonous it brings sickness "in its body. It comes to a house and enters. It enters through the door. It goes into the house and waits until the people return. When they are asleep it spits on them, spitting sickness (*ukukhafula amathe wokugula*). The whole stomach if looked into will be found to be full of spittle. When it has completed spitting, it returns to the one who sent it. That is how it works."[99]

If the snake is found in a homestead it is immediately destroyed and taken out through either a hole explicitly made for the purpose of removing it or through another door. The idea is that, if taken through the door it entered, its "smell of death (*iphunga lokufa*) will be traced by other similar snakes who will come with great anger and avenge its death." In order to prove one's innocence in relation to the snake, all homestead people are expected to gather at the place where it is burnt.[100]

I discussed the snake's not having intestines with a knowledgeable friend. "It is true that it (the snake) has no intestines. The reason for this is that from the beginning it was a snake of a shade. Then it was captured by *umthakathi* and treated in their way. I do not know the treatment, not being *umthakathi* myself. But what I know is that it was a snake of a shade since shades do not eat."

B: "You are using a new word today in speaking of a snake of the shade (*inyoka yedlozi*). Is this a shade manifestation (*idlozi uqobo*, lit. a shade itself)?"

"No. I am not saying a shade itself. I am saying a snake of the shades. It is like the shades. It does not bite, killing people like other snakes. It is like the shades but not a shade itself."

B: "So all snakes associated with shades are not shades themselves?"

"That is so. This is one of them. The very one you are asking about."

B: "Are there other snakes of this type which belong to the shades but are not shades?"

"It is this one snake which is common here. Of other places I do not know. But with us it is this one."

B: "Have I understood correctly if I say that it has no bowels because of its being a snake of the shades?"

"You have understood it correctly. The shades do not eat. That is the reason why it has no bowels."

B: "When there is slaughtering for the shades, do they not eat?"

"Who has ever said that they eat with their teeth? Is there then only this one way of eating by way of teeth? Just tell me, how does your father, being a man without teeth now, eat?"

B: "You must tell me of the shades and food. Perhaps there is something that I have not understood well."

"You and I, we have teeth. Young children just drink, having no teeth. The shades even lack the lips of sucking. They consume by means of licking. They simply lick. Likewise this snake does not eat nor suck. It licks."

B: "Do not misunderstand me, asking further. But lacking lips, do the shades have tongues with which they lick?"

"Being lickers of food it is clear that they must have tongues with which they lick."

B: "Why do you say that they lick?"

"Because that is how they bring blessings (*izibusiso*). When they eat meat they bless it by licking."

B: "This animal also licks?"

"It licks."

B: "What is the difference between this licking and the licking of the shades?"

"If shades lick, then it is good fortune. But when these snakes lick, then it is death."

B: "Once you told me that shades are white like white ants. Are the snakes of shades also white?"

"They are white. Sometimes they are seen in pools. They are always white. All the things that pertain to the shades are white. Their snakes are also white."

B: "But this snake is dark (*nsundu*)?"

"Since the treatment by *umthakathi* it became dark. It was changed from white to a dark colour."

B: "That is the colour which is opposite to white?"

"Yes."

B: "The people of Zululand are also of this colour. I am not thinking of anything special that the people of Zululand should be related or like the snake. But I would like to hear your words on this matter."

(Very hearty laughter.) "You white man! You remember what I said about the ants! Now you are speaking about this thing being dark! Then you speak about men being dark! What do you want to know?"

B: "I want to know about the colour of the snake and the colour of men and the shades."

"Just listen quietly. I will tell you. The fathers are white. That is so. Men are black. That is so. They are opposites. That is one opposite. Then there is the other one. The opposite of evil. This thing is black because it is evil, the shades being white of their own account of being white (uncertain of the meaning of Zulu here). That is another opposite."

B: "So there are two opposites of colour. One is the opposite between the shades and their children. That is the first. The second is the opposite of the shades and their enemies. That is the second. Have I understood it correctly?"

"You have understood it correctly."

B: "Books say that this snake has a protruding spine. Is that so?'

"They speak correctly. It is because of the famine with the owners. The bones stick out because of the hunger. The place of the witches is the place of great hunger. They suffer much in that place, also the animals. *Imikhovu* are ever crying. '*Maye!*' That is because of the famine. This snake, not being able to speak, shows its suffering in this manner."

B: "But in that place of witches it is said that there is eating of human flesh. *Imikhovu* are the very ones indicated when the cows are dry in the morning."

"Since when do those without stomachs eat? Have we not agreed that this snake has no intestines? Further, who eat in that place? Is it not *abathakathi* alone? Why do *imikhovu* suck the cows? Is it not because they are suffering from hunger, their owners never giving them food. That is why they suck the cows."

B: "This snake is thin, having no stomach. But when it still was a snake of the shades, did it then eat normally?"

"Why do we slaughter our cattle and goats? Just tell me so that I can hear the reply from your own mouth. Just tell me the reason for slaughtering?"

B: "For communion."

"Well then. You say communion. You speak well. What father, except those there (the witches) eats alone? Is it not so that when eating, there is happiness in that people are of one spirit (lit. one heart, i.e. harmonious with each other). When the man eats, being happy, even the children eat. Is it not so? Even at the slaughterings, is it not so that the seniors eat first, thereafter the children? It is so. The children having eaten, the dogs. Even these dogs eat the bones (he pointed as his two dogs sleeping in our vicinity). Do you think that there is hunger with the shades having us as suppliers of meat? No, friend, there is no hunger! That is the differences between them (the witches) and the shades. With the shades there is sharing, even the dogs eating something."

Characteristics of both *umhlangwe* and *inyoka yosinga* is that they like other familiars have split tongues. Zulu claim that all poisonous snakes have split tongues as a natural phenomenon "because they are bad animals."[101] Also the lizard that brought the message of death is said to have a split tongue and is associated with evil.[102] Forked lightning is related to the anger of the sky.[103] Comparing the tongue of the chameleon with that of the lizard, the diviner in the uMhlatuze valley said: "The chameleon was not of itself evil. Its tongue is round. It is not split. It is long; the length is another matter. The split tongue has another interpretation. The chameleon stands for unreliability (*ukungathembeki*). Even its tongue gives evidence to this effect in its length. But animals with two tongues (i.e. split tongues) stand for destruction and killing."[104] The split tongue is quite clearly a symbol of evil in Zulu society.

5. Baboons, Dogs and Owls

Beside familiars with split tongues a witch can also have baboons, dogs and sometimes owls as familiars. The latter, however, do not have the sexual associations that the former, together with other familiars, so often have. It is possible that this is the reason for the limited interest given to owls. There are people who claim that they do not think of owls when they speak of familiars.[105]

Baboons, *imfene,* are occasionally associated with male witches "although women also have this animal." Some people claim that *umkhovu* is a tamed and treated male baboon while others say that all baboons are suspect and potential familiars. Trained baboon familiars are regarded as being naked or bald on the back, the hair having been worn away by the riding witch.

Baboons are particularly associated with evil among cattle and are said to suck cows. In order to harm both the calf and a homestead in that the cow will not allow the calf to suck or the herd-boys to milk it, the udder is scratched and bitten by the baboon familiar. Male baboons are said to have intercourse with the cows and the offspring are the monstrosities which sometimes occur among cattle. They also trouble the bull, either by harming its reproductive organs or by causing it to become very tired. Oxen are chased so that they are unable to pull ploughs and sledges the following day.[106]

Dogs which sleep much during the day and are very active without barking at night, are suspect.[107] Dogs that deliberately urinate on huts or on vital equipment such as pots, vessels, ploughs, water-containers, etc. or on the hedge surrounding the byre "have been sent to do this thing. Then there is alarm, because its urine is not just water from animals. It is *ubuthakathi*. It (the dog) has been sent by its owner to do this thing (*umhlolo*)." Homestead dogs can be trained by witches to be their agents while remaining dogs of the home without the senior or anybody else of the homestead knowing about it.

Dogs that are found eating faeces of a person or seen to show interest by sniffing at homestead occupants, especially their reproductive organs, are inevitably taken to be familiars. "They eat this thing. Then they return to the owner. They vomit it up. Then *umthakathi* takes the vomit and uses it in his work of *ubuthakathi*." At a home at C a dog which licked the organ of a small boy (c:a six years old) was immediately destroyed by the senior of the home because he was convinced that it was a familiar. He said that if a dog has been treated by *umthakathi* "it works for him/her at night. The dog works with *umthakathi* (sexual relations). That is why it does this thing also in the day-time with us."

Little information was obtained about owls, although the fear of them as familiars is found especially with rural people. "We just know that this bird is of the night. It works with *abathakathi*. That is all I know about it. The old people do not know either."[108]

On the other hand owls are sometimes said to warn people of the presence of familiars and their masters. "When we hear it, we know that they (witches) are near to us. The owl warns us when it cries. It cries because it sees animals of the night. God put them there as the policemen of the night. They guard the children of God against *ubusathane*."[109]

6. Lovers

Some witches are said to have lovers, *amagxebe* (lit. confidential lovers, not known to anybody) who are not termed familiars but are comparable with them.

Again, it is a female witch in particular who has *igxebe*, although thought-patterns in theory allow also for female lovers who associate with male witches: The lovers are described as being particularly beautiful (resp. handsome) and "always inclined towards satisfying their masters/mistress." As an illustration of the chaotic conditions which characterise witchcraft a man said: "You see for yourself how evil this place of *abathakathi* is. Also men there simply obey the female as if she were *induna* (headman). Where else do you find such things?"

Lovers are said to be light-coloured. "I could compare them with whites. They are of the same colour," said an informant who very hesitantly spoke of *igxebe*. *Amagxebe* are sometimes said to be whites who unlawfully practice intercourse with Africans. A man who expanded, again reluctantly, on the subject said that "whites who do this, do it without knowing what they are doing. They do it because they have been bewitched. That is the reason that I know." Many people said that they had heard of *amagxebe* but never seen one.

Like familiars, *amagxebe* are active at night and are naked. "If a man sleeps naked, then people are suspicious. Is he *igxebe*? Why does this man sleep like this?" That a man shares room/dwelling with a wife is no evidence that he is not a lover of a witch "because at night he leaves the room. It is the power of *ubuthakathi* that carries him (*amandla wobuthakathi ayamthwala*) to

285

umthakathi. They are together very much. Then he returns." One Zulu suggested that people who do not rise early but are tired in the morning must of necessity be *igxebe*.

Some people think that witches work witchcraft through their lovers. "When they are doing the thing, the witch is all the time putting evil into him, whispering his name softly in the ear and saying, 'So-and-so, you are doing the thing so nicely!' She says this, encouraging him. Then the desire comes often to him to come back again to the witch and he comes willingly when *ubuthakathi* carries him away in the night. She (the witch) puts more sickness into him. He does not know it, but it (the evil) is inside. When he goes to his wife to do this thing of men, he puts the sickness into his wife. She develops pains in that region, blood coming out and other things of bad odours. So the witch wishes to kill the wife, being jealous of her because of the husband." Another described how, through the power of *ubuthakathi*, the witch sends the lover to a woman with whom the man is known to have relations, and through her cause the sickness to enter the man. "The witch wishes to kill a man. So she puts evil into the lover. He goes to a woman known by that man. He puts the sickness into her. It stays there in the woman until the man comes to her. Then it enters him through the organ. He develops great pains in passing water. Sometimes he cannot pass water at all. Sometimes there comes blood. At last he dies of great wounds. He does not know where the sickness came from. But that is the way that it came."[110]

The Techniques of *Ubuthakathi*

Theoretically and practically, there are three methods of implementing *ubuthakathi*, i.e. through witchcraft, sorcery, and, thirdly, a combination of the two.[111] The third possibility is that which is most vividly entertained by people, witches being thought to make use of materia in causing harm and distruction. There is no technical term for witchcraft, it generally being referred to simply as *ubuthakathi*. Sorcery is spoken of as *ukudlisa* (lit. cause to eat) while the combination of witchcraft and sorcery is called *ukuphonsa* (lit. to throw).[112]

1. Witchcraft
A man described how his home had been burnt down. "It was in the time of the new moon in winter. That is the time when they (witches) are most active. It is dark then. I dreamt that there was something (amiss) in this place. I woke up and rose, saying, 'I am amazed at this thing I have seen in the dream. Sometimes I dream, but since when does a man dream at this time of the night (Zulu claim that normally people dream in the early hours of the morning), I just having gone to rest? I am amazed at the thing I saw in the dream, seeing the dog bark at this woman.' (He had previously described a quarrel with a sister of his wife. She had been deserted by her husband on his return to work in Johannesburg four years previously. They were constantly quarreling and he, the husband, had ultimately accused her of being *umthakathi* because of her inability to keep quiet and always being on bad terms with people. Due to lack of food and poverty the woman had eventually sought refuge in his home.) So I went outside. I saw her leaving the storage hut. The dog was barking very much. Why did it bark at a person known in this homestead where we

are living all together? While she was running away from the storage hut which I mentioned, I said to her, 'What are you doing there with the food?' She simply fled to her hut and then fled again through the gateway. Then I saw the fire. It was burning everywhere in the whole homestead that night. I carried things the whole night, carrying and saving from hut to hut. In the morning there was nothing left. The people said, having come to see the ashes, 'Did we not warn you concerning this woman?' She ran away. I have never heard of her since that night, even the diviners failing (to trace her). It is clear that she was *umthakathi*."

Subsequent discussions with both the narrator and people who knew of the disaster showed that they were all fully convinced that the wife's sister had become *umthakathi*. The senior who related the destruction of the homestead by fire said that the woman had set fire to the home because of brewing anger, the anger and the ability of *ubuthakathi* traced to the time when she still lived with her husband. "That is the time when she became *umthakathi*." He drew his evidence partly from her continuous quarrelling with her husband and partly from the warnings given him by other people who were suspicious but who "did not speak openly, just being suspicious that there was something (happening) in the woman". He argued that setting a homestead on fire required great strength and that "only *abathakathi* have such great power". He found it characteristic that she had started the fire in the storage-hut, this being the place "where the food is stored. They kill men by destroying the food first, so that men suffer from lack of something for the mouth." He was convinced that the woman had used no medicines in her act. "There were no medicines. She did it herself with the power of *ubuthakathi*. That is all. Her evil was the power she used to burn the place."

Witches are able to cause sickness, bad dreams, sufferings and other devastating happenings merely by mentioning the name of the person whom they wish to harm or the place they wish to destroy. The name is believed to be mentioned to the familiar which is to carry out the evil deed. "Then the familiar leaves. It carries nothing, simply the name and the power given it by *umthakathi*. It goes to that person mentioned by its owner. There it does the evil with that person. The person becomes sick, possibly even to death. That which killed the person is the mentioning of the name by the witch when it sent the familiar with the evil."

A man at H described how his first wife had died. "She was a favourite with many men. Z also desired her. But she was not willing. Also he courted her before we married. But she did not like him. Then, because she refused marriage, he asked for the thing of men and women. She refused, saying that there was no *ukuhlobonga* any more.[113] She refused everything that he proposed in that she did not love him. After some time we married. When we were doing it (intercourse) there was much pain. So much so that she did not wish for it any more. For five months she did not wish for it. During all these months I wasted my money on herbalists. There was no improvement. Then I inquired (with a diviner). He said that she had been bewitched. It was that very man who had thrown his power on her (*umponse ngamandla akhe*). She ate medicines. It became better. In her giving birth the whole matter became relevant again. It became clear that she was closed (*Ekubeletheni kwakhe yavuka indaba yonke. Kwabonakala ukuthi uvalekile*). She could not give birth. She died in giving birth. The child died. They died both, the mother and the child.

It was that man that bewitched her. Even the diviner agreed, seeing him at that place in Durban where he is (the diviner in divination saw the man at the place where he worked). It is clear that he hated her with a great hatred, even killing her because of his hatred. He hated her because she was not willing." My informant, filled with indignation, agony and sorrow over the death of a wife to whom he was deeply attached, was concerned about his own future. He felt that the evildoer would now direct his attention to him (the widower). Being a Christian, he denied emphatically the presence and activities of familiars. But he was convinced that "*ubusathane* had killed my wife and the child" and that *ubusathane* had been manipulated by the former suitor. "That is the thing they do with the power they receive from Satan. They use it in this way." We discussed how the man in Durban, being some 210 kilometers distant, could have exercised his power. The widower suggested two possibilities. "This man (the accused) is not a believer (i.e. not a Christian). So perhaps he just pointed his finger in this direction, mentioning the name." I' asked whether he thought this probable. "Nobody knows the ways of *ubusathane*. It can come in any way it likes. I do not know what way he chose to kill us." The widower claimed that he, being a Christian, could himself not consider "using the ways of *iqaba* (an unsympathetic term denoting a heathen). This thing I cannot do. It is the way of heathens. I am not a heathen. I am a believer." His second suggestion was that the accused could have written a letter to the deceased and through it bewitched her. The letter must have arrived before the marriage. On second thoughts he changed his mind and suggested a possible second letter during the time of pregnancy but dismissed the thought again as his wife, who feared the accused very much, would have shown her husband such a letter. He ruled out any possibility of the accused having used medicines. "She (the woman) took only medicines of doctors that *sindisa abantu* (restore/save people). No, there were no medicines. What he used was *ubusathane* and *ubuhedheni* (heathenism). That is the only thing that he could have used." Later in the discussion he made it quite clear that he attributed to the accused powers which "no ordinary people have. It is the powers of Satan. That is actually what he used. How otherwise could he kill her?" There was no possibility of trying to say that her death could have been caused by a physical ailment or other cause. This one belief he would not discuss, the conviction that the former admirer had killed his wife.

Although there is evidence which shows that Christians tend to deny the activities of familiars, the great majority of Zulu are convinced that witches generally, if not always, use familiars when they are to work evil at some distance. Some give as the reason for the great amount of evil that witches carry out at various places, the number of familiars that witches keep. Some say that witches are cowards and choose to send familiars in their places to do evil acts, and a number said that familiars are sent because witches "are very lazy, just working at home".

Familiars are sent to obtain *insila* (lit. dirt, i.e. faeces, urine, vomit), hair and nail-parings from people who are to be bewitched. They are also sent to find out the names of people to be harmed and on other occasions they are sent with destructive powers to homesteads, cross-roads, and people with evil. Very often they take with them medicines with which they carry out their evil, but the medicines are not, in theory, a necessity. Their harm to people and property, e.g. cattle, can be done without the aid of material powers.

Because the throat of a human being is the seat of feelings which are peculiar to man, the invisible familiars enter huts at night and suffocate people. "When everybody is asleep, a man feels that there is something at his throat, grabbing him and holding him tightly. He fights with this thing, the sweat running over his whole body. He works very hard at releasing himself. When he becomes free he shouts out, waking up the others. This is *ubuthakathi wokumklinya umuntu* (the witchcraft of strangling a human)."

B: "That is what white people call night mares."

"I am glad that even white people believe in this. I have only met whites who have denied the witchcraft of throttling people. But I am glad that they now are admitting it. So they know this thing also! Indeed, it is a good thing that we believe the same thing now and do not only confuse each other."

Familiars are sent to frighten people and cause them not to sleep. Purposely, because they know that they are feared by men, they move about in homesteads, upsetting water-containers, knocking over paraffin-tins and in various manners making themselves heard in order to cause anxiety, uncertainty and unrest. They also cause people to be tired and thus decrease their resistance. "That is their way of making a man weak. He cannot work, being tired the whole day. The boss (employer) becomes annoyed. After a few days the man is dismissed from his work. He finds no work. The police chase him out (of Durban). He returns (to his rural home) bringing with him only famine and death."

In rural settings the familiars likewise fatigue cattle; in the ploughing season their attention is particularly directed to oxen. These are chased around in the byre so that they become tired and do not pull the plough. Sometimes they are bewitched so that they totally refuse to do any work at all. Cows are sucked dry by familiars. *Tikoloshe* is believed to be so desirous of milk that he even approaches them in broad day-light. I have on several occasions been told by people that herdboys, on bringing the cattle back in the evening for milking, found that *Tikoloshe* has already removed the milk from the cows. Snake familiars enter both women and cows and cause them to be infertile as long as the snakes are in them.

2. *Ukudlisa*, sorcery

A sorcerer who has obtained destructive *imithi*, generally poisonous, has many possibilities of mixing these with either the enemy's food or beverage. If the hated person is a male, beer is a favourite vehicle whereby evil may be inflicted.[114]

Sorcerers generally arrange for their medicines to be consumed. Hence the idiom *ukudlisa* (lit. to cause to eat). Some Zulu, however, say that sorcerers can spread out their medicines on a person's sleeping-mat and cause him/her to suffer thereby. "Sometimes it is put in the clothes. I know a man who was given medicines in a handkerchief. When he blew his nose he drew the medicines into the body. Some entered through the nose. He commenced bleeding. First the blood came out only of the nose. Then it came out also through the mouth. He bled a great deal until it was stopped by a doctor." People listening to the description were equally convinced that the medicines had entered the man through the handkerchief. "It (the medicine) was put into the handkerchief by somebody who hated him because of his car. The w'   e car was filled with blood." (The victim was a taxi-owner who drove regularly between Y and Durban.)

Whilst renowned and skilled herbalists[115] are very much admired and respected because of their wide knowledge of the powers embedded in materia, they are also very much feared. "They heal with strength. But I tell you, they also kill with strength. Their medicines are fearful." Their abilities of combating and through the powers of materia resisting evil can, when circumstances invite such action, be swung into achieving evil with equal efficiency. The distance between trust in their abilities to bring health and prosperity and one of profound fear is not far at all.

3. Ukuphonsa

People fear *ukuphonsa* (lit. to throw) far more than *ukudlisa*. "With *ukudlisa* the medicines are merely eaten. If a man is suspicious he excuses himself (from eating), saying some words of explanation and thanks. He may say, 'Just today I have taken medicines of cleansing. Therefore I cannot eat.' Or he may say, 'Forsooth, had I but dreamt of such delicious food I would not have eaten previously. But I cannot take even a small morsel because of the great quantity I have just eaten.' So he does not eat, having certain fears. If there were medicines that he should have eaten and which would have killed him, he avoids them. They do not trouble him at all. But with *ukuphonsa* it is fearful in that nobody knows its ways. It just comes from somewhere, a person being smitten and having had no suspicions at all."

Like all other methods of achieving harmful aims, *ukuphonsa* is thoroughly evil. Also, like witchcraft, it makes use of faeces, urine and, sometimes, spittle,[116] these being symbols of evil. *Ukuphonsa* also makes use of the symbols of life, nail parings and hair. Failing either of these categories it can make use of practically all personal belongings owned by the person who is to be harmed. Soil from footprints and things with which he/she will come into contact are also used in order to achieve the evil. It is, however, important to note the significant role the name of the person/place is given also in *ukuphonsa*.

I discussed *ukuphonsa* with the diviner at eThelezini. As usual his views proved to be both trustworthy and representative.

B: "Why must *umthakathi* make use of such vile things (faeces and urine)?"

"Everything with *abathakathi* is evil. These things are evil. So evil takes the hand of evil, working death (*ukufa*) together."

B: "If they did not use these vile things, would their *ubuthakathi* be less active?"

"It would be less effective. But oxen of the same strength pull best if they are inspanned together."

B: "Are you comparing vileness and medicines with ox and ox?"

"I am comparing them. The same always works best together."

B: "Both oxen that pull have power. Would it be correct to say that both the vile and the medicine have power?"

"It may be that vileness has power. I do not know. In this discussion I am not comparing the powers. What I am talking about is vile and evil medicines. The things that you mention are vile. The work of the medicines is to kill. It is these that I am discussing when I say that the same oxen pull best."

B: "Why must there be something from the man whom the medicines are to harm in order to be able to harm?"

"So that the medicines may kill that man from whom the things come."

B: "Would the medicines not kill anybody else but that man?"

"They would kill only that man. Others remain untouched."

B: "How does this happen, seeing that the power of destruction is in the medicine?"

"The things come from the man. They are his things. They are not the things of anybody else. They are his. He produced them (the vile things). So the vileness knows him in that it came from him. It knows no other man. That is how it happens."

B: "I have heard that other *abathakathi* who do not find vile things from a man seek his hair-clippings and nail parings. How are these used?"

"Sometimes these are even better than vileness. It depends on *umthakathi*, what he wants to do. If he wants to kill a man from within, he uses vileness that comes from within. But if he wants to harm him in another way he uses hair and nails."

B: "What is the difference between nails and hair on the one hand, and vileness on the other?'

'Vileness is waste produce. That is why we say that vileness is dirt. It is dirt, useless, being waste from the body. It is the unclean matter that comes from a man. But hair and nails are not waste. With them it is in another way."

B: "What are they (nails and hair)?"

"They are *impilo* (health, life) of a man. When a man lives, these grow. When he dies they cease to grow. That is what they are. They are his life."

B: "So vileness and hair and nails are two very different things?"

"Very much so! *Au!* Very much!"

B: "But why then, if *umthakathi* is evil and works with evil, does he seek these things that are the life of a man, as you say?"

"Do you not see it for yourself?"

B: "I could guess. But I do not wish to guess. I prefer to hear it from one who knows these things."

"I will tell you. What is the thing that *umthakathi* wants in a man when he seeks that man? He seeks his life, the life of that man. That is the thing that he seeks. If he can get it, then he kills that man. If he has the things of life of a man, I am speaking of those things that you yourself mentioned, then he has captured that man. He mixes them with medicines of death and returns them (*ukubuyisa*) to the man. They kill that man, the medicines being a mixture of those things and medicines of death."

Our discussion continued in terms of the name of the person who was to be harmed.

B: – – – "Everywhere I am told that *umthakathi* mentions the name of the person who is to be killed. Why does *umthakathi* mention the name?"

"It is the name of that person."

B: "Is it important that the name should be mentioned?"

"It is very important. It is the important thing in *ubuthakathi*. If a man can hide his name from people, then he can hide from much evil. *Umthakathi* can kill a man if he lacks vileness and hair, but has the name. So the name is very important."

B: "Why is the name of the person so important?"

"The name is that person. They are the same, the name and the person. It is the word whereby that person is known. That is the name. So the person and the name are one. *Umthakathi* kills a man by combining the words of death with the name. He throws (*ukuphonsa*) these at the man and they kill him."

B: "Is *isibongo* (clan name, surname) the same as the name?"

"Since the coming of the whites the surname is becoming the name. But *umthakathi* does not use the surname. That is the name of the people (i.e. the clan). It is not the name of the person (to be harmed)."

B: "*Ubuthakathi* is always against a certain person?"

"It is always against a certain person. Sometimes it can be against a home. But in general it is against an individual."

B: "Could *abathakathi* attack a whole clan?"

"It is possible. (Time for thought.) No, perhaps not. It would require much power. They disagree too much among themselves. They could not unite to kill a whole clan. That is why they always attack a person. One *umthakathi* attacks one person."

B: "You mentioned the words of death. What are those words?"

"Those are the words mentioned by *umthakathi* saying that he desires the death of So-and-so. Those are the words of death. Like in court. When the judge passes judgment, those are the words of punishment. When a man begs pardon, those are the words of pardon. So *umthakathi*, when he says some words concerning the man whom he wishes to destroy, he says the words of death."

B: "What does he say?"

Laughter. "I have never heard him. As I said, I am not *umthakathi*. I do not know what words he says. But he says words, being the words of death."

B: "If he should not say those words of death, would nothing happen?"

"It is different. Those who use medicines only (sorcery), sometimes do not use words. But nearly all other kinds of *ubuthakathi* have words of death. That is how the medicines know their purpose, being combined with the words of death. *Umthakathi* combines his evil desires with the name of the man and certain medicines. That is the general way of killing with us black people."[117]

Two details in our discussion need expanding on. Firstly, the spittle and secondly, "the words of death", i.e. the intention to harm expressed in words. The diviner argued that spittle could be used in *ubuthakathi* not only because it had been in a persons's body and subsequently ejected. Spittle is associated with cleansing from anger, an angry man spitting out his anger. Like vomit and the result of emetics, spitting in this sense is an ejection "of something bad inside a man. Spitting is throwing out anger. Vomiting is ejection of the bad inside. Emetics is the same as vomiting, these two coming from inside the stomach of a man." It is in this capacity that spittle plays an important part in Zulu thought-patterns and hence is more than just simply "something from the person". It is that which is both good and bad. The positive aspect of spitting is, like vomiting, emetics and other ejections of vileness, in "the bringing out of the bad in the man," whether this is emotional as in anger, or materialised as in vomit. The badness is in the materia which is ejected from the body. "When the spittle comes out, it comes with anger. When a man has spat out his anger, it is in the spittle." Ngema of Mapumulo put it very plainly when he said: "With a man's spittle *umthakathi* kills the cleaning (i.e. the ejection of anger). He awakens the anger again (*ukuvusa inzondo kabusha*) so that it burns in the man as previously. That is how they work with spittle."

Secondly, the importance of "the words of death" must be underlined. The use of the symbols of vileness and/or life is not in itself sufficient for executing *ubuthakathi*. The addition of the person's name, although an important detail, is not in itself sufficient either. There must be an expression and intention of evil which accompanies both the name, the materia (medicines) and the produce from the human who is to be harmed. For it is the expression of intended evil in words that puts into effect and sets into motion the bad desires of a witch into witchcraft. This is comparable to confession and expression of goodwill which are so important in the restoration of harmonious relationships within a community, lineage and clan. While in confessions "everything is said" and there is either an act which expresses goodwill or words wich cover this detail, evil intention is expressed in "the words of death". A friend said: "That is why a man must never say to another, '*Ngizokuthakatha*,' (i.e. I will bewitch you). Then he is already speaking the words of death. It means that he is already killing in that he has spoken the fearful words of intention."

Although not directly associated with *ukuphonsa*, the importance of expressed evil intent is seen very clearly in thoughts which describe how a witch exhumes a dead person in order to transform him into a familiar. I quote a man's description of an exhumation: "*Umthakathi* smites on the grave with the stick. He calls the person, saying, 'So-and-so, I am calling you up. Come out so that I can cause you to work (*puma ngikusebenzise*).' Then the person comes, hearing his name." Asked what would happen if the name and the intention of evil was not mentioned my informant answered: "*Abathakathi* do not play. They know their work well. They know that if these two words (i.e. these two details) are not mentioned, then nothing happens. They do not waste time playing. They say them quickly while they smite so that the man can come up quickly and be treated there in the vicinity of the grave." Another man said thus: "When those words have been said, the words of the work to be done, then there is indeed trouble (*isipelile indaba*, lit. the matter is done with, i.e. there is no hope of a return)." The importance attached to both a definable person who is attacked by anger through his name and the expressed intention of harming him/her is quite evident.

Like witchcraft, *ukuphonsa* is applied when angry people make use of suitable opportunities to harm (*ukubamba ithuba*). The following will illustrate this implementation of immoral anger.

A man at F had fallen ill and the attending diviner indicated a hungry shade. Seven weeks lapsed during which time a letter was written to a relative in S asking for money to buy a goat. The letter also described the illness and the necessity for slaughter. Before anything else was done the patient's condition deteriorated alarmingly. Money was borrowed from a school teacher and a goat bought. On the afternoon of the ritual killing the patient was in a state of unconsciousness and died the following night. The consulted diviner was approached again as the deceased's brother felt that the diviner had deceived them. "Since when do the shades kill?" When the relatives of the deceased arrived at the diviner's home, she claimed that she had dreamt of the death the previous night and expressed her symphaties. Without giving the consulting party a chance to state their business, she continued, indicating that her dream had also revealed that "there was too much time wasted. They (the shades) had become tired of waiting. So they left. There was not even a promise. It is clear that you did not care much about the patient, there not even being any words or steps taken. They (*abathakathi*) came. They took their opportunity. That is when the sickness became worse. The bad sickness which was worse than the sickness of the shades was the sickness caused by medicines. Even now they (the medicines) are there. I see them. They are in the roof. Also the thrower (*umponsi*). I see him in that place where he is. I see him just where he is." (Quotation from a man who quoted the diviner.) The diviner's novice is said to have confirmed the diviner's further diagnosis, claiming that "the mother said all these things early in the morning, even saying that they would come from that very homestead with hot hearts (i.e. the consulting party)." Certain that the diviner's claim and diagnosis were true and urged to accept the claim of the novice that the diviner had revealed the dream to her prior to their arrival, the deceased man's brother apologized for "our hot hearts" with a twenty-cent piece, paid the fee of fifty cents claimed by the diviner, and left. On arrival at the homestead the roof of the hut which had been occupied by the deceased was searched. A metal 35 mm Kodak film container with a yellow lid was found stuck into the thatching. Everyone, including the teacher who had lent the people the money to buy the goat, was convinced that the film-container had been thrown at the homestead by the bewitching party and that it held destructive medicines, referred to by the diviner. My informant expanded on *ukuphonsa* in this particular case: "We do not know how this thing came to be put into the thatching, but it is clear that it was thrown (*ukuphonsa*). We were not present when it was done and the diviner did not explain it. It may be through a familiar. It may just have been thrown." The fact that the contents of the container suggested snuff and a Kodak film capsule having been the deceased's snuff-container was no valid argument against *ukuphonsa*. "That is the very place where they would put their medicines. Indeed, did he not cough badly just before dying? So it may be that you speak correctly, seeing that there was snuff in the box. But what else was with the snuff? You did not see it?"

Many are convinced that *abathakathi* watch for a suitable occasion when they fruitfully can attack and with greater ease achieve their immoral aims. "It was because of the weakness in the man that just a little medicine was needed to kill him. We did not suspect anything. Suddenly we found him dying. So it is clear that they did it with ease."[118]

Not only are the presence and the activities of *abathakathi* ever in the minds of people. Their undoubted success preoccupies thinking to a very large degree. Evidence of the successful manipulation of powers towards evil ends is ever available. Abnormal and unexpected deaths, particularly untimely deaths, are the most conspicuous evidence of successful witchcraft and/or sorcery. Sickness not attributed to the shades or characterised as *umkhuhlane* (ailments accepted as the normal things of the day)[119] are clear indications of successfully manipulated evil powers; dreams which visualize being chased by a naked being, handling by familiars, attending one's own funeral, being beaten by people with sticks (especially branches from *umdlebe*[120]), or seeing one's corpse being harnessed by having a stake driven through the body are all frightening evidence of the success of witchcraft and sorcery. Sexual dreams which involve one's relationships with unknown beings who are filled "with heat that is too hot"; a host of omens (e.g. dogs urinating on one's leg or on a hut, cats not burying their faeces, fowls ascending huts, goats mounting sheep or even calves, birds' droppings falling on homesteads or people, etc.) and the many disasterous accidents which may befall a homestead—fires, deaths of animals, drought, excess rain, violent thunderstorms, accidents with homestead tools such as ploughs, saws, axes, knives, etc., quarrels and disagreements, bad temper—these and very many more are all clear indications of not only the presence and activity of *abathakathi*, but they are also proof of their success in evil enterprise. Ultimately *ubuthakathi* is the manipulation and expression of anger and a desire to destroy.

Notes

[1] See pp. 230 f. Also Samuelson, *Zululand, its Trad., Legends,* etc., p. 131, writes, quoting a representative prayer to this effect, "– – – come into the hut tonight and feast on it, I pray. Then let your anger be returned from us, and let us keep our child."

[2] Bryant, *Dict.,* p. 7, defines *amandla* as "strength; power; might; moral strength; authority; authorisation; as far as doing anything; ability, capability as for doing any work; exertion, labour, expended on any work; euphem. for semen virile (=*amalota*)." Cf. Doke–Vilakazi, *Dict.,* p. 9: Colenso, *Zulu-Engl. Dict.,* p. 8. See also Tempels' study on Luba concepts of power in *Bantu Philosophy.* Baumann, 'Nyama, die Rachemacht', epitomises the notion of a supernatural force in the Mandingo idiom *nyama* connected to the widespread Bantu word *nyama,* meaning animal, game and/or flesh. Tracing the concept to an ancient "Eurafrican steppehunters' culture", Baumann argues that it is inherent in animals as well as humans and in cases of violent death can, if strong and concentrated, become a force of vengeance. Sometimes it is regarded as a life substance and localised in blood, internal body organs and the extremities of the body, i.e. head, ears, tails, hair, male organ, elephant tusks and trunk (particularly the tip), whiskers of cat-species, penis and nipples.

[3] When the word power (*amandla*) is used in the following, it will be limited to involve merely power as expressed in anger (wrath, hatred) and fertility (vitality, ability of growth).

[4] See pp. 35 ff.

[5] See p. 36.

[6] Related pp. 33 f.

[7] See pp. 37 ff.

[8] See p. 40.

[9] Bryant, *Dict.,* p. 692.

[10] Krige, *SSZ,* p. 361. See also Farrer, *Zululand and the Zulus,* pp. 142 ff.: Gardiner, *Narrative of a Journey to the Zoolu Country,* p. 178: Shooter, *The Kafirs of Natal,* p. 159: Callaway, *The Religious System of the Amazulu,* p. 3 and p. 138: Merensky, *Beiträge zur Kenntniss Südafrikas,* p. 124: Döhne, *A Zulu-Kafir Dict.,* p. 247: Leslie, *Among the Zulus and Amatongas,* p. 51: Fritsch, *Die Eingeborenen Süd-Afrikas,* p. 138: Samuelson, *Some Zulu Customs and Folk-Lore,* p. 66: Wanger, The Zulu Notion of God, pp. 665 & 351: Speckmann, *Die Hermannsburger Mission in Afrika,* p. 164.

Note that both Döhne and Speckman refer to anger as the cause for the creator's sending the lizard with news of death after his having sent the chameleon with news of life.

For the wider African context on the origin of death see Abrahamson, *The Origin of Death.*

[11] Note again the deliberate choice of a particular animal which, because of its specific characteristics, would accomplish its mission as required.

[12] Malcolm, 'Zulu Literature', p. 33, says that the reason for anger was the chameleon's delay in executing its duty. "It did not think there was any hurry with the message and delayed so long that Nkulunkulu got angry and sent off another message."

[13] In a Sunday-school class an eleven-year old girl was asked to describe what was meant with the commandment "Thou shalt not kill!" She said: "It was written in the book of commandments that there should be no killing. God read this commandment. Then he sent the chameleon to his children whom he had created, saying, 'You will live for ever and ever. Further, you shall not kill each other.' It went to the children, walking slowly. Then he thought, 'But no! There are all these other people round about who will eat up my children, throwing them into prison, fighting with them and taking their money. How can this commandment be correct? So he looked for a quick runner. He looked, and looked. Then he found the lizard. He said to it, 'Lizard, just hurry with great speed with all your might, running very fast, to my children and say to them that they may kill, especially all the wicked and bad people.' It ran with great speed. It arrived at the place of the children, finding them very much troubled because of the many enemies. It gave the message to them. They became very happy and commenced arranging armies and preparing weapons with which to fight. Shaka was the greatest one in warfare. Then *abafundisi* (missionaries) came and saw what was happening to the blood of men, just running everywhere, even in the houses where they were killed. So they wrote down in a book the commandment, "Thou shalt not kill!"

[14] See pp. 45 f.

[15] See pp. 151 ff.

[16] Women say that should they conceive while feeding a previous baby, they must immediately wean the baby. "The shades cannot be divided, feeding in the womb and in the breast at the same time. That is why the breast-milk becomes poison. It can even kill the child if it is not weaned. but generally they just become sick. It is not the sickness of *abathakathi*. It is another sickness. Then the father (of the children) apologizes for causing confusion and the baby is released from the breast."

[17] Compare a shade's reaction to incest, pp. 221 f.

[18] See e.g. Krige, *SSZ*, pp. 62 ff.

[19] See e.g. Krige, *SSZ*, pp. 81 ff.

[20] Chiefs and authority at large are expected to have a greater capacity than commoners for anger with which they are to uphold law and order.

A school-master was reprimanded by a group of parents because he did not attend to the children's general conduct at the school. One parent, possibly feeling that the others had been unnecessarily harsh against the teacher, said after the meeting: "There is nothing wrong with him. It is only that he has been too soft." Another immediately added: "That is correct. He is soft. He lacks anger. That is the only complaint."

See also Hoffman, 'Witchcraft Among the Zulus', p. 14.

[21] Bryant, *Dict.*, p. 345: Colenso, Zulu-Engl. *Dict.*, p. 307: Doke–Vilakazi, *Dict.*, p. 445.

[22] Bryant, *Dict.*, p. 707. The Zulu word *inhliziyo*, translated as heart in English, is located not in the physical heart. Feelings, according to Zulu thought-patterns, are localised in the throat. Cf. Kohler, Die Krankengeschichte eines zulukaffern, p. 588, who says: "*intliziyo* befindet sich im Hals."

[23] Bryant, *Dict.*, p. 659: Doke–Vilakazi, *Dict.*, p. 805.

[24] Bryant, *Dict.*, p. 414. Cf. Doke–Vilakazi, *Dict.*, p. 543. Note that *ngitshelwa umphimbo* means to have a good conscience.

[25] Bryant, *Dict.*, p. 502: Doke–Vilakazi, *Dict.*, p. 662.

[26] Discussing *unembeza* and *ugovana* Norenius writes: They speak of two hearts; one white which strives for that which is good and the other black which desires that which is bad. They say that these two inner powers are in constant strife with one another and desire (the individual in whom they reside). People are led at one time by one of these, at another time by the other. Of themselves they cannot assist in the strife. They experience themselves as balls being tossed between the influence of the two. – – –. They are not responsible if they from time to time are caught up by the influence of evil. This is (when it happens) their misfortune and not their responsibility. *Ugovana* is stronger than *unembeza*." (See Norenius, *Bland Zuluer och Karanger*, Vol. I, p. 45.) Zulu agree with the above discussion but maintain that too much emphasis is given to man's personal inactivity in the struggle between the two.

Cf. Wangemann, *Die Berliner Mission im Zulu-Lande*, pp. 76 f.

[27] Bryant, *Dict.*, p. 194. Cf. also Doke–Vilakazi, *Dict.*, p. 259.

[28] Bryant, *Dict.*, p. 435: Doke–Vilakazi, *Dict.*, p. 575.

296

²⁹ The Zulu idiom *ePitoli* (in Pretoria) often refers to executions when speaking of convicts and court-cases, Pretoria being the place in the Republic where capital punishment is effected. In South Africa hanging is the method of execution.

³⁰ Bryant, *Dict.*, pp. 625 f.: Doke–Vilakazi, *Dict.*, p. 794. Medicine, in the English understanding of the word, is far too narrow and exclusive a translation for the wide range and inclusive understanding of the Zulu equivalent *(imithi)*. But medicine is used to translate *imithi* for lack of a better expression. The Zulu includes every possible source of power attributed to the elements/materials used, including witchcraft, sorcery and charms.

³¹ In the manipulation of powers in materia it is important to note that it is not the particular techniques in the use of the medicines that are evaluated as either good or bad. It is the purpose and the aim of their usage that makes them either harmful or strengthening.

³² Medicines, i.e. materia of various kinds and species, are taken e.g. to give a young man courage and handsomeness when he courts, to give a person in a position of authority the dignity he requires to execute his duties, to give self-confidence to those who are to face difficult situations, to give majesty to those who are to represent the nation/clan, to give fearfulness to those that are to fight and thus frighten the enemy on sight, etc...

³³ The potency of *imithi* can be further underscored by adding to it potent parts of animals and, if the needs arise, of human beings. Hence "ritual murder". The subsequent medicine is regarded as extremely powerful, being a combination of power tapped from different sources, and the manipulation of it requires skill. It can, as all medicines, be used to work either good or bad.

³⁴ It is characteristic that Zulu creation narratives, as is also the case among other African peoples, are not concerned in the first instance with the creation of materia. The attention is directed on the coming of man firstly, then animals, especially the domestic animals with preference to cattle.

Asked from where the earth came, an informant who otherwise proved to be very well versed in thinking among Zulu, was rather amazed at the question and said after some hesitation: "It has always been there!"

See further Baumann, *Schöpfung und Urzeit des Menschen im Mythus der Afrikanischen Völker*.

³⁵ On legitimate anger among Nyakyusa see Wilson, *Divine Kings and the 'Breath of Men'*, particularly pp. 8 ff. There does not appear to be an equivalent idiom in Zulu to that of the 'Breath of Men' found among Nyakyusa.

³⁶ The case is related fully p. 122. The grandfather refused to speak on the subject saying that he did not wish "to speak on things that had caused anger in his heart". The old lady, on the other hand, was exceedingly well inclined to giving me any information I wanted. She proved to be both very talkative and sometimes a little difficult to keep to the subject, authentic and representative of Zulu ideas. Meeting her was an encounter in which one met a dignified and respectable Zulu lady.

³⁷ See further on becoming a witch, pp. 273 ff.

³⁸ Innocent in the sense that it would not lead to death on its own merits.

³⁹ Writing in the middle of the 19th century, Krantz relates that in connection with the illness of a man a diviner claimed that his indisposition was caused by a shade-snake living in the homestead, and suggested a ritual slaughtering. However, the patient's condition deteriorated. A child of the home also became ill. The diviner was again consulted, and, on divining, found that the illness was no longer caused by the shade, "sondern auch eine ganze Anzahl von anderen Geistern erzürnt wären". A second ritual slaughtering followed in order to convince the shades of their responsibility to step in and defend their survivors. Nevertheless, the child died, apparently in connection with the killing and was therefore buried with the beast's flesh which was not eaten. Shortly afterwards the sick man also died. (Krantz, *Natur- und Kulturleben der Zulu*, p. 107.)

Discussing Krantz' description with a group of friends, nobody doubted the details related by Krantz. Everybody was certain that the diviner was correct in attributing the first illness to the shade and the continued illness of the senior plus the illness of the child to another source. I quote one of the men's reactions: "That was long ago when diviners spoke only the truth. They were all truthful in those days. So his words of divination (i.e. diagnosis) were correct. It is clear that they (*abathakathi*) saw the

297

weakness (*ubuthakathaka*) of the man and took their opportunity. They continued the sickness. The shades were too weak for them. They continued the sickness to the condition that they desired (i.e. death). This is their custom. I am not amazed that they also killed the child. Perhaps it (the child) was *inkosana* (heir). Did the book not say that it was he?"

Note that the flesh of the beast killed in the ritual slaughter on the second occasion was not eaten. If a person dies at the time of a ritual celebration it is a sign that the shades cannot participate in food. This is representative of the whole concept of ritual killings in which the slaughtered animal's flesh is geared towards a communion, i.e. a sharing of food, with the shades and with kinsmen in the first place. The underlying and basic presumption for participation in the sharing of food as visualised in a communion is harmony, mutual agreement and a total absence of anger, hatred, suspicion and envy. Death, being a realization of exercised anger, cannot allow for communion in terms of the slaughtered beast. Hence the burying of the flesh.

[40] The term sickness includes sterility, usually associated with the female.

[41] Tyler, *Forty Years Among the Zulus,* p. 106, refers to misfortune in hunting caused by an angry shade.

[42] Compare in this context Goody, 'Legitimate and Illegitimate Aggression in a West African State', who, thought-provokingly, discusses in terms of "the question of why mystical aggression should be permitted under some conditions and treated as illegitimate under others" (p. 207). She speaks of "four major functions of aggressive behaviour" (p. 207) and of "male witches (who) are expected to have sought witchcraft powers in able to protect their dependants against the attacks of evil witches. By virtue of his powers a male witch who is head of a compound will be able to see witches – – –" (p. 211). This compares favourably to what among Zulu is defined as legitimate anger in this study and which is supposed to be more abundant in chiefs and people of authority in view of their responsibility to defend their juniors and uphold "the good life". However, in Zulu society men with anger cannot automatically be said to be witches, for they have no intention of harming for the sake of destruction. If they harm, then it is done in view of a good purpose and not to destroy.

[43] It is quite clear that the moral anger of the shades expresses itself within the lineage of which the shade was a kinsman. But with men it is different. Although the anger of seniors is feared primarily by such who are either juniors within the lineage and the clan or juniors by virtue of age and are known by the elder people, that of chiefs is expressed among those who today live in their geographically definable chieftainship.

[44] Note Marwick, 'African Witchcraft and Anxiety Load', pp. 123–129, who, convincingly, argues that the function of African witchcraft is a resolution of anxiety, conflict being the cause of anxiety and witchcraft as an institution catering for reactions to it. He relates "the African's increasing preoccupation with witchcraft beliefs" to the "increasing conflicts arising from the modern culture-contact situation", and, drawing on material from East and Southern Africa, speaks of anxiety in terms of i) belief in the efficacy of witchcraft, ii) an expression of hostility, iii) the aggressiveness of witchcraft, and, iv) the general disorganisation of intelligent behaviour that witchcraft brings about.

[45] Bryant, *Dict.,* p. 607: Doke–Vilakazi, *Dict.,* p. 781.

[46] Cf. Wilson, 'Witch Beliefs and Social Structure', pp. 88 f.

[47] Cf. White, 'Witchcraft, Divination and Magic among the Balovale Tribe', p. 83, who says that "the essence of *kulowa* and so of *uloji* is that the accusation of the injury is not explicable by any known cause and no rational explanation can be given. Hence we arrive back at the point that a belief in *uloji* is essentially a belief in a theory of causation to explain that which is incapable of any other explanation."

[48] Note the very clear distinction made among e.g. Venda (Stayt, *The Bavenda,* pp. 273 ff. and 276 ff.) and Nyakyusa (Wilson, *Good Company,* p. 92), who speak of *ubulosi* and *ubutege,* while Swazi allow for overlapping (Kuper, *An African Aristocracy,* pp. 173 f. and Kuper, *The Swazi,* pp. 65–67). See also White, 'Witchcraft, Divination and Magic among the Balovale Tribes', pp. 82–84: Rose, 'African and European Magic'. Jenkinson, *Amazulu,* p. 29, noted the two distinctions and the overlapping among Zulu when writing that "they have a superstitious dread for witchcraft and charms and secret poisoning which is no doubt practised to a large extent, as they are great herbalists and skilled in the knowledge of poisonous plants."

[49] This distinction between witchcraft and witches on the one hand and sorcery and sorcerers on the other was first clearly made by Prof. Evans-Pritchard. See his study *Witchcraft, Oracles and Magic among the Azande*, pp. 8 ff.. J. D. Krige, 'The Social Function of Witchcraft', has elaborated on the two distinctions among Lovedu and shown the differences in that society quite clearly. Schapera, 'Sorcery and Witchcraft in Bechuanaland', distinguishes between "night witches" who are mainly elderly women who gather in smaller groups at night and cause injury, and "day sorcerers" who inflict harm by causing the enemy to eat and consists of putting poisons into food to be eaten by the enemy. The night witches are included into the group of witches by causing the death of a close relative, preferably that of her own first born child."

Allowing for the distinction in Zulu society, the idioms *ubuthakathi* and *abathakathi* (witchcraft/sorcery and witches/sorcerers) will be used fairly extensively, partly in the many instances where Zulu assume overlapping, partly where the emphasis is, in the first instance, on evil as such and not primarily as definition of what kind or the sort of manipulation and/or manipulator. Also, the expressions are so frequently used in ethnographic records and have, to some extent, become terminus technicus as is e.g. *ilobolo*.

Middleton and Winter, *Witchcraft and Sorcery in East Africa*, p. 3, "suggest that the word wizard may usefully be used for both types of practitioners. Wizards may then consist either of witchcraft or sorcery, or of both practices." Note the further discussion in search for suitable terminology and the complexity of the question at stake, particularly in the French records, in Froelich, 'Sorciers et Magiciens: question de mots'.

[50] Jackson, 'Native Superstition and Crime', p. 259, relates the belief that witches can keep meat fresh, in order to be used in witchcraft, for three months. Describing witchcraft he says (p. 252): "There would be no magic in it if the danger could be seen, if physical violence were feared. It is the inherent dread of the unknown and illegitimate power of witchcraft which creates that fear – – – a power held accountable for every untoward incident."

[51] MacKenzie, *Mission Life among the Zulus*, p. 279, says that "a condemned *umtakathi* is looked upon as a condemned criminal is in civilized countries".

[52] Bryant, *Zulu Medicine and Medicine-Men*, p. 18, writes: "the most skilled medicine-man (i.e. herbalist) is with them invariably suspected of being also the greatest *umthakathi*".

[53] Whereas the overwhelming majority of diviners in Zulu society are females, practically all herbalists are males. Two reasons stand out clearly for this division. Firstly, the society being patrilineal and polygynous in set-up, a woman who shows explicit interest in *imithi* (and is not a diviner) runs the immediate risk of being suspected of practising sorcery, if not witchcraft *and* sorcery, women often being associated with witchcraft. Secondly, the herbalist's wanderings and scouring in search of medicines, contacts with strangers who seek medicines, is in keeping with the social behaviour of men rather than of women.

Similarly, in the realm of *ubuthakathi*, it is the females who are chiefly the witches and the familiars with whom they live intimately being of male sex, while men are the sorcerers. As expected, *abathakathi yemithi*, sorcerers, are not associated with familiars. In the frequent cases of overlapping between witchcraft and sorcery, either sex is suspect.

[54] Bryant, *Dict.*, p. 595: Colenso, *Zulu-Engl. Dict.*, p. 555: Doke–Vilakazi, *Dict.*, p. 763. According to the diviner an *umsokoco* is worse than *umthakathi*. Some Zulu agreed to this, others said that they had not heard of the distinction.

[55] Cf. Norenius, *Bland Zuluer och Karanger*, Vol. I, p. 52: Jenkinson, *Amazulu*, p. 30: MacKenzie, *Mission Life among the Zulu-Kafirs*, pp. 63 and 279.

[56] Compare timely and untimely deaths, pp. 79 ff.

[57] Cf. *The Collector*, p. 131, no. 679.

[58] White, 'Witchcraft, Divination and Magic among Balovale Tribes', p. 81, writes that "it is a theory of the causes of misfortunes which the believer finds to have origins in the enmity of people possessed of evil powers". This description is applicable to Zulu society also.

[59] Scotch, 'Magic, Sorcery and Football among the Zulu', pp. 70–74, gives a representative description of Zulu views and reactions to football, Scotch showing how the game, particularly to the urbanised, has become an occasion where tensions may find

their release and hostility towards people may be legally expressed. Scotch further describes how divination, ritual acts, sorcery and the powers of medicines are extensively used in order to win the game. A team that consistently looses matches replaces the diviner, and a team-mate who is the target of *ubuthakathi* also is replaced. At the beginning of the foot-ball season a goat is slaughtered and the team sleeps naked after having been attended to ritually the night prior to a match. A herbalist strengthens the players with medicines which are rubbed into the body in incisions and, in order to avoid witchcraft and/or sorcery from their counter-players and their supporters, the team keeps together until the players enter the field. A successfully played match is explained by successfully manipulated medical powers and avoidance of witchcraft and sorcery.

[60] Evans-Pritchard, *Witchcraft, Oracles and Magic among the Azande*, p. 107.

[61] Already Callaway, *The Religious System of the Amazulu*, p. 353, noted that envy excited hatred, and, p. 367, that quarrelling led to hatred.

[62] See details under becoming a witch, pp. 273 ff.

[63] Bryant, *Dict.*, p. 633: Doke–Vilakazi, *Dict.*, p. 312.

[64] A similar thought-pattern is described by Stayt, *The Bavenda*, pp. 273–4: "They (*vhaloi*) destroy property – – –, often entirely without provocation, to satisfy their inherent craving for evil-doing."

[65] Jackson, 'Native Superstition and Crime', p. 253: "The reputation of being possessed of the powers of witchcraft – – – (no Zulu)—will voluntarily seek to acquire."

[66] Every child is believed to be born with a natural defect called *isigwemba* (see further in Krige, *SSZ*, p. 67) which, if not treated will cause malformation of the legs, uncontrollable desire for meat, excess sexual abilities and a bad temper. It is treated by the mother winding the leaf of *umsenge* (Cussonia spicata) around a stick, inserting it into the rectum of the child when the baby is about three months old and twirling the stick between her hands until blood appears. The blood is collected and thrown into a running stream or buried in moist soil "so that it is carried away". Sometimes it is buried in the floor of the hut, especially if the operation was done in the hut.
Fuze, *Abantu Abamnyama*, pp. 51–53, gives a detailed description of the custom.

[67] Junod, 'The Theory of Witchcraft Amongst South African Natives', p. 231, describes similar thought-patterns among Tsonga. Notice that women give birth to witches, that witches form societies and that they eat human flesh (p. 231), their activities are nocturnal (p. 232), and that they aim at killing, the inspiring motives being hatred and jealousy (p. 234).

[68] Although women in theory also can give birth to male witches, it is always through females that witches breed, the initiative being taken by them. Informants are convinced that if he is a witch, a male cannot consciously father a future witch.

[69] Also the breeding of *abathakathi* is a breach of customary approach to childbirth in which a proper spacing of children is regarded as not only good but ethically the only legitimate way of using the power of fertility.

[70] Norenius, *Bland Zuluer och Karanger*, Vol. I, p. 52, suggests that *abathakathi* are also fallen diviners who use their secret knowledge to harm men.

[71] "The place of *abathakathi*" is by many located in an undefined area in northern Zululand "between Nongoma and Swaziland" which is said to have been given them by king Mpande, thinking that "they would all go to that place and not trouble people any more".
See also Samuelson, *Zululand, its Traditions, Legends*, etc., p. 32–33.

[72] Note the large number of men accused of witchcraft and sorcery in Jackson, Native Superstition and Crime: Mackenzie, *Mission Life among the Zulu Kaffirs*.

[73] Cf. Mpondo concepts of *izithunzela* in Hunter, *Reaction to Conquest*, p. 289.

[74] Other informants have confirmed this belief and claim that the Zulu proverb *ukwanda kwaliwa umthakathi* (family increase is opposed to by *umthakathi*) expresses this view. See also Studhardt, 'A Collection of Zulu Proverbs', p. 65.

[75] On familiars see also Krige, *SSZ*, pp. 324 ff.: Kohler, *The Isangoma Diviners*, pp. 35–40: Sibeko, 'Imilingo nemithi yokwelapha', pp. 248 ff.

[76] Cf. Mpondo concepts of familiars in Hunter, *Reaction to Conquest*, pp. 275 ff. Zulu concepts differ essentially in approach to Mpondo *izulu* (pp. 282 f.).

[77] Doke–Vilakazi, *Dict.*, p. 484.

[78] Doke–Vilakazi, *Dict.*, p. 393.

[79] Doke–Vilakazi, *Dict.*, p. 882.

[80] Also known as *izidwabakazana* (lit. little-woman's-leather-kilt-beings). They are given this name because *umthakathi* is said to dress them in leather-kilts (married female dress) as a disguise when sent to homesteads. See also Norenius, 'Något om magi och annan vidskepelse bland zuluerna', p. 82.

[81] Zulu associated the watching of graves after a burial with the fear of the corpse being removed by witches and being turned into familiars. Watching of graves is mentioned by Tyler, *Forty Years among the Zulus*, p. 94: Farrer, *Zululand and the Zulus*, p. 119: Grout, *Zululand*, p. 147: Wilkinson, *A Lady's Life in Zululand*, p. 158 (king).

[82] Hoffman, 'Witchcraft among the Zulus', p. 10, says that a reason for burying in the homestead is the fear "that the bodies may be dug up by witches". Hoffman indicates that hyenas also act as familiars (p. 10). Zulu accept his statement. "They (witches) have any animal of the night as familiars. Some are common, others are not so common. This one is not so common."

[83] Callaway, *The Religious System of the Amazulu*, pp. 421 ff. Zulu say that the smell of the flowers causes immediate death. The tree, like witches, is regarded as altogether evil, the evil indwelling in the branches, stem, leaves, roots and the flowers. It is subsequently said to be very poisonous. Any associations with this tree are not only dangerous, but also suspect. Only diviners of standing are said to have greater power than these trees.

[84] Grout, *Zululand*, p. 151, says that *abathakathi* "burn a hole in the head, cut out the tongue, then reduce the monster to the form of a cat, wolf or owl; and so make it a servant, and set it to do their work". Informants are hesitant about the matter of making the deceased into a familiar by burning a hole in the head, although they immediately add that "*umthakathi* can do anything". The idiom *ukuklwaya* is used to describe the splitting of the tongue.
See also Kohler, *The Isangoma Diviners*, pp. 35 f.

[85] Cf. *The Collector*, No. 683, p. 131.

[86] Braatvedt, *Roaming Zululand with a Native Commissioner*, p. 182: Norenius, 'Något om magi och annan vidskepelse', etc., p. 82.

[87] Hunchbacks, *izifumbu*, and monstrosities are said to be the offspring of male familiars and women. Although sometimes greatly feared, hunchbacks need not necessarily be associated with *ubuthakathi* themselves, although their mothers often are suspect.

[88] Bryant, *Dict.*, pp. 41 & 480. Note that the correct idiom in Zulu for a domestic cat is *umangobe*. *Ikathi*, which is commonly used today, is a zuluised form of the English word cat.

[89] *The Collector*, No. 193, p. 21. See also Brownlee, 'A Fragment of Xhosa Religious Beliefs', p. 41.

[90] Callaway, *The Religious System of the Amazulu*, p. 348. Also Isaacs, *Travels and Adventures*, Vol. II, p. 250.

[91] Because of the close associations between cats and *impaka*, cats are said not to give birth (*ukuzala*), but *ukuhlanza* (lit. vomit, as one vomits evil). See Bryant, *Dict.*, p. 243, and Doke–Vilakazi, *Dict.*, p. 321. "It (the cat) brings out evil (*ukukhipha ububi*) when it gives birth. Its kittens are not known from where they come. This is the reason why it is said that cats do not give birth."

[92] Samuelson, *Zululand, its Traditions, Legends*, etc., p. 7, says that *Tikoloshe* is "very friendly with the servants of the evildoers (*abathakathi*) namely baboons, owls, wild cats, jackals and evil spirits (*umkovu*). All these serve the *abathakathi* on land, whilst the Intkolotshe serves them under the water."

[93] On *Tikoloshe* as i) a mischievous character who steals food, throws stones at people, etc., see *The Collector*, p. 133, no. 684; and p. 64, no. 383: Krige, *SSZ*, p. 89: Norenius, 'Något om magi och vidskepelse' etc., p. 83: Sibeko, 'Imilingo nemithi yokwelapha yabantu', p. 248.

ii) haunting certain rivers see *The Collector*, p. 133, no. 684: Krige, *SSZ*, p. 354.

iii) fond of children and women, youth under puberty age, but fearful of men, see *The Collector*, p. 64, no. 383.

iv) associated with love (fat of *Tikoloshe* making a girl "soft") see *The Collector*, p. 42, no. 317; and p. 133, no. 684.

v) beating men unexpectedly see *The Collector*, p. 64, no. 383.

vi) also known as *uGiligaqwa* and *uMantindane*, see *The Collector*, p. 133, no. 684: Callaway, *Nursery Tales*, etc., p. 351.

vii) milking cattle mischievously (or getting others to do so), see Norenius, 'Något om magi och annan vidskepelse', etc., p. 83.

Samuelson, *Zululand, its Traditions, Legends*, etc., p. 7, says that *Tikoloshe* is invisible and "herdboys lived in continual fear of its sucking the milk cows. – – –. Another name for this spirit is Intoyetshe (things of stone)."

Callaway, *Nursery Tales, Trad. and Hist. of the Zulus*, pp. 349–352, describes in some detail *Tikoloshe* as visualised by Zulu in the mid-19th century. He suggests, quoting Zulu informants, that concepts of *Tikoloshe* came to the Zulu from the Xhosa "for among the Amazulu there is no Utikoloshe", (p. 349). He bases his argument partly on informants, partly on the "many Kxosisms" used by his narrators.

Further on Tikoloshe see Kohler, *The Isangoma Diviners*, pp. 37–40: Lee, Social Influences in Zulu Dreaming, pp. 269–271.

Herbalists of reputation are said to be able to catch *Tikoloshe* and extract fat from him while he is alive and sell it in liquid or solid forms as a very effective love medicine. One herbalist said that his wife "who saw *Tikoloshe* at the river in the shadow" would catch him for her husband and that, having caught him, he (the herbalist) would "put *Tikoloshe* to sleep as is done in hospitals" while he removed the fat. When *Tikoloshe* woke up the operation was over and the wound healed.

[94] Bryant, *Dict.*, p. 591: Doke–Vilakazi, *Dict.*, p. 758: Döhne, *Dict.*, p. 327: Norenius, 'Något om magi och annan vidskepelse', etc., p. 79.

[95] Gordon, 'Izindaba Zamadlozi, "Words about Spirits"', p. 103, relates what is done when a shade-snake is accidentally killed, i.e. ritual slaughter and expressions of pardon are said.

[96] Zulu claim that for this reason poisonous snakes that are killed should not be buried or simply thrown away. They should be burnt.

[97] The name of the snake is associated with a number of symbolic ideas. i) *Ulusinga* refers to the ailment in cattle which causes them to rush blindly about as though mad. ii) *Umsinga* is the sense of fullness, with pain, in the abdomen of a girl at the menstruation periods, when somewhat disordered. *Isilumo*, on the other hand, is the unbearable pain experienced by a male who, on having illegitimate intercourse with a woman, is regarded as suffering justly. He is not associated with *ukuthakatha* as is the woman who experiences *umsinga*. Cf. Bryant, *Dict.*, p. 367.

[98] Bryant, *Dict.*, p. 243. Cf. also Doke–Vilakazi, *Dict.*, p. 320.

[99] Whilst *abathakathi* are believed to be unable to vomit or spit, thought-patterns allow for this ability with familiars.

[100] Krige, *SSZ*, p. 324: *The Collector*, p. 66, no. 385.

[101] Cf. *uNqanumdolo*, a sea-monster with a split tongue, p. 179.

[102] See p. 251.

[103] See pp. 37 ff. on *elesifazane*. Another tradition, explaining forked lighting, relates how two birds "belonging to the sky", become angry with each other and subsequently, in a fight, one, overcome by the other, is thrown down to earth. "When it comes down it is still very angry and scratches the clouds with its claws. That is why forked lightning is bad. It comes from anger."

See Samuelson, *Zululand, Its Tradition, Legends*, etc., p. 71.

[104] It is characteristic that reptiles with split tongues are regarded as evil omens. See Gordon, Izindaba Zamadlozi, "Words about Spirits", p. 103.

[105] Jenkinson, *Amazulu*, p. 116, refers to familiars as being cats, panthers, jackals, and owls. See also Cory, *The Diary of the Rev. Francis Owen*, p. 58, who enumerates cats, wolves, panthers, jackals and owls.

[106] I recall an incident at a dipping tank. A local Zulu farmer pleaded with the dip-inspector to allow him not to dip a cow, the udder of which he claimed had been badly damaged by familiars. Inspection of the beast revealed that the cow was indeed badly damaged on the udder and at places the wounds were deep. The inspector, a sympathetic gentleman, explained that bats and baboons indeed trouble cows and that they actually scratch the cows, especially if there are several of them trying to get at the one beast. The cow was not dipped either on this specific occasion or the following.

[107] Dogs that bark at night are said sometimes to bark at *abathakathi*. Cf. Mackenzie, *Mission Life among the Zulu Kafirs*, p. 342.

[108] Samuelson, *Zululand, Its Traditions, Legends*, etc., p. 31 and Brownlee, 'A Fragment of Xhosa Religious Beliefs', p. 41.

[109] The owl which is said to warn people of the presence of witches is called *umshuele* (Strix capensis). Bryant, *Dict.*, p. 585: Doke–Vilakazi, *Dict.*, p. 752.

[110] Evidence shows that between 1959 (when collecting material towards a thesis commenced) and 1970 there has been an increase in ideas related to "white lovers". Ethnographic records not referring to them at all suggest that this thought-pattern is of recent date. South African legislation which does not allow mixed marriages and sexual relations across race barriers has probably boosted this thought-pattern considerably and, being illegal, has given it pointed relevance in relation to witchcraft which, according to Zulu, is another way of expressing illegal actions. Evidence shows that, firstly, it is in the urban settings where these ideas are particularly cherished, it being in towns in the first place where white and black meet illegally. Secondly, it is males who to a very great extent are said to be *amagxeba* which would correspond to the large number of white males (in relation to females) who are prosecuted in terms of forbidden relations with black/coloured/Asian women.

Prof. Wilson suggests similar tendencies among Mpondo. See Wilson, 'Witch Beliefs and Social Structure', p. 309.

[111] On medicines used, technical methods employed and general activities of witches and sorcerers see Krige, *SSZ*, pp. 321–323.

[112] Hunter, *Reaction to Conquest*, pp. 275–295 offers comparative material on Mpondo concepts of witchcraft, familiars and evil omens. Swazi material is described by Kuper, *An African Aristocracy*, pp. 172–176.

[113] Bryant, *Dict.*, p. 251.

[114] Hoffman, 'Witchcraft in Zululand', p. 10, says that "poisoning is a well developed art in Zululand – – –. Poisoning is common, but its fatal consequences are invariably attributed to the evil spell invoked by some witch." Experience supports Hoffman's statement.

[115] The term herbalist is used in the widest sense to include knowledge not only of botanical vegetation but also that multitude of materia that are ingredients in *imithi*.

[116] When spittle is associated with confessions it is said to be filled with evil. Cf. Expelling fluid in foll. chapter.

MacDonald, *Light in Africa*, p. 209.

[117] Kohler, 'Die Krankengeschichte eines Zulukaffern', pp. 585 ff., describes a case of witchcraft, apparently without the accused making use of a familiar but only medicines.

[118] Jackson, 'Native Superstition and Crime', pp. 253–259, enumerates a number of cases which illustrate the three types of *ubuthakathi* referred to.

[119] Berglund, 'African Concepts of Health, Sickness and Healing', p. 45.

[120] See further on this tree under *umkhovu*, p. 279.

Chapter VIII

Resisting evil

Hitherto the study has discussed, as far as evil is concerned, how immoral and illegitimate anger releases the powers of *ubuthakathi*. Left uncontrolled, anger inevitably will express itself in corrupt activity. "Wherever there is anger, there you will find *ubuthakathi*."

While very stern measures are taken against people who become involved in *ubuthakathi*, Zulu society offers outlets and safety-valves which aim at checking and resisting commencing anger. This combating of evil is expressed by individuals who feel a need to expose anger in themselves and, if not done of their own will, pressure may be put on individuals to bring about a desired confession. Various people in society have a duty to resist evil in different ways. While diviners expose evildoers, the duty of herbalists is to treat and strengthen the afflicted. Society also offers various occasions when anger is spoken out and purification from evil takes place.

The task of this section of the study is to examine and describe thought-patterns and symbols which allow for the outlet and control of evil in the struggle against it as expressed in *ubuthakathi*.[1]

The Field of Operation and Destruction of *Abathakathi*

The Field of Operation

Accusations of witchcraft and sorcery are not simply thrown out commonly in society. As anger is directed towards a particular individual or a special group of individuals, likewise suspicion, and very often subsequent accusations, are directed towards specific individuals.

It is among people with whom one lives, communicates and labours that tensions arise. In polygynous homes quarrels arise among jealous wives more often than misunderstandings between husband and wives.[2] In monogamous unions the problem of co-wives is eliminated and gives more room for tensions between husband and wife. In traditional homes half-brothers whose ambitions of inheritance could give rise to suspicions are, in the modern setting with schools and westernized patterns of earning a living, replaced by jealousy over against those more successful in examinations and in obtaining work. Misfortunes and calamities that befall daughters- and sons-in-law that live with their inlaws certainly gives a wider possibility for tensions, than had they not been there. Within any given home where people exist together there will be constant cause for frictions. The more crowded and less satisfied they are, the greater the chances of irritation and misunderstandings.

Experience shows, however, that suspisions and accusations of witchcraft and sorcery are not frequently directed to members of one's own lineage or clan.

The theoretical possibility is always open and readily admitted by all inforuments. The test for a witch to be accepted into the community of witches is the killing of, preferably, a kinsman! But "people do not like to think of their own blood (i.e. kinsmen) as *abathakathi*. That is why one looks outside if there is something happening in a home, the responsible person being an enemy outside (the lineage). So there is very great amazement if *umthakathi* who causes trouble is of the lineage".[3] Within a homestead accusations are invariably against a wife or other resident woman outside the lineage and/or clan. Other common accusations outside the home are against former lovers or against rivals in courtship and love, and against neighbours.

Anger may be expressed at work. Successful businessmen cause envy which leads to hatred. A labourer's good standing with the employer gives rise to jealousy and hatred. All kinds or rivalry, ranging from love-affairs to business and prosperity may lead to expressions of anger and cause people to manipulate against each other. The occasions of friction and tension are indeed manifold. It is in these that anger develops, breeds and is eventually realized in the immoral use of power.

Relations between families and homesteads may be impaired by many things. Cattle stray into one another's gardens and fields. Women gather firewood in each other's areas. In times of drought the scarce water-supplies are known to have caused anger. In all walks of life where people meet and associate in a manner that gives room for discord, arguments, jealousy and misunderstandings, there is room for suspicions in terms of sorcery and witchcraft.[4]

The Destruction of *Abathakathi*

"As snakes are killed because they are poisonous, so also *abathakathi* ought to be killed. They are bad, like snakes." Although people accused of being associated with *ubuthakathi* are not killed today, people are convinced that destroying *umthakathi* is "cleaning the land of evil".

"When snakes have been killed they must be burnt with fire on the garbage-heap outside the homestead because fire destroys them totally. They are rubbish. Snakes and *abathakathi* are the same. Both are just rubbish. So that is why *abathakathi* ought to be treated with fire (i.e. burnt)." The quotation is taken from a discussion which arose from ethnographic records referring to the burning of homesteads of suspected *abathakathi*, the burning generally taking place at night.[5] "That was the proper treatment of *abathakathi* in the days when they still were controlled. Today they are no longer controlled, doing what they wish and nothing being done. Not even frightening them. That is the reason for the great increase of evil in the land. It is because *abathakathi* are not checked. That is the only reason." My informant continued: "Yes, there was a reason for the burning of *abathakathi* like rubbish. It was the shade. If a person was burnt with fire, like the fire from the sky (i.e. lightning), there could never be a shade of that person. So if a person was *umthakathi* that person must be destroyed totally (*ukuqedwa*), nothing remaining (*kungasali nokunci*). His medicines and familiars together with all his things must be destroyed."

My resource-person, an aged man, claimed that he had once witnessed the burning of a homestead of a person accused of *ubuthakathi*. He associated the death of a snake and that of *umthakathi* with each other. As snakes wriggle when they are burnt "although the head has been crushed and the back broken, so *abathakathi* shout and throw the body this way and that, when they feel the heat of the fire. If they behave in this way, the people burning the homestead agree, saying, 'So it is clear that we have worked nicely tonight, killing this bad person.' They say so seeing the death of *umthakathi*."

Informants agree that *abathakathi* were also killed by impalement.[6] This method of execution was used because "the blood of *umthakathi* does not flow out. Also with hanging. That is why people are hanged. It is because of the fear of blood. It must not come out." People claim that if evildoers obtain the blood of a destroyed *umthakathi*, they could do endless harm. "The blood is the seed of *abathakathi*. The seed resembles *abathakathi* in bringing forth evil." Another Zulu said: "It is like faeces (of *abathakathi*). Like the faeces, it (the blood) must not come out. It must remain inside. It does not come out when *umthakathi* is treated with sticks (i.e. impalement). If it did come out, who would remove it, touching the vile from *abathakathi*? So this method is used so that nothing evil from within comes out. Not blood. Not faeces." *Abathakathi* are not buried. "They are eaten up by their friends of the night (i.e. animals of the night)."

Discussing *ukugwemba*,[7] one friend claimed that people who, in infancy, had been treated and blood allowed to flow freely, could not be impaled. Only those that had not undergone *ukugwemba* were "not strong enough to resist the sticks when inserted. If the sticks enter the person, then those doing the work are sure that it is *umthakathi* that they are treating. They insert sometimes three sticks, sometimes four. Each one inserts a stick that he has prepared. If the first stick does not enter easily, the man having to work hard, they fear because perhaps it is not *umthakathi* they are treating."

Although imputation of witchcraft is an offence today, there are still numerous accusations. These need not necessarily be declared openly or the accused be treated according to traditional methods of dealing with witches and evildoers. But the pressure of public opinion is very much dreaded, suspect people being shunned and avoided. Until quite recently, accused were driven away from homes and accepted by nobody, unless they fled very far away. Some people claim that the ear-lobe would be cut off from convicted *abathakathi* "so that they would be known". No case of this has, however, been traced.

The destruction of people accused of witchcraft and sorcery was traditionally regarded as a good service rendered society by ridding it of evildoers. Present legislation has, sometimes, been misunderstood to be a protection of *abathakathi* and hence also an encouragement for evil to continue and increase. An old woman put it thus: "It was different in the days of Shaka. Then there was prosperity. That was the time when *abathakathi* were killed. Shaka killed many. The land was nearly cleaned of them in those days. That is why he was so powerful in war. He had no enemies who hated him. They were all killed. But today the evil is very great. People die everywhere and there is no food. Where are the cattle of the Zulu people today? Where are the children of the nation today? There is nothing of it all." In view of the very carefree days associated with Shaka by the old woman, I asked her whether there were no difficulties in those days. "Difficulties? The ones that had difficulties were *abathakathi*. As for good people there was only prosperity (*ukuthuthuka*). He (Shaka) defended the whole nation (*walivikela izwe lonke*)."

The Defenders

The idiom defender[8] refers to those in Zulu society whose aim and purpose it is to defend goodness and resist evil. There are a number of defenders who require attention.

The Shades

There is no doubt that the shades are believed to protect and defend their survivors against the forces of evil.[9] Zulu are emphatic that one of the main concerns of the shades is to guard both their lineage and its individuals against the onslaughts of *ubuthakathi*.

The shades not only discover witches and reveal their intentions; they also fight them. G at Rorkes Dirft described the activity of the shades thus: "You must not think that they (the shades) simply sit there in their place, doing nothing. They are working all the time. They work like men. What work do men accomplish? They do two important things. Firstly, they build the homes. When the houses are few, they increase their numbers. They prepare the fields for planting. They look after the cattle, attending to the dipping, the herding, the byre, the milking, the bull and the things that pertain to cattle. That is the first work of men. The second work is fighting. A man has weapons. Those are the weapons of fighting. He guards his home against enemies. He buys medicines, consulting the diviner and the herbalist. He places them at certain places in order to fight certain bad people. He prepares also for the heaven-herd, paying him money to guard the home against lightning. He is always looking this way and that for the enemy, ready to fight. With the shades it is the same as with men. They are working their work, helping people so that everything goes well. That is the first thing. Then they do the second. They fight like men. Whom do they fight? They fight the bad ones who trouble their children. They take their weapons. They steal upon them. They thrust the spear deeply (into them). They thrust it still deeper, turning it. Then they pull it out, killing *umthakathi*."

A man said that the shades of old and jealous women were particularly active. "In the same way that they ever were ready to argue and discuss, so they are ever ready to fight. Their zeal (*ukushisekela*) is kindled against the enemy. When they are angry, then indeed there is something happening!"

The shades' resistance of evil is directed also to those in whom they trace visible evil or growing anger. What in the previous chapter was referred to as the legitimate and moral anger of the shades can be a warning to men that something is amiss and requires attention.[10] Allowing for their greed and egoistic characteristics, experience shows quite clearly that the shades are the ethical examples, "sometimes comparable to angels" in Christian circles. "When they are hungry or angry, giving us signs of their indignation, then we look at ourselves, trying to find the cause. Sometimes the hunger is caused by something they see in their children. Then they warn them, so that steps may be taken towards warding off the growth of evil in that it does not break out and harm greatly. That is why the sickness of the shades is a good sickness." My informant argued that "the sickness of the shades" gave the afflicted a chance to restore what had gone astray.

Besides their personal intervention, the shades operate chiefly through their servants, the diviners.

The Diviners

Among other duties a diviner's function "is to expose *umthakathi*" and his "energies are directed against *umthakathi*".[11] Jackson's statement was read to a Zulu and his immediate reaction was: "This man knows diviners! Who is he that knows them so well, speaking so clearly of their work?"

In very close co-operation with the shades, diviners are said to be defenders of men. "A diviner is called by the shades for this very purpose. They (the shades) work with men through diviners. All the work of diviners is good work. They (the shades) want their people who can reveal the secrets of the shades (*izimfihlakalo zamadlozi*). That is the work of divination. To reveal to us what the shades say. Then we know their words. Also the powers of *abathakathi*, where they are working. They (the shades) see them. Then they reveal them to us by way of the diviners."

Contrary to witches who have the power of destruction innate in themselves, the diviners operate wholly through the shades.[12] No diviner of any standing claims to have a power of his own. Divination is the work of the shades through the diviner. Although particularly renowned diviners are enveloped in an awe-inspiring atmosphere and are referred to as having a great deal of *amandla*, it is the concentration of symbols and their associations with the shades that is feared—not an innate power in the diviner. Also the social status and dignity ascribed influential diviners add to their prestige and position in society. One diviner whose home was very much respected by the local community described the approach to himself thus: "What they fear are the things of divination. They feel the power in the equipment. When all these things of divination are in one place, then that place is very heavy with power."[13]

Diviners themselves are proud of their close associations with the shades, their lack of innate power and, on the other hand, their ability and respected place in society. "It is clear whom we are, seeing that we take from the fathers the things we speak. So people do not doubt, knowing the words we speak (i.e. knowing that our words are valid because they come from the shades)." It is against this background we are to understand the immense self-confidence that diviners have. Backed up by it, they stand forth in society as symbols of morality and the control of evildoers.

Besides revealing witches and sorcerers, diviners are expected to indicate suitable herbalists or administer medicines themselves which will counteract ongoing evil. A diviner's obligations were described thus: "First the diviner reveals the cause of the troubles. There are many causes. A man cannot of himself know them. The diviner assists him. Secondly, the diviner indicates medicines. That is the medicines of treatment. If the sickness is not treated, it eats the man up. But if the diviner indicates suitable medicines, then he may get well again."

Diviners are consulted in all matters in which people require advice or have to make a choice. Unsuccessful achievements, misfortunes of all kinds, omens and various happenings which suggest a manipulation of powers may lead to consulting a diviner. For behind all these happenings and omens there is a reason. Sometimes it is traced to envious family members or neighbours, sometimes unethical life among lineage kinsmen, sometimes angered shades. In all cases diviners are expected to expose the cause or reveal the forbidden deeds. They must indicate whether familiars have excercized *ubuthakathi*, point out the place where the destructive medicines have been placed, or, if the cause of the misfortune is not *ubuthakathi* but legitimate and moral anger, they must explain this to the inquirers and give acceptable reasons.[14]

Seniors and Authority

While diviners, the distinguished members of society, resist evil with the aid of the shades, lineage seniors and people of authority do so by virtue of the power embedded in humanity. They do so by expressing moral and legitimate anger. Assuming that they are men of experience in the various walks of "the good life", they are in a position to guide and direct their juniors and subjects.

"When we say that a chief should have much power, we are speaking of authority and heat. These go together. If a man is given authority and lacks heat, how does he uphold good order? He fails. He must have heat if he is to be an authority and not just play. Then he can burn the mischievous in the land. Then he is doing his work properly."

Authority is expressed in terms of moral anger and suppression of evil. Speaking on this issue with a group of people one Sunday after a church service in which the preacher had claimed that if people were more reliable, then church authorities would not have to "be angry all the time, merely scolding from the morning to the evening, every day", I asked whether authority would be required if all people were good and caused no harm. A church warden in the group replied immediately: "There is no place where there is no evil. Do you think that the evil people have become less in numbers since Christianity (*amasonto*) came to this land? Do you think that evildoers are few like the policemen are few? No!" We discussed the issue of evildoers, the group very consciously avoiding words which would associate ideas with *ubuthakathi*, choosing to speak of *abantu ababi* (bad people). Another in the group continued: "It is as has been said previously, they (the bad people) are everywhere. This very day I am sure we have seen many bad people without knowing it. Even in church." "Yes, even in church. I agree, even in church," added another. The former continued, encouraged by the latter's comment: "Perhaps there was one in the very bench I was sitting in for all I know. Who knows before you start feeling the effects of the bad people. So it is clear that there must be authority who watch over people so that they are law-abiding."

Besides expressing legitimate anger over tresspasses and immoral actions, seniors and authority conduct court-cases and punish evildoers. In arguments they defend their minors and speak on behalf of their subjects. They listen to complaints and give advice. They settle disputes and pass new laws which regulate "the good life" and relationships between subjects and subordinates. Previously, when the Zulu nation was a warfaring people, leading the men in battle was the concern of the king or his appointed men. Also this was a resisting of evil entrusted the nation's highest authority.

Herbalists

Herbalists,[15] the manipulators of the powers embedded in materia, are able to use these powers for defending people and society against *ubuthakathi*.[16]

The herbalist (*enyanga yemithi*, lit. the authority on medical materia) manipulates the power embedded in materia on the basis, firstly, of his knowledge of the properties and capacity of the materia. This knowledge he acquires partly from his tutor in the use of medicines, partly by either exchanging secret information with other herbalists or buying it from them. Secondly, although this aspect is not always emphasized as being of particularly great importance, there is a formula which the herbalist utters in connection with his manipulating medicines. Herbalists of standing claim that it is the popular diviners and herbalists that use formulae, whilst "with us such a thing is not necessary."[17]

Medicines are used partly to ward off evil, partly to restore health once an individual has been stricken by *ubuthakathi*. Human beings as well as animals and homes, byres and fields may be defended with medicines.[18]

Different herbalists use different methods. One method of treatment was described thus: "A man goes to the herbalist. They sit down, speaking about the work that is to be done. The herbalist agrees. The man returns home. The herbalist begins to prepare himself. He gathers the medicines, going this way and that, finding all those things that pertain to the treatment of that place. (The herbalist was to treat a homestead.) He collects all the medicines in one place in his hut. When everything is collected he sits down to prepare the medicines. He says to his wives, 'As you have seen, there have been people here inquiring about some work at their homestead. So do not expect me.' (i.e. abstention from sexual activity.) He prepares his medicines in his hut, abstaining from food and women. He prepares the medicines in the ways that he knows that they should be prepared. On a certain day he comes to the homestead, carrying his medicines with him. First he works with *inthelezi*. That is the medicine of warding off. This medicine wards off people who are not desired (in the homestead). They (the people) bounce off when touching this medicine. He goes to a certain secluded spot in the homestead and sits down. He opens the bag. He calls for water. It is brought. He takes some medicines in the mouth, taking also water in his mouth. He rises and walks about. He blows out (*ukuchinsa*) medicines everywhere. On the huts, on the yard, on the whole homestead. He blows at the gates and even outside. He fills the mouth with water and medicines, blowing it out everywhere. That is the first medicine he uses. The second is that of the pegs. That is the medicine of *ukubethela*. He opens the bag again. He calls for the pig that they (he and the man) agreed upon. It is brought. The man is instructed by the herbalist to kill it. He cuts the throat. The herbalist takes fat from the throat of the pig. He spits, complaining of the bad smell from the pig. He puts the fat on the pegs. He proceeds by putting on medicines from the bag on the fat.[19] He drives the pegs into the ground. Pegs are put into the ground everywhere. They are placed in the ground at the gateways, around the homestead, in the yard at certain places known by the herbalist. He puts pegs into the ground at the doorway to the huts, even at the storage huts. He puts them in to the right of the doorway. That is the work of the pegs. Others, again, use horns. As for us (in this homestead) we know only of pegs. The third medicine is that of burning. The herbalist takes a potsherd and goes inside a hut. If there is no fire he makes fire, complaining that there has been no preparation for the medicines. Then he puts medicines into the potsherd. It burns. The smell is powerful. He smokes that whole hut. He takes the potsherd and goes to all the huts, smoking them, one by one. He returns to the hut with the fire. He sits down, having worked with strong medicines. He speaks, saying, 'Do not sweep today. Nor tomorrow. Only the third day can you sweep. Furthermore, do not receive visitors these days. Just remain quiet' (lit. peaceful, i.e. avoid quarrels and disputes). Then he rises, having worked with strong things. He returns home. The people do as they have been instructed."

The medicines blown out over the homestead are to ward off witches, sorcerers and familiars. Several informants said that they bounce off when they come in contact with this particular medicine. The smoking of huts is believed to ward off evil that is thrown (ukuphonsa) at the home and to be particularly disagreeable to familiars that enter the huts through the thatching. Most powerful of the medicines used by the herbalist are those related to pegs "because they contain blood and fat".[20] The power radiated from the pegs checks the movements of both abathakathi and their familiars. Hence their being driven into the ground particularly at the doors to huts/houses and at gates.

Lightning is also warded off with medicines. If a heaven-herd is not available, a herbalist with knowledge pertaining to warding off lightning is approached. Medicines, including pounded black stone taken from places where lightning frequently strikes, is buried at the right-hand doorpost as one enters a hut and at each gateway to the homestead. Sticks, smeared with sheep-fat and sprinkled with medicine, known as abafana are stuck into the thatching of the hut above the doorway, above umsamo and sometimes in the middle of the thatching. Laduma Madela explained the position of the sticks thus: "They are put there because of the frightfulness of lightning. It (the lightning) is more powerful than all the medicines. It is more powerful than the shades. They (the medicines and the shades) combine at those places. That is where they prepare to guard the home together, meeting at that place of the shades and the medicines (i.e. they meet at the place where the sticks are inserted into the thatching)." Madela associated the black of the medicines used in connection with defending a homestead against lightning with the light which he claimed is with the Lord-of-the-Sky and the sheep-fat with the thunder, marking the antagonistic opposites.[21]

A herbalist's immunizing people against ubuthakathi was described thus: "He (the herbalist) rises early in the morning and comes to the homestead. He brings with him the medicines which he is to use in treating the people of that home. First he treats the senior (umnumzane). Then he treats the women. Last he treats the children. The treatment is this. He takes the person to a hut or to a secluded spot. He tells them to remove the clothing. They do so. He takes medicines in his mouth and chews them. He chews them until they are a mash. He takes water in the mouth and mixes the medicines. He blows medicines over the body, covering it totally. Thereafter he makes incisions. They are made at the wrists, just below the throat and sometimes at other places, according to what doctor is treating the people. He has the medicines just close by. He takes some and rubs them into the incisions. He rubs until the blood has dried. Then he gives the person he is treating medicines to chew. The medicines are chewed until they become like a paste. He gives water to swallow the medicines. They (the medicines) are swallowed. Then he addresses the person saying, 'Do not wash today!' The people do not wash. They remain quietly in the homestead. The following day they wash their bodies, removing the dry blood from their bodies. All the time they have just remained quietly in the home, not doing any work or speaking much. That is how a herbalist treats people, making them strong against ubuthakathi."

Herbalists give isilambalala as a prophylactic particularly against idliso (sorcery in the form of poisoning). The treatment is said to contain dung from lizards and is, hence, suggestive. A renowned herbalist who specialized in this type of treatment indicated why it was so effective and, naturally, expensive. "The lizard is the animal of death. It is the animal that brought death to us. Dung (*ubulongwe*) is vile. But if the animal is vile, its refuse is good. So the medicine is good. It is very good indeed. It disagrees with death. If people are playing with death at celebrations (*umsebenzi*), then this medicine expels (*ukuchitha*) the medicines of death." The herbalist's wife described the reaction people experienced when treated with *isilambalala*. "First the person feels the trouble in the stomach. There are feelings of unrest in the bowels and much noise comes from them (the bowels). Then he feels the food wishing to come out. He goes outside. There he vomits, vomiting until everything has been brought up. He returns. He does not eat food at the homestead again seeing that he has not *isilambalala* in the stomach. So he refrains from eating, knowing that there is somebody who hates him. He returns home again, giving thanks to *isilambalala*."[22]

Medicines used in combating physical illness, pains, disorders, etc. vary a great deal, depending on the herbalist, diagnosis, cause of the ailment, the herbalist's previous experience, etc.[23] Whatever method of treating his patient the herbalist chooses, and, disregarding the choice of medical materia to be used, the herbalist, the patient and society are fully convinced that the herbalist's healing the afflicted is a resisting of evil experienced by the patient. Although the herbalist is feared and very much respected, and the step between the healer and the destroyer as far as the manipulation of medicine is concerned is not great, in this particular situation he is definitely the defender of men.

A major concern in the defence against evil is the treatment of barren women, for childlessness "is the worst sickness of all the sufferings of women". As in the case of physical ailments, treatment depends largely on a herbalist's knowledge and experience, the cause of the suffering, etc. Evidence indicates a very great variety of medicines used. Equally great in variety are the medicines given pregnant women in order to strengthen the unborn child, make birth less risky, and ward off the many possible evils that endanger the expectant mother in a critical period.[24]

Herbalists not only treat fields and gardens and render them secure from thieves, stray cattle, etc. They also fortify and encourage fertility in them. Likewise they defend domestic animals, particularly cattle, against *abathakathi* and their familiars, as they are believed to encourage fertility and increase in them.

Confessions

If by confessions we mean a disclosing of something previously kept to oneself, a declaring and an acknowledgement of an evil deed or immoral act, and particularly in the Zulu setting, a declaration of envy, suspicion, grudges, and brooding anger, it is beyond doubt that confession in Zulu society plays a far greater role in life than ethnographic records hitherto have suggested.[25] Confessions are, consciously or unconsciously, regarded as essential, if harmonious relations between people are to be retained. Confessions are the legitimatized safety-valves for speaking out grievances, grudges, envy, etc. which lead to anger and subsequent expressions of witchcraft and sorcery.[26]

Examples of confessions are recorded in the ethnographic literature, but they have not been recognized as confessions. Other interpretations have been given the rituals in which confessions are included. We have seen how Zulu underline the difference in meaning between *ukuthetha* and *ukuthethisa*,[27] and claim that scolding the shades is not possible. "Who are we to scold our seniors?" I suggest that *ukuthetha* includes confession and that in all rituals confessions play a part. Much of what Professor Gluckman refers to as "rituals of rebellion", at least in the Zulu setting, appears to involve confession rather than rebellion.[28]

Terminology

Several Zulu words are used to express the English term confession. Technically, confession in the Christian setting is spoken of as *ukuvuma*, confession of sin being *ukuvuma isono*. It is probable that Christian influence has given the use of this particular idiom a pointed relevance in Zulu society of today. Yet, because of basic differences in approach to Christian understanding of confession and those of traditional Zulu society, there is no commonly accepted interpretation of the word. Circumstances, the people one is talking to, the subject matter, etc. will have to be taken into account when interpretating the word *ukuvuma*. In the Mapumulo district the use of the word is far more significant where the Roman Catholic Church has worked than it is in areas where Christian. are predominantly of the Congregationalist tradition. Zulu themselves say that *ukuvuma* in its strict and traditional sense is to concent, to give permission, as well as to concede to a truthful fact.[29] Dictionaries underscore this claim.[30]

Outside Christain circles *ukuvuma* as a ritual word occurs extensively in divination, at times being substituted with *yizwa* (hear)! In the process of divination clients agree (*ukuvuma*) loudly when a diviner is assumed to be on the correct track, less audibly and enthusiastically when they think him/her to be off course. In the setting of divination *ukuvuma* is an agreement with those hidden facts, the revelation of which one has called upon the diviner; an acknowledgement of the findings. It is important to note that the people who agree and acknowledge in divination are the ones who have come to inquire. But the active role in divination is played by the diviner who answers for the revealing. The agreements voiced in *ukuvuma*, are, in a sense, an acknowledgement of the diviner's proper and justified revelation, an indication that his/her word in the matter fits into the larger context as experienced by the inquirers. This understanding of *ukuvuma* in a Zulu setting is very different from the Christian context in which confession, if defined as a penitential expression of a person's failings and sinfulness, assumes the confessing person to be the active party and not the confessor.

In Zionist and other independent groups the idiom *ukuvuma* is used extensively. But evidence among them suggests that there is a shift in terminology used to describe purification from *ukuvuma* to *ukuhlanza* (lit. cleanse oneself, purify oneself) and, occasionally, to *ukuziphilisa* (lit. to cause life in oneself).[31]

Ukuhlanza (refers to a number of symbolically suggestive actions for the expulsion of evil. Besides meaning to clear a person of ill-feeling, to clear away an unpleasant misunderstanding, *ukuhlanza* is vomiting, expulsion of faeces after taking an emetic or a purgative and a cleansing with water or chyme, the latter particularly in ritual celebrations.[32] Vomiting is not limited to experiences in illness only, but includes also the bringing up of water when drunk in large quantities in cleansing rituals and to vomiting in ordeals in times when such were more common than is the case today.

The idiom *ukuphumisa* is equally suggestive and rich in symbolic associations. Linguistically, *ukuphumisa* has its root in *phuma*, come out, *ukuphumesela* expressing an enunciation, speaking out clearly (both linguistically and by way of contents).[33] *Ukuphimisela* means to speak very clearly and to make a plain statement (linguistically and figuratively) as well as to spit on or spit at.[34] Bryant says that *ukuphumisa*, besides meaning to come out or to go out, indicates bring, or put out, eject, as a man from a hut, ejection of spittle from the mouth and giving utterance to. He adds, convincingly supported by evidence, that *ukuphumisa* also means a miscarriage, *ukuphumisa isisu* meaning the expulsion of a dead foetus from the womb.[35]

Zulu agree that it is correct to relate *ukuthetha* with confession. The idiom *ukuthetha* is generally assumed to be associated with ritual celebrations which are symbols of communion with the shades. An informant said: "We simply speak (*ukuthetha*) with them, telling them everything (*ukubika konke*, lit. give information on everything)." Our subsequent discussion made it perfectly clear that my informant included in the word *ukuthetha* what in English is understood by confession. His relating *ukuthetha* to *ukubika* which means to give information, underlines this conclusion.

The Zulu expression *shele* is equivalent to the English 'I beg your pardon!' or 'Sorry!'[36] The verb *ukushweleza* (sometimes, particularly among old people, *ukusheleza*) is the act of expressing regret, asking forgiveness and an expression of goodwill.[37]

Goodwill, harmony, calm, forgiveness, are understood in the term *xolo*, *ukuxolisa* being the act of causing goodwill and *xola* the condition of harmony which characterizes the atmosphere between people when a matter has been confessed and goodwill restored.[38]

The Confession

Zulu thought-patterns do not allow for chance, fortune or fate. "There is always somebody (responsible)."[39] Either the responsible person has had illegitimate and immoral anger as the driving motive towards activating evil. Or the anger has been moral and legitimate and hence the happening which, although painful, does not have destruction as its aim. In both cases the ultimate cause of encounters is anger and, if illegitimate, hatred.[40]

Evidence shows quite clearly that if a patient is to recover from the effects of anger, the cure must begin with confession and be followed by an expression, either by way of a spoken word or a symbol indicating it, of goodwill and a desire for harmony. Without these there can be not restoration of disrupted balance. This is applicable to both legal and illegal anger.

Since Zulu thought-patterns so strongly stress the role played by anger and hatred, it is evident that confession presupposes admission of these. This is what confessions contain—a speaking out of envy, suspicion, jealousy, etc. which all are stepping stones to hatred and anger. Expressed anger naturally assumes a confession not only of the roots which nourish anger, but also anger itself, if the hatred already has materialized in action. Only after confession do good relations return.

The aim of divination is not only to discover the ultimate origin and cause of the suffering experienced. The procedure is also addressed to the responsible persons, making it possible for them to confess. If they do not speak of themselves, it gives people a chance to convince them of the necessity to confess, the persuasion of the accused sometimes being both dramatic, violent and involving torture.

Confession leads not only to restored health of the afflicted. It also halts the expression of hatred and anger itself. Seen from the angle of the angered, confession is a control of one's feelings and an outlet which by-passes the evolution of growing anger towards *ubuthakathi*, halting further harmful development of the anger. It is a cooling off of the heat "of anger that has bad plans", a control that halts the growth of an irritation that may develop into *ubuthakathi*.

In the case of the young man who was troubled by dreams traced to his paternal grandfather and whose anger was deemed legitimate, there was a confession. "– – – he apologized, saying that he had forgotten that we recognized the smell of meat and referring to the lack of teeth – – –."[41] It was after this confession that the grandfather's anger ceased to be active.

Commenting on the relation between healing and confession, another informant said: "It is so even with shades. If there is sickness and the diviner finds the cause to be the anger of the shades against a certain person, then that person must confess. He must speak, clarifying everything. If he leaves out something, then there will be no restoration of health. Everything must be mentioned. Then they become peaceful again. The animal (the victim at the ritual killing) falls nicely. The sick person recovers and there is no more trouble."

I attended a confession in a polygynous home in which the second wife was in difficult labour. A female diviner had been called early on Saturday and arrived immediately. She indicated jealousy in the first wife who, due "to heat against the (second) wife, had closed the womb." There was general amazement in the homestead. Attending women had previously suggested misgivings about the moral life of the woman in labour. She had been compelled to confess to having had lovers, two women actually telling her what to confess in order to make birth possible. She confessed to having had lovers prior to the marriage, but her confession had not resulted in delivery. The diviner who was a kinsman to the husband, had been called on his instructions. Soon after the diviner's verdict, the woman in labour was taken to the nearby mission hospital by ambulance. Some of the attending women protested against the patient's being removed from the home, others agreed. One of the latter, quietening a representative of the opposing group, said: "It does not matter now, since the cause has been revealed."

After the departure of the ambulance the women, still arguing as to the wisdom of sending the woman off, assembled in the hut in which the woman in labour had been. Immediately the first wife, sitting at the door of her own hut, was called in and instructed to sit in front of the diviner. The diviner, sitting in *umsamo* of the hut and facing the doorway, smacked the woman in the face with her switch. "What is it I see?" The accused who, after the accusation had assumed a most distressed attitude, said nothing. She stared into the floor and did not move. Scornfully another woman said: "So there is a killer here in this home, we thinking that there would be birth!" The diviner interrupted her with: "Shut up!" Turning to the accused again, the diviner shouted out in a frightening and altogether unpleasant manner: "Where are the words?" The accused replied: "I can remember nothing."

D: "Whom did I see?" Smack again with the switch across the shoulder.

A: "It is said that it is I."

D: "Since when do I deceive? Who am I?"

A: (After some time.) "It is clear what has been said by *ingoma*."

D: "Where are the words?"

A: "There must be something."

D: "What?"

A: "Something bad."

D: "What bad thing?" Long silence. Slap across the face. "Speak!"

A: "Perhaps some thoughts."

D: "Thoughts! What thoughts?"

A: "I do not know. Perhaps desire (*uthando*)."

D: "Do not say 'perhaps'. Say desire."

A: "It was desire."

The questioning by the diviner under the perfect and murderous silence of the women present continued for an hour, the diviner breaking down, step by step, the accused woman's statements. The accused's chances of ever being released from this iron grip by the diviner were non-existent. With an amazing ability and untiring alertness she drove the accused further into a corner in which she already was trapped. Eventually the accused broke down, totally worn out by fatigue and under the gruesome pressure of the diviner and the other women. She said that she had been envious and jealous because she was not pregnant herself and had therefore "closed the womb". "That is the thing that I did, not knowing what I did. Even now, it appears fearful. Surely this thing from my heart was a fearful thing. I cannot even speak of it, so evil it is. This is what I am saying in this house of pains." There was general and marked relief among the other women. Their attitude toward the accused changed dramatically. From having nearly brought her to despair by their watchful silence and tense atmosphere of arrogance, they held her, crying hysterically, and comforted her. One of them slipped out of the door and returned with a small basin of water. The accused was given a mouthful and instructed by the diviner to spit it out through the door. She rinsed her mouth thoroughly with water and spat it out. Water was poured into her cupped hands, she washed her face and arms, and the water was allowed to spill over the floor. Then water was poured into an enamel mug and the accused woman given it to drink. While this was being done, the diviner had remained seated, saying nothing other than giving necessary instructions. She maintained a dignified and solemn atmosphere but was relaxed, having the situation in her hands all the time. The attending women listened attentively to her and went about their business in assisting the accused with reverence and sincerity. When the accused had emptied the mug, silence fell over the women and a somewhat tenser atmosphere could be felt. After about ten minutes the diviner retired through the hut doorway. The rest of the women sat where they were, watching the accused, who utterly fatigued, leaned against the hut wall and said nothing. I followed the diviner, keen to speak to her. Three details emerged from our discussion.

Firstly, "the child will come out of the womb as the spittle came out of her (the accused's) mouth." We talked about the spitting through the door and the diviner claimed that the woman who fetched the water had been indicated to her (the diviner) by the shades. "She left the door open. The shades forced her (to leave it open). Then I knew that the womb would open." Conversation with the woman in question later in the day revealed that she was not at all conscious of having left the door open!

Secondly, the diviner claimed that had the accused not confessed everything, then "there would have been vomiting of the water [she had drunk]. But there was no vomiting. So she had confessed everything." The diviner claimed that the water was not an ordeal "because it had no medicines. It was just water. I do not know the things of ordeals. All I know is the shades. I pray that they guide me. Even today they have helped me in exposing this woman." It proved difficult to obtain any further information about associations with the water and innocence and their relations to vomiting. But certainly the accused's not vomiting the water was taken as a good sign both by the diviner and the other women.[42]

Thirdly, we discussed the frightening atmosphere of arrogance and contempt assumed by the attending women and the fearful questioning of the accused by the diviner. The onlooker's sympathy in the gruesome encounter was with the accused, whether she was guilty or not. Her experience was nothing short of mental torture, geared towards a forced confession. The diviner, as did the other women later in the day, assured me of the woman's guilt. To them all, she was guilty. There was no doubt about this and further discussion of this issue was refused. The diviner readily admitted that she had been angry and the women agreed that the diviner was correct in being angry. The women also admitted being angry. Asked whether they thought that their anger was moral and legitimate, they were amazed at my even questioning the validity of their reactions against the accused. "Anybody would have been angry, seeing such things in our midst."[43]

The attitude of both the diviner and the assisting women was that they expressed legitimate and moral anger; they also defended the torture, gruesome and fearful as it was. They claimed that it was necessary in order to bring about a confession. "We were angry. That is true. But this atmosphere (umoya) you are speaking about helped her to confess everything." All were convinced that they had "just talked nicely, not showing the heat of the anger". If this had not been so, there would have been no confession. All were equally convinced that the accused's hysterical weeping and their comforting her after her breaking down were expressions of goodwill and renewed bonds of harmony.

At the hospital the woman in labour was safely delivered and returned to the home after her recovery. Wishing to know how she would be received, I drove her home. She was received most heartily by all, including the woman who had been accused of "closing the womb". There was no sign whatsoever of the confession. There were several moving signs of how welcome the woman was; the children and the other womenfolk of the homestead crowded around the mother and her baby, fire-wood had been collected outside her hut and the water-barrel outside it was filled. The yard had been swept and a fowl killed. A chance to discuss the confession with the woman accused was given me, and raising the issue with her she indignantly answered: "I did nothing. I was just helping her to give birth. Do not trouble me with things of the past now."[44]

The recorded incident, as a number of others witnessed, shows quite clearly how confessions stand for healing of the afflicted. Zulu are convinced that confessions inevitably lead to restoration, a recovery from sufferings. Hence forced confessions of the type related above. Hence also, to a far greater extent previously, the use of ordeals in order to disclose the guilty and convince a suspect of the necessity of confessing, if not voluntarily, then through torture.

The number of recanted confessions is remarkable, this being particularly common among women, who, fearing childbirth or an unhappy ending of pregnancy, have admitted, quite frankly and without any hesitation, sexual relations with lovers, immoral dreams and, in two cases on record, relations with men of the same clan as themselves which is regarded as incest. But after the birth of the child an amazing number of confessions are withdrawn or denied.

Recanted confessions could, at the first glance, suggest that accusations of witchcraft and sorcery are not taken seriously and that the confessions are a mere formality: to quote the woman referred to above, "just helping". Yet this is not so. People accused of witchcraft and sorcery take the accusation very seriously. There was nothing to indicate that the woman who confessed jealousy in relation to her co-wife was not sincere when she assumed her distressed attitude. Neither was there anything that suggested her being dishonest in her confession. Everything indicated that she was quite convinced of being guilty.

A number of thought-patterns are closely associated with ideas concerning accusations and subsequent confessions on the one hand, conviction of guilt on the other.

Firstly, witchcraft and sorcery are realities in Zulu thinking. Certainly there is evidence to show that poisoning does take place. A number of confessions involving poisoning may be genuine also according to Western concepts of truth and reality. In view of thought-patterns which describe witches as not always being conscious of their involvement in illegal activity, accusations—practically always backed by overwhelming and convincing arguments against the accused—are simply another way of exposing evildoers. Experience shows that the revealing of the evildoer is as much an unpleasant surprise to the accused as to those related to the accused.

Secondly, although people express suspicions and misgivings, it is often the diviner who has the final word. The assurance that diviners, and particularly those of standing, speak what is revealed to them by the shades, is taken as proof enough that they speak the truth. Not all diviners carry conviction, hence therefore the advice of two, sometimes three, is sought. If their findings agree, their advice is generally accepted as true and valid.

The pressure of society, based on suspicion, must not be underestimated. It was felt very dramatically in the case of the confession related above in which the atmosphere created by the attending woman over against the accused was overwhelming. Because the emphasis in immoral acts is not, in the first instance, a matter of personal conscience, but rather a concern of socially involved and concerned people, immorality of all kinds is a social matter. Hence the weight and pressure of society, its thinking and reasoning, is convincing to both the accused, the accusers, and the community as a whole.

Fourthly, although the pressure of society and the words of the diviner exercise overwhelming pressure on a suspect, there is room for a sense of guilt in all people. "If there is trouble, there must be a cause," is the point of departure. "There is always somebody (responsible)." Because the area of involvement is limited to those with whom one is liable to quarrel and disagree, the number of possible candidates for accusations is restricted. It is in this limitation and under the pressure of thought-patterns that take evil as real that the sense of guilt in individuals plays its role. A Zulu man convicted for an offence and serving sentence in prison said: "I cannot remember doing it, but who else could it have been?"

Recanting confession must not be judged as being a by-passing the truth in all instances. In many cases the recanting is not a withdrawal of confession but a denial of the actual facts expressed in the confession. It appears that although great care is taken to obtain details in view of confessions and particularly so in serious cases, e.g. incest and murder,[45] the greater emphasis is placed on the act of confession. Once, having listened to a young wife confessing previous lovers before her marriage to her husband by whom she now expected her first child, I asked her whether she indeed had lived the extravagant life she described in her confession. She admitted quite frankly that this was not the case, although she had been in love with several young men. "Of some I spoke the truth. Sometimes I dreamt of men. These I also confessed. All those were the truth. Others I imagined (*ukuqamba*). That is what is required in *isivumo* (confession)."

Confessions are expected to be followed by expressions of goodwill. Sometimes the expression is accomplished in a single word, *uxolo* or *ngiyaxolisa* (I beg pardon). Sometimes not even this is said. But it is assumed. "Many things are not said with words. If the person is sorry, we see it."

On one occasion a person confessing took out a five-cent piece from a purse containing a few coins and placed it on the floor. It was received by the man who listened to the confession with the words: "Now everything is complete." Experience has shown on many occasions how goodwill has expressed itself in little acts and gifts given each other after a quarrel has been settled. Two men working in a park in Durban settled a dispute during a lunch-hour rest, the two men seated opposite each other on the pavement. After settling their matter, the confessing man prepared a cigarette of tobacco and brown paper torn from a bag and handed it to the other together with the match-box. The latter received the cigarette and the match-box very graciously, saying: "I see that we agree with each other again." He lit the cigarette and smoked in great relaxation, giving the former a chance to draw from it also. They continued chatting about a number of things as if nothing had happened previously and returned to work gaily.

Confessions are regarded as being an outlet and hence an emptying of evil in oneself. Confession and emptiness are associated with each other, while withheld anger can be described as *ukusinda* (being heavy) or even *ukucwala* (being full). "When a person has spoken out, there is emptiness. That is the emptiness that is good." People say, '*Anginalutho* (I have nothing).' Or they say, '*Akukho okungisindayo* (there is nothing that burdens me).' They say this meaning that they are empty (*ukungenalutho*). But if they carry the thing inside themselves, then it festers (*ukwanda*). The person becomes heavy with it (anger) inside."

Unwillingness to let people speak out is taken very seriously and may be regarded as an indication of action being taken against them. No such case could be traced, although people agreed that not allowing a person to purify himself/herself was a serious offence.

Conditions of life today offer a variety of approaches to confessions and mis-understandings that cause anxiety. The following will illustrate the issue at stake which involved a Christian woman living with her inlaws who were pa-gans. She spoke of her anxiety and the difficulties that arose when trying to live up to expectations from two different life approaches. She said: "The trouble is that among Christians one thing is true while among pagans (*abanga-koliwe*) another thing is true." She spoke of her constantly recurring sexual dreams and feared very much that these would affect her forthcoming labour. Christian women had advised her to confess the dreams to her minister. This she had done. After her telling him about the dreams he had suggested a psychological explanation for her dreams, describing how dreams came about and why she was dreaming as she was. His attempts to explain caused further anxiety in the woman. "So the dreaming just continued and became more and more. Even now, I do not know what to do because at home they expect to hear something so that the birth may go well. But with Christians it is another thing." Asked what she had expected of her minister, she said: "I was con-fessing sins (*bengivuma izono*). But he said it was not sinful to dream." The minister's explanation of dreams was taken by the woman to be a refuting of confession. What she wanted and expected was a condemnation of the sinful-ness of her sexual dreams and a chance to show goodwill by fulfilling her fi-nancial commitments to the parish by having her congregational fee entered into her membership card. Whilst the minister did not understand her confes-sion of dreams as a confession of sin he added to the burden by sending her to the parish treasurer with her money. For in her mind, the settling of her mem-bership fee was a symbol of goodwill.

Occasions and those concerned

All happenings within a homestead and a lineage which give rise to ritual cele-brations are occasions of speaking out and expressing goodwill. Of necessity the times of crisis are included in these, as are the celebrations in connection with sickness, misconduct, and offences against the shades and kinsmen. In rituals related with the call, training and coming out of a diviner there is also confes-sion. Of recent date celebrations at Christmas-time are becoming increasingly prominent. Commencing a few days before Christmas day, the celebrations may continue until the New Year after which date the men generally return to their work in the towns.[46]

The study has hitherto indicated that no ritual celebration is conducted with-out a reason. Ritual beer-drinking and slaughtering is always called for. The importance of the address given in the byre has also been underlined[47] and, as far as the shades are concerned, I suggest that the speech contains a confes-sion. In it the senior who acts as officiant, addresses the shades, "clarify-ing everything". "So today we are washing ourselves. There is nothing that is hidden. Everything has been mentioned. Even the hatred (*inzondo*) and the suspicions (*izingabazo*) which were there have been mentioned here today. So we are washing ourselves."[48] It is quite clear that the circumstances bringing about the ritual celebration will define the contents of the confession, no con-fession being valid so that it covers all the various reasons for celebrating a ritual.

Because the shades are the seniors and because their anger, if expressed either as hunger or motivated by indignation, always is valid and legitimate anger, it is always the survivors who are expected to be the confessing party. "No shade can purify himself (*ukuhlamba*). From what would they purify themselves? There is no *ukuvuma* with shades. The words are spoken by their children (i.e. confessions is made by their survivors)."

Goodwill is sometimes expressed quite clearly in *isicelo* of the address. If not expressed verbally, which Zulu claim is not essential, "it is shown in another way". It is demonstrated in the willingness to slaughter and in the labour, planning, anxiety and expenditure, etc. which precedes a ritual celebration. That the shades accept this indication of goodwill is reflected in the symbols whereby they reveal their subsequent goodwill, i.e. the animal's groaning, falling on the right side, etc. . .

Confession is not limited to the speech made in the byre and directed to the shades. At ritual celebrations survivors, neighbours and friends are given an opportunity which is recognised by society to speak out. This takes place in various ways. Sometimes little groups form where people speak out. Or the officiant is challenged in view of the poor quality and small quantity of beer. Sometimes the host at a celebration actually invites people to speak out against him, a device also used by hosts at large meetings and gatherings where irritation can arise. "If there is anything in your hearts, friends and guests, I am asking you to speak it out. Do not take it home with you. Just speak it out. That is why I am here." Strained relationships of a great many kinds are ventilated at ritual celebrations, for also among men there must be harmony before there can be a sharing of food. The speaking out is necessary before eating.

At a Christmas party to which I had been invited by a friend, I was struck by the many visitors who, sitting in a large room, accused each other of a host of trivial and petty actions; accusations which, to the unaccustomed, sounded quite out of place at a Christmas celebration. I was accompanied by another white who, irritated by what he referred to as the waste of time and inability to keep to the time set (we were invited to come at noon, but did not commence the meal until after three o'clock), suggested that we leave this unpleasant atmosphere. I was on the verge of agreeing with him. Later experience taught me how wrong we were in thoughts about waste of time and of inability to keep time. The celebration had started at noot but not, as we thought, with eating. There were important matters to be dealt with before eating was possible. I was to learn that the accusations fitted in perfectly with what in Zululand is understood by communion in eating. Excited by the plentiful flow of "the food of men", this "fire of the shades", people indeed spoke out! The beer which brought about a talkative mood had its legitimate place in that Christmas celebration in that it excited people "to speak out their anger", and people who were not embarrased by talking to a missionary about beer, claimed that the excitement "is the heat of the shades, encouraging men to talk". The talking in this setting was not only a desire to argue and share different views—it was confession.

Practically everybody talked on some occasion. People spoke when they felt the need to do so, sometimes several men speaking out quite excitedly at the same time. The visitors accused each other of the small and insignificant gifts they had received from each other: one accused another of having occupied the best seat in the taxi that drove them from Durban to their homes without paying more than those who sat less comfortably: a third accused another of having been dishonest at card-games in the city. Another had taken a bottle of spirits that was not his, etc. . . . There was no end to the matters that were ventilated. One was struck by the willingness of the accused to accept the accusations. Seldom have I heard the idiom *ngiyaxolisa* (I beg pardon) used as frequently as on this occasion.

What in the first place appeared to be a tumult of bad and unfriendly relationships in the lives of the visitors at the party proved to be an occasion of uttermost importance in the lives of the people gathered—an opportunity to confess envy, suspicion, jealousy, slander, hatred, anger. Amazing, again, was the very abrupt change in atmosphere when the prepared meal was to be eaten. From having rather drowsy and nearly unpleasant to each other, visitors became happy and exalted in spirit. With enthusiasm one shared in eating the food. Reading notes taken at the Christmas party four years later in the same house with many of the same visitors present, I added to the notes of the previous occasions: "This is communion in Zululand!"

The host, on the occasion four years later commented: "Everybody must speak. Only if everybody speaks out what is in his heart will it be a nice party. But if there is one who does not speak, then people say, 'No, but this person is not speaking. Why does he close it (envy, anger, suspicion, etc.) inside?' Then they do not feel at ease because of the one that is quiet, wondering what kind of man he is that has nothing to speak out."[49]

Accusations and confessions of the type described above take place prior to birth in order to make delivery easy,[50] at puberty rites, marriages, and deaths. They are particularly evident at times prior to births and play, in cases of difficult labour, an essential role. Before a burial, people gather in the hut of e.g. the widow and accuse each other in low and grieved tones of various causes of anger. Many of them are addressed to the widow (or widower). At marriages "relatives of the bride and groom insult and threaten each other and conduct mock battles that sometimes become heated,"[51] while others, less dramatically, sit around and discuss family quarrels and personal grievances they hold against each other. "If they do not do this thing, then the eating is difficult", said a man when commenting on a group of women arguing and accusing each other quite excitedly at a marriage. Probably unconsciously he put his finger on the very nerve of confessions and their relationships to participation in eating.

There is an important connection between participation, participants and confessions at the various occasions in which speaking out takes place. Evidence has shown the great pains taken to celebrate ritual communions at such times when at least kinsmen and clan relatives can take part in the festivity. The concern is first and foremost a family concern.[52] The presence of kinsmen assumes more than just being there. It takes for granted a participation in the activities. Of these, confessions is a major concern. For it is in the speaking out that suspicion of *ubuthakathi* between kinsmen is removed. Professor Gluckman has pointed out the importance attached to presence and participation at burials— a detail that experience underlines very strongly.[53] The thought-pattern underlying this need for participation, particularly in cases of death, is an inner experienced need to assure kinsmen of innocence in relation to the death. "There is no death that is not caused by *ubuthakathi*." Again, "no *umthakathi* confesses of himself/herself". Hence the great importance attached to both presence and participation in confession at ritual celebrations.

Experience suggests that neighbours and friends also take pains to attend ritual celebrations, sometimes at considerable costs and inconveniences. Also with them the motive is a desire to free oneself of suspicions. A Zulu clergyman defined the difference between parties arranged by whites and Zulu participation in ritual celebrations thus: "With us, there are never invitations because of suspicion. If we invite people we are telling them that we suspect their not attending. This is the same as saying that we suspect them of being evildoers. With whites, friends are invited simply because they are friends and the absence of an invitation is judged as broken friendship."

Mutual trust is expressed in speaking out between authority and counsellors. Callaway relates that prior to an army's setting out the warriors spoke out against a chief.[54] Old Zulu men who are acquainted with army procedures agree that this was so. One of them commented: "It was done in order that leaders could trust them in battle." The same attitude is expressed by counsellors toward authority. "Wise men of authority will listen to their counsellors because that shows that he will trust them." Without doubt the "listening to their counsellors" refers to the latter's speaking out, and "the trust" (note that it is placed in the future!) is a conviction that there are no suspicions of growing anger which at a later stage may express itself in *ubuthakathi*. Two counsellors to the late chief Nkanthini Zulu put the issue very boldly when one of them, speaking on behalf of them both, said: "The work of counsellors is to speak to the chief. They speak of the things they hear are in the hearts of the people. They speak openly when the chief calls on them to do so, because then he need not have any fears. The fears are removed by their speaking."

Disturbances and growing anger among kinsmen are settled in the ritual, called *ukuthela ngamanzi* (to cool with water, lit. to pour over water),[55] *ukuthelelana amanzi* (to patch up a difference, become friends after a quarrel, lit. to pour water over each other),[56] or *isidlo senhlanzeko* (the communion of purification). The latter idiom underlines the ritual importance of the occasion. "It is given this name because after *inhlanzeko* (purification) the people can again come together and eat." The purification is, naturally, a cleansing from anger, as the following account illustrates.

A man described the ritual thus: "This work of *ukuthela ngamanzi* is done when kinsmen are very angry, fearing that one will kill the other. When the people are troubled by this anger, they speak to a third person who knows them well. Perhaps it is the father. He goes to them, one by one, saying, 'This heat burning within you is the heat of death. I see clearly that there will be death. This is my word to you, when I say that you must cool. Is there no water of cooling?' They agree. Then he appoints a day. The men with heat just remain quiet. They do nothing because of the words of the father and the agreement (i.e. they do not contemplate *ubuthakathi*). Beer is brewed. It is stored away until the day agreed upon. On that day they meet at a certain place. It is somewhere known to the people of that lineage where the brewing of beer for the celebration has been done. All the people having heat in their hearts come to that place. So on that day they all meet at that spot known by everybody. There is nobody who does not know that place. The father comes to that spot, carrying a goat's skin. The women bring the beer. It is placed in a cool place. Water is brought. It is also put away in the shadow. The angry men just remain quiet all the time, saying nothing. One sits in one place and the other in another place. They do not look at each other because of the heat

323

in their hearts. Then the father speaks. He calls them. They come forward. Then everybody becomes quiet. He says to the first man, 'Just sit here, my child.' He sits down. He says the same thing to the second one. They find themselves sitting opposite each other, facing the father. He (the father) calls for water. He calls for ash and the things for the water. He pours the ash and *imithi* into the water. The medicines are the medicines of washing, for this day is the day of purification. He stirs the water until the medicines are well mixed. He says to the first man, 'Here is water containing ash.' The man rises and washes in the water (washes his hands). He speaks to the second man, saying, 'Even you.' Also he rises and washes (his hands). The men are seated, the water remaining where it was placed by the father. He says to the first man, *'Kipha okusenhliziweni yakho* (Speak out what is in your heart).' He relates the whole matter according to his point of view, how it started, its growth and the present state. He speaks for a long time, describing everything. If he had plans of something (*ubuthakathi*), he will mention it, adding words about not doing it because of the agreement. He concludes his speaking by saying, 'I have completed my speaking. As for me I am grateful for this opportunity of placing this disturbance before you openly today. There is nothing that is not placed openly as far as I am concerned.' The second man commences speaking, relating the same thing at length from his point of view. All the time everybody is silent. He concludes his speaking with words of gratitude for the opportunity to speak openly. The father speaks, summarizing the words of the first man and the words of the second. All the time the people are silent. He turns to them both, asking whether they are willing to forget this matter, having now openly spoken in heavy and hot words. They agree. He instructs the first man to wash his mouth. He rises and takes a mouthful of water from that place where the water with the ash is placed. He puts down the container and spits out forcefully over his left shoulder, himself not looking backwards. He spits as if spitting out poison. He indicates with his whole face how bad it tastes, this thing that he is spitting out, adding *'Twi!'* to the spitting out. He wipes his mouth. He sits down. The father says to the second man, 'Even you.' He rises and does the same thing, saying, *'Twi!'* He wipes his mouth and sits down. The father rises and praises them for working this matter of *inhlanzeko* like men, saying that it is good when matters are clarified in the proper way. All the people agree, giving thanks that the men worked legitimately (*ngomthetho*). Then he (the father) takes the goat-skin and puts it on the grass. The two men rise and sit down on it together, facing each other. They mention the water and its taste (i.e. the bad they spat out), complaining of the bitterness. Beer is brought. The water with medicines is thrown out. A calabash of beer is placed between them (the men). The father drinks, praising the men for their work, saying that it is good that matters are dealt with nicely. Then he gives the container to the first. He drinks deeply and gives the second. Even he drinks deeply. They both speak, praising the taste of the beer and saying that they have not eaten the food of men for a long time. They laugh, joking all the time and drinking. They stand up and go to the people. Then others with hot hearts come forward, each one speaking the thing that is burdening him, speaking out everything. The container is filled with beer for each one that speaks with his partner. They drink from it, leaving the skin (i.e. the goat-skin on which they sat) being friends. So at the end all have spoken who wish to speak, all now drinking beer and laughing. That is what happens when people drink beer for the first time after the disturbances of the hearts have been settled."[57]

Zulu terminology underlines the role played by water in the ritual. Informants are emphatic that although washing in water sometimes (although seldom) is omitted, the expulsion of water from the mouth cannot be by-passed. "If there is no *ukuphimisa amanzi* (expulsion of water), there cannot be peace between the two. The speaking out and the blowing out of the water go together (*ukuhambisana*)."[58]

It is, further, important to note the close associations between the ritual of purification from anger and the common participation in beer (and sometimes meat). *Isidlo senhlanzeko*, like all other ritual celebrations, underlines the necessity of harmonious relationships in connection with communion. While celebrations described previously in the study suggest the emphasis being on communion and hence the necessity of first settling disturbances (e.g. the hunger of the shades), the ritual of *ukuthela ngamanzi* puts its emphasis on the need of reconciliation. The speaking out and spitting of water as symbols of purification from the evil of anger is confirmed in the communion on the goat's skin from one and the same beer container.

All informants agree that men who are disturbed cannot speak to each other. Asked whether they could eat or drink beer together, people refuted any such possibility emphatically, some finding the question startling. Some said that angry men sometimes did not eat at all until the matter had either been resolved or something had been done to separate the disturbed from each other for fear that poisoning might take place. The importance of mutual good relationships are once again underlined as a necessity for participation in food, even if the food is not eaten at the same time or from the same containers. Food stands for life and anger stands for heat in its negative sense. These two cannot be united without considerable self-discipline.

The First Fruits Festival

Although now obsolete as a national event, the festival of the first fruits must, in the past, have played a significant role in Zulu society.[59] Because of the relevance of the subject-matter at stake, the fairly detailed descriptions of the occasion in ethnographic records and the importance attached to the celebration among surrounding people (particularly Swazi),[60] the festival will be studied from the point of view of confessions. I suggest that the humiliating songs of hatred directed to the king and his lineage shades were institutionalized forms of confession which gave commoners and subordinates a recognized opportunity of participation in speaking out.[61]

Professor Gluckman, arguing in terms of what he calls "rituals of rebellion", propounds that "every social system is a field of tension, full of ambivalence, of co-operation and contrasting struggle. This is true of relatively stationary— what I call repetitive—social systems as well as systems which are changing and developing. In the repetitive system particular conflicts are settled not by alternations in the order of offices, but by changing the persons occupying those offices." Drawing on material from Zulu among other South-Eastern African peoples, he states that "in virtue of their social position princes and people hate the king, but nevertheless they support him – – –. This is the social setting for rituals of rebellion."[62] As far as the celebration of the first fruits is concerned, the hatred expressed by brothers to the king and by soldiers in their humiliating songs is interpreted by Gluckman as a dramatizing of conflict between the king and his rival brother/s in the first place, and, secondly, to a lesser degree, between the king and his subjects.

Gluckman draws special attention to the hatred expressed in the songs and relates this hatred to his concept of conflict and rebellion. Professor O. F. Raum, analysing both Gluckman's and Marwick's approaches to conflict, suggests a third alternative to conflict, viz. "regularized opposition, when representatives of certain interests express these in a constitutional manner in appropriate institutions". Raum does not, however, indicate that he assumes the hate songs to be related to a regularized opposition,[63] adding that "we may, in fact, assert that of all rituals, the first fruit ceremony was the least suitable for a ritual rebellion even with integrative effect".[64]

It is clear that the occasion of celebrating the first fruits was one which embraced a number of important aspects of Zulu society. These included, among others, fertility in agriculture, military involvements ranging from an army review and enrolment of new soldiers to persuading the king to undertake new campaigns, strengthening and renewal of the king, and the proclamation of new laws. There was also the ritual slaughtering of cattle at the royal graves, and, mindful of the important role played by the shades—and in particular the shades of the royal clan—this no doubt played a significant role. Allowing for the many and various aspects of the first fruit celebrations in Zulu society, I take the ritual killings at the royal graves as a point of departure and relate them to confession.

In his critique of Gluckman, Norbeck points out that the hatred expressed in the songs is *"They* hate you!", not *"We* hate you!", as argued by Gluckman[65] and he relates the hatred to external enemies. Norbeck's argument that the hatred is to be sought among external enemies is not altogether convincing if he excludes hatred from the army's own ranks. Having listened to Zulu expressing hatred and anger, I note that the confessing party often uses the third person, but includes himself in the confession. This is the idiom. The following phrases, taken from the address given by an officiant in the byre before the victim is stabbed will suffice to illustrate the point: *"Bathi nilambile! Bathi nifuna okuthile okuhambisana namazinyo! – – –. Yebo, uma kunjalo njengokukhomba kwabho, buyiselani imphilo!* (They say that you are hungry! They say that you wish to have something in terms of your teeth, i.e. something to eat! – – –. Indeed, if it is as they have spoken, then bring back health again!)" The use of the third person becomes pointed when it is not only a personal thought that is expressed, but one shared by a large number of people, or, put into a ritual setting, one expressed in what Raum describes as "a constitutional manner in appropriate institutions". It is true that critique of the king in the second person and outside a given frame in Zulu society is hardly possible, as Norbeck indicates. But it is also true that in a setting which has been legalized and in accepted terminology as that used at the first fruits celebration, there is room for expressing hatred of the king. It is in the light of the legalized, ritual and non-personal expression of hatred that the third person is to be understood.

Ritual killings presuppose that communion with the shades and with men takes place in an atmosphere of mutual understanding and with good feeling between the participants. If the songs of hatred are occasions of speaking out against authority[66] it is quite natural that the anger should refer not only to the reigning king, but also to his lineage shades. For the king, like commoners, cannot be separated from the shades or placed out of context from them. In Zulu society the shades and their lineage survivors live very closely and intimately with each other.[67]

In view of the well-being of the nation, fertility and success, it is imperative that the goodwill of the royal shades be secured. Hence the importance attached to the ritual killings at the royal graves and, prior to the slaughtering, the importance of the speaking out as done by the warriors and the prince/s in the ritual setting offered by the occasion. It is comparable to the address given by the officiant at ritual celebrations, the officiant on this occasion being the one that speaks out.

Speaking out at annual celebrations need not of necessity presuppose a personal grievance held against the victim of the accusation. Sometimes a confession is done to ease the mind of the accused that nobody is carrying within himself grievances against the victim. It is, in a sense, an expression of confidence. On other occasions it is an act of purification in general, the particular occasion being one which lends itself to a cleansing of oneself from brooding anger, which may not always be a conscious entertainment of anger. Describing a similar institutionalized and ritualized form of confession of sin, a woman belonging to the Lutheran tradition of the Church in which confession of sin follows immediately after the opening hymn and Introit, said: "Confession of sin in the church is the first thing that is done. It is done first so that everybody may sit at ease (lit. quietly, in peace) without fears. Then we listen nicely to the other things of the service and the things that are said. But if there was no confession of sin, then we would be afraid, not knowing if we have heat or not."

The importance attached to the eating of the first fruit requires attention. It may well be true that "quarrels may arise because of the sudden access of energy from the new food", as Gluckman puts it.[68] But people underline that food from the fields was (and still today among Swazi is) not to be eaten until the rituals of the festival have been completed, including the speaking out in the hatred songs. An informant from Swaziland said in January 1969: "Those words of hatred are spoken before there is eating. If a person eats before everything is done (i.e. the rituals), he is behaving very badly. He is called *umtsakatsi* (equivalent to Zulu *umthakathi*) because he behaves in a very bad way. The eating of the food is the last thing done."

Christmas Celebrations

It is possible that the increasingly important role played by the party in connection with the Christian festival of Christmas in Zulu society may have roots in the obsolete festival of the first fruits. The party, if nothing more, is found everywhere, including among pagans. Parallels between the Christmas celebration, ritual celebrations and the annual feast of the first fruits of old are not lacking.

Much importance is attached to the fact that people get together at Christmas, particularly relatives and kinsmen. The annual holiday granted people who work in urban areas, industry and mines makes it possible for them to assemble. The presence of the men is a significant part of the Christmas party. "That is why Christmas is a great occasion. It is because of the getting together of all the people of the family."

Secondly, besides the fact that Christmas occurs at the time of the year when traditionally the first fruits festival was celebrated, much attention is given to the preparation of a meal to which many assemble. Everywhere possible either a goat or some other animal is slaughtered. In Christian homes where importance is no longer attached to the choice of animal, a sheep may be slaughtered and, occasionally, even a pig.

The speaking out ritual which occurs at most Christmas parties has already been described. Along with the meat eaten at the festival, vegetables are served. It may be a coincidence that greens are obtainable at this time of the year, but I could not but make a note of a hostess once stressing very emphatically that the maize cobs which were placed before us on the table "are the first of the fields". I also made a note of the fact that the cobs were already fairly well ripened, many people eating fresh maize at a far earlier stage.

Zulu do not attend to graves as do many whites. Besides Easter, it appears that Christmas is one of the few occasions when flowers are placed on the graves.

Expelling Fluid

As there are close relations between confession and ritual celebrations in which communion forms a part, likewise there are thought-patterns and symbols which associate confessions with the expulsion of fluid.[69] The blowing out of fluid is a symbol of purification from evil in confessions. It is also a symbol of innocence when evil has been expressed. Thirdly, expelling liquid is an engagement in the interests of fertility and hence the opposite to witchcraft and sorcery which aim at killing and annihilation.

As a Purification from Evil

1. Vomiting and Emetics

The Zulu idiom *ukuhlanza* refers to vomiting and an expulsion of faeces after an emetic or purge.[70] *Ukuphumisa* is negative in that it refers to a woman's miscarriage while *ukuphumisa isisu*, equally negative and unhappy in meaning, describes the expulsion of a dead foetus.[71]

All bodily excess, particularly faeces, which is vile, must be disposed of outside the homestead and, preferably, be buried. "This thing is vile. A home is good. They do not agree. That is why it must be concealed somewhere at a distance from the homestead." Zulu accept this expulsion of something vile as normal.

Evil which, on the other hand, is not expelled normally, must be cast out through aids such as enemas and vomiting. Today castor-oil and a large number of other purges are obtainable in chemist shops and are made use of extensively. There are Zulu who "cleanse the stomach from poison" regularly every week, some even more frequently, sometimes making use of both laxatives and enemas. In cases of sickness, disregarding the type, enemas, laxatives and vomiting are often automatically administered to the patient, especially if the sickness causes a rise in temperature. "If the sick person is hot (i.e. runs a temperature), it is certain that there is a great medicine (i.e. sorcery) inside (him/her). Where does it (the medicine) enter? Is it not through the mouth? So

Fig. 20. The ritual of *ukuphalaza*, vomiting. The man illustrated claimed that men ought to vomit daily if they work at places where many people meet. He was a labourer on road works. He vomited daily at dawn outside the fence surrounding his homestead.

it is in the stomach. That is why there must be vomiting and enemas. These things remove the poison which causes the sickness."[72]

People who fear having been exposed to sorcery cause vomiting by drinking quantities of water and bringing it up by either inserting their fingers as far into the mouth as possible or causing it to be brought up by means of a feather. If vomiting does not take place, more water is drunk.[73] "It is clear that if they have suspicions that there is something, then they must remove that poison. Water cleanses. So it is brought out with water. If the poison is strong, much water must be used. When a man drinks a second or third time, then surely he is correct in his suspicions. The thing that holds back the water in vomiting is *ubuthakathi*. It does not wish the poison to come out. It holds it back. If there is no vomiting quickly, then it is known that *abathakathi* indeed wish to see a corpse today." We discussed the statement further.

B: "If he vomits soon, is it a sign that there was only a little poison?"

"It could be like that. Perhaps the man was just suspicious without having poison within him."

B: "You mean that if he vomits soon after drinking only a little water, then there was perhaps no *ubuthakathi*?"

"It could be like that. Maybe there was no *ubuthakathi*."

329

B: "So the man rejects no evil then?"

"It will be seen in the water. The water just cleanses. If there is nothing in the water when it comes out, then there was nothing."

B: "What is the difference between vomiting out *ubuthakathi* and ordeals?"[74]

"There is no difference. They are the same."

B: "But there is a difference between *abathakathi* and people?"

"That is true. A very great truth. But the water fulfils the same purpose in both. If it comes into the stomach and finds evil, being able to master it (the evil), it takes the evil with it and comes out again. If it does not master it, *ubuthakathi* being stronger, then *ubuthakathi* eats it up. It remains there in the stomach."

B: "So water has power?"

"Yes! Water! Yes, it has power! (Prolonged smile of amusement.) Yes, it has power. Water is a thing of great power, doing this work and that."

B: "In ordeals it is the one who is not *umthakathi* that vomits the water. *Umthakathi* does not vomit it."

"That is true. That is the difference you asked about *abathakathi* and people. Innocent people vomit the water. *Umthakathi* cannot vomit."

B: "Tell me why *abathakathi* cannot vomit."

"*Umthakathi* is heavy (with evil) whereas the innocent is empty.[75] The water has no power when it comes inside *umthakathi*. It is simply eaten up inside the stomach. Even the medicines in the water, they are just eaten up by *umthakathi*."

B: "What medicines are there in the water?"

"Medicines given by the herbalist. If there is the ordeal with water, the medicines are poisonous. That is why the innocent vomit quickly, throwing out the evil medicines. They are not evil inside, so the evil of the medicines does not agree with them. But with *abathakathi* it agrees. Then they do not vomit. The medicines agree with the evil. It is just eaten nicely by *abathakathi*."

B: "What about the other ordeal?"

"That is the one of *imithi yokuphila* (lit. life-giving medicines, i.e. the opposite to poison). When they eat this medicine, then the innocent just remain quiet, feeling no pains anywhere. The medicines agree with them. But with *abathakathi* it does not agree. They become very sick, groaning and feeling great pain within. That is because the medicines do not agree with them. *Abathakathi* are the people of death whereas this medicine is known as *eyemphilo* (that of health)."[76]

B: "Cannot *abathakathi* vomit this medicine?"

"As I said previously, *umthakathi* cannot vomit."

B: "Why not?"

"Because vomiting is purification (*Ngoba ukuhlanza kungukuhlambuluka*). How can *abathakathi* be cleansed? There is no purification with *abathakathi*."

Our discussion proceeded with interpretations of *ukuhlanza* which is used for cats giving birth to kittens.

B: "But this word (*ukuhlanza*) is the birth of cats. Also, familiars do not give birth. They *hlanza*. How do you relate this to the inability of *abathakathi* to vomit?"

(Hearty laughter.) "Today we are speaking of great things! Even cats! (A few moments for thought.) Now we are speaking of familiars. Yes, they do not give birth. They *hlanza*. The meaning is that they bring out evil. *Ukuhlanza* is to bring out (*ukukhipha*) evil. So when we say that familiars *hlanza*, we are saying that they are producing small ones by bringing out more evil."

B: "With regard to birth, women who give birth to dead children are said to *ukuphumisa isisu*. What is the difference between this and that of *ukuhlanza*?"

"There is no difference. Both things that come out are bad."

B: "Is the child bad?"

"What corpse is not bad? All dead bodies are bad things."

B: "But a child comes out, even if it is dead, with water."

"That is correct. All evil comes out with water from humans. Since when do cats give birth with water? Are not the kittens dry when they come out of the cat?"

B: "I think that they are moist when they are born."

"Moist! That is one thing. You must look carefully at cats. There is no water. (Time for thought.) The difference between familiars and people is that they (familiars) have the evil inside them. If a child dies, it has been killed. There is somebody doing this killing. The dead child comes with water. That is the water of salvation (*amanzi yensindiso*) in that it cleanses the mother from the evil of the dead child."

B: "If the mother gives birth to a dead child and it comes out of the water as we have been saying, is the mother then not evil?"

"She is not evil. The evil thing has come out. She is strengthened (with medicines). But she is not bad."[77]

2. Spitting

Angered people who speak out in the presence of the person against whom they have had a grudge or a witness spit "so that they may get the evil out of themselves".[78] Occasions when spitting in connection with purification of anger and other evils takes place are numerous.[79]

At the Christmas party described above, a number of visitors, having spoken out, some addressing their grudges to people present and others speaking generally, rose and walked to the door, spat through it and returned to their seats again. Without exception, people who had spat did not continue speaking out but remained silent. Spitting is common when people, gathered at a ritual celebration, sit around in the homestead and speak out before eating and drinking. It is to be seen at court-cases when either angered people have defended themselves or given witness. A man who had been unjustly humiliated by his employer, on arrival at his home over the weekend, took a piece of burning fire-wood from the stove of the house, related the incident in detail to his wife who sat on the floor, spat on the glowing coal, saying, *"Twi!"* and returned the fire-wood to its place in the stove. His wife rose to fetch a jug of *amahewu* (fermented porridge) and poured cups for her husband and herself, and spoke of the wickedness of the employer. She placed the two cups on a tray and, offering her husband, still seated next to the stove, said: "That is the way of living today, H. But it is good to remove it (*ukukhipha*) and forget it, for what is a man without work (reference to possible dismissal from the job should he object to the treatment). That is the trouble today. What else can be done than *ukuzithulula* (unburden oneself)."[80]

Zulu are explicit that spitting is the expulsion of anger in a man.[81] A friend, describing the relation between speaking out and spitting, said: "First the man speaks out his anger with words. That is the first thing, the matter of words. Then he spits. That is the next thing. That is the sign that he has spoken to the end and that the evil has come out. When he spits, the evil comes out. There is nothing left in his heart. He washes his speaking with the spittle. The spitting is the sign that evil is cast out (*ukucitha*). Then he feels nice again, having removed something bad."[82]

People who have had unpleasant dreams spit when they rise in the morning. "When a man dreams, seeing fearful things, he says on rising, 'What was this that I saw in the night? Is there something (wrong)?' He thinks about the dream. Then he spits outside (the hut), not looking at the spittle. He does it to spit out the evil of the bad dreams. If he dreams the same thing again, he becomes worried, even considering to inquire (from a diviner). If he does not dream of those things again, he is happy, knowing that the bad came out in the spitting on the rubbish-heap."[83]

Spitting is also a symbol of a curse. A school-child was severely reprimanded by a teacher for negligence in connection with her studies, and, on her describing the encounter with the angered teacher, said: "He scolded me fearfully. I accepted all the words. Then he spat on the ground, being very angry. I was very much afraid because of the spitting. First, while he was scolding, I thought he was just angry. But when he spat it became clear that he was going to fail me. He was swearing that I would be failed." The girl took the teacher's spitting as a sign not only of anger and contempt, but finally, as a symbol of a curse with forthcoming failure in the examinations.[84]

Formerly, when the elder women inspected girls from time to time to see whether their virginity was intact, spitting was a sign that the girl was found no longer to be a virgin. The inspecting women would spit in disgust in front of either the girl's mother or her female senior. "When they (the old women) saw that the virginity was broken, they would sit silently, not saying anything. Then somebody would remark, saying, 'Why do they sit thus, saying nothing?' That is when they would spit, having seen something bad. The people would know from the spitting that they had seen something not being in order." Some informants have indicated that sometimes the inspecting women would spit on the girl's organ to indicate to her that her condition had been discovered and that it would be made known.[85]

3. Male Emission

Expulsion of fluid as a symbol of purification is also to be found in male emission, particularly in polygynous homes. Men who have a single wife or lover with whom they live together, may approach other women in order to purge themselves.

"When a man fears that he has been treated secretly with medicines which work on his water (i.e. semen) he does not sleep with his wife. The water can cause sickness in her. So he does not put it into her. He goes to another woman. He tells her of his desire for her and her beauty. She agrees. He puts the water into her. Perhaps the water does not affect her because it was directed towards his wife. So he expells it in this other woman. Then he goes away. He comes to his home, being light (i.e. empty of evil). He cohabits with his wife and there is nothing that is seen (i.e. she does not get sick). The darkness of those medicines was thrown somewhere else."

Asked whether emission of male fluid in this sense is the same as *uku-hlanza*, practically everybody interviewed agreed that this was so. Some claimed that, traditionally, if a man openly told his wives that he intended to *hlanza* before having union with them, they would automatically know that he feared having been treated. Others have stressed the need for men to expel semen "outside the byre" (i.e. not with a wife) if he has associated with angry competitors, attended court-cases, on returning from prison, labour in towns, dangerous enterprises, etc., and particularly with e.g. corpses, medicines and dubious persons whom one does not trust. For in all the various walks of life he could be contaminated with *isifo sesisu* (sterility in the wife, i.e. *ubuthakathi* directed towards destruction of the homestead's fertility).

In traditional polygynous homes, seniors who held positions of authority would have one wife, neither the first nor the main wife, who was known as *umsizi* (the defender) or *umsulamithi* (the remover of medical powers). With her the senior would cohabit when suspicious of *ubuthakathi* and *cit' ubumnyama bemithi emibi* (expel the dark of evil medicines) into her. Not being either the first or the main wife, the medical powers were believed not to affect her as *ubuthakathi* would be aimed at harming either the heir or senior children born by the other two women. The male fluid having been deposited elsewhere, the husband assumed himself cleansed from the power of *ubuthakathi* and could resume normal relations with all his wives. Some say that *umsizi* would be treated medically by a herbalist in order to make her immune from the effects of the medicines deposited in her by her husband.[86]

The importance attached to the expulsion of water in vomiting and enemas, spitting and the ridding oneself of evil medicines in male emission are all quite obvious. It is beyond doubt that these expulsions of fluid, in the Zulu idiom expressed by *ukukhipha amanzi* (to expel water) and *ukuhlanza* are symbols that express a cleansing and purification from evil which, in turn, is related to *ubuthakathi*.

It is important to note that the symbol is attached to either a speaking out of anger or to the expulsion of immorally manipulated powers of materia. Anger, as the study has suggested hitherto, is the stage of developing evil which releases *ubuthakathi*, whilst immorally manipulated powers in *imithi* are already activated *ubuthakathi*. With anger which has been halted and confessed with expulsion of either spittle or water, the active role is taken by the angered. Anger, experienced in activated *ubuthakathi*, requires purification which is expressed through vomiting, enemas and emission of semen. In the latter case action is taken by the harmed. But in both cases, the expulsion of fluid is a symbol for the riddance of evil which works against well-being.

As a Symbol of Innocence

In ordeals, people who were suspected of being associated with *ubuthakathi* proved their innocence by vomiting. The expulsion of water was an accepted symbol of innocence. "If the person is not innocent the water remains inside." "*Abathakathi* cannot vomit."

Spitting, like vomiting, is also a symbol of innocence. At funerals people present will pick up a small sod of earth and, having spat on it, throw it into the grave immediately prior to the grave being filled in.[87] The custom is generally referred to as *ukuvalelisa* (taking farewell). Commenting on spitting on the sod of earth, Ngema said: "When this thing is done, the person who spits says in his heart, 'There is nothing. This death comes from elsewhere. There is nothing in my heart.' So people spit, taking farewell in a nice manner without there being any suspicions."

Our subsequent discussion revealed that people who consciously would not participate in taking farewell by spitting on a sod of earth and throwing it into the grave would be suspected of evil intention and no doubt be regarded as responsible for the death. Ngema related an instance when a diviner indicated a neighbour as responsible for the death of a young man in a homestead. He commented: "Even before the diviner had pointed him out, everybody knew that it was he." He had been present when the body was lowered into the grave but when the grave was being filled in and people commenced to *valelisa*, the man was no longer at the graveside. "Why did he leave? Because he could not spit on the sod! That is the reason."

When omens which indicate the presence of *ubuthakathi* occur, people express innocence by spitting. If a bird's droppings fall on a homestead or on people, fowls ascend huts, shade snakes lie on their backs, calves lie down behind the cow during milking, moles appear on the surface of the earth, cocks crow in the evening, etc., one spits to the left or over the left shoulder. Sometimes a phrase such as "*savelelwa indaba* (lit. there is something appearing among us, i.e. there is evil in our midst)" may be added. On other occasions nothing is said, merely the expression of contempt, "*Twi*", being said. *Twi* expresses disgust or badness. "People spit to show that they are surprised to find evil around. They are amazed to find such things happening, thinking that everything is well." "When they spit, they say, 'No, we do not know of this evil which is revealed in this way.' They say it in the heart, asking what the cause of such things can be." The underlying declaration of innocence is plainly reflected in both attitude and explanations given.[88]

One also spits when seeing improper or disagreeable behaviour, particularly if the person concerned is a kinsman or a close friend. I recall an occasion when a mentally defective girl sat in an unbecoming manner. When her father entered the house and saw her, he immediately spat on the floor and called a sister to remove her from the room. Asked to explain his spitting, he said: "This thing that I saw (reference to the girl's genital organs) must not be seen by a father. But I assured myself that I have nothing to do with it." His latter sentence referred to possible suspicion of incest that might have arisen in people who witnessed the incident. I asked whether I would have acted correctly had I also spat on the floor. The man remarked: "She is not your daughter. If you loved her perhaps you could marry her, if you were black."

A woman, attending to the tidying up of dormatories, happened to enter the room by mistake while a male occupant was dressing. Embarrassed by finding him in the dormitory, she closed the door quickly, spat on the ground and shouted loud enough for him to hear her: "I beg your pardon! I did not know that you were in." Explaining her spitting, she said: "I just wished to show that I had no intentions (*imicabango ethile*)." Instances of spitting as symbols of innocence could be enumerated at length.

When experiencing vile smells or when one sees something vile (faeces) with which one disassociates oneself, one spits and either expresses resentment or combines one's disapproval of it with a wry face.

I suggest that spitting on a stone and throwing it on *isivivane* (cairns) is a symbol of innocence, the heaps themselves probably being traditional roadsigns as they are found alongside frequented paths and located so that they can be recognised.[89]

Passing a cairn in the company of a group of men going to a local farmer with the object of settling a dispute with him I saw each of the men, except he whose cattle had been confiscated by the farmer because of their trespassing into his fields, pick up a small stone, spit on it and throw it on the heap. Everybody readily accepted that the owner of the cattle did not throw a stone on the heap, although I, on the other hand, was graciously told of the heap before we reached it and instructed what to do. Passing the cairn later in the afternoon after successfully negotiating with the farmer, all, again, threw a small stone on the heap after spitting on it. On this occasion the owner of the cattle did so also. He described his behaviour thus: "When we passed it (the cairn) the first time I was hot because of the cattle. Also the men (accompanying us) knew that I was hot. So I could not throw a stone." We discussed his heat, and from our discussion it was quite plain that he had been angry. "It (the anger) was burning inside me. That is why I could not throw a stone, not even speaking along the whole way, the heat burning strongly." But with the successful negotiations, both parties speaking out their points of view and the subsequent promise by the cattle-owner that the responsible herdboys could be punished, and the angered man whose fields had been trespassed agreeing to return the cattle without a fine (expressions of goodwill), the anger was "cooled". "So I was nice when we returned. Then I could throw a stone." The men in the party stressed that the behaviour of the cattle-owner had been correct.

On the way we discussed the issue of luck in connection with spitting on and throwing a stone on the cairn. I told the party that books emphasize this point. After a short discussion one of the men said: "The books speak correct. If a man has something inside (envy, jealousy, hatred, etc.), then he himself knows that there is something wrong. There is, as we say it, no luck in that man who has something within. He has no *inhlanhla* (prosperity). So anger and *inhlanhla* do not agree. They disagree."

As a Symbol of Healing and Fertility

When herbalists defend a homestead by spreading medicines on the huts and in the yard, their fortifying the homestead is said to be *ukukhwifa* or *ukuchinsa*.[90] The expressions imply a forcible spitting out or blowing out of medicines.[91] The medicines are, if not in liquid form, mixed with water, hence making a spirting of them possible. They are known as *intelezi*.[92]

Herbalists spit out medicines on both cattle[93] and people whom they treat. "The medicines are taken in the mouth. Also water is taken. It is chewed, the chewing being done until the medicines are like porridge. When the chewing is completed, the herbalist takes water in the mouth and mixes the medicines with the water. Then he blows it out (*ukukhafula*) on the sick person. Sometimes he squirts it out on the whole body, on other occasions only on certain places. It depends on the sickness. He blows out the medicines until the medicines have been deposited on the patient. The patient lies down again. There is no washing of the patient because medicines have been blown out on the body."[94]

The diviner of uMhlatuze had the following to say about medicines and a herbalist's ability to blow it out. "If there are some bad thoughts in the mind (*inhliziyo*) of the herbalist, and he mixes it with water, it would not come out. It would just remain in his mouth and not come out. That is why he mixes *intelezi* with water, so that it is clear what his intentions are when it comes out."

B: "Are you comparing him with *abathakathi* who are said not to be able to expel water by way of the mouth?"

"That is what I am saying. The water mixes with the medicines and makes it possible to blow it out."

B: "But angry men spit out their anger. Cannot evil come out of the mouth?"

"It (evil) comes out. But the intention (*inhliziyo*) of those who purify themselves says, 'Do this thing so as to be purified', whilst in *abathakathi ugovana* says, 'Do this so as to kill.'[95] Then that person is *umthakathi* and not a human being. Human beings can blow out (*ukukhafula*)[96] anger as you say. But not *umthakathi*."

B: "Is the blowing out of medicines by herbalists and good men always a good thing?"

"It is always a good thing when it comes from the mouths of men. It brings health (*imphilo*) in that *ubuthakathi* is removed."

B: "I have read in a book that if a man wishes to make another man a long distance away ill, then all that is done is to squirt water in the direction of the sun, saying words of illness. Then that person becomes ill. But you say that *umthakathi* cannot spit water. These two statements do not agree very well. What do you say?"[97]

"I stand by the words that I have spoken, that *umthakathi* cannot blow water. If that man wishing to cause illness uses water, he would not harm. He is just deceiving himself, not harming, whereas he thinks he is harming. There are many that act in this manner. Since when does water harm? I do not know of the water that harms."

B: "Can *umthakathi* spit medicines?"

"Without water?"

B: "Yes, without water?"

"That is another question. Without water! That is another thing. Indeed! *Umthakathi* spits like a snake. Snakes and *abathakathi* are alike in that they spit very bad medicines. But that is another thing totally."

B: "Is not the spittle of snakes the same as water?"

"No! (Very marked disagreement.) No! That is medicines of killing. Those are the snakes of killing that spit poison.[98] But the snakes of the pools spit another thing. They (the former) spit to kill. They bring the sickness of blindness and darkness. That is not water. That is death."

B: "In the same manner *umthakathi* can spit medicines?"

"He can spit medicines like snakes spit poison. I agree. But I do not agree with water."

B: "So it is possible for a man to harm another at a distance by spitting medicines in his direction?"

"Yes. That man who spits is *umthakathi*. If he also mentions the words of death, wanting to kill, then he can do it."

B: "Allow me to ask you about the king in Zululand. He used to spit in the direction of the enemy at *umkosi* (first fruit ceremony). What was this spitting?"[99]

"That spitting is the same as *ukuchinsa* (blowing out medicines)."

B: "Tell me more about this thing of spitting in connection with the king."

"The king prepared the medicines by chewing. They were given him by the great herbalists of the whole land. They collected the medicines, obtaining them from everywhere. These are the medicines of warding off the enemies and bad people from the land (*izwe*). Then he took medicines which he had in his mouth with water (i.e. mixed them with water) and spat it out in the direction of the enemies of the land and the bad people. That is the thing that he did."

B: "What is the difference between *ukukhwifa* (spitting out medicines as a resistance against *abathakathi* by a herbalist) and the spitting of the king?"

"There is no difference. They are the same. Are not enemies and bad people all *abathakathi*? They all desire to kill people. So the spitting of the king is the strengthening of the land against *abathakathi*."

B: "Were the medicines he spat out the same as those used by a herbalist against *abathakathi* in a homestead?"

"The whole land is very great. Again, the land has many people whereas a home has only some people. So the medicines of the herbalist used at *umkosi* must be very strong. But I do not know. As for me, I am not a herbalist. I do not know the medicines they use today. That is all I can say on medicines. What are medicines today are nothing tomorrow. That is what they say."[100]

B: "The same book says that if a man wishes to send love-dreams to a girl, then he must squirt out water at the sun.[101] What do you say about this?"

"What I know is that they squirt out water in the direction of the girl. That is so. That is the thing that men do."

B: "Is this the same thing as blowing out medicines by a herbalist?"

"Since when are all men herbalists?"

B: "No, not all men are herbalists. But if the man has received medicines from a herbalist, could he squirt water in the direction of the girl?"

"That is one thing. He can do it if the herbalist gives him the correct (lit. good) medicines."

B: "Is it correct to say that this squirting of water with the correct medicines is a good thing, seeing that it is done with water?"

"Which love is not good? Perhaps he has seen (i.e. fallen in love with) the girl. So he is just awakening love (*uthando*) in her by way of dreams so that she loves him. That is a good thing."

B: "What happens if she is in love with another man?"

"Then he is a thief (i.e. the lover is a thief). He is bad. Then he is just playing."

B: "You said that this was one thing. Is there another?"

"Do you not know the squirting of men? Is there not the thing of men and water?"

B: "You are referring to the emission of male fluid?"

"What else is there in men?"

B: "I understand what you are saying. I was just thinking of the man blowing out water by way of the mouth at the girl."

"Today you are amazing me! Just tell me, what is the squirting of men? Just tell me."

B: "*Amalotha* (lit. ashes, i.e. semen)."

"*Haw!* Why are you afraid of the word when it comes to squirting out?"

B: "Water."

A number of issues which arise from the discussion quoted require our further attention.

The role played by water and its relation to the blowing out of medicines in a moral sense on the one hand, and the absence of water when medicines are spat out by *abathakathi* on the other, appears to be a general thought-pattern among Zulu. Discussing water, thirst, and the belief that *abathakathi* cannot vomit in quite a different setting from that described above (we were talking about familiars), an informant said that familiars suck cows because "there is no water in that place of *abathakathi*. They drink only blood." Evidence makes it clear beyond doubt that water as a fertility symbol is the opposite to evil. Certainly, in its moral sense, water is not only a symbol and medium of purification from evil. It is also a carrier of life itself in that semen is described as water and it is from "the water of the womb" that the child is born.

The blowing out of medicines as a resisting of evil is done by commoners if they have the required materia, by herbalists who are the experts, and by authority (the king in a ritual setting in former times). This is understandable in view of the emphasis which is placed, in the first instance, on the powers embedded in the materia which is used in medicines. But the ability to manipulate the powers must, however, not be underestimated, for it is this knowledge that determines the species of medicines to be used and the exact method and procedure to be followed.

The wide range of medicines used in the defence of people, their possessions, and land against the onslaughts of *ubuthakathi* is impressive. Not only do the medicines which are blown out heal the sick. They act as a 'fence' precaution against the Lord-of-the-Sky's anger expressed in lightning which kills, and against *abathakathi* and their familiars. They "bounce off when they touch these medicines". Also national enemies were warded off and controlled by the king at the festival of the first fruits.

In its legal and moral sense, male emission is a resisting of evil. While witchcraft and sorcery strive for annihilation, the sexual act and the expected pregnancy, birth, growth of the child is an assertion of life. It is important to note that symbols of expulsion of anger, resistance of *ubuthakathi* through medicines, purity, and fertility, have, in common, the emission of fluid, the blowing out of pure and/or medicated water, vomiting, or emission of semen.[102] These symbols are predominantly associated with men.

Water, male fluid, and spittle are classed together. Sometimes they are not only associated with each other—they are regarded as identical.[103] It is men in their capacity as males that are chiefly concerned. The diviner at eThelezini and the ventriloquist so closely associated the blowing out of medicines by a herbalist with males that they held that only men could be proper herbalists. "Only men can *chinsa* medicines nicely." "Men blow out water. They do it in their work of men (sexual act), in curing (*ukuphilisa*, i.e. giving medicines), and in spitting. Those are the things of men. As for women, they do not blow out. They are sucked (*ukuncelwa*). So you can see for yourself that women cannot be *izinyanga zemithi* (herbalists)." Experience shows that well-behaved women do not spit unless specific occasions calls for it (although sometimes aged women well past childbearing age do it).[104]

A herbalist abstains from his wives prior to treating homesteads, fields, and people through *ukuchinsa*,[105] a requirement in a herbalist's preparation which

338

was mentioned again and again as important. The same abstention is required of an officiant before a ritual celebration,[106] as well as that of abstaining from the warmth of a fire and refraining from beer and meat. The herbalist's work as well as that of the officiant's at ritual celebrations are all parts of efforts in restoring healing, well-being and prosperity to men, animals and land. Their work and actions are, either directly or indirectly, associated with sexuality to a greater or less degree and play an important role in the minds of both themselves and the people among whom they work. It is because of this pointed interest and great importance attached to sexuality and related symbols that these require what the ventriloquist called "*ihlelo elingadidi umsebenzi* (a programmed order which does not bring about confusion in the work)" in the lives of herbalists and officiants, particularly when they are to operate. Different sexual symbols and the sexual act itself must be kept apart to avoid confusion. At a time when attention and concentration is required in the preparation and manipulation of medicines or in the rituals of a celebration, then priority must be given to those aspects of sexuality and related thought-patterns which are required at that time. When medicines are to be prepared and distributed or when a ritual celebration is to take place, then one's own sexual desires must give way for such that at that time are of greater concern. Hence the abstentions.

Yet, after fulfilling their duties, the officiant at the ritual celebration and the herbalist not only are permitted to return to their wives. They are, in fact, required to do so. For if they do not have union they "become insane. The male fluid (*amalotha*) must be expelled. Then he becomes healthy again, being cool." The underlying thought-pattern is the close tie and, frequently, identification, between semen and the shades. As excess brooding of the shades is feared because "it causes insanity and other sicknesses that come from the shades when they are too near for too long a time", so also the presence of the shades in semen may cause insanity. The expulsion of the fluid is a means of driving off the shades, a process which is regarded as both normal and natural for well-being.

Milk is another fluid either spat out or squirted out as a symbol of fertility. A man said that herd-boys are sometimes instructed to suck milk from cows in order to increase the milk in them. Boys who had not yet reached puberty were to be preferred to older ones, and they were told to spit out the milk on the ground. "The boys suck each teat in turn. When all the teats have been sucked, the mouth being full of milk, the boys spit it (the milk) out. Then the milk in that cow will become plenteous because of the thing done." Although this practice and the reason for it was confirmed by a number of other men, few attached importance to the age of the boy who did it. Practically all, however, agreed that the boy ought to be of the cattle-owner's lineage.[107]

A number of Zulu mothers have said that if they wish to increase their own supply, they will squirt milk from each breast into the hearth of the hut in which they reside. "Sometimes, if the milk is not plentiful, the mother may do it often. She does it when the child has sucked. She does it until the milk has increased." Mothers who have been away from their babies also squirt milk from the breast before suckling the child.[108] "She does it so that the milk may remain plentiful. She returns from the journey with the breast heavy since the child has not sucked. Then she goes into the hut. She does this thing saying in her heart, 'May it ever remain plentiful as it is now.' Then she lets the baby suck. That is the thing she does when she has been away and returns heavy."

Kidd reports that mothers who leave their babies "under bushes while they themselves work in the fields in the sun – – – protect them – – – by squirting a ring of their own milk on the earth round the sleeping babe. It is thought that neither snakes nor passers-by can cross the charmed circle."[109] Many Zulu mothers agree that this custom is still observed, some of my informants themselves having practised it. While nobody referred the practice directly to the driving away of snakes or undesired persons (as does Kidd), various other reasons were given. One woman, a school teacher, said thus: "When a mother has fed the baby and it has fallen asleep, she spreads out a blanket in a cool place. She puts the sleeping baby on the blanket. Then she does this with the breast. She does it so that the baby sleeps long. If the work in the fields is heavy she hopes that there nevertheless may be milk for it (the baby) when she (the mother) returns. That is why the mother does this thing." Another woman, an elderly lady, said that if there was not a ring of the mother's milk around the child it might forget the breast and not suck on the return of the mother. A third said that if the mother expressed milk thus, "making the breast empty and returning with it heavy, it means that on another occasion she will return carrying heavy burdens from the field". She very consciously and closely related the milk with the forthcoming harvest of the field, adding that this was one reason why suckling mothers with a plentiful flow ought to till fields. "But now our fields do not yield any more as they used to do. It is because this *isiko* (custom) is not done any more. The women do not know their work any more."

No doubt the absence of harm is also a symbol of prosperity. When mothers squirt a few drops of milk on their sleeping babies in the huts "so that they may continue sleeping nicely",[110] they are resisting evil which may disturb their child through a symbol of well-being and fertility, which is the contradiction of harm.

Notes

[1] For comparative material on resisting evil from Mpondo see Hunter, *Reaction to Conquest*, pp. 295 ff., 335 ff. and 341 ff., and from Bhaca see Hammond-Tooke, *Bhaca Society*, pp. 263 ff.

[2] Le Vine, 'Witchcraft and Co-Wife Proximity in South-Western Kenya', p. 43, shows that within a limited area witchcraft and sorcery pre-occupation differs among Luo, Gusii and Kipsigis, depending on the geographical distance and spacing between wives.

[3] Cf. Berglund, 'African Concepts of Health, Sickness and Healing', p. 45.

[4] On Mpondo accusations of witchcraft and sorcery see Hunter, *Reaction to Conquest*, pp. 306–310.

[5] See Jackson, 'Native Superstition and Crime' for several instances. Also White, 'Notes on Some Metaphysical Concepts of the Balovale', p. 147, on burning of witches and snakes.

[6] Although the past tense is used, I do not suggest that impalement is not practised today. Evidence does, however, suggest that it is done secretly when carried out.

[7] See p. 274.

[8] The term 'defenders' was coined by Godfrey Wilson. See Wilson, *Good Company*, pp. 96 ff., particularly p. 97, footnote 2.

[9] Callaway, *The Religious System of the Amazulus*, pp. 348 ff. "But the spirits of your people would not allow you to be killed" (p. 353). Also Samuelson, *Zululand, its Traditions*, etc., pp. 184 ff. Krige, *SSZ*, p. 325, quoting Isaacs.

[10] See pp. 266 ff.

[11] Jackson, 'Native Superstition and Crime', pp. 253–254. See also Liljestrand, 'Något om zulufolkets samfundslif och husliga lif', p. 20.

[12] See example p. 269.

[13] Cf. Asmus, *Die Zulu*, pp. 97 f.

[14] See Hoffman, 'Witchcraft Among the Zulus', p. 3.

[15] Herbalists among Mpondo are described in Hunter, *Reaction to Conquest*, pp. 296 ff. and among Swazi in Kuper, *An African Aristocracy*, pp. 162 ff.

[16] Junod, 'The Theory of Witchcraft Amongst South African Natives', pp. 236 ff. describes resisting evil through diviners and herbalists among Tsonga.

[17] On methods of approaching a herbalist and his reactions see Krige, *SSZ*, pp. 298 f.

[18] On Mpondo usage of medicines see Hunter, *Reaction to Conquest*, pp. 296 ff.

[19] The slaughter of a pig has been mentioned on several similar occasions in connection with treating a homestead against lightning, but no satisfactory explanation could be obtained for the use of a pig. Madela claimed that he did not use a pig but a fat fowl instead. But also fowls, like pigs, have previously been shunned by Zulu.

[20] All informants without exception claim that fat and blood of a slaughtered animal (on one occasion on record a dog was said to have been killed) has nothing to do with ritual celebrations.

[21] On defending a homestead against lightning see Krige, *SSZ*, pp. 315–317: *The Collector*, No. 469, p. 78.

[22] Cf. Bryant, *Dict.*, p. 347.

[23] On medicines and the treatment of diseases see Bryant, *Zulu Medicine and Medicine-Men:* Krige, *SSZ*, pp. 327 ff.

[24] On the levirate, ghost-marriage, and the sororate as institutions to prevent the annihilation of a lineage, see Krige, *SSZ*, p. 181: Bryant, *The Zulu People*, pp. 599 f.

[25] Note the limited scope of material on which e.g. Jeffreys bases his study "Confessions by Africans".

Professor Sundkler has drawn attention to the important role of confessions in the Independent movements and given a detailed description and analysis of the concept in these groups. See Sundkler, *Bantu Prophets in South Africa*, pp. 209–213 particularly.

Fernandez, *Divination, Confessions, Testimonies*, especially pp. 21 ff. discusses confessions among Amakhehleni (Roman Catholic Background) and various Zionist groups with fundamentalistic and pentecostal origins. See also Berglund, 'Rituals of an African Zionist Church', pp. 4 f.

[26] Drawing on material from pre-literate societies Webster, *Taboo: A Sociological Study*, has drawn thought-provoking attention to the question of speaking out in his chapter "Sin and Ritual Defilement", pp. 311–321.

[27] See further pp. 197 f. and 220 f.

[28] See e.g. Krige, *SSZ*, p. 289.

[29] It is important that Christian understandings of confession, private confession, absolution, confessor, etc. not be assumed in the following discussion.

[30] Bryant, *Dict.*, p. 686: Doke–Vilakazi, *Dict.*, p. 481.

[31] Cf. Fernandez, *Divination, Confessions, Testimonies*, p. 23.

[32] Bryant, *Dict.*, p. 243: Doke–Vilakazi, *Dict.*, pp. 321 f.: Döhne, *A Zulu-Engl. Dict.*, pp. 128 f.

[33] Doke–Vilakazi, *Dict.*, p. 674.

[34] Doke–Vilakazi, *Dict.*, p. 662.

[35] Bryant, *Dict.*, p. 515.

[36] Bryant, *Dict.*, p. 573: Doke–Vilakazi, *Dict.*, p. 737.

[37] Bryant, *Dict.*, p. 574: Doke–Vilakazi, *Dict.*, p. 752.

[38] Bryant, *Dict.*, p. 707: Doke–Vilakazi, *Dict.*, pp. 867 f.

[39] See p. 270. Petty bodily ailments and *umkhuhlane* which are accepted as normal physical weaknesses and not ascribed to a definite cause are by-passed here.

[40] For comparative material on confessions from Nguni and other Bantu peoples see: Hunter, *Reaction to Conquest*, pp. 283 f. (Mpondo): Hammond-Tooke, *Bhaca Society*, p. 73: Kuper, *An African Aristocracy*, pp. 168 and 190 (Swazi): Junod, *The Life of a South African Tribe*, Vol. II, pp. 398 ff. (Tsonga): Wilson, *Rituals of Kinship among Nyakyusa*, pp. 186 and 266 ff.: Wilson, *Communal Rituals of the Nyakyusa*, pp. 134 and 160. Also Wilson, *Divine Kings and the Breath of Men*, pp. 12 ff.

Note also Webster, *Taboo, a Sociological Study*, p. 311, who argues that "confession acts as a real purgation, an elimination of evil matter in the patient's body. As such it is comparable to the cathartics, emetics, and the purges so often employed for the same purpose."

[41] See pp. 258 ff.

[42] Cf. vomiting, pp. 328 ff.

[43] The technical term for pressure put on a person and geared towards confession is *ukugazinga*. See Doke–Vilakazi, *Dict.*, p. 234.

[44] Having related the above to a knowledgeable informant, I asked him whether the accused was not a witch. He answered: "The child lived, so there was no death. Furthermore, she confessed everything. Witches never confess everything."

[45] See p. 221 and pp. 231. The case related required details because it was a confessional celebration.

[46] The Christmas festival plays a significant role in Zulu society today. See pp. 327 f.

[47] See p. 230 f.

[48] See also p. 231.

[49] Cf. Callaway, *The Religious System of the Amazulu*, pp. 430 f., who says that attempts made to get a man to confess guilt but who by-passes the accusation with cunning is not relied on in the future.

[50] See descriptions of similar confessions among Mpondo in Hunter, *Reaction to Conquest*, p. 148.

[51] Hoernlé, 'The Importance of the Sib in the Marriage Ceremonies of the South-Eastern Bantu', p. 285.

[52] See p. 219 f.

[53] Gluckman, 'Mortuary Customs among the South-Eastern Bantu', p. 119.

[54] Callaway, *The Religious System of the Amazulu*, p. 440.

[55] Doke–Vilakazi, *Dict.*, p. 790.

[56] Doke–Vilakazi, *Dict.*, p. 790: Krige, *SSZ*, p. 59.

[57] Many informants underlined the use of *ilala* as described by Professor Krige, while Zulu living inland where *ilala* is not as commonly found as along the coast do not emphasize it equally much. The narrative given in the text is from Rorkes Drift where *ilala* is not common. Evidence shows that *ilala* is associated with the shades and with men. It is avoided by women, particularly in ritual connections. Beer may be brewed of *ilala* and baskets made of it are the produce of men only.

Some informants have said that a beast is killed, although this is not essential. Some informants also said that the third party must get the men together within seven days, indicating that after this number of days they were no longer obliged to honour the promise of not doing anything. Although this fact was mentioned on several occasions, I could not get a satisfactory explanation of the statement. No doubt, however, there must be a connection between seven days and brooding anger. When discussing brooding anger a man said that it took seven days for a person to become a witch. Asked whether this referred to the seven days of the calendar, he said that it was "on the day of the pointing finger", i.e. the index finger of the right hand, that was "the day of *abathakathi*".

[58] Cf. Junod, 'The Sacrifice of Reconciliation Amongst the Ba-Ronga' for comparative material.

[59] See Krige, *SSZ*, pp. 250 ff.

[60] Swazi celebrations are described by Marwick, *The Swazi*, pp. 182 ff. and by Kuper, *An African Aristocracy*, pp. 197 ff.: Bhaca by Hammond-Tooke, *Bhaca Society*, pp. 405 f.

[61] Note the expressions of hate recorded by Delegorgue, *Voyage dans l'Afrique Australe*, Vol. II, p. 237: Samuelson, *Long, Long, Ago*, p. 386: Bryant, *The Zulu People*, p. 517.

[62] Gluckman, *Order and Rebellion in Tribal Africa*, pp. 127 f. See also Gluckman, 'Social Aspects of First Fruit Ceremonies among the South-Eastern Bantu': Gluckman, *Custom and Conflict in Africa*.

The hatred of the king is also mentioned by Asmus, *Die Zulu*, pp. 184 ff.: Bryant, *The Zulu People*, p. 517: Bryant, *Olden Times in Zululand and Natal*, pp. 633 ff.: Kück, 'Annual Festival of the Zulus'.

[63] Raum, 'The Interpretation of the Nguni First Fruits Ceremony', pp. 153 ff.

[64] Raum, 'The Interpretation of the Nguni First Fruits Ceremony', p. 158. See also Krige, 'Girls' Puberty Songs and their Relation to Fertility', etc., pp. 173 & 175.

[65] Norbeck, 'African Rituals of Conflict', p. 1261.

[66] See pp. 246 ff.

[67] Cf. Raum, 'The Interpretation of the Nguni First Fruits Ceremony', p. 156.

[68] Gluckman, *Order and Rebellion in Tribal Africa*, p. 132.

[69] For examples of confessions and expulsion of water see pp. 230 f., 323 ff., and 328 ff.

[70] Bryant, *Dict.*, p. 243: Doke–Vilakazi, *Dict.*, pp. 321 f.: Döhne, *A Zulu-Kafir Dict.*, pp. 128 f.

[71] Bryant, *Dict.*, p. 515.

[72] Cf. Ross, 'A Fictitious Native Disease', pp. 371 ff., who describes, from a scientific medical point of view, how enemetics and enemas as an "initial treatment of most acute diseases and especially of specific fevers among Zulu" are used very commonly and results of this use (p. 374). Enemas are "often followed by a suppository" (in the case of *isiqwebedhla* it is mud and red chillies) which in combination with fevers causes dilatation of the anus and is, hence, a secondary ailment arising from fever and its subsequent treatment (pp. 375–377).

[73] See Hoffman, 'Witchcraft among the Zulus', p. 16, who gives an account of drinking water for the purpose of vomiting. Cf. also Kohler, 'Die Krankengeschichte eines Zulu-kaffern', p. 586, who quotes a Zulu's description of a herbalist's treatment: "uma kukona umuntu onesifo semilenze izinyanga zimgcaba, zibuye zimhlanzisa (If a person has disease of the leg, the herbalist makes incisions and causes him to vomit)."

[74] Ordeals in the traditional sense are not practised today. If they at all are in use, this is done in secrecy.

[75] Note that the innocent, like those who have spoken out in confessions, are regarded as being empty while *abathakathi* are heavy (or full) with evil.

[76] Accounting for Swazi ordeals, Kuper, *An African Aristocracy*, p. 168, has described this particular ordeal. It corresponds to the Zulu parallel. Zulu informants claim that the ordeal is done in sunshine because the warmth and light of the sun "helps to expose *umthakathi*. They are of the night. So the sun helps to expose them."

[77] The Nyakyusa symbolism as far as vomiting in ordeals is concerned, is very similar. See Wilson, *Good Company*, p. 115.

[78] Several people have claimed that it is not absolutely essential to speak out in the presence of the person who has caused the anger, although often desirable, particularly if the angry man might contemplate an evil. It is, on the other hand, important that an angered person speaks out in the presence of "somebody who is a witness. If there arise difficulties, that witness can testify that the accused has purified himself (*ukuzihlanza*). So the suspicion against him is not valid. He carries no hatred (*inzondo*) inside (himself), having purified."

[79] See Junod, *The Life of a South African Tribe*, Vol. II, pp. 398–400 and 405 on Tsonga concepts of confession and spitting.

[80] Junod, *The Life of a South African Tribe*, Vol. II, p. 391, relates a case of spitting on charcoal also.

[81] Callaway, *The Religious System of the Amazulu*, p. 435, speaks of "the custom of spitting in contempt". Krige, 'Girls' Puberty Songs and their Relation to Fertility', etc., p. 175, speaks of "throwing out or spurting out evil or disease" as common in Zululand.

[82] See further on spitting and purification in relation to *ubuthakathi*, p. 292 f. The expression *amathe nolimi* (lit. spittle and tongue) meaning intimate friendship was explained thus: "As two people are friends, their friendship is like the speaking of the tongue and spittle. If a man confesses everything and all the evil comes out, he spits. Then there is only goodness. So is close friendship. It is only goodness."

[83] Cf. Callaway, *The Religious System of the Amazulu*, p. 160.

[84] Cf. Callaway, *Nursery Tales, Trad. and Hist. of the Zulus*, p. 163, n.

[85] MacDonald, Manners, Customs, Superstitions, etc., p. 118, says that when a girl is found not to be a virgin, women spit on her pudenda.

[86] Kuper, *An African Aristocracy*, p. 84.

Experience suggests rather emphatically that men who are isolated from their wives due to the effect of the migrant labour system believe that through masturbation they can expel veneral disease which, they think, is caused by another lover to a common girl-friend. "If we cast out the semen in this way the sickness of that place (i.e. veneral disease) is thrown out. It comes out with the water. That is the cure we know.

Then the women (at home) will not be affected of it (lit. be troubled by it)." Note that the evil comes out with water.

Bryant, *Dict.*, p. 593: Doke–Vilakazi, *Dict.*, p. 761: Colenso, *Zulu-Engl. Dict.*, p. 553 (extensively). All associate *umsizi* with both legitimate and illegitimate use of medical powers. Their information is verified by evidence also from today.

[87] Krige, *SSZ*, p. 162, mentions the picking up of the sod, but not the spitting. Spitting on the sod is very common today, there hardly being a single funeral where it is not done.

[88] Tsonga spit on the ground when they see a shooting star, this being an omen indicating a chief's death (Junod, *The Life of a South African Tribe*, Vol. II, pp. 309 f.), as do also Masai (Hollis, *The Masai*, p. 316). Kidd, *Savage Childhood*, p. 149, also mentions spitting when seeing a shooting star, adding that "at the sight of it they will spit on the ground as a mark of friendly feeling towards the dead man". Unfortunately Kidd does not state from which people he has this information.

[89] Bryant, *The Zulu People*, p. 732: Callaway, *The Religious System of the Amazulu*, p. 66: Bryant, *Dict.*, p. 682: Doke–Vilakazi, *Dict.*, p. 836: Leslie, *Among the Zulus and Amatongas*, p. 146: Kidd, *The Essential Kaffir*, pp. 263 f.: Jenkinson, *Amazulu*, p. 33. Spitting on the stone is mentioned by Bryant, Callaway and Kidd.

[90] Cf. pp. 310 f. See also Krige, *SSZ*, pp. 250 f. and 329.

[91] Bryant, *Dict.*, p. 76: Doke–Vilakazi, *Dict.*, pp. 112 f.

[92] Krige, *SSZ*, p. 329.

[93] Shooter, *The Kaffirs of Natal and the Zulu Country*, p. 36, describes the squirting of medicine on a firebrand which is held in front of the head of cattle.

[94] Cf. Carbutt, 'Some Minor Superstitions and Customs of the Zulus', p. 11.

[95] See pp. 255 f. on *ugovana*. Note that my informant speaks of *inhliziyo* as the opposite to *ugovana* and not, as is traditional and usual, *unembeza*.

[96] Bryant, *Dict.*, p. 286: Doke–Vilakazi, *Dict.*, p. 374.

[97] Krige, *SSZ*, p. 251.

[98] The black cobra spits poison into its victim's eye.

[99] Krige, *SSZ*, pp. 250–252 and 255 ff.

[100] Callaway, *The Religious System of the Amazulu*, p. 435, describes how men pick *intelezi*, and, adding water, squirt it out in the direction from where he has received an injury. This the diviner said was *ukubuyisa isifo* (returning the injury) and not *ubuthakathi*.

Kidd, *The Essential Kaffir*, p. 309, describes how flesh taken from a defeated chief conspicuous for bravery, after being chewed, is spat in the direction of the enemy. He relates (p. 310) how wounded soldiers used to chew medicines, spit on a stick and throw it in the direction of the enemy. Both instances were said by the diviner to be "*ukubuyisa ububi* because of the sufferings of those who had been beaten".

See also Bryant, *Dict.*, p. 76: Doke–Vilakazi, *Dict.*, pp. 112 f. and Colenso, *Zulu-Engl. Dict.*, p. 80 (*cinsa*).

[101] Krige, *SSZ*, p. 251.

[102] Cf. the spittle as an expression of fertility with the python associated with the shades in the river pool, pp. 140 ff.

[103] See pp. 94 ff., 115 ff., 140 ff.

[104] It is possible that of the three, emphasis lies on male emission and its associations with the blowing out of medicines in the first instance. Expulsion of spittle does allow, although seldom done, also for women.

[105] See p. 310.

[106] See pp. 225 and 227.

[107] Wilson, *Good Company*, p. 99, records a similar thought-pattern from Nyakyusa.

[108] Kidd, *Savage Childhood*, p. 42.

[109] Kidd, *Savage Childhood*, p. 41 and 43.

[110] Kidd, *The Essential Kaffir*, p. 274.

Chapter IX

Medicines

Experience shows the extensive use of materia for medical purposes in Zulu society. In the lives of all individuals medicines play essential roles, and medical powers are manipulated in the interests of fertility and well-being in a lineage, clan, and society as such, as well as a security and encouragement to homesteads, domestic animals (particularly cattle) and fields.

The goal of this section of the study is not, in the first instance, either to enumerate medicines used by Zulu or to assess their medical values from a scientific and empirical point of view. Besides demanding extensive botanical, archeological, zoological, and chemical knowledge, an enumeration which would be representative is hardly possible due to the very wide range of materia used as medicines and the vast field in which they are manipulated. The aim of the chapter is rather to give an idea of thought-patterns related to medicines and symbols attached to their use. For the medical powers embodied in materia are believed to operate not only on their own merits. With them and interwoven into their powers are symbols related to shape, colour, sound, etc. . . Associated to the powers and symbols is also morality, an essential factor which cannot be excluded from medical treatment of any kind.[1]

Medicine and Manipulators

The Western rational, empirical, and scientific approach to medical services rendered by doctors and nurses in hospitals and clinics, etc. is not applicable to Zulu traditional society. Among Zulu the powers embedded in materia are not applicable only to sickness or useful as tonics when an individual is weak. They are put into activity among all men, both sick and healthy, and cover all walks of life. The point of departure is the conviction that material substances of many, if not all, kinds, particularly the various species in vegetation, contain *amandla*, which, because it generally is believed to be neutral, can be used either morally and legitimately, or, on the other hand, to harm. Lawfully, smiths use *ingcino* (Scilla rigidifolia) to glue spear-blades to the handle because "it has the power to close the opening in the handle with the shaft of the spear for always". Yet illegitimately the glueing property of the plant is used in *ubuthakathi* "to close the woman's womb so that she cannot be penetrated". (In each case *ukuvala umlomo*, to close the mouth, was used to describe the glueing property.) Another informant said that dogs that copulated and were not able to part had most probably been treated with *ingcino*.[2]

The powers embedded in materia are used legally for fertility of all kinds, healing, for success in risky undertakings (e.g. examinations, operations), in courtship, for the favourable outcome of court-cases, for protection of homesteads, fields and property as well as protection against the dangers of travel, police raids, dangerous jobs and ill-tempered employers. Medicines also fortify and strengthen teachers in their duties, make servants adaptable to conditions of work in the variety of homes where sometimes unintelligible things are done, fortify lawyers, make lovers more attractive, etc. . .

On the other hand medicines react also on the personality of an individual. A novice to a heaven-herd is treated "to become a heaven-herd", equipped with those distinct characteristics which are required of a heaven-herd.[3] The dignity, prestige and wisdom (*isithunzi sokuhlakanipha*) of authority are increased by way of medicines.[4] Unreliable people are not only revealed through *imithi*, but they are treated with medicines against this characteristic so that they may become honest (*ukuguqula ubusela*). Through medicines cowards become brave. Brides take medicines not only to become fertile, but also well-behaved and adaptable to their new environment in the homes of their future husbands, thereby avoiding the host of difficulties that would arise should they be obstinate or self-willed.[5] Widows make use of medicines to become independent and courageous, particularly if they have minor children who depend on them, or they are courted by the deceased's brothers without themselves desiring re-marriage.

Because medicines are prepared from a vast variety of different materia and because it is believed that the medical powers can be put into action in practically all spheres of life, the field in which *imithi* is activated covers a wide range. A pebble placed in a water-container when the water is carried from a river to the homestead is termed *umuthi* "because it wards off stumbling and spilling the water".[6] The castor-oil bush (*umhlakuva*, Ricinus communis)[7] often found growing around homesteads, is used extensively in the preparation of hides and, in this capacity, is known as *umuthi*.

Although the great majority of *imithi* are believed to be neutral in character, there are a limited number of medicines, prepared of certain poisonous materia (particularly vegetation), which work only evil. *Umdlebe* (Synadenium arborescens) is wholly vile and its branches are used by witches in treating a corpse to become *umkhovu*.[8] Not only is the smell of its flowers said to cause death, but any association with it is proof enough that the person in question is an *umthakathi*.[9] *Umzilanyoni* (lit. avoided by birds, Croton sylvaticus), a hard wood, is said to be so poisonous that "even birds die if they should sit on its branches". A few herbalists have said that the bark of the tree, believed to be less poisonous than the wood itself and the leaves, is used to prevent nose bleeding. But the diviner at eThelezini claimed that "not all bleeding from the nose is bad. Sometimes it is good. The bad blood comes out. When *abathakathi* wish a man to keep the evil blood inside himself, they give this medicine. Then the man becomes very ill because the bad blood does not come out." Euclea natalensis (*idungamuzi*, lit. the home destroyer) is believed to cause quarrelling in a home and is hence removed totally; informants say that, like *abathakathi* who grow the species in order to bring about disharmony among men, it must be destroyed by burning.[11]

The wide field in which *imithi* operate allows for a range of operators who are the manipulators of the power embedded in materia. Evidence shows quite clearly that practically every Zulu has some knowledge of the use of medicines. Even herd-boys sometimes reveal considerable insight into the local fauna and flora, and collect medicines for their seniors.

Heaven-herds are the specialists in matters pertaining to thunder, lightning and violent storms, and, as a general rule, do not manipulate medical powers outside their own specialization. (One heaven-herd, however, combined his occupation with that of a smith and proved to be well versed in thought-patterns and symbols related to a smithy. He also acted as herbalist, though not regularly or with many patients.) There are those who specialize in treating snake-bite and/or rendering homes safe from venomous snakes. Those who specialize in the treatment of barrenness in women practise particularly in towns where venereal disease appears to be more widespread than in rural areas as yet. Diviners also manipulate the powers embedded in materia as medicines, thereby combining their office of divination with that of a herbalist. Conservative diviners who operate only as diviners work with such medicines as are related to their divination, e.g. *imphepho*.

Besides the above there are those in society who are the experts and who have the knowledge of both the properties of *imithi* in general as well as the method of how these properties are to be handled to achieve the best results. It is these that are known as *izinyanga zemithi* (lit. experts on medicines) or *izinyanga zokwelapha* (lit. the experts on healing). The English idiom herbalist is used to identify them.[12]

In principle anybody can become a herbalist. In practice the profession is hereditary, a father passing his methods and secrets to his son, or, although very seldom, to a daughter.[13] While serving under a senior herbalist, an apprentice is known as *impakatha* or *uhlaka*.[14] Whereas diviners look back to their calling and their coming out as the important occasions in their lives as diviners, and relate their activities in divination to the shades, a herbalist is schooled in the manipulation of powers residing in materia and relies solely on this for his knowledge. Experience with *imithi* plays an essential role in a herbalist's practice and ability. Further, while diviners to a great extent are bound to traditional views on divination, herbalists constantly experiment with new materia and mixtures of these, the demand for medicines in varying fields constantly changing.[15]

But in the many cases in which divination and medical practice are combined in one and the same person, there is overlapping. Diviners who also are herbalists claim that the shades reveal suitable medicines. A patient suffering from what appeared to be tuberculosis said that because herbalists (in the conservative sense of the word) no longer could help him, he turned to diviners who practised in medicine because he thought that if the shades revealed the medicines, he would be healed.

Among popular diviners who do not distinguish closely between divination and medicines, the boundary between the realm of the shades and the powers embedded in materia tends to be undefined. Although strongly opposed by a great number of people, one of these popular diviners once said: "If the shades do not give power to medicines, they (the medicines) are useless." While people were arguing about the validity of the statement, the diviner without further personal comment proceeded to give the patient the medicine he had prepared and which had given rise to the discussion. In a few days time the patient was better. Discussing the issue further with him a week later he said: "You see for yourself what I did. It was the shades that saved him (the patient)."

New herbalists launching new treatments are popular in Zulu society. While Zulu reluctantly and with great hesitation approach non-Zulu diviners, herbalists of another nation have a high reputation. There are people who will go to great inconvenience in order to obtain medicines from Tsonga, Swazi or Sotho herbalists. A man returning from Johannesburg described one of the positive aspects of mixing with other Africans on the Reef thus: "The thing that is good is that doctors are just close by. There is not much travelling (required)." My informant was referring to costs involved in having to travel far in order to consult non-Zulu herbalists. Sotho herbalists operating in the Nqutu district admit that they attend to large numbers of Zulu patients who ignore local herbalists and travel to consult them. Indian practitioners in Stanger claim that many of their patients are Zulu who have, occasionally, said that they approached Asian doctors because they were Indian and not Zulu!

The popularity of a herbalist increases with distance. While Zulu living along the Natal coast are convinced that it is *inyanga* from inland that most effectively treats homesteads against violent storms and lightning, the people living inland suppose that it is the experts from the coastal regions who fruitfully treat fields against birds that eat the ripening ears of millet or successfully fertilize poor gardens. In the latter case the fertile soil of the coastal belt may account for the popularity associated with herbalists from that region. And in the former, evidence shows that violent storms and hail cause more harm inland in Natal than along the coast. Mentioning this fact to friends in the Mapumulo district in connection with the treatment of homes against storms, a woman, assuming that local people at the foot of the Drakensberg mountains made use of heaven-herds from that area in defending their homes, said: "It is clear that this man must be powerful, seeing that there still are people there (in the Drakensberg area)." Asked to explain further, she said: "If he did not do his work well, then the storms would have wiped out (lit. killed totally) those people. Did you not say that the storms there are much worse than the storms here? Well! So he must be powerful. That is why he works our homes too."[16]

Herbalists who specialize in the treatment of certain ailments, e.g. snake-bite, and heaven-herds are particularly secretive about their medicines. Zulu accept this and do not, like some Westerners who are eager to know what they take, insist on knowing what medical materia they receive. The secrets are professional ones, and patients willingly submit to treatment with trust and expectation of restored health or effective protection. "That is why they are known as *izinyanga*. Whereas we would die, not knowing medicines, they know the medicines and their use. They give us medicines and we live."

Medicines and Morality

Two essential moral issues pertain to medical treatment. Firstly, there is the tracing of the cause of the suffering that has brought about the need for medical attendance. This is particularly important when medicines are used to treat sickness. Secondly, the effective capacity of medicines is related to good moral standing. If there is anger or other illfeeling, misconduct, etc. medicines are believed to lose their effectiveness.

Unless the source of illness and affliction can be traced, there cannot be full recovery of normal health in the patient. This conviction is based on the belief that the ultimate cause of suffering and sickness, unless it is common *umkuhlane*, is to be traced to friction and tension in social relationships. These, in turn, are always a breaking of moral standards of living and are, therefore, antisocial and destructive in character. It is for this reason that suffering of all kinds, medical treatment and morality are intimately associated with one anether. Further, tracing of the source of suffering is connected with a speaking out and an expression of goodwill and harmony, as has been illustrated in the chapter dealing with resisting evil. Not until this has taken place will one feel freed from the burden of suffering. Revealing evil, has therefore, this double function, i.e. to bring about confession and expression of goodwill on the one hand, and, on the other, a restoration to health.

A tuberculosis patient, treated for a period of time at a hospital, was readmitted after spending some time at home. His condition had deteriorated during his stay at home. Discussing tuberculosis with him and trying to explain to him the need of proper food, the patient exclaimed: "Yes, that is correct! The hunger is caused by somebody who hates me (*ongizondayo*). That is the person who is working against us! I am happy today in that you are agreeing that there is no food in our homes! *Hrrh!* Indeed, there is somebody eating me up, causing hunger!" Quite excited, the patient who, previously was very unhappy at the prospects of having to stay at the hospital, turned to the two who had accompanied him to the hospital, saying: "You have heard for yourselves! This man agrees that there must be divination (*ukubula*)! Let *umthakathi* be exposed! This is a good day in that also *umfundisi* (minister of religion) agrees with divination!" To the patient one step beyond medical treatment appeared necessary if his ailment was to be halted—a tracing of the ultimate cause of his sickness. For if the accused would confess anger, the patient would surely recover.

If medicines are to function effectively, illwill and disharmony within the homestead or the community which uses them must be cleared before medicines are administered. Also, the effect of medicines is dependent on the retaining of harmonious relationships during the time they are expected to be active. K, living near Rorkes Drift, had had his home treated against lightning early in November by a renowned heaven-herd. Only a few days after the treatment of the place, a beast and a tall tree underneath which the animal had been standing were struck. K, shocked and disturbed, called on the heaven-herd. The latter advised him to consult a diviner "because there must be mischief". K, describing what took place, related how the diviner had come and found the reason to be with the women of the homestead. His lengthy description revealed that on the day the heaven-herd had treated the homestead, K's wife and mother had quarrelled, although not seriously. Neither K nor the heaven-herd were conscious of the tension between the two women, and the women admitted that they had soon forgotten their argument. But, according to the diviner, the quarrel had been sufficient cause to make the treatment of the homestead ineffective. Markedly satisfied with the diviner's findings, the heaven-herd said: "When lightning strikes where I have worked (i.e. treated a place), then I know for sure that there is trouble in that home. That is the only thing that disturbs my medicines. Only trouble."

B, a man with a fair number of cattle, was troubled by bats and baboons that sucked the cows at night, damaging the animals' udders and teats. Fully convinced that it was familiars sent by *abathakathi* to cause harm, he called on the assistance of a herbalist who, after treating the homestead and the byre in particular, advised B to tie his two dogs in the cattle-enclosure at night. In order to keep them awake, he was to feed them in the morning and not in the evening. For a number of nights the cattle were not troubled and the tense anxiety which had prevailed in the home relaxed considerably. About a week after the treatment of the homestead by the herbalist, there was a violent quarrel between the wives of two sons of the senior. The younger of the two wives had visited the local shop and had bought a few things for the elder of the two women. The quarrel arose from differing views on the change the younger wife should have returned to the elder. In the evening the quarrel continued in a heated manner, the elder wife accusing the younger of theft, and the younger saying that the elder was both lazy and greedy. During the night the dogs in the byre barked on several occasions, and the cattle were heard running in the cattle-enclosure as they did before the herbalist had treated the homestead. B was both awe-stricken and furious, and, on calling the women to himself in the morning, scolded them thoroughly for arguing and not settling their quarrel. The experience of the night was pressure enough to cause the two women to beg each other pardon, the elder giving the younger a small pumpkin as a sign of goodwill and the younger giving the other the change she had expected plus a cupful of white sugar. B, the homestead senior, was explicit that "the anger of the women made the medicines weak. That is the trouble with women. They often become very hot with anger. Then the medicines die." He claimed, with no little enthusiasm, that after settling their dispute, order had been restored in the cattle-byre again.

Initiated herbalists and heaven-herds maintain that the annual renewal of protective medicines which resist evil and drive off violent storms is done because of anger. "The medicines become weak. They do not protect (as they ought) because of the quarrels of the year. That is why they must be renewed." Informants suggest that it is not the medicine as such that lose their embedded powers. But the power is made ineffective through anger and quarrels. The diviner at eThelezini claimed that this is the reason for the king's having to renew curses against enemies and bad people annually. "It is because people cannot remain quiet without arguing and becoming angry. The medicines become ineffective because of the wickedness (*ulaka*) of people."[17]

Medical Treatment and Symbolism

The rich experience of past generations handed down from father to son, personal experiments with new medicines and knowledge obtained either by way of exchange of information or purchase, has taught herbalists that certain medicines, particularly those prepared from vegetation, produce favourable reactions in many sicknesses and restore health. Because the treatments restore health, they become fixed. It is not by way of ritual or social compulsion that they become accepted means of treating certain sufferings. It is through experience.

While symbols related to ritual are rooted in society and the shades, and, hence, conservatively tied down, symbols connected with medicines are more free. They are often interpreted individually, different herbalists emphasizing different symbols in their practice with *imithi*. There is room for the individual herbalist to use his imagination. Yet, there are symbols which run through the practice of various specialists and appear to be a characteristic of all those who work in that particular field.

Examination of medicines and symbols attached to them by their manipulators, three different heaven-herds (Laduma Madela at Ceza, the second in the Ngwibi-Louwsberg area and the third in the Kranskop district), showed that each had different medicines, but the symbols attached to the materia used in the medicines were remarkedly alike. Naturally, all medicines and symbols were, in one way or another, connected to thunder and lightning, but, as I shall be showing, symbols were not only related to their common interest, i.e. the violent storms. They were, in fact, similar. There was, on the other hand, a difference in emphasis attached to the different symbols, the tendency being that the more difficult a particular materia was in obtaining, the more emphasis attached to it. Laduma Madela gave pointed attention to the sound of the crack of lightning, his symbol for this sound being feathers from the wings of *ingqungqulu* (Terathopius ecaudatus) which is not easily procured.[18] But with Z at Kranskop the sound of thunder was not an essential although it of necessity must be there. He, in turn, symbolized thunder with the sound produced by hitting one stone against another. In the area where he operated there was an abundance of stones.

One heaven-herd took a clear and glistening white ore found in the iNqathi range (where lightning is supposed to strike frequently) to be the symbol of "the white of lightning",[19] a second used milk from a white cow as a symbol for the white of the flash of lightning and the third produced a spark by throwing one stone onto another, the spark being the symbol of the flash. The latter gave particular attention to the importance of the spark and described quite elaborately how he sometimes had to work at length before he produced the necessary spark. But the heaven-herd who used milk for the similar symbol hardly gave any attention to this symbol at all and chose to speak more about the white cow and how he had paid a large sum of money for it, than talk about the white of lightning. Laduma Madela, on the other hand, underlined the importance of the fat of *ingqungqulu* eagle which he said was the colour of lightning together with the ore from the iNgqathi range. Both the fat and the ore were, according to Madela's views, very difficult to obtain. Throughout, the symbols of the heaven-herd were constant, although the materia used were different and emphasis varied.[20]

Although the three heaven-herds used different medicines in their practice and apparently treated homesteads and people differently, the differences were not many or significant. Neither of the three underestimated each other's ability. There was nothing to suggest competition or rivalry between them as is the case frequently with diviners and, sometimes, with herbalists. The heaven-herd at Kranskop, on my relating to him what his colleague at Ceza did and describing the symbols which he attached to various materia when he warded off storms, said: "That is the way that he does it, the way that you have spoken of. That is his way of doing his work. I do it the way that I have told you. (He had given me interesting insights into his practice.) But we do the same thing in warding off fire from heaven."

Thirdly, although the choice of materia used in medicines is different, symbols related to medical treatment are not illogical. Neither are they isolated from the general thought-patterns which describe Zulu society. This accounts for the three heaven-herds accepting each other's procedures as intelligible and acceptable, for the different methods of safe-guarding a homestead against lightning and storms were valid in each other's views. Allowing for the fact that renowned heaven-herds are not many and the role played by competition therefore considerably reduced, the fact remains that they accepted each other's methods as effective and true, once the underlying symbols were understood. To this may be added that two of the heaven-herds were men of dignity and truly Zulu, giving considerable importance to the fact that they were very conscious of *why* they did things in a particular manner and *how* they were to go about their duty to make it meaningful to at least themselves if not a wider circle of people. The third could not be characterized as being particularly traditional in his total view of either himself or his work, being something of a new thinker in many aspects. Yet his views as far as his business of being a heaven-herd are concerned, were not out of place. They fitted into the ideas of the other two very well indeed.

With all three heaven-herds the importance given the symbol by far outweighed the importance given the materia which carried the symbol. This does not imply that no importance was given the materia and its choice, for without careful choice, *imithi* would not have symbolized that which one wished it to typify. The main concern was not the materia. It was the symbol. Once the symbol required had been identified, one took the next step—to find the materia which would carry the symbol. I found the opinion of the heaven-herd in the Kranskop district quite revealing on this matter. We had talked about the practise of other heaven-herds and compared these thoughts with his own. Challenging him to say what he thought of the various things used by e.g. Madela at Ceza in his manipulation of powers, my friend at Kranskop said: "It depends on his (Madela's) views (i.e. his interpretation of symbols) (*Kuhambisana ngemibono yakhe*)."

Because symbols related to medicines and healing fit into the generally accepted patterns of thought in Zulu society, many of the associations and relations within the symbolic understanding are common with those which make ritual symbols intelligible. There is the importance attached to the blowing out of medicines which is similar in use by all herbalists of standing, although some may emphasize it more than others. Vomiting and expulsion of water stand for purification and innocence everywhere. Strength and togetherness are symbolized by the python, and "strong medicines are kept in horns".

Allowing for extensive overlapping, there appear to be four basic different approaches to the symbolic understanding of medicines and medical treatment in Zulu society.

Antagonistic Associations

One principle on which symbols are based is that of association. Like things and similar behaviour, as well as similar sounds and colours are associated with each other and thought to act against each other. They are antagonistic *because* they are similar. It is along this thought-pattern one argues when black medicines (*imithi emnyama* or *ibulawo elimnyama*) are used to drive off the darkness of evil. The blackness of the medicines, experienced both in colour and in taste, drives off evil which, typically, is expelled from the body outside the homestead in a secret place.[21]

The reverse is equally true. Because certain colours and sounds are similar and hence associated with each other, they are thought to produce the same effects. In this sense they are sympathetic. Zulu medical practice has evidence which shows how both these approaches to symbols of likenesses are used.[22]

As the sky, "when it is dark, being angry", produces lightning, so also "black stones (granite?) thrown (against other stones) causes lightning (i.e. sparks)". My informant, a heaven-herd, who used soot and flint from black stones in medicines for protection against lightning, associated not only the spark obtained when one stone struck another with lightning. The colour of soot and the stone was associated with thunderstorms. He claimed that he deliberately chose soot and black stones when preparing the medicines because "they are like the sky when it is angry". The difficulty experienced in chipping off small portions of black stone from a larger was related to the difficulty by throwing one stone on the other. If a spark was not produced, the medicine would be ineffective. Only after the spark had been produced could the chips be ground into the required powder. Again, if there was not a cracking sound in the process of chipping off the stone, similar to that of lightning when it strikes in one's neighbourhood, the medicine would be of no avail. He attached some importance also to the smell experienced when the stone split. He claimed that it smelt like thunder and lightning.

We looked at the stone the heaven-herd kept in his hut. It very much resembled both in colour and form a stone that previously had been shown to me as being the colour of the rock which is believed to be of the sky.[23] I thought that the heaven-herd's choice of stone might have associations with this also, and asked him if this were so. He refuted the idea immediately. He said that stones sometimes did fall from heaven, but anybody, including heaven-herds, who touched or even came in the close vicinity to these would become insane and eventually die. But he had no reason for this. "It is thus. Everybody working with this medicine knows that the things from the sky cause people to become *izinhlanya* (insane). ·That is all I know." His information on insanity in relation to things from the sky was verified by a number of people.

The association between the darkness of the sky during thunderstorms and the black stone (actually the stone was a dark grey-blue colour, but the heaven-herd throughout said that it was black, *mnyama*) is obvious. The emphasis lies on the similarities being antagonistic towards each other. The dark stone drives away the dark sky, the spark from the stone reacts against the lightning, the hardness of the stone is related to the difficulty in controlling the heavens, the crack of the stones diverts the crack of thunder, the smell of the chipped stone disassociates itself with the smell of sulphur when lightning has struck nearby.

The thought-pattern that like things are antagonistic to each other covers a large range of details in life. When women carry containers with water or even beer a small pebble is placed in the vessel "so that it may not fall and break". Women returning from the fields with baskets of maize may place a pebble with a small lump of earth from the garden in the basket for the samer purpose. The diviner at eThelezini explained: "Dead people are stones. The stone in the vessel means that it (the calabash containing water) must not die." (The idiom *ukufa* was used to describe both the dead people and the breaking of the vessel, the dead people being referred to as *abafileyo*.) Not for a moment did the diviner hesitate to classify the pebble as *umuthi*. To him this was perfectly natural in that "it has work to do".

If dogs appear to sleep too much, medicine is prepared from *imfinyezi* (a beetle that curls up when touched) and given the animal to prevent it from being like the beetle. Insanity, believed to be caused by excessive brooding of the shades and, frequently today, the nearness to God, is treated with medicines prepared of feathers and skin from a vulture because these fly very high up in the sky.[24] "They come very close to the sky." Another herbalist used fat and parts of common moles to treat mental disorder because "these animals live in the earth". His explanation puzzled me until I had realized the very close relations between earth and the shades. Another herbalist said that he used the bones of moles because "they are white". Mindful of the belief that the shades are white in Zulu concepts, the symbol becomes fully intelligible.

Men who are unable to attain erection are given infusions of *inthwalabombo* (Rubia cordifolia, a species of climbing plant said to be soft and bendable without breaking off, associated with the male member).[25] "The medicine enters the body. It goes to that place (male member). It does its work there. The man goes to his wife and finds that he can work nicely."

A man refused by girls because he is considered ugly becomes handsome in their eyes if he is treated with a decoction prepared by boiling *ibhuma* (the common bulrush, Cyperus sp.) in milk, preferably that of a goat. Bulrushes are believed to have no flowers (Zulu who recognize the flower say that it is ugly) and goats, particularly females with elongated udders, are also said to be ugly. The ugliness of the growth and the animal produce handsomeness in the male. (There were herbalists who laughed when they heard of this treatment and said that it was just the common things used by young people when courting and themselves claimed that they had better treatment.)

Previously, when warfare was common, a soldier carried a thorn or needle (*usungulo*) with him in battle, thereby making him invulnerable to the sharp spears of the enemy. But after the battle, when seeking refuge and food among the local population, the thorn or needle would be removed, lest it affect the goodwill of friends.[26] Today, medicines prepared with thorns and carried as charms or taken internally prior to parties and social gatherings, etc., are believed to be protective against knives and spears should fighting arise during the party. The extensive use of pins in various ways by a great number of people is evident to all who associate with Zulu. Diviners sometimes have pins attached to the gall-bladders, others wear them fixed to bangles, etc. around the arms and legs "so that no sharp thing may hurt them".[27]

Sympathetic Associations

The principle of association works also the other way. Like things produce like. The herbalist who gave me the information about *ithwalabombo* with regard to men, immediately added that the same plant is used in treating women who gave birth to girls only. Describing his method of treatment and relating the use of the plant to men and women, the following emerged: whilst the bark of the plant was used in treating men, the wood was used in the case of women; women drink the medicine daily for a period of two weeks after the menstrual period has ceased, some medicine also being poured over the genitals prior to intercourse. Men were treated by drinking the medicine and, if drinking proved unsatisfactory, incisions would be made on the body and the medicine rubbed into them (two herbalists once said that incisions were like women, comparing them to the female genital organs, but this could not be verified in wider Zulu circles). Men stand and drink the medicines, an approach that my informant associated with alertness (*ukuvuka*, which is also related to the erection of the male member), while women are treated sitting to the right of the hearth, i.e. the men's side of the hut. But while the effect of the soft and bendable plant's bark with men is the opposite to the growth's characteristic, the reverse is true with women. Women who use the wood medically are believed to bear male children.

Whilst *imithi emnyama* expel evil because of the character of blackness in the medicines, *imithi emhlophe* (or *ibulawo elimhlophe*), white medicines, produce similarity in the human. The white froth of the medicines is smeared on the body and taken internally because "it brings about whiteness". Generally, the ingredients of *imithi emhlophe,* although of a great variety and depending partly on the herbalist who prepares them and partly on the purpose for using them, are lightcoloured and always referred to as being white. These medicines are associated with fortifying and strengthening. Hence, whereas treatment with *imithi emnyama* requires abstinence from food, certain people, etc., *imithi emhlope* presuppose eating and drinking. The aim of taking them and food is similar.[28]

Besides black and white medicines, there are also green *imithi, amakhambhi.* This medicine is prepared of green leaves, roots, and herbs freshly collected from fields, the word *amakhambhi* implying greenness and associated with growth. *Amakhambhi* are given children as a tonic "to make them strong" and to convalescent patients for the same purpose. Sometimes they are also given to domestic animals. "These medicines are the same as the grass they (the animals) eat." The associations of similarity are obvious.[29]

Dignity and the characteristic of fearfulness are acquired by men of authority through pounding certain heavy stones into a fine powder. Fat and the ground eyes of snakes which are feared are mixed with the powder and, if at all obtainable, also quicksilver. The face and limbs of the man are anointed with the mixture. He is believed to develop the required dignity and awesomeness. The symbolism lies with weight and its relation to dignity. For heavy people (*abasindayo*) are prosperous and dignified. Hence the heavy stone, fat, and quicksilver. Awesomeness goes with the ability to see things and grasp them quickly, quick reactions and intellectual alertness. Snakes are believed to have these characteristics, particularly ill-tempered species. Hence the eyes which symbolize seeing and understanding.[30]

Bald men are believed to be infertile and their ailment is treated with medicines from gardens with a profuse growth. "Hair is like life. If there is no life on the head, then there is no life in the thing of men. (The word *imphilo* was used to describe the life of the hair on the head and the life of the male member.) This sickness in men is treated with medicines from gardens with much life, (*imphilo*). This medicine is called *amakhambhi.* It has this name because it brings life to men."

Talkativeness is treated with parts from a sheep, the animal being a symbol of quietness. A man with particularly short legs was once treated with bones obtained from a stork, the bird itself being procured with great difficulty. Fear and anxiety are treated with flesh from animals which are said to have no fear (previously lions, elephants, today bulls, puff-adders, and wild cats).[31]

Symbols Accepted

Some symbols used in medical treatment are related to accepted symbols in society. Pythons stand for togetherness ("the snake that holds together"),[32] and fat from the reptile is used "to keep the sickness in one place in the body". Two prominent herbalists claimed that medicines containing flesh from pythons was used effectively against leprosy (*uchoko*), "not allowing the flesh to fall off (the body)". It was also used for people whose thoughts tended to stray.

Skin shed by snakes in early spring is used medically to treat women with irregular menstrual periods or who tend to give birth either earlier or later than in the tenth lunar month; the underlying symbol being that the regularity with which snakes change their skin will bring about regularity in the women.[33]

Iron, on the other hand, stands for productivity in women, animals and fields. Ngema was convinced that the reason for the plentiful harvest obtained from fields and gardens surrounded by barbed wire was the presence of iron in relation to the field. He by no means discounted compost, manure, frequent tilling, watering, etc... I argued that the barbed wire only prevented animals from entering the fields, but Ngema, accepting this function, would not be totally convinced. He changed the theme of discussion from the barbed wire to the stands and droppers. I pointed out the destruction of wooden poles brought about by the presence of termites in the area. Ngema pointed out the use of treated poles, adding that farmers of the Greytown and Kranskop area increasingly used iron standards and droppers, despite the fact that the ground is largely covered by wattle from which good poles could be obtained and the presence of a factory from which treated poles could be obtained in the district![34]

Red, the colour of blood and frequently related to menstruation and pregnancy, as a symbol, plays an important role in fertility and pregnancy.[35] Red medicines are prepared from the large and red roots of *intolwane* (Elephantorhiza burchellii) and given expectant women at regular intervals during the time of pregnancy. "This medicine is like blood. It makes the child strong. Even the bitterness of the medicines makes it (the child) strong." The root of *isikhubadende* (Indigofera sp.), also red but not equally large as that of *intolwane*, is used for the same purpose.[36] If a woman does not conceive although she has regular menstruations, the red root of *isinama esibomvu sehlathi* (Pupalia atropurpurea)[37] is pounded and prepared into a paste. Of this paste two balls "like a man (i.e. testicles) are prepared". One is eaten by the husband and the other inserted into the vagina by the woman prior to intercourse. "That night the blood mixes nicely. She will conceive of this medicine. It is the medicine of blood (*imithi yegazi*)."[38]

Informants claim that *isidwa* (Gladiolus ludwigii) and particularly its nut-like roots are placed as a medicine in baskets containing seed when women plant. "This thing (the root) is hard. Evil (lit. rot) does not penetrate into it. So it makes the seed hard (i.e. resistant) against rot." A herbalist who supplied *isidwa* to customers in early spring explained its ability thus: "They (the customers) know that it is hard. They wish the maize seeds to be hard. Rot and insects must not come into the seed. It must be hard. Then the radicle bursting from the inside (of the seed) can grow nicely until it bursts the outer skin. Seed is like all other things which are alive. The life comes from the inside. Destruction comes from outside. So the skin of the seed must be hard (resistant)."

Visually suggestive symbols

There are, fourthly, symbols in medical treatment which may be termed visually suggestive. The roots of *ihlamvu lomfana nentombazana* (Glorioso vires-

356

cens)[39] resemble partly the male organ, partly the female. The symbolism is utilized in various ways. Men, whose wives have given birth to girls and who desire male children, are treated with the root resembling the male, while, if they desire girls, the female root is administered. On the other hand, women who have only girls are treated with roots resembling the female organ while if they have only boys and wish to have a girl are treated with the male-resembling root. "They (women) are treated in this way so that the womb knows that this child (i.e. the sex represented by the root) is no longer desired." I am told that the treatment is applicable to cattle also.

One herbalist claimed that he prepared love-medicines used by girls who had no lovers from scrapings collected from the fork of trees "because it is like a woman". To this he added honey, a few hairs plucked from the pudenda of the woman and scrapings from the porridge-pot containing food that she had prepared. The medicine was used to interest a man to whom the girl chose to give the medicine.

Women with underdeveloped mammary glands and/or with an unsufficient supply of milk are treated with medicines prepared of the common paw-paw. The fruit is plucked while still green but fully developed, preference being given to the round ones rather than the elongated. "It (the paw-paw) is like the breast. Even the nipple is there on this fruit." Others emphasized the milky sap which emerges when the fruit is plucked and associated it with female milk. Barren women are treated with the leaves of the paw-paw because "it is like the hand of a human". Men, on the other hand, who have various sexual ailments are treated with the stem or branches of paw-paw as these are hollow "like men and the sap is like the water (of men)".

Bananas are identified with men and pregnant women should not eat this fruit. Conservative Zulu women avoid the fruit altogether, one old lady once stating: "This (a banana which was offered her) is not food. It is something else. It must not be eaten." Medically, banana shoots are used to cure impotency in men; the method used has, unfortunately not been ascertainable.[40]

Illegitimately, crabs are used medically in *ukuthakatha* to cause the eyes to fall out because the eyes of a crab stick out. Legitimately, crabs eyes are used to draw out the eyes of a person who has them set deeply in the head, a characteristic which is looked upon as ugly and ridiculed.

The Symbol in Treatment

Experience seems to suggest that the emphasis is often not on the medicine as such. It is rather the symbol typified by the medicine that is the important aspect. In some instances this suggestion is fully evident. It is two such occasions which I wish to draw attention to in this section of the chapter.

I witnessed an old woman preparing seed to be planted in a maize-field, she not knowing that I would be present, and I not knowing that I was to see her do it. She was preparing the seed while her son, the male senior of a homestead, was preparing to plough the field that was to be planted. The incident took place on a Saturday morning after good spring rains had fallen.

In a secluded spot, hidden from sight by bushes and tall dry grass and low down on the slope of the field to be tilled, not very far from a stream of water, the woman, about sixty-five years old (possibly more) had scraped out earth to form a small hollow in the field. The cavity in the soil was about fifteen centimeters in diameter and equally deep. Covering the hole, she placed a plastic sheet over it, pressed down the middle and flattened out the plastic against the edges of the hole, taking care that no earth fell into the plastic. The outer edges of the plastic reached well over the edges of the hole. A boy was called from a group of herding youngsters, playing a short distance away. He was sent to fetch a stone which the woman said was to be found in a certain place in the stream nearby. The boy returned with a bored stone, dripping wet. The woman received the stone from the boy and gave him a billy-can lid, instructing him to fetch water from the stream in it. (She had apparently scooped out the earth to make the hole with the lid as there was a little loose earth attached to the lid.) The boy returned with the lid nearly full of water and walking carefully so as not to spill any.

On receiving the lid with water, the old lady poured about half of the contents out behind herself (apparently there was too much water in the lid), placed the lid in the hole on the plastic after she had taken a mouthful of water from it, and placed the bored stone over the lid. From her clothing she produced a brown paper-packet containing a powdered medicine, about a teaspoon full, which she poured into her left hand and then took into the mouth and mixed it with the water as one would do when rinsing one's teeth after brushing. From a basket containing seed which was to be planted she took a handful in her right hand and let the seeds run into the hole of the bored stone, falling into the lid with water. Having emptied her hand, she bent down over the hole and blew some medicine into the hole. This was repeated three times, the third handful of maize seed filling the hole in the bored stone. On this occasion she blew out the remaining medicine and water in her mouth.

She lifted the stone from its position and called for the boy again, instructing him to return the stone to its place in the homestead. The billy-can lid was lifted from its position and the maize in it with medicine and water was emptied into the basket with maize seed. Carefully she lifted the plastic sheet by the four corners and poured the seeds and water which had run over into the basket. Thereafter she mixed the seed in the basket with her right hand, the left holding the basket in position. On lifting the basket, one saw that water had trickled out through the basket, but this did not disturb the woman. She lifted the basket, and prepared to commence planting. The hole in the ground was left uncovered, the plastic and the brown paper-packet returned to a pocket (presumably) in her clothing.

The stone, on examination in the home, proved to have some red paint on it. Although I was fairly convinced that it was either red roof-paint or something similar, the old lady insisted that is was *igazi*, blood. Asked what blood it was, she merely smiled. No further information could be obtained on this issue from anybody. The bored stone was kept underneath the storage-hut in the homestead and when seen on several occasions later, always had its two openings blocked with maize cobs. At least on two occasions I was convinced that they had been changed and on inquiring whether this was so, was told that the children had been playing with it and removed the cobs that had been inserted previously. The old lady complained, saying that the children were mischievous and caused trouble by not returning the stone where it belonged. Practically no further information could be obtained either from the old lady or the men who ploughed other than that the rite was done to give fertility to the seed.[41]

Fig. 21. The bored stone used in fertility rituals lying underneath the storage hut in the homestead. The openings have been plugged with maize cobs.

The diviner at eThelezini was informed, however, although he claimed that he had no bored stone in his homestead. From the discussion with the diviner the following emerged: Sometimes no medicines are used. But the water is regarded as essential. The diviner did not know whether the water always is blown out by way of the mouth into the hole in the stone, but he thought that would be the case. "That is the way with medicines." Without hesitation he associated the water in the billy-can lid with the water of the womb and said: "From where do children come if not from water? So this is the water of children." Asked whether there was any symbolism in the hole constructed in the field, my informant, after some hesitation, said that the field is "the mother from whom we eat", suggesting that it is female. He was quite explicit that the ritual could only be done by an old woman. On the other hand, he also insisted that no male could do it. "Men do not sow. They slaughter the animals when there is to be meat. But they do not sow." Asked whether children could do it, he said that children do not know "how to do this thing", clearly indicating sexual symbolism. He was equally convinced that a pregnant woman could not do it "because she is hot with water and blood (menstrual blood and semen)". On the other hand, a woman who was not menstruating and not pregnant he thought could also do it.

Sometimes the symbolic element in the preparation of medicines is an important factor. We were discussing the awe with which a smith is regarded by the local population, when the man related that "it is because of the medicines which come from the place of iron". We took up the matters related to the smelting of iron and the smithy.

Our discussion revealed a very close relationship between the red-hot molten iron that trickled out from the furnace and the sexual symbols of the forge.

359

The smith took up some red soil in his hand and stretching out his open hand towards me said: "Why is this earth red? It is because it is blood. The blood of the earth." He closely associated the ore from which the iron is obtained with the earth, adding that the red iron ore came from the earth. "The earth is the mother of iron. Iron comes from its mother." The red iron ore that trickled out was, in the eyes of the smith, a symbol and likeness to a woman's monthly periods. He insisted that he could work in the smithy only a few days each month "when the iron flows out nicely", very clearly associating this time to that when women experience their menstrual flows. He claimed that personally he chose to work in his workshop just after the full moon, for a period of about four or five days. "After those days I am tired. The power has left my limbs. I cannot any longer smite the iron. It does not form nicely and the flowing (from the forge) is poor."

We discussed the black of cool iron. This colour, the smith claimed, was the colour of dried blood. "When the blood is red, it is hot. When it is black, it is cool. So iron and blood are the same." I suggested that dried blood was in form the same as iron and asked whether this was so. He agreed immediately and related this aspect to the dross of the forge which we had been discussing previously. Dross from the forge is pounded into a powder and used as a medicine to cure painful menstruation.

My informant put his case for having a forge in these times when metal tools are obtainable in all shops strongly in terms of the medicines that came from the smithy; the medicines were the cause of his being a smith, not in the first place tools he made. These were of secondary importance. What was essential to him were the medicines. "The sickness of women can only be treated with iron. Why do I travel far sometimes? Because of these medicines! Even if I do not travel, people travel to me. Even from Johannesburg. Also Pretoria. They come to this place X to get these powders. Here are the letters of people writing for them. (He placed his hand on a large brief-case he had in his hut.) They write to me for this medicine."[42]

Notes

[1] Classifications of medical materia, forms of materia and treatment, approaches to ailments, symtoms and general approaches to sufferings are discussed by Bryant, *Zulu Medicine and Medicine Man:* Bryant, *Dict.,* contains some 770 entries on Zulu uses of vegetation in terms of healing: Jackson, 'The Medicine-man in Natal and Zululand': *The Collector* has many useful hints on concepts of sickness and healing: Krige, *SSZ,* pp. 327–335 carries a systematized approach.

Jenkinson, *Amazulu,* p. 29, refers to a Zulu pharmocopoeia of 290 medicines drawn up by Callaway. This list has not been available for consultation and is most probably lost.

See also Bews, 'List of Zulu Plant Names': Watt and Breyer-Brandwijk: *Medicinal and Poisonous Plants of South Africa.*

Keen, *Western Medicine and the Witch-doctor* offers a popular description of healing concepts.

The approach to material in this chapter has been influenced by Wilson, *Communal Rituals of the Nyakyusa,* pp. 142–153 who gives a symbolic analysis of Nyakyusa concepts of medicines.

An extensive account of Tsonga concepts is to be found in Junod, *The Life of a South African Tribe,* Vol. II, pp. 452–505.

[2] Cf. pp. 256 ff. and Doke–Vilakazi, *Dict.*, p. 236.

[3] Cf. pp. 46 ff.

[4] Cf. McCord, 'Zulu Witch Doctors and Medicine-Men', p. 310. Chips from heavy stones are mixed with fat (stands for greatness), eyes of a snake (a symbol for fearfulness, majesty) and quicksilver (symbol for togetherness and of weight which is dignity). Lacking the latter, filings from a magnet are used instead.

[5] These medicines are mixed with *ujiba* beer which plays a significant role in Zulu women's lives.

[6] Cf. Liljestrand, 'Något om zuluernas samfundslif och husliga lif', p. 28.

[7] Doke–Vilakazi, *Dict.*, p. 314.

[8] See pp. 279 and 301, note 83. Also Doke–Vilakazi, *Dict.*, p. 155.

[9] Krige, *SSZ*, p. 290, note 1. Bryant, *Zulu Medicine and Medicine Men*, p. 44, says that *umdlebe* is used against catarrh, but this has not been verified.

[10] Cf. Bryant, *Zulu Medicine and Medicine Men*, p. 68: Doke–Vilakazi, *Dict.*, p. 892.

[11] Doke–Vilakazi, *Dict.*, p. 174.

[12] On herbalists see Krige, *SSZ*, pp. 298–299: Bryant, *Zulu Medicine and Medicine Men*, pp. 9–18.

[13] Bryant, *Zulu Medicine and Medicine Men*, p. 10, says: "One of the medicine-man's songs being compulsorily introduced by him (the father) into the trade, as his assistant, during life, and inheriting his legacy of the bags and bundles of medicines after his death."

[14] Jackson, 'The Medicine Man in Natal and Zululand', p. 197.

[15] See further pp. 257 f. and 267 ff.

[16] McCord, 'Zulu Witch Doctors and Medicine Men', p. 309, relates that herbalists operating in the Mapumulo district of Natal obtained medicines from Gasaland and Swaziland. McCord gathered his information in the Mapumulo district.

[17] Cope, *The Rainmaker*, particularly chapter 18, pp. 195 ff. describes, in novel form, how a rain-maker's ability to produce rain is brought to naught by moral misconduct in his immediate social neighbourhood. Note especially pp. 200 ff.

[18] Doke–Vilakazi, *Dict.*, p. 811.

[19] Cf. Sayce, 'Lightning Charms from Natal'. See also Samuelson, *Long, Long, Ago*, p. 307, and Krige, *SSZ*, p. 315 f.

[20] Cf. pp. 48 ff. and Radcliffe-Brown, *Structures and Function in Primitive Society*, pp. 155 ff.

[21] Cf. Callaway, *The Religious System of the Amazulu*, pp. 142 ff. and Krige, *SSZ*, p. 328 ff.

[22] Cf. also a pregnant woman who by all means avoids a barren woman during her time of expectation for fear that the unborn child may die in the womb and eventually cause sterility. Also, pregnant women avoid each other for fear of giving birth to twins.

[23] Cf. Krige, *SSZ*, p. 410.

[24] On vulture feathers and skin see McCord, 'The Zulu Witch Doctor and Medicine Man', p. 308.

[25] Doke–Vilakazi, *Dict.*, p. 811.

[26] *The Collector*, p. 8, no. 89.

[27] Cf. McCord, 'The Zulu Witch Doctor and Medicine Man', p. 309, who says: "If the blood of the body comes through the nose or the mouth, it is necessary to take the bark of trees which have the juice like blood, and parts of an animal which has much blood in its body." Informants of the Mapumulo district say that the bark of *umdlebe* (identity not clear, but certainly of the Euphobia family), growing in the lowlands of the Thugela valley and said to bleed blood, and the tree known as *igazi* (species not clear), also claimed to bleed a sap resembling blood profusely when the bark is damaged are mixed with the blood of, generally, a goat.

Popularly, snake-bite is treated with medicine prepared from the head and bile of preferably the reptile which harmed the victim. See also Jackson, 'The Medicine Man in Natal and Zululand', p. 202.

[28] On *imithi emnyama* and *imithi emhlophe* see Krige, *SSZ*, pp. 328 f.

[29] Bryant, *Zulu Medicine and Medicine Men*, p. 20.

[30] McCord, 'The Zulu Witch Doctor and Medicine Man', p. 310.

[31] McCord, 'The Zulu Witch Doctor and Medicine Man', p. 309.

[32] McCord, 'The Zulu Witch Doctor and Medicine Man', p. 309.

[33] Cf. pp. 94 f.

[34] Bryant, *Zulu Medicine and Medicine Men*, p. 63, mentions iron being used as a cure for dysmenorrhoea.

[35] Cf. particularly the growth of the unborn child as being dependent on blood from the mother, i.e. menstrual blood believed to encourage growth, and water from the father, i.e. the father's seminal emission during pregnancy, which is believed to also encourage growth of the foetus.

[36] Bryant, *Zulu Medicine and Medicine Men*, p. 39, says that these are used in treating dysentery and diarrhoea.

[37] Doke–Vilakazi, *Dict.*, p. 521.

[38] The red berries of *uthothovane* (Solanum auriculatum) (Doke–Vilakazi, *Dict.*, p. 803) are said to cause profusely bleeding wounds and hence associated with *ubuthakathi*.

[39] Doke–Vilakazi, *Dict.*, p. 318.

[40] Both paw-paw and bananas play a role in Zulu medical symbolism. The former is a recent introduction among Zulu, the latter was previously made use of by royalty only. Both appear to have fertility symbols attached to them.

Abortive medicines are prepared of the light- and dark-coloured seeds of the paw-paw, these being obtained preferably from the fruit of both male and female trees. The seed is said to cause confusion in the womb and thereby bring about abortion.

On the other hand the stem of the paw-paw tree is hollow and spongy, "like men", and used accordingly. Some people have said that the fruit of the male trees is "like bulls", and hence administered to them when bull calves are desired.

Fruit of the female tree is compared with breasts.

Zulu distinguish bananas from other fruit in that banana-plants become pregnant (*ukumitha*) when carrying fruit while other trees *khahlela* or *twala*, carry. Fruit trees in general are said to be *izithelo* (fruit), but bananas have *amazinyane* (lit. offspring, related to living species).

[41] For similar practice in Transvaal see Dart, 'The Ritual Employment of Bored Stones by Transvaal Bantu Tribes'.

The incident related was observed in the Nqutu district in which there is Sotho cultural influence. It is possible that this particular use of bored stones has been introduced by Sotho into the area and adopted by Zulu. The ritual does not appear to be commonly known among other Zulu, although there are several who claim that they have heard of it. The ventriloquist did not doubt the validity of the ritual, once I had described it to him. But he did not intend doing it himself!

[42] For descriptions of traditional Zulu smithies and work in them see Bryant, *The Zulu People*, pp. 386 ff.: Bodenstein-Raum, 'A Modern Zulu Philosopher': Krige, *SSZ*, pp. 209–211.

Chapter X

Inversions and funerary reversals

Inversions

In Zulu society are found at least three different kinds of inversions. There is, firstly, the opposites related to the sexes.

Women are generally associated with the left, men with the right. Women occupy the left side of the hut as one enters through the doorway, men sit to the right and opposite the women. Men generally carry bangles of skin from animals slaughtered on their behalf at ritual celebrations around the right arm, women wearing them around the left.

In the sex act the man lies, traditionally, on his right side while the female lies on her left.[1] Also traditionally, the umbilical cord is buried immediately to the right of *umsamo* seen from the doorway of the hut in the case of a male child, and to the left if a girl.[2] At the rite in which a new-born baby is passed through smoke believed by Kidd to be the ceremony in which the child receives *ithongo* of the clan, the father scrapes sweat from his right arm and shoulder if the child to be treated is a male. If it is a girl, he will take sweat from his left arm.[3] A pregnant woman who experiences a twitching of her right eye will take this as an omen that her child will be a boy, while twitching of the left eye indicates a girl baby. Women who are not pregnant take the twitching of the left eye as indications of visits by female relatives while twitching of the right eye is related to the arrival of male relatives, the relatives in both cases coming from the woman's clan by birth.

When the lobe of the ear is pierced, the right ear is pierced first in the case of boys, followed by the left. In the case of girls, the left ear is treated first, thereafter the right. When milking a cow, the milker sits to the right of the cow "because milking is the work of men".

General household tools used by men, e.g. hunting and defence weapons, yokes and ploughs, saws, hammers, etc. are stored to the right of a hut as one enters through the doorway. Tools used by women are found to the left. Sleeping mats which are rolled out by the women in the evening are also stored to the left of the hut.

Cooking huts are generally situated to the left of living quarters, this tradition being retained by Zulu who also build square houses and fit them with westernized furniture. If a kitchen is attached to the main building, it will undoubtedly be found on the left hand side of the building as one enters. Among schooled Zulu who have an office, e.g. school teachers, clerks, chiefs, etc., this room will usually be found to the right of the building, assuming that the occupant of the office is a male.

Zulu claim that women, and therefore the left side, are not regarded as necessarily inferior to men and the right side. Nor are men superior to women. It is rather a matter of opposites which complement each other. Relating women to men, Ngema said: "There are two hands, the right one and the left, in order that a man may work properly. There are two eyes. Close one eye and you do not see properly. There are two ears: close one and where is the hearing? There are two feet. What is a man with only one foot? That is what men and women are like. They must be two so that things may work nicely without disturbances."

On the other hand, people generally agree that men are stronger physically than women. Likewise they are well aware of the fact that the left arm frequently is weaker than the right. "That is why the left side is that of women and the right that of man. It is because men are stronger than women." But there was not a qualitative comparison between men and women attached to this difference. Ngema said: "That is the way of living. Sometimes strength (physical) is required. That is the time when the men must work. Sometimes there is required tenderness. That is the work of women. So it is clear men and women have each their work to do."

Secondly, there are the opposites related to ethical values. Evil, and associated things, are generally related to dark and the left side, while good things are spoken of *ezimhlophe*, the white ones.

Witches are believed to practise their evil devices particularly at night, this also being the time when familiars are active.[4] During the day there is the possibility of being attacked by sorcerers, but as a whole the daytime is regarded as generally safe in comparison with the night and darkness.[5]

Snakes associated with witchcraft are believed to be of a dark colour.[6]

Faeces are removed with the left hand "because we do not eat with this hand. Faeces are vileness. It must be removed with the left hand." The left side is also associated with the expulsion of anger in ritual celebrations where there is a speaking out, for it is over the left shoulder that angry men spit out. This is emphatically the case in the ritual of *ukuthela ngamanzi*.[7]

The third category of opposites are reversals which, with Professor Jeffreys, I refer to as funerary inversions. Adopting Professor Jeffreys' definition, "by inversions or reversals is meant the reversal of ordinary custom or procedure. Thus if it is customary to dance with the sun, i.e. 'go the deasel' then the funeral dance will be danced 'widershines' or against the sun."[8]

Funerary Inversions

Burials at night are recorded in the relevant literature from practically the whole of Africa,[9] including from among Zulu.[10] Interment at night has practically fallen into disuse among Zulu today, but on record I have a case dating from 1962. The deceased was an old man whose age I estimated to about ninety years. A relative to the deceased who had attended the funeral said of it: "We did it at night because of his age. That is how he was honoured." It was difficult to obtain any further information beyond reference to traditional custom. But nobody reacted negatively to the funeral being conducted at night.

Equally well documented from the whole of Africa is the use of an especially constructed exit for the body at the back of the hut, opposite the doorway. Although not equally noted in literature describing Zulu, especially constructed exits are used also among them, the opening being closed when the burial has been completed. Informants have not been able to give reasons for the use of this exit beyond reference to custom. But evidence indicates that the exit is made by men who attend to the digging of the grave while nearly always it is women who close the exit after the body has been removed from the hut. (See illustration.)[11]

While customary procedure would regard a person's leaving a hut backwards as suspect and rude, carriers of a corpse may carry the body out with their faces towards the entrance of the hut, thus leaving the hut backwards. Zulu who are aware of this reversal have added that sometimes the carriers of the corpse will enter the hut backwards "so that their footprints face outwards all the time".[12]

At the funeral of chief Isak Zulu pictures on the walls in the hut where the corpse lay in state had been reversed to face the wall.[13] At the funeral of a distinguished minister at Eshowe the antependium of the altar had been reversed to hang back-to-front. A church warden commented: "We did it because we have a burial", the warden claiming that this was the procedure in that particular church at funeral services. He was not able to give another place where this was done nor where the particular inversion had originated. A leader of a Zionis group in Durban reversed his clerical collar back-to-front on occasions when he conducted funeral services. (See illustration.) He claimed that he always did this when burying members of his group and that he had adopted the practice from other group leaders. Neither he nor any other Zionist leader who knew of the custom could give an acceptable reason for reversing the collar other than "this is done when we bury".

On a number of occasions on record when a polygamous man was being buried, his *ingqadi* wife (i.e. the right hand side wife) carried her husband on the left hand side while the *ikhohlwa* wife (left hand side wife) carried on the right hand side, when the body was being carried to the grave, thereby reversing their traditional positions in the family.[14] Qedizwe Ngema who was familiar with this custom said that it was done "so that the husband may leave his home nicely".

At the burial of chief Nkantini Zulu, the cattle in the royal byre are claimed to have been milked from the left side of the cow immediately after the funeral instead of the customary right side. On speaking to one of the herd-boys who milked the cattle in this manner, he immediately recalled the occasion, associating it with the difficulty of getting the cow to stand still because it, in turn, was unaccustomed to the procedure. He claimed that he had been instructed to do the milking thus by a senior member of the royal clan, but could give no further information about the milking from the left side.

One informant claimed that the senior wife, whose duty it is to wash her husband's body prior to interment, will be instructed to do so with the left hand instead of the right. Another friend claimed that the eyes of the deceased ought to be closed with the fingers of the left hand, so that "the deceased may not be troubled."

At a funeral attended at Appelsbosch the terrace into which the corpse had been placed was to be closed up with a barrier of prepared logs. These logs had been placed some three meters from the grave prior to the funeral service. When the body had been placed into the cavity by attending women (the deceased was a girl about ten years old), they were helped out of the grave and a church warden entered to place the logs in position. He was assisted by a second warden who handed him the logs. Both men used only their left hands throughout this stage of the burial, and did so with consider-

Fig. 22. A special exit made for a corpse at the back of a hut, opposite the doorway. After the corpse had been removed the opening was partially closed off with the roof-iron. The stones removed to make the exit had been heaped up to the left of the exit. The exit was repaired the following day.

Fig. 23. As soon as the corpse had been taken out of the hut through the special exit constructed in the hut's *umsamo*, an elderly woman closed up the exit temporarily with a sheet of old roof-iron, holding it in position with a three-legged pot the bottom of which had been destroyed with a hearth stone from the hut occupied by the deceased.

Fig. 24. While the corpse is being taken out of the hut through an opening constructed for the purpose in *umsamo* of the hut, women leave the hut through the door backwards.

Fig. 25. Immediately after the burial people walked in and out through the doorway in the normal way.

Fig. 26. Lowering logs into the grave with the left hand.

able and noticeable inconvenience. There were fourteen logs to be placed into position. After the funeral the two men were approached and asked to comment on their using the left hands only. Both knew of no other reason than that this was customary procedure (see illustration).

Frequently seeds will be put into the hands of the deceased after the corpse has been placed in position in the grave. On several occasions note has been made to the effect that seeds have been placed in the right hand of women, while they are placed in the left hand of men. While the placing of the seeds in the hands of the deceased generally is associated with future fertility, there are no acceptable explanations of the reversal other than that this is customary procedure. The church membership card, in Lutheran circles known as *ithikithi,* is frequently placed in the left hand of a male deceased while a woman will have the ticket stuck into her right hand. Generally, the emphasis, when discussing the presence of *ithikithi* in connection with the burial, being placed on the deceased being a church member, has been regarded as a valid reason for its being placed in the coffin, nobody could explain why there was an inversion in the placing of it in the hands of the deceased.

While the grave of a local mininster's son at Appelsbosch was being filled in I greeted a church elder who stood a little distance from me. On asking him

Fig. 27. Zionist group leader with his clerical collar turned back-to-front while conducting a funeral service.

about his health, he answered: "*Yebo, sisekhona!*" During the funeral service poems written by the deceased had been read and I commented on them, asking whether the poems had been published or were known by others. The elder answered to the effect that he did not know whether the poems had been published, he himself not having heard of them previously. But he introduced his reply with *yebo*, meaning yes. On both occasions the man used the idiom *yebo*, when traditionally he should have used the term *ca*, meaning no. After the funeral I asked the elder about his reversal of speach. He was amazed that it had been noticed, claiming that he had been taught it by his father who had been a Christian. He claimed the reason for the inversion to be "that it may go well with the deceased and he come to God's place safely". Other congregation members were conscious of the reversal, some claiming that they practised it if it was a relative or close friend who was the deceased. They all agreed that the reversal ceases when all the earth has been placed on the grave, because "then the funeral is over". At the funeral of the late king Cyprian, this language reversal was overheard when a group of women, seated underneath a tree at some distance from the actual place of burial talked. But all were unwilling to comment on their speach when approached.

Widows sometimes turn their skirts inside out on the occasion of their husband's death. Again, while it is customary to drape *ingubo* (body covering) around the body with the knot on the right shoulder of the women, the clothing is turned around so that the knot is on the left shoulder when women attent their husbands' burials.[15]

Reversals and the Underworld

Ethnographic records show that Zulu, as many other African peoples, have a notion of an underworld, inhabited by the shades. It is true that ideas often are vague and hence also unsystematic. But there are informants who have had clearer notions. The following, related by a secondary school boy, was told to him by his paternal grandmother who lived with his parents. The description has subsequently been verified by several people.[16]

He stretched out his left hand and said: "She (the paternal grandmother) says that the world is like this. The inner part of the earth is *izwe* (the mainland). Here are the mountains, rivers, trees, gardens, pasture-land and hunting grounds. Around *izwe* is the ocean. Where it starts we do not know. Above *izwe* is *izulu* (the sky). It is where the stars and the clouds are found. In *izulu* there is also the path of the sun, the path on which it moves. In the morning it rises in the East, wanders over the sky and sets in the West. When the sun wanders along this path it is light on the mainland. This side of the hand is the earth." Thereafter he turned his hand so that the inside of it faced downwards and the back of the hand faced upwards. "They say that this side is the side of *abaphansi* (lit. those below, the shades). We do not know this place, but it is said that *izwe* is found there also. There are mountains, trees, fields, pastures and hunting grounds. They say that everything there faces downwards. The trees grow like this (he pointed downwards) and the mountains point in the same direction. The sun also has its path here, but it rises in the West and sets in the East. This is the land of *amathongo*. The cattle are herded by the small *amathongo*. The grown-up (*amathongo*) hunt, eat and drink. One would think that they are just ordinary people. He who has been a good person while living will be a good *ithongo* in that place. That is what the old people say about the place of the departed."[17]

Thought-patterns describe the underworld as one where things are reversed in comparison with the upper world. The nether world is, further, the bottom section of a flat pancake-shaped surface which constitutes the world and around which the sun circulates. A school teacher who took great pride in traditional Zulu life, commented on this idea: "Well, in the class-room I read in books that the world is like a ball. So then I believed it because the books speak the truth. When I come home and hear the people saying something else, then I believe them, because the old people speak from experience and knowledge. My father has been told these thing by authorities. (The father was a diviner of some fair reputation. The authorities are the shades.) They (the shades) have said that the world is like a piece of plank (i.e. flat). So that is also the truth."

Tyler states that cattle in the underworld were thought to be white. Evidence from Zulu of today indicates that this thought-pattern is still prevalent among traditionalists.[18]

370

Shades, Diviners and Inversions

Shades, like the cattle of the underworld, are thought to be white,[19] a concept found generally on the African continent and sometimes associated with the presence of whites in former times.[20] No Zulu whose thinking on shades is representative doubts that they are white. A conservative diviner said: "That is why we can see them at night. If they were like us, they would not be seen." My friend at eThelezini added: "The difference between shades and *abathakathi* is that *abathakathi* cannot be seen at night. That is why they are so fearful, not being seen. But shades are seen by people. They are not feared because they appear openly to us."

Shades are believed to be active at night. Some people have associated the shades with the night because the hours of dark are the reverse of day-time.[21] At night the shades reveal coming events through dreams, these being interpreted in the reverse to what the dreamer experiences, because "they (the shades) always say the opposite".[22]

Shades like the taste of gall, simply because this to the survivors is bitterness. "But this thing of bitterness is honey on their tongues. That is why they like this thing so much, always desiring it. It is because it tastes like honey."[23]

Zulu diviners often carry the bag containing divination equipment in the left hand. Fully conscious of doing this, they will go out of their way to take the bag in the left hand, carrying the shield and sticks, which traditionally ought to be carried in the left hand, in the right. Very frequently the divination bones are cast out with the left hand. (See illustration.)

The set-up of some diviners' homesteads has been the reverse to that of ordinary homes. The main entrance to the homestead is found behind the main hut (*indlunkulu*) instead of opposite the cattle-enclosure gate. Laduma Madela had reversed his wives' huts so that his *ingqadi* wife (right hand wife) occupied a hut to the left of *indlunkulu*, while his *ikhohlwa* wife lived to the right of *indlunkulu* as seen from the gateway at the byre and facing *indlunkulu*.

Conservative male diviners pass much time in the lower section of the homestead in the vicinity of the cattle-gate, and not in the regions of *indlunkulu* as would be expected of men. They will also entertain guests in a hut set aside for the purpose in the lower end of the homestead, frequently situated to the left of the cattle-gate, if the diviner is a male. In the case of female diviners their huts have been situated in the upper regions of the homestead, in some cases being *indlunkulu* itself.[24] The diviner at eThelezini had a tuft of grass in the roof-thatching above *umsamo* reversed.[25]

Entering a diviner's hut for consultation, the diviner often sits to the left of the entrance if the diviner is a male, to the right if the diviner is a female. Likewise, some male diviners sleep on the left side of the hut, i.e. the women's side, female diviners sleeping on the right side.[26] The diviner of the uMhlatuze valley consciously faced the left side when divining, he himself seated in *umsamo* of the hut because "their (the shades') place, if they were men (i.e. like the survivors physically), would be the right hand side of the hut. So I face the other side."[27] Also during the important *ingoma yokuvumisa* during the training of a novice, male diviners and novices sit to the left in the hut in which the dance is conducted, women sitting to the right seen from the doorway of the hut.[28]

Many diviners claim that they see things upside-down. This is said to be the

Fig. 28. The diviner, having covered his shoulders with *ingubo yamadlozi*, throws out the divining "bones" with the right hand.

reason for their often leaning their head over to one side "so that we may see the things straight". The diviner at eThelezini said that he saw things upside-down continually. When he saw things the right way up he would get worried and irritated, take excessive quantities of *imphepho* and call on the shades to restore good order, until he saw things "in the manner of truthful diviners again". The diviner at uMhlatuze said that some diviners continually saw things upside-down. But he for one only did so during divination. To him seeing things upside-down was a sign that he was divining "according to the revelation given by the shades. Then it is clear that I am not just dreaming, but seeing the things of the shades very clearly."

Omens which to ordinary people are bad signs are interpreted by diviners as good signs when they occur in relation to the diviners. Shade snakes which lie on their backs are bringers of fearful news to commoners, but to diviners this is a very good and welcome omen. "When we see this happen (i.e. shade snakes on their backs) it is a sign that they have some good news for us. So we are very happy." One diviner, whose second wife had no children, claimed

Fig. 29. Bones that fell outside the mat are collected with the left hand.

that on a particular occasion a shade-snake had been seen on its back close to the hut occupied by this wife. The following night he had dreamt of her becoming pregnant. Accordingly he spent the following nights with this wife and as a result she became pregnant and gave birth to a son, the first of four children.

While swallows and their nests are disliked in the homesteads of commoners because they build their nests upside-down, diviners welcome the birds into their homes. It was with marked enthusiasm that Laduma Madela showed me a swallow-nest in his reception hut, saying that he regarded the presence of the birds as a special favour and blessing of the shades.

I discussed the question of swallows with the ventriloquist diviner.

B: "King Shaka is claimed to have said when his brother killed him, 'You are killing me hoping that you will rule in my place. But swallows will rule instead.' A book says that Shaka said this because the white people build houses like swallows with mud."[29]

"That is so. He was thinking of swallows that build with mud."

Fig. 30. The divination starts. The *ingubo yamadlo*
is hung over the knees "to give darkness to the wor
of the shades", the "bones" collected in the left han
and thrown out on the mat.

Fig. 31. The position of the "bones" is noted by pointing with the left fore finger.

374

Fig. 32. The inquirer is given the verdict by the diviner, the latter pointing with his left hand. Throughout the divination the diviner used the left hand, but when the inquirer left, the "bones" were collected in the container with the right hand.

B: "So there was a connection between swallows and the white men?"

"Yes, there was a connection."

B: "The connection was the similarity in building their houses?"

Amusement. "It was the houses."

B: "What was it that Shaka thought of that brought his mind to think of white people and swallows in connection with their houses that they build?"

"He thought of them because they build in that way which is not common."

B: "You mean upside-down?"

Laughter, indicating approval.

B: "But white people do not build upside-down?"

"No, they do not build upside-down." Pause. "But they were also not common. That is what Shaka saw. They were not common in those days as they are known by all today."

B: "What was so uncommon with them? Surely also Zulu knew that there were other nations than Zulus?"

"They knew that there were other nations, indeed. But the thing that was uncommon was the whiteness of the skin. That is the thing that Shaka saw. It was strange (to him)."

B: "What do you think that he thought when he saw white men?"

Pause and amusement. "You are asking what he thought? He thought, 'From where do these fathers come, being here with us?' That is what he asked."

B: "What do you indicate when you say 'fathers'?"

"*Haw!* You are amazing me today! Who are fathers here with us?"

B: "You mean the shades?"

"Those are the ones."

B: "So Shaka thought there was a connection between white people and swallows because the white people came from a certain place (below)?"

"That is what he thought."

B: "Because swallows build upside down and white people have the reverse colour to Zulu?"

"Now you are saying it properly. That is the truth. That is where the connection between swallows and white men lies."

Analysis of Funerary Inversions

Professor Krige has convincingly shown the role of kinship in terms of the clan and the lineage in Zulu society.[30] She has also drawn attention to the importance of age-sets within society, indicating that the age-set itself is the basis of social organisation. The significant role played by the formation of regiments, a fact that continued long after the breakdown of Zulu military power and dignity, is a reflection of the role played by age-sets. Age-sets group people together already from childhood, and throughout physical life one is bound to belong to some age-set within society.[31] The emphasis on age-sets differs today from what it was at the time when Professor Krige wrote her book, but basically the pattern of age-sets remains. Today there are age-sets of class-room mates, cattle-herding groups, people who travel together to work and are of a similar background and age, confirmation groups, etc. who tend to stick together rather rigidly.

As classificatory systems and age-sets are applicable to survivors, so they are also among the shades. The shades form a separate and distinguished age-set of their own in a clan, along with that of the unborn, the children, the youth. Although most intimately connected to the survivors both morally, sentimentally and otherwise, the shades are regarded as having moved out of the physical life to that of the shades, adopting the characteristics and conditions of being which are descriptive of the shades.

Mindful, first, of the all-important function and role played by the shades in Zulu concepts, and, secondly, of the role played by the age-sets in a clan, I suggest that funerary inversions have their explanation partly in the emancipation of a deceased person from an age-set within the lineage, partly an integration of the departed into the age-set of the shades of that particular lineage. This involves the moving of the deceased from the land of the survivors on the upper surface of the flat world to the nether realms of the underworld.

Miss Bendann, who discusses funerary inversions, offers a psychological explanation, basing her argument on what she calls "the principle of oppositions". She says: "This relation (between the corpse and the survivors) which we regard of vital importance is responsible for the shock which the living must experience when they become aware of the deceased, who has been so near and clear to them, cannot speak, or move, or become a participant in those activities with which he has ordinarily associated. This spontaneous reaction on the part of the survivors brings with it a change from the positive to an indifferent or negative attitude towards the corpse, and positive customs become a thing of the past for the same being or are eliminated entirely. A different action which is associated with the shock is now the outcome, and, as a result, all the values affected. Then the actions of the survivors become standardized since they are no longer charged. In all probability, the attitude towards the corpse which we find in so many areas is primarily caused by the shock of death followed by the break-up of kinship bonds and social relations."[32]

Miss Bendann's argument in terms of the "break-up of kinship bonds and social relations" could be applicable to the Zulu situation. But pursuing her discussion on a change "from a positive to an indifferent or negative attitude towards the corpse", this would not be applicable to the Zulu setting. If it were, how is one to account for the elaborate rites in connection with funerals on the one hand and the intimate bonds expressed in communion with the shades on the other?

Professor Radcliffe-Brown builds his explanation of funerary inversions on an assumed "notion of hostility between the society of the living and the world of the spirits".[33] Discussing material from the Andamann Islanders, Professor Radcliffe-Brown argues that the society in which an individual is a link will act as a protector to the individual, protecting him from the dangers and hardships which are caused by the deceased. He says: "The society itself is the source of protection of the individual; the spirits are the chief source of danger. Hence all protection tends to be referred to the society and all danger to the spirits."[34] He develops this view so far that he finds the solution to funerary inversions in the assumed hostile relationships between the living and the deceased. He continues: "By the action of the principle of opposition the society—the world of the living—comes to be opposed to the spirits—the world of the dead."[35]

Had Professor Radcliffe-Brown been discussing material from Zulu society, two basic objections would be made to his views. Firstly, Zulu society does not regard itself as a society of the living alone, with little or no regard to the individual. I suggest that it is not a question of either a collective approach or an individual one. Rather, it is a matter of both—and. It is the individual Zulu who, in togetherness, constitute society. Secondly, it is true that also Zulu society allows for strained relations between the shades and their survivors. The study has given ample examples of this. But the strained relationships are thrashed out in the various rituals and discussed with the shades in order to bring about an atmosphere in which communion can take place. For without the shades no survivor can visualize the future.

In his contribution on funerary inversions Professor Jeffreys does not seek a reason for reversals. He limits his study to a suggestion that inversions came to the Bantu from the Hamites. He does, however, in the course of the discussion suggest that inversions at funerals are "characteristic of the people of the land of the dead", referring his argument to the behaviour and expressions of the masker or clown.[36]

Rosalind Moss discusses inversions found in Oceania and A. C. Kruijt takes up the phenomenon in the Indian Archipelago. W. C. Willoughby refers to funerary inversions in Africa. All three authors associate inversions with the existence of the deceased after their earthly life, connecting inversions closely to reversals in the land of the deceased.[37]

Dr. Needham, in taking up reversals with diviners among Nyoro, argues that the diviner in this particular society appears to be associated with the feminine. He arrives at this conclusion after a lengthy discussion in which he attempts to prove that the left hand side, colour symbolism, odd numbers and the voice of the diviner all point to his being feminine. He closes the discussion, saying: "The left hand connects the diviner not only with the feminine but also with values which themselves are connected, either by direct association or by analogy, with the feminine. Black, evil, danger, the inauspicious, and death (perhaps, too, the destructive and impure aspect of sexuality) all conjoin to make the diviner what the Nyoro themselves may well conceive as an agent of darkness, and the left hand is the readiest symbol of this condition."[38]

Dr. Beattie, discussing Needham's contribution, produces evidence which he claims disassociates itself with Needham's theory. In his lengthy discussion, Beattie offers "two possible lines of explanation which might help us to understand the matter, so far as the available information allows it".[39] First, he says: "It might reasonably by argued that diviners, especially those who divine by spirit mediumship, are 'marginal' people, at least while they are divining, for they stand in a special relationship to the unseen world of non-human, 'mystical' powers. In Nyoro culture, . . . marginal people and events are in some degree anomalous, and the anomalous is often associated with ritual danger which is expressed and dealt with through symbolism. One kind of symbolism which is held to be appropriate in such situations is symbolic reversal."[40] Adding, however, that cowry-shell divination is not thought to be at all dangerous and hence the argument not applicable to this particular instance, Beattie offers us his second suggestion, namely, that 'certain anomalous acts and situations as having a certain potency (mahano), simply because they are anomalous. In certain contexts this potency may be, as it were, put to use; anomalous, out of the ordinary, actions may be performed, by persons specially qualified to perform them, in order that, by this means, such persons may enhance their own power. It would be consistent with this way of thinking that the diviner's anomalous use of the left hand should be thought by Banyoro in some measure to enhance his power as a diviner."[41]

Well realizing that neither Needham nor Beattie take their material from Zulu, I suggest that neither the feminine aspect nor the two solutions offered by Beattie would answer issues raised by the presence of inversions among Zulu diviners.

Needham correctly argues that the left hand often is associated with the feminine and that evil also is associated with the left. But it does not follow that as a consequence the left hand side throughout is a symbol of the feminine or of evil. For a symbol requires an interpretation related to its context. Sometimes similar things, acts, colours, etc. are symbols with different meanings in different settings and evaluation of the symbol depends on the context in which it functions. Among Zulu the left hand side is associated with three things: the feminine, evil, and the shades.

Zulu diviners can hardly be classified as 'marginal' people, if by marginal is meant people who are at the border between what is human and non-human, or, as I suggest, one who moves from one age-set within a lineage to another—in this particular case between the age-sets of the survivors and the age-set of the shades. A marginal person would rather be somebody who is on the verge of passing from one age-set to another, e.g. a person about to die.

In Zulu society one would have to define precisely what is visualised when speaking of "non-human, 'mystical' powers", especially when relating such terminology to one so closely attached and associated with the shades as is the diviner. It would not be descriptive of Zulu thought-patterns to refer to the power of the shades as being mystical or non-human, if one thereby isolates the shades from their lineage. For it is in their capacity of being just lineage seniors that the shades exercize power within their lineage.[42]

Lastly, is there indeed a ritual danger in divination? I have raised the question with a number of Zulu diviners. They agree that there is a danger in divination. But the danger is not with the ritual of divination itself. The danger is that of the diviner not being able to listen carefully enough to the shades or understand that which they say to them through their symbols. Sometimes the danger lies in the diviner's inability to maintain the necessary close ties with the shades in order to be able to fulfil his duties. It is for these reasons that the life of a diviner may be regarded as risky. It requires constant abstentions from such things that by many are regarded as luxuries and desireable but which would disassociate a diviner from the shades. To quote an informant on this particular issue: "The difference between a diviner and us is that we eat much, sleep much, and drink much. We talk much gossip. But he eats only certain things in limited quantities, takes *imphepho* and medicines. He does not drink beer, nor does he talk much. But he talks very much at night (i.e. speaks with the shades), not sleeping. This is the difference between them and us."

As far as Zulu diviners are concerned, it would appear correct to associate reversals in the life and work of a diviner with the inversions characteristic of the shades. For diviners are the servants of the shades, called by the shades and very closely associated with them. The shades, in turn, are associated with inversions because they are the inhabitants of the nether world where everything is reversed.

In funerary inversions which form parts of funeral rituals, the deceased is thought to leave his/her old relationships within the age-set, immediate family ties and the upper world. Through the rituals he/she is released from previous bonds, and, in order to avoid the fearfulness of being outside a social engagement in an age-set, the person is incorporated into the next. Expanding on these rituals of reversals, the diviner of uMhlatuze said: "If you bury without these things (i.e. reversals), then you are simply putting the person into the earth like a dog. What will become of him, if nothing is done that will assist him? He just remains there without anything taking place." Another said: "Doing the things that pertain to a funeral is like accompanying a man on the way. If you go with the man, especially if he is going through an unknown land, then you are helping him to find the way. So this is done so that the man may find his way, being on the journey to that place (the nether world)."

B: "How do you know that doing just these things helps the man on the way?"

"You are talking about these things of reversals?"

B: "Yes. In what way do these help a man on his way?"

"They have been revealed."

B: "By whom?"

"By those who know."

B: "Who knows?"

"Those that have been instructed."

B: "Who are they? Could you mention them by name?"

"They are the diviners."

B: "From where did they get the information?"

"It was revealed to them."

"By whom?"

"Those who already are in that place. The ones that they talk to, getting information."

B: "The shades?"

"Those are the ones."

Reversals and Rites of Passage

A. M. Hocart, who has observed that inversions are found elsewhere besides funerals, says that "inversions should not be restricted to death if all ritual is death and rebirth".[43] Relating Hocart's statement to A. van Gennep's contribution on rites of passage at occasions of crisis in life (birth, puberty, marriage and death in particular, but also the coming out of a diviner), one could expect to find reversals at these various occasions.

A Zulu midwife said that if traditional procedure was followed, the navel string of a baby boy ought to be buried in the floor of the hut where the confinement took place, to the left of the hearth seen from the entrance of the hut, and to the right in the case of a girl. She gave as the reason, the hope of long life both for the mother and the child. "They (the shades) see that everything was done nicely, in the proper way. Then they give long life, looking after their children."

Although not applicable to Zulu, there is ethnographic evidence to the effect that a special doorway is sometimes used at puberty rites.[44] One informant said that at the ear-piercing of boys, the patients are instructed to turn their loinskins inside out immediately before the operation, he himself with his mates having done this when they were treated.[45]

M. M. Fuze and D. Leslie state that Zulu bridal parties are expected to arrive at and enter into the bridegroom's home at night.[46] Again, prior to a bride's being accepted fully into the home of her husband a bride walks in front of her new homestead huts. But after the marriage the bride walks behind the huts, which is the normal thing to do.[47] In the important *ukuqhubushela* singing and dancing during which also *ihubo* of the bride's clan is sung, *ikhetho* (bridegroom's party) occupies the left hand side of the lower section of the homestead seen from the main entrance to the home and facing the byre. The bridal party, *umthimba*, will appear on the right hand side of the homestead. The reversal is obvious in that men and women have changed positions in the homestead, the bridegroom being found in the lower left end of the home whereas he otherwise would be expected to occupy himself in the upper right end of it.[48] Records from elsewhere in Africa describe inversions at marriage.[49]

Assuming that van Gennep is correct in arguing that transition takes place through the medium of a death rite in which an individual ritually dies from one stage of life and is born, ritually, into the next, it appears that reversals in connection with birth, puberty, marriage, etc. are rituals through which persons cut off from one age-set are integrated into the next. At least the occasions of crisis of life which, in their rituals, contain reversals are definite experiences of change in the lives of individual Zulu, whereby the foetus becomes the born child, the childless one becomes the parent, the unmarried becomes the married, the child becomes the maturing youth. According to Zulu thought-patterns these are occasions of no small significance, both to the individual and his/her lineage as well as to society as a whole.

Notes

1 Bryant, *The Zulu People*, p. 620, says that the male lies on the left side and the woman on her right. Zulu are emphatic that this is a misconception in Bryant's description of Zulu.

2 *The Collector*, No. 643, p. 113.

3 Kidd, *Savage Childhood*, p. 12.

4 See pp. 276 ff., 278 ff., 281.

5 For a discussion on Nyoro concepts of day and night, dark and light, see Needham, 'Right and Left in Nyoro Symbolic Classification', pp. 433 f. and Beattie, 'Aspects of Nyoro Symbolism', pp. 417 ff.

6 See pp. 281 ff.

7 See pp. 323 ff.

8 Jeffreys, 'Funerary Inversions in Africa'; p. 26.

9 Holleman, 'Die Twee-eenheidsbeginsel in die sosiale en politieke samelewing van die Zulu', pp. 31–75, offers a thorough and convincing description with analysis of Zulu dualistic concepts.

Berglund, Some African Funerary Inversions, accounts for ethnographic records on inversions, opposites, and reversals in Africa.

10 Braadvedt, *Roaming Zululand with a Native Commissioner*, p. 185, and Krige, *SSZ*, p. 161. See also Kidd, *The Essential Kafir*, p. 253.

11 Holden, *The Past and Present of the Kafir Races*, p. 384. Compare also Mac-Donald, 'Manners, Customs, Superstitions and Religions in South African Tribes', p. 275.

12 *The Collector*, No. 529, p. 87.

13 Frostin, 'Korset och Oxhuden', p. 264.

14 See Krige, *SSZ*, pp. 41 f. for description and relationships between *ingqadi* and *ikhohlwa* wives.

15 Bleek, *Zulu Legends*, p. 16.

Turner, *The Lozi Peoples of North-Western Rhodesia*, p. 46, states that at a Lozi funeral skin'cloaks are worn with the hair outside, the reversal of normal fashion.

16 Cf. Krige, *SSZ*, p. 284.

17 Cf. Ludlow, *Zululand and Cetewayo*, p. 146: Norenius, 'Något om zuluernas religiösa föreställningar och bruk', pp. 265 ff.: Also Molema, *The Bantu*, p. 143, and Kidd, *Savage Childhood*, p. 147, which all verify the account recorded.

For comparative material from the lower Congo see Westlind, 'Religiösa begrepp och föreställningar bland kongofolket', p. 59.

See also illustration showing Laduma Madela's concept of the world in Schlosser, *Wandgemälde des Blitz-Zauberers Laduma Madela*, p. 52.

18 Tyler, *Forty Years Among the Zulus*, p. 97.

19 See pp. 90 and 167 f. Straube, 'Gedanken zur Farbensymbolik in Afrikanischen Eingeborenen-Kulturen', argues convincingly that white is associated with the shades and the underworld of the departed. He claims, further, that the opposite of white is red which colour symbolizes this world and its earthly life.

[20] The idea that the shades are white appears to be widespread in Africa. See e.g. Shropshire, 'The Bantu Conception of the Supra-mundane World', p. 64: Lindblom, *Notes Ethnographiques sur le Kavirondo Septentrional*, p. 417: Tylor, *Primitive Culture*, Vol. II, p. 5, quoting Brun-Rollet: Baumann, *Durch Massailand zur Nilquelle*, pp. 80 f.: Pechuel-Loesche, *Volkskunde von Loango*, p. 211: Nassau, 'Spiritual Beings in West Africa', p. 117: Junod, *The Life of a South African Tribe*, Vol. II, p. 350.

[21] See pp. 87 f. and 89 ff.

[22] See p. 101 f.

[23] See also pp. 110 f.

[24] See pp. 174 f. For reversals in Laduma Madela's homestead see Bodenstein and Raum, 'A Present Day Zulu Philosopher', pp. 160–180.

[25] See p. 175.

[26] See p. 175.

[27] See p. 104 f. See also Hunter, *Reaction to Conquest*, p. 498, for a Mpondo parallel.

[28] See p. 152. See also de Jager and Getywa, 'A Xhosa Umhlwayelelo Ceremony in the Ciskei', p. 114, for a Xhosa parallel.

[29] Lugg, *Historic Natal and Zululand*, p. 83.

[30] Krige, *SSZ*, pp. 23 ff.

[31] Krige, *SSZ*, pp. 36 ff.

[32] Bendann, *Death Customs*, pp. 185 f.

[33] Radcliffe-Brown, *The Andamann Islanders*, p. 300.

[34] Radcliffe-Brown, *The Andamann Islanders*, p. 307.

[35] Radcliffe-Brown, *The Andamann Islanders*, p. 307.

[36] Jeffreys, 'Funerary Inversions in Africa', pp. 35–37.

[37] Willoughby, *The Soul of the Bantu*, p. 64, and Willoughby, 'The Bantu Conception of the Soul', p. 346: Rosalind Moss, *Life and Death in Oceania*, p. 39: Kruijt, *Het Animisme in den Indischen Archipel*, p. 380.

[38] Needham, 'Right and Left in Nyoro Symbolic Classification', pp. 436 f.

[39] Beattie, 'Aspects of Nyoro Symbolism', p. 439.

[40] Beattie, 'Aspects of Nyoro Symbolism', pp. 439 f.

[41] Beattie, 'Aspects of Nyoro Symbolism', p. 400. I have bypassed Beattie's presumably conscious oversimplification of the problem when he says that the cowries are thrown with the left hand simply because the diviner's right hand is already occupied, p. 416.

[42] Cf. pp. 253 ff. on power in a clan and lineage.

[43] Hocart, *The Progress of Man*, p. 182. See also van Gennep, *Les Rites des Passage*, chs. IV–VII, and Eliade, *Birth and Rebirth*, ch. 3.

[44] For references to the use of a special doorway at puberty rites see Hoernlé, 'Certain Rites of Transition', pp. 70–73: MacCulloch, 'Door', p. 851.

[45] Krige, *The Realm of a Rain-queen*, p. 119, says that a Lovedu boy wears his loincloth backwards during initiation rites.

[46] Leslie, *Among the Zulus and Amatonga*, p. 195, and Fuze, *Abantu Abanyama*, p. 47.

[47] Braatvedt, 'Zulu Marriage Customs and Ceremonies', p. 563.

[48] Krige, *SSZ*, p. 139 f.

[49] On marriage at night and anti-clockwise movements at the occasion see Murray, 'The Northern Beja', pp. 44 f.

Chapter XI

Conclusion

The rituals and celebrations described in this study have been commented upon by the people among whom the rituals are practised and function. The thought-patterns reflected have, as far as possible, been interpreted as seen by Zulu men and women, the people in whose ranks the rituals have meaning and, therefore, are functional.

The approach in the study has been influenced primarily by a desire to know how Zulu men and women themselves view their life-pattern and its means of expression. Hitherto there has been an abundance of guess-work with assumptions made in terms of evaluating the "primitives", rather than a study of their own understanding of themselves. We have come to realize that our evaluations and understanding of each other demands a respect *for* each other and *of* each other. This pre-supposes a willingness to listen to each other, rather than assuming an understanding which may lack realistic evidence.

No society is static. Zulu society has in the course of two centuries changed through both internal and external pressures acting on it. Internally, the national pride, centred chiefly on the now royal clan, has some of its roots in the nation's history and the achievements of famous Zulu kings. Externally, there is the pressure of Western cultural systems, so different from that of the Zulu. Western pressures have brought to Africa two specific cultural characteristics, viz. a dominating desire to accumulate wealth, and markedly so in the South African setting, colour discrimination. There is also the conscious pressure of Christian missions, pre-occupied with bringing about change in faith and an implementation of Christian principles. Also, particularly among Zulu living south of the Thugela river, there is a distinct influence brought about by the presence of people whose roots were in India. It is evident that these pressures all have influenced Zulu life.

Evidence collected shows very clearly that among Zulu there is a conception of heavenly divinities. There exists today a clear idea of God, quite distinct from a first ancestor and from the shades. If there has been hesitation on the issue previously—early literature seems to suggest this—no Zulu today hesitates to accept and dogmatise on a belief in "God who is in heaven". Although old people still maintain that *uMvelingqangi*, the Lord-of-the-Sky, must be avoided lest one become insane, God has become approachable to the Zulu. His having become available, dogma and rituals related to him are introduced and adjusted to fit into the general patterns descriptive of Zulu. This shows a flexibility which is inclusive and adoptive in character. Professor Monica Wilson convincingly argues that previously "no rituals were celebrated for God, and he was not consistently distinguished from a first ancestor who dwelt beneath". (Monica Wilson, *Religion and Transforma-*

tion of Society, pp. 32 ff.) However, among Zulu today there is definitely the transcendental and vertical worship of the Lord-of-the-Sky, particularly in times of extreme crises. Certainly there is no hesitation whatsoever in regard to his presence in the sky.

The increasingly important role played by the Lord-of-the-Sky in the lives of men and women does not appear to affect the all-important role attributed to the shades. Several issues pertaining to the shades stand out quite clearly. The shades are not worshipped. There is, rather, *ukuthetha amadlozi,* a speaking relationship with the shades. They are the seniors of the lineage, and without communication with them there is a breakdown of normal and harmonious togetherness with them. Without their constant activity and nearness there cannot be a happy future. To the Zulu the shades are in the home and among their descendants. There is no distance to them. Living in the far back of the hut (*umsamo*), in the doorway, in the cattle enclosure, in their descendants, and in the earth, indeed sometimes identified with the earth, they are ever present, revealing themselves mainly through dreams, diviners, and certain omens. It is, therefore, quite natural that people are pre-occupied with the shades and matters related to them. Hence the important role played by diviners in the life of Zulu.

There being basically no difference between still living seniors and the shades of a lineage, both are honoured with ritual beer-drinking and/or ritual slaughtering. Like seniors, the shades are believed to feed in the main hut of a homestead. Evidence shows clearly that, like living seniors, the shades are believed to exercise legitimate anger in support of the moral code of law that lineage survivors are expected to observe. If, therefore, the anger of the shades is indicated as having been brought about by a breach of morals and hence necessitates a ritual celebration, there must be a speaking out, a confession, of evil. Without a revealing of all anger and unexposed ill-feelings, there cannot be an atmosphere of mutual understanding and harmony. And short of mutual trust and restored good relationships, there cannot be an "eating of food together". Ritual celebrations are, primarily, occasions of communion in the full and deepest sense of the word.

When life flows normally, the shades are held at a healthy distance from their survivors, as the Lord-of-the-Sky is kept distant from men. But in times of crises, occasioned by the various interruptions in life that naturally occur in the lives of men and women, it is thought that the shades brood over their descendants as a hen broods over her chickens. This brooding is regarded as most necessary for a good outcome from the crisis. But a prolonged brooding, it is argued, develops into a smothering relationship that leads to insanity. Hence, after the brooding of the shades, one throws off the intimate condition experienced with the shades, exchanging it for a fruitful togetherness and partnership at a healthy distance.

There is also the notion that the world of the shades is the opposite of that of their descendants still living on earth. This belief is expressed in a series of reversals and opposites, noticeable particularly on occasions and in circumstances when the shades are intimately concerned, e.g. with diviners and in divination, at birth, at marriage, and particularly at death and funerals. In the world of the shades dark stands for light and light for dark—hence the shades are active at night, and reveal themselves in a light (or white) complexion, while men are active by day and dark in complexion: the left hand stands for the right hand—hence male diviners occupy the left-hand side of the hut as seen from the doorway and the diviner, even if he is a male, throws the divination bones with the left hand, though in the every-day world it is women who keep to the left: up stands for down—hence diviners claim to see things upside-down, and the shades are thought to move in the underworld as do flies on ceilings of modern homes: bitterness stands for sweetness—hence the shades' delight in the gall of a slaughtered beast.

Two further opposites are, firstly, difference in sex, male and female being regarded as complementary to each other and necessary for the upholding of life; and, secondly, good as opposed to evil. Zulu ideas about witchcraft and sorcery are a reply to the presence of evil in the world. Annihilation is the reverse of well-being and fertility. While the shades stand for prosperity and future, witches and sorcerers stand for destruction and a general break-down of good order, with the ultimate end annihilation. Thought-patterns on witchcraft and sorcery are nothing short of recognition of evil and its reality among men: a denial of them is regarded as a denial of the presence of evil. Because of the experience of evil in the lives of Zulu and their dogmas about it, there is a very lively preoccupation with fertility and health.

It is immoral anger, rooted in jealousy, slander, suspicion, envy, and quarrels, that expresses itself practically in *ubuthakathi*, witchcraft and/or sorcery. Salvation from anger within is through speaking out, confession, of what is within one. Because of the very great importance attached to witch-craft and sorcery, society offers opportunities when anger or its preliminaries may be revealed in confessions and expressions of goodwill which lead to restored good and harmonious conditions.

Four issues related to the understanding of symbols have emerged in the study. Firstly, a symbol and its interpretation must be seen in relation to the context in which that symbol is found. In one instance water is a cleans-ing and purifying symbol, as is the case in the ritual of *ukuphalaza:* in another it is the symbol of origin and birth, as in the coming out of a diviner: in another it is equated with male fluid and stands for the masculine and the shades. And further, herbalists and heaven-herds who treat people and/or homesteads by blowing out medicines mixed with water on them, *ukukhwifa* or *ukuchinsa,* use water and the ritual of blowing out as symbols of healing and protection. Spitting is the expulsion of anger in a man and so is a symbol of innocence. But it is also a symbol of a curse or of disgust. Spittle can stand for either male fluid and thus be equated with fertility and life, or be poison directed against life and represent destruction. Which it is depends on the context in which it is used. Practical experience while collecting material for this book has shown abundantly how careful one must be when talking about symbols and attempting an exegesis.

Secondly, in a society such as that of the Zulu, symbols appear to remain similar though not necessarily identical. Throughout the country Zulu feel a need to symbolise the corpse with stones at funerals. For "dead people are like stones". In areas where stones are available, these are used, although there does not appear to be any particular type of stone in demand for the symbol of the corpse. But in regions where stones are not available, sods of earth are used, and, sometimes, chips from calabashes. With the introduction of bricks, these have been used on a limited number of occasions (Ekuthuleni and Ceza). Whether chips from clay vessels, or sods of earth, or bricks were used, these were very clearly associated with stones.

Similarly, heaven-herds use different methods to symbolise the crack of lightning, sometimes feathers from the wings of Terathopius ecaudatus, sometimes the sound produced by hitting one stone against another. To typify lightning one heaven-herd used milk from a white-coloured cow, another a glistening white ore, and a third the spark produced by throwing one stone onto another. Careful examination of the three heaven-herds revealed a wide variety of medicines used, but there was an amazing similarity in thought-patterns and in what it was deemed essential to symbolize.

Thirdly, evidence shows quite clearly that the importance ascribed to a symbol often outweighs the attention given the materia which carries the symbol. This applies particularly in symbols related to medicines and healing. Zulu believe that one of the three channels of power is that which is enveloped in materia. (The other two are the Lord-of-the-Sky and the clan lineage.) No doubt the experience of generations and personal experimentation has taught herbalists that the properties of certain *imithi*, materia, produce favourable reactions on their patients. Such treatments, therefore, become fixed. But where this experience is lacking, the tendency is that the symbol outweighs the value given the materia. To heaven-herds it was irrelevant whether the blackness of thunder-clouds was symbolised by soot or by chips from black stones; far more important than the materia used was the facial expression and a symbol typifying blackness. Because a python sometimes stands for togetherness, its fat is used to cure people whose thoughts tend to stray. Talkative people are treated with sheep's tongue, not because a sheep's tongue in itself has the ability to cure the ailment but because sheep are symbols of quietness. Fear in men is cured with flesh of a bull because bulls stand for fearlessness.

Lastly, symbols found among Zulu and interpreted by Zulu in a particular manner, have parallels elsewhere in Africa. Confession of anger accompanied by spitting or blowing out of water to express forgiveness, or as symbols of ridding oneself of suspicion, anger and tension; these are the symbols used by Nyakyusa for the same purpose (Cf. Monica Wilson, *Religion and the Transformation of Society*, pp. 28 f.). Snakes, fire and water are symbols of sex and fertility, whilst the python "is a symbol of ultimate power down the eastern side of Africa from the Sudan to the Cape" (Monica Wilson, ibid., p. 57). These, and many further examples, illustrate that in a family of languages such as that of Bantu-speaking Africa, there is a continuity of symbolism. This continuity does not, however, of necessity imply the same emphasis everywhere.

It was Ruth Benedict who first pointed out that a society has interests and orientation which give that particular society its specific configuration or pattern (Ruth Benedict, *Patterns of Culture*. See also Margaret Mead, *Sex and Temperament*). Zulu society has its specific pattern, distinct to a greater or lesser degree from the patterns of neighbouring Nguni societies (Swazi, Mpondo, Thembu, Bhaca and Xhosa). Comparison of experience among Zulu with descriptions of other Nguni societies reveal certain differences. But on the whole rituals, symbols and thought-patterns are remarkably similar within the Nguni family; frequently they are identical. This is true particularly in regard to major issues such as those that involve the shades, health and well-being, evil and its expressions, and the overall world view. It is mainly in the details and the localised issues that the specific Zulu configurations have been noticeable. These have often been conditioned by geographical and historic facts, and, consequently, become that which is specifically and particularly just Zulu.

Abbreviations

A Africa (London)
AA American Anthropologist (Menasha, Wisconsin)
AeA Afrique et Asie (Paris)
AER African Ecclesiastical Review (Masaka, Uganda)
Af.Af. African Affairs (London)
AJC The American Journal of Sociology (Chicago)
An Anthropos (Wien)
ANM Annals of the Natal Museum (Pietermaritzburg)
ANN Africana Notes and News (Johannesburg)
AS African Studies (Johannesburg)
AQ Anthropological Quarterly
ATMP Annals of Tropical Medicine and Parasitology (Liverpool)
AV Archiv für Völkerkunde (Wien)
BAGS Bulletin of the American Geographical Society
Bryant, *Dict.*, Bryant, A. T., *A Zulu-English Dictionary* (Mariannhill 1905).
BS Bantu Studies (Johannesburg)
Doke–Vilakazi, *Dict.*, Doke, C. M. and Vilakazi, B. W., *Zulu-English Dictionary* (Johannesburg 1949).
E Ethnology
EA The Eastern Anthropologist (Luchnow)
ERE Encyclopaedia of Religion and Ethics (Edinburgh)
ESA The Ethnographical Survey of Africa (London)
FKL Folk-Lore (London)
FL Folk-Lore (Cape Town)
GA Geneve—Afrique (Geneve)
HAS Harvard African Studies (Cambridge, Mass.)
IJVS Innsbrucher Jahrbuch für Völkerkunde und Sprachwissenschaft (Innsbruck)
IRM International Review of Mission (London)
JAS Journal of the African Society (London)
JCR Journal of Conflict Resolution (Ann Arbor)
JRA Journal of Religion in Africa (Leiden)
JRAI The Journal of the Royal Anthropological Institute (London).
JSI Journal of Social Issues (Ann Arbor, Michigan)
JPS The Journal of Social Psychology
M Man (London)
NADA The Southern Rhodesia Native Affairs Department Annual (Salisbury).
NH Natural History: The Journal of the American Museum of Natural History (New York)
NTJ Native Teachers' Journal (Pietermaritzburg)
P Paideuma (Frankfurt a. M.)
RSA Report on the South African Association for the Advancement of Science (Cape Town)
SAAB South African Archeological Bulletin (Cape Town)
SAFJ South African Folklore Journal (Cape Town)
SAJS South African Journal of Science (Cape Town)
SAMJ South African Medical Journal (Johannesburg)
SG Studium Generale (Berlin, Göttingen and Heidelberg)
SJA Southwestern Journal of Anthropology
SKMT Svenska Kyrkans Missions Tidning (Uppsala)
SMT Svensk Missionstidskrift (Uppsala)

SN Santa News (Johannesburg)
SSZ Krige, Eileen Jensen, *The Social System of the Zuluz* (Pietermaritzburg 1936)
TDR Tillkomme Ditt Rike: Svenska Kyrkans Missions Årsbok (Uppsala)
Th Theoria (Durban)
Z Zaire
ZE Zeitschrift für Ethnologie (Berlin)

Bibliography

Abrahamsson, H., *The Origin of Death* (Uppsala 1951).

Anell, B., and Lagercrantz, S., *Geophagical Customs* (Uppsala 1958).

Asmus, G., *Die Zulu* (Essen 1939).

Barker, Lady, *A Year's Housekeeping in South Africa* (London 1879).

Barter, Charlotte, *Alone Among the Zulus* (London, SPCK, n. d.).

Bartels, M., 'Die Würfelzauber Südafrikanischen Völker' (*ZE*, 1903, pp. 344–348).

Baumann, H., 'Nyama die Rachemacht: Über einige mana-artige Vorstellungen in Afrika' (*P*, Vol. 4, 1950, pp. 191–230).

— *Schöpfung und Urzeit des Menschen im Mythus der Afrikanischen Völker* (Berlin 1936).

Baumann, O., *Durch Massailand zur Nilquelle* (Berlin 1894).

Beattie, J., 'Aspects of Nyoro Symbolism' (*A*, Vol. 38, 1968, pp. 413–442).

Becken, H.-J., *Am Buschbockfluss: Die Speer der Ahnen* (Hermannsburg 1961).

Beemer, Hilda, 'The Swazi Rain Ceremony' (*BS*, Vol. 9, 1935, pp. 273–281). (See also Kuper, Hilda).

Beidelman, T. O., 'Pig (Guluwe): an essay on Ngulu sexual symbolism and ceremony' (*SJA*, Vol. 20, 1964, pp. 359–392).

— 'Right and Left among the Kaguru: a note on symbolic classification' (*A*, Vol. 31, 1961, pp. 250–257).

— 'Three Tales of the Living and the Dead' (*JRAI*, Vol. 94, pp. 109–137).

Bendann, E., *Death Customs* (London 1930).

Benedict, Ruth, *Patterns of Culture* (London 1935).

Berglund, A.-I., 'African Concepts of Health, Sickness and Healing (In *The Healing Ministry of the Church*, Miss. Inst., Lutheran Theol. College, Mapumulo, 1967, pp. 37–50).

— 'Church and Culture Change in a Zulu Tribal Community' (In *Lux Mundi*, No. 3, Pretoria).

— 'Fasting and Cleansing Rites' (In *Concepts of Death and Funeral Rites*, Miss. Inst, Luth. Theol. College, Mapumulo, 1969, 101–116).

— 'Rituals of an African Zionist Church' (African Studies Programme, Occasional Paper No. 3, 1967, Johannesburg).

— Some African Funerary Inversions (Unpublished Thesis, Uppsala 1957).

Bews, J. W., 'List of Zulu Plant Names' (*ANM*, Vol. 4, 1919–1923, pp. 455–467).

Binns, C. T., *Dinuzulu* (London 1968).

Birkby, C., *Native Life in South Africa* (Pretoria 1956).

Bleek, Wm. H. I., *Zulu Legends* (Pretoria 1952).

Bodenstein, W., and Raum, O. F., 'A Present Day Zulu Philosopher' (*A*, Vol. 30, 1960, pp. 166–181).

Braatvedt, H. P., *Roaming Zululand with a Native Commissioner* (Pietermaritzburg 1949).

— 'Zulu Marriage Customs and Ceremonies' (*SAJS*, Vol. 24, 1927, pp. 553–565).

Braatvedt, N., *Erindringer fra mitt misjonsliv* (Stavanger 1930).

Brown, J. T., *Among the Bantu Nomads* (London 1926).

Brownlee, Ch., 'A Fragment on Xhosa Religious Beliefs' (*AS*, Vol. 14, 1955, pp. 37–41).

Bryant, A. T., A Series of Public Lectures at the University of Witwatersrand (In Killie Campbell Library, Marriott Road, Durban. Series 21073).

— *A Zulu-English Dictionary* (Mariannhill, 1905).

— *Olden Times in Zululand and Natal* (London 1929).

— 'Some Aspects of Zulu Social Life' (*NTJ*, April 1920, pp. 102–107).

— 'The Religion of the Zulus' (*NTJ*, Jan. 1920, pp. 44–50).

— 'The Zulu Cult of the Dead' (*M*, Vol. 17, 1917, pp. 140–145).

— *The Zulu People* (Pietermaritzburg 1949).

— *Zulu Medicine and Medicine-men* (Cape Town 1966).

Bullock, C., *The Mashona* (Cape Town 1927).

Burgess, A., *Unkulunkulu in Zululand* (Minneapolis, 1934).

Callaway, H., *Izinganekwane: Nursery Tales, Traditions, and History of the Zulus.* (London 1868).

— *The Religious System of the Amazulu* (London 1870).

Carbutt, Mrs. E. G., 'Some Minor Superstitions and Customs of the Zulus connected with Children' (*FL*, Vol. 2, 1880, pp. 10–13).

Chinyandura, 'Spirit Cattle (Ngombe yoMudzimu)' (*NADA*, Vol. 16, 1939, pp. 92–93).

Coertze, P. J., *Dolosgooiery in Suid-Afrika* (An. Univ. Stellenbosch, 1931).

Colenso, J. W., *Ten Weeks in Natal* (Cambridge 1855).

— *Zulu-English Dictionary* (Pietermaritzburg 1861).

Collector, The, (ed. W. Wanger, Marriannhill, 1911–1913).

Cope, J., *The Rainmaker* (London 1971).

Cory, G. E. (ed.), *The Diary of the Rev. Francis Owen, Missionary with Dingaan in 1837–1838* (Cape Town 1926).

Dammann, E., 'A Tentative Philological Typology of some African High Deities' (*JRA*, Vol. 2, 1969, pp. 81–95).

Dart, R. A., 'The Ritual Employment of Bored Stones by Transvaal Bantu Tribes' (*SAAB*, Vol. 3, 1948, pp. 61–66).

Delegorgue, A. M., *Voyage dans l'Afrique Australe, Vol I and II*, (Paris 1847).

Doke, C. M., and Vilakazi, B. W., *Zulu-English Dictionary* (Johannesburg 1948).

Dornan, S. S., 'Divination and Divining Bones' (*SAJS*, Vol. 20, 1923, pp. 504–511).

Douglas, Mary, 'Animals in Lele Religious Symbolism' (*A*, Vol. 27, 1957, pp. 46–58).

— *Purity and Danger* (London 1966).

— 'Social and Religious Symbolism of the Lele of the Kasai (*Z*, Vol. 9, 1955, pp. 385–402).

— 'The Lele of Kasai' (In *African Worlds*, ed. by D. Forde, London 1954, pp. 1–26).

Duggan-Cronin, A. M., *The Bantu Tribes of South Africa, Vol. III, Section III, The Zulu with an Introductory article on the Zulu* by D. McK. Malcolm (Cambridge 1938).

Döhne, J. L., *A Zulu—Kafir Dictionary* (London 1857).

Eiselen, W. M., 'The Art of Divination as Practiced by the Bamasemola' *BS*, Vol. 6, 1932, pp. 1–29 and 251–263).

Eiselen, W. M. and Schapera, I., 'Religious Beliefs and Practices' (In *The Bantu-Speaking Tribes of South Africa*, ed. I. Schapera, London 1953).

Eliade, M., *Birth and Rebirth* (New York 1958).

Evans-Pritchard, E. E., *Witchcraft, Oracles and Magic among the Azande* (Oxford 1937).

Farrer, J. A., *Zululand and the Zulus* (London 1879).

Faye, C., *Zulu References* (Pietermaritzburg 1923).

Fernandez, J. W., *Divinations, Confessions, Testimonies—Zulu Confrontation with the Social Superstructure* (Occasional Paper No. 9, Inst. for Social Research, Durban, 1967).

Fortes, M., 'Some Reflections on Ancestor Worship in Africa' (In Fortes, M. and Dieterlen, G., *African Systems of Thought*, pp. 122–142, London 1965).

Fristedt, F. L., *Tjugofem År i Sydafrika* (Lund 1905).

Fritsch, G., *Die Eingeborenen Süd-Afrikas* (Breslau 1872).

Froelich, J. C., 'Sorciers et Magiciens: question de mots' (*AeA*, Vol. 83/84, 1968, pp. 74–79).

Frostin, Signe, 'Korset och Oxhuden' (*SKMT*, No. 19, 1957, 264–266).

Fuze, M. M., *Abantu Abamnyama, lapa bavela ngakona* (Pietermaritzburg 1922).

Fynn, H. F., *The Diary of Henry Francis Fynn* (Pietermaritzburg 1950). (See Stuart, J. and Malcolm, D. MacC.)

Gardiner, A., *Narrative of a Journey to the Zoolu Country in South Africa* (London 1836).

Gennep, van, A., *Les Rites de Passage* (Paris 1909).

Gibson, J. Y., *The Story of the Zulus* (London 1911).

Gluckman, M., *Custom and Conflict in Africa* (Oxford 1955).
— 'Mortuary Customs among the South Eastern Bantu' (*BS*, Vol. 11, 1937, pp. 117–136).
— *Order and Rebellion in Tribal Africa* (London 1963).
— 'Social Aspects of First Fruit Ceremonies among the South-Eastern Bantu' (*A*, Vol. 11, 1938, pp. 25–41).
— 'Some Processes of Social Change Illustrated from Zululand' (*AS*, Vol. 1, 1942, pp. 243–260).
— 'Zulu Women in Hoecultural Ritual' (*BS*, Vol. 9, 1935, pp. 255–271).
Goody, Esther, 'Legitimate and Illegitimate Aggression in a West African State' (In *Witchcraft, Confessions and Accusations*, ed. Mary Douglas, London 1970, pp. 207–244).
Gordon, W. R., 'Izindaba zaMahlozi, Words about Spirits' (*FL*, Vol. 2, 1880, pp. 100–103).
Griaule, M., *Conversations with Ogotemmeli* (Oxford 1965).
Grout, L., *Zululand; or, Life Among the Zulu-Kafirs of Natal and Zululand, South Africa* (Philadelphia 1864).
Hammond-Tooke, W. D., *Bhaca Society* (Oxford 1962).
— 'Some Bhaca Religious Categories' (*AS*, Vol. 19, 1960, pp. 1–13).
— 'The Initiation of a Bhaca Isangoma Diviner' (*AS*, Vol. 14, 1955, pp. 17–21).
Hartland, E. S., 'Travel Notes in South Africa' (*FKL*, Vol. 17, 1906, pp. 472–487).
H. M. G. J., 'Odds and Ends of Matabele Customs and Customary Law' (*NADA*, 1928, pp. 7–10).
Hocart, A. M., *The Progress of Man* (London 1933).
Hochegger, H., 'Die Vorstellungen von Seele und Totengeist bei Afrikanischen Völkern' (*An*, Vol. 60, 1965, pp. 273–339).
Hoernlé, A. Winifred, 'Certain Rites of Transition and the conception of !Nau among the Hottentots' (*HAS*, Vol. 2, 1918, pp. 65–82).
— 'The Importance of the Sib in the Marriage Ceremonies of the South Eastern Bantu' (*SAJS*, Vol. 22, 1925, pp. 481–492).
Hoffman, von, C., 'Witchcraft Among the Zulus' (*NH*, Vol. 35, 1935, pp. 3–16).
Holden, W. C., *The Past and Future of the Kafir Races* (London 1871).
Holleman, J. F., 'Die Twee-eenheidsbeginsel in die Sosiale en Politieke Samelewing van die Zulu' (*BS*, Vol. 14, 1940, pp. 31–75).
Hollis, A. C., *The Masai* (Oxford 1905).
Holub, E., *Sieben Jahre in Süd-Afrika, Vol. I and II* (Wien 1881).
Hughes, A. J. B. and van Velsen, J., 'The Ndebele' (In *The Shona and Ndebele of Southern Rhodesia*, by Kuper, Hilda, Hughes, A. J. B. and van Velsen, J., Ethnographic Survey of Africa, London 1955).
Hulme, Mairn, *Wild Flowers of Natal* (Pietermaritzburg 1954).
Hunter, Monica, *Reaction to Conquest* (London 1936).
— (See also Wilson, Monica).
Isaacs, N., *Travels and Adventures in Eastern Africa, Vol. I and II* (London 1836).
Jackson, C. G., 'Native Superstition and Crime' (*SAJS*, Vol. 13, 1917, pp. 251–263).
Jager, de, E. J. and Gitywa, V. Z., 'A Xhosa Umhlwayelelo Ceremony in the Ciskei' (*AS*, Vol. 22, 1963, pp. 109–116).
Jeffreys, M. D. W., 'Confessions by Africans' (*EA*, Vol. 6, 1952, pp. 42–57).
— 'Funerary Inversions in Africa' (*AV*, Vol. 3–4, 1948–49, pp. 24–31).
— 'Lobolo is Child-price' (*AS*, Vol. 10, 1951, pp. 145–184).
Jenkinson, Th. B., *Amazulu. The Zulus, their Past History, Manners, Customs, and Language* (London 1884).
Joest, W., 'Reise in Afrika im Jahre 1883' (*ZE*, Vol. 17, 1885, pp. 472–487).
Jordan, A. C., *Ingqumbo Yeminyanya* (Lovedale 1946).
Junge, D., 'Im Zululande. Aus Geschichte und Religion' (In *Und die Vögel des Himmels wohnen unter seinen Zweigen*, ed. W. Wickert, Hermannsburg 1949, pp. 110–124).
Junod, H. A., 'Some Features of the Religion of the Ba-Venda' (*SAJS*, Vol. 17, 1921, pp. 207–220).
— *The Life of a South African Tribe, Vol. I and II* (Neuchatel, 1913).
— 'The Magic Conception of Nature amongst Bantus' (*SAJS*, Vol. 17, 1920, pp. 76–85).

— 'The Sacrifice of Reconciliation Amongst the Ba-Ronga' (*SAJS*, Vol. 7, 1911, pp. 179–182).

— 'The Theory of Witchcraft Amongst South African Natives' (*RSA*, 1905/6, pp. 230–241).

Junod, H.-P., 'Essai sur les notions fondamentales de la pensée africaine bantoue' (*GA*, Vol. 7, 1968, pp. 83–90).

Kay, S., *Travels and Researches in Caffraria* (London 1833).

Keen, P., *Western Medicine and the Witchdoctor* (ISMA Publication, Johannesburg, n.d.).

Kenyatta, J., *Facing Mount Kenya: The Tribal Life of the Gikuyu* (London 1938).

Kidd, D., *Savage Childhood* (London 1906).

— *The Essential Kafir* (London 1904).

Kohler, M., 'Die Krankengeschichte eines Zulu-kaffern' (*An*, Vol. 26, 1931, pp. 585–593).

— *The Izangoma Diviners* (Pretoria 1941).

Kopytoff, I., 'Ancestors as Elders in Africa' (*A*, Vol. 41, 1971, pp. 129–142).

Kranz, M., *Natur- und Kulturleben der Zulus* (Wiesbaden 1880).

Krauss, F., 'The Zulu' (translated and edited by O. H. Spohr and A. W. Crowhurst, *ANN*, Vol. 18, No. 5, 1969, pp. 201–220).

Krige, Eileen Jensen, 'Girls' Puberty Songs and their Relation to Fertility, Health, Morality and Religion among the Zulu' (*A*, Vol. 38, 1968, pp. 173–198).

— *The Social System of the Zulus* (Pietermaritzburg 1936).

Krige, Eileen Jensen and J. D., *The Realm of a Rain-queen* (London 1943).

Krige, J. D., 'The Social Function of Witchcraft' (*Th*, 1947, pp. 8–21).

Kropf, A., *A Kaffir English Dictionary* (Lovedale 1899).

Kruijt, A. C., *Het Animisme in den Indischen Archipel* (Gravenhage 1906).

Kück, H., 'Annual Festival of the Zulus' (*SAFJ*, Vol. I, 1876).

Kuper, Hilda, *An African Aristocracy* (Oxford 1947).

— *The Swazi: A South African Kingdom* (New York 1963).

— (See also Beemer, Hilda).

Lagercrantz, S., *African Methods of Fire-Making* (Uppsala 1954).

— *Contribution to the Ethnography of Africa* (Uppsala 1950).

— (See also Anell, B., and Lagercrantz, S.).

Laubscher, B. J. F., *Sex, Custom and Psychopathology* (2nd ed., London 1951).

Laydevant, F., 'The Praises of the Divining Bones among the Basotho' (*BS*, Vol. 7, 1933, pp. 341–373).

Lee, A. W., *Once Dark Country* (London 1949).

Lee, S. G., 'Social Influences in Zulu Dreaming' (*JSP*, Vol. 47, 1958, pp. 265–283).

— 'Spirit Possession Among the Zulu' (In *Spirit Mediumship and Society in Africa*, ed. J. Beattie and J. Middleton, London 1969).

Leinhardt, Y., *Divinity and Experience* (Oxford 1961).

Leslie, D., *Among the Zulus and Amatongas* (ed. by W. H. Drummond, London 1875).

Levine, D. N., 'The Flexibility of Traditional Culture' (*JSI*, Vol. 24, 1968, pp. 124–141).

Le Vine, R. A., 'Witchcraft and Co-wife Proximity in South-western Kenya' (*E*, Vol. I, 1962, pp. 39–45).

Lévy-Bruhl, L., *The 'Soul' of the Primitive* (London, 1965).

Liljestrand, A., 'Något om zulufolkets samfundslif och husliga lif' (In Liljestrand, A., and Hallendorf, K., *Zulufolket och Zulumissionen*, Uppsala 1930, pp. 9–30).

Lindblom, G., *Notes Ethnographiques sur le Kavirondo Septentrional* (Tucuman, 1932).

Livingstone, D. and Ch., *Narrative of an Expedition to the Zambezi and its Tributaries* (London 1865).

Ludlow, W. R., *Zululand and Cetewayo* (London 1882).

Lugg, H. C., *Historic Natal and Zululand* (Pietermaritzburg 1949).

— 'The Practice of Lobolo in Natal' (*AS*, Vol. 4, 1945, pp. 23–27).

MacCulloch, J. A., 'Abode of the Blest' (*ERE*, Vol. 2, pp. 680–687).

— 'Door' (*ERE*, Vol. 4, pp. 846–852).

— 'State of the Dead' (*ERE*, Vol. II, pp. 817–828).

MacDonald, J., 'Manners, Customs, Superstitions, and Religions of South African Tribes' (*JRAI*, Vol. 19, 1890, pp. 264–296 and Vol. 20, 1891, pp. 113–140).

MacKenzie, Anna, *Mission Life Among the Zulu Kafirs—Memorials of Henrietta Robertson* (Cambridge 1866).

Makhathini, D. D. L., Ancestors, Umoya, Angels (In *Our Approach to the Independent Church Movement in South Africa,* Missiological Inst., Luth. Theol. College, Mapumulo, 1965, pp. 154–159).

Malcolm, D. McK., 'The Zulu' with introductory article by . . . See Duggan-Cronin.

— 'Zulu Literature' (*A,* Vol. 19, 1949, pp. 33–39).

Marwick, B. A., *The Swazi* (Cambridge).

Marwick, M. G., 'African Witchcraft and Anxiety Load' (*Th, 1948, pp. 115–129*).

Matthews, J. W., *Incwadi Yami* (London 1887).

Mayr, F., 'The Zulu Kafirs of Natal' (*An,* Vol. 1, 1906, pp. 453–472).

Mbatha, Ph., Witchcraft and Ancestor-Worship (*The Net,* London, August 1955 pp. 18–20).

Mbiti, J. S., *Concepts of God in Africa* (London 1970).

— *African Religion and Philosophy* (London 1969).

McCord, J. B., 'The Zulu Witchdoctor and Medicine Man' (*SAJS,* Vol. 15, 1919, pp. 306–324).

Mdladla, M. E., 'Ukohlonipha kwabantu nemikhuba esikelene nako' (*NTJ,* Vol. 13, July, 1934, pp. 164–167, and Oct. 1934, pp. 46–49).

Mead, Margaret, *Sex and Temperament* (London 1935).

Merensky, A., *Beiträge zur Kenntniss Südafrikas* (Berlin 1875).

Middleton, J., *Myth and Cosmos* (New York, 1967).

Middleton, J., and Winter, E. H., (ed.), *Witchcraft and Sorcery in East Africa* (London 1963).

Mofolo, Th., *Chaka, An Historical Romance* (London 1931).

Mohr, E., *To Victoria Falls of the Zambezi* (London 1876).

Molema, S. M., *The Bantu, Past and Present* (Edinburgh 1920).

Moore, R. O., 'God and Man in Bantu Religions: the theories of Malinowski and of Durkheim and two points of Bantu Religion' (*AER,* Vol. 9, 1967, pp. 149–160).

Moss, Rosalind, *Life after Death in Oceania and the Malay Archipelago* (Oxford 1925).

Murray, G. W., 'The Northern Beja' (*JRAI,* Vol. 57, 1927, pp. 39–53).

Nassau, R. H., 'Spiritual Beings in West Africa: Their Classes and Functions' (*BAGS,* Vol. 35, 1903, pp. 115–124).

Ndamase, V. P., *Ama-Pondo Ibali ne-Ntlalo* (Lovedale, n.d.).

Needham, R., 'Right and Left in Nyoro Symbolic Classification' (*A,* Vol. 37, 1967, pp. 425–452).

Nieuwenhuijsen, van, J. W., 'The Witchdoctor Institution in a Zulu Tribe' (*SN,* Vol. 7, No. 3, 1968, pp. 4–5).

Norbeck, E., 'African Rituals of Conflict' (*AA,* Vol. 65, 1963, pp. 1 254–1 279).

Norenius, J. E., *Bland Zuluer och Karanger, Vols. I and II* (Stockholm 1924).

— 'Izanusi' (*TDR,* No. 7, 1912, pp. 34–48).

— *Izita Zohlanga* (Dundee, Natal, 1908).

— 'Något om magi och annan vidskepelse bland zuluerna' (*TDR,* Vol. 12, 1917, pp. 57–86).

— 'Något om zuluernas religiösa föreställningar och bruk' (*SMT,* Vol. 1, 1913, pp. 97–107 and Vol. 2, 1914, pp. 263–282).

— 'Något om zuluernas stammar och hövdingar' (*TDR,* Vol. 23, 1928, pp. 34–58).

Pechüel-Loesche, E., *Volkskunde von Loango* (Stuttgart 1907).

Pettazoni, R., *Dio* (Rome 1922).

Pheko, S. E. M., *African Religion Rediscovered* (Bulawayo 1965).

Pettersson, O., *Chiefs and Gods* (Lund 1953).

Plant, R., *The Zulu in Three Tenses* (Pietermaritzburg 1905).

Radcliffe-Brown, A. R., *The Andamann Islanders* (Cambridge 1933).

— *Structure and Function in Primitive Society* (London 1952).

Raum, O. F., 'The Interpretation of the Nguni First Fruits Ceremony' (*P,* Vol. 13, 1967, pp. 148–163).

Reader, D. H., *Zulu Tribe in Transition* (Manchester 1966).

Richards, Audrey, *Chisungu* (London 1956).

Rigby, P., 'Dual Symbolic Classification among the Gogo of Central Tanzania' (*A,* Vol. 36, 1966, pp. 1–17).

— 'Some Gogo Rituals of Purification (In *Dialectic in Practical Religion*, ed. by E. R. Leach, Cambridge 1968).

Roberts, Ester L., Shembe, the Man and his Work (Unpublished MA Thesis, University of South Africa, 1936).

Roberts, N., 'A few notes on "To Kolo", a system of divination practiced by the superior natives of Malaboch's Tribe in Northern Transvaal' (*SAJS*, Vol. 11, 1915, pp. 367–370).

Rose, B. W., 'African and European Magic: A First Comparative Study of Beliefs and Practices' (*AS*, Vol. 23, 1964, pp. 1–9).

Ross, G. P. A., 'A Fictitious Native Disease—Isigwebedla' (*ATMP*, Vol. 7, 1913, pp. 371–376).

Sahlins, M. D., *Tribesmen* (Foundations of Modern Anthropology Series, Prentice-Hall, New Jersey, 1968).

Samuelson, Miss L. H., 'Some Zulu Customs' (*JAS*, Vol. 10, 1910/1911, pp. 191–199).

— *Some Zulu Customs and Folk-lore* (London 1912).

— *Zululand, its Traditions, Legends, Customs and Folk-Lore* (Mariannhill 1930).

Samuelson, R. C., *Long, Long, Ago* (Durban 1929).

Sawyer, H., *God: Ancestor or Creator?* (London 1970).

Sayce, R. U., 'Lightning Charms from Natal' (*M*, Vol. 26, 1926, pp. 69–70).

Schapera, I., 'Sorcery and Witchcraft in Bechuanaland' (*Af.Af.*, Vol. 51, 1952, pp. 41–52).

Schebesta, P., 'uNkulunkulu' (*A*, Vol. 16/17, 1921–1922, pp. 525–526).

Schimlek, F., *Mariannhill. A Study in Bantu Life and Missionary Effort* (Mariannhill, Natal, 1953).

Schlosser, Katesa, *Wandgemälde des Blitz-Zauberers Laduma Madela* (Kiel 1971).

— 'Die Ahnen des Blitz-Zauberers Laduma Madela' (In *Christiana Albertina*, Kieler Universitäts-Zeitschrift, Part 10, Neumünster 1970).

— 'Zulu Mythology as Told and Illustrated by the Zulu Lightning Doctor Laduma Madela' (In *Proceedings of the VIIIth International Congress of Anthropological and Ethnological Sciences*, Vol. III, pp. 76 ff., Tokyo and Kyoto 1968).

— *Zauberei im Zululand — Manuskripte des Blitz-Zauberers Laduma Madela* (Kiel (1972).

Schmidt, W., *Der Ursprung der Gottesidee, Vols. I–VII* (Münster in W. 1912–1949).

Schoeman, P. J., 'The Swazi Rain Ceremony' (*BS*, Vol. 9, 1935, pp. 169–177).

Scriba, F., 'Die Naturerscheinungen im Glauben der Zulu' (*Die Eiche*, Beilage 3, Printed Moorleigh, Natal, 1948).

— 'Hexenwesen bei den Zulu' (*Die Eiche*, Beilage 24, n.d., printed as above).

Scotch, N. A., 'Magic, sorcery and football among urban Zulu: a case of reinterpretation under acculturation' (*JCR*, Vol. 5, 1961, pp. 70–74).

Shaw, W., *The Story of my Mission in South-Eastern Africa* (London 1860).

Shooter, J., *The Kafirs of Natal and the Zulu Country* (London 1857).

Shropshire, D., 'The Bantu Conception of the Supra-mundane World' (*JAS*, Vol. 30, 1931, pp. 58–68).

Sibeko, A. Violet, 'Imilingo nemithi yokwelapha yaBantu' (*NTJ*, Vol. 11, 1932, pp. 197–203 and pp. 244–253).

Sicard, H. von, 'The Hakata Names' (*NADA*, Vol. 36, 1959, pp. 26–29).

Sikakana, J. M. A., Review of *Zulu Woman* (*AS*, Vol. 9, 1950, p. 97).

Speckmann, F., *Die Hermannsburger Mission in Afrika* (Hermannsburg, 1876).

Stayt, H. A., *The Bavenda* (London 1931).

Straube, H., 'Gedanken zur Farbensymbolik in afrikanischen Eingeborenen-Kulturen' (*SG*, Vol. 13, 1960, pp. 391–418).

Stuart, J., *uKulumetule* (London 1925).

— *uBaxoxele* (London 1924).

— *Kwe Sukela* (London 1926).

— *uTulasizwe* (London 1923).

— *uVusezakiti* (London 1934).

— *Zulu Proverbs and Popular Sayings with Translation* (ed. by D. McK. Malcolm, Publ. by T. W. Griggs & Co., Durban, n.d.).

Stuart, J. and Malcolm, D. McK., (ed.), *The Diary of Henry Francis Fynn* (Pietermaritzburg 1950).

Studhardt, J. G., 'A Collection of Zulu Proverbs' (*NADA*, Vol. 8, 1930, pp. 62–69).

Sundkler, B. G. M., *Bantu Prophets in South Africa* (London 1948).

Swantz, Marja-Liisa, *Ritual and Symbol in Transitional Zaramo Society* (Uppsala 1970).

Tempels, P., *Bantu Philosophy* (transl. from original French by C. King, published by Presence Africaine, Paris, 1958).

Toit, B. M. du, 'Some Aspects of the Soul-Concept among the Bantu-Speaking Nguni-Tribes of South Africa' (*AQ*, Vol. 23, 1960, pp. 134–142).

— 'The Isangoma: An Adaptive Agent Among the Urban Zulu' (*AQ*, Vol. 44, 1971 pp. 51–65).

Tracey, H., 'What are Mashawi Spirits?' (*NADA*, Vol. 12, 1934, pp. 39–52).

Tromp, Th. M., *De Stam der ama-Zoeloe, (Zoeloes)*. (Leiden 1879).

Turner, V. W., 'The Lozi People of North-Western Rhodesia' (*ESA*, West Central Africa, Part 3, London 1952).

— *The Drums of Affliction* (Oxford 1968).

— *The Forest of Symbols* (New York 1967).

— 'Ritual Symbolism among the Mdembu' (In *African Systems of Thought*, ed. by M. Fortes and G. Dieterlen, London 1965).

Twala, Regina G., 'Beads as Regulating the Social Life of the Zulu and Swazi' (*AS*, Vol. 10, 1951, pp. 113–123).

Tyler, J., *Forty Years Among the Zulus* (Boston 1891).

Tylor, E. B., *Primitive Culture, Vols. I and II* (London 1871).

Vilakazi, A., *Zulu Transformations* (Pietermaritzburg 1962).

Wangemann, D., *Ein Reise-Jahr in Süd-Afrika* (Berlin 1868).

Wangemann, H. Th., *Die Berliner Mission im Zulu-Lande* (Berlin 1875).

Wanger, W., 'The Zulu Notion of God' (*A*, Vol. 18/19, 1923–1924, pp. 656–687, and Vol. 21, 1926, pp. 351–385).

— 'Totenkult (Ahnenkult) bei den zulusprechenden Völkern' (*IJVS*, Vol. 1, 1926, pp. 10–21).

Wanger, W., (ed.), *The Collector* (Mariannhill, 1911–1913).

Warmelo, N. J. van, *Kinship Terminology of the South African Bantu* (Pretoria 1931).

Watt, J. M., 'The Native Medicine Man' (*South African Nursing Record*, Vol. 18, 1931, pp. 265–266).

Watt, J. M. and van Warmelo, N. F., 'The Medicines and Practice of a Sotho Doctor' (*BS*, Vol. 4, 1930, pp. 47–63).

Webster, H., *Taboo, a Sociological Study* (London 1942).

Werner, Alice, 'Some Notes on Zulu Religious Ideas' (*KFL*, Vol. 32, 1921, pp. 28–48).

Westlind, P. A., 'Religiösa begrepp och föreställningar bland kongofolket' (*Dagbräckning i Kongo*, Stockholm, n.d., pp. 58–94).

White, C. M. N., 'Notes on Some Metaphysical Concepts of the Balovale' (*AS*, Vol. 7, 1948, pp. 146–156).

— *Elements in Luvale Beliefs and Ritual* (Rhodes-Livingstone Papers, No. 32, Manchester 1961).

— 'The Supreme Being in the Beliefs of the Balovale Tribes' (*AS*, Vol. 7, 1948, pp. 29–35).

— 'Witchcraft, Divination and Magic Among the Balovale Tribes' (*A*, Vol. 18, 1948, pp. 81–104).

Willoughby, W. C., 'Some Conclusions concerning the Bantu Conception of the Soul' (*A*, Vol. 1, 1928, pp. 338–348).

— *The Soul of the Bantu* (London 1928).

Wilson, G., Nyakyusa Conventions of Burial (*BS*, Vol. 13, 1939, pp. 1–31).

Wilson, Monica, *Communal Rituals of the Nyakyusa* (Oxford 1959).

— *Divine Kings and the 'Breath of Men'* (Cambridge 1959).

— *Good Company* (Boston 1963).

— 'Nyakyusa Ritual and Symbolism' (*AA*, Vol. 56, 1954, pp. 228–241).

— *Religion and Transformation of Society* (Cambridge 1971).

— *Rituals of Kinship among the Nyakyusa* (London 1957).

— 'Witch Beliefs and Social Structure' (*AJS*, Vol. 56, 1951, pp. 307–313).

Wilson, G. and Monica, *The Analysis of Social Change* (Cambridge 1965).

Winick, Ch., *Dictionary of Anthropology* (New Jersey 1964).

Woods, G. C. B., 'Extracts from Customs and History; Amandebele' (*NADA*, Vol. 9, 1931, pp. 16–23).

Xuma, A. B., 'Native Customs and Folklore' (*SAMJ*, 1932, pp. 234–239).

INDEX